Arnulfo L. Oliveira Memorial Library

Ethnocultural Aspects
of Posttraumatic Stress Disorder
Issues, Research, and Clinical Applications

Ethnocultural Aspects
of Posttraumatic Stress Disorder
Issues, Research, and Clinical Applications

EDITED BY

Anthony J. Marsella

Matthew J. Friedman

Ellen T. Gerrity

Raymond M. Scurfield

AMERICAN PSYCHOLOGICAL ASSOCIATION
WASHINGTON, DC

First printing February 1996
Second printing September 1996

Published by
American Psychological Association
750 First Street, NE
Washington, DC 20002

Copies may be ordered from
American Psychological Association
Order Department
P.O. Box 92984
Washington, DC 20090-2984

In the UK and Europe, copies may be ordered from
American Psychological Association
3 Henrietta Street
Covent Garden, London
WC2E 8LU England

Typeset in Goudy by PRO-IMAGE Corporation, Techna-Type Div., York, PA

Printer: Port City Press, Baltimore, MD
Cover and Jacket Designer: Minker Design, Bethesda, MD
Jacket Illustrator: Stephanie Shieldhouse, Jacksonville, FL
Technical/Production Editor: Sarah J. Trembath

Library of Congress Cataloging-in-Publication Data
Ethnocultural aspects of posttraumatic stress disorder : issues,
   research, and clinical applications / edited by Anthony J. Marsella
   . . . [et al.].
      p.   cm.
   Includes bibliographical references and index.
   ISBN 1-55798-319-4 (acid-free paper)
   1. Post-traumatic stress disorder—Cross-cultural studies.
2 Psychiatry, Transcultural.   I. Marsella, Anthony J.
RC552.P67E83   1996
616.85'21—dc20   95-40252
                                                                CIP

British Library Cataloguing-in-Publication Data
A CIP record is available from the British Library.

Printed in the United States of America

CONTENTS

CONTRIBUTORS

Francis R. Abueg, PhD, Trauma and Alcohol Clinic, National Center for PTSD, Palo Alto VA Health Care System, and Stanford University School of Medicine, California

Irving M. Allen, MD, Harvard University, Cambridge, Massachusetts

Dora Anderson, RN, BSN, Department of Psychiatry, UCLA Harbor Medical Center, Torrance, California

Janette Beals, PhD, National Center for American Indian and Alaskan Native Mental Health Research, Colorado Health Sciences University, Denver, Colorado

Donald Bechtold, MD, National Center for American Indian and Alaskan Native Mental Health Research, University of Colorado Health Sciences University, Denver, Colorado

Dudley David Blake, PhD, Veterans Affairs Palo Alto Health Care System, Palo Alto, California

Glorisa J. Canino, PhD, Medical Sciences Campus, University of Puerto Rico, San Juan, Puerto Rico

Barbara Chester, PhD, The Hopi Foundation, Tucson, Arizona

Kevin M. Chun, MA, University of San Francisco, California, and National Research Center on Asian American Mental Health, University of California, Los Angeles

Giovanni de Girolamo, MD, Servizio Sanitario Nazionale, Bologna, Italy

Vincenzo F. DiNicola, MD, MPhil, Dip. Psychiatry, FRCPC, Division of Child/Adolescent Psychiatry, Queens University, Ontario, Canada

Juris G. Draguns, PhD, Department of Psychology, Pennsylvania State University, University Park, Pennsylvania

John Fairbank, PhD, Research Triangle Institute, Research Triangle Park, North Carolina

Alan F. Fontana, PhD, Evaluation Research Division, National Center for PTSD, Westhaven, Connecticut

Matthew J. Friedman, MD, PhD, National Center for PTSD, Veterans Administration Medical Center, White River Junction, Vermont

Ellen T. Gerrity, PhD, Emergency and Violence Research Program, National Institute of Mental Health, Rockville, Maryland

David Goldman, MD, Laboratory of Neurogenetics, NIAA/NIH, Tucson, Arizona

Bonnie Green, PhD, Department of Psychiatry, Georgetown University Medical School, Washington, DC

Fred D. Gusman, MSW, Veterans Affairs Palo Alto Health Care System, Palo Alto, California

Bruce Hiley Young, LCSW, Veterans Affairs Palo Alto Health Care System, Palo Alto, California

Richard Hough, PhD, Homeless Research Project, Department of Sociology, San Diego State University, California

E. Huland Spain, PhD, Eastern Virginia Medical School, Norfolk, Virginia, and Eastern State Hospital, Williamsburg, Virginia

Janis H. Jenkins, PhD, Department of Anthropology, Case Western Reserve University, Cleveland, Ohio

Monica Jones, MS, National Center for American Indian and Alaskan Native Mental Health Research, Colorado Health Sciences University, Denver, Colorado

Daniel G. Kaloupek, PhD, National Center for PTSD, Boston Veterans Administration Medical Center, Boston, Massachusetts

Ellen Keane, MSPH, National Center for American Indian and Alaskan Native Mental Health Research, Colorado Health Sciences University, Denver, Colorado

Terence M. Keane, PhD, National Center for PTSD, Boston Veterans Administration Medical Center, Boston, Massachusetts

Laurence J. Kirmayer, MD, Department of Psychiatry, McGill University, Montreal, Canada

Ira M. Lesser, MD, Department of Psychiatry and Behavioral Sciences, UCLA Harbor Medical Center, Torrance, California

Keh-Ming Lin, MD, Department of Psychiatry, UCLA Harbor Medical Center, Torrance, California

Spero Manson, PhD, National Center for American Indian and Alaskan Native Mental Health Research, Colorado Health Sciences College, Denver, Colorado

Anthony J. Marsella, PhD, Department of Psychology, University of Hawaii, Honolulu

Alexander C. McFarlane, MD, Department of Rehabilitation and Community Psychiatry, Glenside Hospital, Eastwood, South Australia

Theresa O'Nell, PhD, National Center for American Indian and Alaskan Native Mental Health Research, Colorado Health Sciences University, Denver, Colorado

Joan Piasecki, PhD, National Center for American Indian and Alaskan Native Mental Health Research, Colorado Health Sciences University, Denver, Colorado

Russell E. Poland, PhD, Department of Psychiatry, UCLA Harbor Medical Center, Torrance, California

Sherry J. Riney, MSW, Veterans Affairs Palo Alto Health Care System, Palo Alto, California

Robert W. Robin, PhD, Laboratory of Neurogenetics, NIAA/NIH, Tucson, Arizona

Maria P. Root, PhD, American Ethnic Studies Department, University of Washington, Seattle

Robert Rosenheck, PhD, Evaluation Research Division, National Center for PTSD, Westhaven, Connecticut

William Schlenger, PhD, Research Triangle Institute, Research Triangle Park, North Carolina

Raymond M. Scurfield, DSW, National Center for PTSD, Veterans Administration, Honolulu, Hawaii

Susan D. Solomon, PhD, Violence and Traumatic Stress Research Branch, National Institute of Mental Health, Rockville, Maryland

Judith Stewart, PhD, Veterans Affairs Palo Alto Health Care System, Palo Alto, California

Frank W. Weathers, PhD, National Center for PTSD, Boston Veterans Administration Medical Center, Boston, Massachusetts

PREFACE

What sets worlds in motion is the interplay of differences, their at-
tractions and repulsions. Life is plurality, death is uniformity. By suppressing differences and peculiarities, by eliminating different civilizations and cultures, progress weakens life and favors death. The ideal
of a single civilization for everyone, implicit in the cult of progress and
technique, impoverishes and mutilates us. Every view of the world that
becomes extinct, every culture that disappears, diminishes a possibility
of life.

—*Octavio Paz (1967)*
The Labyrinth of Solitude

Within the last decade, posttraumatic stress disorder (PTSD) has
emerged as one of the most popular areas of clinical and scientific inquiry
and concern among mental health professionals and academics. Reference
to the experience of stress-related disorders is centuries old (e.g., the Ho-
meric legends), but it has only been in recent years that PTSD has been
identified and acknowledged as a distinct clinical dysfunction and disorder
with its own set of diagnostic criteria (American Psychiatric Association
[APA], *DSM–III*, 1980; *DSM–III–R*, 1987; *DSM–IV*, 1994).

As a result, today there is an extensive body of clinical knowledge
and scientific research on PTSD. There are scientific and professional societies (e.g., The International Society for Traumatic Stress Studies) and
scientific and clinical research journals (e.g., *Journal of Traumatic Stress*)

specifically concerned with the topic. Interest in PTSD has become so widespread that the mass media has referred to PTSD as "the disorder of the 1990s."

As the concept of PTSD captured the attention and concern of clinicians and scientists, emphasis was initially placed on the identification and assessment of reliable and valid diagnostic criteria. Once these goals seemed to have been achieved, emphasis shifted to epidemiological studies, especially among high-risk populations such as refugees, Vietnam War veterans, and victims of adult and childhood sexual abuse and natural and technological disasters. A clearinghouse for publications of PTSD[1] noted that more than 8,000 articles on various aspects of PTSD have been published around the world in the scientific, medical, and popular literature, most of which have appeared in the last decade.

According to the *DSM–IV* (APA, 1994), PTSD refers to a disorder that may occur when a person has been exposed to a traumatic event in which

> the person experienced, witnessed, or was confronted with an event or events that involved actual or threatened death or serious injury, or a threat to the physical integrity of self or others, [and] the person's response involved intense fear, helplessness, or horror. (p. 209)

The *DSM–IV* also posits that the traumatic event is persistently re-experienced in any of a number of ways, which later chapters will specifically detail, and that other symptoms include a persistent avoidance of stimuli associated with the trauma, a numbing of responsiveness, and symptoms of arousal. Furthermore, the duration of symptoms is more than one month, and the disturbance causes significant distress or impairment in various important areas of life functioning.

The *DSM–IV* definition and description of PTSD has been the subject of controversy and debate—some of which is captured in the present volume—because some researchers and practitioners find its definitional or operational clarity problematic. Some critics of the *DSM–IV* definition have suggested that PTSD constitutes a rather broad-based human response that can assume a variety of individual and societal forms, expressions, and dimensions with multiple degrees of severity and disability.

Although there is discord over definitional matters, many researchers and practitioners seem to agree that exposure to traumatic events, in the absence of psychological and social resources that may mediate their severity and effects, may result in both immediate and long-term pernicious and destructive consequences for individuals, families, communities, and nations.

---

[1] The reader is referred to the PILOTS Database at the National Center for PTSD, VAM and ROC, White River Junction, Vermont 05009.

Current research supports the universality of many of the biologically determined components of the PTSD experience. This is not surprising, for the human response to trauma is fundamentally shaped by psycho-physiological and neurobiological mechanisms and adaptive response to a perceived threat, initially conceptualized as the primitive flight–fight response. Researchers have pointed out that PTSD appears to be associated with a stable and consistent pattern of changes involving hyperarousal of the sympathetic system; augmentation of the acoustic startle reflex; sleep abnormalities; and system-wide changes in the noradrenergic, endogenous opioid, and hypothalamic–pituitary–adrenal axis. There have also been suggestions that the locus coeruleus, limbic system, and other areas of the brain are critical parts of the trauma response complex, and that severe or chronic traumatic experiences can alter homeostatic neurobiological processes (e.g., Pitman, 1993).

Although a universal neurobiological response to traumatic events most likely does exist, there is considerable ethnocultural variation in the expressive and phenomenological dimensions of the PTSD experience, especially the intrusive, avoidant/numbing, and arousal pattern aspects. In addition, it is also likely that there are ethnocultural variations in co-morbidity patterns; somatic, hysterical, substance-abuse, and paranoid symptoms may vary as a function of the ethnocultural context of the patient. Furthermore, if there are significant cross-cultural variations in the experience of PTSD, the implications for ethnocultural variations in preferred treatment alternatives and prevention activities must be addressed.

One of the many aspects of PTSD that has provoked interest and debate recently is the issue of ethnocentric bias in conceptualization, diagnosis, measurement, and treatment. There also has been an increased interest in the study of other ethnocultural aspects of PTSD, which is evident in the numerous books, technical reports, and journal articles published on a broad spectrum of ethnic populations and ethnic aspects of PTSD. However, there have been few literature reviews[2] on the topic, and those literature reviews that have been published have been limited to either specific topics (e.g., assessment), specific traumas (e.g., refugee status) or ethnic groups (e.g., Indochinese). The absence of systematic coverage of the topic is one of the primary motives behind the publication of this volume.

The purpose of this volume is to explore and examine the role of ethnocultural aspects of PTSD through a thorough and comprehensive discussion of current theory, research, and practice on the topic. The chapters in this edited volume have been prepared by many of the visible leaders in the field of PTSD research and practice. Every effort has been made by

---

[2]See Marsella, Friedman, & Spain, 1993; and Wilson & Raphael, 1993 for literature reviews of ethnocultural research.

editors and chapter authors to provide detailed and scholarly coverage of the subject matter. However, the nature of the topic is such that socio-political interests and inclinations cannot be ignored. Thus, the reader will find that the content of many of the chapters flows between scientific and historical fact and informed political opinion.

This volume should prove useful to researchers, practitioners, and administrators because it articulates our current knowledge of the many issues, findings, and applications associated with ethnocultural aspects of PTSD. The ethnocultural study of PTSD is immensely significant in understanding the etiology, phenomenology, epidemiology, treatment, and prevention of the "disorder of our time." Chapter authors represent a spectrum of disciplines and professions, and include anthropologists, epidemiologists, pharmacologists, psychologists, psychiatrists, social workers, and sociologists. The multidisciplinary approach to PTSD has now become popular because of the many dimensions of PTSD.

Each of the chapters was first presented at the International Conference on Ethnocultural Aspects of PTSD held in Honolulu, Hawaii from June 28 to July 1, 1993. The conference was sponsored and supported by the following groups: The National Center for PTSD,[3] The Pacific Center for War-Related Disorders, the Refugee Mental Health Program and the Violence and Traumatic Stress Research Branch of the National Institute of Mental Health, the College of Social Sciences, University of Hawaii, and the Department of Psychiatry of the Karolinska Institute, Stockholm.

At this conference, more than 40 mental professionals, medical and behavioral scientists, and administrators gathered to discuss ethnocultural factors related to PTSD. The participants represented a variety of academic disciplines and professional specialties, and included representatives from diverse governmental and academic institutions. Many participants were women, and represented various ethnocultural groups.

In the period between the conference and the publication of this volume, the chapters were extensively revised to accommodate the discussion and debate that characterized the Honolulu conference. Chapters were then further reviewed by other experts. Because of space limitations, a number of the original conference papers could not be included. The editors are grateful to the authors of those paper, and are encouraged by the fact that these authors' papers are being published in other forums.

What the volume cannot capture is the spirited discussion and debate that accompanied all of the conference presentations, and the interstitial commentary that occurred at coffee breaks and in informal talks among participants. It is the editors' hope, however, that the revised and edited versions of the papers that constitute the present volume's chapters will

---

[3]The address for the National Center for PTSD is VAMROC, Department of Veterans Affairs, White River Junction, Vermont, 05009.

adequately reflect ideas, thoughts, and conclusions that were the essence of the Honolulu conference, and the inspired insight and scholarship that can only occur within the context of a true multidisciplinary and multicultural encounter.

REFERENCES

American Psychiatric Association (1980). *Diagnostic and statistical manual of mental disorders* (3rd ed.). Washington, DC: Author.

American Psychiatric Association (1987). *Diagnostic and Statistical manual of mental disorders* (3rd ed., rev.). Washington, DC: Author.

American Psychiatric Association (1994). Diagnostic and Statistical manual of mental disorders (4th ed.). Washington, DC: Author.

Pitman, R. (1993). Biological findings in PTSD. In J. Davidson & E. Foa, Eds. *Posttraumatic stress disorder: DSM–IV and beyond* (pp. 173–190). Washington, DC: American Psychiatric Press.

ACKNOWLEDGMENTS

The editors would like to express their deep appreciation and gratitude to a number of individuals and agencies that helped make the publication of this volume possible. Anthony J. Marsella and Matthew J. Friedman conceived and organized the International Conference on Ethnocultural Aspects of PTSD from which this volume is derived. Ellen Gerrity, Susan Solomon, Raymond Scurfield, and Thomas Bornemann were tireless sources of strength and commitment in the planning and conduct of the conference. All were also major resources for funding the conference through their respective agencies. Richard Rohde offered many services to help make the conference a success.

Special thanks are owed to Frederick Goodwin for his support of the conference from its inception to its completion. His early recognition that such a conference would be helpful to scientists and clinicians around the world was a constant source of inspiration. The editors would also like to express their deep appreciation to Jeffrey Nathan who contributed to the production of the manuscript by scanning chapter drafts, correcting bibliographic errors, translating computer software programs, and doing a score of other tasks that helped make our task easier. Jonathan Davidson and Frederick Leong offered numerous suggestions to improve both the content and expressive dimensions of the book, for which we are grateful.

Lastly, the editors would like to express their deep gratitude to the following staff of the American Psychological Association books Department for their patience and their tireless efforts in bringing the manuscript to publication: Susan Reynolds, Acquisitions Editor; Mary Lynn Skutley, Manager, Acquisitions and Development; Judy Nemes, Development Editor; Sarah J. Trembath, Technical/Production Editor; and Julia Frank-McNeil, Director, APA Books. What we most admire and respect about this talented group and what we are most grateful for, are their uncommon creative energies and technical skills, and their unspoken commitment to excellence.

INTRODUCTION

ANTHONY J. MARSELLA, MATTHEW J. FRIEDMAN,
ELLEN T. GERRITY, and RAYMOND M. SCURFIELD

Anyone interested in posttraumatic stress disorder (PTSD) must eventually confront the role of ethnocultural factors in the etiology, distribution, expression, course, outcome, and treatment. This fact should not be surprising because PTSD is a dysfunction that implicates biological, psychological, and social aspects of functioning—all of which are influenced by ethnocultural factors such as cultural conceptions of health and disease, perceptions and definitions of trauma, conceptions of the person, and standards concerning normality and abnormality.

To the extent that non-Western cultural groups are similar to Western populations in their basic epistemological assumptions, language, activity contexts, reward systems, and other fundamental variables involved in the social construction of reality, it is likely that there will be less difference in the relevance of the PTSD construct. However, if more profound cultural differences exist, then it is clear that care must be taken in applying the PTSD construct. This does not mean that it is impossible to make use of the PTSD construct, but rather that every effort should be made to develop sensitivities to possible cultural influences on the clinical experience and expression, as well as the treatment process.

As scientists and clinicians approach the ethnocultural study of PTSD, a number of questions emerge: (a) Is the PTSD construct valid across cultures? Can PTSD be diagnosed successfully across cultural boundaries? If so, under what circumstances and conditions? (b) Are there ethnocultural variations in the rates and distribution of PTSD? If so, what conditions and procedures are necessary to conduct valid epidemiological studies? (c) Are certain ethnocultural groups at greater risk for the development of PTSD? If so, what factors contribute to this vulnerability, and what can be done to reduce it? (d) Does culture impact interpretations of trauma, resulting in different responses? What are the implications of differential interpretations of traumatic experiences? (e) Are there ethnocultural variations in expression, manifestation, experience of PTSD? Are there universal and culture-specific responses to trauma? If so, what factors may account for these differences? (f) Are there ethnocultural variations in the course and outcome of PTSD? Are there special problems related to the assessment of PTSD across cultures? If so, how can these problems be addressed so the validity and reliability of assessment can improved? (g) Are there ethnocultural variations in the response to any of the biological, psychological, or social treatments of PTSD? Is it possible to render successful treatments independently of the patient's cultural construction of their illness experience, or are there alternative therapies that may be appropriate for particular ethnocultural groups? (h) Are there specific research strategies for the ethnocultural study of PTSD that should be considered in our efforts to investigate this disorder?

For the impatient reader, the reader who cannot bear the tension of not knowing the answers to these questions, there is a summary chapter at the end of the book that addresses the contributions of the chapters toward answering these questions. But, to the reader willing to defer knowing and willing to spend the time to carefully read the chapters of this book, the answers will unfold with greater detail, precision, and intellectual delight.

OVERVIEW OF THIS BOOK

The editors have organized the chapters of this book into five major sections. Section I: Foundations offers a general introduction to the topic of PTSD, with specific attention given to clinical epidemiological and treatment-research overviews. Section II: Ethnocultural Research on PTSD includes a series of chapters that address the relationship between ethnocultural factors and PTSD as these are implicated in somatoform and dissociative disorders, emotional experience, and assessment and measurement issues. Section III: PTSD Among Specific Ethnocultural Groups, is devoted to analysis and discussion of current theory and research regarding African Americans, American Indians, Asians and Asian Americans, and Hispanic Americans. Section IV: PTSD Among Specific Victim Populations looks at the topic another way, by examining groups that have been exposed to natural and human-made disasters. The penultimate section, Section V:

Ethnocultural Considerations in Therapies and Mental Health Services for PTSD includes chapters devoted to counseling and psychotherapy, crisis care and management, ethnopsychopharmacology, and the delivery and evaluation of mental health services. As noted earlier, Section VI: Conclusions offers some closing thoughts regarding the questions raised in the introductory chapter.

As a group, chapter authors address the topic of ethnocultural variations and similarities in the etiology, distribution, expression, clinical diagnosis, and treatment of PTSD and related stress disorders. Thus, the present volume constitutes a unique resource for scientists, professionals, administrators, and policy planners—a single book that summarizes and reviews the extensive clinical and research literature on ethnocultural aspects of PTSD.

The following paragraphs summarize some of the major themes and directions of each of the book's chapters. These chapters summaries provide the reader with a brief overview of the volume without detracting from the careful scholarship, discussion, and conclusions of each chapter. Indeed, the editors have intentionally sought to whet the reader's appetite by presenting pithy commentaries rather than exhaustive and detailed summaries of each chapter.

Section I: Foundations

"Posttraumatic Stress Disorder: An Overview of the Concept," by Matthew Friedman, a psychiatrist and pharmacologist, and Anthony Marsella, a psychologist, offers the reader a brief overview of the PTSD concept, including a table summarizing the new *DSM–IV* diagnostic criteria. Chapter 1 identifies and discusses current knowledge and issues related to the epidemiology, classification and diagnosis, etiology, and clinical parameters (e.g., comorbidity, course, outcome) of PTSD. Chapter 1 provides readers a starting point for understanding the interface between ethnocultural factors and PTSD.

Psychiatrist and epidemiologist Giovanni de Girolamo, M.D., and psychiatrist Alan McFarlane, in their chapter, "The Epidemiology of PTSD," offer the reader a comprehensive summary and overview of the epidemiology of PTSD from an international perspective. The literature review on the epidemiology of PTSD offered by these two scholar–clinicians is unduplicated in its size and scope among current publications. Special attention is given to the difficulties of comparing results from the diverse array of published studies due to variations in methods and assumptions. Despite these difficulties, the authors cautiously reach some important conclusions on the distribution of PTSD and related stress disorders that help illuminate the challenges that clinicians and scientists will face in improving our understanding of the topic.

In chapter 3, "The Treatment of PTSD and Related Stress Disorders" psychologists Ellen Gerrity and Susan Solomon summarize what is known about the treatment of PTSD based on the research literature. They begin by identifying the methodology necessary for valid treatment studies, and then evaluate the studies that have been published. The gaps in our knowledge about the efficacy of alternative treatment approaches to PTSD (i.e., different kinds of therapy) suggest that there is still much to learn about the successful treatment of PTSD. This conclusion raises interesting possibilities about the value of approaches to treatment that are emerging from different ethnocultural traditions (e.g., sweat-lodge ceremonies, tai chi).

Section II: Ethnocultural Research On PTSD

Anthony Marsella, Matthew Friedman, and E. Huland Spain offer an overview of current knowledge regarding ethnocultural aspects of PTSD in chapter 4. This chapter, "Ethnocultural Aspects of PTSD," which was previously published in slightly different form, was praised for its clarification of terms, extensive review of the literature, and recommendations for future research. The chapter in the current volume offers a useful introduction to the state of research today and the issues associated with understanding ethnocultural aspects of PTSD.

In chapter 5, Laurence Kirmayer, a transcultural psychiatrist, offers readers a detailed and scholarly analysis of the relationship between somatic and dissociative disorders and PTSD through a discussion of the cross-cultural literature on these topics. His careful review of the literature, "Confusion of the Senses," highlights the importance of understanding the ways that ethnocultural factors affect the expression, display, and experience of stress-related behaviors. He argues that somatic and dissociative disorders may coexist with PTSD and may complicate PTSD in different cultures. Furthermore, he suggests these disorders may actually represent more appropriate conceptualizations of posttraumatic related distress than PTSD per se.

A similar contribution is made by medical anthropologist Janis H. Jenkins in chapter 6. She addresses the complex interplay between culture, emotions, and PTSD, and what emerges is the fact that the cultural construction of reality requires consideration of ethnocultural variables in every effort to understand health and disease. In "Culture, Emotion, and PTSD," Jenkins argues that the cultural nature of emotion development, experience, and expression demands we reassess many of our assumptions about the causes and nature of emotional disorders such as PTSD.

Clinical psychologists Terence Keane, Daniel Kaloupek, and Frank Weathers, authored chapter 7, "Ethnocultural Considerations in the Assessment of PTSD." Each of these scientist–practitioners has been active in the development of valid instruments to measure PTSD, and their chapter addresses the many complex issues and challenges involved in the assessment of PTSD when cultural boundaries are crossed. Clearly, if symptomatology varies among cultures, if emotional experiences have different cultural constructions, and if there are differences in language, concepts, scales, and norms, clinicians must be cautious in assessing clients.

Section III: PTSD Among Specific Ethnocultural Groups

Chapter 8, by clinical psychiatrist Irving Allen, is a passionate discussion of PTSD and related stress disorders among African American populations. Allen offers broad historical, social, and political arguments to support his contentions regarding the extent and nature of PTSD among African Americans. In "PTSD Among Afican Americans," the author provides a scholarly account of the African American experience, and the reasons that this often tragic and sorrowful experience may influence the health and well-being of the African American individual. Allen, who has authored a number of publications on PTSD, addresses the difficulties encountered in treating PTSD in African Americans; he contends that treatment difficulties are often rooted in the constant stress to which Black Americans are exposed as a result of historical and contemporary racism.

Chapter 9, addresses PTSD among American Indian populations. It is authored by cultural anthropologist Robert Robin, psychologist Barbara Chester, and research psychiatrist David Goldman, all of whom have been involved in behavioral genetic and psychocultural studies of American Indian mental health problems—especially alcoholism and substance abuse. In "Cumulative Trauma and PTSD in American Indian Communities," the authors emphasize the importance of understanding the prevalence of PTSD and cumulative trauma from a historical framework incorporating chronic social and political abuse. They contend that the current definition of PTSD fails to describe the nature and impact of severe, multiple, repeated, and cumulative aspects of trauma among American Indians, and suggest other frameworks for conceptualizing the experience.

Chapter 10, another chapter addressing the topic of PTSD among American Indians, was written by members of the American Indian and Native Alaskan Mental Health Research Center in Denver, Colorado. The authors of "Wounded Spirits, Ailing Hearts" are Spero Manson, a cultural anthropologist, Jan Beals, a social psychologist, Theresa O'Nell, a medical anthropologist, Joan Piasecki, a research psychologist, Donald Bechtold, a psychiatrist, Ellen Keane, a public health specialist, and Monica Jones, a research psychologist. These authors approach the problem of PTSD among American Indians through a thorough analysis of research studies conducted at the their center. Chapter 10 carefully analyzes the relationship between cultural factors and a spectrum of PTSD dimensions, giving special attention to the validity of the PTSD construct, its assessment, its diagnosis, and its treatment within the context of American Indian cultural traditions.

In chapter 11, "Traumatization Stress Among Asians and Asian Americans," clinical psychologist Frances Abueg, and Kevin Chun, a graduate student in psychology, summarize studies of PTSD among Asian and Asian American populations. They note that much of the research on PTSD in these groups is based on refugees, and they call for increased research directed toward other traumatized groups. Furthermore, in their review of research on refugees, they point out the traumas associated with the premigration, migration, and postmigration aspects of refugee life. They also discuss some of the research related to Asian American Vietnam veterans, pointing out that much of what we know in this area is anecdotal and in need of formal research support.

Chapter 12, by sociologist Richard Hough, psychiatrist and epidemiologist Glorisa Canino, clinial psychologist Frances Abueg, and social worker Fred Gusman, offers the most thorough and detailed analysis of the PTSD literature to date among Hispanic populations. In "PTSD and Related Disorders Among Hispanics," the authors carefully summarize the literature, dividing it into different categories of traumatic experience, pointing out the difficulties in conducting valid research in these areas. Among the groups they discuss are refugees, victims of natural disasters, and veterans. They also carefully evaluate and summarize results from the Los Angeles Epidemiologcial Catchment Area study.

Section IV: PTSD Among Specific Victim Populations

Chapter 13, by Bonnie Green, a clinical psychologist, provides a clear and comprehensive summary of the international literature on disasters, giving special attention to the complex methodological problems involved in reaching valid conclusions in such studies. In "Crossnational and Ethnocultural Issues in Disaster Research," she points out that ethnocultural differences may influence (a) the likelihood that events will be perceived as traumatic, (b) the capacity of risk factors to predict postdisaster outcomes, and (c) individual beliefs about the nature and possibility of recovery.

In chapter 14, Maria P. P. Root, a clinical psychologist, calls attention to the sociopolitical context of violence directed toward women of color. She suggests that the "marginalization" of women of color is shaped and determined through a complex process that serves to deny them opportunities to experience change, access resources, and alter the "domestic captivity" in which many must live. Root points out in "Women of Color and Traumatic Stress in 'Domestic Captivity'" that the combination of racial and ethnic and female subordination in our society creates a context for

PTSD and other forms of trauma-related disorders to flourish and destroy women's lives.

Transcultural child psychiatrist Vincent DiNicola traces some of the problems inherent in cross-cultural studies of PTSD among children in chapter 15. DiNicola first discusses the developmental issues related to PTSD in youth and the difficulties of assessing the various dimensions of traumatic experience. "Ethnocultural Aspects of PTSD and Related Disorders Among Children and Adolescents" also explores cross-cultural studies of PTSD among children and adolescents, citing some clinical cases that demonstrate the problems in diagnosis and treatment. Lastly, the author calls attention to some principles of "cultural family therapy," a method he believes can be helpful in healing the scars of trauma in youth.

Chapter 16 authors William Schlenger and John Fairbank, both clinical psychologists, present epidemiological data from The National Vietnam Veterans Readjustment Study on African American, Hispanic, and White/other male Vietnam War veterans. "Ethnocultural Considerations in Understanding PTSD and Related Disorders Among Military Veterans" examines variations in PTSD rates according to premilitary, military, and postmilitary experiences.

Section V: Ethnocultural Considerations in Therapies and Mental Health Services for PTSD

Chapter 17 is concerned with ethnocultural aspects of crisis care and management for PTSD through the use of a multicultural and developmental model of intervention. "A Multicultural Developmental Approach for Treating Trauma" was written by members of the National Center for PTSD Educational and Clinical Research Team, social worker Fred Guzman, clinical psychologist Judith Stewart, social worker Bruce Hiley Young, research assistant Sherry Riney, and clinical psychologists Francis Abueg, and Dudley David Blake. The authors present a developmental–constructionist model of crisis care that emphasizes multicultural knowledge and negotiation of the PTSD experience. They suggest that this model is particularly useful for ethnocultural minority group members who must live in ethnoculturally pluralistic milieus.

In chapter 18, Juris Draguns, a professor of psychology, offers a conceptual framework for understanding some of the challenges that emerge when psychologists offer services across cultural boundaries. In "Ethnocultural Considerations in the Treatment of PTSD" Draguns suggests that there are both universal and culturally variant aspects of PTSD that can be identified and used in the therapy process. He also calls attention to the possibility of using emic therapies in the treatment of PTSD.

Keh-Ming Lin, a professor of psychiatry, Russell E. Poland, a research scientist, Dora Anderson, a research assistant, and Ira Lesser, a psychiatrist, authored chapter 20, "Ethnopsychopharmacology and the Treatment of PTSD." They offer a scholarly summary of the ethnopsychopharmacological research literature showing how ethnocultural and racial factors may interact with metabolism and the actions of medications commonly used to treat PTSD, such as antidepressants, neuroleptics, benzodiazepines, and lithium. The authors offer several hypotheses to account for these differences, and discuss the potential applicability of their findings to clinical practice.

Chapter 19, "Ethnocultural Variations in Service Use Among Veterans Suffering From PTSD" was written by psychiatrist Robert Rosenheck, and research psychologist Allan Fontana. Rosenheck and Fontana provide a thorough discussion of their data on ethnocultural elements of service use in VA clinics, with a special focus on African American, Hispanic, and Euro-American populations. They conclude that variations in service use that appear may be due to (a) epidemiological differences in type and severity of disorders among different groups, (b) differences in receptiveness and responsivity to treatments offered, and (c) differences in the quality, quantity, and acceptability of services provided by clinicians.

Section VI: Conclusion

In Chapter 21, written by the editors, a summary and overview of conclusions derived from the various chapters is offered according to the questions first raised in the introduction. For those seeking a quick overview, "Some Closing Thoughts" may be a good place to begin. However, for those seeking an intellectually exciting experience—put your feet up, sit back, and begin at the beginning. The journey to the end of the book offers a scholarly and provocative experience filled with fascinating facts, theories, and possibilities that serve to reaffirm the need to consider ethnocultural variables in any effort to understand the nature, etiology, clinical parameters, and treatment of PTSD. Happy journey!

I

FOUNDATIONS

1

POSTTRAUMATIC STRESS DISORDER: AN OVERVIEW OF THE CONCEPT

MATTHEW J. FRIEDMAN and ANTHONY J. MARSELLA

He tried to make love to her. . . . until he was defeated by sadness, or shame, and pushed her away. . . . But darkness was not good; he needed the rectangle of light from the street, because without it he felt trapped again in the abyss of the timeless ninety centimeters of his cell, fermenting in his own excrement, delirious . . . he knew that he was coming apart, as he had so often before, and he gave up the struggle, releasing his last hold on the present, letting himself plunge down the endless precipice. He felt the crusted straps on his ankles and wrists, the brutal charge, the torn tendons, the insulting voices demanding names, the unforgettable screams of Ana, tortured beside him, and of the others, hanging by their arms in the courtyard.

From "Our Secret," by Isabelle Allende

When he came home [from Vietnam] though, Henry was very different, and I'll say this: the change was no good. You could hardly expect him to change for the better, I know. But he was quiet, so quiet, and never comfortable sitting still anywhere but always up and moving around. . . . now you couldn't get him to laugh, or when he did it was more the sound of a man choking, a sound that stopped up the throats of other people around him. They got to leaving him alone most of the time, and I didn't blame them. It was a fact: Henry was jumpy and mean.

From "The Red Convertible," by Louise Erdrich

THE PTSD CONCEPT

Exposure to trauma has been a risk of the human experience throughout human history. Emotional reactions to extreme stress have been noted by historians and literary authors for 4,000 years (e.g., Figley, 1993; Veith, 1965). Homer's Ulysses (and probably Achilles) and Shakespeare's Henry

11

IV experienced profound posttraumatic stress reactions after exposure to war. Charles Dickens also experienced a traumatic stress reaction as a result of a major train wreck (Figley, 1993; Shay, 1991; Trimble, 1981).

However, it has only been since 1980, when the American Psychiatric Association's *DSM–III* (American Psychiatric Association; [APA] 1980) included the category of posttraumatic stress disorder (PTSD) in its official diagnostic and statistical manual that mental health clinicians had a suitable diagnostic option for the symptoms characteristic of survivors of traumatic and catastrophic stress. PTSD has provided a very new and useful conceptual and therapeutic approach to the psychological impact of trauma. Studies on adult victims of crime, war veterans, natural disaster survivors, and traumatized children (see Davidson, 1993) have shown that the revised (*DSM–III–R*) PTSD symptom clusters show good internal cohesiveness as a group.

> On the basis of multivariate and frequency studies in four different United States populations, the *DSM–III–R* symptom criteria for PTSD appear to bear out the constructs, traditions, and clinical wisdom embodied in the description. (Davidson, 1993, p. 151)

The same can be said for *DSM–IV* diagnostic criteria for PTSD because these same symptom clusters have been essentially preserved.

Ethnocultural Aspects of PTSD

Most research and clinical experience validating PTSD as a diagnostic category was carried out in Western industrialized nations. Although there are many evocative literary accounts depicting posttraumatic intrusion and avoidant/numbing and arousal symptoms in non-Western protagonists, such as political torture survivors from South America (Allende, 1991) or a Chippewa Vietnam veteran (Erdrich, 1984), there has been little methodologically sound cross-cultural research on PTSD among people from non-Western ethnocultural backgrounds (e.g., Marsella, Friedman, Gerrity, & Scurfield, this volume; Marsella, Friedman, & Spain, 1993).

Furthermore, Chakraborty (1991), has actually objected to applying the PTSD diagnosis to people from non-Western traditional societies. He argues that PTSD is a Western culture-bound syndrome that should be restricted to Euro-American individuals. We believe that Chakraborty's conclusion may be too extreme, and that there are many aspects of posttraumatic stress that are universal even in the face of what appear to be ethnocultural variations. Because most studies of non-Western cohorts lack the requisite cross-cultural methodological rigor (Marsella, Friedman, & Spain, 1993), it is unclear whether PTSD per se is the most appropriate diagnostic construct to apply universally. But this does not mean that the construct lacks applicability or meaning across cultures.

The authors have argued elsewhere (a) that we must remain open to the possibility that ethnocultural differences in the expression of traumatic stress may not strictly conform to *DSM–IV* diagnostic criteria; (b) that ethnocultural tendencies may alter clinical phenomenology to such an extent that highly traumatized cohorts will exhibit surprisingly low rates of PTSD; and (c) that following traumatic exposure, members of some ethnocultural groups may exhibit a traumatic stress syndrome that overlaps with PTSD but features symptoms idiosyncratic to individuals from specific ethnocultural traditions (Friedman & Jaranson, 1994; Marsella, Friedman, & Spain, 1993).

It is important to note that because ethnocultural differences among people are tied to variations in the social construction of reality, the perception of what constitutes a traumatic exprience, as well as the individual and social response to it, may vary considerably. For example, among followers of religions in which individual responsibility for acts and their consequences is limited, the perceptions, expressions, and treatment of exposure to trauma may differ from individuals of religions in which individual responsibility is emphasized.

Diagnostic precision and cross-cultural methodology notwithstanding, a number of recent studies have demonstrated profound posttraumatic psychiatric sequelae among non-Westernized individuals such as Southeast Asian refugees (Kinzie, 1993); Sri Lankans exposed to civil war (Somasundaram, 1993); civilian survivors of the war in Afghanistan (Wardak, 1993); cyclone survivors in Fiji and Sri Lanka (Fairley, 1984; Patrick & Patrick, 1981); earthquake victims in Mexico, Ecuador, Japan, and China (Conyer, Amor, Medina-Mara, Caraveo, & De la Fuentes, 1987; Lima, et. al., 1989; McFarlane & Hua, 1993; Odaira, Iwadate, & Raphael, 1993); volcano survivors in Colombia (Lima, Pai, Santacruz, Lozano, & Luna, 1987); and political torture detainees in South Africa (Simpson, 1993).

We will set the stage for the following chapters by reviewing PTSD with respect to the following factors: epidemiology, diagnostic criteria, theoretical issues, diagnostic issues, research issues, and clinical issues. We will discuss pretraumatic, traumatic, and posttraumatic risk factors for developing PTSD. Finally, we will mention a few cultural factors that might influence vulnerability to or resistance against the development of PTSD following exposure to extreme stress.

OVERVIEW OF THE RESEARCH LITERATURE

Epidemiology

In both the *DSM–III* (p. 236) and *DSM–III–R* (p. 247) formulations of PTSD, the risk of exposure to a traumatic event was characterized as "outside the range of usual human experience." A number of epidemiologic surveys have shown that exposure to trauma with subsequent development of PTSD was not uncommon. Among civilian residents of a large American city (Breslau, Davis, Andreski, & Peterson, 1991), and among veterans of the Vietnam War (Kulka, et al., 1990), lifetime prevalence rates of PTSD were approximately 9% and 30% respectively. One attempt to determine PTSD in the general population (Helzer, Robins, & McEvoy, 1987) of the St. Louis portion of the Epidemiologic Catchment Area Survey estimated a prevalence rate of 1 to 2%. Although there are instrumental and methodological reasons for rejecting this projection as a serious underestimation (Keane & Penk, 1988), even if we accept the Helzer et al. study's 1–2% figure, it yields an estimate of 2.4 to 4.8 million cases of PTSD in the United States alone. As noted by Keane (1990), with high rates of rape, criminal victimization, natural disaster, technological disaster, and war contributing to the development of PTSD, it is likely that the true prevalence rate of PTSD may substantially exceed the Helzer, et al. (1987) estimate. As a result, the latest revision of PTSD diagnostic criteria, the *DSM–IV*, no longer describes trauma as an event that is "outside the range of usual human experience." A detailed review of the epidemiology of PTSD and related stress disorders is presented in the chapter by DeGirolamo and McFarlane in Chapter 2 of the current volume.

Current Diagnostic Criteria

The appendix to this chapter summarizes the *DSM–IV* diagnostic criteria (American Psychiatric Association, 1994). The *stressor* criterion, or Criterion A, specifies that a person has been exposed to a catastrophic event such as war, torture, rape, a natural disaster, or an industrial accident, for example. During such exposure the person has been confronted with actual or threatened death or injury, or a threat to the physical integrity of himself or herself, or others. Green (1993, p. 138) has proposed eight "generic" dimensions of trauma:

1. Threat to life and limb;
2. Severe physical harm or injury;
3. Receipt of intentional injury/harm;
4. Exposure to the grotesque;
5. Violent/sudden loss of a loved one;
6. Witnessing or learning of violence to a loved one;
7. Learning of exposure to a noxious agent;
8. Causing death or severe harm to another.

In addition to exposure per se, many investigators now believe it is important to emphasize that during traumatic exposure, an individual's subjective response was marked by intense fear, helplessness, or horror. As is shown in the appendix, there is an emphasis on the subjective response to extreme stress, which has resulted in an expansion of the stressor criterion in *DSM–IV*. Criterion A–1 states that an individual has "experienced, witnessed, or been confronted by a catastrophic event (as in *DSM–III–R*)," whereas criterion A–2 is a new addition that addresses the person's emotional response to such traumatic exposure. Furthermore, Foa, Zenberg, & Rothbaum, (1992) have recently proposed that to qualify as traumatic, a stressor must not only be perceived as a potential threat to survival but must also be experienced as uncontrollable or unpredictable. Expansion of the stressor criterion to include such subjective components opens the door for consideration of psychological, experiential, and ethnocultural factors that mediate emotional responses to stressful events. Such factors also include the individual's subjective response to the historical, social, and political context in which stressful events occur.

The presence of an etiological factor in a diagnostic category, as with traumatic stress in PTSD, is relatively uncommon in the *DSM–III–R* and *DSM–IV*, and there is some controversy about where to draw the line between traumatic events and painful stressors that constitute the common vicissitudes of life such as divorce, failure, rejection, serious illness, and so on. Furthermore, the subjective appraisal of an historical event may determine whether an individual perceives a stressful episode as traumatic or merely difficult. After all, the subjective experience of trauma is a process by which information about an historical event is filtered through cognitive and emotional psychological processes.

Because of individual differences in this appraisal process, people appear to have varying trauma thresholds; some are more protected and some more vulnerable to developing clinical symptoms after exposure to extremely stressful situations. In this regard, there are some data suggesting that among people exposed to a traumatic stressor, those with a personal or family history of psychiatric illness are more likely to develop PTSD (Breslau, et al., 1991; Kulka, et al., 1990).

Criterion B, the *intrusive recollection* criterion, includes symptoms that are perhaps the most distinctive and readily identifiable symptoms of PTSD. For individuals with PTSD, the traumatic event remains— sometimes for decades or a lifetime—a dominating psychological experience that retains its power to evoke panic, terror, dread, grief, or despair in daytime fantasies, nightmares, and psychotic reenactments known as *PTSD flashbacks*. The only B-criterion change in the *DSM–IV* is that Symptom D–6 in *DSM–III–R* has now been moved to B–5.

The opening passage by Allende evokes an intrusive recollection about incarceration that escalates rapidly into a flashback about torture. Symptoms B–4 and B–5 reflect well-known clinical observations that traumamimetic stimuli can trigger recollections of the original event and have the power to evoke mental images, emotional responses, and physiological reactions associated with the trauma. Because of this, researchers can reproduce PTSD symptoms in the laboratory by exposing affected individuals to auditory or visual traumamimetic stimuli (Blanchard, Kolb, Pallmeyer, & Gerardi, 1982; Malloy, Fairbank, & Keaner, 1983; Pitman, Orr, Forgue, de Jong, & Clairborn, 1987). Such symptoms can also be provoked pharmacologically by the adrenergic alpha-2 receptor antagonist, yohimbine, that acts directly upon the locus coeruleus in the brain (Southwick, et al., 1992).

The *avoidant/numbing* criterion, Criterion C, consists of symptoms reflecting behavioral, cognitive, or emotional strategies by which PTSD patients attempt to reduce the likelihood that they either will expose themselves to traumamimetic stimuli or, if exposed, will minimize the intensity of their psychological response. Behavioral strategies include avoiding any situation in which patients perceive a risk of confronting such stimuli. In its most extreme manifestation, avoidant behavior may superficially resemble agoraphobia because the person suffering from PTSD is afraid to leave the house for fear of confronting reminders of the traumatic event(s). Dissociation and psychogenic amnesia are included among avoidant/numbing symptoms by which individuals cut off the conscious experience of trauma-based memories and feelings.

Finally, because individuals with PTSD cannot tolerate strong emotions, especially those associated with the traumatic experience, they separate the cognitive from the emotional aspects of psychological experience and perceive only the former. Robert Lifton, observing this phenomenon in Hiroshima atom bomb survivors and later in Vietnam combat veterans, labeled it *psychic numbing* (1976; 1979). Psychic numbing is an emotional anesthesia that makes it extremely difficult for people with PTSD to participate in meaningful interpersonal relationships. There has been no change between *DSM–III–R* and *DSM–IV* for C symptoms.

Symptoms included in the D or *hyperarousal* criterion most closely resemble those in panic and generalized anxiety disorder. Whereas symptoms such as insomnia and irritability are generic anxiety symptoms, hypervigilance and startle are more unique. The hypervigilance in PTSD may sometimes become so intense as to appear like frank paranoia. The startle response has a unique neurobiological substrate (Davis, 1990) and may actually be the most pathognomonic PTSD symptom (Ornitz & Pynoos, 1989). D symptoms have remained unchanged in *DSM–IV*, except for that *DSM–III–R* D–6 has become *DSM–IV* B–5.

The E or *duration* criterion specifies how long symptoms must persist in order to qualify for the chronic or delayed PTSD diagnosis. In *DSM–III* the mandatory duration was 6 months. In *DSM–III–R* the duration was shortened to 1 month. This has remained the criterion in *DSM–IV*. The "F" or *functional impairment* criterion is a new addition to the PTSD diagnosis in *DSM–IV*. Also new are definitions of *acute* (duration of symptoms for less than 3 months) and *chronic* (duration of symptoms for greater than 3 months) PTSD.

Theoretical Issues

PTSD differs from most other psychiatric disorders because there is a wealth of experimental literature from both psychology and neurobiology that appears pertinent to the clinical syndrome. Indeed, unlike most other psychiatric disorders, a number of animal models have been proposed for PTSD including learned helplessness/inescapable stress (Seligman & Beagley, 1975; van der Kolk, Greenberg, Boyd, & Krystal, 1985); fear potentiated startle (Davis, 1990); kindling (Friedman, 1988; van der Kolk, 1987); and time dependent sensitization (Yehuda & Antelman, 1993).

Because the hallmark of PTSD is the response to a traumatic event, and because PTSD symptoms can be triggered by exposure to traumamimetic stimuli, no other psychiatric syndrome can be conceptualized in terms of classic learning theory as well as PTSD. Keane, Zimmering, and Caddell (1985) have proposed a two-factor model of PTSD that invokes the seminal work of Mowrer (1939). Foa, et al. (1992) proposed an unpredictable/uncontrollable stress model of PTSD that is a modern extrapolation from Masserman's (1943) paradigm used to produce experimental neurosis in animals.

Other significant theoretical issues in psychology that have spurred ongoing PTSD research are a reformulation of James' (1890) model of arousal-based behavior (Blaskovich, 1990) and a reinterpretation of Lang's (1977) information processing theory of fear and anxiety (Creamer, Burgess, & Pattison, 1992; Litz & Keane, 1989). Finally, research on the appraisal process by which individuals decide whether a stressful event presents a threat or a challenge (Lazarus & Folkman, 1984) is, in our opinion, extremely relevant to cognitive processing of posttraumatic reactions as shown by Fairbank, Hansen, and Fitterling (1991). A review of this literature, however, is beyond the scope of this chapter.

As with the psychological literature, there is a wealth of pertinent neurobiological literature starting with the classic works of Cannon (1929) and Selye (1956) on adrenergic and hypothalamic-pituitary-adrenocortical (HPA) responses to stress, which has been reinterpreted by Dienstbier (1989). More recent animal research has shown that exposure to stress can produce alterations in a least seven different neurobiologic systems: adrenergic, HPA, dopaminergic, GABA-benzodiazepine, opioid, serotonergic, and NMDA (see reviews by Bremner, Davis, Southwick, Krystal, & Charney, 1993; Charney, Deutch, Krystal, Southwick, & Davis, 1993). As noted earlier, Kardiner (1941) was the first to suggest that World War I veterans with war neurosis were suffering from a central nervous system disorder that he labeled a *physioneurosis*. It has also been suggested that the cardiovascular and other medical abnormalities (e.g., neurocirculatory asthenia) seen in World War II veterans (Cohen, White, & Johnson, 1948) may have actually reflected the underlying pathophysiology of PTSD (Friedman, 1991).

Recent findings in patients with PTSD suggest that the disorder may be associated with stable neurobiological alterations in both the central and autonomic nervous systems. Patients with combat-related PTSD have been shown to exhibit physiologic hyperarousal manifested by cardiovascular hyperactivity (Blanchard, et al., 1982), increased sensitivity and augmentation of the acoustic-startle eyeblink reflex (Ornitz & Pynoos, 1989), a reducer pattern of auditory evoked cortical potentials (Paige, Reid, Allen, & Newton, 1990), and sleep abnormalities (Ross, Ball, Sullivan, & Caroff, 1989). Stable neurobiological abnormalities have also been detected in the central noradrenergic, HPA, and endogenous opioid systems. These studies are reviewed extensively elsewhere (Bremner, et al., 1993; Charney, et al., 1992; Friedman, 1991; Friedman, Charney, & Deutch, 1995).

A number of animal models have been invoked to account for the observed stability of PTSD symptoms over time (Bremner, Southwick, & Charney, 1991; Friedman, 1988; van der Kolk, 1987; Yehuda, & Antelman, 1993). Many of these models postulate that exposure to trauma produces significant alteration and sensitization of crucial brain mechanisms that are not only responsible for the persistence of PTSD symptoms but also for increased vulnerability to the impact of subsequent traumatic events.

Diagnostic Issues

Since PTSD has been an official diagnosis, there has been much greater clinical sensitivity to the impact of trauma on other psychiatric disorders. For instance, recent research has shown that childhood sexual or physical abuse is the rule rather than the exception in borderline personality disorder, multiple personality disorder, and somatization disorder (Davidson, 1993; Herman, 1992). Other DSM–IV disorders in which prior exposure to extreme physical or psychological stress appears to be instrumental include brief reactive psychosis, dissociative fugue, dissociative amnesia, conversion disorder, depersonalization disorder, dream anxiety disorder, and antisocial personality disorder (Davidson, 1993). There is also emerging evidence to suggest that at least some cases of attention deficit hyperactivity disorder in children can be ascribed to exposure to trauma before the age of 3 (Perry, 1994). In other words, although PTSD may be the most unequivocal and most easily diagnosed consequence of traumatic exposure, there are a number of other psychiatric disorders that may be caused or exacerbated by extreme stress.

The most important diagnostic controversy in the trauma field revolves around the fact that the PTSD syndrome does not include those symptoms most often seen in victims of prolonged interpersonal violence such as childhood incest, repeated domestic violence, prolonged captivity, or protracted torture. A new syndrome, proposed by Herman (1992), has had several named: victimization disorder, complex PTSD, or disorder of extreme stress not otherwise specified (DESNOS). Herman has proposed an alternative diagnostic formulation that emphasizes excessive somatization, dissociation, changes in affect, pathological changes in relationships, pathological changes in identity, self-injurious or suicidal behavior, and revictimization. She has argued that diagnoses such as borderline personality disorder, multiple personality disorder, and somatization disorder can be more appropriately conceptualized and treated as manifestations of DESNOS. However, data from field trials on the prevalence of DESNOS conducted by the *DSM–IV* PTSD Task Force did not result in the inclusion of DESNOS in the *DSM–IV*. Clearly, additional studies are needed.

Research Design Issues

According to King and King (1991), much of the PTSD research is questionable because of numerous flaws in research design and statistical analysis. In their detailed review of validity issues in research on Vietnam War veteran adjustment, King and King (1991) concluded that

> the full causal network of factors regarding Vietnam veteran status is yet to be understood; and the accumulated literature, literally hundreds of studies, is fraught with threats to validity. Although recognizing that the methodological sophistication of Vietnam veteran studies has certainly improved over the past two decades, we maintain that many discrepant findings and conclusions can be attributed to differences in methodological approaches and certain weaknesses in the logic on which causal inferences are based. (pp. 107–108)

King and King (1991) offer a careful and detailed analysis of issues related to Cook and Campbell's (1979) classic monograph on design and analysis issues in quasi-experimental research designs typical of field research strategies in which the rigors of laboratory experimentation cannot be met. King and King (1991) discuss statistical conclusion validity, internal validity, construct validity of cause and effect, and external validity issues. Furthermore, the problems noted by King and King (1991) are compounded when ethnocultural differences are the topic of research. This is because of the rigorous requirements of cross-cultural research designed to limit ethnocentric bias in such areas as sampling, clinical criteria, measurement, and data analysis (see Marsella, Friedman, & Spain, 1993).

Clinical Issues

Comorbidity

If an individual meets diagnostic criteria for PTSD, it is likely that he or she will meet *DSM–IV* criteria for one or more additional diagnoses (Davidson and Foa, 1993; Kulka, et al., 1990). Most often, these comorbid diagnoses include major affective disorders or personality disorders. There is a legitimate question whether the high rate of diagnostic comorbidity seen with PTSD diagnoses is an artifact of our current decision rules for making the PTSD diagnosis because there are no exclusionary criteria in the *DSM–IV*. For example, Yehuda et al., (1993) have shown that the major depressive disorder (MDD) that often accompanies PTSD is a very different biological abnormality than primary major depression. These results suggest that the MDD seen with PTSD is actually a part of the PTSD syndrome itself rather than a comorbid depressive disorder as it currently must be classified by *DSM–IV*. The same argument may apply to other comorbid diagnoses such as panic disorder, generalized anxiety disorder, and obsessive–compulsive disorder. At the present time, however, high rates of comorbidity complicate treatment decisions concerning patients with PTSD because the clinician must decide whether to treat the comorbid disorders concurrently or sequentially. This is especially true when PTSD is comorbid with alcoholism or substance abuse (Kofoed, Friedman, & Peck, 1993).

Longitudinal Course and Chronicity

Longitudinal studies have shown that PTSD can persist for decades and sometimes for a lifetime. In their 20-year follow-up of World War II veterans, Archibald and Tuddenham (1965) found that veterans with PTSD ("war neurosis" [sic]) not only continued to exhibit such symptoms but, in many cases, exhibited a worsened clinical status over time. Studies of World War II American military veterans, prisoners of war, and Dutch resistance fighters have shown that PTSD was present and virulent after 40 years (see review by Schnurr, 1991).

Longitudinal outcomes are variable, however. Whereas some trauma survivors may become free of most or all PTSD symptoms previously exhibited, others may remain seriously affected (Blank, 1993). Patients with persistent PTSD may manifest a chronic mental disorder with a longitudinal course marked by remissions and relapses (Friedman & Rosenheck, in press). Unlike schizophrenia and affective disorders, however, the triggers for relapse in PTSD are more readily identifiable. Such relapses often appear to be precipitated by further exposure to traumatic stimuli and situations. For example, during the massive 1990–91 deployment of troops to the Persian Gulf, American print and broadcast media bombarded the public with information about the war. It appears that such war-related stimuli may have precipitated or exacerbated PTSD symptoms in older veterans because there was a marked increase in the number of veterans seeking treatment for PTSD from VA facilities (Gelsomino, Hayman, & Walker, 1992; Wolfe, Brown, & Buscela, 1992).

Although PTSD is not inherently a persistent mental disorder, there are patients with PTSD who are severely and chronically incapacitated. Like people with schizophrenia, these patients are severely ill, their social functioning is markedly restricted, and they often rely heavily on public housing, community support, and public mental health services. For some patients, PTSD is severe enough to result in repeated hospitalizations over many years and to require ongoing outpatient treatment as a persistent mental disorder (Friedman & Rosenheck, in press).

Treatment

Solomon, Gerrity, and Muff, (1992) reviewed recent treatment literature and showed that out of 255 published articles on treatment for PTSD only 11 can be considered satisfactory randomized therapeutic trials (see also chapter 3 by Gerrity & Solomon in this volume). These include five drug trials, four studies on behavioral treatment, one study on cognitive–behavioral therapy, and one study comparing psychodynamic therapy, behavioral therapy, and hypnotherapy. Results from drug trials were inconsistent, whereas findings with behavioral treatment were more encouraging.

The most dramatic clinical improvement was reported by Foa and colleagues (Foa, Rothbaum, Murdock, & Riggs, 1991), who demonstrated the efficacy of cognitive–behavioral treatment for rape victims with PTSD in a randomized clinical trial. In addition, there are numerous reports on the effectiveness of cognitive–behavioral, psychodynamic, pharmacotherapeutic, group, and other treatments for PTSD (Marmar, Foy, Kagan, & Pynoos, 1993; Williams & Sommer, in press). However, as noted previously (Solomon et al., 1992; Gerrity & Solomon, this volume) there are few published randomized clinical trials to back-up claims of therapeutic efficacy.

Herman (1992) asserts that most treatment approaches for PTSD consist of three stages. In Stage 1, the emphasis is on establishing a safe environment, stabilization, and building trust. In Stage 2, the patient tells the story of the trauma. The major therapeutic task at this stage is to explore, reexperience, and integrate the traumatic memories and feelings that continue to intrude on the present. Stage 3 is devoted to integration of the trauma, personality rehabilitation, development of coping skills, and reconnection to family and society.

There are particular problems in assessment and treatment of patients from non-Western backgrounds. Most of the writing on this subject covers treatment of refugees and is reviewed in detail elsewhere (Friedman & Jaranson, 1994; Kinzie, 1989; Marsella, Borneman, Ekblad, & Orley, 1994; Owan, 1985; Westermeyer, 1989). Some therapeutic issues that need to be considered with regard to refugees are that treatment is often avoided until the patient is severely ill, and has multiple somatic complaints, severe depression or dissociative and paranoid symptoms. Building trust and establishing a safe therapeutic environment may be especially difficult when the therapist is from a different cultural or racial background than the patient. Futhermore, language problems or the need to use interpreters may compound these difficulties. In addition, culturally-based willingness to accept different therapeutic formats (e.g., individual vs. group) may have a decisive impact on the therapeutic process. And of course, the cultural sensitivity and sophistication of the therapist is of paramount importance when discussing pertinent aspects of the trauma, such as those related to sexual matters or to death.

Risk Factors

The original *DSM–III* formulation emphasized that exposure to the traumatic event itself was primarily responsible for the later development of PTSD. It rejected the psychodynamic concept of war neurosis that was predicated on pretraumatic vulnerability. It was asserted that whereas individual differences, with regard to vulnerability or resilience, might have a major impact in mediating the consequences of ordinary stress, they were of little value when it came to mediating the impact of traumatic stress. Support for this position came from numerous studies showing that the best predictor of developing PTSD was the intensity of the trauma itself rather than personal psychological factors. For example, higher levels of PTSD were repeatedly found among Vietnam veterans who had experienced the highest levels of exposure to extreme events in the war zone (Kulka, et al., 1990). A similar dose–response relationship between trauma intensity and PTSD prevalence rates has been found in physically injured sexual assault victims (Winfield, George, Swartz, & Blazer, 1990), children exposed to a school yard sniper attack (Pynoos, et al., 1987), survivors of the Mount St. Helens volcanic eruption (Shore, Tatum, & Vollmer, 1986), and Australian firefighters who battled a large bush fire (McFarlane, 1988).

Despite this strong relationship, exposure to trauma is not a sufficient condition for the later development of PTSD. Many people exposed to war, interpersonal violence, or other trauma never develop the full PTSD syndrome (Breslau et al., 1991; Kulka et al., 1990). This has prompted research on risk factors for PTSD. Such research has focused on pretraumatic, traumatic, and posttraumatic factors.

Summarizing a number of studies, Davidson (1993) lists the following as risk factors for PTSD: positive history of psychiatric illness among first-degree relatives, early sexual or other childhood trauma, parental poverty, behavior disorder in childhood or adolescence, separation or divorce of parents before 10 years of age, high neuroticism, introversion, prior psychiatric disorder, poor self-confidence before age 15, life stress before and after the trauma, and being female. Fontana and Rosenheck (1993), focusing on Vietnam veterans, add the following pretrauma variables to Davidson's list: a background of academic difficulty, an unstable or problematic family, a father who had been in combat, problems with authorities, illegal drug use, and ethnic minority status. Finally, researchers have shown that among Dartmouth College graduates who later served in Vietnam freshman MMPI scores were predictive of later development of lifetime PTSD (Schnurr, Friedman, & Rosenburg, 1993).

In addition to severity and pretraumatic factors, the nature of the traumatic experience may affect the likelihood of developing PTSD. For veterans, being wounded in combat, witnessing or participating in abusive violence or atrocities, or receiving a disciplinary action such as a court martial has been reported to be related to the severity of PTSD (Fontana & Rosenheck, 1993). For rape victims, important factors appear to be prior acquaintance with the perpetrator, or threat to life (Herman, 1992).

Finally posttraumatic factors may have an important influence on facilitating recovery or promoting the development of PTSD. For instance, because the first 24 to 72 hours following traumatic exposure are particularly decisive, rapid therapeutic intervention such as critical-incident stress debriefing within this crucial period can often prevent the later development of PTSD (Mitchell, 1983). The quality of the posttrauma recovery environment may also determine the long-term clinical outcome (Williams & Summer, 1994). There is also reason to believe that social support, availability of help, and availability of someone in whom to confide about the trauma can reduce the likelihood of developing PTSD (Fontana & Rosenheck, 1993).

Ethnocultural Traditions and Vulnerability to PTSD

There are many possible interactions between ethnocultural traditions and vulnerability to PTSD. For instance, given evidence that a number of neurobiological systems are affected by exposure to trauma and altered in individuals who suffer from PTSD, it is possible that genetic differences may confer greater or less vulnerability to PTSD on people from different ethnocultural backgrounds (see chapter 20 in the present volume by Lin, Poland, Anderson, & Lesser).

Through historical events and accidents of geography, some ethnocultural groups have had more exposure to trauma than others. In some cases cultures have developed institutions or rituals for addressing the impact of traumatic exposure For example, the Navajo Enemy Way ceremony represents that culture's ritualized attempt to cleanse returning warriors from the deleterious impact of war trauma and to help them readjust to a peace-time society (see Manson et al., this volume). The ceremony is predicated on Navajo society's understanding that warriors may experience profound psychological consequences because of their exposure to the trauma of war. Family and the tribe accept responsibility for the impact of trauma on their courageous young men. The healing ceremony, the Enemy Way, is a ritual in which the extended family, clan, and surrounding community members actively join the warrior. Such collective acceptance of ceremonial participation facilitates processing of war trauma and reintegration into peacetime Navajo society.

Religion and cultural beliefs may differentially influence the meaning and subjective experience of trauma. For example, a terrifying physical ordeal might be appraised as a rite of passage in one cultural setting and as a traumatic event in another. Eastern versus Western beliefs about individual responsibility and the capacity of individuals to influence events may have profoundly different effects on the appraisal, meaning, and psychological impact of traumatic events. Futhermore, different ethnocultural practices may have a direct bearing on PTSD symptoms themselves as defined by the *DSM–IV*. For example, the meaning, experience, and subjective context for stress-induced dissociation may be very different for a Zen Buddhist monk than for an adult incest survivor of the Western world.

Finally, current information regarding risk factors for PTSD (Fairbank, Schlenger, Saigh, & Davidson, 1995) suggests that individuals from cultures that provide family stability, environmental safety, community support, and low rates of drug use might be less vulnerable to PTSD than others. Likewise, we would predict better long-term outcomes for traumatized individuals who are enmeshed in a culture where open discussion of the trauma is encouraged, where survivorship is honored, where victimization is not stigmatized, and where posttraumatic problems are normalized. The remainder of this volume is devoted to exploring some of these issues through more detailed discussions.

REFERENCES

Allende, I. (1991). Our secret. *The stories of Eva Luna* (pp. 184–187). New York: Bantam.

American Psychiatric Association (1980). *Diagnostic and statistical manual of mental disorders* (3rd ed.). Washington, DC: Author.

American Psychiatric Association. (1987). *Diagnostic and statistical manual of mental disorders* (3rd ed., rev.). Washington, DC: Author.

American Psychiatric Association. (1994). *Diagnostic and statistical manual of mental disorders* (4th ed.). Washington, DC: Author.

Archibald, H. C., & Tuddenham, R. D. (1965). Persistent stress reaction after combat: A 20-year follow-up. *Archives of General Psychiatry, 12*, 475–781.

Blanchard, E. B., Kolb, L. C., Pallmeyer, B. A., & Gerardi, R. J. (1982). A psychophysiological study of post-traumatic stress disorder in Vietnam veterans. *Psychiatric Quarterly, 54*, 220–229.

Blank, A. (1993). The longitudinal course of posttraumatic stress disorder. In J. R. T. Davidson & E. B. Foa (Eds.), *Post-traumatic stress disorder: DSM–IV and beyond.* Washington, DC: American Psychiatric Press.

Blascovitch, J. (1990). Individual differences in arousal and somatic self-perception: Missing links in Jamesian notions of arousal-based social behaviors. *Personality & Social Psychology Bulletin, 16*, 665–674.

Bremner, J. D., Davis, M., Southwick, S. M., Krystal, J. H., & Charney, D. S. (1993). Neurobiology of post-traumatic stress disorder. In J. M. Oldham, M. B. Riba, & A. Tasman (Eds.), *Review of psychiatry: Vol. 12.* Washington, DC: American Psychiatric Press.

Bremner, J. D., Southwick, S. M., & Charney, D. S. (1991). Animal models for the neurobiology of trauma. *PTSD Research Quarterly, 2*(4), 1–7.

Breslau, N., Davis, G. C., Andreski, P., & Peterson, E. (1991). Traumatic events and post-traumatic stress disorder in an urban population of young adults. *Archives of General Psychiatry, 48*, 216–222.

Cannon, W. B. (1929). *Bodily changes in pain, hunger, fear, and rage* (2nd ed.). Boston: Branford.

Chakraborty, A. (1991). Culture, colonialism, and psychiatry. *Lancet, 337*, 1204–1207.

Charney, D. S., Deutch, A. Y., Krystal, J. H., Southwick, S. M., & Davis, M. (1993). Psychobiologic mechanisms of post-traumatic stress disorder. *Archives of General Psychiatry, 50*, 294–305.

Cohen, M. E., White P. D., & Johnson, R. E. (1948). Neurocirculatory asthenia, anxiety neurosis, or the effort syndrome. *Archives of Internal Medicine, 81*, 260–281.

Conyer, R. C. T., Amor, J. S., Medina-Mora, E. M., Caraveo, J., & De la Fuente, J. R. (1987). Prevalence of post-traumatic stress syndrome in survivors of a natural disaster. *Salud Publico de Mexico* [Public Health of Mexico], *29*, 406–411.

Cook, T., & Campbell, D. (1979). *Quasi-experimentation: Design and analysis issues for field settings. Chicago: Rand-McNally.*

Creamer, M., Burgess, P., & Pattison, P. (1992). Reaction to trauma: A cognitive processing model. *Journal of Abnormal Psychology, 101*, 452–459.

Davidson, J. (1993). Issues in the diagnosis of posttraumatic stress disorder. In J. M. Oldham, M. B. Riba, & A. Tasman (Eds.), *Review of psychiatry: Vol. 12.* Washington, DC: American Psychiatric Press.

Davidson, J., & Foa, E. (Eds.). (1993). *Post-traumatic stress disorder: DSM–IV and beyond*. Washington, DC: American Psychiatric Press.

Davis, M. (1990). Animal models of anxiety based on classical conditioning: The conditioned emotional response and fear potentiated startle effect. *Pharmacology & Therapeutics, 47*, 147–165.

Dienstbier, R. A. (1989). Arousal and physiological toughness: Implications for mental and physical health. *Psychological Review, 96*, 84–100.

Erdrich, L. (1984). The red convertible. *Love medicine* (pp. 147–48). New York: Holt, Rinehart, & Winston.

Fairbank, J. A., Hansen, D. J., & Fitterling, J. M. (1991). Patterns of appraisal and coping across different stressor conditions among former prisoners of war with and without post-traumatic stress disorder. *Journal of Consulting and Clinical Psychology, 59*, 274–281.

Fairbank, J. A., Schlenger, W. E., Saigh, P. A., & Davidson, J. R. T. (1995). An epidemiologic profile of post-traumatic stress disorder: Prevalence, comorbidity, and risk factors. In M. J. Friedman, D. S. Charney, & A. V. Deutch (Eds.), *Neurobiological and clinical consequences of stress: From normal adaptation to post-traumatic stress disorder*. Philadelphia/New York: Lippencott–Raven.

Fairley, M. (1984). *Tropical cyclone Oscar: Psychological reactions of a Fijian population*. Paper presented at the meeting of the Disaster Research Workshop, Mt. Macedon, Victoria, Australia.

Figley, C. R. (1993). Foreword. In J. P. Wilson & B. Raphael (Eds.), *International handbook of traumatic stress syndromes* (pp. xvii–xx). New York: Plenum Press.

Foa, E. B., Rothbaum, B. O., Murdock, T., & Riggs, D. S. (1991). The treatment of PTSD in rape victims. *Journal of Consulting and Clinical Psychology, 59*, 715–723.

Foa, E. B., Zenberg, R., & Rothbaum, B. O. (1992). Uncontrollability and unpredictability of post-traumatic stress disorder: An animal model. *Psychological Bulletin, 112*, 218–238.

Fontana, A., & Rosenheck, R. (1993). A causal model of the etiology of war-related PTSD. *Journal of Traumatic Stress, 6*, 37–62.

Friedman, M. J. (1988). Towards rational pharmacotherapy for post-traumatic stress disorder. *American Journal of Psychiatry, 145*, 281–285.

Friedman, M. J. (1991). Biological approaches to the diagnosis and treatment of post-traumatic stress disorder. *Journal of Traumatic Stress, 4*, 67–91.

Friedman, M. J., Charney, D. S., & Deutch, A. Y. (1995). *Neurobiological and clinical consequences of stress: From normal adaptation to PTSD*. Philadelphia/New York: Lippencott–Raven.

Friedman, M. J., & Jaranson, J. M. (1994). The applicability of the PTSD concept to refugees. In A. J. Marsella, T. H. Borneman, S. Ekblad, & J. Orley (Eds.), *Amidst peril and pain: The mental health and well-being of the world's refugees* (pp. 207–228). Washington, DC: American Psychological Press.

Friedman, M. J., & Rosenheck, R. A. (in press). PTSD as a persistent mental illness. In. S. Soreff (Ed.), *The seriously and persistently mentally ill: The state-of-the-art treatment handbook*. Seattle, WA: Hogrefe & Huber.

Gelsomino, J., Hayman, P., & Walker, J. (1992). ODS clinical activities. *NCP Clinical Newsletter, 2*(2), 14–18.

Green, B. L. (1993). Identifying survivors at risk: Trauma and stressors across events. In J. P. Wilson & B. Raphael (Eds.), *International handbook of traumatic stress syndromes* (pp. 135-144). New York: Plenum Press.

Helzer, J. E., Robins, L. N., & McEvoy, L. (1987). Post-traumatic stress disorder in the general population: Findings of the epidemiologic catchment area survey. *New England Journal of Medicine, 317*, 1630–1634.

Herman, J. L. (1992). *Trauma and recovery*. New York: Basic Books.

James, W. (1890). *The principles of psychology*. New York: Holt.

Kardiner, A. (1941). The traumatic neuroses of war. *Psychosomatic Medicine, Monograph (I-II)*. Washington, DC: National Research Council.

Keane, T. M. (1990). The epidemiology of post-traumatic stress disorder: Some comments and concerns. *PTSD Research Quarterly, 1*, 1–7.

Keane, T. M., & Penk, W. E. (1988). The prevalence of post-traumatic stress disorder. *New England Journal of Medicine, 318*, 1690–1691.

Keane, T. M., Zimering, R. T., Caddell, J. M. (1985). A behavioral formulation of posttraumatic stress disorder in Vietnam veterans. *Behavior Therapy, 8*, 9–12.

King, D., & King, L. (1991). Validity issues in research on Vietnam veteran adjustment. *Psychological Bulletin, 109*, 107–124.

Kinzie, J. D. (1989). Therapeutic approaches to traumatized Cambodian refugees. *Journal of Traumatic Stress, 2*, 75–91.

Kinzie, J. D. (1993). Posttraumatic effects and their treatment among Southeast Asian refugees. In J. P. Wilson & B. Raphael (Eds.), *International handbook of traumatic stress syndromes* (pp. 311–320). New York: Plenum Press.

Kofoed, L., Friedman, M. J., & Peck, R. (1993). Alcoholism and drug abuse in patients with PTSD. *Psychiatric Quarterly, 64*, 151–171.

Kulka, R. A., Schlenger, W. E., Fairbank, J. A., Hough, R. P., Jordan, B. K., Marmar, C. R., & Weiss, D. S. (1990). *Trauma and the Vietnam War generation*. New York: Brunner/Mazel.

Lang, P. J. (1977). Imagery in therapy: An information processing analysis of fear. *Behavior Therapy, 8*, 862–886.

Lazarus, R. S., & Folkman, S. (1984). *Stress, appraisal and coping*. New York: Springer.

Lifton, R. J. (1976). *Death in life*. New York: Touchstone.

Lifton, R. J. (1979). *The broken connection*. New York: Touchstone.

Lima, B. R., Chavez, H., Samaniego, N., Pompei, M. S., Pai, S., Santacruz, H., & Lorenzo, J. (1989). Disaster severity and emotional disturbance: Implications for primary mental health care in developing nations. *Acta Psychiatrica Scandinavica, 79,* 74–82.

Lima, B. R., Pai, S., Santacruz, H., Lozano, J., & Luna, J. (1987). Screening for the psychological consequences of a major disaster in a developing country: Armero, Colombia. *Acta Psychiatrica Scandinavica, 76,* 561–567.

Litz, B. T., & Keane, T. M. (1989). Information processing in anxiety disorders: Application to the understanding of post-traumatic stress disorder. *Clinical Psychology Review, 9,* 243–257.

Malloy, P. F., Fairbank, J. A., & Keane, T. M. (1983). Validation of a multimethod assessment of post-traumatic stress disorders in Vietnam veterans. *Journal of Consulting & Clinical Psychology, 51,* 488–494.

Marmar, C. R., Foy, D., Kagan, B., & Pynoos, R. S. (1993). An integrated approach for treating posttraumatic stress. In J. M. Oldham, M. B. Riba, & A. Tasman (Eds.), *Review of psychiatry: Vol. 12.* Washington, DC: American Psychiatric Press.

Marsella, A. J., Bornemann, T., Ekblad, S., & Orley, J. (1994). *Amidst peril and pain: The mental health and well-being of the world's refugees.* Washington, DC: American Psychological Association.

Marsella, A. J., Friedman, M. J., & Spain, H. (1993). Ethnocultural aspects of PTSD: An overview of issues, research and directions. In J. M. Oldham, M. B. Riba, & A. Tasman. *Review of Psychiatry: Vol. 12* (pp 157–181). Washington, DC: American Psychiatric Press.

Masserman, J. H. (1943). *Behavior and neurosis: An experimental psychoanalytic approach to psychobiologic principles.* Chicago: University of Chicago Press.

McFarlane, A. C. (1988). The longitudinal cause of post-traumatic morbidity: The range of outcomes and their predictors. *Journal of Nervous & Mental Disease, 176,* 30–39.

McFarlane, A. C., & Hua, C. (1993). Study of a major disaster in the People's Republic of China: The Yunnan earthquake. In J. P. Wilson & B. Raphael (Eds.), *International handbook of traumatic stress syndromes* (pp. 493–498). New York: Plenum Press.

Mitchell, J. T. (1983). When disaster strikes: The critical incident stress debriefing. *Journal of Medical Emergency Services, 8,* 36–39.

Mowrer, O. H. (1939). A stimulus–response analysis of anxiety and its role as a reinforcing agent. *Psychological Review, 46,* 553–565.

Odaira, T., Iwadate, T., & Raphael, B. (1993). Earthquakes and traumatic stress: Early human reactions in Japanese society. In J. P. Wilson & B. Raphael (Eds.), *International handbook of traumatic stress syndromes* (pp. 487–492). New York: Plenum Press.

Ornitz, E. M., & Pynoos, R. S. (1989). Startle modulation in children with post-traumatic stress disorder. *American Journal of Psychiatry, 146,* 866–870.

Owan, T. (1985). *Southeast Asian mental health: Treatment, prevention, services, training, and research.* Washington, DC: U.S. Department of Health & Human Services.

Paige, S., Reid, G., Allen, M., & Newton, J. (1990). Psychophysiological correlates of PTSD. *Biological Psychiatry, 27,* 419–430.

Patrick V., & Patrick, W. R. (1981). Cyclone 78 in Sri Lanka—The mental health trail. *British Journal of Psychiatry, 138,* 210–216.

Perry, B. (1994). Neurobiological sequelae of childhood trauma: Post-traumatic stress disorders in children. In M. M. Murburg (Ed.), *Catecholamine function in PTSD: Emerging concepts.* (pp. 233–255). Washington, DC: American Psychiatric Press.

Pitman, R. K., Orr, S. P., Forgue, D. F., de Jong, J. B., & Clairborn, J. M. (1987). Psychophysiologic assessment of post-traumatic stress disorder imagery in Vietnam combat veterans. *Archives of General Psychiatry, 44,* 970–975.

Pynoos, R., Frederick, C., Nader, K., Arroyo, W., Steinberg, A., Eth, S., Nunez, F., & Fairbanks, L. (1987). Life threat and post-traumatic stress in school-age children. *Archives of General Psychiatry, 44,* 1057–1063.

Ross, R. J., Ball, W. A., Sullivan, K. A., & Caroff, S. N. (1989). Sleep disturbance as the hallmark of post-traumatic stress disorder. *American Journal of Psychiatry, 146,* 697–707.

Schnurr, P. P. (1991). PTSD and combat-related psychiatric symptoms in older veterans. *PTSD Research Quarterly, 2,* 1–6.

Schnurr, P. P., Friedman, M. J., & Rosenberg, S. D. (1993). Premilitary MMPI scores as predictors of combat-related PTSD symptoms. *American Journal of Psychiatry, 150,* 479–483.

Seligman, M. E. P., & Beagley, G. (1975). Learned helplessness in the rat. *Journal of Comparative & Physiological Psychology, 88,* 534–541.

Selye, H. (1956). *The stress of life.* New York: McGraw-Hill.

Shay, J. (1991). Learning about combat stress from Homer's Iliad. *Journal of Traumatic Stress 4,* 561–579.

Shore, J. H., Tatum, E. L., & Vollmer, W. M. (1986). The Mount St. Helens stress response syndrome. In J. H. Shore (Ed.), *Disaster stress studies: New methods and findings.* Washington, DC: American Psychiatric Press.

Simpson, M. A. (1993). Traumatic stress and the bruising of the soul: The effects of torture and coercive interrogation. In J. P. Wilson & B. Raphael (Eds.), *International handbook of traumatic stress syndromes* (pp. 667–684). New York: Plenum Press.

Solomon, S. D., Gerrity, E. T., & Muff, A. M. (1992). Efficacy of treatments for post-traumatic stress disorder: An empirical review. *Journal of the American Medical Association, 268,* 633–638.

Somasundaram, D. J. (1993). Psychiatric morbidity due to war in Northern Sri Lanka. In J. P. Wilson & B. Raphael (Eds.), *International handbook of traumatic stress syndromes* (pp. 349–364). New York: Plenum Press.

Southwick, S. M., Krystal, J. H., Johnson, D. R., & Charney, D. S. (1992). Neurobiology of posttraumatic stress disorder. In A. Tasman (Ed.), *Annual review of psychiatry* (pp. 347–370). Washington, DC: American Psychiatric Press.

Trimble, M. (1981). *Post-traumatic neurosis: From railway spine to the whiplash*. New York: John Wiley.

van der Kolk, B. A. (1987). The drug treatment of post-traumatic stress disorder. *Journal of Affective Disorders, 13*, 203–213.

van der Kolk, B. A., Greenberg, M., Boyd, H., & Krystal, J. (1985). Inescapable shock, neurotransmitters, and addiction to trauma: Toward a psychobiology of post-traumatic stress. *Biological Psychiatry, 20*, 314–325.

Veith, I. (1965). *Hysteria: The history of a disease*. Chicago: University of Chicago Press.

Wardak, A. W. H. (1993). The psychiatric effects of war stress on Afghanistan society. In J. P. Wilson & B. Raphael (Eds.), *International handbook of traumatic stress syndromes* (pp. 349–364). New York: Plenum Press.

Westermeyer, J. (1989). Psychiatric care of migrants: A clinical guide. In J. H. Gould (Ed.), Washington, DC: American Psychiatric Press.

Williams, M. B., & Sommer, J. F. (Eds.). (1994). *Handbook of post-traumatic therapy*. Westport, CT: Greenwood Press.

Winfield, I., George, L. K., Swartz, M. S., & Blazer, D. G. (1990). Sexual assault and psychiatric disorders among women in a community population. *American Journal of Psychiatry, 147*, 335–341.

Wolfe, J., Brown, P. J., & Bucsela, M. L. (1992). Symptom responses of female Vietnam veterans to Operation Desert Storm. *American Journal of Psychiatry, 149*, 676–679.

Yehuda, R., & Antelman, S. (1993). Criteria for rationally evaluating animal models of posttraumatic stress disorder. *Biological Psychiatry, 33*, 479–486.

Yehuda, R., Southwick, S. M., Krystal, J. H., Bremner, D., Charney, D. S., & Mason, J. W. (1993). Enhanced suppression of cortisol following dexamethasone administration in post-traumatic stress disorder. *American Journal of Psychiatry, 150*, 83–86.

APPENDIX
DSM–IV CRITERIA FOR PTSD
(American Psychiatric Association, 1994)

A. The person has been exposed to a traumatic event in which both of the following were present:

    (1) the person experienced, witnessed, or been confronted with an event or events that involved actual or threatened death or serious injury, or a threat to the physical integrity of self or others

    (2) the person's response involved intense fear, helplessness, or horror. Note: In children, this may be expressed instead by disorganized or agitated behavior.

B. The traumatic event is persistently reexperienced in one (or more) of the following ways:

    (1) recurrent and intrusive distressing recollections of the event, including images, thoughts, or perceptions. Note: In young children, repetitive play may occur in which themes or aspects of the trauma are expressed.

    (2) recurrent distressing dreams of the event. Note: In children, there may be frightening dreams without recognizable content.

    (3) acting or feeling as if the traumatic event were recurring (includes a sense of reliving the experience, illusions, hallucinations, and dissociative flashback episodes, including those that occur on awakening or when intoxicated. Note: In young children, trauma-specific reenactment may occur.

    (4) intense psychological distress at exposure to internal or external cues that symbolize or resemble an aspect of the traumatic event

    (5) physiological reactivity on exposure to internal or external cues that symbolize or resemble an aspect of the traumatic event

C. Persistent avoidance of stimuli associated with the trauma and numbing of general responsiveness (not present before the trauma), as indicated by three (or more) of the following:

    (1) efforts to avoid thoughts, feelings, or conversations associated with the trauma

    (2) efforts to avoid activities, places, or people that arouse recollections of the trauma

    (3) inability to recall an important aspect of the trauma

    (4) markedly diminished interest or participation in significant activities;

    (5) feeling of detachment or estrangement from others

    (6) restricted range of affect (e.g., unable to have loving feelings)

From *Diagnostic and Statistical Manual of Mental Disorders, Fourth Edition.* Copyright 1994 by the American Psychiatric Association. Reprinted with permission of the publisher.

(7) sense of a foreshortened future (e.g., does not expect to have a career, marriage, children, or a normal life span)

D. Persistent symptoms of increased arousal (not present before the trauma), as indicated by two (or more) of the following:
   (1) difficulty falling or staying asleep
   (2) irritability or outbursts of anger
   (3) difficulty concentrating
   (4) hypervigilance
   (5) exaggerated startle response

E. Duration of the disturbance (Symptoms in B, C, and D) is more than one month.

F. The disturbance causes clinically significant distress or impairment in social, occupational, or other important areas of functioning.

Specify if:
   Acute: if duration of symptoms is less than three months
   Chronic: if duration of symptoms is three months or more

Specify if:
   With Delayed Onset: if onset of symptoms at least six months after the stressor

2

THE EPIDEMIOLOGY OF PTSD: A COMPREHENSIVE REVIEW OF THE INTERNATIONAL LITERATURE

GIOVANNI DE GIROLAMO and ALEXANDER C. MCFARLANE

THE IMPORTANCE OF EPIDEMIOLOGICAL STUDIES

Since posttraumatic stress disorder (PTSD) was first included in the *Diagnostic and Statistical Manual of Mental Disorders, Third Edition* (*DSM–III*) in 1980 (American Psychiatric Association [APA], 1980), the study of the epidemiology of the disorder has become a field of growing interest for researchers and clinicians. *Epidemiology*, the study of the distribution and determinants of disorder in populations (Last, 1983), is a particularly important discipline in understanding the etiology of PTSD because it provides a methodology for investigating the relative contribution of exposure and individual vulnerability.

Such information can only be obtained from studies that examine entire populations exposed to a particular trauma or representative samples. The role of the *intensity of exposure* is demonstrated by comparing prevalence rates to intensity of exposure. In contrast, the role of *vulnerability* is highlighted by determining the distinguishing characteristics of individuals who do and do not develop PTSD with similar levels of exposure.

These epidemiological investigations are also valuable in the design of treatment services after large-scale traumatic events because they provide prevalence estimates that help define the size of the affected populations. Studies conducted a significant period after the trauma also provide essential information about the chronicity of symptoms and disability, which are critical issues in arguing the case for service provision and prevention in the immediate aftermath of traumatic events.

Studying treatment-seeking populations and other unrepresentative samples provides information that answers a different set of questions. The extent to which PTSD defines and characterizes the pattern of psychological symptoms in those seeking treatment is valuable information in understanding the specificity of the trauma response and the nature of the treatment required. However there are a number of problems that arise when extrapolating from these studies, because a variety of factors influence treatment-seeking other than suffering from PTSD. The study of Brom, Kleber, and Hoffman (1993) suggests that those seeking treatment may be only 10% of a traumatized population.

This review examines the epidemiological studies of PTSD with these issues in mind and proposes the questions that epidemiological studies could usefully address in the future. Before an examination of the existing studies, the nature and prevalence of the different types of traumatic events, namely natural disasters and man-made violence will be reviewed. This is a necessary background, because the disaster and violence data define the possible size of populations at risk for developing PTSD, in contrast to specific studies of defined events that give estimates of the prevalence within exposed populations. Information about the nature and prevalence of traumatic events helps define the size of the populations qualifying for the stressor criterion in the diagnosis of PTSD—the first step in diagnosis. This information also has both political and social ramifications when considering the differing ability of health services in different countries to provide optimal interventions and rehabilitation of communities following traumatic events.

Although many studies investigating the frequency and consequences of different types of events on human behavior have been conducted, their findings are hardly comparable because of the use of different concepts, competing diagnostic systems and assessment methodologies, and the investigation of selective and nonrepresentative samples. Only the identification of operationally defined PTSD diagnostic criteria and the refinement of assessment methodologies has made it possible to carefully investigate the epidemiology of PTSD.

Against this background, the aim of this contribution is to present a comprehensive review of the main studies of the frequency of PTSD in the general population, in clinical populations, and among subjects at risk.

TRAUMATIC EVENTS

There is a need to circumscribe the populations in whom PTSD can be considered as an important mental health issue. The stressor criteria in *International Classification of Disease, 10th Edition* (*ICD–10*) (World Health Organization [WHO], 1992a, p. 147) defines an event that may lead to PTSD as one that is either short or long-lasting and is of "an exceptionally threatening or catastrophic nature, which is likely to cause pervasive distress in almost anyone." These traumas can be divided into natural disasters and man-made violence for practical purposes.

The definitions of extremely distressing events therefore are examined to ensure that the boundaries that they define are applicable when considering the possible prevalence of PTSD. These definitions of disasters also focus on the issue that within traumatized populations there will be significant variations in the levels of exposure and the intensity of threat experienced. Therefore, the prevalence data from any study of a disaster will be partially determined by the level of exposure required before a subject can be included, given that studies of populations with high levels of exposure are likely to have higher prevalence estimates.

Definition and Taxonomy of Disasters

One conceptualization of disaster defines it as a severe disruption, ecological and psychosocial, that greatly exceeds the coping capacity of the affected community. However, such a notion implies that what is a disaster for one community might not necessarily be so for another. The difficulties of conceptualization arise because, that "upwards a disaster is unlimited, downward one has to draw a line somewhere" (Korver, 1987). Moreover, a disaster is a very complex, multidimensional phenomenon. An event may be a disaster along certain dimensions (ecological, economic, material, psychological, or social) without being one along all of these dimensions for any specific event (WHO, 1992b). The determination of the complexity of a disasterous event either may be dependent on the nature of the event itself or primarily on the consequences of the event.

There are many possible ways to classify disasters, which may have important consequences for the way people react. A recent meeting of international organizations proposed the following taxonomy of disasters (International Federation of Red Cross and Rec Crescent Societies [IFRC], 1993):

Natural and Industrial Disasters

The International Federation of the Red Cross (IFRC, 1993) has recently released a *World Disaster Report 1993*, which provides a large dataset

TABLE 1
Disaster Taxonomy

Sudden natural: e.g., avalanches, cold waves, earthquakes, floods, dam collapses, high-wind cyclones, hail storms, sand storms, storm surges, thunderstorms, tornados, landslides, earth flows, tsunamis, and volcanic eruptions.

Long-term natural: e.g., epidemics, droughts, desertification, and famine.

Sudden man-made:

- structural accidents, e.g., structural collapse, building collapse, mine collapse
- transport accidents, e.g., air, land, or sea transport disasters
- industrial technological accidents
- explosions (chemical or nuclear)
- pollution, e.g., acid rain, chemical pollution, atmosphere pollution, oil pollution
- fires

Long-term man-made: e.g., civil strife, civil war, international war, or displacement.

Note. Taxonomy proposed in the *World Disasters Report 1993* of the International Federation of Red Cross and Red Crescent Societies.

---

for the period 1967–1991. In these statistics, only those disasters that killed 10 or more or affected 100 or more people have been included. Table 2 lists the total number and percentages of events for each type of disaster occurring internationally over these 25 years, the numbers of deaths by each type of disaster, and the number of people affected. These statistics on people killed include all confirmed deaths as well as those missing and presumed dead.

Most frequent disasters

Floods (17.5%), accidents (16.5%), and storms (10.6%) have been the most frequent types of natural and industrial disaster, accounting for more than 44% of the total number of disasters. The total number of deaths due to any type of disaster is higher than 7 million; civil strife (41%) and droughts (18%) are responsible for almost 60% of that total. It is likely that the number of deaths represents an underestimate, because of underreporting, definitional problems, and difficulty in the follow-up of many affected subjects. Thus the most frequent disasters are not those that account for the most deaths.

The IFRC (1993) report points out that the estimation of the number of people affected by a particular type of disaster is extremely difficult, because there are many different standards for inclusion in such a category. The report points out that, in the case of famines and civil strife, major socioeconomic structural breakdowns are responsible for the human impact, thus numbers of the affected are almost impossible to calculate.

If one bears in mind this limitation, drought (48%) and floods (36%) have affected the largest numbers of people (approximately 2.5 billion),

TABLE 2
Types and Numbers of Disasters, Number of People Killed, and Number
of People Affected, 1967–1991

Type of Disaster	Number/ Percentage*	Number of People Killed**	Number of People Affected
Accidents	1,284 (16.5%)	71,745	418,557
Avalanche	29 (0.4)	1,237	500,000
Chemical accident	271 (3.5)	15,787	1,202,536
Civil Strife	207 (2.7)	3,007,154	135,653,524
Cold wave	92 (1.2)	4,926	71,000
Cyclone	394 (5.1)	846,240	80,485,116
Displaced persons	97 (1.3)	68,741	25,611,475
Drought	430 (5.5)	1,333,728	1,426,239,250
Epidemic	291 (3.8)	124,338	5,791,234
Earthquake	758 (9.8)	646,307	42,943,009
Famine	15 (0.2)	605,832	12,950,000
Fire	729 (9.4)	81,970	814,341
Flood	1,358 (17.5)	304,870	1,057,193,110
Food shortage	22 (0.3)	252	28,320,267
Hurricane	120 (1.6)	15,139	6,028,833
Insect infestation	66 (0.9)	—	446,000
Landslide	236 (3.0)	41,992	3,603,580
Power shortage	5 (0.1)	—	1,825,000
Storm	819 (10.6)	54,500	68,122,580
Tsunami	20 (0.3)	6,390	918
Typhoon	380 (4.9)	34,684	63,321,930
Volcano eruption	102 (1.3)	27,642	1,938,270

Note. Data taken from IFRC (1993) World Disaster Report 1993.
*Percentage of total number of disasters.
**Dashes indicate missing data.

whereas civil strife has affected more than 135 million individuals. In total, for the period 1967–1991, about 3 billion people were affected by various types of disasters, demonstrating that psychological trauma is a major public health issue. On a global level, disaster data reveal two important variations: an increase over time and a geographical correlation.

Increases in Mortality Rates

In terms of trends over time, Figure 1 clearly shows that, although numbers vary greatly from year to year, there is a definite rising trend in the number of people being affected by disasters. The mortality rate per 1,000 people exposed has increased significantly over the past three decades for all types of disaster except floods, with the highest increase for drought-related famines.

Geographical Locations. The geographical distribution of disasters is uneven: Asia has suffered from the largest number (42%), followed by the Americas (22%), Africa and Europe (each 15%), and finally Oceania (6%).

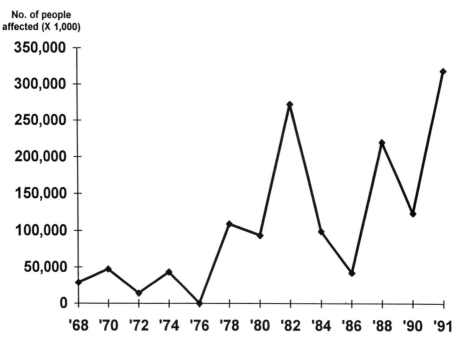

No. of people affected (X 1,000)

Figure 1. Annual number of people reported affected by disasters according to IFRC (1993) estimates. Years 1968–1991.

The spread between developed and developing countries merits special attention, not only because disasters of any type tend to be much more frequent in developing countries, but also because there is a relationship between the location of a disaster and mortality rates.

The United Nations Disaster Relief Coordinator (UNDRO, 1984) noted that the smallest and most economically disadvantaged countries are most severely affected by natural disasters and that, within individual communities, the most impoverished and disadvantaged people experience the gravest consequences. This concept is particularly apparent in droughts in the developed world where deaths are extremely uncommon because of the protection provided by government agencies and social welfare organizations, whereas these resources are often overwhelmed in times of disaster in developing nations.

For the period 1967–91, in fact, an average of 117 million people living in developing countries were affected by disaster each year, compared to about 700,000 people living in developed countries; the ratio of people affected in developing to developed countries is a striking 166:1 (IFRC, 1993). This general imbalance is also reflected in the number of people killed, which is estimated at three or four times higher in developing countries. This imbalance probably reflects the ability to both contain a disaster as it unfolds and rescue those in danger. The most striking difference, however, is in the number of survivors affected (exposed), estimated to be some 40 times higher in developing countries. One must presume that the high rates of survivors affected by disasters in developing countries indicates a massive psychosocial as well as physical need.

The Glickman, Golding, and Silverman (1992) Review

Another worldwide overview of disaster statistics has been published by Glickman et al. (1992). The authors have analyzed the data for natural and industrial disasters for the period 1945–1987, and have highlighted the relative dangerousness and destructiveness of natural disasters. Natural disasters with 25 or more deaths (a) have occurred 4 times more frequently than major industrial accidents with 5 or more deaths; (b) took over 150 times as many lives each year; and (c) claimed over 30 times as many lives per event than industrial disasters.

These authors have also noted that, worldwide, the number of less severe natural disasters (those that kill between 25 and 100 people per event) has increased over the past four decades (Glickman et al., 1992). This increase may reflect both growing population densities in hazard-prone areas and increasing vulnerability to less extreme geological and meteorological phenomena; it may also reflect improved reporting. The number of major industrial accidents followed a similar upward trend through the late 1970s, although it has declined more recently. The largest number of major industrial accidents occurred in the United States, although most deaths occurred in the least developed countries. Thus disasters create huge populations at risk of developing PTSD when considered on a global scale—an issue likely to have major long-term implications for the mental health of these populations.

Man-Made Violence

Large-Scale Violence. One of the most common sources of PTSD is man-made violence, which can be categorized as individual, small group, or large-scale. War represents the most ancient and the most important form of man-made violence in terms of the magnitude of its effects. Since World War II, there have been 127 wars and 21.8 million war-related deaths (Zwi, 1991). The Red Cross estimates a total twice as high, or about 40 million people killed in wars and conflicts since WWII (IFRC, 1993).

As with natural disaster, the consequences of wars have worsenened over time and there is also a striking geographical imbalance. Civilian deaths have increased as a proportion of war-related deaths from 5% in WWI, to 50% in 1950, to approximately 84% of recorded deaths in current conflicts, and up to 90% in Lebanon (Zwi, 1991). Today, in conflicts such as Somalia and the former Yugoslavia, 9 out of every 10 people injured or killed are civilians (IFRC, 1993).

In terms of geographical distribution, all but 2 of the 127 wars have taken place in developing countries. War and political violence not only cause direct psychosocial health problems in the exposed populations, but in the refugees who attempt to flee the fighting. According to official United Nations High Commissioner for Refugees (UNHCR) estimates, 20 years ago the refugee population stood at just under 2.5 million; by 1980 it had risen to 8.2 million. At the end of 1992, the number of refugees cared for by the UNHCR approached 19 million (Toole & Waldman, 1993), in addition to 2 million Palestinians assisted by the United Nations Relief and Works Agency.

Overall the number of refugees and internally displaced people has increased from 30 million in 1990 to more than 43 million in 1993 (Marsella, Bornemann, Orley, & Ekblad, 1994; Toole & Waldman, 1993). Several reports have shown that refugees and displaced populations are at high risk for suffering from various forms of violence and trauma; physical and sexual abuse; starvation; and lack of food, shelter, and medical care; in addition, crude death rates for refugees and internally displaced people are between 5 and 25 times the baseline crude death rates in the countries of origin (Toole & Waldman, 1993).

Small-Scale Violence. The magnitude of small-scale violence and crimes is just as alarming but more difficult to define because of different thresholds of reporting in different studies. A recent survey coordinated by the United Nations Interregional Criminal Justice Research Institute investigated this question in 18 developed countries and 2 Eastern European countries (van Dijk & Mayhew, 1993). A large sample of approximately 55,000 people was interviewed either in 1988, 1991, or both years (in 8 countries) using a standardized questionnaire (in most cases on the telephone). Results of this study are summarized in Table 3.

Although the van Dijk and Mayhew (1993) survey included different types of crimes and levels of severity (e.g., thefts, robberies, burglaries, various types of physical assaults, etc.), in this chapter only the most stressful types of crime that are likely to be associated with PTSD, namely physical assaults and threats and sexual assaults, will be considered. The latter (rapes, attempted rapes, and indecent assaults) are considered only in women.

Physical and Sexual Assaults. Table 3 shows the one-year reported victimization rate for these two types of crime for one of the two years considered. (For countries that took part in both the 1989 and 1992 surveys, the two annual counts have been averaged in the original report of the study.) On average, the total victimization rates across countries for physical assaults and sexual assaults were 3.0% and 1.1% respectively. Rates of physical assaults and threats were higher in New Zealand (5.7%), the United States (5.0%), Australia (5.0%), and Canada (4.4%); in 40% of the incidents the offender actually used force, as opposed to threatening

TABLE 3
One-Year Victimization Rates for Physical Assaults/Threats and for Sexual Assaults in 20 Counties, 1988–1991

Country	Percentage Reporting Physical Assault Threats	Percentage of Women Reporting Sexual Assaults*
England	2.8	0.3
Scotland	1.8	0.8
Northern Ireland	1.8	0.4
The Netherlands	3.7	0.9
West Germany	3.1	1.7
Switzerland	1.2	0
Belgium	1.9	0.6
France	2.0	0.6
Norway	3.0	0.6
Finland	3.5	0.5
Spain	3.1	0.7
Sweden	2.7	0.8
Italy	0.8	1.0
USA	5.0	1.5
Canada	4.4	1.8
Australia	5.0	1.9
New Zealand	5.7	1.5
Japan	0.6	—
Poland	4.2	2.0
Czechoslovakia	3.4	2.4
Average, all countries	3.0	1.1

Note. Data taken from van Dijk & Mayhew (1993) "Criminal Victimization in the Industrialized World: Key Findings of the 1989 and 1992 International Crime Surveys," based on the survey coordinated by the United Nations Interregional Criminal Justice Research Institute.
*Dash indicates missing data.

behavior. For sexual assaults, rates were highest in Czechoslovakia (2.4%), Poland (2.0%), Australia (1.9%), Canada (1.8%), and West Germany (1.7%).

For most types of crimes the young tended to be more at-risk than the elderly, men more than women, subjects of high socioeconomic status more than subjects of low socioeconomic status, and city dwellers more than inhabitants of rural areas or of small towns. Rates for women tended to be substantially higher (similar to those of men) in the countries where female employment levels are more equal, such as the United States. Aggressive crimes seemed more prevalent in North America, Australia, New Zealand, and Poland than in Western European countries and in Japan.

Within Western Europe, violent crimes seemed more frequent in West Germany, the Netherlands, and Finland—the more northern countries. The authors (Van Dijk and Mayhew, 1993) speculate that aggressive criminality seems to be a feature of beer-drinking countries, though they recognize that drinking patterns may represent only one provoking factor. Interestingly, the authors of the survey note that they found higher rates of crime than expected. It should be noted that the comparative rates reviewed so far might be strongly affected by differences in reporting, as other studies have shown much higher rates of physical and sexual violence (Dahl, 1989; Kilpatrick et al., 1989). In other words, the prevalence of reported violence may have as much to do with the receptiveness of legal agencies to documenting these issues and their sensitivity of dealing with the victims as it is to the true occurrence of these events, as well as victims' willingness to report violent crimes.

Violent Deaths. Recent WHO statistics, based on data from various countries, provide further support to the results of the previouly discussed UN survey: Bourbeau (1993), analyzed crude death rates, specifically rates of violent deaths (e.g., motor vehicle accidents, falls, suicides, homicides, and deaths from various other types of violent behaviors) for a large number of developed and developing countries. His research has shown that violent deaths rank third among the major causes of death, after diseases of the circulatory system and malignant tumors, in most developed countries and in some developing countries. He has also found a substantial variation in the level and structure of rates for violent deaths, with the highest rates being three or four times greater than the lowest. Countries in Latin America showed a very high mortality rate due to homicide.

Intentional Violence. In another analysis of global data on intentional violence among adolescents and young adults, Jeanneret and Sand (1993) found that intentional violence is taking on worrying proportions among adolescents and young adults (10–25-year olds). For instance, in the United States, homicide is the leading cause of death among Black males 15–24 years old and the third leading cause (after motor vehicle injuries and suicide) among White males in the same age group (Fingerhut & Kleinman, 1990).

Finally, an epidemiological survey recently carried out in the United States has provided additional data about the frequency and impact of 9 potentially traumatic events on different demographic groups (Norris, 1992).[1] Drawn from four southwestern cities, the sample ($N = 1,000$) was half Black and half White, half male and half female, and evenly divided among younger, middle-aged, and older adults. Over their lifetimes, 69% of participants experienced at least one of the events, with 21% reporting such an event in the past year alone. The 9 events varied in importance, with tragic death occurring most often but sexual assaults yielding the highest rate of PTSD. Motor vehicle accidents presented the most adverse combination of frequency and impact. The prevalence and vulnerability to the effects of trauma was influenced by social and demographic characteristics, with lifetime exposure being higher among Whites and men than

---

[1]The 9 traumatic events are robbery, physical assault, sexual assault, tragic death, motor vehicle crash, combat, fire, other disorder, and other hazard.

among Blacks and women. Past-year exposure was highest among younger adults. Black men appeared to be most vulnerable to the effects of the events, but young people showed the highest rate of PTSD.

The data reviewed demonstrate the extent of exposure to man-made violence in most communities. The public health importance of this phenomenon is usually presented in terms of the mortality and physical morbidity rates. However, its relevance in terms of the prevalence of PTSD occurrence will be appreciated on the basis of the following literature review. In particular, these data give an indication of the numbers of survivors of these events who are clearly at risk of developing PTSD but when the relatives of those affected are also taken into account, the true magnitude of the issue becomes apparent.

REVIEW OF EPIDEMIOLOGICAL STUDIES

Literature Review Strategy

To review the available literature on the epidemiology of PTSD, an extensive search was made using the Excerpta Medica Psychiatry CD-ROM 1980–1993 (October). Using "posttraumatic stress disorder" as a key phrase, a total of 1,057 papers published in this timespan were retrieved. A more extensive search was made using the same key phrase with MED-LINE CD-ROM 1988–1993. A manual search was also performed for all issues of the *Journal of Traumatic Stress*—the leading publication in this field—up to September 1993. Finally, a few additional papers listed in recent literature reviews (e.g., Smith and North, 1993) were retrieved and considered for inclusion.

Inclusion criteria were the following: (a) The study had to report explicit PTSD prevalence rates, or had to provide data that made it possible to calculate those rates among general population samples, clinical population samples, or at-risk subjects (all adults); (b) *DSM–III* or *DSM–III–R* PTSD diagnostic criteria had to be used (no studies have so far been conducted according to *ICD–10* diagnostic criteria for PTSD); and (c) an assessment instrument tailored to generate *DSM–III* or *DSM–III–R* diagnoses had to have been employed. Studies that assessed the overall amount of psychopathology or the rate of "stress-related disorders" without any clear reference to PTSD or means to define and assess PTSD, were not included. Studies that used other self-report measures designed to evaluate the general degree of psychological distress (e.g., the General Health Questionnaire, Hamilton Depression Scale) also are not mentioned in this review because they are not directly related to PTSD assessment.

A total of 135 studies met the inclusion criteria and were selected for this review. They are shown in the Appendix to this chapter. The columns show the main study features, the PTSD prevalence rate, and some selected findings. Almost two thirds ($n = 86$; 64%) of these studies were carried out in the United States, demonstrating the great interest in the United States resulting from the Vietnam War and the large number of veterans suffering from stress-related disorders.

Developed Versus Developing Country Populations

Although several studies were conducted among subjects (mostly refugees) originally from developing countries and subsequently resettled in developed countries, only 8 (6%) studies have actually been conducted in developing countries. This observation is especially noteworthy considering the disproportionately high number of disaster-affected people living in developing countries as compared to those who live in developed countries.

Sample Size Issues

The sample size ranges from a low of 11 subjects, as in two studies, up to a high of 22,463 subjects in the study by Blow et al. (Blow, Cook, Booth, Falcon, & Friedman, 1992), who reviewed the clinical diagnoses made for all alcoholics seeking outpatient care in any Veteran Affairs mental health facility during a one-month period in 1986. The mean sample size is 500, and the median value is 108.

Alternative Assessment Methods

In one third ($n = 45$; 33%) of the studies the investigators used a PTSD symptom checklist (either self-administered or administered by a research assistant) based on DSM criteria to generate a PTSD diagnosis. In one third of the studies ($n = 44$; 33%) of the studies, a structured interview was administered (e.g., the DIS, generally with the addition of the Disaster Supplement [DIS/DS]; the SCID; the SADS; the CIS; or the PSE-9), whereas in the remaining surveys the diagnostic evaluation was based either on an unstructured clinical assessment or on the administration of other specific assessment instruments (e.g., the Mississipi Combat Scale [M-PTSD], the Impact of Event Scale [IES], the Symptom Checklist-90-R [SCL-90-R], or others).

What Diagnostic Criteria?

In 77 studies (57%) the investigators based their assessment on *DSM–III* diagnostic criteria for PTSD, whereas in 55 studies (41%) *DSM–III–R* criteria were applied; in one study (Hryvniak, 1989) either *DSM–III* or *DSM–III–R* criteria were used for different patients, whereas in another study (Creamer, 1989) both criteria were applied to the same subjects. Schwarz and Kowalski (1991) applied *DSM–III*, *DSM–III–R*, and the proposed *DSM–IV* criteria to a sample of adults and children exposed to a school shooting, thus making possible a comparison between the rates of the disorder as per the different criteria employed.

Prevalence Rates of PTSD

The prevalence rate of PTSD will be now discussed separately for the various populations surveyed. Unbiased estimates of prevalence and risk factors can best be investigated in nonhigh-risk general population studies (Davidson & Fairbanks, 1993). The second group that has been studied most rigorously is populations at risk, such as disaster victims and combat veterans.

General Population Studies

Six studies have assessed the prevalence of PTSD in the general population, independent of the exposure to specific stressful events; of these, three have been carried out in the framework of the Epidemiological Catchment Area Program (Robins & Regier, 1991). These studies provide information about the total number of cases in different communities, which reflects both the prevalence of various traumas affecting members of the community in question and the potency of the individual traumatic events to trigger PTSD. Four studies—those carried out in St. Louis, North Carolina, Detroit, and Iceland—are reviewed here.

In the first study, carried out in a sample of 2,493 people living in St. Louis, a lifetime PTSD rate of 0.5% among men and 1.3% among women was found; however, the number of those who experienced some symptoms after a trauma was substantially higher (15% among men and 16% among women), with an average of 2.4 symptoms per person among those affected (Helzer, Robins, & McEvoy, 1987). In half of those with symptoms, the symptoms lasted less than six months.

In the St. Louis study, the rate of the disorder was also investigated in two samples exposed to specific stressors. The first group, which consisted of civilians exposed to physical attack, had a PTSD prevalence rate of about 3.5%. The second group consisted of Vietnam veterans, who had a 6.3% prevalence rate. The rate of comorbidity with other psychiatric disorders (e.g. obsessive–compulsive disorders, dysthymia, and manic depressive disorder) was also high. The PTSD rates found in these subgroups are less than would be expected from the studies that have specifically examined these at-risk populations, such as the NVVRS (Kulka et al., 1990), which raises questions about the sensitivity of case detection in this and other general population samples.

At the St. Louis site, additional data were collected as part of the second wave of the same survey (Cottler, Compton, Mager, Spitznagel, &

Janca, 1992). The overall rate of PTSD was very similar to that found in the first wave (1.35%). One of the main aims of this study was to assess the association between PTSD and substance use. Data showed that cocaine/opiate users were over three times more likely than controls to report a traumatic event. They were also more likely to report symptoms and stressful events and to meet diagnostic criteria for PTSD.

At the Duke site of the Epidemiological Catchment Area Program, lifetime and six-month PTSD prevalence rates were investigated among 2,985 people, yielding rates of 1.30% and 0.44% respectively (Davidson, Hughes, Blazer, & George, 1991). In comparison with subjects without any history of PTSD, those with PTSD reported significantly more job instability, family history of psychiatric illness, parental poverty, experiences of child abuse, and separation or divorce of parents prior to the age of 10. PTSD was also associated with greater psychiatric comorbidity (e.g., somatization disorders, schizophrenia, and panic disorders). Interestingly, similar PTSD lifetime rates, on the order of 1.5%, have been found in two studies that employed control groups randomly selected from the general population (Kulka et al., 1990; Shore, Vollmer, & Tatum, 1989).

A fourth survey was carried out in a random sample of 1,007 young adults (aged 21–30 years) from a large health maintenance organization in Detroit (Breslau, Davis, Andreski, & Peterson, 1991). The lifetime exposure to traumatic events was 39% among the sample surveyed. The rate of PTSD in those who were exposed was 23.6%, yielding an overall lifetime prevalence rate in the total sample of 9.2%. PTSD is among the most common psychiatric disorders for this age-specific population group, preceded only by phobia, major depression, and alcohol and drug dependence.

Among those who were exposed to a traumatic event, there was a significant gender difference in the rate of the disorder, with 30.7% of women meeting PTSD criteria compared to 14% of exposed men. PTSD rate and the frequency of exposure to traumatic events were higher among people with lower educational levels. Those with PTSD were at increased risk for other psychiatric disorders, especially anxiety and affective disorders. Risk factors for PTSD following exposure included early separation from parents, neuroticism, preexisting anxiety or depression, and a family history of anxiety. It is unclear why the rates in this study were higher than in the St. Louis ECA samples, given that the population was not markedly different than the general population of similar age.

Finally, Lindal and Stefansson (1993) have reported the lifetime prevalence rates of anxiety disorders, including PTSD. The authors assessed disorder prevalence rates by administering the DIS in a cohort consting of one half of those born in the year 1931 and living in Iceland ($N = 862$). The overall prevalence of anxiety disorders was 44% and the lifetime prevalence of PTSD was 0.6%; however, the disorder was found only in females

(1.2%), and had a mean onset of 39 years. Women with a diagnosis of PTSD had an average of 3.2 additional diagnoses.

Finally, epidemiological studies can examine the prevalence of traumatic events as well as the prevalence of PTSD. The study of Kessler et al. (in press) used CIDI in the National Comorbidty Study to examine these questions in a USA population of 8,098 subjects. These data demonstrate that the original *DSM–III* criteria that traumatic events were outside the range of normal human experience severely underestimated the prevalence of traumatic stress in civilian populations. Among the male sample, 60.3% had experienced a qualifying trauma and 17% had experienced a trauma that produced intrusive recollections but was not covered by the stressor criterion. In contrast, 50.3% of women had experienced a traumatic stressor. There were significant sex differences in the types of event experienced. For example 25% of men had had an accident in contrast to 13.8% of women, and 9.2% of women had been raped in contrast to 0.7% of men. These data also demonstrate that there is little doubt that many people experience the threat and distress of these events without being disabled or developing longterm psychological symptoms.

This study found that there was a lifetime prevalence of 6.5% of PTSD with the 30-day prevalence being 1.8%. The male to female ratio was 1:2. The most common causes of PTSD in men are combat and witnessing death or severe injury, whereas rape and sexual molestation are the most common in women. The capacity of these events to produce PTSD varied significantly ranging from 48.4% of female rape victims developing PTSD to 10.7% of men witnessing death or serious injury. Survival analysis of the data suggested that more than one third of subjects with PTSD run a chronic course. The greatest recovery occurs in the first year, although even after 2 years the average person with PTSD still has a 50% chance of recovery.

Natural and Technological Disaster Prevalence Studies

A total of 16 studies assessed the prevalence of PTSD among victims of natural and technological disasters; among them, 9 were carried out in the United States, and the remaining 6 in other countries, including three developing countries (Colombia, Fiji, and Mexico). In these 16 studies the sample size ranges between a low of 42 subjects up to a high of more than a thousand in the study by Shore et al. (1989).

Shore et al. (1989) examined the impact of the Mount St. Helens volcanic eruption and compared the exposed population with a control group. The lifetime prevalence in the Mount St. Helens group was 3.6% in contrast with 2.6% in the controls. McFarlane (1988) studied a representative sample of 469 volunteer firefighters exposed to a severe natural disaster in Australia. This study found a rate of 16% of PTSD, less than half of which had gone into remission at 42 months (McFarlane, 1992). McFarlane's study is one of the most in-depth follow-ups conducted in order to evaluate the course of PTSD over time, and the relationship of PTSD to a number of variables.

A series of studies examining nonrepresentative samples has demonstrated a wide variation in prevalence rates. Lima and coworkers (Lima, Pai, Caris, et al., 1981; Lima, Pai, Santacruz, & Lozano, 1991) surveyed the victims of the Armero eruption in Colombia living in two shelters (N = 102) or attending two primary care clinics (N = 500). They found a PTSD rate of 32% and 42% respectively. In Mexico, Conyer et al. (Conyer, Sepulveda Amor, Medina Mora, Caraveo, & De La Fuente, 1987) have conducted a study among the victims of a large Mexican earthquake, and found a similar prevalence rate (32%). On the other hand, in Puerto Rico, Canino, Bravo, Rubio-Stipec, & Woodbury (1990) found a substantially lower PTSD rate (4%) among 321 victims of a flood, compared with 0.7% in the unexposed control group.

The Buffalo Creek disaster, is one of the best-studied disasters.[2] Several follow-ups have been conducted, making possible the investigation of disaster psychopathology over time. Green et al. (Green, Lindy, Grace, & Leonard, 1992) have found a 59% PTSD lifetime rate among the victims; 25% still met PTSD diagnostic criteria at the 14-year follow-up assessment. Children aged 2 to 15 who were exposed to the disaster have also been investigated, revealing a 37% prevalence rate (Green et al., 1991).

A similarly high prevalence rate (59%) has been found by Madakasira and O'Brien (1987) among the victims of a tornado living in a rural community. Steinglass and Gerrity (1990) have found a PTSD rate of 15% at 4 months and of 21% at 16 months among the victims of a tornado and of a flood from two communities. On the other hand, North et al. (North, Smith, McCool, and Lightcap, 1989) and Smith et al. (Smith, Robins, Przybeck, Goldring, & Solomon, 1986) found low rates, ranging from 2% to 5%, among victims of natural disasters.

Six studies have studied the PTSD rates among victims of various technological disasters (Green et al., 1992; Palinkas, Petterson, Russell, & Downs, 1993; Realmuto et al., 1992; Silverman et al., 1985; Smith et al., 1986; Weisaeth, 1989), giving point prevalence rates ranging from a low of 5% (e.g., Smith et al.) up to a high of 80%, as in the study by Weisaeth.

War Veterans and Victims

A relatively large number of studies (n = 34) have been carried out among samples of war veterans; 24 have been conducted in the United

---

[2]The Buffalo Creek disaster occured in February 1972 when a coal mining dam collapsed, and millions of gallons of water and sludge flooded the valley below. Thousands were homeless and 125 people were killed. The community and the environment were devastated.

States and 20 included or were entirely made up of Vietnam veterans. Sample size and composition; study setting; assessment methods; prevalence period (point, period, or lifetime); and inclusion of a comparison group are remarkably different among various studies. These differences are reflected in a marked variation in prevalence rates, ranging from a low of 2% (current prevalence) in the Centers for Disease Control (CDC) Vietnam Experience Study (1988) to over 70%, found in 5 studies.

Prevalence rates higher than 20% among the subjects surveyed were reported in 19 studies, many of which examined subpopulations of veterans. Some studies included very large samples, as in the study carried out by Blow et al. (1992) among alcoholics seeking outpatient care in the VA system. Similarly, several studies have been conducted among clinical samples of veterans seeking different types of medical care. In recent years, four major studies have been carried out among large random samples of Vietnam veterans.

The National Vietnam Veterans Study (NVVRS)

The National Vietnam Veterans Readjustment Study (NVVRS) is probably the most in-depth investigation of the overall psychological and psychosocial consequences of the Vietnam war among veterans (Kulka et al., 1990). It included an overall sample of 3,016 participants, assessed with a variety of standardized instruments. This study reported that 15% of all male veterans who were involved in active war operations were currently diagnosed with PTSD, and an additional 11% suffered from partial PTSD; these rates must be compared to a PTSD rate of 2.5% among Vietnam era veterans who did not serve in Southeast Asia, and of 1.2% among civilian controls who were matched on age, sex, race/ethnicity, and occupation. Among the women who served in Vietnam, the PTSD prevalence estimate was 9%. In the same study it was found that there were few differences in the rate of other psychiatric disorders among the three groups (Jordan et al., 1991).

Vietnam Experience Study (CDC)

The CDC Vietnam Experience Study (1988) investigated 2,490 Vietnam veterans and 1,972 soldiers who did not serve in Vietnam, and found that about half of the veterans reported experiencing one or more symptoms related to a traumatic combat event, whereas 15% met diagnostic criteria for PTSD at some time during or after service; 2.2% of the Vietnam veterans were still suffering from the disorder during the month prior to the interview.

In addition, Vietnam veterans were more likely than non-Vietnam veterans to meet diagnostic criteria for alcohol abuse or dependency (13.7% vs. 9.2%), generalized anxiety (4.9% vs. 3.2%), and depression

(4.5% vs. 2.3%). The rate of psychiatric comorbidity among the veterans suffering from PTSD was also high. In contrast, the results of the medical examinations showed few current objective differences in physical health between the two groups.

Identical Twin Studies

Another study evaluated the influence of military service during the Vietnam era on the occurrence of PTSD among a sample of over 2,000 male–male monozygotic veteran twin pairs (Goldberg, True, Eisen, & Henderson, 1990). A PTSD prevalence of almost 17% was found in twins who served in Southeast Asia compared with 5% in cotwins who did not. There was a ninefold increase in the rate of PTSD among twins who experienced high levels of combat compared to those who did not serve in Vietnam.

Finally, the study by Snow et al. (Snow, Mager-Stellman, Stellman, & Sommer, 1988), which assessed a random sample of 2,858 Vietnam veterans, found different PTSD rates depending on whether *exposure to combat* was defined relatively narrowly or broadly. Among those exposed to a median level of combat, the rate of PTSD was 28%, whereas the rate was 65% among those exposed to the highest level. Therefore, changing the threshold for the definition of exposure to combat changes reported prevalence rates.

In addition to the studies now mentioned, several others, listed in Table 3, have confirmed high psychological morbidity among Vietnam veterans, or veterans of other wars. Most studies have found an association between severity and duration of combat exposure on one hand and prevalence and persistence of PTSD on the other (Solomon & Mikulincer, 1987). Having been wounded or involved in some highly traumatic experiences (e.g., handling dead bodies, witnessing mutilation or atrocities) was also generally strongly associated with PTSD. High comorbidity rates have also been found, showing that PTSD is only one of the possible psychopathological outcomes following exposure to combat and highly stressful situations.

Prisoner of War and Other Prisoner Studies

Ten studies have been carried out among former prisoners of war and other types of prisoners, generally those imprisoned for political reasons (Basoglu et al., 1994; Bauer, Priebe, Haring, & Adamczak, 1993; Burges Watson, 1993; Crocq, Hein, Duval, & Macher, 1991; Eberly & Engdahl, 1991; Kluznik, Speed, Van-Valkenburg, & McGraw, 1986; Kuch & Cox, 1992; Mellman, Randolph, Brawman-Mintzer, Flores, & Milanes, 1992; Speed et al., 1989; Sutker, Allain, & Winstead, 1993). Among these, six have been conducted in the United States, and one each in Germany, Turkey, Australia, and France. In all these studies, the PTSD rate was quite substantial, with the prevalence rate in six studies being equal to or higher than 50%, and with three studies showing prevalence rates of 70% or more. Former prisoners of war and political detainees appear to be a group at high risk for developing PTSD. However, a more recent survey in the former East Germany by Bauer et al., (1993) found a somewhat lower rate of 22%.

In almost all of these prisoner studies, there were patients who suffered from PTSD symptoms for the first time decades after the end of their imprisonment; many others were still suffering decades after the end of detention and the first appearance of the disorder. Some studies have found an association between the appearance and the severity of PTSD and the length and the severity of the imprisonment, the latter being mainly evaluated by the experience of torture and by percentage of body weight lost (e.g., Eberly & Engdahl, 1991; Speed et al., 1988).

Victims of Terrorist Attacks

Five studies focused on victims of terrorist attacks (Abenhaim, Dab, & Salmi, 1992; Bell, Kee, Loughrey, Roddy, & Curran, 1988; Curran et al., 1990; Shalev, 1992; Weisaeth, 1993), and one assessed the PTSD rate among residents in Lockerbie who claimed compensation after the aircraft disaster caused by a terrorist explosion. The rate of PTSD was substantial, exceeding 20% of the subjects studied and in two cases being higher than 40% (Curran et al., 1990; Weisaeth, 1993).

In a study carried out in France among 254 survivors of terrorist attacks occurring between 1982 and 1987, the PTSD rate among the uninjured victims was 10.5% compared with 31% among the severely injured (Abenhaim et al., 1992). In contrast, in one of two Irish studies carried out following the Enniskillen bombing, no correlation was found between physical injury and the degree of psychological disorders (Curran et al., 1990). In both Irish studies, women showed higher PTSD rates.

Refugee Studies

Of the twelve studies assessing the rate of PTSD among samples of refugees, nine were carried out in the United States among samples of resettled refugees, mostly Southeast Asians (Carlson & Hogan, 1991; Cervantes, Salgado de Snyder, & Padilla, 1989; Hauff & Vaglum, 1993; Hinton et al, 1993; Kinzie et al., 1990; Kinzie, Sack, Angell, Manson, & Rath, 1986; Kroll et al., 1989; Mollica et al., 1993; Mollica, Wyshak, & Lavelle, 1987; Moore & Boehnlein, 1991; Ramsay, Gorst-Unsworth, & Turner, 1993; Summerfield & Toser, 1991). The remaining three have studied diverse populations, with Mollica et al. (1993) studying Cambodian refugees living on the Thai–Cambodian border; one being conducted in Nicaragua by Summerfield and Toser (1991) and the survey by Ramsay et al. (1993)

that looked at a British sample. Of these studies six have found a PTSD rate equal to or higher than 50%, demonstrating that refugees who seek treatment and have usually faced very difficult circumstances (e.g., torture, starvation, witnessing killings) represent a highly traumatized population, displaying a substantial rate of PTSD and other psychiatric disorders.

Victims of Violence

A number of studies ($n = 21$) have assessed the prevalence rate of PTSD among victims of different types of violence; they include victims of crime, people exposed to multiple homicides, police officers involved in shooting experiences, children and adults exposed to sniper attacks, battered women, and finally victims of rape or other sexual violence. The latter topic has been investigated in six studies (Bownes, O'Gorman, & Sayers, 1991; Burge, 1988; Dahl, 1989; Lopez, Piffaut, & Seguin, 1992; Riggs, Dancu, Gershuny, Greenberg, & Foa, 1992; Rothbaum, Foa, Riggs, Murdock, & Walsh, 1992), and in four of them the rate of PTSD was over 70%. The rate of PTSD was substantial in most investigations of rape and sexual violence; in three studies the PTSD prevalence rate was lower than 25% of the victims. The degree of life threat and of physical injury was generally correlated with both the occurrence and the severity of PTSD.

Other At-Risk Groups

Of the studies listed in Table 2, one fourth ($n = 34$) have investigated the prevalence of PTSD in a variety of samples of at-risk subjects. They include, for the largest part, (a) medical patients hospitalized or treated for different reasons (e.g., major burns or accidental injuries, including road accidents); (b) pain sufferers (e.g., Aghabeigi, Feinmann, & Harris, 1992; Benedikt & Kolb, 1986; Feinstein, 1993; Hickling & Blanchard, 1992; Malt, 1988; Mayou, Bryant, & Duthie, 1993; Patterson, Carrigan, Questad, & Robinson, 1990; Perry, Difede, Musngi, Frances, & Jacobsberg, 1992; Roca, Spence, & Munster, 1992; Schottenfeld & Cullen, 1985); (c) victims of technological disasters or aircraft accidents (e.g., Newman & Foreman, 1987; Palinkas et al., 1993; Realmuto et al., 1991; Silverman et al., 1985; Sloan, 1988; Smith, North, McCool, & Shea, 1990; Weisaeth, 1989); (d) psychiatric patients with other baseline diagnoses (e.g., Craine, Henson, Colliver, & MacLean, 1988; Davidson & Smith, 1990; Hryvniak, 1989; McGorry et al., 1991; McNally & Lukach, 1992; Rudd, Dahm, & Rajab, 1993; Warshaw et al., 1993); and (e) rescuers of disaster victims (e.g., Durham, McCammeron, & Allison, 1985; Ersland, Weisaeth, & Surd, 1989).

Across these studies the rate of PTSD varies, depending on a number of factors related to the type, severity, length, and consequences of the stressor, and on the psychiatric status of the subjects prior to the traumatic event. In particular, a substantial rate of PTSD has been found among psychiatric patients specifically evaluated on measures of PTSD symptomatology and among burn patients.

DISCUSSION AND CONCLUSION

Several general conclusions can be drawn from this review. There has been a remarkable increase in the number and quality of studies examining the prevalence of PTSD over the past decade. These studies have addressed the frequency of PTSD among both unbiased population samples and among at-risk subjects, and have investigated vulnerability factors, common symptom patterns, and natural history of this disorder. However, a number of important issues exist.

The Need for Research in Developing Countries

The first important limitation in the PTSD literature is that many of the most traumatized populations have not been studied, and the relevance of much of the available information to these populations is unclear. Of 135 studies, only eight (6%) have been carried out in developing countries. However, as the review of traumatic events demonstrates, developing countries are far more commonly the sites of natural disasters, wars, crimes, and other large-scale or small-scale disasters—the events that typically trigger PTSD. It is therefore probable that *disaster subcultures* may exist among populations living in developing countries with a lengthy experience in coping with natural disasters, wars, and other traumatic events.

The relevance of findings from research carried out among populations living in countries only uncommonly affected by large-scale disaster is unclear. The difference between the cultural patterns, social structures, and coping behaviors of developed and developing countries may significantly influence the incidence, severity, and psychosocial outcome of PTSD. There is an urgent need for specific research on these populations. The trauma perspective has the potential to provide a series of valuable insights into the dynamics of social strife and individual behavior in these settings, as well as the health needs of these populations.

Variations in Diagnostic Criteria

Within the groups that have been studied, a series of problems exist in making direct comparisons between studies even of similar populations. Firstly, the revisions of the *DSM* diagnostic criteria and the subsequent publication of criteria for PTSD in *ICD–10* (WHO, 1992a) mean that different diagnostic criteria have been used in different studies, which is an important limitation in generalizing any results. Two studies (Creamer, 1989; Schwarz & Kowalski, 1991) have clearly shown the diagnostic criteria set selection influenced rates of diagnosis. Creamer (1989) found that the application of *DSM–III–R* criteria more than halved the rate of the disorder as diagnosed by the *DSM–III* (from 74% to 33%). Similarly, the application of *DSM–III–R* criteria in the study by Schwarz and Kowalski (1991) lowered the diagnostic rates as compared to both *DSM–III* and proposed *DSM–IV* criteria.

However, diagnostic agreements between *DSM–III–R* and proposed *DSM–IV* criteria were good to excellent for both adults and children at all thresholds, whereas patterns of agreement between *DSM–III* and its successors were problematical. The results of these two studies highlight the crucial importance of the diagnostic criteria employed for the identification of the disorder and consequently for the epidemiological study of clinical and nonclinical populations.

Diagnostic Sensitivity of Instruments

Concern about diagnostic criteria variations raises the critical question of the diagnostic sensitivity of the different instruments used to detect PTSD, which again have the potential to create substantial differences in prevalence rates. As noted, in approximately one third of the studies surveyed in this chapter, investigators used a PTSD-symptom checklist (either self-administered or administered by a clinician) based on *DSM* criteria to generate a PTSD diagnosis. In another third of the studies a structured interview was administered (e.g., DIS, DIS/DS, SCID, or SADS), whereas in the remaining surveys the diagnostic evaluation was based either on an unstructured clinical assessment or on the administration of other specific assessment instruments (e.g., M-PTSD, IES, SCL-90-R, or others). Generally speaking, studies conducted with structured interviews tended to report lower rates of PTSD than studies using less structured data collection.

The Diagnostic Interview Schedule

Among structured interviews, the DIS has shown reasonable diagnostic accuracy in clinical samples of veterans, but inadequate validity in a general population sample (Green, 1991). For instance, the DIS identified only about one in five cases of PTSD as diagnosed by expert clinicians (Kulka et al., 1991) in the NVVRS. Solomon and Canino (1990) demonstrated that many subjects fail to report the symptoms of PTSD when asked to anchor their onset to the traumatic event, which creates a high number of false negative responses with DIS. This is an important issue because the DIS was used in the ECA study; and this may mean that the population estimates for PTSD, which are largely derived from this study, may represent significant underestimates of the prevalence.

The Structured Clinical Interview for Diagnosis (SCID)

The SCID, used in 24 studies (18%), has been considered the "gold standard" in terms of diagnosis in clinical samples, and has shown promising discriminate validity when administered to clinical samples of veterans (Green, 1991). However, more research on the use of this instrument in other clinical samples is needed. In addition, it seems that the SCID gives twice the prevalence rates of the DIS, which might explain the difference in prevalence rates between the CDC (1988) and the NVVRS (1990) surveys of Vietnam veterans.

IES and SCL-90-R

The IES and the SCL-90-R have been used extensively, probably because of the ease of administration. Strictly speaking, they are not diagnostic instruments, but rather measures that document only some of the phenomena of PTSD and provide thresholds above which the probablity of being diagnosed with PTSD can be defined. Thus, these instruments have shown good psychometric properties in a number of studies (Green, 1991), but the extent to which they are able to generate reliable PTSD diagnoses is questionable. Rather, they are useful to screen subjects likely to be suffering from the disorder who should then evaluated with a structured interview. The intended purposes of the IES and SCL-90-R should be considered when the data from studies using these methodologies are interpreted.

PTSD Checklists

Similarly, the reliability of diagnoses generated using PTSD symptom checklists (especially self-administered), which were widely employed in the studies reviewed here, is still unclear. As Green points out (1991), "The extent to which such measures represent a satisfactory substitute for interview measures or may under- or overestimate the proportion of people with the diagnosis is not known"(p. 543). Because these checklists have never been validated against clinical diagnostic interviews, appropriate data on their diagnostic validity and reliability should be urgently gathered and made available to other researchers. On the whole, it seems justified to conclude that we still lack an assessment instrument that has both satisfactory reliability and validity combined with ease and rapidity of administration. These features are of special importance in assessing victims in the aftermath of a disaster, which are characteristically busy and difficult settings.

When Should the Diagnosis Be Made?

Another important point related to the assessment of the disorder has to do with the timing of the diagnostic evaluation: no particular standard has been defined so far to be used in epidemiological research, and the studies discussed in this chapter vary widely in their timing. This variability represents an additional limit to meaningful comparisons across studies and to the ability to generalize their results.

Clearly, studies conducted in close temporal proximity to a trauma are likely to yield higher prevalence rates than when a significant time period has elapsed during which a significant number of cases may have gone into remission. As already noted by Smith and North (1993), studies in which researchers were able to obtain and compare pre- and postdisaster data on the prevalence of psychiatric disorders prospectively are very rare and restricted to samples limited in size. This is an area that certainly deserves more attention in future investigations.

Difficulties in Making Comparisons

Numerous difficulties arise when attempting to make comparisons in PTSD rates. The roots of those difficulties include the relative lack of prevalence studies in general populations, methodological variations, sampling and response rates, exposure level differences, and lifetime prevalence estimates. For all the reasons discussed so far, and considering the differential impact of different types of traumatic experiences on the victims, it is difficult to draw meaningful averages, in terms of prevalence rates, from the studies previously discussed. Wide range in rates from study to study and the fact that only very few among the studies listed in Table 3 can be called truly epidemiological studies further complicate the issue. In fact the studies that looked at the PTSD rate in samples of the general population are very few, and are represented mostly by subsets of the ECA study. Some of these studies also have been met with some criticism (e.g., Haber-Schaim, Solomon, Bleich, & Kottler, 1988; Keane & Penk, 1988) becasue PTSD rates within the ECA study were derived from data that originally were not intended to diagnose this type of disorder.

Most of the other studies have been carried out in highly selected populations, and differences in findings between them could be explained by differences in sampling methods, diagnostic criteria, assessment methodologies, timing of the investigation, types of disasters under study, degree of exposure to a traumatic event, and a number of other intervening and moderating factors. Perhaps the greatest problem is sample selection in which a range of factors can have a significant impact on the prevalence rates defined and apparent determinants of etiology.

Many of the studies reported are of treatment-seeking groups, which means that they are not representative of the exposed victim groups. This makes interpretation of prevalence rates difficult, and it is similarly problematical to separate the determinants of treatment seeking from the etiology of the disorder. Many studies also arbitrarily recruit from at-risk samples with little or no definition of how they represent the population exposed to the traumatic event.

Response rates can be a critical issue. Those studies reporting very low response rates due to the avoidance among traumatized populations can have a major impact on apparent prevalence rates. For example, the study of the Beverley Hills Supper Club fire has indicated that only 2% of those approached in an intervention study agreed to participate (Lindy, Green, Grace, & Tichner, 1983); a recent study by Brom et al. (1993) looking at motor accident victims demonstrates similar low response rates.

There is also a need to define the level of exposure within a sample in comparison to the total victim population. For example, if high-exposure subjects are overrepresented, the prevalence rates of PTSD for that type of traumatic event will not reflect the full range of exposure and will be artifically high. These biases can also modify the apparent importance of the etiological role of exposure against a range of vulnerabilty factors. Despite these general difficulties, we will try to indicate some general points worth of consideration.

Lifteime Prevalence Estimates

Concerning the lifetime prevalence of PTSD in the general population, the studies carried out so far show a remarkable consistence, giving rates in the region of 1–3% when using the DIS to assess prevalence. This percentage shows a predictable and moderate increase in PTSD in various risk groups exposed to distressing traumatic experiences, in contrast to those studies examining nonrepresentative samples of victims with higher prevalence rates. This suggests that the potency of exposure as an etiological factor may be overestimated when nonrepresentative samples are examined. Representative studies of at-risk samples similarly demonstrate the interaction between vulnerability factors and exposure, with prevalence rates of 30% (e.g., for war veterans the NVVRS study, Kulka et al., 1990) being typical.

Rates are substantially higher among people exposed to higher levels of stress (e.g., people exposed to combat stress, refugees, prisoners of war, victims of rape and other violent crimes, etc.), often approaching 50% of exposed subjects. Being wounded, held in captivity, or tortured can further increase the overall prevalence rate of PTSD among people involved in combat. The significance of these findings is difficult to establish for the methodological reasons discussed. It remains to be established whether these findings are validated by studies that use more representative samples.

The Impact of Method of Assessment

The impact of method of assessment and sampling has been particularly graphically demonstated in the more rigorous studies of Vietnam veterans. Among four of the most important surveys (CDC, 1988; Goldberg et al., 1990; Kulka et al., 1990; Snow et al., 1988), Kulka et al. and Goldberg et al. found a current PTSD prevalence rate among Vietnam veterans in the range of 15% of the studied subjects. In the Centers for Disease Control study the current prevalence rate was lower (2.2%), while in the Legion study by Snow et al. the rate was as high as 28% and approached 65% among those exposed to the highest level of combat, a finding similar to the NVVRS data (Kulka et al., 1990). This demonstrates the need for care in making any definitive conclusions about the prevalence and etiology of PTSD on the basis of the currently available data without careful analysis of the methodology employed.

Natural Versus Technological Disasters

Concerning the differential impact of natural disasters as compared to technological disasters on PTSD prevalence rates, Smith & North (1993), in a recent review of 13 studies reporting PTSD rates in the context of disaster by using well-established criteria, have concluded that technological disasters were associated with higher rates of PTSD.

On the other hand, a recent metaanalysis that analyzed the relationship between disasters and subsequent psychopathology for 52 studies using quantitative measures (Rubonis & Bickman, 1991) found higher impairment estimates for naturally caused disasters (e.g., volcano eruptions) as opposed to those caused, at least in part, by humans (e.g., industrial or nuclear accidents). The authors, however, included a large number of studies related to nuclear accidents ($n = 19$) in their metaanalysis and considered various categories of psychopathology, sometimes nonspecific (for instance, "stress"). The present literature review does not allow any firm conclusion on this point because of the noted methodological limitations for most studies reviewed.

Cormorbidity Issues

As noted by Davidson and Fairbank (1993), the epidemiological data are consistent with the conceptualization of PTSD as a prolonged or even chronic disorder rather than an acute or self-limited one. In many of the studies reviewed, PTSD emerges with a variety of other psychiatric disorders, in particular depression, anxiety disorders, alcohol and drug abuse, and somatization disorders following the experience of trauma, suggesting that trauma does not have a unique role in triggering PTSD.

Another possibility is that comorbid psychiatric disorders may have preceded the traumatic experience, and their causation and onset inappropriately attributed to the traumatic event. This raises the important issue that is seldom addressed in retrospective epidemiological studies of trauma, namely the relationship between PTSD and the significant prevalence of background psychiatric morbidity that is present in any community.

The interaction between preexisting psychiatric disorders and the onset of PTSD is a critical research agenda. It is important to clarify whether PTSD mainly arises in those who have been suffering from some other psychiatric illness, and consequently to estimate the size of the sample developing a new disorder following traumatic exposure. Only a few studies (e.g., Solomon & Canino, 1990) have provided any real insight into this question, and they emphasize the importance of looking at comparative rates of psychiatric diagnosis in general community samples as against the rates of PTSD in the disaster affected group.

The Dose–Response Issue

The dose–response relationship between stressors and PTSD is an issue that can be addressed particularly in randomly selected population samples. The available data is not as clear cut as often suggested (Mc-Farlane, in press). The results of population samples often seem to be at variance with the studies of selected at-risk samples. Green (1991, 1993) has suggested that general stressor factors that increase the risk for PTSD include violent loss, life threat, exposure to grotesque death, receipt of intentional harm, injury, witnessing violence, exposure to noxious agents, and being responsible for the death of another person. Multiple traumas also seem to increase the risk of suffering from PTSD.

In this review, only studies that generated specific PTSD prevalence rates have been considered. However, it should be noted that there are several studies in the current literature that did not use specific measures of PTSD, but provide valuable information about rates of psychiatric morbidity other than PTSD following traumatic events that are extremely important for those concerned with the field of traumatic stress. For a detailed review of these studies, readers are referred to Smith and North (1993).

In conclusion, Keane (1990) has stated the following:

> In trying to integrate the exact information on the epidemiology of PTSD, perhaps the most challenging task was to interpret sensibly the outcomes of studies that used very different subjects, stressors, dependent measures, sampling strategies, independent variables, and data analytic procedures. (p. 3).

To this statement, it has to be added that much of the research into PTSD has been done among Western populations, which is reflected in the very limited number of contributions from non-English speaking countries (de Girolamo, 1993; Marsella, Friedman, & Spain, 1993). It is therefore imperative to carry out extensive research with populations from developing countries, which are most affected by natural and man-made disasters of large and small scale. This research will allow the study of cross-cultural variations in frequency, symptomatology, temporal patterns, and outcome of PTSD and related disorders and will clarify the moderating effect of culture on this disorder (de Girolamo, 1993). The prevalence of trauma in these communities emphasizes the potential magnitude of the public health consequences of PTSD, an issue that is only just emerging.

REFERENCES

Abenhaim, L., Dab, W., & Salmi, L. R. (1992). Study of civilian victims of terrorist attacks (France 1982–1987). *Journal of Clinical Epidemiology, 45*, 103–109.

Aghabeigi, B., Feinmann, C., & Harris, M. (1992). Prevalence of posttraumatic stress disorder in patients with chronic idiopathic facial pain. *British Journal of Oral and Maxillofacial Surgery, 30*, 360–364.

American Psychiatric Association (1980). *Diagnostic and Statistical Manual of Mental Disorders* (3rd ed.). Washington, DC: Author.

American Psychiatric Association (1987). *Diagnostic and Statistical Manual of Mental Disorders* (3rd ed., rev.) Washington, DC: Author.

Amick McMullan, A., Kilpatrick, D. G., & Resnick, H. S. (1991). Homicide as a risk factor for PTSD among surviving family members. *Behaviour Modification, 15*, 545–559.

Basoglu, M., Paker, M., Ozmen, E., Marks, I., Incesu, C., Sahin, D., & Sarimurat, N. (1994). Psychological effects of torture: a comparison of tortured with nontortured political activists in Turkey. *American Journal of Psychiatry, 151*, 76–81.

Bauer, M., Priebe, S., Haring, B., & Adamczak, K. (1993). Long-term sequelae of political imprisonment in East Germany. *Journal of Nervous and Mental Disease, 181*, 257–262.

Bell, P., Kee, M., Loughrey, G. C., Roddy, R. J., & Curran, P. S. (1988). Posttraumatic stress in Northern Ireland. *Acta Psychiatrica Scandinavica, 77*, 166–169.

Benedikt, R. A., & Kolb, L. C. (1986). Preliminary findings on chronic pain and posttraumatic stress disorder. *American Journal of Psychiatry, 143*, 908–910.

Blake, D. D., Keane, T. M., Wine, P. R., Mora, C., Taylor, K. L., & Lyons, J. A. (1990). Prevalence of PTSD symptoms in combat veterans seeking medical treatment. *Journal of Traumatic Stress, 3*, 15–27.

Blow, F. C., Cook, C. A. L., Booth, B. M., Falcon, S. P., & Friedman, M. J. (1992). Age related psychiatric comorbidities and level of functioning in alcoholic veterans seeking outpatient treatment. *Hospital and Community Psychiatry, 43,* 990–995.

Boon, S., & Draijer, N. (1993). Multiple personality disorder in The Netherlands: A clinical investigation of 71 patients. *American Journal of Psychiatry, 150,* 489–494.

Bourbeau, R. (1993). Analyse comparative de la mortalité violente dans les pays développés et dans quelques pays en developpement durant la période 1985–1989. [A comparative analysis of violent deaths in developed and developing countries during the period 1985–1989]. *World Health Statistics Quarterly, 46,* 4–33.

Bownes, I. T., O'Gorman, E. C., & Sayers, A. (1991). Assault characteristics and posttraumatic stress disorder in rape victims. *Acta Psychiatrica Scandinavica, 83,* 27–30.

Brawman-Mintzer, O., Lydiard, B., Emmanuel, N., Payeur, R., Johnson, M., Roberts, J., Jarrell, M. P., & Ballenger, J. C. (1993). Psychiatric comorbidity in patients with generalized anxiety disorder. *American Journal of Psychiatry, 150,* 1216–1218.

Breslau, N., & Davis, G. C. (1987). Posttraumatic stress disorder: The etiologic specificity of wartime stressors. *American Journal of Psychiatry, 144,* 578–583.

Breslau, N., Davis, G. C., Andreski, P., & Peterson, E. (1991). Traumatic events and posttraumatic stress disorder in an urban population of young adults. *Archives of General Psychiatry, 48,* 216–222.

Brom, D., Kleber, R. J., & Hoffman, M. C. (1993). Victims of traffic accidents: Incidence and prevention of post-traumatic stress disorder. *Clinical Psychology, 49,* 131–140.

Brooks, N., & McKinlay, W. (1992). Mental health consequences of the Lockerbie disaster. *Journal of Traumatic Stress, 5,* 527–543.

Burge, S.K. (1988). Post-traumatic stress disorder in victims of rape. *Journal of Traumatic Stress, 1,* 193–209.

Burges Watson, I. P. (1993). Post-traumatic stress disorder in Australian prisoners of the Japanese: A clinical study. *Australian and New Zealand Journal of Psychiatry, 27,* 20–29.

Buydens-Branchey, L., Noumair, D., & Branchey, M. (1990). Duration and intensity of combat exposure and posttraumatic stress disorder in Vietnam veterans. *Journal of Nervous and Mental Disease, 178,* 582–587.

Caldwell, M. F. (1992). Incidence of PTSD among staff victims of patient violence. *Hospital and Community Psychiatry, 43,* 838–839.

Callen, K. E., Reaves, M. E., Maxwell, M. J., & McFarland, B. H. (1985). Vietnam veterans in the general hospital. *Hospital and Community Psychiatry, 36,* 150–153.

Canino, G., Bravo, M., Rubio-Stipec, M., & Woodbury, M. (1990). The impact of disaster on mental health: Prospective and retrospective analyses. *International Journal of Mental Health, 19,* 51–69.

Card, J. J. (1987). Epidemiology of PTSD in a national cohort of Vietnam veterans. *Journal of Clinical Psychology, 43,* 6–17.

Carlson, E. B., & Hogan, R. (1991). Trauma experiences, posttraumatic stress, dissociation, and depression in Cambodian refugees. *American Journal of Psychiatry, 148,* 1548–1551.

Centers for Disease Control Vietnam Experience Study (1988). Health status of Vietnam veterans, I: Psychosocial characteristics. *Journal of the American Medical Association, 259,* 2701–2707.

Cervantes, R. C., Salgado de Snyder, V. N., & Padilla, A. M. (1989). Posttraumatic stress in immigrants from Central America and Mexico. *Hospital and Community Psychiatry, 40,* 615–619.

Chemtob, C. M., Bauer, G. B., Neller, G., Hamada, R., Glisson, C., & Stevens, V. (1990). Posttraumatic stress disorder among special forces Vietnam Veterans. *Military Medicine, 155,* 16–20.

Collins, J. J., & Bailey, S. L. (1990). Relationship of mood disorders to violence. *Journal of Nervous and Mental Disease, 178,* 44–47.

Conyer, R. C., Sepulveda Amor, J., Medina Mora, M. E., Caraveo, J., & De La Fuente, J. R. (1987). Prevalencia del sindrome de estrés postraumático en la población sobreviviente a un desastre natural [The prevalence of posttraumatic stress syndrome in a population following a natural disaster]. *Salud Publica Mexicana* [Mexican Public Health], *29,* 406–411.

Cottler, L. B., Compton, W. M. III, Mager, D., Spitznagel, E. L., & Janca, A. (1992). Posttraumatic stress disorder among substance users from the general population. *American Journal of Psychiatry 149,* 664–670.

Craine, L., Henson, C. E., Colliver, J. A., & MacLean, D. G. (1988). Prevalence of a history of sexual abuse among female psychiatric patients in a state hospital system. *Hospital and Community Psychiatry, 39,* 300–304.

Creamer, M. (1989). Posttraumatic stress disorder: Some diagnostic and clinical issues. *Australian and New Zealand Journal of Psychiatry, 23,* 517–522.

Crocq, M. A., Hein, K. D., Duval, F., & Macher, J. P. (1991). Severity of the prisoner of war experience and post traumatic stress disorder. *European Psychiatry, 6,* 39–45.

Curran, P. S., Bell, P., Murray, A., Loughrey, G., Roddy, R., & Rocke, L. G. (1990). Psychological consequences of the Enniskillen bombing. *British Journal of Psychiatry, 156,* 479–482.

Dahl, S. (1989). Acute response to rape a PTSD variant. *Acta Psychiatrica Scandinavica Supplementum, 80,* 56–62.

Davidson, J. R., & Fairbank, J. A. (1993). The epidemiology of postttraumatic stress disorder. In J. R. Davidson & E. B. Foa (Eds.), *Posttraumatic stress disorder. DSM–IV and beyond* (pp. 147–172). Washington, DC: American Psychiatric Press.

Davidson, J. R., Hughes, D., Blazer, D. G., & George, L. K. (1991). Posttraumatic stress disorder in the community: An epidemiological study. *Psychological Medicine, 21,* 713–721.

Davidson, J. R., & Smith, R. (1990). Traumatic experiences in psychiatric outpatients. *Journal of Traumatic Stress, 3,* 459–475.

de Girolamo, G. (1993). International perspectives in the treatment and prevention of post-traumatic stress disorders. In J. Wilson & B. Raphael (Eds.), *International handbook of traumatic stress syndromes* (pp. 935–946). New York: Plenum.

De Groen, J. H. M., Op den Velde, W., Hovens, J. E., Falger, P. R. J., Schouten, E. G. W., & Van Duijn, H. (1993). Snoring and anxiety dreams. *Sleep, 16,* 35–36.

den Velde, W. O., Falger, P. R. J., Hovens, J. E., de Groen, J. H. M., Lasschuit, L. J., Van Dijn, H., & Schouten, E. G. W. (1993). Posttraumatic stress disorder in Dutch resistance veterans from World War II. In J. Wilson & B. Raphael (Eds.), *International handbook of traumatic stress syndromes* (pp. 219–230). New York: Plenum.

Durham, T. W., McCammon, S. L., & Allison, E. J., Jr. (1985). The psychological impact of disaster on rescue personnel. *Annals of Emergency Medicine, 14,* 664–668.

Eberly, R. E., & Engdahl, B. E. (1991). Prevalence of somatic and psychiatric disorder among former prisoners of war. *Hospital and Community Psychiatry, 42,* 807–813.

Ersland, S., Weisaeth, L., & Sund, A. (1989). The stress upon rescuers involved in an oil rig disaster: "Alexander Kielland" 1980. *Acta Psychiatrica Scandinavica Supplementum, 80,* 38–49.

Fairley, M., Langeluddecke, P., & Tennant, C. (1986). Psychological and physical morbidity in the aftermath of a cyclone. *Psychological Medicine, 16,* 671–676.

Famularo, R., Kinscherff, R., & Fenton, T. (1992). Psychiatric diagnoses of abusive mothers. A preliminary report. *Journal of Nervous and Mental Disease, 180,* 658–661.

Farmer, R., Tranah, T., O'Donnell, I., & Catalan, J. (1992). Railway suicide: The psychological effects on drivers. *Psychological Medicine, 22,* 407–414.

Feinstein, A. (1993). A prospective study of victims of physical trauma. In J. Wilson & B. Raphael (Eds.), *International handbook of traumatic stress syndromes* (pp. 157–164). New York: Plenum.

Fierman, E. J., Hunt, M. F., Pratt, L. A., Warshaw, M. G., Yonkers, K. A., Peterson, L. G., Epstein-Kaye, T. M., & Norton, H. S. (1993). Trauma and posttraumatic stress disorder in subjects with anxiety disorders. *American Journal of Psychiatry, 150,* 1872–1874.

Fingerhut, L. A., & Kleinman, J. C. (1990). International and interstate comparisons of homicide among young males. *Journal of the American Medical Association, 263,* 3292–3295.

Fisher, N., & Jacoby, R. (1992). Psychiatric morbidity in bus crews following violent assault: A follow-up study. *Psychological Medicine, 22,* 685–693.

Frye, S., & Stockton, R. A. (1982). Discriminant analysis of posttraumatic stress disorder among a group of Viet Nam veterans. *American Journal of Psychiatry, 139,* 52–56.

Gersons, B. P. R. (1991). Intensive treatment of post traumatic stress disorder; experiences with policemen. *Tijdschrift Psychiatry, 33,* 244–261.

Glickman, T. S., Golding, D., & Silverman, E. D. (1992). *Acts of God and acts of man. Recent trends in natural disasters and major industrial accidents.* Washington, DC: Resource for the Future.

Goldberg, J., True, W,. R., Eisen, S. A., & Henderson, W. G. (1990). A twin study of the effects of the Vietnam war on posttraumatic stress disorder. *Journal of the American Medical Association, 263,* 1227–1232.

Green, B. L. (1991). Evaluating the effects of disasters. *Journal of Consulting and Clinical Psychology, 3,* 538–546.

Green, B. L. (1993). Identifying survivors at risk. Trauma and stressors across events. In J. Wilson & B. Raphael (Eds.), *International handbook of traumatic stress syndromes* (pp. 135–144). New York: Plenum.

Green, B. L., Korol, M., Grace, M. C., Vary, M. G., Leonard, A. C., Gleser, G. C., & Smitson-Cohen, S. (1991). Children and disaster: Age, gender, and parental effects of PTSD symptoms. *Journal of the Academy of Child and Adolescent Psychiatry, 30,* 945–951.

Green, B. L., Lindy, J. D., Grace, M. C., & Gleser, G. C. (1989). Multiple diagnosis in posttraumatic stress disorder. The role of war stressors. *Journal of Nervous and Mental Disease, 177,* 329–335.

Green, B. L., Lindy, J. D., Grace, M. C., & Leonard, A. C. (1992). Chronic posttraumatic stress disorder and diagnostic co-morbidity in a disaster sample. *Journal of Nervous and Mental Disease, 180,* 760–766.

Haber-Schaim, N., Solomon, Z., Bleich, A., & Kottler, M. (1988). The prevalence of PTSD. *New England Journal of Medicine, 318,* 1691.

Hauff, E., & Vaglum, P. (1993). Vietnamese boat refugees: The influence of war and flight traumatization on mental health on arrival in the country of resettlement. *Acta Psychiatrica Scandinavica, 88,* 162–168.

Helzer, J. E., Robins, L. N., & McEvoy, L. (1987). Post-traumatic stress disorder in the general population: Findings of the epidemiologic catchment area survey. *New England Journal of Medicine, 317,* 1630–1634.

Hendin, H., & Haas, A. P. (1991). Suicide and guilt as manifestations of PTSD in Vietnam combat veterans. *American Journal of Psychiatry, 148,* 586–591.

Hickling, E. J., & Blanchard, E. B. (1992). Posttraumatic stress disorder and motor vehicle accidents. *Journal of Anxiety Disorders, 6,* 285–291.

Hinton, W. L., Chen, Y. C. J., Du, N., Tran, C. G., Lu, F. G., Miranda, J., & Faust, S. (1993). DSM–III–R disorders in Vietnamese refugees: Prevalence and correlates. *Journal of Nervous and Mental Disease, 181,* 113–122.

Hough, R. L., Vega, W., Valle, R., Kolody, B., Griswald del Castillo, R., & Tarke, H. (1990). Mental health consequences of the San Ysidro McDonald's massacre: A community study. *Journal of Traumatic Stress, 3*, 71–93.

Houskamp, B. M., & Foy, D. W. (1991). The assessment of posttraumatic stress disorder in battered women. *Journal of Interpersonal Violence, 6*, 368–376.

Hryvniak, M. R. (1989). Concurrent psychiatric illness in inpatients with posttraumatic stress disorder. *Military Medicine, 154*, 399–401.

International Federation of Red Cross and Red Crescent Societies (1993). *World disasters report 1993.* Dordrecht, Holland: Martinus Nijhoff.

Jeanneret, O., & Sand, E. A. (1993). Intentional violence among adolescents and young adults: An epidemiological perspective. *World Health Statistics Quarterly, 46*, 34–52.

Jordan, B. K., Schlenger, W. E., Hough, R., Kulka, R. A., Weiss, D., Fairbank, J. A., & Marmar, C. R. (1991). Lifetime and current prevalence of specific psychiatric disorders among Vietnam Veterans and controls. *Archives of General Psychiatry, 48*, 207–215.

Keane, T. M. (1990). The epidemiology of posttraumatic stress disorder: Some comments and concerns. *PTSD Research Quarterly, 1*, 1–3.

Keane, T. M., & Penk, W. E. (1988). The prevalence of PTSD. *New England Journal of Medicine, 318*, 1690–1691.

Kemp, A., Rawlings, E. J., & Green, B. L. (1991). Post-traumatic stress disorder (PTSD) in battered women: A shelter sample. *Journal of Traumatic Stress, 4*, 137–147.

Kidson, M. A., Douglas, J. C., & Holwill, B. J. (1993). Post-traumatic stress disorder in Australian World War II veterans attending a psychiatric outpatient clinic. *Medical Journal of Australia, 158*, 563–566.

Kilpatrick, D. G., Saunders, B. E., Amick-McMullan, A., Best, C. L., Veronen, L. J., & Resnick, H. S. (1989). Victim and crime factors associated with the development of crime-related post-traumatic stress disorder. *Behaviour Therapy, 20*, 199–214.

Kinzie, J. D., Boehnlein, J. K., Leung, P. K., Moore, L. J., Riley, C., & Smith, D. (1990). The prevalence of post-traumatic stress disorder and its clinical significance among Southeast Asian refugees. *American Journal of Psychiatry 147*, 913–917.

Kinzie, J. D., Sack, W. H., Angell, R. H., Manson, S., & Rath, B. (1986). The psychiatric effects of massive trauma on Cambodian children: I. The children. *Journal of the Academy of Child and Adolescent Psychiatry, 25*, 370–376.

Kluznik, J. C., Speed, N., Van-Valkenburg, C., & Magraw, R. (1986). Forty-year follow-up of United States prisoners of war. *American Journal of Psychiatry, 143*, 1443–1446.

Korver, A. I. H. (1987). What is a disaster?. *Prehospital and Disaster Medicine, 2*, 152–153.

Kozarick-Kovaclc, D., Folnegovic-Smalc, V., & Marusic, A. (1993). Psychological disturbances among 47 Croatian prisoners of war tortured in detention camps. *Journal of the American Medical Association, 270,* 575.

Kroll, J., Habenicht, M., Mackenzie, T., Yang, M., Chan, S., Vang, T., Nguyen, T., Ly, M., Phommasouvanh, B., Nguyen, H., Vang., Y., Souvannasoth., L., & Cabugao, R. (1989). Depression and posttraumatic stress disorder in Southeast Asian refugees. *American Journal of Psychiatry, 146,* 1592–1597.

Kuch, K., & Cox, B. J. (1992). Symptoms of PTSD in 124 survivors of the Holocaust. *American Journal of Psychiatry, 149,* 337–340.

Kulka, R. A., Schlenger, W. E., Fairbank, J. A., Hough, R. L., Jordan, B. K., Marmar, C. R., & Weiss, D. S. (1990). *Trauma and the Vietnam war generation.* New York: Brunner and Mazel.

Kulka, R. A., Schlenger, W. E., Fairbank, J. A., Jordan, B. K., Hough, R. L., Marmar, C. R., & Weiss, D. S. (1991). Assessment of PTSD in the community: Prospects and pitfalls from recent studies of Vietnam veterans. *Psychological Assessment: A Journal of Consulting and Clinical Psychology, 3,* 546–559.

Last, J. M. (1983). *A dictionary of epidemiology.* New York: Oxford University Press.

Lima, B. R., Pai, S., Caris, L., Haro, J. M., Lima, A. M., Toledo, V., Lozano, J., & Santacruz, H. (1991). Psychiatric disorders in primary health care clinics one year after a major Latin American disaster. *Stress Medicine, 7,* 25–32.

Lima, B. R., Pai, S., Santacruz, H., & Lozano, J. (1991). Psychiatric disorders among poor victims following a major disaster: Armero, Colombia. *Journal of Nervous and Mental Disease, 179,* 420–427.

Lindal, E., & Stefansson, J. G. (1993). The lifetime prevalence of anxiety disorders in Iceland as estimated by the US National Institute of Mental Health Diagnostic Interview Schedule. *Acta Psychiatrica Scandinavica, 88,* 29–34.

Lindberg, F. H., & Distad, L. J. (1985). Post-traumatic stress disorders in women who experienced childhood incest. *Child Abuse and Neglect, 9,* 329–334.

Lindy, J. D., Green, B. J., Grace, M., & Tichner, J. (1983). Psychotherapy with survivors of the Beverly Hills Supper Club Fire. *American Journal of Psychiatry, 37,* 593–610.

Long, N., Chamberlain, K., & Vincent, C. (1992). The health and mental health of New Zealand Vietnam war veterans with posttraumatic stress disorder. *The New Zealand Medical Journal, 105,* 417–419.

Lopez, G., Piffaut, G., & Seguin, A. (1992). Prise en charge psychologique des victimes d'agressions sexuelles. [Psychological treatment of victims of rape.] *Psychologie Médicale [Medical Psychology], 24,* 286–288.

Madakasira, S., & O'Brien, K. F. (1987). Acute post-traumatic stress disorders in victims of a natural disaster. *Journal of Nervous and Mental Disease, 175,* 286–290.

Malt, U. (1988). The longterm psychiatric consequences of accidental injury. A longitudinal study of 107 adults. *British Journal of Psychiatry, 153,* 810–818.

Manolias, M. B., & Hyatt-Williams, A. (1993). Effects of post-shooting experiences on police-authorized firearms officers in the United Kingdom. In J. Wilson & B. Raphael (Eds.), *International handbook of traumatic stress syndromes* (pp. 385–394). New York: Plenum.

Marsella, A. J., Bornemann, T., Orley, J., & Ekblad, S. (Eds.). (1994). *Amidst peril and pain: The mental health and wellbeing of the world's refugees*. Washington, DC: American Psychological Association.

Marsella, A.J., Friedman, M., & Spain, H. (1993). Ethnocultural aspects of PTSD. In J. Oldham, M. Riba, & A. Tasman (Eds.). *Review of psychiatry* (pp. 157–182). Washington, DC: American Psychiatric Press.

Mayou, R., Bryant, B., & Duthie, R. (1993). Psychiatric consequences of road traffic accidents. *British Medical Journal, 307,* 647–651.

McFall, M. E., MacKay, P. W., & Donovan, D. M. (1991). Combat-related PTSD and psychosocial adjustment problems among substance abusing veterans. *Journal of Nervous and Mental Disease, 179,* 33–38.

McFarlane, A. C. (1988). The phenomenology of posttraumatic stress disorders following a natural disaster. *Journal of Nervous and Mental Disease, 176,* 22–29.

McFarlane, A. C. (1992). Avoidance and intrusion in posttraumatic stress disorder. *Journal of Nervous and Mental Disease, 180,* 439–445.

McFarlane, A. (in press). The severity of the trauma: Issues about its role in PTSD. In R. Kleber & C. Figley (Eds.). *Perspectives in the study of PTSD.* New York: Brunner/Mazel.

McGorry, P. D., Chanen, A., McCarthy, E., Van-Riel, R., McKenzie, D., & Singh, B. S. (1991). Posttraumatic stress disorder following recent onset psychosis: An unrecognized post-psychotic syndrome. *Journal of Nervous and Mental Disease, 179,* 253–258.

McNally, R. J., & Lukach, B. M. (1992). Are panic attacks traumatic stressors? *American Journal of Psychiatry, 149,* 824–826.

Mellman, T. A., Randolph, C. A., Brawman-Mintzer, O., Flores, L. P., & Milanes, F. J. (1992). Phenomenology and course of psychiatric disorders associated with combat-related posttraumatic stress disorder. *American Journal of Psychiatry, 149,* 1568–1574.

Mollica, R. F., Donelan, K., Tor, S., Lavelle, J., Elias, C., Frankel, M., & Blendon, R. J. (1993). The effect of trauma and confinement on functional health and mental health status of Cambodians living in Thailand-Cambodia border camps. *Journal of the American Medical Association, 270,* 581–586.

Mollica, R. F., Wyshak, G., & Lavelle, J. (1987). The psychological impact of war trauma and torture on Southeast Asian refugees. *American Journal of Psychiatry 144,* 1567–1572.

Moore, L. J., & Boehnlein, J. K. (1991). Posttraumatic stress disorder, depression, and somatic symptoms in U.S. Mien patients. *Journal of Nervous and Mental Disease, 179,* 728–733.

Newman, J. P., & Foreman, C. (1987). Traumatic stress. Presentation to the Society for Traumatic Stress, Baltimore, Maryland.

Norris, F. H. (1992). Epidemiology of trauma: Frequency and impact of different potentially traumatic events on different demographic groups. *Journal of Consulting and Clinical Psychology, 60,* 409–418.

North, C. S., & Smith, E. M. (1992). Posttraumatic stress disorder among homeless men and women. *Hospital and Community Psychiatry, 43,* 1010–1016.

North, C. S., Smith, E. M., McCool, R. E., & Lightcap, P. E. (1989). Acute postdisaster coping and adjustment. *Journal of Traumatic Stress, 2,* 353–360.

North, C. S., Smith, E. M., McCool, R. E. & Shea, J. M. (1989). Short-term psychopathology in eyewitnesses to mass murder. *Hospital and Community Psychiatry, 40,* 1293–1295.

North, C. S., Smith, E. M., & Spitznagel, E. L. (1994). Posttraumatic stress disorder in survivors of a mass shooting. *American Journal of Psychiatry, 151,* 82–88.

O'Brien, L. S., & Hughes, S. J. (1991). Symptoms of post-traumatic stress disorder in Falklands veterans five years after the conflict. *British Journal of Psychiatry, 159,* 135–141.

Orner, R. J. (1993). Posttraumatic stress syndromes among British veterans of the Falklands war. In J. Wilson & B. Raphael (Eds.), *International handbook of traumatic stress syndromes* (pp. 305–310). New York: Plenum.

Palinkas, L. A., Petterson, J. S., Russell, J., & Downs, M. A. (1993). Community patterns of psychiatric disorders after the Exxon Valdez oil spill. *American Journal of Psychiatry, 150,* 1517–1523.

Patterson, D. R., Carrigan, L., Questad, K. A., & Robinson, R. (1990). Posttraumatic stress disorder in hospitalized patients with burn injuries. *Journal of Burn Care and Rehabilitation, 11,* 181–184.

Perez-Jimenez, J. P., Graell-Berna, M., Perez-Sales, P., & Santodomingo, J. (1993). Severe burn injuries and PTSD. *American Journal of Psychiatry, 150,* 1276.

Perry, S., Difede, J., Musngi, G., Frances, A. J., & Jacobsberg, L. (1992). Predictors of posttraumatic stress disorder after burn injury. *American Journal of Psychiatry, 149,* 931–935.

Pitman, R. K., Altman, B., & Macklin, M. L. (1989). Prevalence of posttraumatic stress disorder in wounded Vietnam veterans. *American Journal of Psychiatry, 146,* 667–669.

Ramsay, R., Gorst-Unsworth, C., & Turner, S. (1993). Psychiatric morbidity in survivors of organised state violence including torture. A retrospective series. *British Journal of Psychiatry, 162,* 55–59.

Raphael, B. (1986). *When disaster strikes.* London: Hutchinson.

Realmuto, G. M., Masten, A., Carole, L. F., Hubbard, J., Groteschulen, A., & Chun, B. (1991). Adolescent survivors of massive childhood trauma in Cambodia: Life events and current symptoms. *Journal of Traumatic Stress, 5,* 589–599.

Resnick, H. S., Kilpatrick, D. G., Best, C. L., & Kramer, T. L. (1992). Vulnerability, stress factors in development of post-traumatic stress disorder. *Journal of Nervous and Mental Disease, 180,* 424–430.

Riggs, D. A., Dancu, C. V., Gershuny, B. S., Greenberg, D., & Foa, E. B. (1992). Anger and post-traumatic stress disorder in female crime victims. *Journal of Traumatic Stress, 5*, 613–624.

Roberts, W. R., Penk, W. E., Gearing, M. L., Robinowitz, R., Dolan, M. P., & Patterson, E. T. (1982). Interpersonal problems of Vietnam combat veterans with symptoms of posttraumatic stress disorder. *Journal of Traumatic Stress, 91*, 444–450.

Robins, L. N., & Regier, D. A. (1991). *Psychiatric disorders in America.* New York: The Free Press.

Roca, R. P., Spence, R., & Munster, A. M. (1992). Posttraumatic adaptation and distress among adult burn survivors. *American Journal of Psychiatry, 149*, 1234–1238.

Rothbaum, B. O., Foa, E. B., Riggs, D. S., Murdock, T., & Walsh, W. (1992). A prospective examination of post-traumatic stress disorder in rape victims. *Journal of Traumatic Stress, 5*, 455–476.

Rubonis, A. V., & Bickman, L. (1991). Psychological impairment in the wake of disaster: The disaster–psychopathology relationship. *Psychological Bulletin, 109*, 384–399.

Rudd, M. D., Dahm, P. F., & Rajab, M. H. (1993). Diagnostic comorbidity in persons with suicidal ideation and behavior. *American Journal of Psychiatry, 150*, 928–934.

Schnurr, P. P., Friedman, M. J., & Rosenberg, S. D. (1993). Premilitary MMPI scores as predictors of combat-related PTSD symptoms. *American Journal of Psychiatry, 150*, 479–483.

Schottenfeld, R. S., & Cullen, M. R. (1985). Occupation-induced posttraumatic stress disorders. *American Journal of Psychiatry, 142*, 198–202.

Schwarz, E. D., & Kowalski, J. M. (1991). Malignant memories: PTSD in children and adults after a school shooting. *Journal of the Academy of Child and Adolescent Psychiatry, 30*, 936–944.

Shalev, A. Y. (1992). Posttraumatic stress disorder among injured survivors of a terrorist attack. Predictive value of early intrusion and avoidance symptoms. *Journal of Nervous and Mental Disease, 180*, 505–509.

Sherwood, R. J., Funari, D. J., & Piekarski, A. M. (1990). Adapted character styles of Vietnam veterans with posttraumatic stress disorder. *Psychological Reports, 66*, 623–631.

Shore, J. H., Vollmer, W. M., & Tatum, E. L. (1989). Community patterns of posttraumatic stress disorders. *Journal of Nervous and Mental Disease, 177*, 681–685.

Silverman, J. J., Hart, R. P., Garrettson, L. K., Stockman, S. J., Hamer, R. M., Schulz, S. C., & Narasimhachari, N. (1985). Posttraumatic stress disorder from pentaborane intoxication: Neuropsychiatric evaluation and short-term follow-up. *Journal of the American Medical Association, 254*, 2603–2608.

Skre, I., Onstad, S., Torgensen, S., Lygren, S., & Kringlen, E. (1993). A twin study of *DSM–III–R* anxiety disorders. *Acta Psychiatrica Scandinavica, 88*, 85–92.

Sloan, P. (1988). Post-traumatic stress in survivors of an airplane crash-landing: A clinical and exploratory study. *Journal of Traumatic Stress, 1,* 211–229.

Smith, E. M., & North, C. (1993). Post-traumatic stress disorder in natural disaster and technological accident. In J. Wilson & B. Raphael (Eds.), *International handbook of traumatic stress syndromes* (pp. 9–22). New York: Plenum.

Smith, E. M., North, C. S., McCool, R. E., & Shea, J. M. (1990). Acute postdisaster psychiatric disorders: Identification of persons at risk. *American Journal of Psychiatry, 147,* 202–206.

Smith, E. M., Robins, L. N., Przybeck, T. R., Goldring, E., & Solomon, S. D. (1986). Psychosocial consequences of a disaster. In J. Shore (Ed.), *Disaster stress studies: New methods and findings* (pp. 50–76). Washington, DC: American Psychiatric Press.

Snow, B. R., Mager-Stellman, J., Stellman, S. D., & Sommer, J. F., Jr. (1988). Post-traumatic stress disorder among American legionnaires in relation to combat experience in Vietnam: Associated and contributing factors. *Environmental Research, 47,* 175–192.

Solomon, S. D., & Canino, G. J. (1990). Appropriateness of *DSM–III–R* criteria for posttraumatic stress disorder. *Comprehensive Psychiatry, 31,* 227–237.

Solomon, Z., Laor, N., Weiler, D., Muller, U. F., Hadar, O., Waysman, M., Koslowsky, M., Yakar, M. B., & Bleich, A. (1993). The psychological impact of the Gulf War: A study of acute stress in Israeli evacuees. *Archives of General Psychiatry, 50,* 320–321.

Solomon, Z., & Mikulincer, M. (1987). Posttraumatic stress disorder among front-line soldiers with combat stress reactions: The 1982 Israeli experience. *American Journal of Psychiatry, 144,* 448–454.

Southwick, S. M., Morgan, A., Nagy, L. M., Bremner, D., Nicolaou, A. L., Johnson, D. R., Rosenheck, R., & Charney, D. S. (1993). Trauma-related symptoms in veterans of Operation Desert Storm: A preliminary report. *American Journal of Psychiatry, 150,* 1524–1528.

Speed, N., Engdahl, B., Schwartz, J., & Eberly, R. (1989). Posttraumatic stress disorder as a consequence of the POW experience. *Journal of Nervous and Mental Disease, 177,* 147–153.

Steinglass, P., & Gerrity, E. (1990). Natural disasters and post-traumatic stress disorder: Short-term versus long-term recovery rates in two disaster-affected communities. *Journal of Applied and Social Psychology, 20,* 1746–1765.

Streimer, J. H., Cosstick, J., & Tennant, C. (1985). The psychosocial adjustment of Australian Vietnam veterans. *American Journal of Psychiatry, 142,* 616–618.

Stretch, R. H. (1990). PTSD and the Canadian Vietnam Veteran. *Journal of Traumatic Stress, 3,* 239–253.

Stretch, R. H. (1991). Psychosocial readjustment of Canadian Vietnam Veterans. *Journal of Consulting and Clinical Psychology, 59,* 188–189.

Stretch, R. H., Vail, J. D., & Maloney, J. P. (1985). Posttraumatic stress disorder among army nurse corps Vietnam veterans. *Journal of Consulting and Clinical Psychology, 53,* 704–708.

Summerfield, D., & Toser, L. (1991). "Low intensity" war and mental trauma in Nicaragua: A study in a rural community. *Medicine and War, 7,* 84–99

Sutker, P. B., Allain, A. N., Jr., & Winstead, D. K. (1993). Psychopathology and psychiatric diagnoses of World War II Pacific theater prisoner of war survivors and combat veterans. *American Journal of Psychiatry, 150,* 240–245.

Sutker, P. B., Uddo, M., Brailey, K., & Allain, A. N. (1993). War-zone trauma and stress-related symptoms in operation Desert Shield/Storm (ODS) returnees. *Journal of Social Issues, 49,* 33–49.

Toole, M. J., & Waldman, R. J. (1993). Prevention of excess mortality in refugee and displaced populations in developing countries. *Journal of the American Medical Association, 263,* 3296–3302.

United Nations Disaster Relief Coordinator. (1984). *Disaster prevention and mitigation, Vol. II: Preparadness aspects.* New York: United Nations.

van Dijk, J. J. M., & Mayhew, P. (1993). Criminal victimization in the industrialized world: Key findings of the 1989 and 1992 international crime surveys. In A. Alvazzi del Frate, U. Zvekic, & J.J van Dijk (Eds.), *Understanding crime: Experiences of crime and crime control* (pp. 1–5). Rome, Italy: United Nations Interregional Crime and Justice Research Institute, Publication # 49.

Warshaw, M. G., Fierman, E., Pratt, L., Hunt, M., Yonkers, K. A., Massion, A. O., & Keller, M. B. (1993). Quality of life and dissociation in anxiety disorder patients with histories of trauma or PTSD. *American Journal of Psychiatry, 150,* 1512–1516.

Weisaeth, L. (1989). A study of behavioural responses to an industrial disaster. *Acta Psychiatrica Scandinavica Supplementum, 80,* 13–24.

Weisaeth L. (1993). Torture of a Norwegian ship's crew: Stress reactions, coping and psychiatric aftermath. In J. Wilson & B. Raphael (Eds.), *International handbook of traumatic stress syndromes* (pp. 743–750). New York: Plenum.

Wolfe, J., Brown, P. J., & Kelley, J. M. (1993). Reassessing war stress: Exposure and the Persian Gulf war. *Journal of Social Issues, 49,* 15–31.

World Health Organization. (1992a). *International classification of diseases—10th Edition. Chapter V (Mental and behavioural disorders including disorders of psychological development). Clinical descriptions and diagnostic guidelines.* Geneva, Switzerland: Author.

World Health Organization. (1992b). *Psychosocial consequences of disasters: Prevention and management.* Geneva, Switzerland: Author, WHO/MNH/PSF/91.3.

Zwi A. B. (1991). Militarism, militarization, health and the third world. *Medicine and War, 7,* 262–268.

APPENDIX
Prevalence Rates of Posttraumatic Stress Disorder

Author & Year	Country	Sample Studied	Sample Size (N)	Assessment Methods	Diagnostic System	Prevalence Rate of PTSD	Notes
Abenhaim, Dah, & Salmi, 1992	France	Survivors of terroristic attacks 1982–87	254	Self-administered questionnaire	DSM–III	10.5% (uninjured) 8% (moderately injured) 31% (severely injured)	Major depression was found in 13% of the victims.
Aghabeigi, Feinmann, & Harris, 1992	UK	Patients with chronic idiopathic orofacial pain	34	SCID	DSM–III–R	15%	The history of PTSD coincided with the onset of pain. Most PTSD sufferers also had a personality disorder.
Amick-McMullan et al., 1991	USA	Family survivors of criminal homicide victims (group 1) and alcohol-related vehicular homicide victims (group 2)	206	Clinical assessment	DSM–III–R	19% (lifetime) & 5% (current) (group 1) 27% (lifetime) & 4% (current) (group2)	Survivors who experiences the homicide during their childhood, adolescence, or adulthood also showed equal likelinood of PTSD.
Basoglu et al., 1994	Turkey	Former political prisoners	55	SCID.M-PTSD. PTSD symptom checklist (administered by a clinician)	DSM–II–R	33% (lifetime) 18% (point)	Despite the severity of their torture experiences, the survivors had only a moderate level of psychopathology. Several factors proved to be protective from the risk of suffering frm PTSD.
Bauer, Priebe, Haring, & Adamczak, 1993	Germany	Former political prisoners imprisoned for at least 6 weeks	55	Clinical assessment, PTSD symptoms checklist.	DSM–III–R	22%	In most patients there was a characteristic syndrome including symptoms of depression and anxiety, with vegetative complaints and increased arousal. Eight out of twelve patients with PTSD also had another diagnosis.
Bell, Kee, Loughrey, Roddy, & Curran, 1988	Northern Ireland	Adults seeking compensation for "nervous shock" and referred for a medico-legal assessment	643	Clinical assessment	DSM–III	23%	People with PTSD tended to be older, of female sex, to have more depressive symptoms, and more severe, prolonged disturbance.
Benedikt & Kolb, 1986	USA	Patients attending a Veterans Administration pain clinic	225	Clinical assessment	DSM–III	10%	Many of these patients had current or past histories of depression, anxiety, or substance abuse.
Blake et al., 1990	USA	Combat veterans seeking medical treatment	161	M-PTSD, SCL-90-R, CES	DSM–III–R	24%	There were no differences in combat exposure among the three different veteran groups; however, PTSD rate was higher among Vietnam veterans. A combination of psychological and demographic factors predicted PTSD status.
Boon & Draijer, 1993	The Netherlands	Patients with multiple personality disorders	71	SCID-D, STI	DSM–III–R	81%	95% of the patients reported a history of sexual and / or physical abuse. Patients presented many different symptoms.

DE GIROLAMO AND MCFARLANE

Study	Location	Sample	N	Assessment	Criteria	Prevalence	Findings
Bownes, O'Gorman, & Sayers, 1991	Northern Ireland	Rape victims referred for medico-legal assessment	51	Clinical assessment	DSM-III	70%	Being raped by strangers, subjected to physical force and weapons, and having suffered from injuries were all associated with higher risk of PTSD.
Blow, Cook, Booth, Falcon, & Friedman, 1992	USA	Alcoholics seeking outpatient care in any Veterans Affairs mental health facility during a one-month period in 1986	22,463	Clinical assessment	DSM-III	8%	PTSD peaked in patients of the age of 30–39, rates decreased with increasing age.
Brawman-Mintzer et al., 1993	USA	Patients with a primary diagnosis of generalized anxiety disorder	109	SCID-P	DSM-III-R	3%	The mean age at onset of PTSD was 19 years.
Breslau, Davis, Andreski, & Peterson, 1991	USA	Adults from a large health maintenance organization in Detroit	1,007	SCID-III-R	DSM-III-R	9% (lifetime rate in the overall sample) 24% (among those exposed to traumatic events)	The lifetime prevalence of exposure to traumatic events was 39.1%. Risk factors for PTSD after exposure included early separation from parents, neuroticism, preexisting anxiety or depression, and family history of anxiety.
Breslau & Davis, 1987	USA	Vietnam veterans being inpatients in a VA psychiatric facility for a period of 3 months	69	DIS	DSM-III	77%	Participation in atrocities and the cumulative exposure to combat stresses increased the risk of PTSD
Brooks & McKinlay, 1992	UK	Residents in Lockerbie who claimed for compensation after the aircraft disaster	66	PTSD symptom checklist (administered by a clinician), IES.	DSM-III-R	44%	An additional 29% had mild or remitted PTSD. There were no significant predictors of the presence or severity of the diagnosis, but a number of predictors (age, death of friends, exposure to distressing sights) of questionnaire scores. An additional 59% had a moderate PTSD disorder.
Burge, 1988	USA	Rape victims who had sought support at two women's helping centers	29	IES, BSI	DSM-III	28%	All but two would have probably satisfied the criteria for PTSD at some time following their release.
Burges-Watson, 1993	Australia	Prisoners of Japanese during WW II admitted to a general hospital	11	Clinical assessment, IES.	DSM-III-R	27% (current)	
Buydens-Branchey, Noumair, Branchey, 1990	USA	Vietnam veterans attending an orthopedic clinic formerly exposed to combat	34	SCID	DSM-III	73% (lifetime)	PTSD associated with longer combat exposure, more intense combat experience and particularly with war injuries.
Caldwell, 1992	USA	Mental health workers from two facilities	224	PTSD symptom checklist (self-administered).	DSM-III-R	10%	62% reported experiencing a critical incident involving a serious threat to life or physical safety or witnessing a serious injury or death.
Callen, Reaves, Maxwell, & McFarland, 1985	USA	Vietnam veterans admitted to a general hospital	300	PTSD symptom checklist (self-administered)	DSM-III	50%	About 50% had high levels of PTSD symptoms, or depression, or both. Combat veterans were more symptomatic.
Canino, Bravo, Rubio-Stipec, & Woodbury, 1990	Puerto Rico	Victims of a flood	321	DIS/DS	DSM-III	4%	The PTSD prevalence rate in the unexposed control group (n = 591) was 0.7%. Other common disorders among the exposed included depression and anxiety.
Card, 1987	USA	Vietnam veterans randomly sampled on the basis of their high school attendance	481	PTSD symptom checklist (self-administered)	DSM-III	19%	PTSD was associated with other family, mental health, and social interaction problems. The presence of a spouse or the religious affiliation were associate with reduced levels of PTSD.
Carlson & Hogan, 1991	USA	Cambodian refugees resettled in the USA	50	PTSD symptom checklist (self-administered)	DSM-III-R	86%	A relationship was found between the amount of trauma experienced and the severity of PTSD symptoms.

(continued)

APPENDIX (Continued)
Prevalence Rates of Posttraumatic Stress Disorder

Author & Year	Country	Sample Studied	Sample Size (N)	Assessment Methods	Diagnostic System	Prevalence Rate of PTSD	Notes
Centers for Disease Control Vietnam Experience Study, 1988	USA	Random sample of Vietnam veterans who entered the U.S. army between 1965–71	2,490	DIS, MMPI	DSM–III	15% (lifetime) 2% (current)	Veterans who met DSM–III criteria for PTSD were also more likely to meet DSM–III criteria for other psychiatric disorders.
Cervantes, Salgado de Snyder, & Padillo, 1989	USA	Immigrants from Central America and Mexico	258	SCL-90-R, CES-D, PTSD symptom checklist (self-administered).	DSM–III	49–52% (among Central Americans) 25% (among Mexican immigrants)	Individuals with PTSD also showed a high rate of other symptoms including anxiety, depression, somatization.
Chemtob et al., 1990	USA	Special-forces Vietnam veterans	57	IES, PTSD symptom checklist (self-administered)	DSM–III	25%	PTSD symptoms were associated with poorer preservice relationships, being wounded, having friends missing in action, feeling guilt over the death of a friend, lack of emotional preparation to leave the unit or service, and failure to discuss feelings upon return from Vietnam.
Collins & Bailey, 1990	USA	Incarcerated male felons	1,140	DIS	DSM–III	2% (lifetime)	A relationship of PTSD violence and its symptoms to arrest and incarceration for expressive violence was found when other factors were controlled.
Conyer, Sepulveda Amor, Medina Mora, Caraveo, & De La Fuente, 1987	Mexico	Victims of an earthquake	524	DIS, SCID	DSM–III	32%	Women were more affected than men.
Cottler, Compton, Mager, Spitznagel, & Janca, 1992	USA	Respondents surveyed at the St. Louis site in the second wave of the ECA study	2,663	DIS	DSM–III	1%	16% reported ever experiencing a symptom-related stressful event. 38% of the sample met the criteria for substance use. Female gender and use of cocaine/opiates predicted PTSD.
Craine, Henson, Colliver, & MacLean, 1988	USA	Female psychiatric hospital patients sexually abused as children or adolescent	54	PTSD symptom checklist (administered by a psychiatrist)	DSM–III	66%	None of these patients had received a PTSD diagnosis before the study assessment. Adults patients sexually abused were more likely to have several symptoms commonly linked with sexual abuse.
Creamer, 1989	Australia	Subjects exposed to a multiple homicide and seeking treatment	42	Clinical assessment	DSM–III DSM–III–R	74% (using DSM–III criteria) 33% (using DSM–III–R criteria)	The symptoms aded in the DSM–III–R were the least frequently reported, while guilt, which has been excluded from the DSM–III–R, was endorsed by 38% of the sample.
Crocq, Hein, Duval, & Macher, 1991	France	Former WW II Prisoners of war	817	Mailed self-report questionnaire	DSM–III–R	71%	The presumptive diagnosis of PTSD was significantly associated with longer internment and with higher scores on a severity of POW experience index.

Study	Country	Sample	N	Assessment	DSM	Prevalence	Comments
Curran et al., 1990	Northern Ireland	Survivors of the Enniskillen bombing (1987)	26	PTSD symptom checklist (administered by a psychiatrist)	DSM–III–R	50% (at 6-month follow-up)	More females were suffering from PTSD. No correlation was found between physical injury and psychiatric disorders.
Dahl, 1989	Norway	Victims of rape and attempted rape	55	Clinical assessment, CPRS, IES, SSL, STAI	DSM–III	47%	77% had high levels of intrusion, and 57% high levels of avoidance on the IES.
Davidson & Smith, 1990	USA	Newly referred psychiatric outpatients with a history of traumatization	44	Clinical assessment	DSM–III–R	22%	Factors related to PTSD included early trauma, more traumatic events, incest, perceiving the event as frightening or life threatening, being physically injured, and seeing a physician and being hospitalized.
Davidson, Hughes, Blazer, & George, 1991	USA	Respondents surveyed at the Duke site of the ECA study	2,985	DIS	DSM–III	1.3% (lifetime) 0.4% (6 months)	Subjects with PTSD reported job instability, family history of psychiatric illness, parental poverty, child abuse, and separation or divorce of parents prior to age 10.
De Groen et al., 1993	The Netherlands	WW II veterans	98	SCID	DSM–III–R	56% (current)	Current PTSD was highly associated with anxiety dreams and with snoring.
den Velde et al., 1993	The Netherlands	WW II Dutch Resistance fighters	147	SCID, 21-item Maastricht Questionnaire to assess vital exhaustion	DSM–III	84% (lifetime) 56% (current)	Many cases had a very delayed onset (up to more than 35 years after the events). Vital exhaustion was frequent among PTSD subjects. High rate of marital breakdown.
Durham, McCammon, & Allison, 1985	USA	Rescuers who treated victims of an apartment building explosion.	53	PTSD symptom checklist (self-administered)	DSM–III	21%	Rescuers who worked at the scene of the disaster were more likely to report symptoms of adjustment difficulty than were hospital-based workers.
Ersland, Weisaeth, & Sund, 1989	Norway	Rescuers involved in an offshore oil rig disaster	134	Self-report questionnaire (including IES scale)	DSM–III	14%	52–64% reported discouragement, restlessness, uncertainty, anxiety, and irritation. Nine months after the disaster 24% of the rescuers reported poor mental health conditions.
Eberly & Engdahl, 1991	USA	Former WW II prisoners living in Minnesota	426	Clinical assessment SADS-L and PTSD Symptom checklist (administered by a psychiatrist) on 65% of the sample	DSM–III	71% (lifetime)	Those who lost more than 35% of the body weight during captivity had higher rates of PTSD and other psychiatric disorders.
Fairley, Langeluddecke, & Tennant, 1986	Australia	Victims of a cyclone in the Fiji islands	75	PTSD symptom checklist (self-administered)	DSM–III	66% (partial PTSD)	Two months after the cyclone both psychological and physical morbidity was 2–3 times greater in the affected community compared to controls. By the third month morbidity had resolved to levels similar to the control population.
Famularo, Kinscherff, & Fenton, 1992	USA	Mothers of abused children either before a justice court or having the abused child admitted to a pediatric ward	54	SCID	DSM–III–R	43%	The rate of PTSD was significantly higher as compared to a control group (n=37; PTSD rate=13%). Abusing mothers also had higher rates of mood disorders, alcohol abuse, and personality disorders.

(continued)

APPENDIX (Continued)
Prevalence Rates of Posttraumatic Stress Disorder

Author & Year	Country	Sample Studied	Sample Size (N)	Assessment Methods	Diagnostic System	Prevalence Rate of PTSD	Notes
Farmer, Tranah, O'Donnell, & Catalan, 1992	UK	London Underground train drivers witnessing railway suicides	43	PSE-9, PTSD symptom checklist (administered by a psychiatrist). IES, PTSS-10	DSM–III–R	16% (at one month)	39% of the drivers showed depression or phobia one month after the accident. All PTSD subjects had taken some substantial time off work following the accident.
Feinstein, 1993	UK	Patients admitted to an orthopedic ward because of a leg fracture due to a motor vehicle accident	48	CIS. IES. BDI.	DSM–III	25% (at 6 weeks) 14% (at 6 months)	Scores on the IES were the single most important predictor of psychiatric morbidity at 6 months
Fierman et al., 1993	USA	Patients enrolled in a prospective, longitudinal, naturalistic study on anxiety disorders	711	SCID	DSM–III–R	10%	Subjects reporting sexual trauma were significantly more likely to have PTSD. The rate of PTSD was not higher in subjects with panic disorder than in those with other anxiety disorders.
Fisher & Jacoby, 1992	UK	Bus crew victims of physical assault	22	CIS. PTSD symptom checklist (administered by a psychiatrist). IES.	DSM–III–R	23%	PTSD was largely associated with the severity of the index assault, although this did not always equate with serious physical injury. At 18-month follow-up psychiatric distress and impairment persisted.
Frye & Stockton, 1982	USA	Vietnam veterans trained together	88	PTSD symptom checklist (self-administered)	DSM–III	24%	Veterans with PTSD experienced a higher level of combat, a more immediate discharge after the war, a negative perception of their family's helpfulness on return home and an external locus of control.
Gerson, 1991	The Netherlands	Police officers involved in a serious shooting accident	37	PTSD symptom checklist (administered by a psychiatrist)	DSM–III	46% (lifetime)	None of the policemen had looked for help or treatment.
Goldberg, True, Eisen, & Henderson, 1990	USA	Monozygotic twins discordant for military service during the Vietnam War	1,430 (715 sets of twins)	PTSD symptom checklist (self-administered).	DSM–III	17% (among those who served in Vietnam) 5% (among cotwins who did not serve in Vietnam)	There was a ninefold increase in the rate of PTSD among twins who experienced high levels of combat compared to those who did not serve in Vietnam.
Green, Lindy, Grace, & Leonard, 1992	USA	Victims of the Buffalo Creek disaster surveyed at 14-year follow-up	193	SCID. PEF. SCL-90R. IES.	DSM–III–R	59% (lifetime) 25% (current)	The stressors of life threat and bereavement were most strongly associated with mental health outcome measure. Major depression was also very common and was highly associated with PTSD.
Green, Lindy, Grace, & Gleser, 1989	USA	Vietnam veterans recruited from different sources in Ohio	191	SADS-L (with a PTSD additional schedule)	DSM–III	30%	Being active in a unit patrol, or being exposed to grotesque and mutilating death was strongly associated with PTSD.

Study	Country	Sample	N	Assessment	Criteria	Prevalence	Findings
Hauff & Vaglum, 1993	Norway	Adult resettled Vietnamese boat refugees	145	Clinical assessment. SCL-90-R. DIS	DSM–III	9% (current)	Nearly all war trauma variables but none of the escape or refugee camp variables were related to mental health 7 years after the end of the war.
Helzer, Robins, & McEvoy, 1987	USA	Respondents surveyed at the St. Louis site of the ECA study	2,493		DSM–III	1% (in the general population) 3.5% (among civilians physically affected) 20% (in Vietnam veterans wounded in action)	PTSD was associated with a variety of disorders. 15% of men and 16% of women reported only some PTSD symptoms. Behavioral problems before the age of 15 predicted adult exposure to physical attack.
Hendin & Haas, 1991	USA	Vietnam veterans attending VA hospital or informed about the research.	122	Clinical assessment. PTSD symptom checklist (self-administered). RCS.	DSM–III	82%	19 out of 100 veterans with PTSD had made a postservice suicide attempt. Severe PTSD was significantly related to suicide attempt.
Hickling & Blanchard, 1992	USA	Victims of motor vehicle accident referred to a clinical psychologist becasue of headache or other pain problems.	20	Clinical assessment	DSM–III–R	50%	Most of the victims also presented mood and anxiety disorders.
Hinton et al., 1993	USA	Vietnamese refugees resettled in the USA undergoing mandatory health screening	201	SCID, ADIS-PTSD.	DSM–III–R	3.5%	19% of the refugees reported traumatic events. PTSD was more frequent among refugees exposed to heavier traumatic events.
Hough et al., 1990	USA	Poor Mexican American immigrant women from an area where a shooting took place	100	DIS. CES-D	DSM–III	12%	Women most affected had relatives or friends involved in the massacre and were socially more vulnerable.
Houskamp & Foy, 1991	USA	Battered women attending a domestic violence clinic	26	SCID. IES.	DSM–III–R	45%	Dividing the group into high and low exposure groups based on degree of life threat, 60% of the high exposure group had PTSD compared to 14% in the low exposure group.
Hryvniak, 1989	USA	Inpatients admitted to a VA general psychiatry ward during a 18-month period	375	Case record review.	DSM–III or DSM–III–R	17%	Patients with PTSD had on average 2.9 diagnoses each, compared to 1.4 for the non-PTSD group. Alcohol and substance abuse, and depression were most common in the PTSD group.
Kemp, Rawlings, & Green, 1991	USA	Battered women from a shelter	77	IES, SCL-90-R, PTSD symptom checklist (self-administered)	DSM–III	84%	Extent of the abuse was positively correlated to presence and degree of PTSD and other psychiatric disturbances.

(continued)

Prevalence Rates of Posttraumatic Stress Disorder

Author & Year	Country	Sample Studied	Sample Size (N)	Assessment Methods	Diagnostic System	Prevalence Rate of PTSD	Notes
Kidson, Douglas, & Holwill, 1993	Australia	WW II veterans attending a psychiatric outpatient clinic	108	IES, PTSD symptom checklist (administered by a psychiatrist)	DSM–III–R	45% (current)	PTSD rate was siginificantly associated with physical injuries, and with degree of combat stress. Anxiety and depressive disorders were more common among PTSD veterans.
Kilpatrick et al., 1989	USA	Female victims of crime	294	DIS, IRI	DSM–III	28% (lifetime)	Life threat, physical injury, and completed rape were associated with PTSD. Victims who had all these three features were 8.5 times more likely to suffer from PTSD.
Kinzie, Sack, Angell, Manson, & Rath, 1986	USA	Cambodian refugees resettled in the USA (yrs 14–20) and attending a high school	40	DIS (some parts), SADS (some parts)	DSM–III	50% (current)	Mild but prolonged depressive symptoms were also common.
Kinzie et al., 1990	USA	Southeast Asian refugees attending a psychiatric clinic	322	Clinical assessment. PTSD symptom checklist (administered by a psychiatrist)	DSM–III–R	75% (lifetime) 70% (current)	PTSD symptoms were highly chronic (traumas usually occured 10–15 years before). Most cases never diagnosed before the start of the study.
Kluznik, Speed, Van-Valkenberg, & Magraw, 1986	USA	WW II Prisoners of war	188	SADS-L, BPRS, PTSD symptom checklist (administered by a psychiatrist).	DSM–III	67% (lifetime)	29% had fully recovered; 39% still had mild symptoms; 24% had improved but still had symptoms; 8% had not improved or had deteriorated. PTSD was not significantly associated with other mental disorders.
Kozarick-Kovak, Folnegovic-Smalc, & Marusic, 1993	Croatia	POWs	47	Clinical assessment. MMPI	DSM–III	34%	All POWs had at least two and on average eight to nine symptoms of psychological disturbance.
Kroll et al., 1989	USA	Southeast Asian refugees seen at a community mental health clinic during a 18-month period	404	Clinical assessment	DSM–III	14%	15–30% of the surveyed subjects reported specific traumatic experiences either in their homeland or during their escape.
Kuch & Cox, 1992	USA	Survivors of the Holocaust	124	Case record review.	DSM–III–R	46%	Auschwitz survivors had significantly more symptoms and were three times more likely to meet diagnostic criteria for PTSD.
Kulka et al., 1990	USA	(1) Vietnam veterans who served in Vietnam theater of operations; (2) veterans who served in the military during the Vietnam conflict but who did not serve in the Vietnam theater; (3) matched controls	3,016	SCID, M-PTSD. MMPI	DSM–III	(1) current: 15% (men); 8.5% (women) lifetime: 31% (men); 27% (women) (2) current: 2.5% (men); 1% (women) (3) current: 1% (men); 0.3% (women)	There was a strong relationship between PTSD and other postwar readjustment problems. There were substantial differences in PTSD prevalence rates by minority status. PTSD had a very negative impact on veterans' families. There were few differences between the veterans and the control groups in the rate of other psychiatric disorders.

Study	Country	Sample	N	Instrument	Criteria	Rate	Comments
Limaet al., 1991	Colombia	Consecutive patients attending two primary health care clinics from a disaster area (Armero eruption)	500	Clinical assessment.	*DSM–III*	24%	Among the victims the rate was 32%, as compared to 11% among the nonvictims.
Lima, Pai, Santacruz, & Lozano, 1991	Colombia	Victims of the Armero eruption from two shelters	102	Clinical assessment. PTSD Symptom checklist (administered by a clinician).	*DSM–III*	42%	PTSD and major depression accounted for 80% of all diagnoses made.
Lindberg & Distad, 1985	USA	Women who experienced childhood or adolescent incest and entered in psychotherapy	17	Clinical assessment.	*DSM–III*	100%	All regarding their incest experience as the most damaging event of their lives.
Lindal & Stefansson, 1993	Iceland	Cohort represented by half of those who were born in 1931	862	DIS	*DSM–III*	0.6%	PTSD was found only in women. The mean for onset of PTSD was 39 years, and the women with PTSD had on average other 3.2 additional diagnoses.
Long, Chamberlain, & Vincent, 1992	New Zealand	New Zealand Vietnam veterans	573	M-PTSD	*DSM–III–R*	12%	The PTSD group differed from the non PTSD group on all measures of physical and mental health. Significant differences were also found in terms of demographic and service measures.
Lopez, Piffaut, & Seguin, 1992	France	Victims of rape	436	PTSD symptoms checklist (self-administered).	*DSM–III*	37%	71% also showed a significant depressive disorder.
Madakasira & O'Brien, 1987	USA	Victims of a tornado from a rural community	116	Clinical assessment. HSCL (modified). CPRS. IES. STAIX-1.	*DSM–III*	59%	Demographic factors, degree of injury or property damage were not related to the occurance of PTSD.
Malt, 1988	Norway	Hospitalized victims of accidental injuries	107		*DSM–III*	0.9%	The overall incidence rate of any psychiatric disorder caused by the accident was 22%. Depressive disorders were the most frequent disorders.
Manolias & Hyatt-Williams, 1933	UK	Policemen involved in a shooting experience	25	Clinical assessment. Reaction Index.	*DSM–III*	12%	67% had a marked emotional reaction after the accident and 60% of the officers reported perceptual distortions during it. Appearance in court to render testimony increased PTSD symptoms.
Mayou, Bryant, & Duthie, 1993	UK	Victims of road traffic accidents	171	PTSD symptom checklist (administered by a psychiatrist)	*DSM–III–R*	8% (3 months) 8% (1 year)	PTSD was not associated with a neurotic predisposition but was strongly associated with horrific memories of the accident. It did not occur in subjects who had been briefly unconscious and were amnesic for the accident.

(continued)

APPENDIX (Continued)
Prevalence Rates of Posttraumatic Stress Disorder

Author & Year	Country	Sample Studied	Sample Size (N)	Assessment Methods	Diagnostic System	Prevalence Rate of PTSD	Notes
McFall, MacKay, & Donovan, 1991	USA	Veterans consecutively contacting a VA medical center substance abuse treatment facility	489	MASI. RCS. M-PTSD	DSM-III	11%	46% of the subsample of combat-exposed Vietnam veterans with substance abuse problem had significant PTSD symptoms. Degree of combat exposure distinguished Vietnam veterans with PTSD from those without PTSD.
McFarlane, 1992	Australia	Firefighters exposed to a severe natural disaster	147	DIS	DSM-III	22% (at 8 months) 36% (at 42 months)	Ad additional 13% received a diagnosis of borderline PTSD. Avoidance had no direct relationship with the onset of symptoms and appeared to be a defensive strategy to control the distress due to the reexperiencing of the disaster.
McGorry et al., 1991	USA	Patients recovering from am acute psychotic episode	36	PTSD symptom checklist (slef-administered). IES.	DSM-III	46% (at 4 months) 35% (at 11 months)	A significant correlation was found between depressive symtomatology and PTSD.
McNally & Lukash, 1992	USA	Subjects suffering from panic attacks	30	SCID.	DSM-III-R	17% (lifetime) 7% (current)	PTSD was less severe than PTSD produced by either rape or combat in two control groups.
Mellman, Randolph, Brawman-Mintzer, Flores, & Milanes, 1992	USA	Subjects exposed to severe combat stress (including Vietnam veterans or WWII veterans or POWs)	60	SADS–L. SCID (parts)	DSM-III-R	82%	High rates of psychiatric morbidity (anxiety and affective disorders) were found in the sample. The mean onset of phobias, major depression, and panic disorder occurred later than PTSD.
Mollica, Wyshak, & Lavelle, 1987	USA	Southeast Asian refugees attending an Indochinese psychiatric clinic	52	DIS	DSM-III	50%	Each patient had experienced a mean of 10 traumatic events and 2 torture experiences. Many had a concurrent major affective disorder.
Mollica et al., 1993	Cambodia	Cambodian displaced people living on the Thai–Cambodian border	993	Harvard Trauma Questionnaire. Hopkins Symptom Checklist-25	DSM-III-R	15%	A large number of respondents reported lack of food, water, shelter, and medical care, and brainwashing and high levels of trauma and symptoms, social and work functioning were well preserved in the majority of respondents.
Moore & Boehnlein, 1991	USA	Laotian refugees attending an Indochinese Psychiatric Program	84	Clinical assessment	DSM-III	88%	All patients with PTSD also had a diagnosis of major depression. Many patients had a somatic presentation of complaints.
Newman & Foreman, 1987	USA	Victims of a plane crash in a shopping mall	50	Questionnaire. HIES.	DSM-III	50–100%	Rate of PTSD widely varied in the different subgroups studied.
North, Smith, McCool, & Shea, 1989	USA	Eyewitnesses to mass murder	11	DIS / DS	DSM-III	18%	There was a clear dose-relationship in the amount of distress shown by the eyewitnesses
North, Smith, McCool, & Lightcap, 1989	USA	Victims of a tornado	42	DIS / DS.	DSM-III	2%	PTSD prevalence rates, were particularly low. Subjects turned to family and friends for support as their most frequent coping method.

Author, year	Country	Sample	N	Assessment	Diagnostic criteria	Prevalence	Comments
North, Smith, & Spitznagel, 1994	USA	Survivors of a mass shooting	136	DIS/DS	DSM–III–R	20% (males) 36% (females)	Most subjects who developed PTSD had no history of psychiatric illness. Rates of preexisting PTSD were relatively high and did not predict the presence of PTSD after the disaster. One half of the women and one fourth of the men with PTSD also met criteria for another postdisaster psychiatric diagnosis, especially major depression.
North & Smith, 1992	USA	Homeless men and women living in St. Louis	900	DIS/DS	DSM–III–R	18% (males) 34% (females)	Most subjects with PTSD had an additional lifetime psychiatric diagnosis. In 3/4 of cases PTSD had preceded the onset of homelessness.
O'Brien & Hughes, 1991	UK	Falkland War veterans	64	SEQ	DSM–III	22%	An additional 28% had only some PTSD symptoms. PTSD was associated with intensity of combat experience and the report of emotional difficulties in the initial period of return from the war.
Orner, 1993	UK	Falkland War veterans	53	PTSD symptom checklist (self-administered)	DSM–III	60%	The rate of PTSD was significantly associated with physical injury suffered during the war.
Palinkas, Petterson, Russell, & Downs, 1993	USA	People exposed to the Exxon Valdez oil spill and living in 13 Alaska communities	599	DIS/DS	DSM–III–R	9%	Members of the exposed group were 2.9 times likely to have PTSD as compared to the unexposed group. Women were particularly vulnerable
Patterson, Carrigan, Questad, & Robinson, 1990	USA	Patients hospitalized for a major burn	54	Clinical assessment. PTSD symptom checklist (administered by a clinician)	DSM–III	30%	PTSD was related to patients' total body surface area burn, length of hospital stay, female sex, and lack of responsibility for the injury.
Perry, Difede, Musngi, Frances, & Jacobsberg, 1992	USA	Patients hospitalized for a major burn	51	SCID. IES	DSM–III–R	35% (at 2 months) 40% (at 6 months)	Severity of burn injuries and presence of facial disfigurement were not predictors of PTSD.
Perez-Jimenez, Graell-Berna, Perez-Sales, & Santodomingo, 1993	Spain	Patients hospitalized for a major burn for at least 7 days	35	SCID-P. IES.	DSM–III–R	38% (at 7 days) 20% (at 2 months)	There were no differences in the total body surface burned between PTSD and non-PTSD patients.
Pitman, Altman, & Macklin, 1989	USA	Vietnam veterans formerly wounded in action	156	SCID. M-PTSD	DSM–III–R	32% (current) 40% (lifetime)	A high rate of psychiatric morbidity was found in the sample.
Ramsay, Gorst-Unsworth, & Turner, 1993	UK	Refugees surviving state organised violence, including torture, and attending a torture treatment centre	100	Review of case records using a PTSD symptom checklist	DSM–III–R	51%	20% of the subjects met diagnostic criteria for both major depression and PTSD. PTSD showed a strong association with torture.

(continued)

APPENDIX (Continued)
Prevalence Rates of Posttraumatic Stress Disorder

Author & Year	Country	Sample Studied	Sample Size (N)	Assessment Methods	Diagnostic System	Prevalence Rate of PTSD	Notes
Realmuto et al., 1991	USA	Victims of a technological disaster	24	PTSD symptom checklist (administered by a clinician)	DSM–III–R	12%	Victims experiencing PTSD symptoms were more likely to be of female sex, older, and have a history of psychiatric treatment. Some PTSD symptoms were the most frequent.
Resnick, Kilpatrick, Best, & Kramer, 1992	USA	Community sample of female victims of crime	295	DIS. IRI. PTSD symptom checklist (administered by a psychiatrist)	DSM–III–R	35% (high crime stress group) 13% (low crime stress group)	The rate of PTSD in the high crime stress group was 35%, as compared to 13% in the low crime stress group. The rate of PTSD was substantially higher in association with precrime depression only in the high crime stress group.
Riggs, Dancu, Gerhuny, Greenberg, & Foa, 1992	USA	Female victims of sexual or nonsexual assaults	86	PTSD symptom checklist (administered by a psychiatrist)	DSM–III–R	51%	Elevated levels of anger were positively related to the development of PTSD.
Roberts et al., 1982	USA	Vietnam veterans seeking treatment for substance abuse	86	Figley VVS. MMPI. HIPI.	DSM–III	44%	The PTSD group scored higher on clusters of problems dealing with intimacy and sociability and on a number of MMPI scales.
Roca, Spence, & Munster, 1992	USA	Patients hospitalized for a major burn	43	SCID. BDI. MCMI-II.	DSM–III–R	7% (at discharge) 22% (at 4 months)	PTSD symptoms were associated with symptoms of depression, while they were not associated with psychosocial adjustment to illness.
Rothbaum, Foa, Riggs, Murdock, & Walsh, 1992	USA	Rape victims from different referrals	95	PTSD symptom checklist (administered by a psychiatrist) IES	DSM–III–R	94% (at 1 week) 65% (at 35 days) 47% (at 94 days)	PTSD status at 3 months could be predicted very well by two brief self-report measures administered at the first assessment
Rudd, Dahm, & Rogah, 1993	USA	Outpatients who had attempted suicide or were at high risk for continued suicidal behavior or eventual suicide	209	DIS	DSM–III–R	31%	There was a highly significant association between PTSD, phobias, and mood disorders.
Schnurr, Friedman, & Rosenberg, 1993	USA	Male Vietnam and Vietnam-era veterans who had taken the MMPI in college	131	SCID	DSM–III–R	8%	Hypochondriasis, psychopathic deviate, masculinity–feminity, and paranoia scales on the MMPI predicted PTSD symptoms.
Scottenfeld & Cullen, 1985	USA	Patients who were disabled by medically unexplained symptoms following occupational exposure to toxic substances	21	Clinical assessment	DSM–III	14%	33% met only in part PTSD diagnostic criteria. Patients with typical PTSD had experienced acute, life-threatening occupational injury or exposure.

Study	Country	Sample	N	Instrument	Diagnostic criteria	Prevalence	Findings
Schwarz & Kowalski, 1991	USA	Adults exposed to a shooting in a school	66	Reaction Index.	DSM-III, DSM-IV	DSM-III: 52%-16%-4% DSM-III-R: 39%-19%-3% DSM-IV: 54%-24%-6% (diagnostic frequency according to liberal-moderate-conservative symptom thresholds)	Compared with DSM-III and proposed DSM-IV, DSM-III; R generally diagnosed fewest cases. Agreements between DSM-III-R and proposed DSM-IV were good, while agreements between DSM-III and its successors varied for children and adults.
Shalev, 1992	Israel	Injured survivors of a terrorist attack on a civilian bus	12	IES. BSI. PTSD symptom checklist (self-administered)	DSM-III-R	33%	Symptoms of intrusion and denial at admission did not predict PTSD, and were not significantly correlated with psychiatric symptoms on follow-up.
Sherwood, Funari, & Piekarski, 1990	USA	Vietnam veterans admitted to a specialized inpatient unit	189	MCMPI. MMPI.	DSM-III	72%	Most of PTSD patients had passive-aggressive schizoid, avoidant, and boderline personalities.
Shore, Vollmer, & Tatum, 1989	USA	Subjects living in two rural communities, of which one suffered from the consequences of an eruption (1980)	1,016	DIS	DSM-III	4.5% (men, 3% (women) (in the affected community) 1.5% (men), 4% (women) (among controls) (lifetime rates)	The total rate of new psychiatric disorders in the affected population in the first year after the eruption was 11.3% for men and 20.9% for women.
Silverman et al., 1985	USA	Individuals briefly exposed to a toxic industrial compound	14	Clinical assessment	DSM-III	50%	Patients suffered from a combination of organic brain insult and psychological trauma.
Skre, Onstad, Torgensen, Lygren, & Kringlen, 1993	USA	Twins of anxiety disorders probands	49	SCID-I	DSM-III-R	16%	PTSD was significantly more frequent in co-twins of anxiety probands than in co-twins in a control group and was more prevalent in monozygotic than in dizygotic twins.
Sloan, 1988	USA	Male survivors of an airplane crash landing	30	IES. BDI. SCL-90R. STAI. MMPI. PTSD symptom checklist (administered by a psychiatrist)	DSM-III	54% (after the accident) 10-15% (at 1 year)	There was a marked variability in the type of stress responses.
Smith, North, McCool, & Shea, 1990	USA	Victims of flood and dioxin exposure	172	DIS.	DSM-III	5%	Initial status and particularly prior psychiatric history overwhelmed disaster exposure in predicting outcome for disorders other than PTSD.
Smith, Robins, Przybeck, Goldring, & Solomon, 1986	USA	Hotel employees who survived to a jet airplane crash into the hotel	17	DIS/DS	DSM-III	29%	17% among the off-site employees also met DSM-III criteria for PTSD. More than 2/3 of the cases of acute postdisaster psychiatric disorders were predicted by predisaster psychopathology.
Snow, Mager-Stellman, Stellman, & Sommer, 1988	USA	Random sample of Vietnam veterans	2,858	VVQ, PTSD symptom checklist (self-administered)	DSM-III	28% (among those exposed to a median level of combat stress; n=1,524) 65% (among those exposed to the highest level of combat stress; n=78)	The rate varied depending on whether exposure to combat was defined relatively narrowly or broadly. A distinct linear dose-relationship between combat stress and a quantitative measure of PTSD intensity was observed.

(continued)

APPENDIX (Continued)
Prevalence Rates of Posttraumatic Stress Disorder

Author & Year	Country	Sample Studied	Sample Size (N)	Assessment Methods	Diagnostic System	Prevalence Rate of PTSD	Notes
Solomon & Mikulincer, 1987	Israel	Soldiers participating in the 1982 Lebanon war	716	PTSD symptom checklist (self-administered)	DSM–III	59% (among soldiers with combat stress reactions) 16% (among soldiers without combat stress reactions)	Older age was associated with an increased rate of PTSD in the combat stress reactions group. Most cases in both groups were chronic.
Solomon et al., 1993	Israel	People evacuated because of bombings during the Gulf War	51	IES. PTSD symptom checklist (self-administered)	DSM–III–R	80%	The authors point out that they did not intend to make a formal diagnosis but only to indicate a constellation of symptoms consistent with DSM–III–R criteria for PTSD.
Southwick et al., 1993	USA	Veterans of Operation Desert Storm	84	M-PTSD, PTSD symptom checklist (self-administered)	DSM–III–R	2% (at 1 month) 5% (at 6 month)	Level of exposure to combat, as reflected by the Combat Exposure Scale and a trauma questionnaire, was significantly associated with score on M-PTSD. There were no significant differences in combat exposures and PTSD symptoms between males and females.
Speed, Engdahl, Schwartz, & Eberly, 1989	USA	World War II Prisoners of War	62	SADS-L, PTSD symptom checklist (administered by a psychiatrist)	DSM–III	50% (in the year following repatriation)	29% still met DSM–II criteria for PTSD 40 years later. The strongest predictors of PTSD were proportion of weight loss and the experience of torture during captivity.
Steinglass & Gerrity, 1989; 1990	USA	Victims of a tornado and a flood from two communities (a and b)	39(a) 76(b)	DIS. HIES.	DSM–III	15%a (at 4 months) 21%b (at 16 months)	In the first community (a) significant decrements in PTSD morbidity occured by 16 months. Women were significantly more affected both short and long term.
Streimer, Cosstick, & Tennant, 1985	Australia	Australian Vietnam veterans admitted to a psychiatric unit.	126	Case records review	DSM–III	19%	PTSD was a primary diagnosis in 10.3% of the overall sample; it was found only among combat veterans. There was a high rate of comorbidity.
Stretch, Vail, & Maloney, 1985	USA	Vietnam army nurse veterans	361	PTSD symptom checklist (self-administered)	DSM–III	3% (among Vietnam nurse veterans)	Danger and degree of exposure to violence was associated with PTSD diagnosis. Social support was an important moderator in the attenuation of PTSD.
Stretch, 1990; 1991	Canada	Canadian veterans who served in Vietnam	164	VEVAS	DSM–III	65%	PTSD rates are up to 2.5 times higher than in similar studies of US veterans.

Study	Country	Sample	N	Assessment	Criteria	Prevalence	Findings
Summerfield & Toser, 1991	Nicaragua	Former refugees still living in a war area	43	Clinical assessment.	DSM-III-R	25% (men), 50% (women)	62% of men and 91% of women were positive on the GHQ. Sustained sleep distrubance, hyperalertness, and other anxiety-based symptomatology and poor concentration were frequently found.
Sutker, Allain, & Winstead, 1993	USA	WWII Pacific combat veterans, some of whom had been Japanese POWs	51 (23 POW)	DIS. PTSD symptom checklist (administered by a psychiatrist)	DSM-III-R	29% (lifetime, combat veterans) 78% (lifetime, POW)	PTSD was more frequent among the veterans who had been subjected to the most severe trauma, showing a dose-dependant relationship between the two variables.
Sutker, Uddo, Brailey, & Allain, 1993	USA	Soldiers who served in the Operation Desert Shield and who did not seek mental health care	215	M-PTSD	DSM-III-R	19%	The prevalence was higher among those who described high (36%) versus low (5%) war zone stress. In general, as war-zone stress exposure increased, the frequency and severity of psychological symptoms were enhanced.
Warshaw et al., 1993	USA	Subjects enrolled for a prospective study on anxiety disorders	688	SCID	DSM-III-R	9%	Subjects with PTSD had the worst functioning on all of the measures examined except social life. Those with histories of trauma but no PTSD differed from subjects who reported no history of trauma, primarily in high rates of alcoholism and minor depression.
Weisaeth, 1989	Norway	Survivors of an industrial disaster	125	Clinical assessment. SAI.	DSM-III	80% (high stress group) 71% (medium stress group)	The rate refers to posttraumatic anxiety reaction. Only 19% of the control group (employees off-site) showed a specific posttraumatic anxiety reaction.
Weisaeth, 1993	Norway	Norwegian ship crew victims of torture	13	Clinical assessment. STAI. PTSS-10.	DSM-III	46% (first assessment) 54% (at 6-months)	The two men who were exposed to the most extreme stress had the most severe disorders.
Wolfe, Brown, & Kelley, 1993	USA	Troops who participated in Operation Desert Storm	2,344	M-PTSD	DSM-III-R	4% (males) 9% (females)	Female sex, lack of college education, lower (nonofficer) rank, and marital separation or dissolution were generally associated with poorer psychological outcome.

3

THE TREATMENT OF PTSD AND RELATED STRESS DISORDERS: CURRENT RESEARCH AND CLINICAL KNOWLEDGE

ELLEN T. GERRITY
and SUSAN D. SOLOMON

The purpose of this chapter is to review the empirical evidence for the efficacy of a range of treatments for posttraumatic stress disorder (PTSD). As noted in an earlier article on this topic (Solomon, Gerrity, & Muff, 1992), the most common treatments offered to trauma victims include pharmacotherapy; individual psychotherapy, typically involving either behavioral techniques, cognitive approaches, crisis intervention, or psychodynamically oriented approaches; and group therapy, including mutual self-help groups and family therapy. These treatments have been applied to a variety of trauma populations, including victims of combat, rape, child abuse, accidents, terrorism, and disaster.

NATURE OF PTSD AND RELATED STRESS DISORDERS

Although the formal concept of war neurosis has been in use in various forms since World War I, the episodic nature of catastrophic events was seen to prevent any systematic or programmatic research effort until recent years. Prior to the 1980s, events such as combat were seen as unconnected in any conceptual way to other traumatic events, such as accidents, disaster, or rape. The beginning of systematic research and treatment for the mental sequelae which often follow exposure to extreme events has been linked to the inclusion of posttraumatic stress disorder as a diagnostic category in the third edition of the Diagnostic and Statistical Manual of Mental Disorders (American Psychiatric Association [APA] 1980, 1987). Prior to *DSM–III*, responses to traumatic events were classified as "transient situational disturbances"; more persistent reactions were presumed to indicate the presence of another disorder.

In the *DSM–IV* (APA, 1994), diagnostic criteria for PTSD include (a) exposure to a traumatic event that involved actual or threatened death or serious injury, and the person's response involved intense fear, helplessness, or horror; (b) the traumatic event is persistently reexperienced in one or more ways, including recollections, dreams, distress at exposure to cues, physiological reactivity to cues, or acting as if the event were reoccurring; (c) persistent avoidance of stimuli associated with the trauma and numbing of general responsiveness; and (d) persistent symptoms of increased arousal. The definition of PTSD now used in the *ICD-10* (World Health Organization, 1992) describes it as a "delayed and/or protracted response to a stressful event or situation . . . of an exceptionally threatening or catastrophic nature, which is likely to cause pervasive distress in almost anyone" (p. 147).

Another important difference between the two classification systems is that the *DSM–IV* now contains the classification *acute stress disorder*, resulting in a diagnosis of illness even for the most immediate reaction to an extreme event, occurring within 4 weeks of the event. The predominant symptomatology required for this diagnosis is dissociative in nature, accompanied by some reexperiencing, avoidance, anxiety, or arousal, and lasting for a minimum of 2 days.

Thus, even a transient strong reaction to an extreme event results in a *DSM–IV* psychiatric diagnosis. In contrast, the *ICD-10* classification system includes a category called *acute stress reaction*, whereby a person can experience "a transient disorder of significant severity. . .in response to exceptional physical and/or mental stress and which usually subsides within hours or days" (p. 146). This diagnostic classification requires an immediate and clear temporal connection between the impact of an exceptional stressor and the onset of symptoms. Because the *ICD-10* system is applied more frequently worldwide, it may be more likely to have a direct impact on the future of cross-cultural research. But these classifications of what is and is not a traumatic reaction continue to be hotly debated.

As violence, war, terrorism, and other extreme events become increasingly more common throughout the world, these issues of definition, diagnostic criteria, and applicability across cultures become even more salient. Recent research (Breslau, Davis, Andreski, & Peterson, 1991; Norris, 1992) suggests that serious, traumatic events happen to the majority of people, which may be why both the *DSM–IV* and the *ICD-10* no longer describe the stressor as an event outside the range of usual human experience.

In a study by Norris (1992), the frequency and impact of 10 different traumatic events were examined in a sample of 1,000 adults of mixed age, sex, and race living in the southeastern part of the United States. Over their lifetimes, 69% of the sample experienced at least one of the events, including tragic death (30%), robbery (25%), injury-related motor vehicle accidents (23%), and physical assault (15%). In the previous year alone, 21% of the sample had experienced one or more of these traumatic events.

Several studies using different measures and different sample populations estimated lifetime prevalence rates of between 9 and 11% for PTSD, suggesting that PTSD rates may well be higher than rates reported in the Environmental Catchment Area studies of drug abuse (5.9%), schizophrenia (1.3%), affective disorders (mania, major depression and dysthymia, 8.3%), panic disorder (1.6%), somatization (0.1%), obsessive–compulsive disorder (2.5%), and antisocial personality disorder (2.5%) (Regier, Boyd, & Burke, 1988).

EMPIRICAL LITERATURE REVIEW

The present review of PTSD treatment research is based on literature searches with the PsycInfo, Medline, and PILOTS PTSD databases. The authors also contacted traumatic stress investigators known to have conducted treatment research, and scanned the proceedings from the 1991–1994 International Society for Traumatic Stress Studies Annual Meetings to learn of any treatment studies currently in progress.

The literature since 1967 reflects the tremendous interest in discovering an effective cure for PTSD. For the earlier review (Solomon et al., 1992), 255 original published reports (excluding an additional 63 articles written in languages other than English) describing the efficacy of various treatments for the effects of exposure to traumatic events were identified. In the 2 years since that first search, almost 200 additional articles have been published. But the vast majority of these reports are descriptive case histories or, in a few instances, uncontrolled open trials. For this chapter, our selection was again restricted to randomized clinical trials of treatments for PTSD. To date, there are only 11 published reports of these controlled studies across all trauma groups. Clearly more controlled studies of PTSD are needed.

Although traumas such as rape, combat, assault, and tragic bereavement may appear quite different on the surface, victims of all these events share what Horowitz (1974, 1986) has characterized as a violation of pre-existing schemata of the self and the world. Janoff-Bulman and her colleagues characterized trauma as shattering three basic assumptions: (a) the belief in personal invulnerability; (b) the perception of the world as meaningful; and (c) the view of the self as positive (Janoff-Bulman, 1992; Janoff-Bulman & Frieze, 1983). Regardless of the type of trauma experience, all victims must deal with the mental distress caused by the violation of these basic beliefs. Ongoing discussion and additional research is needed to establish the link among one's basic beliefs, cultural identity, and the treatment of PTSD and other traumatic stress reactions with a particular culture (Herman, 1992).

Regarding cross-cultural applications, however, the present comparison is limited by virtue of the fact that a particular treatment is more likely to be tested for and offered to a very specific victim population. Furthermore, 8 of the 11 controlled studies were conducted in the United States, primarily on male Vietnam veterans. The available literature on treatments for rape and bereavement victims is also problematic in that most victims did not receive a clinical diagnosis or when they did, it was often not used as a basis for inclusion in or exclusion from the study.

To be included in this review, the study design had to meet the following strict criteria: (a) restricted inclusion of subjects to those both exposed to a traumatic event and systematically assessed as having PTSD (using *DSM–III* or *DSM–III–R* criteria); and (b) random assignment to the treatment of interest, with either an alternative treatment or a no-treatment (or wait-list) control group.

Pharmacotherapy

Several recent literature reviews of the biological aspects of PTSD have suggested that trauma is a psychobiological event that not only produces adverse psychological effects, but also potentially long-term neurobiological changes in the brain (Davidson, 1992). PTSD appears to be associated with biological alterations in noradrenergic and serotonergic functioning; the hypothalamic-pituitary-adrenocortical axis; the endogenous opioid system; and the diurnal sleep cycle. This pattern of biological abnormalities appears to be unique to PTSD, and suggests that drug therapy should be effective in treating PTSD symptoms (Davidson, 1992; Friedman, 1991).

Almost every type of psychotropic agent has been described as efficacious in case reports, resulting in prescribing practices that differ widely from one place to another (Friedman, 1991). However, there have been to date only five double-blind, placebo-controlled trials of drug therapies for PTSD—two on Israeli participants from varied trauma populations

(Braun, Greenberg, Dasberg, & Lerer, 1990; Shestatzky, Greenberg, & Lerer, 1988) and three on United States male veteran samples (Davidson, et al., 1990; Frank, Kosten, Giller, & Dan, 1988; Reist, Kauffman, & Haier, 1976). Of these studies, four have been of antidepressants.

The rationale for the efficacy of antidepressants is posited to result from a reduction in noradrenergic response to aversive environmental stimuli (Charney, Menkes, & Heninger, 1981), a dysregulation in serotonin neurotransmission (McDougle, Southwick, Charney, & St. James, 1991), or an inhibition of REM sleep (Wyatt, Fram, & Kupfer, 1971). The antidepressants that have been subjected to randomized controlled trials consist of tricyclics (amitriptyline, imipramine, desipramine) and phenelzine, a monoamine oxidase (MAO) inhibitor.

Whereas short-term drug therapy appeared to have no effect, the two controlled drug studies that lasted 8 weeks (Davidson et al., 1990; Frank et al., 1988) showed a modest but clinically meaningful effect on PTSD and clearly superior effects over the placebo when used in combination with psychotherapy. The tricyclic therapy appeared to be well-tolerated without causing major side effects. One study found phenelzine to be more effective than imipramine, but phenelzine is contraindicated with patients who cannot comply with the substance abuse and dietary restrictions required for its use (Frank et al., 1988).

A study of alprazolam found this drug to be no more effective than placebo in the treatment of PTSD symptoms (Braun et al., 1990). Other drugs have shown early promise in open trials, and may be worthy of further testing (e.g. propranolol, Famularo, Kinscherff, & Fenton, 1988), but it is clear that much more research is needed before any strong conclusions can be drawn about the efficacy of pharmacotherapies for PTSD.

Comorbidity issues are also critical in the treatment of PTSD with pharmacotherapy; individuals exposed to traumatic events seldom display symptoms of PTSD alone. Typically, the diagnosis is accompanied by symptoms of several other psychiatric disorders (e.g., depression, generalized anxiety, substance abuse, personality disorder, (Keane & Wolfe, 1990; Steketee & Foa, 1987), each of which will affect the decision about which medication is most appropriately prescribed.

Furthermore, victims of traumatic events may display potentially severe problems of adjustment including grief, guilt, suicide ideation, somatic complaints, poor self-esteem, social impairment, and sexual dysfunction. Some of these other reactions may not respond to medication in the same way as symptoms of PTSD. In general, drug treatment for PTSD has been recommended primarily as a useful adjunct to psychotherapy, for which it may serve a facilitative effect (Bleich, Siegel, Garb, Kottler, & Lerer, 1986; Friedman, 1991; Silver, Sandberg, & Hales, 1990).

Psychotherapy

As with pharmacotherapy, almost every form of psychotherapy has been attempted in the clinical care of those suffering from PTSD (Dye & Roth, 1991; Foa, Olasov, Rothbaum, & Steketee, 1987). For example, Dye and Roth (1991) note that Vietnam veterans are commonly treated with behavioral techniques, hypnosis, gestalt therapy, psychodynamic therapy, and "rap" groups. Rape victims are most commonly treated with group psychotherapy and crisis intervention techniques (often seen as less a treatment for PTSD than a prevention of PTSD in the acutely traumatized; Foa et al., 1987), but also have been given behavioral and cognitive treatments, as well as psychodynamic psychotherapy.

Other psychotherapies used with individuals with PTSD include biofeedback, relaxation techniques, self-help groups, family therapy, and multimodal approaches that combine elements of several of these techniques. Although almost all of these have been reported as efficacious in case reports, few have been subjected to systematic testing (see Abueg & Fairbank, 1992; Allodi, 1991; Dye & Roth, 1991; Foa et al, 1987; Olasov Rothbaum, & Foa, 1992).

Behavior Therapy

Psychosocial treatments for PTSD have grown out of disparate theoretical foundations. Several researchers have drawn on behavioral theory to explain PTSD symptoms (Becker, Skinner, Abel, Axelrod, & Cichon, 1984; Keane, Zimering, & Caddell, 1985; Kilpatrick, Veronen, & Best, 1985; Mowrer, 1960). According to this theory, fear and avoidance are acquired first when a neutral stimulus is paired with an innately frightening one. The previously neutral stimulus thereby becomes aversive and capable of producing higher-order conditioning, wherein many stimuli (words, thoughts, images) will also produce anxiety.

This conditioning is followed by the development of avoidance responses that decrease the anxiety associated with the presence of the conditioned stimuli. Some (Foa, Steketee, & Olasov Rothbaum, 1989) have argued that a strictly behavioral explanation for PTSD is incomplete, suggesting that it cannot account for many of PTSD's most important symptoms (e.g., startle response, nightmares). Noting that perceived threat is a better predictor of the development of PTSD than is actual threat (Kilpatrick, Best, Veronen, Villeponteaux, & Amick-McMullan, 1986; Sales, Baum, & Shore, 1984), Foa et al. (1989) argued that it is necessary to adopt a theoretical position that can accommodate the meaning associated with stimuli. Cognitive theories, such as information processing theory, have been advanced to more fully address the array of PTSD symptomatology.

Interventions based on behavioral theory are designed to reduce anxiety by means of repeated or extended, real or imaginary exposure to objectively harmless but feared stimuli (Boudewyns & Shipley, 1983). Both systematic desensitization (gradually increasing intensity of exposure) and flooding (extended high intensity of exposure) forms of behavior therapy have been used as treatments for PTSD.

Several (six) studies have examined the efficacy of behavioral techniques consisting of different forms of systematic desensitization or flooding (Boudewyns & Hyer, 1990; Brom, Kleber, & Defares, 1989; Cooper & Clum, 1989; Foa, Olasov Rothbaum, Riggs, & Murdock, 1991; Keane, Fairbank, Caddell, & Zimering, 1989; Peniston, 1986). The five behavioral studies that included indices of intrusive symptoms as a part of their outcome measures all showed clear improvement on this cluster of symptoms.

It should be noted that cases of severe complications have been recently reported in the use of flooding for PTSD (Pitman, Altman, & Greenwald, 1991), including exacerbation of depression, relapse of alcoholism, and precipitation of panic disorder. Foa et al. (1989) note that prolonged exposure, which adjusts the severity of the stimuli to the patients' ability to tolerate the stress, is more effective and less likely to cause harmful side effects than is true flooding. Similar to pharmacotherapy, flooding has been primarily recommended for use as an adjunctive treatment (Cooper & Clum, 1989).

Cognitive Therapy

Although still untested, behavioral techniques may prove to be most effective when combined with cognitive forms of therapy, as noted above. Whereas behavioral techniques are designed to activate fear and promote habituation, several cognitive therapies have been developed to reduce anxiety by providing patients with skills to control fear (Foa, Steketee, & Olasov Rothbaum, 1989; Kilpatrick et al., 1986; Pitman, Altman, & Greenwald, 1991).

To date, the only cognitive therapy subjected to systematic study is stress inoculation training (SIT) (Foa et al., 1991) Immediately following treatment, SIT was found to be superior to prolonged exposure, counseling, and a wait-list control; however, after 3 months prolonged exposure appeared superior to SIT in reducing the symptoms of PTSD.

Psychodynamic and Hypnotherapies

According to psychodynamic theory, traumatized individuals are faced with the task of integrating the traumatic event into their understanding of the meaning of life, self-concept, and world image. The emotional reactions of traumatized individuals are viewed as the result of discrepancies between internal and external information (Horowitz, 1974, 1986; Horowitz & Kaltreider, 1980; Schwartz, 1990; Widom, 1989). These discrepancies serve as motives for defense and control, as evidenced in PTSD by the symptom clusters of intrusion and avoidance. Like psychodynamic therapy in general, the goal of hypnotherapy is to allow the traumatized person to release unconscious material and to integrate the traumatic event.

The only controlled study of either psychodynamic or hypnotherapy approaches to PTSD treatment is a study of Dutch resistance fighters (Brom, Kleber, & Defares, 1989). They compared psychodynamic therapy, hypnotherapy, and systematic desensitization to a wait-list control group. As noted, all three treatments showed more improvement in symptom scores than the control group. The psychodynamic group appeared to achieve a greater reduction in avoidance symptoms, with a lesser change in intrusion symptomatology. The other hypnotherapy and the desensitization groups showed the reverse pattern: a greater reduction in intrusive symptoms, with a lesser change in avoidance symptomatology.

Group Therapy

Psychotherapy is often provided to victims of traumatic events through a variety of types of support groups. The assumption with support group therapy is that the bonding of survivors of the same kind of traumatic event can be conducive to the recovery and adjustment process. To date, there are no systematic and controlled studies of PTSD support groups. Clearly, more systematic research is needed in an area of treatment that is so widespread.

METHODOLOGICAL LIMITATIONS AND CONSIDERATIONS

Because of methodological limitations of even these controlled clinical trials, the interpretation and generalizability of these results is restricted. One important methodological limitation arises from the fact that in many of these studies the subjects were also receiving concurrent treatments. There is no way to know if these additional treatments influenced the results in unintended ways. In other words, it may have been the combination of treatments, rather than the focal treatment of interest, that accounted for any results showing the effectiveness of, say, a particular pharmacological approach.

For instance, taken by itself, the same drug may well have proven completely ineffective in treating PTSD symptoms. Furthermore, many participants are likely to have received other forms of treatment in the years preceding the controlled trial. However, past treatment was seldom noted in the reports, and never controlled for in the analyses. Whereas randomization hopefully minimized any bias resulting from these and other major differences among subjects (e.g., substantial variability in time since trauma, or in types of trauma, etc.), most of these studies had so few subjects that other factors could easily have overwhelmed the treatment effects, thereby lowering the chances of detecting between-treatment differences.

Another limitation affecting interpretability of the findings is that many of these studies also experienced substantial attrition between initial screening and follow-up. Some studies based their analyses on everyone entering treatment, whereas others based theirs on treatment completers, a less rigorous test of treatment effects. Studies using a wait-list control group (as opposed to an untreated control group) were limited in what could be concluded at long-term follow-up, because by then the wait-list group had also received some form of treatment.

Finally, almost all of these studies have been conducted on patient populations, or individuals seeking treatment, and may therefore be atypical of individuals with PTSD in the general population. Furthermore, the vast majority of subjects were suffering from chronic PTSD resulting from traumatic events that occurred as long ago as a decade or more, leaving open the question of whether the same treatment might be more effective on a more recently traumatized population.

CROSS-STUDY DIFFERENCES

All of the pharmacological studies, and most of the flooding studies, were conducted using male participants (primarily combat veterans) as subjects. In contrast, the studies of stress inoculation training, hypnotherapy, psychodynamic therapy, and group therapy were conducted on primarily female samples. In addition, the latter studies most often focused on survivors of rape or tragic bereavement, traumas that tended to be somewhat more recent.

If one accepts the conventional (though untested) wisdom that the acute effects of recent trauma are more easily treatable than the chronic effects resulting from events in the distant past (Schwartz, 1990), one would expect to see greater success in studies of these populations, regardless of therapy type. Unfortunately, event recency, gender, type of trauma, and type of therapy are all confounded in these studies. And even without this confound, cross-study comparisons of efficacy are virtually impossible to make, because these studies tended to use different follow-up periods and different measures of efficacy as criteria of success.

It should also be noted that the pharmacotherapies have been held to a different and less stringent standard of efficacy than the psychotherapies, in that the proof of efficacy for pharmacotherapy was that the positive effects disappeared when treatment was discontinued (Famularo et al.,

1988), whereas for a psychotherapy to have been considered successful, the positive outcomes were expected to endure after treatment was discontinued.

The study by Foa et al. (1991) suggests the inadvisability of relying too heavily on immediate posttreatment findings for the assessment of efficacy of psychotherapy. For example, in this study the effects of prolonged exposure were found to be superior to that of SIT only at the 3-month follow-up, whereas SIT appeared superior when assessed immediately posttreatment. It is conceivable that SIT might have continued to show superiority over prolonged exposure had the patients in the SIT group been required to continue in an aftercare program designed to keep their cognitive processing skills alive. It may be that psychotherapy, like pharmacotherapy, is most effective when embedded in a long-term program.

FUTURE DIRECTIONS

In many respects, the future is now. What is needed in the area of cross-cultural research is to advance our understanding of treatment effectiveness. The studies described here have shown at least modest effects for several types of treatment, with the strongest evidence for efficacy favoring direct therapeutic exposure (DTE).[1] However, what these studies have demonstrated most clearly is how very much we still need to learn about the effective treatment of PTSD.

At this time, what is needed are studies that explore comparisons of individual versus combined treatment approaches, to gain an understanding of which components in which combinations result in treatment gains. Like pharmacotherapy, flooding has been primarily recommended for use as an adjunctive treatment (Boudewyns & Hyer, 1990). Although it is still untested, exposure therapy may prove to be most effective when combined with cognitive approaches, which are designed to address irrational cognitions and provide the patient with coping skills.

Still untested is the optimal minimum and maximum length of treatment for each treatment approach. Also unknown is the optimal timing for treatment; that is, whether early intervention is in fact superior to later intervention in preventing chronic and severe PTSD. Controlled studies that take into account the comorbidity of PTSD with other diagnoses and examine the effect of this comorbidity on treatment and outcome also remain to be conducted. These other diagnoses can result in harmful con-

---

[1]DTE is a flooding or implosive therapy whereby a patient experiences repeated exposure, either in reality or imagination, to objectively harmless–but feared– stimuli for the purpose of reducing negative emotions.

sequences to the patient, even when the treatment is effective in reducing symptoms of PTSD (Pitman, Altman, & Greenwald, 1991).

Treatments for PTSD resulting from some traumas such as child physical and sexual abuse, disaster, physical assault, and accidents have received little systematic study to date. Indeed, several kinds of traumatized populations have never been subjects of a controlled clinical trial, such as victims of child sexual and physical abuse. Studies of children exposed to violence are particularly to be encouraged because the rate of children's exposure to violence appears to quite high (National Center on Child Abuse and Neglect, 1988). Intervention at an early age holds the promise of breaking the cycle of abuse wherein child victims grow up to be themselves perpetrators of violence (Widom, 1989).

Still undetermined is the most appropriate measure of success in treating individuals suffering from PTSD: reduction of symptoms of distress, decreased rates of individuals meeting diagnostic criteria, or optimal functioning in daily life. Practitioners treating different trauma populations disagree about which of these outcomes is the most appropriate to consider.

Even if one limits oneself to the measurement of PTSD as an outcome, this can be problematic for cross-cultural studies. As mentioned earlier, the problem goes beyond instrumentation to the very definition of PTSD itself. The *DSM–IV* now requires specific symptomatology in the separate areas noted earlier in addition to the requirement of experiencing, witnessing, or being confronted with an event that involves actual or threatened death or serious injury.

In contrast, the *ICD-10* definition of PTSD requires intrusive symptomatology be present, but does not require numbing or avoidance symptoms, and views the arousal and other disturbances as of less that prime importance. The *ICD-10* requires only that the intrusive symptoms be manifest within 6 months of the event for a diagnosis of PTSD to be made. This definitional difference is likely to have important consequences for both research and clinical practice with individuals suffering from PTSD.

The *DSM–IV* (or even *DSM–III–R*) criteria are much more difficult to satisfy than those of the *ICD-10* in that the *ICD-10* does not require the numbing symptoms, thus substantially reducing epidemiological estimate of rates of PTSD in populations measured by this diagnostic classification. Since the *ICD-10* makes no such requirements, reported rates of PTSD are like to be much higher in countries other than the United States, even though the United States now has the unfortunate distinction of being one of the most violent countries in the industrialized world.

Of course there also remains the possibility that these definitional differences are appropriate, and that avoidance and numbing are much more likely to be associated with exposure to traumatic stressors in the United States than in other cultures. This as yet unstudied question highlights the need for a sensitive cross-cultural approach, because ethnocultural and religious factors may have a particularly powerful and differential influence on the expression of PTSD in non-Western nations, especially with respect to avoidant/numbing symptoms that are linked to expression of emotion, stoicism, and individual responsibility.

Discussions often focus on the need for cultural sensitivity specifically in the area of instrumentation. Results may not be comparable with different ethnocultural cohorts when instruments have been used which may not be comparable in their linguistic, conceptual, or normative properties. However, studies that have sensitively dealt with cultural differences have been successful in revealing high levels of PTSD among other cultures exposed to trauma.

For example, a recent study of Cambodian refugees reported a very high rate of PTSD along with documentation that the PTSD was initially missed in early treatment assessments (Kinzie et al., 1990). The investigators reported problems of patient underreporting of symptoms and discussed this in terms of patient shame, loss of face, psychic numbing, and a fatalistic view of life but also in terms of interviewing style and interviewer ethnicity as a factor in the revelation of symptoms. This issue is of critical importance in the application of mental health treatment with the growing refugee population (currently estimated at 40 million people worldwide) (Marsella, Bornemann, Ekblad, & Orley, 1994). The horror of the refugee experience can lead to severe and long-lasting mental health problems, such as posttraumatic stress disorder, anxiety, and depression, which can then exacerbate the serious problems associated with finding food, shelter, and safety.

Arguments have been made that PTSD itself is a culture-bound syndrome that is only expressed among traumatized individuals from Western/industrialized countries or that it is expressed differently in different cultures (e.g., Marsella, Friedman, & Spain, 1993). The findings of treatment studies conducted on American, Dutch, and Israeli populations (all Westernized cultures) need to be replicated with individuals from other countries, who may express PTSD very differently, or may have cultural norms that prohibit help-seeking from formal caregivers for emotional difficulties. Cultural differences may ultimately suggest the need for greater reliance on self-help groups or more innovative forms of therapeutic approaches that may call into question western concepts of treatment itself.

Researchers and treatment providers must be aware of the need for a broader context that integrates an understanding of ethnocultural factors, such as ethnocultural variation in language, metaphors and symbolism, adaptational or acculturation pressures, belief systems, religious ideas, social constraints on behavior, culturally defined notions of shame and help-seeking, and sex roles. The world is getting more, not less, violent and the number of refugees and migrants is rapidly increasing. It is obvious that much more research is needed, as is specialized education and supervision for treatment providers of culturally diverse populations.

REFERENCES

Abueg, F. R., & Fairbank, J. A. (1992). Behavioral treatment of the PTSD-substance abuser: A multidimensional stage model. In P. Saigh (Ed.), *Posttraumatic stress disorder: A behavioral approach to assessment and treatment* (pp. 111–146). New York: McMillan.

Allodi, F. A. (1991). Assessment and treatment of torture victims: A critical review. *Journal of Nervous and Mental Diseases, 179*(1), 4–11.

American Psychiatric Association. (1980). *Diagnostic and statistical manual of mental disorders (3rd ed.).* Washington, DC: American Psychiatric Press.

American Psychiatric Association. (1987). *Diagnostic and statistical manual of mental disorders (3rd ed., rev.).* Washington, DC: American Psychiatric Press.

American Psychiatric Association. (1994). *Diagnostic and statistical manual of mental disorders (4th ed.).* Washington, DC: American Psychiatric Press.

Becker, J., Skinner, L., Abel, G., Axelrod, R., & Cichon, J. (1984). Sexual problems of sexual assault survivors. *Women's Health, 9,* 5–20.

Bleich, A., Siegel, B., Garb, B., Kottler, A, & Lerer, B. (1986). Post traumatic stress disorder following combat exposure: Clinical features and psychopharmacological treatment. *British Journal of Psychiatry, 149,* 365–369.

Boudewyns, P. A., & Hyer, L. (1990). Physiological response to combat memories and preliminary treatment outcome in Vietnam veteran PTSD patients treated with direct therapeutic exposure. *Behavior Therapy, 21,* 63–87.

Boudewyns, P. A., & Shipley, R. H. (1983). *Flooding and implosive therapy.* New York: Plenum.

Braun, P., Greenberg, D., Dasberg, H., & Lerer, B. (1990). Core symptoms of posttraumatic stress disorder unimproved by alprazolam treatment. *Journal of Clinical Psychiatry, 51,* 236–238.

Breslau, N., Davis, G., Andreski, P., & Peterson, E. (1991). Traumatic events and post-traumatic stress disorder in an urban population of young adults. *Archives of General Psychiatry, 48,* 216–222.

Brom, D., Kleber, R. J., & Defares, P. B. (1989). Brief psychotherapy for posttraumatic stress disorders. *Journal of Consulting and Clinical Psychology, 57*(5), 607–612.

Charney, D. S., Menkes, D. B., & Heninger, G. R. (1981). Receptor sensitivity and the mechanism of action of antidepressant treatment: Implications for the etiology and therapy of depression (Letter to the editor). *Archives of General Psychiatry, 38,* 1160–1180.

Cooper, N. A., & Clum, G. A. (1989). Imaginal flooding as a supplementary treatment for PTSD in combat veterans: A controlled study. *Behavior Therapy, 20,* 381–391.

Davidson, J. (1992). Drug therapy of post traumatic stress disorder. *British Journal of Psychiatry, 160,* 309–314.

Davidson, J., Kudler, H., Smith, R., Mahorney, S., Lipper, S., Hammett, E., Saunders, W., & Cavenar, J. (1990). Treatment of posttraumatic stress disorder with amitriptyline and placebo. *Archives of General Psychiatry, 47,* 259–266.

Dye, E, & Roth, S. (1991). Psychotherapy with Vietnam veterans and rape and incest survivors. *Psychotherapy, 28*(1), 103–120.

Famularo, R., Kinscherff, R., & Fenton, T. (1988). Propranolol treatment for childhood posttraumatic stress disorder, acute type: A pilot study. *American Journal of Diseases of Childhood, 142,* 1244–1247.

Foa, E. B., Olasov Rothbaum, B., Riggs, D. S., & Murdock, T. B. (1991). Treatment of posttraumatic stress disorder in rape victims: A comparison between cognitive–behavioral procedures and counseling. *Journal of Consulting and Clinical Psychology, 59*(5), 715–723.

Foa, E. B., Olasov Rothbaum, B., & Steketee, G. S. (1987). *Treatment of rape victims.* Paper presented at the NIMH Conference: State of the Art in Sexual Assault Research, Charleston, SC.

Foa, E. B., Steketee, G., & Olasov Rothbaum, B. (1989). Behavioral/cognitive conceptualizations of post-traumatic stress disorder. *Behavior Therapy, 20,* 155–176.

Frank, J. B., Kosten, T. R., Giller, E. L., & Dan, E. (1988). A randomized clinical trial of phenelzine and imipramine for post traumatic stress disorder. *American Journal of Psychiatry, 145,* 1289–1291.

Friedman, M. (1991). Biological approaches to the diagnosis and treatment of post-traumatic stress disorder. *Journal of Traumatic Stress, 4*(1), 67–91.

Herman, J. L. (1992). *Trauma and recovery.* New York: Basic Books.

Horowitz, M. (1974). Stress response syndromes, character style, and dynamic psychotherapy. *Archives of General Psychiatry, 31,* 768–781.

Horowitz, M. (1986). *Stress response syndromes* (2nd ed). Northvale, NJ: Jason Aronson.

Horowitz, M. J., & Kaltreider, N. B. (1980). Brief psychotherapy of stress response syndromes. In T. Karasu, & L. Bellak (Eds.), *Specialized techniques in individual psychotherapy* (pp. 162–183). New York: Brunner/Mazel.

Janoff-Bulman, R. (1992). *Shattered assumptions: Towards a new psychology of trauma.* New York: Free Press.

Janoff-Bulman, R., & Frieze, I. H. (1983). A theoretical perspective for understanding reactions to victimization. *Journal of Social Issues, 39,* 1–18.

Keane, T. M., Fairbank, J., Caddell, J., & Zimering, R. T. (1989). Implosive (flooding) therapy reduces symptoms of PTSD in Vietnam combat veterans. *Behavior Therapy, 20,* 245–260.

Keane, T. M., & Wolfe, J. (1990). Comorbidity in post-traumatic stress disorder: An analysis of community and clinical studies. *Journal of Applied and Social Psychology, 20,* 1776–1788.

Keane, T. M., Zimering, R. T., & Caddell, J. M. (1985). A behavioral formulation of post-traumatic stress disorder in Vietnam veterans. *The Behavior Therapist, 8*, 9–12.

Kilpatrick, D. G., Best, C. L., Veronen, L. J., Villeponteaux, L. A., & Amick-McMullan, A. (1986). *Predicting the impact of a stressful life experience: Criminal victimization.* Paper presented at the 7th Annual Meeting of the Society of Behavioral Medicine, San Francisco, CA.

Kilpatrick, D. G., Veronen, L. J., & Best, C. L. (1985). Factors predicting psychological distress among rape victims. In C. R. Figley (Ed.), *Trauma and its wake.* (pp. 113–141). New York: Brunner/Mazel.

Kinzie, J. D., Boehnlein, J. K., Leung, P. K., Moore, L. J., Riley, C., & Smith, D. (1990). The prevalence of posttraumatic stress disorder and its clinical significance among Southeast Asian refugees. *American Journal of Psychiatry, 147*(7), 913–917.

Marsella, A. J., Bornemann, T., Ekblad, S., & Orley, J. (1994). *Amidst peril and pain: The mental health and well-being of the world's refugees.* Washington, DC: American Psychological Association.

Marsella, A. J., Friedman, M., & Spain, H. (1993). Ethnocultural aspects of PTSD. In J. Oldham, M. Riba, & A. Tasman (Eds.) *Review of psychiatry* (pp. 29–62). Washington, DC: American Psychiatric Press.

McDougle, C. J., Southwick, S. M., Charney, D. S., & St. James, R. L. (1991). An open trial of fluoxetine in the treatment of posttraumatic stress disorder. *Journal of Clinical Psychopharmacology, 11*, 325–327.

Mowrer, O. H. (1960). *Learning theory and behavior.* New York: John Wiley.

National Center on Child Abuse and Neglect. (1988). *Study findings: The National incidence of prevalence of child abuse and neglect.* Washington, DC: Author.

Norris, F. (1992). The epidemiology of trauma: Frequency and impact of different potentially traumatic events on different demographic groups. *Journal of Consulting and Clinical Psychology, 60*(3), 409–418.

Olasov Rothbaum, B., & Foa, E. B. (1992). Cognitive–behavioral treatment of posttraumatic stress disorder. In P. Saigh (Ed.) *Posttraumatic stress disorder: A behavioral approach to assessment and treatment.* (pp. 85–110). New York: MacMillan.

Peniston, E. G. (1986). EMG biofeedback-assisted desensitization treatment for Vietnam combat veterans post-traumatic stress disorder. *Clinical Biofeedback and Health, 9*(1), 35–41.

Pitman, R., Altman, B., & Greenwald E. (1991). Psychiatric complications during flooding therapy for posttraumatic stress disorder. *Journal of Clinical Psychiatry, 52*(1), 17–20.

Regier, D., Boyd, J., & Burke, J. (1988). One-month prevalence of mental disorders in the United States. *Archives of General Psychiatry, 45*, 977–986.

Reist, C., Kauffman, C. D., & Haier, R. J. (1976). A controlled trial of desipramine in 18 men with post-traumatic stress disorder. *American Journal of Psychiatry, 146*, 513–516.

Sales, E., Baum, M., & Shore, B. (1984) Victim readjustment following assault. *Journal of Social Issues, 40,* 117–136.

Schwartz, L. S. (1990). A biopsychosocial treatment approach to post-traumatic stress disorder. *Journal of Traumatic Stress, 3,* 221–238.

Shestatzky, M., Greenberg, D., & Lerer, B. (1988). A controlled trial of phenezine in posttraumatic stress disorder. *Psychiatry Research, 24,* 149–155.

Silver, J. M., Sandberg, D., & Hales, R. E. (1990). New approaches to pharmacotherapy of posttraumatic stress disorder. *Journal of Clinical Psychiatry, 51,* 33–38.

Solomon, S., Gerrity, E., & Muff, A. (1992). Efficacy of treatments for posttraumatic stress disorder: An empirical review. *Journal of the American Medical Association, 268,* 633–638.

Steketee, G., & Foa, E. B. (1987). Rape victims: Post-traumatic stress responses and their treatment. *Journal of Anxiety Disorders, 1,* 69–86.

Widom, C. S. (1989). The cycle of violence. *Science, 24*(4), 117–264.

World Health Organization. (1992). *The ICD-10 classification of mental and behavioral disorders: Clinical descriptions and diagnostic guidelines.* Geneva, Switzerland: Author.

Wyatt, R. J., Fram, D. H., Kupfer, D. J. (1971). Total prolonged drug-induced REM sleep suppression in anxious–depressed patients. *Archives of General Psychiatry, 24,* 145–155.

II

ETHNOCULTURAL RESEARCH ON PTSD: CONCEPTUAL AND METHODOLOGICAL ISSUES

4

ETHNOCULTURAL ASPECTS OF PTSD: AN OVERVIEW OF ISSUES AND RESEARCH DIRECTIONS

ANTHONY J. MARSELLA, MATTHEW J. FRIEDMAN,
and E. HULAND SPAIN

INTRODUCTION

Interest in ethnocultural aspects of PTSD has grown dramatically in recent years.

Within the last two decades, there has been an increased interest in the study of ethnocultural aspects of posttraumatic stress disorder (PTSD). This interest has manifested itself through the publication of numerous books, technical reports, and journal articles on a spectrum of ethnic populations and ethnic aspects of PTSD. However, during this time period, there have been few literature reviews on the topic, and those literature reviews that have been published have been limited to either specific topics (e.g., assessment); traumas (e.g., refugee status); or ethnic groups (e.g., Indochinese).

Some examples of literature reviews include those by Penk and Allen (1991), who summarized the research literature on clinical assessment among ethnic minority Vietnam War veterans; de Girolamo (1992), who summarized the literature on the treatment and prevention of PTSD among

This chapter was previously published in slightly altered form in J. Oldham, A. Tasman, & M. Riba (Eds.). (1993) *American Psychiatric Association Press Review of Psychiatry*, Volume 12, American Psychiatric Association, Washington, DC. It is included here with the permission of the American Psychiatric Press.

victims of natural disasters in different countries; Friedman and Jaranson (1992), who summarized the literature on PTSD among refugees; and Marsella, Friedman, & Spain, who offered a brief overview of the topic with an accompanying annotated bibliography (1992), and more detailed analysis (1993).

One reason for the limited number of literature reviews on ethnocultural aspects of PTSD is that the information on the topic is distributed across hundreds of publications and is focused on different (a) ethnocultural groups (e.g., Afro-Americans, American Indians, Asian Americans, Cambodians, Hispanics); (b) victim populations (e.g., war veterans, refugees, torture victims, prisoners-of-war, rape and other crime victims, victims of natural and non-natural disasters); (c) traumatic events (e.g., Vietnam War, Afghan War, Northern Ireland Conflict, Buffalo Creek Disaster, Chernobyl, Three Mile Island, San Ysidro Massacre, refugee camp internment, rapes, other criminal assaults); and (d) clinical topics (e.g., epidemiology, measurement, clinical diagnosis, alternative therapies).

In addition to the problematic nature of surveying, organizing, and critically reviewing such a sizable research and clinical literature, there is the issue of research quality. For example, the majority of ethnocultural studies on PTSD have assumed that by studying one or more racial or ethnocultural groups they were, in fact, accounting for the variance associated with ethnocultural factors. However, as will be pointed out in detail in later sections, a comparison of different races or ethnic groups in the absence of a priori criteria for defining meaningful group divisions limits our understanding of any group differences found.

What does it mean, for example, when Whites, African Americans, American Indians, and Hispanics are found to differ in rates of PTSD if the samples studied also differ in educational level, social class, exposure to trauma, regional background (e.g., Cubans, Puerto Ricans, Mexicans), urban–rural residence, and so forth? Using broad categories of ethnocultural group membership as the basis for research studies may, in fact, create more problems than it resolves. It is essential that clinical studies attributing differences in PTSD rates, expression, and treatment responsivity to ethnocultural variables control for, or at least account for, these and other possible sources of variance.

In addition, there are considerable within-group ethnocultural differences among African Americans, Asians, Hispanics, and Whites, and these differences must be considered in valid cross-cultural research. For example, there is no single African American subculture. There are a variety of African American experiences, and these differ from one another in dramatic ways. Consider the contrasts among African American groups such as Haitians, Black Cubans, Jamaicans, Brazilians, and Ethiopians; Southern-rural Blacks, and Northern-urban Blacks; and wealthy professional, and impoverished Blacks. PTSD among these different groups may not have similar causes, expressions, or experiential and social implications because these groups are, in fact, different from one another in numerous ways.

In spite of the many publications addressing ethnocultural aspects of PTSD, relatively little is known about the relationship between ethnocultural factors and the etiology, epidemiology, onset, diagnosis, course, outcome, and assessment and treatment of PTSD. The present chapter has three major purposes: (a) to summarize and critically review the existing cross-cultural PTSD literature, especially as it pertains to veterans and refugees, the two groups most frequently studied; (b) to discuss some of the major conceptual and methodological issues involved in understanding the relationship between culture and PTSD; and (c) to recommend conceptual and research approaches for studying ethnocultural aspects of PTSD.

While a universal neurobiological response to traumatic events most likely does exist, there is room for considerable ethnocultural variation in the expressive and phenomenological dimensions of the experience, especially among comorbidity patterns and associated somatic, hysterical, and paranoid symptoms and experiences. The extensive research literature on ethnocultural variations in psychopathology points to the importance of our understanding the pathoplastic aspects of severe psychopathology and other forms of mental disorder. If more sensitive cross-cultural research and clinical methods are used in the study of PTSD, ethnocultural variations may emerge with greater regularity and clarity. Therefore, at this point in time, a number of research questions remain to be answered regarding the relationship between ethnocultural factors and the etiology, rates, expression, experience, and treatment of PTSD. A purpose of this chapter is to examine some of these questions.

AN OVERVIEW OF THE EPIDEMIOLOGICAL AND CLINICAL LITERATURE

Refugees

There are several reviews that have examined mental disorders among populations considered to be at high risk for PTSD (e.g., refugees, immigrants, veterans, concentration camp survivors) that can shed partial light on possible relationships between traumas and the rates and clinical manifestations of PTSD in different ethnocultural populations (e.g., Arthur, 1982; Beiser, 1991; Friedman & Jaranson, 1992; Garcia-Peltoniemi, 1992a, 1992b; Mollica, 1988; Weisaeth & Eitinger, 1991). In addition, the National Center for PTSD Research Quarterly (NC PTSD, 1991) recently compiled a bibliography of traumatic reactions among Asian and European refugee, concentration camp, and veteran populations.

More recent studies of PTSD, among Indochinese refugees continue to support the close relationship between the traumas associated with refugee status and PTSD and related anxiety and depressive disorders (e.g., Beiser, Turner, & Ganesan, 1989; Boehnlein, 1987a, 1987b; Boehnlein, Kinzie, Rath, & Fleck, 1985; de Girolamo, Diekstra, & Williams, 1989; Friedman & Jaranson, 1992; Goldfeld, Mollica, Pesavento, & Faraone, 1988; Lin, Ihle, & Tazuma, 1985; Kinzie, Boehnlein, Leung, & Moore, 1990; Kinzie, Frederickson, Rath, Fleck, & Karls, 1984; Kroll, Habenicht, MacKenzie, & Yang, 1989; Mollica, 1988; Mollica, Wyshak, & Lavelle, 1987; Moore & Boehnlein, 1991; Nicassio, 1985).

Westermeyer and his coworkers (e.g., Westermeyer, 1988; Westermeyer, Williams, & Nguyen, 1992; Williams & Westermeyer, 1986) have edited and authored a number of books on refugee mental health that contain extensive material on the diagnosis and treatment of PTSD among Indochinese refugees and other groups. Rozee and Van Bomel (1989) looked at the effect of war trauma on older Cambodian women.

An example of the extensive studies on PTSD among Indochinese refugees is provided by Kinzie, Frederickson, Rath, Fleck, and Karls (1984), who surveyed 322 patients at a psychiatric clinic for Indochinese refugees to determine the presence of PTSD. They found that 226 patients met the criteria for a current diagnosis of PTSD, and an additional 15 met the criteria for a past diagnosis. The Mein (Laotian hill people) had the highest rate of PTSD (93%) and Vietnamese refugees had the lowest (54%). The authors concluded that PTSD is a common disorder among Indochinese refugees, but the diagnosis is often difficult to make because of communication difficulties that complicate the diagnostic process.

Cervantes, Salgado de Snyder, and Padilla (1989) investigated self-reported symptoms of depression, anxiety, somatization, generalized distress, and PTSD in a community sample of 258 immigrants from Central America and Mexico and 329 native-born Mexican Americans and Anglo-Americans. Research instruments included the SCL-90-R and the Center for Epidemiologic Studies Depression Scale. The authors found that immigrants had higher levels of generalized distress than native-born Americans. They also found that 52% of Central American immigrants who migrated as a result of war or political unrest reported symptoms consistent with a diagnosis of PTSD, compared with 49% of Central Americans who migrated for other reasons and 25% of Mexican immigrants. Other studies involving Hispanic refugee PTSD victims have been published by Lopez, Boccellari, and Hall (1988); Summerfield and Toser (1991); and Urrutia (1986).

Natural Disasters and Political and Family Traumas

Perry (1986), de Girolamo (1992), and de Girolamo & Orley (1992) summarized much of the literature on the relationship between natural disasters and PTSD across national boundaries. They concluded that natural disasters are an important source of psychiatric adjustment difficulties among survivors regardless of the country in which the disaster occurred. One example of PTSD following a natural disaster was reported by de la Fuente (1990), who evaluated emotional reactions in 573 people (age 18–64 years) associated with the Mexican earthquakes, and found that 32% of the victims displayed PTSD, 19% had generalized anxiety, and 13% had depression. In the same study, he found that of 208 women housed in shelters, 72.3% showed no psychopathological symptoms, 18% displayed some signs of decompensation, and 9.5% suffered severe decompensation.

Holen (1990); Malt (1988); Malt, Blikra, & Hoivik, (1989); and Weisaeth (1989), studied the effects of industrial disasters and civilian accidents among Scandinavian populations. Weisaeth (1989) found a direct relationship between the severity of trauma exposure and PTSD symptoms among survivors of a paint factory explosion in Norway. Immediate PTSD reactions were reported by 80% of the high-stressor-exposure group while only 5% showed a delayed PTSD response. The seven-month-point prevalence of PTSD was 37% among high-stressor-exposure victims but only 4% among low-stressor-exposure victims. The direct relationship between stressor exposure and PTSD among this cultural population is consistent with reports of others around the world and suggests a possible universal relationship between extent of trauma and risk of PTSD symptomatology.

In addition to the work of Holen and Malt and his coworkers on Scandinavian victims of industrial disasters and civilian accidents, there have been many other cross-cultural studies of natural disasters and political and family traumas. For instance, Kim (1987) discussed PTSD-like symptoms among battered housewives in Korea. Solomon (1989) discussed the dynamics of PTSD in South African political detainees. Lima, Pai, Santacruz, and Lozano (1991) evaluated 102 victims of the Armero volcanic eruption and mudslide disaster and found that the majority of the victims met *DSM–III–R* criteria for PTSD and depression.

American Military Veterans

There have also been numerous recent publications on ethnocultural variations in the rates and clinical phenomenology of PTSD among American military veterans. Studies of PTSD among American Vietnam War veterans have reported conflicting PTSD rates. Some studies suggested Blacks have higher rates of PTSD than Whites or Hispanics (e.g., Allen,

1986; Green, Grace, Lindy, & Leonard, 1991; Laufer, Gallops, & Frey-Wouters, 1984; Parson, 1984; Penk, et al.; 1989).

Parson (1985) has proposed a "tripartite adaptational dilemma" among ethnocultural minority Vietnam War veterans in which the veterans must resolve the triple effects of a "bicultural identity, institutional racism, and residual stress from trauma" in dealing with the war. He suggests an increased risk of PTSD and other psychiatric disorders for ethnocultural minority veterans. Penk and Allen (1991), commenting on possible differences in the rates of PTSD among ethnic groups, stated:

> Research has consistently demonstrated that effects of the Vietnam war are more pronounced among the American minorities who served. That is, studies of treatment seeking and non-treatment seeking samples concur in showing higher rates of maladjustment among non-whites than whites. . . . Readjustment needs of any veteran are complex but those of the American minority veterans are compounded by the traditional ethnic minority problems of other stresses produced by prejudice in a segregated and racist society. Racism adds stresses to traumatic experiences. . . . But many clinicians have not comprehended the additional complications experienced by many American minority Vietnam veterans whose stress reactions are increased by their experiences of not being majority culture members. (p. 45)

Marsella, Chemtob, & Hamada (1990) suggested that ethnocultural minority Vietnam veterans might have an increased risk for developing PTSD because of a number of factors, including the following: (a) Ethnocultural minority soldiers were subjected to increased stress because of racial stereotypes, ridicule, and inequitable treatment; (b) they were subjected to increased stress because they were asked to fight against non-white people on behalf of a country that many considered racist; (c) the Vietnamese reminded many of the veterans of family, friends, and other minority groups, thus, they were unable to dehumanize the Vietnamese; and (d) personality and interpersonal style of ethnocultural minority soldiers did not fit in with military preferences. In brief, ethnocultural minority veterans may have had increased levels of stress and reduced coping resources available to them, resulting in a higher risk of PTSD.

However, issues have been raised about the confounding effects of substance abuse problems (e.g., Carter, 1982); early life stressors (e.g., Breslau, Davis, Andreski, and Peterson, 1991); and more severe combat stressors among African Americans. Green, Grace, Lindy, and Leonard (1991) were surprised to find high lifetime PTSD diagnosis probabilities of 42% for Whites and 72% for Blacks, and current PTSD probabilities of 30% for Whites and 47% for Blacks. Linking these differences to the Vietnam War experience, however, was problematic because of confounds arising from status and historical differences between the two groups.

Some studies have suggested that Hispanics are also at increased risk for PTSD (e.g., Becerra, 1982; Escobar et al., 1983). Escobar et al. (1983) noted that PTSD was rarely seen as a discrete entity among Hispanics, but rather was mixed within other *DSM–III* categories. Pina (1985) also noted both increased risks and diagnostic variations in PTSD among Hispanic veterans.

The National Vietnam Veterans Readjustment Study (NVVRS) study of PTSD rates was a comprehensive national epidemiological survey of current and lifetime prevalence rates of PTSD conducted under contract from the Department of Veterans Affairs (see Kulka et al, 1990). This study offered a comparison of PTSD among White, Black, and Hispanic male and female populations. Other ethnocultural groups were considered too small in number to provide comparative data. The NVVRS study found that Hispanic populations suffered higher current rates of PTSD (28%) than Blacks (19%) or Whites (14%). However, it should be pointed out that when data were controlled for war-zone trauma exposure, differences between White and Black prevalence rate differences disappeared, and White versus Hispanic rate-differences became much smaller. In another analysis of NVVRS data, Jordan et al. (1991) reported that Hispanics were at an increased risk for alcohol and other substance abuse and general anxiety disorder, and African Americans for antisocial personality disorder.

Both of these studies are good examples of the importance of accounting for nonethnocultural factors in ethnocultural research. However, on the other hand, the NVVRS made no effort to use culturally sensitive assessment materials in the determination of cases. Furthermore, the study did not sample American Indian, Asian American, or Pacific Island veterans in sufficient sizes to reach conclusions about the prevalence of PTSD among these groups. As a result, the United States Congress has directed the National Center for PTSD of the Department of Veterans Affairs to study rates of PTSD among ethnocultural groups not included in the study, and to develop culturally sensitive instruments for the detection and differentiation of PTSD among these groups. This study is currently in progress (see Friedman, Marsella, Ashcraft, Keane, & Manson, 1992).

There have been few studies of PTSD among American Indian or Asian American Vietnam War veterans. However, several papers have suggested that minority-status stress, racial prejudice, and identification with Vietnamese people and culture may have increased the risk of PTSD among American Indians (e.g., Barse, 1984; Holm, 1982, 1989; Silver, 1984) and Asian Americans (e.g., Hamada, Chemtob, Sautner, & Sato, 1988; Marsella, Chemtob, & Hamada, 1990). It is noteworthy that Parson (1984) and Allen (1986) feel that the risk of PTSD was enhanced among Black veterans because of their identification with the Vietnamese.

In contrast, there have been numerous studies of PTSD among veterans from other nations including Australia (e.g., Streimer, Cosstick, &

Tennant, 1985; Tennant, Streimer, & Temperly, 1990); Canada (e.g., Stretch, 1990, 1991); Israel (e.g., Solomon, K., 1989; Solomon, Z., 1989; Solomon & Mikulincer, 1987; Solomon, Oppenheimer, & Noy, 1986; Solomon, Weisenberg, Schwartzwald, & Mikulincer, 1987); and Sweden (Kettner, 1972). These studies are not methodologically comparable to the American veteran studies of PTSD, so comparisons of data are difficult. However, they do provide additional demonstrations of the link between PTSD and combat experiences.

Tennant et al. (1990) reported that 19% of the Australian Vietnam War veterans suffered from PTSD. However, limitations in sampling and assessment confounded the results. Stretch (1991) reported a prevalence rate of 65% among self-selected Canadian and some American Vietnam War veterans using PTSD symptomatology as the case index rather than clinical diagnoses. He attributed this exceptionally high rate to lack of recognition, lack of PTSD services, and isolation of veterans in Canada. Solomon and her coworkers (Solomon et al., 1987) reported that 59% of a sample of Israeli soldiers who fought in the 1982 Lebanese conflict had PTSD one year after the end of the war. The variations in these rates are a result of different case criteria and research methodologies. However, as a group, they point to the fact that combat experience is closely linked to PTSD. It should be noted that Solomon and her coworkers have published a score of studies on PTSD among Israeli soldiers, of which interested readers should be aware.

Assessment Studies and Issues

There are only a few published ethnocultural studies of PTSD concerned with assessment issues, in spite of the fact that cultural sensitivity in assessment procedures may be a major factor in the determination of PTSD rates and clinical features (e.g., Penk & Allen, 1991; Penk, Robinowitz, Dorsett, Bell, & Black, 1989). Allodi (1991) reviewed some of the assessment methods used with international torture victims; he reported no efforts to accommodate methods to specific ethnocultural populations. Westermeyer and Wahmemholm (1989) commented on the difficulties of assessing the traumatized combat and refugee patient. Mollica et al., (1992) attempted to develop a questionnaire for measuring trauma, torture, and PTSD among Indochinese refugees using refugee experiences rather than Western standards.

However, most studies of non-White PTSD victim populations have tended to use standard clinical methods. As a result, questions arise about the validity of the conclusions reached because many of these instruments were constructed and normalized with White populations. Nevertheless, it is important to note that consistent symptomatology has been reported with the use of a variety of popular Western psychiatric instruments (e.g.,

SCL-90, DIS, MMPI, CED-S, M-PTSD) across a variety of different eth-nocultural groups. A paper by Jaranson and Shiota (1989) is noteworthy because they developed an interview assessment package for specific use with Indochinese refugee PTSD victims.

Therapy Studies

Psychotherapy Studies

There have been no systematic comparisons of therapy outcomes or processes among PTSD victims from different cultures using accepted ex-perimental design procedures (e.g., control groups, alternative therapies, multiple outcome measures). However, there have been a number of reports on various therapy experiences with different ethnocultural groups. Some of these indicate the importance of adjusting therapies to the patient's ethnocultural background.

For example, Parson (1990) discusses a special form of PTSD therapy that he used for Black veterans. He called his therapy approach post-traumatic psychocultural therapy (PTpsyCT). In contrast to other thera-pies, Parson integrated the Vietnam sector, the African/slavery sector, the Eurocentric sector, and the post-Vietnam sector of the Black veterans ex-periential world. He cited ten basic principles that distinguished PTpsyCT from other psychotherapies. Baumgartner (1986) reported success with Black veterans using sociodrama, a form of group therapy that encourages catharsis. However, he did not specify procedures that would be therapeu-tically unique to different ethnic groups, nor did he discuss the biases and problems associated with this method among other populations.

Allen (1986) noted that cross-cultural therapy with Black veterans is complicated by a variety of factors including the tendency to misdiagnose Black patients;, the varied manifestations of PTSD in this group; the Black patient's frequent alcohol and drug abuse; and medical, legal, personality, and vocational problems. Allen acknowledges that these factors make it difficult to treat Black veterans using traditional therapeutic approaches.

Krippner and Colodzin (1989) cited the success of using indigenous healers (American Indian and Asian) in treating PTSD among Vietnam War veterans from these groups. They noted that the traditional practi-tioners used therapies that helped veterans "regain power," "cleanse them-selves," and "decrease shame, guilt, and rage." Among American Indians, sweat lodges, vision quests, and other indigenous practices have been used successfully with American Indian veterans. Holm (1982) and Silver and Wilson (1990) reported success with a variety of American Indian purifi-cation and healing practices.

Lee and Lu (1989) called attention to the importance of considering ethnocultural factors in the treatment of Asian populations. Their article discussed functional and dysfunctional coping strategies of Asian immigrants and refugees and offers some principles for the psychiatric assessment of Asian immigrants and refugees who may have PTSD. Culturally specific treatment strategies were discussed, including (a) crisis intervention; (b) supportive, behavioral, and psychopharmacological approaches; (c) amytal and hypnosis; and (d) folk healing. Niem (1989) also noted some of the problems and possibilities associated with the use of Western psychiatric therapies among Vietnamese refugee populations.

Boehnlein (1987a, 1987b) discussed the importance of considering cultural factors in PTSD therapy with Cambodian women who were concentration camp survivors. He stressed that attention to cultural factors helped provide more comprehensive and valid diagnostic and treatment formulations. Kinzie and Fleck (1987) described their therapy experiences with four severely traumatized refugees from different Indochinese countries. They noted therapeutic problems include the setting in which therapy takes place, reactivation of PTSD, lack of objectivity by the therapist, and the failure of the therapist to provide effective assistance with the immediate social and urgent financial needs of the refugees.

Jaranson (1990); Kinzie, (1985, 1989); Kinzie and Fleck (1987); Kinzie, Tran, Breckenridge, and Bloom (1980); Mollica and Lavelle (1988); Rosser (1986), and Westermeyer (1989) all noted that counseling and psychotherapy adjusted for the ethnocultural traditions of Indochinese refugees can be helpful in reducing traumatic stress. They urge increased sensitivity to cultural factors in treatment procedures.

Dobkin de Rios and Friedmann (1987) used a culturally sensitive hypnotherapeutic intervention for Hispanic burn patients with symptoms of PTSD because of the difficulties that recent monolingual Mexican migrants experience in responding to psychological interventions that are culturally insensitive. A combination of the hypnotherapeutic interventions, systematic desensitization, and other culturally sensitive therapeutic activities helped the effective rehabilitation of Hispanic burn patients. Arredondo, Orjucla, and Moore (1989) discussed the value of family therapy in treating Central American war refugees who have suffered traumas.

Although many countries have torture rehabilitation centers that are heavily concerned with PTSD, there are no comparative reports of the therapeutic effectiveness of different approaches (e.g., psychoanalysis vs. behavior modification) as a function of ethnocultural variables. Research on this topic should be encouraged because of the ready opportunity for well-designed comparative cultural studies.

Psychopharmacology

It is noteworthy that interest in ethnopharmacology has grown considerably in the last decade. Much of the current research on the topic has been generated by Lin and his colleagues at the NIMH-funded research project on ethnopharmacology based at UCLA (see Lin & Finder, 1983; Lin, Poland, & Lesser, 1986; Lin, Poland, Anderson, & Lesser, chapter 20, this volume). Kinzie, Leung, Boehnlein, and Fleck (1987) discussed the use of antidepressants in Southeast Asian patients. Jaranson (1991) also offered a summary of his medication experiences with refugee populations. However, there have no been no carefully controlled experimental studies of psychoactive treatments of trauma victims from different ethnocultural backgrounds.

One of the few clinical studies on the topic was an open trial of clonidine and imipramine in Cambodian PTSD patients conducted by Kinzie and Leung (1989). They reported that 68 severely traumatized Cambodian refugee patients who suffered from chronic PTSD and major depression improved symptomatically when treated with a combination of clonidine, an alpha-2 adrenergic agonist, and imipramine—a tricyclic antidepressant. In addition, a prospective study of 9 Cambodian PTSD patients (aged 31–64 yrs) using this combination resulted in improved symptoms of depression among 6 patients, 5 of whom improved to the point that DSM–III–R diagnoses were no longer applicable.

Kinzie and Leung concluded that clonidine and imipramine reduced, but did not eliminate, hyperarousal symptoms, intrusive thoughts, nightmares, and startle reactions in their Cambodian patients. They felt the imipramine–clonidine combination was well tolerated and should be explored further in treating severely depressed and traumatized patients. Freimer, Lu, and Chen (1989) reported the use of amobarbital interviews with a 23-year-old male Laotian refugee veteran whose symptoms and clinical course fit DSM–III–R criteria for combat-related disorder and PTSD. They noted that the patient was more responsive following three amobarbital interviews, and this provided diagnostic information that helped treatment through expanded use of suggestion and abreaction.

Summary

With the exception of the Parson (1990) report, there have been no systematic efforts to develop alternative forms of psychotherapy that are applicable to distinct ethnocultural groups of PTSD victims. The use of indigenous methods holds some promise for future treatment; however, it will be necessary to conduct rigorous experimental studies (i.e., control groups) to test the efficacy of these methods. Most reports of psychotherapy with PTSD victims from different ethnocultural groups have explored Western methods, making adjustments for certain ethnocultural traditions. Much the same can be said of the psychopharmacology reports on PTSD among different ethnocultural groups. What is needed now are experimental studies with double-blind crossover designs to test the effects of psy-

choactive medications on members of different ethnocultural groups suffering from PTSD. There are no current publications that offer information
on differential treatments (i.e., dosage, medications, side effects, titration
levels).

SOME BASIC CONSIDERATIONS IN CONDUCTING ETHNOCULTURAL RESEARCH ON PTSD

Ethnocentricity

The study of ethnocultural aspects of PTSD can provide insight into
a number of important dimensions of the problem including the role of
ethnocultural variables in the etiology, epidemiology, diagnosis, expression,
treatment, and prevention of PTSD. However, it is critical that the insidious risks of ethnocentricity be closely monitored in cross-cultural studies
of PTSD. As in many other psychiatric disorders, virtually all of the theory,
research, and measurement on PTSD has been generated by Euro-
American, European, Israeli, and Australian researchers and professionals.
When this knowledge is applied to members of these cultural traditions,
issues of cross-cultural validity and reliability are not as serious a problem
because the concepts and approaches are consistent with Western cultural
traditions. However, when these concepts and approaches are applied indiscriminately to members of non-Western cultural traditions, including
ethnic minority members who still practice or are identified with non-
Western cultural traditions, there are serious risks of ethnocentric bias.

Ethnocentricity can be defined in this context as the tendency to view
one's own way of thinking or behaving as the right, correct, or moral way,
and to reject all others as incorrect or of limited accuracy or value. As a
result of ethnocentric bias, concepts and methods of measurement of PTSD
may have only limited cross-cultural relevancy and usefulness. Ethnocen-
trically biased concepts do not encompass or include the experiences of
non-Western people, particularly with regard to their notions of health,
illness, personhood, and normality, as well as their expressions of symptomatology and phenomenological experiences of disorders such as PTSD.

Definition of Culture

Kluckholm & Murray (1957), stated, "Every man is like all other
men, like some other men, and like no other man" (p. 10). The wisdom
of these words is obvious. All human beings share a common biological
heritage that makes them all similar. But, it is also true that human beings

belong to thousands of different ethnocultural groups, each of which shapes both the content and process of individuals' acquired learning. It is also true that each human being is unique because of the specific interactions of their biological, psychological, and cultural natures. Thus, in the process of dealing with PTSD and other psychiatric disorders, we are dealing with at least three different dimensions of human nature—universal, cultural, and personal uniqueness.

Marsella (1988) has defined culture as

> shared learned behavior which is transmitted from one generation to another to promote individual and group adjustment and adaptation. Culture is represented externally as artifacts, roles, and institutions, and is represented internally as values, beliefs, attitudes, cognitive styles, epistemologies, and consciousness patterns. (p. 10).

Ethnocultural Identity

Within the last decade, increased interest in and support for the concept of diversity and cultural pluralism has resulted in a greater use of ethnocultural identity as the principal independent variable in cross-cultural research. Marsella (1990) has defined ethnocultural identity as

> the extent to which an individual or group is committed to both endorsing and practicing a set of values, beliefs, and behaviors which are associated with a particular ethnocultural–cultural tradition. (p. 12)

Among ethnocultural minorities, the variations in behavior within a given ethnocultural group are dramatic and profound, and any effort to group people together for research on the basis of the largest possible ethnocultural dimension (e.g., Arab, Asian, Black, Hispanic) contributes excessive error variance to the design. Even within these larger categories, the shared culture may be minimal because of geographical, genetic, and psychocultural variation. In brief, researchers must emphasize the variations and patterns within an ethnocultural tradition and heritage, and not simply use general racial or national category when conducting cross-cultural research. For instance, researchers should not group data according to large variables such as "Japanese," but rather break the group down into subgroups according to the extent to which they, for example, embrace or endorse traditional practices and behaviors.)

The emergence of highly diverse and pluralistic cultures has led to discontent with older views of ethnocultural identity that posited linear notions of acculturation and assimilation (i.e., each new generation becomes progressively more Euro-American). These views considered the dominant ethnocultural majority as being the end point toward which all ethnocultural minorities were striving. Today, we recognize that there are a number of social statuses for minorities who do not acculturate to the majority culture, including *acculturated, bicultural, marginal, anomic, deviant,* and *multicultural.* In addition, emphasis is now placed on multiculturalism, including multiple identities that emerge in response to situation demands and prerequisites.

If research on ethnocultural identity is to progress and replace or complement our current reliance on broader racial and ethnic categories (i.e., Arab, Asian, Black, Hispanic), it is critical that efforts be made to develop valid and reliable methods for assessing ethnocultural identity. There are a number of different ways for assessing ethnocultural identity (e.g., Marsella, 1991).

Equivalency in Assessment

If measurement concepts and methods are to be valid when applied across cultures, it is necessary to meet certain requirements regarding equivalency in language, concepts, scales, and norms. By equivalency, the authors are referring to the extent to which these topics are similar among the different cultural groups under study. There are four types of equivalency that are important in psychiatric assessment, including linguistic, conceptual, scale, and normative equivalence (e.g., Marsella & Kameoka, 1989). If measures are not equivalent, validity is questionable.

Ethnosemantic Methods

If the measures being used in a study do not meet the equivalency challenges, a researcher may want to consider developing instruments for the culture under study. This can be done through the use of *ethnosemantic methods,* a series of techniques that have long been established in anthropology to reduce ethnocentricity and bias. Marsella (1987) outlined the ethnosemantic procedures and steps for the measurement of depressive affect and experience. However, the procedures and steps are relevant to the study of any concept (e.g., PTSD, emotion, health). The value of this approach is that it begins with the subjective experience of the respondent rather than the assumptions of the researcher. This helps reduce ethnocentricity and bias resulting from the use of culturally insensitive and inappropriate materials and procedures. For example, it cannot be assumed that anxiety, as we define and measure it in the Western world, is applicable to the world of the African tribal member. It is not simply a question of translation, it is a question of worldview and the implications that different worldviews may have for understanding human behavior.

CONDUCTING CROSS-CULTURAL STUDIES OF PTSD

Epidemiology

In assessing the incidence and the prevalence of PTSD and related psychiatric disorders, it is important to consider ethnocultural variations in the definition and expression of the disorders. If standard psychiatric definitions (*DSM–III–R/ICD-10*) are to be used for case inclusion, it is possible that false positives and false negatives will enter into the rates, resulting in erroneous and potentially pernicious conclusions. For example, if researchers are studying traditional American Indian populations living on reservations, and they are using *DSM–IV* standards, they may misdiagnose cases. In such situations it is necessary to use idioms of distress and indigenous concepts to determine an accurate rate of disorder. Several publications have addressed the problems associated with cross-cultural epidemiology (e.g., Marsella, 1978; Marsella, Sartorius, Jablensky, & Fenton, 1986); these offer detailed suggestions for conducting cross-cultural epidemiology studies.

Recommended Clinical Studies of PTSD

There are a number of research strategies that can be used to conduct clinical research studies of PTSD and related disorders across ethnic and racial groups. These include *symptom frequency* (explore symptom frequencies of standard psychiatric and indigenous symptoms among cohorts or samples from different ethnocultural groups); *matched diagnosis* (explore symptom profiles among populations from different ethnocultural groups who share a common diagnosis of PTSD or a related disorder); *international survey* (conduct surveys of symptomatology and other clinical parameters of patients with PTSD from different countries); and *matched samples* (explore symptom profiles and other clinical phenomenology of PTSD by comparing its presence in matched samples from different ethnocultural groups). In this last instance, the emphasis is placed on matching for age, gender, education, social class, and so forth to reduce the variance associated with these variables in general population studies.

Other approaches include *indigenous symptom expressions and folk disorders* (study the symptomatological expressions in non-Western populations via investigations of culture-specific disorders such as *latah*, *koro*, and *susto*, and folk expressions and symptom metaphors such as heavy heart, soul loss, shaking stomach, and brain fag); and *factor analytic approaches* (use factor analysis to empirically derive the structure of symptom patterns among different ethnocultural groups). Furthermore, rather than accepting existing Western notions about symptom clusters, researchers can administer symptom checklists to different ethnocultural groups and then submit the responses to factor analyses for each of the groups studied. The factorial structures or symptom clusters then can be compared using factor-comparison methods to determine the degree of similarity. This method offers the chance to determine ethnocultural variations in symptom patterns empirically rather than accepting a priori notions based on Western assumptions and experiences.

CONCLUSION

Ethnocultural studies of PTSD offer an opportunity to identify the universal and the culture-specific aspects of the PTSD experience by comparing ethnocultural group differences in the distribution, expression, and treatment of PTSD. Identifying these differences can help clinicians adjust their practices and procedures to accommodate to the shared and the unique aspects of the PTSD experience.

There have been numerous studies of PTSD that have examined ethnocultural aspects of PTSD rates, expressions, and treatment regimens. These studies have investigated different (a) ethnocultural groups (e.g., Afro-American, Indochinese); (b) victim populations (e.g., refugees, veterans, victims of natural disaster); (c) traumatic events (e.g., Vietnam War, rapes, and other crimes); and (d) clinical topics (e.g., epidemiology, expression patterns, alternative therapies). The results of these studies are generally consistent with the results of existing biological research that suggests there is a universal biological response to traumatic events that involves psychophysiological activation and disregulation of the adrenergic, opioid, hypothalamic–pituitary–adrenal systems, with attendant clinical symptomatology. It has also been speculated that there are permanent changes in the structure and neurochemical response patterns of the locus coeruleus. However, whereas the response to a traumatic event may share some universal features, especially when a trauma is more severe, ethnocultural factors may play an important role in the individual's vulnerability to PTSD, the expression of PTSD, and the treatment responsivity of PTSD. The sociocultural construction of reality cannot be ignored. Notions of personhood, social support system patterns, and concepts of health and disease are all cultural factors that may mediate PTSD.

Limitations in the cross-cultural sensitivity of much of the existing ethnocultural research constrains our knowledge about culture-specific aspects of PTSD. Some researchers have suggested that whereas intrusive thoughts and memories of a traumatic event may transcend cultural experiences, the avoidance/numbing and hyperarousal symptomatology may be highly determined by ethnocultural affiliation. In addition, ethnocultural factors may be important determinants of vulnerability to trauma (by shaping concepts of what constitutes a trauma); personal and social resources for dealing with traumas; early childhood experiences; exposure to multiple trauma; premorbid personality; disease profiles (e.g., substance abuse and alcoholism); and treatment options that successfully contain and control the trauma experience.

The measurement of PTSD remains a serious problem because the existing instruments often do not include indigenous idioms of distress and causal conceptions of PTSD and related disorders. For example, it is widely known that many non-Western ethnic groups present symptoms somatically rather than psychologically or existentially. Since somatization symptoms are not broadly sampled in many of the PTSD measurement instruments, it is possible that important ethnocultural variations are not being considered. In addition, of course, there are problems of norms, scale formats, translation of materials, and the appropriateness of concepts.

Therapeutic approaches to PTSD have taken a variety of psychotherapeutic and psychopharmacologic forms. While these have generated some interesting hypotheses and some avenues for more extensive exploration, there has been a dearth of well-controlled therapy studies that would enable us to reach scientific conclusions about the treatment of PTSD in different ethnocultural groups. A promising area of inquiry appears to be the use of indigenous healing ceremonies for treating traumas in indigeneous populations.

Existing studies provide an opportunity for generating and testing critical hypotheses about the role of ethnocultural factors in PTSD. With the careful application of accepted crosscultural research methods and the use of more experimentally controlled studies, future research will enable us to understand the role of ethnocultural factors in the etiology, expression, and treatment of PTSD.

Not all victims of trauma develop PTSD. Furthermore, some develop it immediately whereas others develop a delayed syndrome. There is also a need for more research among ethnocultural minority populations to identify the sources of strength and resiliency that somehow mediate the onset, course, and outcome of PTSD. One wonders if there are certain philosophical or religious beliefs, social interaction patterns, or personal dispositions and personality orientations that may be critical mediators of PTSD among certain ethnocultural groups.

Exposure to an extreme and brutalizing traumatic event may override ethnocultural variations. However, there are people exposed to the same traumatic event who do not develop PTSD in any of its forms. Is there something that people who do not develop PTSD have learned—something within their ethnocultural experience—that can provide an inoculating effect? More and better research on ethnocultural aspects of PTSD is needed to answer this question.

REFERENCES

Allen, I. (1986). Post-traumatic stress disorders among Black Vietnam veterans. *Hospital and Community Psychiatry, 37,* 55–61.

Allodi, F. (1991). Assessment and treatment of torture victims: A critical review. *Journal of Nervous & Mental Disease, 179,* 4–11.

American Psychiatric Association (1980). *Diagnostic and statistical manual of mental disorders* (3rd ed.). Washington, DC: American Psychiatric Press.

American Psychiatric Association (1987). *Diagnostic and statistical manual of mental disorders* (3rd ed., rev.). Washington, DC: American Psychiatric Press.

Arredondo P, Orjucla E., & Moore L: Family therapy with Central American war refugee families. *Journal of Strategic and Systematic Therapies,* 8, 28–35, 1989

Arthur, R. Psychiatric syndromes in prisoners of war and concentration camp survivors. In C. Fiemann & R. Faquet (Eds.), *Extraordinary disasters and human behavior.* New York, Plenum Press.

Barse H. (1984, April 19). Post traumatic stress disorder and the American Indian Vietnam Veteran. *Stars and Stripes,* p. 1.

Baumgartner, D. (1986). Sociodrama and the Vietnam combat veteran: A therapeutic release for a wartime experience. *Journal of Group Psychotherapy, Psychodrama, and Sociometry, 39,* 31–39.

Becerra, R. (1982). The Hispanic Vietnam veterans: Mental health issues and therapeutic approaches. In R. Becerra & K. Escobar (Eds.), *Mental Health and Hispanic-Americans.* (pp. 169–180). New York: Grune & Stratton.

Becker, M. (1963). Extermination camp syndrome. *New England Journal of Medicine, 269,* 1145.

Beiser M. (1991). Mental health of refugees in resettlement countries. In W. Holtzman & T. Borneman (Eds.), *Mental Health of Immigrants and refugees* (pp. 51–65). Austin, TX: Hogg Foundation.

Beiser M., Turner, R., & Ganesan, S. (1989). Catastrophic stress and factors affecting its consequences among Southeast Asian refugees. *Social Science & Medicine, 28,* 183–189.

Boehnlein, J. (1987a). Clinical relevance of grief and mourning among Cambodian refugees. *Social Science & Medicine, 25,* 763–762.

Boehnlein, J (1987b). Culture and society in post-traumatic stress disorder: Implications for psychotherapy. *American Journal of Psychotherapy, 41,* 519–530.

Boehnlein, J., Kinzie D., Rath, B., & Fleck, J. (1985). One year follow-up study of post-traumatic stress disorder among survivors of Cambodian concentration camps. *American Journal of Psychiatry, 142,* 958–968.

Breslau N, Davis G, Andreski, P., Peterson, E. (1991). Traumatic events and post-traumatic stress disorder in an urban population of young adults. Archives of General Psychiatry, 48, 216–222.

Carter, J. (1982). Alcoholism in Black Vietnam veterans: Symptoms of post-traumatic stress disorder. *Journal of the National Medical Association, 74*, 655–660.

Cervantes, R. C., Salgado de Snyder, V., & Padella, A. M. (1989). Posttraumatic stress in immigrant from Central America and Mexico. *Hospital and Community Psychiatry, 40*, 615–619.

de Girolamo, G. (1992). International perspectives on the treatment and prevention of post traumatic stress. In J. Wilson & B. Raphael (Eds.), *International handbook of traumatic stress syndromes.* (pp. 935–946). New York: Plenum Press.

de Girolamo, G., Diekstra, R., & Williams C: *Report of a visit to border encampments on the Kampuchea–Thai Border.* Geneva, Switzerland, World Health Organization.

de Girolamo, G., & Orley, J. (1992). *Psychosocial consequences of disasters: Prevention and management.* Geneva, Switzerland: Division of Mental Health, World Health Organization.

de la Fuente, R. (1990). The mental health consequences of the 1985 earthquakes in Mexico. *International Journal of Mental Health, 19*, 21–29.

Derogaitis, L. (1983). *SCL–90–R manual.* Towson, MD: Clinical Psychometric Research.

Dobkin de Rios, M., & Friedman, J. (1987). Hypnotherapy with Hispanic burn patients. *International Journal of Clinical and Experimental Hypnosis, 35*, 87–94.

Eitenger, L. (1960). The symptomatology of mental disease among refugees in Norway. *Journal of Mental Science, 106*, 947–966.

Eitenger, L. (1964). *Concentration camp survivors in Norway and Israel.* London: Allen & Unwin.

Eitenger, L., & Grunfeld, B. (1966). Psychoses among refugees in Norway. *Acta Psychiatrica Scandinavica, 42*, 315–328.

Escobar, J., Randolph, E., Puente, G., Spivak, F., Asamen, J., Hill, M., & Hough, R. (1983). Post-traumatic stress disorders in Hispanic Vietnam vets: Clinical phenomenology and sociocultural characteristics. *Journal of Consulting & Clinical Psychology, 52*, 79–87.

Freimer, N., Lu, F., & Chen, J. (1989). Post-traumatic stress and conversion disorders in a Laotian refugee veteran: Use of amobarbital interviews. *Journal of Nervous & Mental Disease, 177*, 432–433.

Friedman, M., & Jaranson, J. (1992). The applicability of the PTSD concept to refugees. In A. J. Marsella, T. Borneman, S. Ekblad, & J. Orley (Eds.) *Amidst peril and pain: The mental health and social wellbeing of the world's refugees* (pp. 207–228). Washington, DC: American Psychological Association.

Friedman, M., Marsella, A. J., Ashcraft, M., Keane, T., Manson, S. (1992). *The Matsunaga Study: Clinical and epidemiological studies of American Indian, Native Hawaiian, and Japanese American Vietnam War veterans.* Project Technical Report #1. National Center for PTSD, VA ROMC, White River Junction, Vermont, 1992

Garcia-Peltoniemi, R. (1992a). Clinical manifestations of psychopathology in refugees. In J. Westermeyer, C. Williams, & N. Nguyen (Eds.), *Refugee mental health and social adjustment: A guide to clinical and preventive services* (pp. 42–55). Washington, DC. Government Printing Office.

Garcia-Peltoniemi, R. (1992b). Epidemiological perspectives. In J. Westermeyer, C. Williams, & N. Nguyen (Eds.), *Refugee mental health and social adjustment: A guide to clinical and preventive services* (pp. 24–41). Washington, DC: Government Printing Office.

Gaw, A. (1992). *Culture, ethnicity, and mental illness.* Washington, DC: American Psychiatric Press.

Goldfeld, A., Mollica, R., Pesavento, R., & Faraone, S. (1988). The physical and psychological sequelae of torture. *Journal of the American Medical Association, 259,* 2725–2729.

Green, B., Grace, M., Lindy, J. & Leonard, A. (1991). Race differences in response to combat stress. *Journal of Traumatic Stress, 3,* 379–393.

Hamada, R., Chemtob, C., Sautner, R., & Sato, R. (1988). Ethnic identity and Vietnam: A Japanese–American Vietnam veteran with PTSD. *Hawaii Medical Journal, 47,* 100–109.

Hathaway, S., & McKinley, R. (1970). *Minnesota multiphasic personality inventory.* Minneapolis, MN: University of Minnesota.

Holen, A. (1990). *A long-term outcome study of survivors from a disaster.* Oslo, Norway: University of Oslo Press.

Holm, T. (1982). Indian veterans of the Vietnam War: Restoring harmony through tribal ceremony. *Four Winds, 3,* 34–37.

Holm, T. (1989). *Warriors all: 170 American Indian Vietnam Era veterans.* Tucson, AZ: University of Arizona.

Jaranson, J. (1990). Mental health treatment of refugees and immigrants. In W. Holtzman & T. Bornemann (Eds.), *Mental health of immigrants and refugees* (pp. 207–215). Austin, TX: Hogg Foundation.

Jaranson, J. (1991). Psychotherapeutic medication. In *Mental health services for refugees* (pp. 132–145). Washington DC: US Department of Health and Human Services.

Jordan, K., Schlenger, W., Hough, R., Kulka, R., Weiss, D., Fairbank, J., & Marmar, C. (1991). Lifetime and current prevalence of specific psychiatric disorders among Vietnam veterans and controls. *Archives of General Psychiatry, 48,* 207–215.

Kettner, B. (1972), Combat strain and subsequent mental health: A follow-up of Swedish soldiers serving in the United Nations armed forces in 1961–62. *Acta Psychiatrica Scandinavica Supplementum, 230,* 1–112.

Kim, K. (1987). Severely battered wives: Clinical manifestations and problems in Korea. *International Journal of Family Psychiatry, 8,* 387–414.

King, D., & King, L. (1991). Validity issues in research on Vietnam veteran adjustment. *Psychological Bulletin, 109,* 107–124.

Kinzie, D. (1985). Cultural aspects of psychiatric treatment with Indochinese patients. *American Journal of Social Psychiatry, 1,* 47–53.

Kinzie, D. (1989). Therapeutic approaches to traumatized Cambodian refugees. *Journal of Traumatic Stress, 2,* 75–91.

Kinzie, D., Boehnlein, J., Leung, P., & Moore, L. (1990). The prevalence of PTSD and its clinical significance among Southeast Asian refugees. *American Journal of Psychiatry, 147,* 913–917.

Kinzie, D., & Fleck, J. (1987). Psychotherapy with severely traumatized Cambodian refugees. *American Journal of Psychotherapy, 41,* 82–94.

Kinzie, D., Frederickson, R., Rath, B., Fleck, J., & Karls, W. (1984). Post-traumatic stress disorder among survivors of Cambodian concentration camps. *American Journal of Psychiatry, 141,* 645–650.

Kinzie, D., & Leung, P. (1989). Clonidine in Cambodian patients with PTSD. *Journal of Nervous & Mental Disease, 177,* 546–550.

Kinzie, D., Leung, P., Boehnlein, J., Fleck, J. (1987). Tricyclic antidepressant blood levels in Southeast Asians: Clinical and cultural implications. *Journal of Nervous & Mental Disease, 175,* 480–485.

Kinzie, D., Tran K., Breckenridge, A., & Bloom J. (1980). An Indochinese refugee clinic: Culturally accepted treatment approaches. *American Journal of Psychiatry, 137,* 1429–1432.

Kleinman, A, & Good, B. (Eds.). (1986). *Culture and depression.* Los Angeles: University of California Press.

Kluckhohn, C, Murray H. (1957). *Personality in nature, culture and society.* New York: Basic Books.

Krippner, S., & Colodzin, B. (1989). Multicultural methods of treating Vietnam veterans with PTSD. *International Journal of Psychosomatics, 36,* 79–85.

Kroll, J., Habenicht, M., MacKenzie, T., & Yang, M. (1989). Depression and posttraumatic stress disorders in Southeast Asians. *American Journal of Psychiatry, 146,* 1592–1597.

Krupinski, J., Stoller, A., & Wallace, L. (1973). Psychiatric disorders of Eastern European refugees in Australia. *Social Science & Medicine, 7,* 31–49.

Kulka, R., Schlenger, W., Fairbank, J., Hough, R., Jordan, K., Marmar, C., & Weiss, D. (1990). *Trauma and the Vietnam War generation.* New York: Brunner/Mazel.

Laufer, R., Gallops, M., & Frey-Wouters, E. (1984). War stress and trauma: The Vietnam veterans experience. *Journal of Health and Social Behavior, 18,* 236–244.

Lee, E. (1988). Cultural factors in working with Southeast Asian refugee adolescents. *Journal of Adolescence, 11,* 167–179.

Lee, E., & Lu, F. (1989). Assessment and treatment of Asian-American survivors of mass violence. *Journal of Traumatic Stress, 2,* 93–120.

Lima, B., Pai, S., Santacruz, H., & Lozano, J. (1991). Psychiatric disorders among poor victims following a major disaster: Armero, Columbia. *Journal of Nervous & Mental Disease, 179,* 420–427.

Lin, E., Ilhe, L. & Tazuma, L. (1985). Depression among Vietnamese refugees in a primary care clinic. *American Journal of Medicine, 78,* 41–44.

Lin, K., & Finder, K. (1983). Neuroleptic dosages for Asians. *American Journal of Psychiatry, 140* 480–491.

Lin, K., Poland, R., & Lesser, M. (1986). Ethnicity and psychopharmacology. *Culture, Medicine, & Psychiatry, 10* 151–165.

Lin, K., & Shen, W. (in press). Pharmacotherapy for Southeast Asian psychiatric patients. *Journal of Nervous & Mental Disease.*

Lopez, A., Boccellari, A., & Hall, K. (1988). Post-traumatic stress disorder in a Central American refugee. *Hospital and Community Psychiatry, 39,* 1309–1311.

Malt, U. (1988). The long term psychiatric consequences of accidental injuries: A longitudinal study of 107 adults. *British Journal of Psychiatry, 153,* 810–818.

Malt, U., Blikra, G., & Hoivik, B. (1989). The three year biopsychosocial outcome of 551 hospitalized accidentally injured adults. *Acta Psychiatrica Scandinavica Supplementum, 355,* 84–93.

Marsella, A. J. (1978). Thoughts on cross-cultural studies on the epidemiology of depression. *Culture, Medicine, & Psychiatry, 2,* 343–357.

Marsella, A. J. (1979). Cross-cultural studies of mental disorders. In A. J. Marsella, R. Tharp, & T. Ciborowski (Eds.), *Perspectives on cross-cultural psychology* (pp. 233–264). New York: Academic Press.

Marsella, A. J. (1987). The measurement of depressive experience and disorder across cultures. In A. J. Marsella, M. Katz, & R. Hirschfield (Eds.), The measurement of depression (pp. 376–398). New York: Guilford.

Marsella, A. J. (1988). Cross-cultural research on severe mental disorders: Issues and findings. *Acta Psychiatrica Scandinavica Supplementum, 344,* 7–22.

Marsella, A. J. (1991). Ethnocultural identity: The "new" independent variable in cross-cultural research. *Focus: Newsletter of The American Psychological Association Minority Division, 3,* 7–8.

Marsella, A. J., & Kameoka, V. (1989). Ethnocultural issues in the assessment of psychopathology. In S. Wetzler (Ed.). *Measuring mental illness: Psychometric assessment for clinicians* (pp. 229–256). Washington, DC: American Psychiatric Press.

Marsella, A. J., & White, G. (1982). *Cultural conceptions of mental health and therapy.* Boston: G. Reidel.

Marsella, A. J., Chemtob, C., & Hamada, R. (1990). Ethnocultural aspects of PTSD in Vietnam War veterans. *National Center for Post-Traumatic Stress Disorder Clinical Newsletter, 1,* 1–3.

Marsella, A. J., Friedman, M., & Spain, H. (1992). A selective review of the literature on ethnocultural aspects of PTSD. *PTSD Research Quarterly, 2,* 1–7.

Marsella, A. J., Friedman, M., & Spain, H. (1993). Ethnocultural aspects of PTSD: An overview of issues, research, and directions. In J. Oldham, A. Tasman, & M. Riba (Eds.), *Review of psychiatry* (pp. 157–181). Washington, DC: American Psychiatric Press.

Marsella, A. J., Sartorius, N., Jablensky, A., & Fenton, F. (1986). Cross-cultural studies of depression: An overview. In A. Kleinman & B. Good (Eds.), *Culture and depression* (pp. 229–324). Los Angeles: University of California Press.

Mollica, R. (1988). The trauma story: The psychiatric care of refugee survivors of violence and torture. In F. Ochberg (Ed.), *Post-traumatic therapy and victims of violence* (pp. 295–314). New York: Brunner/Mazel.

Mollica, R., & Lavelle, J. (1988). The trauma of mass violence and torture: An overview of psychiatric care of the Southeast Asian refugee. In L. Comas-Diaz & E. Griffith (Eds.), *Clinical practice in cross-cultural mental health* (pp. 262–304). New York: John Wiley.

Mollica, R., Wyshak, G., & Lavelle, J. (1987). The psychosocial impact of war trauma and torture on Southeast Asian refugees. *American Journal of Psychiatry, 144,* 1567–1572.

Mollica, R., Caspi-Yavin, Y., Bollini, P., Truong, T., Tor, S., & Lavelle, J. (1992). The Harvard Trauma Questionnaire: Validating a cross-cultural instrument for measuring torture, trauma, and PTSD in Indochinese refugees. *Journal of Nervous & Mental Disease, 180,* 111–116.

Moore, L., & Boehnlein, J. (1991). Post-traumatic stress disorder, depression, and somatic symptoms in U.S. Mien patients. *Journal of Nervous & Mental Disease, 179,* 728–733.

National Center for PTSD. (1991). Selected Abstracts of European PTSD Literature. *National Center for PTSD Research Quarterly 2,* 1–7.

Nicassio, P. (1985). The psychosocial adjustment of the Southeast Asian refugee. *Journal of Cross-Cultural Psychology, 16,* 153–173.

Niem, T. (1989). Treating Oriental patients with Western psychiatry: A 12 year experience with Vietnamese refugee psychiatric patients. *Psychiatric Annals, 19,* 648–652.

Ostwald, P., & Bittner, E. (1968). Life adjustment after severe persecution. *American Journal of Psychiatry, 124,* 1393–1400.

Parson, E. (1984). The "gook" identification and post-traumatic stress disorders in Black Vietnam veterans. *Black Psychiatrists of America Quarterly, 11,* 14–18.

Parson, E. (1985). Ethnicity and traumatic stress: The intersecting point in psychotherapy. In C. Figley (Ed.), *Trauma and its wake: The study and treatment of PTSD* (pp. 314–337). New York: Brunner/Mazel.

Parson, E. (1990). Post-traumatic psychocultural therapy (PTpsyCT): Integration of trauma and shattering social labels of the self. *Journal of Contemporary Psychotherapy, 20,* 237–258.

Pedersen, P., Sartorius, N., & Marsella, A. J. (1984). *Mental health services: The cross-cultural contest.* Beverly Hills, CA: Sage.

Penk, W. & Allen, I. (1991). Clinical assessment of post-traumatic stress disorder (PTSD) among American minorities who served in Vietnam. *Journal of Traumatic Stress, 4,* 41–66.

Penk, W., Robinowitz, R., Dorsett, D., Bell, W., & Black, J. (1989). Post-traumatic stress disorder: Psychometric assessment and race. In T. Miller (Ed.), *Stressful life events* (pp. 525–552). Madison, CO: International Universities Press.

Perry, R. (1986). *Minority citizens and disasters.* Athens, GA, University of Georgia Press.

Pina, G. (1985). Diagnosis and treatment of PTSD among Hispanic Vietnam veterans. In S. Sonneberg, A. Blank, & J. Talbott (Eds.), *The trauma of war* (pp. 389–402). Washington, DC: American Psychiatric Press.

Rosser, R. (1986). Reality therapy with the Khmer refugees resettled in the United States. *Journal of Reality Therapy, 6,* 21–29.

Rozee, P., & Van Boemel, G. (1989). The psychological effect of war trauma and abuse on older Cambodian women. *Women and Therapy, 8,* 23–50.

Silver, S. (1984). *Worth of the warrior project.* Readjustment Counseling Service, Veterans Administration Central Office, Washington, DC, 20420.

Silver, S., & Wilson, J. (1990). Native American healing and purification rituals for war stress. In J. Wilson, Z. Harel, & B. Kahanal (Eds.), *Human adaptation to stress: From the Holocaust to Vietnam.* New York: Plenum.

Solomon, K. (1989). The dynamics of post-traumatic stress disorder in South African political detainees. *American Journal of Psychotherapy, 43,* 208–217.

Solomon, Z. (1989). Psychological sequelae of war: A three year prospective study of Israeli combat stress reaction casualties. *Journal of Nervous & Mental Disease, 177,* 342–346.

Solomon, Z., & Mikulincer, M. (1987). Combat stress reactions, PTSD, and social adjustment: A study of Israel veterans. *Journal of Nervous & Mental Disease, 175* 277–285.

Solomon, Z., Oppenheimer, B., & Noy, S. (1986). Subsequent military adjustment of combat stress reaction casualties: A nine year follow-up study. *Military Medicine, 151,* 8–11.

Solomon, Z., Weisenberg, M., Schwarzwald, J., & Mikulincer M. (1987). PTSD among frontline soldiers with combat stress reaction: The 1982 Israeli experience. *American Journal of Psychiatry, 144* 448–453.

Streimer, J., Cosstick, J., & Tennant, C. (1985). The psychosocial adjustment of Australian Vietnam veterans. *American Journal of Psychiatry, 142,* 616–618.

Stretch, R. (1990). Post traumatic stress disorder and the Canadian Vietnam veteran. *Journal of Traumatic Stress, 3,* 239–254.

Stretch, R. (1991). Psychosocial readjustment of Canadian Vietnam veterans. *Journal of Consulting & Clinical Psychology, 59,* 188–189.

Summerfield. D., & Toser, L. (1991). "Low intensity" war and mental trauma in Nicaragua: A study in a rural community. *Medicine & War, 7,* 84–89.

Tennant, C., Streimer, J., & Temperly, H. (1990). Memories of Vietnam: Post-traumatic stress disorders in Australian veterans. *Australian & New Zealand Journal of Psychiatry, 24,* 29–39.

Urrutia, G. (1986). Mental health problems of encamped refugees: Guatemalan refugees in Mexican camps. *Bulletin of the Menninger Clinic, 51,* 170–185.

Weisaeth, L. (1989). The stressors and the post-traumatic stress syndrome after an industrial disaster. *Acta Psychiatrica Scandinavica Supplementum, 355,* 25–37.

Weisaeth, L., & Eitinger, L. (1991). Research on PTSD and other post-traumatic reactions: European literature. *National Center for PTSD Research Quarterly, 2,* 1–7.

Westermeyer, J. (1988). *Mental health for refugees and other migrants.* Chicago: Charles C. Thomas.

Westermeyer, J. (1989). Cross-cultural care of PTSD: Research, training, and service needs for the future. *Journal of Traumatic Stress, 2,* 515–536.

Westermeyer, J., & Wahmemholm, K. (1989). Assessing the victimized psychiatric patient: Special issues regarding violence, combat, terror and refuge seeking. *Hospital & Community Psychiatry, 3,* 245–249.

Westermeyer, J., Williams, C., & Nguyen, N. (Eds.). *Refugee mental health and social adjustment: A guide to clinical and preventive services.* Washington DC: Government Printing Office.

Williams, C., & Westermeyer, J. (Eds). (1986). *Refugee mental health in resettlement countries.* Washington, DC: Hemisphere.

World Health Organization (1992). *The ICD-10 classification of mental and behavioral disorders.* Geneva, Switzerland: Author.

5

CONFUSION OF THE SENSES: IMPLICATIONS OF ETHNOCULTURAL VARIATIONS IN SOMATOFORM AND DISSOCIATIVE DISORDERS FOR PTSD

LAURENCE J. KIRMAYER

INTRODUCTION

In current psychiatric nosology, posttraumatic stress disorder (PTSD) is classified as an anxiety disorder; its core symptoms resemble those of generalized anxiety, and it can be understood as the outcome of conditioned emotional responses of fear to external stimuli that become generalized to a range of external cues and, most important, to internal cues including thoughts, images, and other feelings. PTSD is also closely related to depression, both through common underlying neurophysiological systems and because traumatic situations often involve some degree of enduring loss.

Dissociative phenomena also are prominent in PTSD. Indeed, some have argued they are such a common part of both acute and chronic stress response syndromes that PTSD and related problems should be reclassified as dissociative disorders (Spiegel, 1991). Somatic symptoms are also central to PTSD in the form of symptoms of autonomic hyperarousal or hyperreactivity. Thus, the symptomatology of PTSD overlaps with affective, somatoform, dissociative, and anxiety disorders.

In this chapter, I will focus on somatoform and dissociative disorders that have been relatively neglected in recent psychiatry, despite their prominence from a cross-cultural perspective. Although PTSD often is characterized as a disorder uniquely linked to catastrophic stress, it is reasonable to compare it to more common problems associated with milder levels of stress for at least three reasons: (a) to the extent that the effects of stress are cumulative or multiple, these disorders likely coexist with and complicate PTSD; (b) it is possible that PTSD does not represent some unique mechanism activated at higher levels of stressor exposure but is related to or on a continuum with other common disorders; in this case, mechanisms operating at milder levels of distress may be intensified or interact in a specific configuration to give rise to the core symptoms of PTSD; (c) regardless of whether assumptions (a) or (b) prove true, the ways in which culture and ethnicity influence these common disorders is somewhat better understood and may provide models for cultural influences on PTSD.

In the next two sections, I will review some of what is known about ethnocultural variations in somatoform and dissociative disorders. I then will sketch a general model of the relationship between bodily and social processes in symptom experience. This model helps to clarify some of the many different ways in which trauma can be inscribed on the body. Although they often are confounded in the literature, each of these senses of traumatic wounding has different implications for models of pathological process. In the final section, I will consider some questions raised by work on culture, somatization, and dissociation for research and clinical practice with individuals suffering from trauma-related disorders.

SOMATIZATION AND SOMATOFORM DISORDERS

In psychodynamic theory, the term *somatization* originally named a process of converting, transforming, or diverting emotional distress into somatic symptoms. Contemporary use is more uncertain regarding the underlying mechanisms and operationalizes the notion of somatization in three ways (Kirmayer & Robbins, 1991a): (a) as medically unexplained or *functional* somatic symptoms, as in *DSM–IV* Somatization or Conversion Disorders (American Psychiatric Association, 1994); (b) as hypochondriacal worry, bodily preoccupation, and disease conviction; and (c) as somatic presentations of psychiatric disorders conventionally viewed as cognitive or emotional in nature (most frequently, depression and anxiety).

Although these three categories are often conflated in clinical literature that characterizes the "somatizing patient," they are recognized within psychiatric nosology as distinct, and the literature provides evidence that they are substantially nonoverlapping conditions in primary care (Kirmayer & Robbins, 1991b).

A review of cross-national and cross-cultural studies of somatoform disorders identified several problems for existing nosology (Kirmayer & Weiss, 1994): (a) the separation of somatoform disorders from anxiety and mood disorders reflects distinctions between physical and emotional distress that are not made in the same way in other cultures; (b) in many cultures, somatic symptoms and attributions commonly are used as idioms of distress to convey a wide range of personal and social concerns that may or may not indicate individual psychopathology; (c) the nature of physical symptoms varies cross-culturally with ethnophysiological theories, illness models, and previous illness experience.

The first issue has to do with the existence of somatoform disorders as a distinct nosological category that reflects a dualistic ontology in medicine in which distress is partitioned into the physically based—and hence "real"—and the psychological—and hence "imaginary" (Kirmayer, 1988). In fact, somatic symptoms accompany most forms of psychiatric distress. Far from being mutually exclusive alternatives, somatic and emotional symptoms coexist and are substantially correlated in the general population (Simon & Von Korff, 1991). People from many other cultures do not subscribe to the same version of mind–body dualism that informs both Western medicine and the everyday concept of the person (Kirmayer, 1988, 1989). The insistence that distress is exclusively physical or emotional must be understood as a cultural strategy for making sense of experience and for managing its social and moral consequences.

The second issue concerns the pathological significance of observations of widely varying rates of functional somatic symptoms cross-culturally. In many cultures, people use somatic symptoms or talk of bodily illness as *idioms of distress*—that is, commonly experienced symptoms or problems that are recognized within the culture as indicating personal or social difficulties (Nichter, 1981). Self-reported or interview-based rates of somatic symptoms may be higher in some groups not simply because of greater levels of somatic distress but also because somatic symptoms are used to talk about and negotiate matters other than bodily illness. This idiomatic use of symptoms allows people to draw attention to and metaphorically comment on the nature of their quandaries. When reduced to symptoms of a disorder, this meaningful personal and social dimension of distress may be lost.

The third issue concerns the cultural shaping of distress that results in culture-specific symptoms and syndromes. Studies of somatic symptoms have tended to use limited lists that reflect common symptoms in Europe and North America. However, there are many culture-specific symptoms. Some such symptoms are metaphors for expressing distress; others are different interpretations or attributions of vague sensations (Kirmayer, 1984; Mumford, 1989). Efforts to develop culture-specific inventories of somatic symptoms indicate a wide range of symptoms neglected in Western psychiatric nosology that may be relevant to a more comprehensive understanding of psychopathology and the psychophysiology of stress (Mumford et al., 1991). For example, sensations of heat are common nonspecific complaints throughout equatorial Africa and Asia (Ebigbo, 1986; Mumford, 1989). Ethnophysiological ideas also may give rise to culture-specific interpretations of ordinary variations in bodily functions. For example, concerns about loss of semen in the urine are common in South Asia, where the body is perceived to be highly permeable (Bharati, 1985) and where Ayurvedic theory holds that vital essence (*dhatu*) is highly concentrated in blood and still more concentrated in semen (Obeyesekere, 1977). This complex of beliefs gives rise to the *dhat syndrome*, which may be associated with many somatic symptoms, especially fatigue and weakness as well as concerns about sexual functioning. In fact, *dhat* is not so much a syndrome as an explanation that may be used for a wide variety of problems—including somatic, anxiety, and depressive symptoms, as well as difficulties in relationships or at work (Bhatia & Malik, 1991).

Dhat illustrates how a cultural model can influence perception so that sensations or events are noticed and interpreted as symptoms of an illness. As a result of this influence of cognitive models on perception, it is not possible to make a sharp distinction between metaphors, attributions, and sensations. Even a conventional metaphor or attribution may shape perception so that the corresponding symptom is actually felt.

There is a widespread impression that somatization, in any of its definitions, is more common in non-Western populations (Kirmayer, 1984). This claim initially was based on primarily anecdotal studies that used imprecise definitions of somatization, unreliable measures, and noncomparable samples. Patients seen in the community or in primary care in non-Western countries were compared with prototypical patients in mental health clinics or tertiary care psychiatric settings in Europe and North America who had learned to adopt a psychological mode of expressing their distress.

To conduct a meaningful comparison, it is necessary to adopt a consistent definition of somatization and apply it to groups in comparable health care settings. When this is done, it becomes evident that somatization, in each of the three forms outlined previously, is extremely common in North American primary care, affecting about 25% of all patients (Kirmayer & Robbins, 1991b). Somatized presentations contribute to the substantial underrecognition and undertreatment of depression and anxiety in primary care (Kirmayer, Robbins, Dworkind, & Yaffe, 1993). This finding does not mean that sociocultural factors are unimportant in somatization, only that they are also operative in North America within majority ethnocultural groups.

Somatization in all three forms is common among disaster victims (Escobar, Canina, Rubio-Stipec, & Bravo, 1992) and refugees (Hinton et al., 1992; Mollica et al., 1990; Moore & Boehnlein, 1991; Westermeyer, Bonafuely, Neider, & Callies, 1989). Factors that may contribute to medically unexplained symptoms in this population include occult organic disease or nutritional deficiency, prolonged physiological hyperarousal or hyperreactivity, persistent feelings of physical vulnerability, memories tied to bodily injury and scars, and perceptions of what is appropriate to report to the doctor. In the sections that follow, I will consider each of the three forms of somatization in cultural perspective.

Medically Unexplained or Functional Somatic Symptoms

This form of somatization includes somatization disorder, conversion disorder, chronic pain syndromes of unknown origin, and a wide variety of isolated, medically unexplained symptoms and functional somatic syndromes (e.g., irritable bowel syndrome, fibromyalgia, chronic fatigue syndrome) that, depending on current fashion in medical diagnosis, would be classified as physical illness or as somatoform disorder not otherwise specified (NOS) in *DSM–IV*.

Somatization disorder (SD) is the exemplary diagnosis in this group of disorders and applies to patients who have a long history of many unexplained symptoms (13 or more in *DSM–III–R*, at least 8 from 4 different groups in *DSM–IV*) affecting many different functional systems in the body. In epidemiological surveys with the Diagnostic Interview Schedule, the prevalence of SD and subsyndromal levels of medically unexplained symptoms has been found to vary substantially across different regions, cultures, and nations (Escobar, 1987; Swartz, Landerman, George, Blazer, & Escobar, 1991).

In the Puerto Rican parallel to the Epidemiologic Catchment Area (ECA), SD was found to be much more common in Puerto Rico than in the mainland United States (0.7% vs. 0.1%), and the mean level of medically unexplained symptoms was twice that in the United States, despite equal or lower levels of other psychiatric symptoms. Whereas SD is found predominately among women in the United States, equal numbers of male and female cases were found in the Puerto Rican sample (Canino, Rubio-Stipec, Canino, & Escobar, 1992).

Cross-national and cross-cultural differences in somatization have been related to cultural variations in symptom reporting, to culture-specific idioms of distress, and to representations of self (Kirmayer, 1984; Kleinman, 1977, 1986; Marsella, Kinzie, & Gordon, 1973). In the case of Puerto Rico, it has been suggested that the high rates of somatic symptom reporting reflect the effect of the culturally salient idioms of distress of *nervios* and *ataques de nervios* (Guarnaccia, Rubio-Stipec, & Canino, 1989). Among many Hispanic American groups, *nervios* (nerves) is a common symptom of diffuse distress involving anxiety, demoralization, and a wide range of somatic complaints. It is used to express many different social concerns and is woven into commentaries on personal, familial, and political problems (Koss, 1990). As such, it cannot be treated simply as an index of individual pathology and, indeed, it remains to be seen with longitudinal data to what extent the high rates of somatic symptoms found in Puerto Rico and other countries actually indicate the sort of disabling psychopathology presumed to exist in SD.

In a similar way, *ataques de nervios*, a term that covers a wide range of acute episodes of emotional upset and loss of control, is an idiom of distress in common use that may also reflect interpersonal and social concerns more than enduring individual psychopathology (Guarnaccia et al., 1989). It must be emphasized that neither *nervios* nor *ataques* are really syndromes in the sense that they involve a fixed or highly correlated cluster of cooccurring symptoms. Rather, they are folk categories or cultural idioms of distress—that is, modes of explanation and metaphoric expression that are used by people in many different ways to explain, comment on, and adapt to a wide range of problems (Guarnaccia, 1993).

Ethnophysiological models and cultural notions about legitimate forms of illness also may account for cross-cultural variations in the prevalence and nature of *conversion symptoms*, like "hysterical" paralyses, that can change rapidly with shifts in local norms or cultural models for illness behavior. Studies during World War II found much higher rates of conversion symptoms among Indian soldiers than British soldiers (Leff, 1988). Whereas conversion symptoms tended to be found among the less educated and those with low morale among British soldiers, among Indians the afflicted included educated soldiers with good morale.

Leff (1988) reviewed data indicating a dramatic decrease in the prevalence of classical conversion symptoms in England and Wales from 1949 to 1978. Similar declines in the diagnosis of conversion symptoms were found in a hospital outpatient clinic in Athens by Stefanis and colleagues (Stefanis, Markidis, & Christodoulou, 1976). These studies, however, relied on hospital statistics and did not give sufficient attention to the prevalence of conversion symptoms in primary care. It can be argued that conversion symptoms have changed form rather than simply disappearing. Recent European and American episodes of epidemic hysteria have taken the form of "sick building syndrome" or "chronic fatigue syndromes" that are attributed to environmental toxins or viruses, respectively. These attributions serve to legitimate such commonly experienced symptoms as fatigue, weakness, dizziness, headache, and muscular pains (Wessely, 1990).

In many cases, conversion symptoms can be understood as protests of the powerless against intolerable social circumstances (Weller, 1988). Changes in social status and economic and political empowerment, therefore, may reduce their prevalence. For example, Nandi and colleagues (Nandi, Banerjee, Nandi, & Nandi, 1992) observed a dramatic decrease in the prevalence of pseudoseizures in two rural Indian villages over a period of 10 years, following increased availability of wage-earning jobs for women who thus became less economically dependent on their husbands. It remains unclear in this study to what degree changes in spousal abuse and larger social circumstances played a role in both the initially high rates of pseudoseizures and their subsequent decline.

While conversion symptoms currently are attributed to dissociative mechanisms, many other medically unexplained symptoms probably involve disturbances of physiological function that are aggravated by anxiety or depression and by cognitive misattributions (Sharpe & Bass, 1992). Many functional somatic syndromes (e.g., irritable bowel, fibromyalgia, chronic fatigue) clearly are exacerbated, if not caused, by a wide range of stressors (Weiner, 1992). Indeed, in psychosomatic research, it has proven easier to identify stressors as precipitants of the onset of functional syndromes symptoms than of organic disease. Acute abdominal pain, irritable bowel syndrome, and surgery for possible appendicitis with removal of a normal appendix all have been found to be more commonly associated than organic disease with recent life events (Creed, 1993).

Although stressful events contribute to both conversion symptoms and functional somatic syndromes, premorbid characteristics, including personality, also play an important role (Kirmayer, Robbins, & Paris, 1994). Neuroticism, chronic anxiety, or coping deficits may make individuals liable to react with prolonged physiological hyperarousal to stress, anxiety, or strong emotion. High hypnotizability or related personality traits of openness to absorbing experiences or fantasy proneness may make some individuals more likely to dissociate in response to stress and so evidence conversion symptoms or other dissociative phenomena (Spiegel, 1991).

The tendency to suppress emotion may leave individuals unable to resolve and dissipate high levels of physiological arousal or engage them in constant mental effort to contain and control distressing feelings (Pennebaker, 1985). In the same way, difficulty in symbolically expressing or transforming emotional experience, termed *alexithymia*, may contribute to psychophysiological disorders (Taylor, Parker, Bagby, & Acklin, 1992).

Alexithymia is a multidimensional construct and current measures tap dimensions of difficulty discriminating emotional and bodily sensations (a distinction that I already have noted is highly culture-bound), reticence to express emotion, externally oriented, thinking, and a paucity of fantasy or daydreaming (Kirmayer & Robbins, 1993). These factors are related differentially to social class and education and probably to cultural codes of communication and styles of emotional expression (Kauhanen, Kaplan, Julkunen, Wilson, & Salonen, 1993). Social and cultural factors influence the prevalence of alexithymia and may modify its pathological significance (Kirmayer, 1987). In most studies to date, however, alexithymia has not been found to be related to somatization (Kirmayer et al., 1994).

Somatization as Hypochondriasis

The second form of somatization, hypochondriacal worry, appears to be related to anxiety and to a catastrophizing cognitive style. Hypochondriacal worries are common in situations in which attention is focused on the body, there is a heightened sense of vulnerability, a tendency to attribute common sensations to illness, or a corresponding lack of ability to generate normalizing explanations for such distress (Robbins & Kirmayer, 1991).

Cultural factors may influence these mechanisms of somatic amplification (Barsky & Klerman, 1983). For example, in Japanese culture, children receive close monitoring of their physical condition throughout infancy and early childhood (Ohnuki-Tierney, 1985). Prevalent concerns about purity and bodily vulnerability may combine with general heightened self-consciousness and may lead to hypochondriasis and related forms of anxiety in vulnerable individuals. A highly demanding work system with an ethos that views absenteeism because of illness as more acceptable than voluntary vacations also may contribute to what is probably a higher prevalence of hypochondriacal worry in Japan than in the United States.

Although anxiety is viewed sometimes as a consequence of an innately wired fear response, there is much evidence of cross-cultural variations in the causes, symptomatology, and course of anxiety disorders (Good & Kleinman, 1985; Guarnaccia & Kirmayer, in press). Sociocultural factors may influence anxiety through both intrapsychic and interpersonal mechanisms.

This is well illustrated by the syndrome of *taijin-kyofusho* (TKS), a common form of social phobia in Japan (Kirmayer, 1991). Unlike North American patients with social phobia, people with TKS are concerned not only with feelings of personal embarrassment, shame, and humiliation, but also with the fear that through their overly self-conscious and inappropriate interpersonal behavior they may so discomfit others that they cause the others personal injury. This intense preoccupation with one's impact on others fits pervasive Japanese concerns about the correct social presentation of self and the management of hierarchical social relationships.

While social phobias were relatively neglected in American psychiatry until recently, they have received much attention in Japan. In the 1920s, the Japanese psychiatrist Shoma Morita developed a theory of neurosis that grouped together hypochondriacal, obsessive–compulsive, and social phobic syndromes under the broad rubric of *shinkeishitsu* (neurasthenia). According to Morita, what all have in common is a constitutional weakness manifested as a process of excessive self-consciousness (*toraware*) and negative self-evaluation leading to a vicious circle of escalating anxiety, a view quite consonant with contemporary cognitive theories of anxiety (Ishiyama, 1986). A comparative cultural perspective adds to this the observation that interpersonal processes that demand a high degree of attention to relative social status and self-presentation can lead to runaway feedback amplification of self-consciousness. Through this feedback loop, social preoccupation actually may lend delusional intensity to the concerns of the patient with TKS. Yet even the delusional symptoms of TKS often respond to forms of cognitive–behavioral or group therapy.

The interpretation of events as threatening clearly depends on cultural beliefs. As a consequence, the nature of fears associated with panic disorder or generalized anxiety depends on culture. While fear of a heart attack is a common expression of panic disorder in North America (Eifert, 1991), in other societies panic may be manifested as fear of soul loss or of spirit attack. For example, Makanjuola (1987) describes the syndrome of *ode ori* in Africa, characterized by fears of witchcraft attack and parasitic infestation. Seemingly trivial events may be terrifying if they are interpreted as evidence of black magic or the action of malign spirits. Where such beliefs are prevalent they may not, in themselves, indicate individual pathology but may reflect widespread social concerns or conflicts, manifested in particular individuals who are vulnerable not only because of their personal characteristics but also because of their social positions.

Culture also may influence the somatic concomitants of anxiety. For example, Prince (1960) described the syndrome of *brain fag* among African students who were the first generation in their families to receive Western-style education. Brain fag is characterized by symptoms of discomfort located in the head associated with mental effort and resulting in difficulty concentrating and disabling fatigue. The sensations may be described as a hot or peppery feeling or as worms crawling in the head. Coexisting anxiety, depression, psychotic illness, or social conflicts may be found to account for these symptoms (Guinness, 1992b). Although many cases of chronic fatigue syndrome in contemporary North America have been attributed to depression or anxiety, neurasthenia may constitute a third dimension of dysphoria separable from anxiety and depression (Goldberg & Huxley, 1992).

Concerns about environmental safety in industrial societies, or fears of witchcraft and malign magic in many non-Western societies, may combine with interpersonal tensions or larger sociopolitical conflicts to give people reasons to believe they are threatened and may lead to epidemics of anxiety that often take somatic form. Culture-specific forms of epidemic anxiety have been described, including *koro* in China, Malaysia and South Asia (the fear that the penis is shrinking into the body and will result in death) (Tseng et al., 1992) and *magical penis loss* reported in Nigeria (Ilechukwu, 1992). While these epidemic forms of fear affect vulnerable individuals, they also have been linked to wider social threats to the status of specific groups in society (Murphy, 1982).

In Central and South America, many illnesses are attributed to a sudden startle, shock, or fright (often called *susto* or *fright illness* (e.g., Rubel, O'Nell, & Collado-Ardón, 1984). Where fear serves as an explanation for illness, people may search for recent events that were startling or upsetting and retrospectively interpret them both as more intensely fearful and as direct causes of their subsequent symptoms. These attributions make anxiety a more salient feature of many conditions, including both infectious diseases and psychiatric disorders. Such attributional schemas may complicate efforts to identify traumatic precursors for distress.

Somatization as the Somatic Presentation of Depression and Anxiety

The majority of patients with depression, anxiety, and related disorders in Canadian and British primary care present exclusively with somatic symptoms (Bridges & Goldberg, 1985; Kirmayer et al., 1993). While most patients will accept some connection between their emotional states and their somatic symptoms, a significant minority adamantly reject any such connection.

Somatized presentations of anxiety, depression, or other psychiatric disorders are related to both individual and social factors (Bridges, Goldberg, Evans, & Sharpe, 1991; Robbins & Kirmayer, 1991). The intrinsic phenomenology of affective and anxiety disorders includes a prominent somatic aspect so that pain and other somatic symptoms related to muscle tension and autonomic disturbance are present in almost all depressed patients, whereas cardiovascular–respiratory symptoms (e.g., palpitations, hyperventilation) routinely accompany and contribute to anxiety (Sharpe & Bass, 1992).

As discussed previously, cultural idioms of distress may make specific somatic symptoms or illness attributions highly salient and, in conjunction with the widespread stigmatization of emotional conflict and psychiatric illness, lead individuals to deemphasize or suppress the emotional component of their distress and avoid psychological attributions (Fabrega, 1991). Cultural prohibitions against openly confronting interpersonal conflict also may leave oppressed individuals with little alternative than to focus on the somatic aspects of their distress (Racy, 1980).

Somatized presentations also are influenced by cultural theories of emotion that link social and bodily experience in ways that deemphasize or bypass the psychological realm that is the focus of psychotherapeutic theory and practice (Kirmayer, 1989). Finally, the structure of the health care system plays an important role in defining what symptoms or problems are appropriate to take to the doctor who, in most places, is likely to be a primary care provider with limited time for, or training in, the treatment of mental health problems.

What remains less clear is how such somatization influences the course of the underlying disorder. Somatized presentations significantly reduce the likelihood that depression or anxiety will be recognized and treated by the primary care physician (Kirmayer et al., 1993). It has been argued, however, that attributing depressive symptoms to physical illness (e.g., chronic fatigue syndrome) may protect individuals from the lowered self-esteem associated with depression, even though it may prevent them from seeking effective help (Powell, Dolan, & Wessely, 1990). This trade-off may be particularly important for the milder forms of mixed depression–anxiety often seen in primary care, which may remit spontaneously and hence benefit from benign neglect (Katon & Roy-Byrne, 1991). More longitudinal research on primary care populations is needed to clarify this potential trade-off with somatization.

DISSOCIATION AND DISSOCIATIVE DISORDERS

Dissociation involves functional alterations of consciousness, memory, and identity (Spiegel & Cardeña, 1991). After a long period of relative neglect, dissociative phenomena recently have been rediscovered by American psychiatry, and dissociative disorders now seem to have a much higher prevalence than previously appreciated. This neglect and rediscovery demand a cultural explanation because dissociative phenomena are extremely common worldwide—although, in most societies, dissociation is most prominent in healing or religious rituals and does not indicate pathology. Indeed, this has been the major concern voiced by anthropologists in response to efforts to include trance and possession disorders in psychiatric nosology (Boddy, 1992; Leavitt, 1993). This same literature makes it clear that dissociative phenomena take very different forms in different cultures (Lewis-Fernandez, 1992). Dissociative phenomena are commonly part of religious and healing cults that offer oppressed groups (often women) an avenue for protest and a measure of power or leverage within relationships.

Dissociative experiences are common in the general population in North America (Ross, Joshi, & Currie, 1990) but appear to be more frequent in traumatized refugee populations (Carlson & Rosser-Hogan, 1991). Cardeña and Spiegel (1993) reported a high prevalence of dissociative symptoms in two student samples following the October 1989 earthquake in the San Francisco Bay area. Common transient dissociative symptoms included derealization, depersonalization, alterations in time perception, and difficulty concentrating. They cited similar findings from other recent studies of disasters that dissociative phenomena are a prominent part of the pattern of response to acute stress. Symptoms of anxiety and somatic distress (easy fatigability, palpitations, dizziness) also were common in their subjects, and the most frequent experiences, reported by more than 60% of respondents, were hypervigilance, difficulty concentrating, and an exaggerated startle response, which seem more closely related to anxiety than dissociation.

Cultural factors may influence the propensity to dissociate as a response to stress. In some societies, individuals may receive practice using dissociation in religious or artistic performances. Social occasions in which it is appropriate or even expected for one to experience trance allow individuals to maintain these skills and make such behavior more acceptable in other circumstances. For example, Bateson (1975) described how Balinese training for dance performances that employed intense concentration and passive yielding to the molding hands of the dance master made individuals liable to respond to traumatic events with dissociative behavior.

Cultural norms also may sanction the use of dissociation as a coping strategy in times of stress. In a subtler way, cultural variations in the structure of narratives and in the social construction of memory also may contribute to dissociation both by determining the types of gaps in experience and behavior that are acceptable and explicable to others and by altering the deployment of attention in specific contexts, hence influencing dissociation at its roots in mechanisms of attention (Kirmayer, 1992a, 1994). This influence of narrative processes remains an intriguing possibility for future research.

Dissociation, Trauma, and Personality

Researchers contributing to the recent literature on dissociative disorders have emphasized the importance of childhood traumatic experiences, particularly severe and prolonged physical and sexual abuse, as antecedents (Chu & Dill, 1990). In the case of the more severe disorders (i.e., dissociative identity disorder—formerly *multiple personality disorder*), it has been reported that close to 100% of patients report such severe childhood trauma (Ross et al., 1991). However, there are some inconsistent findings that indicate that dissociative experience is not highly correlated with abuse in all samples (Sandberg & Lynn, 1992). For example, Zweig-Frank, Paris, & Guzder (1994) found that dissociative experiences were not correlated with the presence or severity of abuse in a sample of patients with severe personality disorders. This may reflect the fact that, as with hypnotizability, the propensity to experience dissociative phenomena depends on premorbid personality traits that interact with a variety of aspects of personal history, resulting in frequent dissociative symptoms (Tilman, Nash, & Lerner, 1994).

Hypnotizability is a personality trait related to dissociation (Frischholz, Lipman, Braun, & Sachs, 1992). Hypnotizability is correlated with personality measures of openness to absorbing experiences and involves the capacity to become imaginatively involved and focused with great intensity (Frankel, 1990). Developmental studies of hypnotizability indicate that although some patients who are highly hypnotizable come from families that were rigid and authoritarian and used much physical punishment, other such patients come from warm, liberal families in which imaginative play was encouraged strongly (Hilgard, 1979).

While temperamental or personality traits may make individuals more liable to use dissociation as a coping mechanism in situations of great stress, they also may use these strategies to cope with less stressful situations (such as boredom, neglect, parental anxiety, or over-protection) and to regulate physical tension states associated with anxiety, hunger, or dysphoria (for example, as in eating disorders such as bulimia) (Lynn & Rhue, 1988).

The relationship between dissociation, hypnotizability, and openness to absorbing experiences is the object of current efforts to disentangle the dimensions of hypnotic responding and continues to generate controversy (Bowers, 1991; Frankel, 1990). It remains possible that individuals who are highly prone to dissociate deal with hypnotic situations in a qualitatively different way than those who are simply comfortable and skillful with their imaginations. Exposure to trauma involves additional factors of intense emotion and rapid alterations of attention. As Spiegel (1990; Spiegel et al., 1988) has suggested, intense emotion may result in affective state-dependent learning, whereas the narrowing of attention during traumatic events may lead to registration in episodic memory of only a limited range of cues. Both state-dependent learning and the limited registration of cues could then give rise to functional amnesias and other dissociative phenomena.

There is a long-standing controversy in hypnosis research between social psychological versus state models of hypnosis and, by extension, dissociative phenomena. State theorists view hypnotic and dissociative phenomena as reflecting alterations in the mode of information processing by the individual that are sufficiently distinct, both experientially and in terms of underlying mechanisms, to warrant recognizing a special phenomenon. Social psychological theorists argue that hypnotic and dissociative phenomena can be understood as social roles with specific scripts, models, or rules that guide the individual's performance. Some social psychological theorists assume that the dissociative behavior and experience of individuals can be understood completely in terms of consciously available instructions they are following (Spanos & Chaves, 1989). The experiences of involuntariness in hypnosis and dissociation, then, are the results of a misattribution (Lynn et al., 1990). However, many people seem genuinely amnestic for their dissociative actions, experience them as happening *to* them rather than being self-initiated, and find them deeply perplexing and disturbing. Although this can be explained in terms of self-deception and related to other forms of psychological defense, this characterization does not capture the quality of the conflict and confusion experienced with dissociation.

If, however, the scripts for dissociative behavior posited by social psychological theorists are viewed as unavailable to the consciousness of the person, then the two views can be seen to converge. Nonconscious regulation of behavior by scripts or implicit memory need not have the same form as conscious self-direction by explicit memories or accessible self-descriptions. These models allow room for processes of procedural learning, automaticity, and affective state-dependent learning that modify the accessibility of memories, the control of action, and the experience of self (Kirmayer, 1992a).

Cultural Shaping of Dissociative Experiences

Studies of dissociation in ritual contexts indicate how readily dissociation is shaped and controlled by cultural expectations and ongoing social interaction. Contrary to the portrait of dissociative behavior as either neurobiologically patterned or disorganized and capricious, careful ethnographic studies demonstrate a high degree of cultural patterning (Lambek, 1993). This cultural construction of dissociative experience is not so much a matter of fixed scripts for dissociative behavior as it is an interactional or dialogical process in which dissociative behavior emerges in response to, and as an expression of, powerful and contested relationships. This observation suggests that as cultural models for dissociation change, so do the corresponding phenomena.

For example, multiple personality disorder appears to be primarily a Western phenomenon (e.g., Bourguignon, 1989; Kenny, 1981). In many non-Western cultures, when individuals experience autonomous voices or agents within themselves, these are generally believed to be spirits, ancestors, and other culturally determined historical or communal agents rather than episodes or strands of personal history. From a cross-national perspective, possession is a common way of experiencing and describing dissociative phenomena, and multiple personality disorder is a culture-specific way of describing possession, based on the central role of the individual in Euro-American culture. This individualism makes elements of personal history the most natural way to interpret alternative voices of the person and leads to an ethnopsychological theory that describes these voices as split aspects of the self.

A more sociocentric view leads to an experience of dissociative states as voices coming from outside the person, and the individual experiencing them interprets them as embodiments of collective social agents (gods, spirits, ancestors) that are distinct from the person and that convey collective meanings rather than fragments of an idiosyncratic personal history. As Obeyesekere (1991) has argued, culture allows individuals to appropriate these collective symbols to work with personal conflict; at the same time, culture works through individuals as each person contributes to new collective meanings through their own symbolic constructions.

Of course, possessing spirits are not always helpful to people, and dissociations may not always be contained completely or managed smoothly by traditional ritual practices, so it is possible to identify *negative possession experiences* (Bourguignon, 1989). Such patients may be brought to mental health practitioners when conventional methods of help fail, although it is more likely they will be managed within a religious or healing group.

Brief Reactive Psychoses

Brief reactive psychoses are defined as psychotic episodes that are attributed to traumatic life events; they occur within 2 weeks of a stressful event and resolve completely, usually within 1 to 3 months (World Health Organization, 1992). Typically, they involve affective symptoms, difficulty concentrating, confusion, agitation, paranoid ideation or delusions, and less commonly auditory or visual hallucinations. Patients usually do not evidence Schneiderian symptoms or more pervasive thought disorder. Delusions and hallucinations are usually consistent with social position (e.g., paranoia in recent immigrants) or with cultural and religious beliefs (Allodi, 1982). Related terms include *bouffée délirante* (acute paranoid psychosis), psychogenic psychosis, and hysterical psychosis.

Brief reactive psychoses have long been recognized as distinct from schizophrenia; however, diagnostic practices have varied markedly crossnationally and over time (Allodi, 1982). At least four different uses of the term *reactive* have been identified in the literature (Hansen, et al., 1992): (a) as a psychosis distinct from schizophrenia, affective disorder, or paranoia; (b) as a psychosis entirely caused by a psychological trauma; (c) as a psychosis with a good outcome; (d) as a psychosis caused by an interaction between trauma and vulnerability. The Nordic concept of reactive psychosis largely corresponds to the atypical psychosis category in *DSM-III-R* and hence pertains to a psychotic disorder distinct from schizophrenia (Dahl, Cloninger, Guze, & Retterstøl, 1992). In Switzerland, it appears that the term *hysterical psychosis* has been applied primarily to women with histrionic traits who otherwise fit criteria for reactive psychoses (Modestin & Bachmann, 1992). As a result of the different uses of the terminology, it is difficult to make cross-national comparisons.

In several studies conducted in developing countries, it appears the label *reactive psychosis* has been applied to behavior that involves dissociative phenomena (Guinness, 1992a). In this form of brief psychosis, psychotic symptoms can be viewed as socially shaped dissociative experiences rather than manifestations of a primary thought disorder. There is evidence that individuals in the United States with such hysterical psychoses are highly hypnotizable (e.g., Spiegel & Fink, 1979; Steingard & Frankel, 1985).

The higher prevalence of brief reactive psychoses in some cultures may reflect a greater expectation for, or tolerance of, dramatically disorganized behavior as a response to stress. Paranoid ideation and auditory and visual hallucinations are more common in reactive psychoses described in Africa and India than in Europe, while confusion appears less common (e.g., Andrade, Srinath, & Andrade, 1988; Chavan & Kulhara, 1988; Guinness, 1992a).

In the most useful study to date, Guinness (1992a) reviewed hospital records of patients in Swaziland given diagnoses of brief psychoses. He identified three groups. The first presented with a dissociative state involving a culturally sanctioned form of illness behavior. These patients were most often female and had underlying major depressions. Their psychoses were precipitated by relatively minor life events (e.g., quarrels, accusation or fears of bewitchment, religious excitement, school examinations) and recovery was usually complete. The second group, which was predominantly male, had episodes of transient psychosis in response to major life events (e.g., illness or death of a relative, failed job application or labor dispute, financial conflict, refugee status, pass laws restricted mobility). The third group had more psychotic symptoms at the time of presentation and eventually fit diagnostic criteria for schizophrenia. In some cases, their schizophrenia had an insidious onset but presented at one point with a superimposed *hysterical psychosis*. This study suggests that socially sanctioned processes of dissociation may interact with either the combination of mild stress and depression, severe stress alone, or an underlying psychotic disorder to give rise to a brief psychotic episode.

Culture-Related Syndromes and Dissociative Disorders

Many culture-related syndromes might be typified as acute dissociative disorders. DSM-IV groups together *amok, latah, bebainan, pibloktoq, phii pob, vim buza,* and *ataques de nervios* as dissociative disorders not otherwise specified. This nosological largesse is problematic, however, because these syndromes have little in common beyond a tendency to be amnesic for the illness episode. This claim of amnesia may or may not represent dissociation and, in any event, can hardly be viewed as the central feature of each disorder. Most of these terms are folk illnesses or attributions that cut across many DSM-IV categories. In addition, *latah* is not an illness, and some, like *pibloktoq,* are historical curiosities whose prevalence and pathological significance was never adequately established. The enthusiasm for including such variegated syndromes under the dissociative disorders ignores the very powerful effects of social influence and expectation on symptomatic behavior independent of any processes of dissociation.

146   *LAURENCE J. KIRMAYER*

Study of the culture-related syndromes makes it clear that they are a heterogeneous group of problems spanning syndromes, folk illnesses, idioms of distress, and simple attributions. Most of the culture-related syndromes do not fit neatly within one broad category of the *DSM*. For example, *ataques de nervios* is a culturally shaped syndrome that cuts across conventional psychiatric distinctions among anxiety and affective and dissociative disorders and requires rethinking of the relationship between these disorders. The most common symptoms of *ataques* are bouts of uncontrollable shouting and of crying (Guarnaccia, 1993). Dissociative symptoms involving loss or alteration of consciousness and amnesia may accompany *ataques* (Lewis-Fernandez, 1992). In the Puerto Rican Disaster Study, 13.8% of the population reported experiencing *ataques de nervios* and, although fully 91% of these received another Diagnostic Interview Schedule (DIS) diagnosis, these diagnoses cut across the gamut of other *DSM* diagnoses including, in order of frequency of cooccurrence: generalized anxiety disorder (GAD), alcoholism, dysthymia, PTSD, depression, and panic disorder (Guarnaccia, Canino, Rubio-Stipec, & Bravo, 1993).

It is part of the cultural logic of *ataques de nervios* that they are provoked by an upsetting event; as a consequence, the salience and severity of the precipitant must be emphasized by the sufferer to justify or make sense of an episode. This does not mean that *ataques* is simply a stress response syndrome. Whereas *ataques* may occur in the context of individual psychopathology, marital or social conflict, it also serves itself as a legitimating explanation for many other forms of distress.

CULTURE, SOMATIZATION, AND DISSOCIATION: IMPLICATIONS FOR PTSD

In this section, I will consider the implications of work on culture, somatization, and dissociation for theory, research, and clinical practice with PTSD and trauma-related disorders.

How Trauma Is Inscribed on the Body

In clinical practice, patients with PTSD do not usually come with a single discrete disorder; they suffer from a broad mix of forms of distress, including generalized anxiety, depression, dissociative symptoms and somatization. Often some of these problems antecede the traumatic event. The question is, "What does the diagnosis of PTSD add to the clinical understanding of these complex situations?"

The label of PTSD tends to make clinicians think in terms of some wound inflicted on the body-mind through unspeakable fear or horror. Survivors suffer because terror has been inscribed indelibly on their minds and

is replayed relentlessly, derailing thoughts and creating pervasive, and progressively more generalized, anxiety, demoralization, and depression. PTSD
represents some final common pathway in which specific neurobiological
mechanisms are activated (or damaged), giving rise to specific symptoms
(McNally, 1992). It can be argued that the most distinctive PTSD symptom
in current nosology is the reexperiencing of the traumatic event in a vivid
and intrusive way, although in fact this symptom is common in people
exposed to a stressor and is not specific to those who suffer from other
symptoms of PTSD (McFarlane, 1993). Vividness is usually understood in
terms of some special way in which memory is engraved on the mind.
Traumatic memories, while often vivid and intense, are also often vague
in detail. This may be understood in terms of processes of registration and
recall.

The intense emotion associated with a traumatic event may lead to
a narrowing of attention and hence encoding of a limited range of idiosyncratic details of events (Christianson, 1992). Many individuals do not
recall actual events but only feelings or bodily sensations. This might indicate a sort of episodic sensory–affective memory stored not as descriptions
of events or declarative knowledge but as strong emotions or feelings. Research on state-dependent learning suggests that when memories are associated with strong emotions, they may be difficult to evoke unless the
emotion itself is recreated (Spiegel, 1991). At the same time, memories
may be linked to specific trigger stimuli through a conditioned emotional
response and so be involuntarily and intrusively recalled along with painful
affect. Alternatively, individuals who tend to become absorbed in internally
generated images may be more prone to experience overly intense reliving
of events. This would relate vividness to the personality trait of openness
to absorbing experiences or hypnotizability.

Intrusiveness is common to states of high arousal or anxiety in which
the stream of thought is diffuse rather than focused. In addition to anxiety,
intrusiveness also may reflect specific cognitive–attentional processes. For
example, Wegner (1989) shows how efforts to control or suppress specific
thoughts may boomerang, resulting in an increase in their frequency and
salience.

There are many ways in which memory can be said to be inscribed
on the body: (a) psychophysiologically, as conditioned emotional responses,
affective state-dependent learning, persistent states of hyperarousal, or
other enduring changes in neuroregulation; (b) physically, as scars or other
stigmata; (c) as changes in habitus, the posture, stance, or carriage of the
body; (d) as changes in the body–self—that is, in feelings of bodily safety,
comfort, security, and self-esteem; (e) as changes in attention—for example, as heightened attention to the body or as denial of, or distancing from,
the body through isolation of affect or dissociation; (f) in the creation of
images or metaphors that become central to self-depiction and experience;

(g) as narrative accounts of injury, loss, and disfigurement that become part of the person's life story.

These forms of inscription are closely related: Changes in the body influence social stance. Scars from physical injuries may serve as focal points in life narratives; somatic symptoms may be used as a metaphoric language to speak about the unspeakable. In a sense, all of these forms of inscription are forms of memory. Not all forms of inscription are accessible to conscious awareness, however; many remain implicit, vague, and difficult to articulate. It is discouraging for those who put human agency at the center of self-narratives to recognize that Pavlovian conditioning is the stylus that engraves significant portions of our personal history.

But the body on which trauma is inscribed is not only the individual body, it is also the social body. First, and most intimately, it is the body of others who have shared the traumatic experience, but it is also the relationships that have been marked or changed by the trauma and its aftermath and the ever widening circles of response of other individuals and institutions. Stories of trauma arrest attention, and the magnitude of injury and loss becomes the focus of health care providers' explanations for patient's obdurate suffering. Traumatic memory is carried for the survivor by others and replayed throughout local systems of power and health care institutions. If the significance of the traumatic event is to be understood in biological terms, it must be a biology that encompasses not only the nervous system but also relationships, commitments, social position, and wider systems of cultural meaning and value.

Some of the ways in which illness and traumatic experience take on meaning are listed in Figure 1. On the left are actions of the individual body; on the right of the social body. Each arrow represents a relationship of elaboration and embedding, mediated by the processes of translation and interpretation noted within each cycle. We usually think of experience as simply reflecting sensory processes within the individual (represented by the largest arrow going directly from bodily sensation to experience). However, the processes that interpret sensations (based on symptom schemas) to give rise to symptom expression or self-report, illness narratives, and help-seeking are embedded themselves in larger social processes that shape each level through social practices and cultural schemas (collective representations). Thus, experience itself is a social creation, deeply rooted in the systems of interpretation of conventional cultural idioms, local worlds, and the larger social context (Kirmayer, 1992b).

The mechanisms of the cultural shaping of symptomatology presented in Figure 1 differ in some details for somatic, anxiety, and dissociative symptoms. Models of somatization emphasize somatic amplification and symptom attribution (Barsky & Klerman, 1983; Robbins & Kirmayer, 1991); models of anxiety emphasize cognitive evaluation leading to catastrophizing loops (Clark et al., 1988); models of dissociation involve

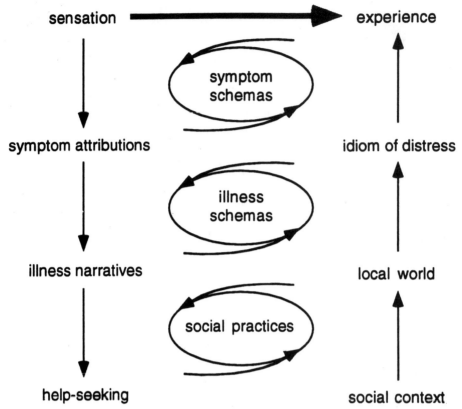

Figure 1. Systems of Meaning in Illness Experience. (Adapted from: Kirmayer, Young, & Robbins, [1994].)

alterations of attention, absorption in imagery, and attributions of involuntariness (Bowers, 1991; Lynn et al., 1990). Some of the specific social mechanisms posited have been discussed previously. However, all involve a hierarchy of attentional mechanisms, attribution and interpretation, narratization, discourse, and praxis in which simpler psychophysiological processes are embedded in more complex levels of social meaning.

Figure 1 suggests that the same interaction of social and bodily processes is involved in symptom formation and the negotiation of illness meanings. Pathophysiology and cultural construction occur at the same time, and researchers must be cautious that efforts to isolate one segment in the circular process do not result in a misleading picture. Thus, the effort in the PTSD literature to isolate a simple cause-and-effect relation between trauma events and specific symptoms ignores the social and cultural embedding of distress that ensures that trauma, loss, and restitution are inextricably intertwined.

Life events are not *episodes*; they are arcs on a trajectory coursing through personal and social time and space that joins events in logical sequence and describes a coherent and intelligible life journey. This trajectory confers meaning on events as it integrates them into a story. Trauma creates a broken narrative, a gap or caesura in which the logic and continuity of one's life is ruptured and the story falters. This rupture is portrayed in Langer's (1991) account of the oral testimonies of Jewish survivors of the Holocaust. In the effort to regain coherence, survivors may try to ignore their traumas or else make them central to their stories. But the very failure or impossibility of the effort to forge a coherent story makes certain events doubly traumatic.

Epidemiological Research

Among the implications of work on somatization for PTSD research is the likelihood that many people with trauma-related disorders initially present to primary care with somatic symptoms and, given time constraints and clinical orientation, may never have their anxiety, depressive, or dissociative symptoms identified or treated. Alternatively, many somatic symptoms, including those that might be attributed to PTSD, may represent cultural idioms of distress that serve to draw attention to and comment on social problems (Kleinman, 1986). Viewing such distress exclusively in terms of individual pathology may undermine patients' efforts to extricate themselves from oppressive circumstances.

Another issue raised by somatization research concerns the possibility of spurious correlations of trauma and illness in clinical studies as a result of what epidemiologists term *Berkson's bias*. Functional somatic symptoms and syndromes are extremely common in the general population, but most people, on most occasions, do not seek help (Kirmayer & Robbins, 1991a). What distinguishes those individuals who seek help may be recent or coexisting life events that are not so much the cause of their somatic distress as reasons to decide they can no longer manage symptoms on their own. This issue is relevant to studies of PTSD and other trauma-related disorders in which identifying a traumatic event is crucial to diagnosis and, at times, is all that prevents patients from receiving a different diagnosis. A traumatic event may lead people to seek help for preexisting or incidental illnesses. Only studies that follow a nonclinical cohort before and after a significant stressor can distinguish between effects of stress on pathophysiology and its effects on help-seeking.

Research on dissociation illustrates the interaction between personality, trauma, and social context in the generation of symptoms and distress and challenges any simple link between trauma and dissociation (Nash, Hulsey, Sexton, Harralson, & Lambert, 1993; Sandberg & Lynn, 1992).

Indeed, although dissociative phenomena commonly accompany and follow frightening events (Cardena & Spiegel, 1993; Guarnaccia et al., 1993; McFarlane, 1993), such responses are not in themselves pathological. Pathological dissociation may be better understood not as a direct manifestation of trauma but as a consequence of intensely painful memories and emotions that interact with attentional and imaginative strategies made salient by past history and personality traits. Without ongoing emotional conflict or affective disturbance, similar dissociative experiences would be transitory and go unnoticed.

Research on dissociation also raises broader issues for PTSD research with regard to the veridicality of traumatic memories and the link between trauma and symptomatology. Far from being a photographic record of experience, memory is a roadway full of potholes, badly in need of repair. There is now much laboratory evidence for the remarkable malleability of memory and for the unreliability of personal accounts of antecedent events on which the diagnosis of PTSD is based (Christianson, 1992; Frankel, 1993). Among highly hypnotizable individuals, memory can be manipulated easily in the laboratory (e.g., Laurence & Perry, 1983). Whether memory for traumatic events is more or less malleable than everyday memory remains a controversial point, but the very existence of dissociative amnesias argues that traumatic memories are just as vulnerable to manipulation and modification. This raises serious methodological problems for self-report or structured interview measures of PTSD.

Cross-cultural work on somatization and dissociation has uncovered a wide range of symptoms neglected in conventional psychiatric nosology. There have been few attempts to tap into this cultural variation in somatoform and dissociative disorders with standardized instruments (Ebigbo, 1986; Guarnaccia et al., 1993; Mumford et al., 1991). There is a need for more work using expanded symptom inventories to explore the dimensional structure of distress cross-culturally. Until broader symptom lists are used to canvas distress, both apparent similarities and differences in the prevalence of disorders may reflect insensitivities of observers or epidemiological measures to cultural variations in symptom patterns and expression.

However, many culture-specific syndromes are better thought of as popular illness labels, explanations or idioms of distress rather than discrete entities that can be mapped one to one to existing nosology. Such labels influence help-seeking and hence the composition of clinical samples. It remains to be seen to what extent they also influence the course and outcome of psychiatric disorders. To the extent that they do, the case can be made for a parallel or multidimensional diagnostic system that acknowledges folk categories as crucial influences on the prognosis and appropriate treatment of distress.

Clinical Intervention

Consideration of cultural variations in somatization and dissociation also raises issues for intervention. Current Euro-American health psychology and treatment interventions are based on culture-specific concepts of the person that are manifested in distinctive notions about: (a) the optimal relationship between public expression and private experience; (b) the value of self-efficacy and interpersonal independence as sources of self-esteem; (c) the symbolic interpretation of symptoms and action in terms of intrapsychic processes and personal history (Kirmayer, 1989).

American values of expressive individualism lead to assumptions that people need to reveal their private concerns to others to relieve the tension of containing secrets and to assert their individuality through emotional expression and personal decisionmaking and choice, that people must assert individual control over their lives through externally oriented instrumental behavior, and that actions are to be interpreted primarily with regard to an idiosyncratic personal history. The results of cross-cultural research raise questions about each of these assumptions. Other cultures approach these dimensions quite differently. For the sake of comparison, we might consider cultures in which: (a) identification with the family, lineage, or social group is the primary source of self-definition and self-worth, hence private conflicts may be kept private to protect social harmony or else assimilated to larger social themes and worked out in collective rituals in concert with others (Wikan, 1990); (b) containment, equanimity, and acceptance are viewed as strengths and marks of distinction, so that control is exercised internally rather than externally by mature individuals (Weisz, Rothbaum, & Blackburn, 1984); (c) events have symbolic meaning that is first and foremost shared and collective rather than personal and idiosyncratic; as a consequence, dreams, symptoms, and actions are interpreted in terms of larger cultural, historical, and mythological themes (Obeyesekere, 1991).

Of course, both poles exist in all cultures and are sources of intrapsychic and interpersonal tension, negotiation, and compromise. The issue for cultural psychiatry is what is valued and dealt with explicitly and what must go underground because it is ignored, derogated, or actively suppressed. Cultural and religious ideals can influence receptivity to, and the ultimate value of, expiation, confession, abreaction, and self-assertion. Telling stories of trauma, while immediately stressful, ultimately may be healing for the individual (Pennebaker, Barger, & Tiebout, 1989); but what is the wider personal and social significance of disclosing traumatic events for Buddhists, for example, who may feel they must maintain equanimity, or that the traumas they (or members of their group) have suffered must be inevitable consequences of prior karma? Our theories of psychopathology and of healing cannot evolve in a culturally sensitive fashion without seriously considering these dilemmas.

CONCLUSION

The broad distinction between affective, anxiety, somatoform, and dissociative disorders enshrined in the *DSM* and, to a lesser extent in the *ICD* reflects the salience of prototypical clinical cases. Prototypes are a natural way to organize cognitive categories and may be extended to cover a wide range of different cases by family resemblance. These prototypes, however, are not simply products of the natural history of psychiatric disorders. Which cases are identified as prototypical also reflects processes of case-finding and definition driven by both popular and professional ethnopsychological theory, as well as by patterns of help-seeking in health care systems with specific divisions of labor. Thus, the received categories of affective, anxiety, dissociative, and somatoform disorders are not natural divisions in the world or in the phenomenology of disease, disorder, or illness. Once established, nosological categories tend to become reified and to obscure the variation and overlap between disorders in patients. When applied to patients who typically have problems cutting across these categories, these divisions force clinicians into all kinds of contortions: the use of laundry lists of diagnoses to characterize comorbidity in patients; the use of ill-defined residual categories such as *not otherwise specified* (NOS), or, more often, the procrustean solution of simply giving a diagnosis that truncates and ignores much of what is going on for the individual.

The stress-related syndromes are distinguished from most other *DSM* diagnoses in that a specific etiological factor (the traumatic event) is intrinsic to their definitions. The general issue of identifying stress as a salient cause or contributor to disorders, as has been noted, is bound up with whether there are prevalent cultural notions about stresses as necessary or sufficient causes for problems so that individuals must find such causes to make their distress coherent and explicable to themselves and others. Indeed, the finding of a stressful cause to account for distress may change the nature of that distress, not only with regard to its explanatory links to behavior and events but in its very experience and manifestations.

Stress is a popular lay explanation for a wide variety of problems and afflictions. Part of its appeal is that it is viewed as outside the person, ubiquitous and inevitable. One cannot help feeling the stress of modern life or of unfortunate circumstances, and too much stress will bend or break both mind and body. The metaphor of stress serves to displace personal responsibility for affliction and protects individuals from more pejorative psychological labels and terms that imply a greater degree of personal culpability or weakness (Kirmayer, 1988). As an externalizing concept, stress works against the fundamental attributional bias in Euro-American culture that leads us to attribute any distinctive, unusual, or pathological features of someone's behavior to some personal trait or characteristic (Ross & Nisbett, 1991).

At the same time, the external attribution made by stress is vague, diffuse, and does not point to any specific social institution or practice as the culprit. The encompassing nature of stress that makes it an imprecise term is part of its social and psychological utility. Everyday explanations in terms of stress thus serve a dual defensive function: Such explanations extend sympathy to sufferers of circumstances beyond their control while evading any clear critique of those damaging social forces (Young, 1980). Whereas these connotations of the metaphor of stress do not obviate its use to call attention to problems in a local world (Barley & Knight, 1992) or its utility in analyzing social structural problems (Aneshensel, 1992), they certainly make such pointed analyses more difficult.

The focus on stress or trauma, and on a unique and expectable response to it, is attractive because it performs three great simplifications: (a) morally, it simplifies the issue of responsibility, guilt, and blame that plagues survivors and authorizes their righteous anger or forgiveness; (b) scientifically, it suggests a linear causal model amenable to animal models and simple experiments; (c) therapeutically, it allows clinicians to attribute a wide range of problems to a single wound and so to organize treatment along clear lines that may include both the moral and scientific models.

When we consider the situation of the people who are the exemplars of PTSD (e.g., veterans of the Vietnam war; victims of rape, trauma, and disaster; or refugees who have undergone torture, dispossession, and displacement), we recognize that not only are these situations immensely complex and simply caricatured as *stressful* or traumatic, the responses of individuals to them are equally complex and varied. Individuals who escaped the killing fields of Cambodia suffered not only from trauma and torture, injury and privation, nor even just from individual loss, but from a collective loss of meaning and social structure—the preconditions for communal life—that puts them in an enduring predicament.

If the complexity of this human predicament is to be respected in research and clinical practice, we must understand the impact of trauma in terms of the disruption of the ongoing construction of a coherent and valued self through participation in communal life. Eisenbruch's (1991) notion of cultural bereavement may be helpful in this regard. Trauma is at once a sociopolitical event, a psychophysiological process, a bodily and emotional experience, an explanation, and a narrative theme. Although trauma is spoken of as though it can be localized at a discrete time and place, the processes of coping and adaptation spread it out over time so that one is faced not with simple linkages of cause and effect, but with feedback loops in which traumatic memories and attributions are used to make sense of experience and sustain social positions. Focusing on trauma exclusively as a wound inflicted on the body–mind is likely to miss the wider dimensions of the predicament and so limit one's therapeutic imagination.

REFERENCES

Allodi, F. (1982). Acute paranoid reaction (*bouffée délirante*) in Canada. *Canadian Journal of Psychiatry, 27*, 366–373.

American Psychiatric Association. (1994). *Diagnostic and Statistical Manual (4th ed.)*. Washington, DC: Author.

Andrade, C., Srinath, S., & Andrade, A. C. (1988). True hallucinations as a culturally sanctioned experience. *British Journal of Psychiatry, 152*, 838–839.

Aneshensel, C. S. (1992). Social stress: Theory and research. *Annual Review of Sociology, 18*, 15–38.

Barley, S. R., & Knight, D. (1992). Toward a cultural theory of stress complaints. *Research in Organizational Behavior, 14*, 1–48.

Barsky, A. J., & Klerman, G. L. (1983). Overview: Hypochondriasis, bodily complaints and somatic styles. *American Journal of Psychiatry, 140*, 273–283.

Bateson, G. (1975). Some components of socialization for trance. *Ethos, 3*, 143–155.

Bharati, A. (1985). The self in Hindu thought and action. In A. J. Marsella, G. DeVos, & F. L. K. Hsu (Eds.), *Culture and self: Asian and Western perspectives* (pp. 185–230). New York: Tavistock.

Bhatia, M. S., & Malik, S. C. (1991). *Dhat* syndrome: A useful diagnostic entity in Indian culture. *British Journal of Psychiatry, 159*, 691–695.

Boddy, J. (1992) Comment on the proposed DSM-IV criteria for Trance and Possession Disorder. *Transcultural Psychiatric Research Review, 29*(4), 323–330.

Bourguignon, E. (1989). Multiple personality, possession trance and the psychic unity of mankind. *Ethos, 17*(3), 371–384.

Bowers, K. S. (1991). Dissociation in hypnosis and multiple personality disorder. *International Journal of Clinical and Experimental Hypnosis, 39*(3), 155–176.

Bridges, K. W., & Goldberg, D. P. (1985). Somatic presentation of DSM-III psychiatric disorders in primary care. *Journal of Psychosomatic Research, 29*(6), 563–569.

Bridges, K., Goldberg, D., Evams, B., & Sharpe, T. (1991). Determinants of somatization in primary care. *Psychological Medicine, 21*, 473–483.

Canino, I. A., Rubio-Stipec, M., Canino, G., & Escobar, J. I. (1992). Functional somatic symptoms: A cross-ethnic comparison. *American Journal of Orthopsychiatry, 62*(4), 605–612.

Cardeña, E., & Spiegel, D. (1993). Dissociative reactions to the San Francisco Bay earthquake of 1989. *American Journal of Psychiatry, 150*(3), 474–478.

Carlson, E. B., & Rosser-Hogan, R. (1991). Trauma experiences, posttraumatic stress, dissociation and depression in Cambodian refugees. *American Journal of Psychiatry, 148,* 1548–1551.

Chavan, B. S., & Kulhara, P. (1988). A clinical study of reactive psychosis. *Acta Psychiatrica Scandinavia, 78,* 712–715.

Christianson, S.-A. (1992). Emotional stress and eyewitness memory: A critical review. *Psychological Bulletin, 112*(2), 284–309.

Chu, J. A., & Dill, D. L. (1990). Dissociative symptoms in relation to childhood physical and sexual abuse. *American Journal of Psychiatry, 147*(7), 887–892.

Clark, D. M., Salkovskis, P. M., Gelder, M., Koehler, C., Martin, M., Anastasiades, P., Hackmann, A., Middleton, H., & Jeavons, A. (1988). Tests of a cognitive theory of panic. In I. Hand & H. U. Wittchen (Eds.), *Panic and phobias* (pp. 149–158). Berlin: Springer-Verlag.

Creed, F. (1993). Stress and psychosomatic disorders. In L. Goldberger & S. Breznitz (Eds.), *Handbook of stress* (pp. 496–510). New York: Free Press.

Dahl, A. A., Cloninger, C. R., Guze, S. B., & Retterstøl, N. (1992). Convergence of American and Scandinavian diagnoses of functional psychoses. *Comprehensive Psychiatry, 33*(1), 13–16.

Ebigbo, P. O. (1986). A cross-sectional study of somatic complaints of Nigerian females using the Enugu somatization scale. *Culture, Medicine, and Psychiatry, 10*(2), 167–186.

Eifert, G. (1991). Cardiophobia: A paradigmatic behavioural model of heart-focused anxiety and non-anginal chest pain. *Behaviour Research and Therapy, 30*(4), 329–345.

Eisenbruch, M. (1991). From postraumatic stress disorder to cultural bereavement: Diagnosis of Southeast Asian refugees. *Social Science and Medicine, 33*(6), 673–680.

Escobar, J. I. (1987). Cross-cultural aspects of the somatization trait. *Hospital and Community Psychiatry, 38*(2), 174–180.

Escobar, J. I., Canino, F., Rubio-Stipec, M., & Bravo, M. (1992). Somatic symptoms after a natural disaster: A prospective study. *American Journal of Psychiatry, 149*(7), 965–967.

Fabrega, H., Jr. (1991). Psychiatric stigma in non-Western societies. *Comprehensive Psychiatry, 32*(6), 534–551.

Frankel, F. H. (1990). Hypnotizability and dissociation. *American Journal of Psychiatry, 147*(7), 823–829.

Frankel, F. H. (1993). Adult reconstructions of childhood events in the multiple personality literature. *American Journal of Psychiatry, 150,* 954–958.

Frischholz, E. J., Lipman, L. S., Braun, B. G., & Sachs, R. G. (1992). Psychopathology, hypnotizability, and dissociation. *American Journal of Psychiatry, 149*(11), 1521–1525.

Goldberg, D., & Huxley, P. (1992). *Common mental disorders: A bio-social model.* London: Tavistock/Routledge.

Good, B. J., & Kleinman, A. M. (1985). Culture and anxiety: Cross-cultural evidence for the patterning of anxiety disorders. In A. H. Tuma & J. Maser (Eds.), *Anxiety and anxiety disorders* (pp. 297–324). Hillsdale, NJ: Erlbaum.

Guarnaccia, P. J. (1993). *Ataques de nervios* in Puerto Rico: Culture-bound syndrome or popular illness? *Medical Anthropology, 15,* 157–170.

Guarnaccia, P. J., Canino, G., Rubio-Stipec, M., & Bravo, M. (1993). The prevalence of *ataques de nervios* in the Puerto Rico disaster study: The role of culture in psychiatric epidemiology. *Journal of Nervous and Mental Disease, 181*(3), 157–165.

Guarnaccia, P., & Kirmayer, L. J. (in press). Cultural considerations on anxiety disorders. In T. A. Widiger, A. Frances, H. Pincus, M. B. First, R. Ross, & W. Davis (Eds.), *DSM–IV Sourcebook.* Washington, DC: American Psychiatric Press.

Guarnaccia, P. J., Rubio-Stipec, M., & Canino, G. (1989). *Ataques de nervios* in the Puerto Rican Diagnostic Interview Schedule: The impact of cultural categories on psychiatric epidemiology. *Culture, Medicine, and Psychiatry, 13,* 275–295.

Guinness, E. A. (1992a). Brief reactive psychosis and the major functional psychoses: Descriptive case studies in Africa. *British Journal of Psychiatry*(Suppl.), 24–41.

Guinness, E. A. (1992b). Profile and prevalence of the brain fag syndrome: Psychiatric morbidity in school populations in Africa. *British Journal of Psychiatry* (Suppl.), 42–52.

Hansen, H., Dahl, A. A., Bertelsen, A., Birket-Smith, M., von Knorring, L., Ottoson, J. O., Pakaslahti, A., Rettersol, N., Salvesen, C., Thorsteinsson, G., & Vflisflnen, E. (1992). The Nordic concept of reactive psychosis: A multicenter reliability study. *Acta Psychiatrica Scandinavia, 86*(1), 55–59.

Hilgard, J. R. (1979). *Personality and hypnosis: A study of imaginative involvement* (2nd ed.). Chicago: University of Chicago Press.

Hinton, W. L., Chen, Y.-C. J., Du, N., Tran, C. G., Lu, F. G., Miranda, J., & Faust, S. (1992). DSM-III-R Disorders in Vietnamese refugees: Prevalence and correlates. *Journal of Nervous and Mental Disease, 181*(2), 113–122.

Ilechukwu, S. T. C. (1992). Magical penis loss in Nigeria: Report of a recent epidemic of a *Koro*-like syndrome. *Transcultural Psychiatric Research Review, 29,* 91–108.

Ishiyama, F. I. (1986). Positive reinterpretation of fear of death: A Japanese (Morita) psychotherapy approach to anxiety treatment. *Psychotherapy, 23*(4), 556–581.

Katon, W., & Roy-Byrne, P. P. (1991). Mixed anxiety and depression. *Journal of Abnormal Psychology, 100*(3), 337–345.

Kauhanen, J., Kaplan, G. A., Julkunen, J., Wilson, T. W., & Salonen, J. T. (1993). Social factors in alexithymia. *Comprehensive Psychiatry, 34*(5), 330–335.

Kenny, M. G. (1981). Multiple personality and spirit possession. *Psychiatry, 44,* 337–358.

Kirmayer, L. J. (1984). Culture, affect and somatization. *Transcultural Psychiatric Research Review, 21*(3), 159–188 & (4), 237–262.

Kirmayer, L. J. (1987). Languages of suffering and healing: Alexithymia as a social and cultural process. *Transcultural Psychiatric Research Review, 24,* 119–136.

Kirmayer, L. J. (1988). Mind and body as metaphors: Hidden values in biomedicine. In M. Lock & D. Gordon (Eds.), *Biomedicine examined* (pp. 57–92). Dordrecht, Netherlands: Kluwer.

Kirmayer, L. J. (1989). Cultural variations in the response to psychiatric disorders and emotional distress. *Social Science and Medicine, 29*(3), 327–339.

Kirmayer, L. J. (1991). The place of culture in psychiatric nosology: *Taijin kyofusho* and DSM-III-R. *Journal of Nervous and Mental Disease, 179*(1), 19–28.

Kirmayer, L. J. (1992a). Social constructions of hypnosis. *International Journal of Clinical and Experimental Hypnosis, 40*(4), 276–300.

Kirmayer, L. J. (1992b). The body's insistence on meaning: Metaphor as presentation and representation in illness experience. *Medical Anthropology Quarterly, 6*(4), 323–346.

Kirmayer, L. J. (1994). Pacing the void: Social and cultural dimensions of dissociation. In D. Spiegel (Eds.), *Dissociation: Culture, mind and body* (91–122). Washington, DC: American Psychiatric Press.

Kirmayer, L. J., & Robbins, J. M. (Ed.). (1991a). *Current concepts of somatization: Research and clinical perspectives.* Washington, DC: American Psychiatric Press.

Kirmayer, L. J., & Robbins, J. M. (1991b). Three forms of somatization in primary care: Prevalence, co-occurrence and sociodemographic characteristics. *Journal of Nervous and Mental Disease, 179*(11), 647–655.

Kirmayer, L. J., & Robbins, J. M. (1993). Cognitive and social correlates of the Toronto Alexithymia Scale. *Psychosomatics, 34*(1), 41–52.

Kirmayer, L. J., Robbins, J. M., Dworkind, M., & Yaffe, M. (1993). Somatization and the recognition of depression and anxiety in primary care. *American Journal of Psychiatry, 150*(5), 734–741.

Kirmayer, L. J., Robbins, J. M., & Paris, J. (1994). Somatization and somatoform disorders: Personality and the social matrix of somatic distress. *Journal of Abnormal Psychology, 103*(1), 125–136.

Kirmayer, L. J., & Weiss, M. G. (in press). Cultural considerations on somatoform disorders. In T. A. Widiger, A. Frances, H. Pincus, M. B. First, R. Ross, R. & W. Davis (Eds.), *DSM–IV Sourcebook.* Washington, DC: American Psychiatric Press.

Kirmayer, L. J., Young, A., & Robbins, J. M. (1994). Symptom attribution in cultural perspective. *Canadian Journal of Psychiatry, 39,* 584–595.

Kleinman, A. M. (1977). Depression, somatization and the "new cross-cultural psychiatry." *Social Science and Medicine, 11,* 3–10.

Kleinman, A. (1986). *Social origins of distress and disease.* New Haven, CT: Yale University Press.

Koss, J. M. (1990). Somatization and somatic complaint syndromes among Hispanics: Overview and ethnopsychological perspectives. *Transcultural Psychiatric Research Review, 27*(1), 5–30.

Lambek, M. (1993). *Knowledge and practice in Mayotte: Local discourses of Islam, sorcery, and spirit possession.* Toronto, Ontario: University of Toronto Press.

Langer, L. L. (1991). *Holocaust testimonials: The ruins of memory.* New Haven, CT: Yale University Press.

Laurence, J.-R., & Perry, C. (1983). Hypnotically created memory among highly hypnotizable subjects. *Science, 222,* 523–524.

Leavitt, J. (1993). Are trance and possession disorders? *Transcultural Psychiatric Research Review, 30*(1), 51–57.

Leff, J. (1988). *Psychiatry around the globe: A transcultural view.* London: Gaskell.

Lewis-Fernandez, R. (1992). Trance and possession as dissociative disorders. *Transcultural Psychiatric Research Review, 29*(4), 301–318.

Lynn, S. J., & Rhue, J. W. (1988). Fantasy proneness: Hypnosis, developmental antecedents, and psychopathology. *American Psychologist, 43*(1), 35–44.

Lynn, S. J., Rhue, J. W., & Weekes, J. R. (1990). Hypnotic involuntariness: A social cognitive analysis. *Psychological Review, 97*(2), 169–184.

Makanjuola, R. O. A. (1987). *Ode Ori:* A culture-bound disorder with prominent somatic features in Yoruba Nigerian patients. *Acta Psychiatrica Scandinavica, 75*(3), 231–236.

Marsella, A. J., Kinzie, D., Gordon, P. (1973). Ethnocultural variations in the expression of depression. *Journal of Cross-Cultural Psychology, 4,* 435–458.

McFarlane, A. C. (1993). PTSD: Synthesis of research and clinical studies: The Australia bushfire disaster. In J. P. Wilson & B. Raphael (Eds.), *International handbook of traumatic stress syndromes* (pp. 421–429). New York: Plenum.

McNally, R. J. (1992). Psychopathology of post-traumatic stress disorder (PTSD): Boundaries of the syndrome. In M. Basoglu (Eds.), *Torture and its consequences* (pp. 229–252). New York: Cambridge University Press.

Modestin, J., & Bachmann, K. M. (1992). Is the diagnosis of hysterical psychosis justified?: Clinical study of hysterical psychosis, reactive/psychogenic psychosis, and schizophrenia. *Comprehensive Psychiatry, 33*(1), 17–24.

Mollica, R. F., Wyshak, G., Lavelle, J., Truong, T., Tor, S., & Yang, T. (1990). Assessing symptom change in Southeast Asia refugee survivors of mass violence and torture. *American Journal of Psychiatry, 147,* 83–88.

Moore, L. J., & Boehnlein, J. K. (1991). Posttraumatic stress disorder, depression, and somatic symptoms in U.S. Mien patients. *Journal of Nervous and Mental Disease, 179*(12), 728–733.

Mumford, D. B. (1989). Somatic sensations and psychological distress among students in Britain and Pakistan. *Social Psychiatry and Psychiatric Epidemiology, 24,* 321–326.

Mumford, D. B., Bavington, J. T., Bhatnagar, K. S., Hussain, Y., Mirza, S., & Naeaghi, M. M. (1991). The Bradford Somatic Inventory: A multi-ethnic inventory of somatic symptoms reported by anxious and depressed patients in Britain and the Indo-Pakistan subcontinent. *British Journal of Psychiatry, 158,* 379–386.

Murphy, H. B. M. (1982). *Comparative psychiatry: The international and intercultural distribution of mental illness.* New York: Springer-Verlag.

Nandi, D. N., Banerjee, G., Nandi, S., & Nandi, P. (1992). Is hysteria on the wane? A Community survey in West Bengal, India. *British Journal of Psychiatry, 160,* 87–91.

Nash, M. R., Hulsey, T. L., Sexton, M. C., Harralson, T. L., & Lambert, W. (1993). Long-term sequelae of childhood sexual abuse: Perceived family environment, psychopathology, and dissociation. *Journal of Consulting and Clinical Psychology, 61,* 276–283.

Nichter, M. (1981). Idioms of distress: Alternatives in the expression of psycho-social distress: A case study from India. *Culture, Medicine and Psychiatry, 5,* 379–408.

Obeyesekere, G. (1977). The theory and practice of psychological medicine in the Ayurvedic tradition. *Culture, Medicine, and Psychiatry, 1,* 155–181.

Obeyesekere, G. (1991). *The work of culture: Symbolic transformation in psycho-analysis and anthropology.* Chicago: University of Chicago Press.

Ohnuki-Tierney, E. (1985). *Illness and culture in contemporary Japan.* Cambridge: Cambridge University Press.

Pennebaker, J. W. (1985). Traumatic experience and psychosomatic disease: Exploring the roles of behavioral inhibition, obsession, and confiding. *Canadian Psychologist, 26,* 82–95.

Pennebaker, J. W., Barger, S. D., & Tiebout, J. (1989). Disclosure of traumas and health among Holocaust survivors. *Psychosomatic Medicine, 51,* 577–589.

Powell, R., Dolan, R., & Wessely, S. (1990). Attributions and self-esteem in depression and chronic fatigue syndromes. *Journal of Psychosomatic Research, 34,* 665–673.

Prince, R. (1960). The brain fag syndrome in Nigerian students. *Journal of Mental Science, 106,* 559–570.

Racy, J. (1980). Somatization in Saudi women: A therapeutic challenge. *British Journal of Psychiatry, 137,* 212–216.

Robbins, J. M., & Kirmayer, L. J. (1991). Cognitive and social factors in somatization. In L. J. Kirmayer & J. M. Robbins (Eds.), *Current concepts of somatization: Research and clinical perspectives.* Washington, DC: American Psychiatric Press.

Ross, C. A., Joshi, S., & Currie, R. (1990). Dissociative experiences in the general population. *American Journal of Psychiatry, 147,* 1547–1552.

Ross, C. A., Miller, S. D., Bjornson, L., Reagor, L., Fraser, G. A., & Anderson, G. (1991). Abuse histories in 102 cases of multiple personality disorder. *Canadian Journal of Psychiatry, 36,* 97–101.

Ross, L., & Nisbett, R. E. (1991). *The person and the situation: Perspectives of social psychology.* Philadelphia: Temple University Press.

Rubel, A. J., O'Nell, C. W., & Collado-Ardón, R. (1984). *Susto: A folk illness.* Berkeley: University of California Press.

Sandberg, D. A., & Lynn, S. J. (1992). Dissociative experiences, psychopathology and adjustment, and child and adolescent maltreatment in female college students. *Journal Abnormal Psychology, 101,* 717–723.

Sharpe, M., & Bass, C. (1992). Pathophysiological mechanisms in somatization. *International Review of Psychiatry, 4,* 81–97.

Simon, G. E., & Von Korff, M. (1991). Somatization and psychiatric disorder in the NIMH Epidemiologic Catchment Area study. *American Journal of Psychiatry, 148,* 1494–1500.

Spanos, N. P., & Chaves, J. F. (Ed.). (1989). *Hypnosis: The cognitive–behavioral perspective.* Buffalo, NY: Prometheus Press.

Spiegel, D. (1990). Hypnosis, dissociation, and trauma: Hidden and overt observers. In J. L. Singer (Eds.), *Repression and dissociation: Implications for personality theory, psychopathology, and health* (pp. 121–142). Chicago: University of Chicago Press.

Spiegel, D. (1991). Dissociation and trauma. In A. Tasman & S. M. Goldfinger (Eds.), *Review of psychiatry* (pp. 261–266). Washington, DC: American Psychiatric Press.

Spiegel, D., & Cardeña, E. (1991). Disintegrated experience: The dissociative disorders revisited. *Journal of Abnormal Psychology, 100*(3), 366–378.

Spiegel, D., & Fink, R. (1979). Hysterical psychosis and hypnotizability. *American Journal of Psychiatry, 33,* 1259–1261.

Spiegel, D., Hunt, T., & Dondershine, H. E. (1988). Dissociation and hypnotizability in posttraumatic stress disorder. *American Journal of Psychiatry, 145,* 301–305.

Stefanis, C., Markidis, M., & Christodoulou, G. (1976). Observations on the evolution of the hysterical symptomatology. *British Journal of Psychiatry, 128,* 269–275.

Steingard, S., & Frankel, F. H. (1985). Dissociation and psychotic symptoms. *American Journal of Psychiatry, 142*(8), 953–955.

Swartz, M., Landerman, R., George, L. K., Blazer, D. G., & Escobar, J. (1991). Somatization disorder. In L. N. Robins & D. A. Regier (Eds.), *Psychiatric disorders in America: The Epidemiologic Catchment Area Study* (pp. 220–257). New York: Free Press.

Taylor, G. J., Parker, J. D. A., Bagby, M. A., & Acklin, M. W. (1992). Alexithymia and somatic complaints in psychiatric outpatients. *Journal of Psychosomatic Research, 36*(5), 417–424.

Tilman, J. G., Nash, M. R., & Lerner, P. M. (1994). Does trauma cause dissociative pathology? In S. J. Lynn & J. W. Rhue (Eds.), *Dissociation: Clinical and theoretical perspectives,* (pp. 395–414). New York: Guilford.

Tseng, W.-S., Kan-Ming, M., Li-Shuen, L., Guo-Qian, C., Li-Wah, O., & Hong-Bo, Z. (1992). *Koro* epidemics in Guangdong China: A questionnaire survey. *Journal of Nervous and Mental Disease, 180*(2), 117–123.

Wegner, D. M. (1989). *White bears and other unwanted thoughts: Suppression, obsession, and the psychology of mental control.* New York: Penguin Books.

Weiner, H. (1992). *Perturbing the organism: The biology of stressful experience.* Chicago: University of Chicago Press.

Weisz, J. R., Rothbaum, F. M., & Blackburn, T. C. (1984). Standing out and standing in: The psychology of control in America and Japan. *American Psychologist, 39*(9), 955–969.

Weller, M. P. (1988). Hysterical behaviour in patriarchal communities: Four cases, one with Ganser-like symptoms. *British Journal of Psychiatry, 152,* 687–695.

Wessely, S. (1990). Old wine in new bottles: Neurasthenia and 'ME'. *Psychological Medicine, 20,* 35–53.

Westermeyer, J., Bouafuely, M., Neider, J., & Callies, A. (1989). Somatization among refugees: An epidemiologic study. *Psychosomatics, 30,* 34–43.

Wikan, U. (1990). *Managing turbulent hearts: A Balinese formula for living.* Chicago: University of Chicago Press.

World Health Organization. (1992). *The ICD-10 classification of mental and behavioural disorders: Clinical descriptions and diagnostic guidelines.* Geneva, Switzerland: Author.

Young, A. (1980). The discourse on stress and the reproduction of conventional knowledge. *Social Science and Medicine, 14,* 133–146.

Young, K. (1989). Narrative embodiments: Enclaves of the self in the realm of medicine. In J. Shotter & K. J. Gergen (Eds.), *Texts of identity* (pp. 152–165). London: Sage Publications.

Zweig-Frank, H., Paris, J., & Guzder, J. (1994) Dissociation in borderline and non-borderline personality disorders. *Journal of Personality Disorders, 8*(3), 203–209.

6

CULTURE, EMOTION, AND PTSD

JANIS H. JENKINS

INTRODUCTION

This chapter is an anthropological examination of relations among culture, emotion, and posttraumatic stress disorder (PTSD). It begins with a review of PTSD constructs and a consideration of the research application of the PTSD category to a sample of Central American refugees. The discussion concludes with reflections on how culture and gender complicate the diagnostic use of the PTSD category and on the importance of conceptualizing collective trauma as the context for individual trauma.

Some Research Issues

Research issues specifically of interest to a culturally informed study of posttraumatic stress disorder include (a) the cultural validity of the construct across sociocultural settings; (b) the nature of eliciting stressors and symptom formation; (c) the relation of trauma to what Janet termed *overwhelming* or *vehement emotion*; (d) phenomenological and manifest differences among anxiety, fear, terror, and horror; (e) experiential specificity of events that symbolize or resemble traumatic events in an afflicted person's subsequent life; (f) the emotional integrity of survivors of extreme circumstances that test the limits of human strength and resilience; (g) perception of an individual's reaction to the traumatic stressor as normal or abnormal; (h) conceptualization of trauma in individual and intrapsychic terms versus collective and sociopolitical terms; and (i) gender variation in the experience and consequences of traumatic events.

Psychic Trauma

Severe psychic trauma has long been considered a functional illness (Archibald, Long, Miller, & Tuddenham, 1962; Brill & Beebe, 1955; Kardiner, 1941). Nevertheless, psychological trauma was only recently introduced to the *Diagnostic and Statistical Manual* (*DSM–III–R*, American Psychiatric Association [APA], 1980 under the label of posttraumatic stress disorder (PTSD) in the revised third edition of the manual). Much of the impetus to delineate a specific diagnostic category came about in the wake of recurring clinical presentations by American Vietnam War veterans.[1]

The prominent symptoms of PTSD in the *DSM–III–R* and *DSM–IV* (APA, 1987, 1994) include sleep disturbance, intrusive memories and feelings associated with the traumatic event, and an avoidance of stimuli associated with the trauma (such as particular thoughts and activities). Autonomic features of increased arousal, irritability, outbursts of anger, and hypervigilant monitoring of the environment also occur. These symptoms are thought to be generated by a wide variety of trauma-related events that are, on the one hand, "outside the range of usual human experience," and that, on the other, would be "markedly distressing to almost anyone." These events include serious threats to life or physical integrity, sudden destruction of one's home or community, or witnessing another person who has been injured or killed through accident or violence (APA, 1987, p. 250).

Pierre Janet and Vehement Emotion

Over a century ago, Pierre Janet (1889) documented the pathological transformation of what he termed *vehement emotion* (e.g., overwhelming anger or fear) into trauma-related psychiatric disorders. Although Janet's studies were historically rooted in the diagnostic idiom of his time—hysteria—his principal concern was with processes of dissociation

---

[1] For an anthropological description of how American psychiatric ideology shapes the moral parameters of PTSD in Vietnam veterans, see Young (1993).

of memory and identity stemming from severe psychic trauma. With the publication of *Automatic Psychological Mechanisms* in 1889, Janet sketched an outline of the dynamics that structure psychic trauma and the specific processes that transform traumatic emotional experience into illness.

Janet advanced the notion that "traumas produce their disintegrating effects in proportion to their intensity, duration, and repetition" (van der Kolk & van der Hart, 1989, p. 1536). The initial response to a trauma combines the vehement emotion and a cognitive interpretation that results in dissociation of memory or identity processes, and attachment to the trauma such that a person is unable to effectively conduct his or her everyday affairs (van der Kolk & van der Hart, 1989).

Janet's clinical studies of psychopathology proved instrumental to his formulation of emotion:

> Emotion is one of the least known of moral phenomena, and its modifications are very difficult to determine. . . . Emotion is not a simple phenomenon, a manifestation of the faculty of sensibility, as was once thought; it is an ensemble of a great number of elementary phenomena, a state of complex consciousness . . . . To be moved, and especially to be moved in a certain way, there must be in one's consciousness the sensations of all kinds of momentary changes which take place in all the organs.
>
> The respiratory apparatus, the heart, the skin, the viscera, the bladder itself, "this mirror of the soul," are modified in a special manner in every emotion. To experience this emotion, is to experience all these modifications. Add to these sensations the images of the remembrance which recalls them into life, the movements of all kinds which are begun, produced, or arrested, and you will have the notion of the complexity of an emotional state. (Janet, 1901, p. 204)

Janet (1901) defined emotion as a complex, total body experience that at once comprises social (moral) and physiological (organ-specific) phenomenal reactions. Much psychocultural study is still needed to specify more precisely the elaborate relationship between traumatic experience of strong, overwhelming emotion and the subsequent development of a psychiatric syndrome such as PTSD. For example, Janet's (1889) notion of *psychological automatisms*—the behavioral phenomena of persons suffering from an extended traumatic reaction—has yet to be fully examined. This complex task entails consideration of psychological defense mechanisms (especially dissociation) developed in response to "vehement" emotional experiences. The specifically maladaptive character of the vehement emotions is their association with semiautomatic behavioral responses that do not take into account new information about the behavioral environment, often leading to dissociation (van der Hart & Horst, 1989).

CULTURE AND THE EXPERIENCE OF EMOTION AND MENTAL DISORDER

The Nature of Culture

Within cultural anthropology there has been general accord that culture is a context of dynamic symbols and meanings that people create and recreate for themselves in the process of social interaction (Geertz, 1973; Sapir, 1961). Recent developments in culture theory have served to expand and refine this generally accepted view. Toward a more expansive view, culture is thought to provide an orientation of a people's way of feeling, thinking, and being in the world—their unselfconscious medium of experience, interpretation, and action (Jenkins & Karno, 1992). This more expansive view of culture is based in part on an appreciation of culture as relevant not merely for cognitive and behavioral features of human worlds but also for experiential orientations of body, self, and emotion (Csordas, 1994; Good, 1994; Kleinman & Kleinman, 1991; Ots, 1990).[2]

Culture and Emotion

Cross-cultural studies of emotion have documented the pervasive extent to which culture mediates the experience and expression of emotion. Rosaldo (as cited in Levy, 1983) has provided an anthropological formulation of emotion as

> self-concerning, partly physical responses that are at the same time aspects of moral or ideological attitudes; emotions are both feelings and cognitive constructions, linking person, action and sociological milieu. Stated otherwise, new views of culture cast the emotions as themselves aspects of cultural systems, of strategic importance to analysts concerned with the ordering of action and the ways that people shape and are shaped by their world. (p. 128)

Emotion, Rosaldo (1984) further urges, can be productively considered as *embodied thoughts*. Emotion in this sense is both a physical response and cognitive construction of the self.

These newly emergent anthropological perspectives have led to a proliferation of contextually specific studies of emotion. Contemporary studies include a wide range of issues such as child-rearing practices and the socialization of emotion (Clancy, 1986; LeVine, 1990; Ochs & Schieffelin, 1986); the cultural engagement of the self (Csordas, 1994; Hallowell, 1955; Marsella, DeVos, & Hsu, 1985; Shweder & Bourne, 1984; White & Kirkpatrick, 1985); cross-cultural variations in the experience and expres-

---

[2] Although these ideas have recently regained new persuasiveness, they can be identified in the work of earlier anthropologists, such as Hallowell (1955).

sion of emotion (Briggs, 1970; Edgerton, 1971; Levy, 1973; Myers, 1979; Shweder & LeVine, 1984); cognitive studies of emotion (D'Andrade, 1987; Holland, 1992; Lakoff & Kovecses, 1987), sociolinguistic approaches to affective elements of speech (Beeman, 1985; Ochs & Schieffelin, 1986); and theoretical treatments of Western scientific discourse on emotion (Lutz, 1988; Lutz & Abu-Lughod, 1990; Rosaldo, 1984).

In contrast, cross-cultural investigations of psychopathology have been pursued for many decades (Hallowell, 1938; Marsella, 1993; Sapir, 1961; Sullivan, 1953). For comparative studies of psychopathology, an explicit conceptualization of culture is crucial because it provides the most generalized baseline from which persons may deviate. To draw a parallel between the constructs of emotion and psychopathology, an earlier conceptualization of mental disorder as socially transacted (Sullivan, 1953) has as its counterpart the contemporary formulation of affect as interactive construction (Jenkins, 1991a; Lutz, 1988).

Examination of the relations among culture, emotion, and psychopathology therefore calls for an exploration of longstanding and new questions such as the following: should issues common to the constructs of emotion and mental disorder be conceptualized (a) as universal autonomic responses or culturally specific evaluative responses? (b) as intrapsychic mental events or intersubjective social processes? or (c) as biologically natural events or sociopolitically produced reactions? (d) Should "normal" and "pathological" emotion be conceptualized in qualitative terms as discontinuous categories or in quantitative terms on a continuum? (e) Is it possible to differentiate cognitively comprised "emotion" from bodily "feeling?" Although each of these issues deserves scholarly attention, the last question is particularly important for the present chapter.

Bodily Feeling and Cognized Emotion

While evolving conceptions of culture have had a significant impact on studies of emotion and psychopathology, critiques of the mind–body dualisms that structure scientific and popular thinking have also emerged (Csordas, 1994; Good, 1994; Kleinman, 1986; Lutz, 1988; Scheper-Hughes & Lock, 1988). Dualisms are evident in customary distinctions between mind and body, affect and cognition, and feeling and emotion. To the extent that such distinctions are premised on Western ethnopsychological categories, their use as research constructs in psychology may unwittingly reproduce cultural assumptions about the scientific nature and parameters of "emotion."

In the case of feeling versus emotion, feeling has been associated with bodily based (and presumedly universally shared) sensation, and emotion has been linked to a cognitively structured (and presumedly culturally interpreted) human phenomenon. Can cognitively comprised emotion be differentiated from bodily feeling or sensation? Such a differentiation may be linked with an assumption that culture influences emotion but not feeling. Thus, whereas emotional expression may be expected to vary cross-culturally, the physicality of emotional experience and expression (Ekman, 1982) would, in the traditional line of thinking, be presumed invariant. The empirical case discussed in the following section casts doubt on the legitimacy of the presumption that it is possible to differentiate biological feeling from cultural emotion. It is possible that such distinctions are informative more of Euro-American ethnopsychology and less of categories useful in interpreting the nature and range of human emotion within and across cultures.

SALVADORAN WOMEN REFUGEES' DISTRESS AND POSTTRAUMATIC STRESS DISORDER

I turn now to consider the relationship of culture, emotion, and post-traumatic stress disorder in light of an ethnographic case of Salvadoran women refugees living in exile in North America. A collaborative study was carried out by a psychiatric anthropologist, a clinical psychologist, and a specialty clinical team serving Latino psychiatric outpatients from the Boston area.[3] Patients' clinical status was assessed by using a modified version of the Schedule for Affective Disorders and Schizophrenia (SADS) as developed by Endicott and Spitzer (1978) to include *DSM–III–R* symptoms of posttraumatic stress disorder. Anthropological interviewing of patients was carried out to explore illness experience and the ethnopsychology of emotion. Observational data from patient households and ethnographic descriptions of neighborhoods and local community were also collected.

Twenty-two women between the ages of 20 and 62 participated in the study. The women were primarily Spanish speakers of peasant background with little formal education. Reasons for fleeing from El Salvador included escape from large-scale political violence, regularized violence by male kin, and impoverished economic conditions. Rather then viewing these as discrete occasions of violence, these conditions are more usefully regarded as coordinate dimensions of a *political ethos* (Jenkins, 1991b). Political ethos in this sense combines Bateson and colleagues' (Bateson, Jackson, Haley, & Weakland, 1956) notion of ethos as a culturally standardized system of emotion of a given social group or culture.

[3] Thanks to Martha E. Valiente, a clinical psychologist with special expertise among the Salvadoran clinical population, who closely collaborated in the present research (see Jenkins & Valiente, 1994). The author worked as anthropological consultant to the Latino Team, The Cambridge Hospital, Department of Psychiatry, Harvard Medical School, from 1986 to 1990. Thanks also to Drs. Pedro Garrido, Mauricia Alvarez, and Sylvia Halperin.

The idea of specifically political ethos is useful here because it incorporates social domains of power and interest into a culturally standardized organization of feeling and sentiment. The political–emotional atmosphere of El Salvador is one of generalized and specific conditions of terror, and has serious mental health consequences for those whose daily experience is so constructed (Jenkins, 1991b).

Nervios and Calor among Salvadoran Women Refugees

During the course of seeking help at the outpatient clinic, all of the women reported they suffered from a serious problem of *nervios*. Within the context of flight from El Salvador, the cultural category of nervios indexes an array of dysphoric affects (anxiety, fear, anger); diverse somatic complaints (bodily pains, shaking, trembling); and often *calor* (heat). Among Salvadorans, "nervios refers at once to matters of mind, body, and spirit and does not make good cultural sense in relation to mind–body dualisms" (Jenkins, 1991b, p. 151).

Calor is of particular interest here for its heuristic value as a form of experience that poses a challenge to the distinction between feeling and emotion. Calor is described as an experience of intense heat that may rapidly spread throughout one's entire body. It may be brief (momentary) or prolonged (several days). Calor was reported among women ages 25 to 56, thus ruling out the interpretation that this phenomenon is reducible to menopause-related experience. Common situations in which calor is experienced include threats to one's physical integrity such as an impending or actual violent event, serious family conflict, or life-threatening illness. In addition, calor may be perceived in relatively mundane circumstances where no immediate threat is apparent.

The following narrative data serve to convey the women's experience of nervios and calor from a 36-year-old married woman and mother of three:

> In my country I had *un susto* (a fright) when a man was dying. Already the man couldn't speak [but] he made signs to me with his eyes. It was during the daytime, and I was going to get some chickens for a Baptism. He could barely move his eyes. He had been shot in the forehead. It was the time of the fair in November. When I came back he was already dead. I returned home with a fever, and it wasn't something I'd ever experienced. Since it was carnival time, strangers came. They kill strangers. They say him throwing away some papers. Yes, I have seen various dead bodies. Since then, I became sick from nervios. Nervios, upon seeing the dead bodies. (Jenkins, 1991b, p. 146)

From 36-years-old Elsa Hemandez, working with a Euro-American family to provide live-in child care and housekeeping, came the following testimony:

Calorias (heat attacks), that's what we call them here in El Salvador, my mother also had them and they say it has to do with the blood, apparently it becomes irritated and well, my hands and neck become . . . as if I had fever and I get real hot, but only in my hands and neck . . . it's a type of heat, yes, that they call "the urge to bathe," yes, it doesn't matter what time, the heat you feel, even though it's cold . . . it comes from worries, more than anything worries about important things, one is startled by one's nervous system and blood that are stirred by bodily memories. . . . (Jenkins & Valiente, 1994)

It may be that calor is better conceptualized as a phenomenon that is intermediate between affects and bodily complaints, or it may be that it is like a type of bodily experience for which distinctions between feeling and emotion are more usefully collapsed. It seems apparent that the phenomenological experience of calor is quite unlike that of ordinary Euro-American experience. Certainly the *DSM–III–R* does not offer nosological guidance for the understanding of these culturally specific forms of illness experience.

Arguably, however, the case can be made that such expressions not be incorporated as a diagnostic category of psychopathology because they may more properly represent normal response to abnormal human conditions within this cultural setting. Indeed, prolonged exposure to political violence and terror is likely to induce elaborated expressions of emotional distress in nearly anyone. For this group of Salvadoran women, the experiences of *nervios* and *calor* are embedded within the context of chronic warfare and exposure to violence.

CULTURAL VALIDITY OF THE PTSD DIAGNOSTIC CATEGORY

In this section, symptomatic markers for determination of posttraumatic stress disorder according to the *DSM–III–R* (APA, 1987) are reviewed and applied to the Salvadoran sample. Apart from criterion A (discussed below), the symptoms are similar to those currently employed in the DSM–IV (1994). Only general patterns can be provided here. At the outset, it is noteworthy that only two *DSM–III–R* categories required an etiologically linked stressor criterion for diagnosis: adjustment disorders and PTSD. Comparatively speaking, the former is generally conceived as more commonplace and less severe whereas the defining stressor criterion for PTSD involves a more serious traumatic event that threatens one's own or another's physical integrity.

Criterion A requires exposure to an event outside the realm of normal human experience that would be highly distressing to nearly anyone, including experiencing serious threat to one's own or a loved one's life or destruction of one's home or community, or witnessing an event of violence (*DSM–III–R*; APA, 1987, p. 250). By virtue of the definition of *la situación*,[4] each of the Salvadoran women studied had experienced systematic destruction of her community, and nearly all spontaneously narrated destructive and threatening everyday encounters in a landscape of violence. This raises the question as to whether and how traumatic events can be construed broadly—as in the case of chronic warfare and terror—or discretely, as in particular instances of traumatizing events such as witnessing an assassination or actually undergoing torture and interrogation.

In the vast majority of cases, the Salvadoran women in our study reported living in conditions that were traumatizing, and were regularly exposed to discrete events of particular violent threat to themselves or others. Thus Criterion A was met for all of the women.

For Criterion B, in which a recurrent or intrusive reexperiencing of the traumatic event must be present, it was very common for women in this sample to report distressing dreams (nightmares). The thematic content of such dreams often involved specific scenes of actual violence from their homeland. Also common were symbolically laden dreams of violence. For example, one woman reported her recurrent dream of being encased in a large blood-filled bubble from which she could not escape. Dreams of knives, blood, and mutilation were also common.

Criterion C concerns avoidance of aversive stimuli associated with the trauma or a numbing of general responsiveness as manifest in a variety of specific ways. Aside from the clinical complexities of observing this set of symptoms (especially the numbing, by definition), we found this cluster of factors not to be particularly common among the women in our sample. Feelings of detachment, estrangement, restricted affect, foreshortened future, or inability or unwillingness to narrative the traumatic situation were not marked. Thus, this whole cluster of symptoms of avoiding and forgetting were not common.

Criterion D requires that symptoms of increased arousal be manifest in such ways as sleep disturbance, irritability, and difficulty concentrating. These were common among the women in our sample; however, these symptoms overlap with those used for major depressive disorder, a diagnostic category for which nearly all the women in the sample made research diagnostic criteria according to the SADS research interview. This raises questions of comorbidity and diagnostic specificity of PTSD. The exaggerated startle response and physiological reactivity upon exposure to events that symbolize the trauma were observable for only one case, and in this instance the woman's experience was not comparable to those of

---

[4] "*La situación* is the most common way of referring to the intolerable conditions within the country, and condenses a set of symbols and meanings that refer to a nation besieged by both devastating economic problems and violence" (Jenkins, 1991a, p. 141).

the others. In this case, the woman had undergone three separate instances of detention and torture. She manifested the full range of symptoms that make up the syndrome of PTSD according to *DSM–III–R* criteria.

To summarize, the PTSD diagnostic category as set forth in *DSM–III–R* and as applied to this particular sample of Salvadoran women refugees does not appear fully applicable. This seems especially true for symptoms that constitute Criterion C. This lack of applicability could be due to (a) diagnostic difficulties inherent in observing these particular features (e.g., numbing, avoiding trauma-related thoughts), or (b) restricted cultural validity of the full syndrome as currently conceived and as applied to this sample. If the latter hypothesis was true, it would mean that the parameters of the syndrome should be differentially constructed for Salvadoran women refugees or that the PTSD construct is simply of limited usefulness in characterizing the nature of the distress existing among this group of refugee women (see also Marsella, Friedman, & Spain, 1993).

Salient bodily experiences of these Salvadoran women as expressed in the nervios and calor idioms are not included in the PTSD symptom list. This appears to present a significant problem of cultural validity.[5] A different problem with respect to cultural validity stems from the cultural specificity and fluidity of symptoms associated with the indigenous category of nervios (Guarnaccia, Good, & Kleinman, 1990; Low, 1985). In this case, the cultural "work" (as defined by Obeyesekere, 1985) of indigenous illness categories and experience is not comparable to the cultural "work" of psychiatric nosological categories for purposes of diagnosis (Jenkins, 1988). In the former case, the cultural lack of diagnostic specificity concerns more the social and moral status of the ill individual than the psychopathological manifestations of illness behavior (Jenkins, 1988).

A compelling case for the productive use of specific DSM diagnostic categories (as opposed to generalized distress) has been made by Good (1992). Good observed that whereas DSM categories are plainly grounded in Western cultural premises, they are sufficiently systematic to be usefully used in cross-cultural work and may be criticized on the basis of empirical research. Because the foregoing discussion has documented that emotions vary cross-culturally both in expression and experience, it follows that we can expect the parameters—even the validity of the PTSD syndrome—to vary substantially across populations to which it is applied. Indeed, in some settings the PTSD construct may be of very limited usefulness.

Failure to appreciate this likelihood may result in what Kleinman (1977) has termed a *category fallacy*, or the presumption that the parameters of a mental disorder (in this case, PTSD) will be similarly constituted cross-

---

[5] Elsewhere, the experience of intense heat has been reported as central to depressive experience in some cultural settings (e.g., Ifabumuyi, 1981), but it is not represented in *DSM–III–R* symptom profiles for depression or PTSD.

culturally. Cross-cultural assessment of the usefulness of the PTSD diagnostic category must therefore await culturally informed empirical investigations. In addition, cross-cultural variation in PTSD and the pathoplasticity of symptom formation and expression may serve as evidence not only of the cultural shaping of the disorder, but also the likelihood that PTSD, like schizophrenia, may not denote a single disease process. PTSD may be better conceived as a plurality of stress-related disorders rather than as a unitary diagnostic category.

CULTURE, GENDER, AND THE COMPLEXITY OF THE DIAGNOSIS OF PTSD SYMPTOMS

The Salvadoran research project has provided an empirical case for caution concerning the degree of difficulty in applying the PTSD symptom criteria. In my view, these problems primarily concern cultural complexity and subtlety. There is diagnostic difficulty, for instance, in identifying events that "symbolize or resemble" the traumatic event. The problem of identification is present in terms of (a) getting to the correct level of psychological abstraction and (b) identifying which of a set of possible circumstances counts as the salient instance(s) in the concrete (but with no necessary or expected symbolic connection). This judgment cannot be adequately made without highly specific cultural knowledge of the group for whom diagnostic assessment is being conducted. Furthermore, the particular admixture of cultural and individual levels of analysis required to make accurate psychiatric or psychological judgment across cultures is particularly complex. Three examples, focusing on psychoculture themes of responsibility, vulnerability, and immobilization of cross-cultural effects on psychiatric and psychological judgment, are discussed in the following section.

Responsibility

In the case of responsibility, a Vietnam veteran who was charged with the responsibility for others but who panicked under the extreme pressure of a warfare situation may currently encounter social difficulties in the area of responsibilities for others economically or domestically after having returned to the United States.

Vulnerability

In cases in which the psychocultural theme of vulnerability is evident, such as the case of a Salvadoran refugee who daily inhabited a landscape of violence (in which it is not uncommon to see dismembered or dead bodies), vulnerability associated with fear of death might be transformed into a daily, generalized sense of vulnerability for one's physical integrity. The particular fear that people in authority will kill or hurt a person may be experienced as overwhelming anxiety concerning dealings with, for instance, the Immigration and Naturalization Service.

Immobilization

Finally, the same refugee might experience immobilization upon threat of physical assault and may neither fight nor flee but be frozen in physical immobility or dissociation. This controverting of the primordial human response to "fight or flight" may originate in a PTSD-generating circumstance, but the particular situations of individual experience of such circumstances may vary cross-culturally in relation to the particular cultural meaning that is attached to the trauma.

Categorizing an emotion even in terms of symbolic representation can be expected to be especially complex. The same event in one setting may mean humiliation, bereavement, just revenge, individual responsibility, vulnerability, or immobility, to different people. Inversion of the cultural meanings associated with emotion was captured by Salvadoran novelist Manlio Argueta, in his book Cuzcatlan: Where the Southern Sea Beats (1987). In an exchange between a Salvadoran army commander and a foreign journalist requesting permission to take a landscape photograph of the face of a mountain, the commander responded, "You think this mountain is beautiful? I hate it. To me it means war. It's nothing but a theater for this shitty war" (p. 1).

Investigation of culture, gender, and PTSD-related symptoms will be important to cross-cultural studies. The relationship between depression and gender is well-known: epidemiological evidence documents that women disproportionately suffer from depression relative to men (Nolan-Hoeksema, 1990). This epidemiological fact with reference to North American women has also been confirmed cross-culturally in nearly every case that has been investigated.

For PTSD-related symptoms, one must consider the nature and complexity of the traumatic stressors in context of overlap and multiplicity. For instance, many of the Salvadoran refugees encountered violence every day, not only through civil warfare by also through brutality of male kin and strangers. This suggests differential exposure to particular kinds of stressors that must be examined in the separate context of gender status, power inequities, and culturally sanctioned misogyny, which generate particular types of socially produced disorders.

Collective Trauma

Because traumatic experience can also be conceptualized collectively, person-centered accounts alone are insufficient to an understanding of traumatic reactions. In addition to the social and psychocultural dynamics surrounding any traumatic response, the collective nature of trauma may be related to what was earlier referred to as the political ethos characterizing an entire society (Jenkins, 1991b). As social psychologist Martin-Baro (1990) observed just prior to his own brutal assassination,[6] an entire nation can be characterized as one where state terror is elaborated and sustained as a mechanism of social control.

Individualized accounts of trauma in the context of long-term political violence never can be fully adequate in understanding traumatized cultures. Although emotional trauma is clearly present in personal psychic suffering (manifest as various forms of psychopathology), it may also be valid to consider psychosocial trauma as "the traumatic crystallization in persons and groups of inhuman social relations" (Martin-Baro, 1988, p. 138). Psychosocial trauma can also be manifest in the collective denial of reality (Jenkins, 1991b). In the context of long-term civil warfare, Martin-Baro (1990) considered the array of state-constructed emotions, maladies, and defenses as a formidable means of psychological warfare.[7]

Another source of collective trauma theorizing comes from scholars who have examined the responses of Nazi Holocaust survivors (Kristeva, 1982; Staub, 1989). Krystal (1968) conducted research on both individual and group responses to massive psychic trauma as the mental health sequelae to massive social pathology. Aside from the compelling need to understand the horror of political campaigns of cultural and ethnic genocide, Krystal argued that examination of extreme situations also serves as a basis for understanding the effects of trauma in everyday life. He identified one type of mental health consequence among survivors of the Holocaust as an *affect lameness*, involving suppression of most or all emotional response to one's social world. Also common are symptoms of depression, somatization, and those used in *DSM–III–R* diagnoses of PTSD.

Although refined understandings of the posttraumatic emotional distortion are needed, it is also clear that accounts of the sustained emotional integrity of people surviving extreme horrific human circumstances must equally compel our attention. This will require not only informed analyses of individual and social dynamics surrounding traumatic situations, but also

---

[6] Ignacio Martín-Baró was one of the six Jesuit priests assassinated by the Salvadoran government during the bloody 1989 rebel offensive in that country's civil war.

[7] For a theoretical introduction to the notion of state-constructed affects, see Good and Good (1988).

a fuller explication of the parameters of human nature (see Edgerton, 1985, 1992).

CONCLUDING REMARKS

I have drawn together two critical but often separate areas within psychology and anthropology—the study of the relation between culture and emotion, and the study of psychopathology in general and PTSD in particular—in order to suggest that there is a great deal of commonality in the conceptual issues raised by each.

This chapter has encompassed intersubjective and sociopolitical accounts of emotion, the conceptual distinction between emotion and feeling, and the problem of continuity and discontinuity between normal and pathological. As the study of PTSD continues, cultural variability in the phenomenology, course, and outcome of PTSD-like reactions will likely emerge. Examination of peoples' reactions to overwhelmingly horrific conditions will require that the parameters of the PTSD construct be expanded considerably to take into account gendered, sociopolitical, and ethnocultural dimensions of experience.

REFERENCES

American Psychiatric Association. (1980). *Diagnostic and statistical manual of mental disorders* (3rd ed.). Washington, DC: Author.

American Psychiatric Association. (1987). *Diagnostic and statistical manual of mental disorders* (3rd ed., rev.). Washington, DC: Author.

American Psychiatric Association. (1994). *Diagnostic and statistical manual of mental disorders* (4th ed.). Washington, DC: Author.

Archibald, H. C., Long, D., Miller, C., & Tuddenham, R. (1962). Gross stress reaction in combat: A 15 year follow-up. *American Journal of Psychiatry, 119*, 317–322.

Argueta, M. (1987). *Cuzcatlan: Where the southern sea beats.* New York: Vintage Books.

Bateson, G., Jackson, D., Haley, J., & Weakland, J. (1956). Toward a theory of schizophrenia. *Behavioral Science, 1*, 251–264.

Beeman, W. O. (1985). Dimensions of dysphoria: The view from linguistic anthropology. In A. Kleinman & B. Good (Eds.), *Culture and depression: Studies in the anthropology and cross-cultural psychiatry of affect and disorder* (pp. 216–243). Berkeley, CA: University of California Press.

Briggs, J. (1970). *Never in anger: Portrait of an Eskimo family.* Cambridge, MA: Harvard University Press.

Brill, A., & Beebe, G. W. (1955). *A follow-up study of war neuroses.* Washington, DC: Veterans Administration Medical Monographs.

Clancy, P. (1986). The acquisition of communicative style in Japanese. In E. Ochs & B. Schieffelin (Eds.), *Language socialization across cultures* (pp. 213–250). Cambridge, MA: Cambridge University Press.

Csordas, T. J. (1994). *The sacred self: Cultural phenomenology of a charismatic world.* Berkeley, CA: University of California Press.

D'Andrade, R. (1987). A folk model of the mind. In D. Holland & N. Quinn (Eds.), *Cultural models in language and thought* (pp 112–150). Cambridge, MA: Cambridge University Press.

Edgerton, R. B. (1971). *The individual in cultural adaptation.* Los Angeles: University of California Press.

Edgerton, R. B. (1985). *Rules, exceptions, and social order.* Berkeley: University of California Press.

Edgerton, R. B. (1992). *Sick societies: Challenging the myth of primitive harmony.* New York: Free Press.

Ekman, P. (1982). *Emotion in the human face* (2nd ed.). Cambridge, MA: Cambridge University Press.

Endicott, J., & Spitzer, R. L. (1978). A diagnostic interview: The Schedule for Affective Disorders and Schizophrenia. *Archives of General Psychiatry, 35,* 837–844.

Geertz, C. (1973). *The interpretation of cultures.* New York: Basic Books.

Good, B. (1992). Culture and psychopathology: Directions for psychiatric anthropology. In T. Schwartz, G. White, & C. Lutz (Eds.), *New directions for psychological anthropology* (pp 181–205). Cambridge, MA: Cambridge University Press.

Good, B. (1994). *Medicine, rationality, and experience: An anthropological perspective.* Cambridge, MA: Cambridge University Press.

Good, B., & Good, M. D. (1988). Ritual, the State, and the transformation of emotional discourse in Iranian society. *Culture, Medicine and Psychiatry, 12,* 43–63.

Guarnaccia, P., Good, B., & Kleinman, A. (1990). A critical review of epidemiological studies of Puerto Rican mental health. *American Journal of Psychiatry, 147,* 1449–1456.

Hallowell, A. I. (1938). Fear and anxiety as cultural and individual variables in a primitive society. *Journal of Social Psychology, 9,* 25–47.

Hallowell, A. I. (1955). The self in its behavioral environment. In A. I. Hallowell (Ed.), *Culture and experience* (pp. 75–111). Philadelphia: University of Pennsylvania Press.

Holland, D. (1992). How cultural systems become desire: A case study of American romance. In R. D'Andrade & C. Strauss (Eds.), *Human motives and cultural models* (pp 61–89). Cambridge, MA: Cambridge University Press.

Ifabumuyi, O. I. (1981). The dynamics of central heat in depression. *Psychopathologie Africaine, 17*, 127–133.

Janet, P. (1889). L'automatisme psychologique [Automatic psychological mechanisms]. Paris: Felix Alcan. (Reprinted: Société Pierre Janet, Paris, 1973)

Janet, P. (1901). *The mental state of hysterics.* New York: Putnam.

Jenkins, J. H. (1988). Ethnopsychiatric interpretations of schizophrenic illness: The problem of nervios within Mexican-American families. *Culture, Medicine, & Psychiatry, 12*, 303–331.

Jenkins, J. H. (1991a). The state construction of affect: Political ethos and mental health among Salvadoran refugees. *Culture, Medicine, & Psychiatry, 15*, 139–165.

Jenkins, J. H. (1991b). Anthropology, expressed emotion, and schizophrenia. *Ethos: The Journal of the Society for Psychological Anthropology, 19*, 387–431.

Jenkins, J. H., & Karno, M. (1992). The meaning of expressed emotion: Theoretical issues raised by cross-cultural research. *American Journal of Psychiatry, 149* (1), 9–21.

Jenkins, J. H., & Valiente, M. (1994). *Bodily transactions of the passions:* El calor *among Salvadoran women refugees.* In T. J. Csordas (Ed.), *Embodiment and experience* (pp 163–182). Cambridge, MA: Cambridge University Press.

Kardiner, A. (1941). The traumatic neuroses of war. New York: Hoeber Press.

Kleinman, A. (1977). Depression, somatization and the new cross-cultural psychiatry. *Social Science & Medicine, 11*, 3–10.

Kleinman, A. (1986). *Social origins of distress and disease. Depression, neurasthenia, and pain in modern China.* New Haven, CT: Yale University Press.

Kleinman, A. (1988). *Rethinking psychiatry.* New York: Free Press.

Kleinman, A., & Kleinman, J. (1991). Suffering and its professional transformation: Toward an ethnography of interpersonal experience. *Culture, Medicine and Psychiatry, 15*, 275–301.

Kristeva, J. (1982). *Powers of horror: An essay on abjection.* New York: Columbia University Press.

Krystal, H. (1968). *Massive psychic trauma.* New York: International Universities Press.

Lakoff, G., & Kovecses, Z. (1987). The cognitive model of anger inherent in American English. In D. Holland & N. Quinn (Eds.), *Cultural models in language and thought* (pp. 195–221). Cambridge, MA: Cambridge University Press.

LeVine, R. A. (1990). Infant environments in psychoanalysis: A cross-cultural view. In J. Stigler, R. Shweder, & G. Herdt (Eds.), *Cultural psychology: Essays on comparative human development* (pp. 454–471). New York: Cambridge University Press.

Levy, R. (1973). *Tahitians: Mind and experience in the Society Islands.* Chicago: University of Chicago Press.

Levy, R. (1983). Introduction: Self and emotion. *Ethos, 11*, 128–134.

Low, S. (1985). Culturally interpreted symptoms of culture-bound syndromes: A cross-cultural review of nerves. *Social Science & Medicine, 22,* 187–196.

Lutz, C. (1988). *Unnatural emotions: Everyday sentiments on a Micronesian atoll and their challenge to Western theory.* Chicago: University of Chicago Press.

Lutz, C., & Abu-Lughod, L. (Eds.). (1990). *Language and the politics of emotion.* Cambridge, MA: Cambridge University Press.

Marsella, A. J. (1993). Sociocultural foundations of psychopathology: A pre-1970 historical overview. *Transcultural Psychiatric Research Review, 30,* 97–142.

Marsella, A. J., DeVos, G., & Hsu, F. L. K. (Eds.). (1985). *Culture and self: Asian and Western perspectives.* London: Tavistock.

Marsella, A. J., Friedman, M., & Spain, H. (1993). Ethnocultural aspects of PTSD: Issues, research, directions. In J. Oldham, M. Riba, & A. Tasman (Eds.), *Review of psychiatry* (pp. 29–62). Washington, DC: American Psychiatric Press.

Martín-Baró, I. (1988). *La violencia política y la guerra como causas del trauma psicosocial en El Salvador* [Political violence and war as causes of psychosocial trauma in El Salvador]. *Revista de Psicología de El Salvador, 31,* 5–25.

Martin-Baro, I. (1990). *De la guerra sucia a la guerra psicológica* [From the dirty war to the psychological war]. *Revista de Psicología de El Salvador, 35,* 109–122.

Myers, F. (1979). Emotions and the self: A theory of personhood and political order among Pintupi Aborigines. *Ethos, 7,* 343–370.

Nolen-Hoeksema, S. (1990). *Sex differences in depression.* Stanford, CA: Stanford University Press.

Obeyesekere, G. (1985). Depression, Buddhism, and the work of culture in Sri Lanka. In A. Kleinman & B. Good (Eds.), *Culture and depression: Studies in the anthropology and cross-cultural psychiatry of affect and disorders.* Berkeley: University of California Press.

Ochs, E., & Schieffelin, B. (Eds.). (1986). *Language socialization across cultures.* Cambridge, MA: Cambridge University Press.

Ots, T. (1990). The angry liver, the anxious heart and the melancholy spleen. *Culture, Medicine & Psychiatry, 14,* 21–58.

Rosaldo, M. (1984). Toward an anthropology of self and feeling. In R. A. Shweder & R. A. LeVine (Eds.), *Culture theory: Essays on mind, self and emotion* (pp. 137–157). Cambridge, MA: Cambridge University Press.

Sapir, E. (1961). (In D. G. Mandelbaum, Ed.), *Culture, language, and personality: Selected essays.* (pp. 66–89). Berkeley: University of California Press.

Scheper-Hughes, N., & Lock, M. (1988). The mindful body: A prolegomenon to future work in medical anthropology. *Medical Anthropology Quarterly, 1,* 6–41.

Shweder, R. A., & Bourne, E.. (1984). Does the concept of the person vary cross-culturally? In R. Shweder & R. LeVine (Eds.), *Culture theory: Essays on mind, self, and emotion* (pp. 158–199). Cambridge, MA: Cambridge University Press.

Shweder, R. A., & LeVine, R. A. (Eds.). (1984). *Culture theory: Essays on mind, self, and emotion.* Cambridge, MA: Cambridge University Press.

Staub, E. (1989). *The roots of evil: The origins of genocide and other group violence.* Cambridge, MA: Cambridge University Press.

Sullivan, H. S. S. (1953). *Conceptions of modern psychiatry.* New York: Norton.

van der Hart, O., & Horst, R. (1989). The dissociation theory of Pierre Janet. *Journal of Traumatic Stress, 2,* 397–412.

van der Kolk, B., & van der Hart, O. (1989). Pierre Janet and the breakdown of adaptation in psychological trauma. *American Journal of Psychiatry, 146,* 1530–1540.

White, G., & Kirkpatrick, J. (Eds.) (1985). *Person, self, and experience: Exploring Pacific ethnopsychologies.* Berkeley, CA: University of California Press.

Young, A. (1993). A description of how ideology shapes knowledge of a mental disorder (posttraumatic stress disorder). In S. Lindenbaum & M. Lock (Eds.), *Knowledge, power and practice: The anthropology of medicine and everyday life* (pp. 108–128). Berkeley: University of California Press.

7

ETHNOCULTURAL CONSIDERATIONS IN THE ASSESSMENT OF PTSD

TERENCE M. KEANE, DANNY G. KALOUPEK,
and FRANK W. WEATHERS

Assessing the occurrence of potential traumatic events and their psychological sequelae, including posttraumatic stress disorder (PTSD), has become an important component of clinical care and research in the field of mental health (Wilson & Raphael, 1993). Since 1980, when PTSD was first included in the diagnostic nomenclature of the American Psychiatric Association (i.e., *DSM–III*; American Psychiatric Association, 1980), the study of this disorder has resulted in a more comprehensive understanding of the effects of major life stressors on adjustment, adaptation, and social functioning.

There also has been a parallel growth in the appreciation of the role of traumatic events in the development of other forms of psychopathology (e.g., substance abuse, personality disorders, and depression). Traumatic events may have a direct etiological link to psychopathology, may serve to precipitate certain problems, or may exacerbate already existing conditions. In addition, as Keane and Wolfe (1990) have pointed out, the development of PTSD can result in a cascade of psychological problems that reach criteria for other diagnostic conditions (e.g., substance abuse, major depressive disorder, panic disorder). Much of the progress and increased understanding of PTSD and its implications for psychopathology can be traced to the development of reliable and valid methods for assessing potential traumatic events and PTSD itself (Keane, Weathers, & Kaloupek, 1992).

The psychological assessment of PTSD and related factors has developed primarily within the context of Western, developed, industrialized countries (DeGirolamo, 1992; see also chapter 4, this volume). The purpose of this chapter is to identify issues related to ethnocultural considerations in the assessment of PTSD. To accomplish this objective we will examine existing models for conceptualizing the PTSD assessment process. Next, we will review fundamental procedures that are used in documenting the psychometric properties of measures of PTSD and then selectively review the literature on PTSD instruments that have taken ethnic and minority issues into consideration during the process of development.

We intend to demonstrate the process that might be considered when undertaking research and clinical work across cultures or across ethnic groups within a society. Marsella, Friedman, and Spain (1992) and Wilson and Raphael (1993) have reported that cross-cultural issues in PTSD are receiving increased attention world wide because of the high rates of war, natural disaster, ethnic conflict, and technological disaster in contemporary society. There is a clear need to develop methods that are suitable for diverse contexts and populations. In this chapter we will attempt to provide a framework for that development.

MULTIDIMENSIONAL ASSESSMENT OF PTSD

Keane, Wolfe, and Taylor (1987) outlined a method for evaluating the psychological effects of trauma exposure that incorporated assessment of the stressor variable (e.g., rape, disaster, combat), broad-based symptom measurement, and the use of multiple indices of PTSD. This methodological approach to assessment included recommendations to obtain information from the affected individual, collateral informants, available records, psychological tests, and psychophysiological indices. While a carefully conducted and sensitive clinical interview was the cornerstone of this approach to assessment, the addition of multiple indicators of symptomatology and adjustment was conceptualized as providing a more comprehensive understanding of the traumatized individuals and the contexts in which they functioned.

Recognizing the fallibility of any single indicator of PTSD and the likelihood that not all indicators would agree, we suggested the use of clinical judgment to reconcile any discrepancies found in the concordance of measures. Under research conditions, clinical judgments could be replaced by statistical algorithms, as was done in the National Vietnam Veterans Readjustment Study (Kulka et al., 1990). However, the benefit of a statistical versus a clinical decision-making process has been debated in multiple arenas.

With respect to targeting goals and objectives for treatment, Keane et al. (1987) recommend the use of clinical input by experienced clinicians to reconcile differences among the indicators and to arrive at a decision regarding the presence, absence, and severity of PTSD symptomatology. With the practice of consensus diagnosis, a patient can be classified optimally according to diagnostic criteria, and through this process of diagnosis, a functional analysis of the individual's problems can occur with suggestions for clinical interventions.

Research on the assessment of trauma exposure and PTSD has progressed remarkably in the past 15 years (Sutker, Uddo-Crane, & Allain, 1991). Clinical interviews for examining the diagnostic criteria have been developed and validated; psychometric measures have been constructed and tested empirically; and measures of psychophysiology have become increasingly accepted as a component of the comprehensive assessment of PTSD (Newman, Kaloupek, & Keane, in press). Because little evidence currently exists regarding ethnocultural measures of trauma exposure and PTSD, we will provide a brief overview of the available literature that has addressed the topic of cross-cultural assessment and trauma work.

There are some notable precedents that have been established for guiding the development of culturally sensitive instruments for trauma exposure and PTSD, and there are numerous ongoing research studies that have employed state-of-the-art methods in identifying and measuring cultural variations in the manifestation of the traumatic response. Our review will attempt to guide researchers and clinicians who wish to extend current knowledge in PTSD assessment to a specific cultural context. Our efforts will be directed toward elucidating scientifically sound methods of constructing measures to be used in PTSD work and the principles that would contribute to the development of sound, empirically based cross-cultural measures of this disorder.

CONSIDERATIONS IN DEVELOPING CROSS-CULTURALLY SENSITIVE PTSD MEASURES

In this section we will identify, define, and explain the many factors that researchers may wish to consider when developing measures of trauma and stress for use in research studies across cultures.

The Importance of Equivalency

To ensure that psychological assessment instruments are measuring the intended constructs across different cultures and societies, researchers and clinicians have employed numerous scientifically based methods, including methods to assess conceptual equivalency (e.g., Dana, 1993; Marsella & Kameoka, 1988) and to assess reliability and validity. Applying these methods will increase the likelihood that a measure will provide the researcher or clinician with the desired information (e.g., the severity of PTSD or its prevalence). Ignoring the need for assessing the cultural relevance for a test or measurement instrument will be reflected in reliability and validity studies. If such studies are not conducted, the results of research may have adverse consequences for the individuals assessed, particularly if public policy is influenced by a study using faulty measures.

For example, a problem might arise if a PTSD measure that was developed in North America was adopted for use in an African culture and was simply insensitive to the cultural experience of trauma for the individuals. It is possible that the presentation of symptoms and the meaning and consequences of trauma could differ in the African culture. Thus, low rates of PTSD might emerge in a study and influence the researchers into erroneously concluding that rates of trauma were low, when in fact the measure itself might not assess the essence of traumatization for the culture under investigation. This hypothetical example amplifies the need for psychometric science in conducting cross-cultural research that has public policy implications.

There is a methodology available that, if applied with rigor, can avert situations such as this. Measures can be developed directly on the population to be studied (e.g., through the use of ethnoscience methods) or the performance of available instruments can be examined, either prior to their use or during the course of their use in research and clinical studies (e.g., pilot studies). In this way researchers and clinicians can be more confident that their instruments are performing in the intended manner, thus avoiding or reducing measurement error.

Kinds of Equivalence

Equivalence of instruments is a central tenet of cross-cultural assessment (Flaherty, et al., 1988; Kleinman & Good, 1985; Marsella, 1987; Marsella & Kameoka, 1988). It refers to the extent to which an assessment instrument fulfills its promise across different cultures and subcultures within a society. As specified by Marsella and Kameoka (1988), equivalence has many forms, and documenting equivalence increases the confidence that one has in the instrument to be used. The various forms of equivalence include (a) content equivalence, (b) linguistic and semantic equivalence, (c) conceptual equivalence, (d) scale and technical equivalence, and (e) normative equivalence.

Content Equivalence

Individuals in different cultures experience life and its vicissitudes in a variety of ways. If researchers were interested in response to rape across two distinct cultures, developing instruments for such a research project would involve a complex process because *rape* may be defined differently across cultures because of variations in gender relationships, sexual behavior, and perceptions of violence.

To construct an instrument for measuring PTSD within a culture, one needs to consider the various ways in which an individual in that culture might perceive, evaluate, and experience a high-magnitude stressor. To assist in this process, one might consider the creation of focus groups, a common contemporary method for assisting behavioral scientists in understanding a social problem and its implications for targeted populations.

A focus group for creating an instrument to understand the broad behavioral and psychological effects of rape in a society, for instance, might include people who have been raped, professional or respected leaders who have been involved in ministering to these people, and professionals familiar with the culture, language, and mores of the society. This group would attempt to generate a comprehensive list of the signs and symptoms associated with rape in that culture. Items from this list could be included in the development of an assessment instrument for measuring the effects of rape in that society.

If two societies vary in the way in which their citizens respond to rape, the items in the content domain will vary accordingly. It may prove difficult to devise a single instrument that would measure rape reactions fairly and equitably across both societies. If one were intent on developing a single instrument, the final product would at least need to reflect the specific reactions of the members of both cultures to properly measure and compare the adverse effects of rape for each group. The measure would include those items the cultures held in common as well as those items that were unique to one culture.

In theory, measures might need to be completely different to accomplish such goals across two cultures if the two cultures' responses to rape were completely different. However, if content equivalence is high for two cultures, then the same instrument would be acceptable. If content equivalence is low for two cultures, then separate instruments would be required.

Linguistic and Semantic Equivalence

If the same instrument is to be used in different cultures, as is often the case for expediency, researchers must establish semantic equivalence. This might involve translating an instrument from the parent language and then back-translating to see if the original meaning is retained. Translators would work together to understand the concept under discussion and the various means of expressing the concept in the different languages. Grammar, denotative meanings, and connotative meanings should be similar or equivalent in the final product. One-way translation simply does not offer the opportunity to generate semantically or linguistically equivalent instruments that are capable of comparably measuring the construct under investigation in two cultures. The ultimate objective of semantic equivalence is to have the meaning of the statement in the test be the same across the two languages.

Conceptual Equivalence

Determining whether a concept is equivalent across different cultures is a difficult task. Marsella (1987) has described a series of steps that investigators can employ to increase the conceptual equivalence of their measurement tools across societies. These steps include, but are not necessarily limited to: (a) eliciting the domain of the concept (e.g., rape responses) through interviews with appropriate members of the society to be studied; (b) categorizing the items through an acceptable means of sorting, ranking, and scaling; (c) examining and rating the meaning of the items that have been generated through word association and antecedent–consequent methods; and (d) identifying the behavioral referents of the concept being examined.

Concepts such as anxiety, depression, aggression, anger, intrusive thoughts, and emotional numbing are central to understanding the psychological response to high-magnitude stressors. These characteristics have different meanings, and their presence has different implications for societies the world over. To assume cross-cultural conceptual equivalence of items measuring these constructs and symptoms surely would lead to mismeasurement of the important concepts related to traumatization in different societies. Even concepts that are related to traumatization—such as intimacy and love, suicide, death, and social support—may vary in different cultures so that variables that are known risk factors and correlates of traumatization in Western culture pose a major challenge for cross-cultural assessment.

Scale and Technical Equivalence

Scale and technical equivalence refers to the use of comparable metric methods in measuring a construct. Western cultures employ Likert scaling procedures and true/false methods from the time children are taught to read and write. As a result, there is a familiarity with this type of measurement of attitudes, behaviors, and experiences. This is less true for other societies. The types of options available for responding simply may not reflect the experience or the view of life of individuals from other cultures.

This problem is compounded by the predilection of the members of some cultures to respond in deference to the interviewer, rather than to avoid responding to items that seem unacceptable or that invalidly represent their personal experience.

Scales are not necessarily the same throughout the world; a seven-point Likert scale may function perfectly well in France and Sweden yet be incomprehensible in an African or Southeast Asian country. For this reason, efforts to ascertain the technical equivalence of a test will enhance the quality of the data obtained in a research or clinical setting.

Normative Equivalence

Norms are often the bases for determining abnormality and normality in specific cultures. Normative standards developed in one society may not necessarily generalize to other societies, however. Attempting to generalize norms across societies that differ in known ways on many characteristics can lead to inaccurate conclusions regarding the presence, absence, or severity of symptoms.

More to the point, making comparisons between non-Western individuals' performance on tests or instruments developed with Western norms risks two major problems. First, it gives precedence to the Western way of experiencing life. Second, it does not inform the investigator of the relative status of individuals compared to their ethnic and cultural peers.

Summary of Cross-Cultural Equivalence

The concept of cultural equivalence in personality testing is more a hope than a reality. Nonetheless, it remains an important objective for all researchers to attempt to reach equivalence on each of the dimensions discussed previously. The use of culturally fair tests is indicative of a thoughtful research program that is likely to yield valuable and maximally useful information. This is true whether the research is across Eastern and Western cultures or within a multiethnic country such as Australia, Canada, or the United States.

Recent modifications of the Minnesota Multiphasic Personality Inventory (MMPI-2; Hathaway & McKinley, 1989) have highlighted the importance of considering ethnicity, language, and experience in the revision of specific questions in the test. In addition, the restandardization samples also included normative groups from major ethnic subsections of society. This effort is a clear improvement over previous development methods used for the MMPI.

However, using a single variable such as ethnicity on which to draw conclusions regarding a group of people (e.g., African Americans, Hispanic Americans, Asian Americans) presents as many problems as it solves. The primary difficulty is that such clustering ignores individual differences within such groupings in experience, constitution, and acculturation, while assuming homogeneity among large groups of people. Careful attention to the specific factors that underlie the ethnicity variable and contribute to observed differences between groups ultimately may prove to be a more fruitful approach to understanding individual differences in psychological status (e.g., discrimination, poverty, religious beliefs, educational sophistication, etc.).

STRATEGIES FOR CROSS-CULTURAL RESEARCH

Universality or Relativism in Psychopathology

There are two strategies recommended for making valid comparisons across cultures in the study of psychopathology. Neither strategy is entirely satisfactory, and the field is still struggling to address methodological issues and problems inherent in each. The demands of society and the need for public policy often drive cross-cultural research, although the field's research methods may not be up to the task yet.

One strategy has been to employ standard research instruments across cultures, translating them into the best format possible. The premise of this approach is that there are fundamental characteristics of mental disorders that transcend culture, race, and ethnicity. The instrument, if carefully translated for maximal equivalence, is assumed to be able to detect cases of the disorders targeted for study.

However, the assumption of universality of psychopathology has been shattered by numerous researchers over the years (Kleinman, 1977; Kleinman & Good, 1985; see also chapter 4, this volume). Perhaps this premise of universality is wishful thinking on the part of researchers. An alternative approach is to examine the statistical and psychometric properties of measures used across cultures to estimate the degree to which instruments are working in comparable ways across societies through techniques such as factor analysis (Kameoka, 1985; Marsella & Kameoka, 1988; Marsella, Kinzie, & Gordon, 1973).

For example, in a pioneering study of cross-cultural depression, Marsella, Kinzie, and Gordon (1973) submitted a depression checklist administered to Caucasian Americans, Chinese Americans, and Japanese Americans to a factor analysis according to each ethnic group and found variations in factor structure across the groups. The Chinese group showed a strong somatic factor; the Japanese a strong interpersonal factor; and the Caucasians a strong existential factor orientation. These were interpreted to reflect primary dimensions of self-construction and presentation. Although this is a reasonable first step, it is simply the first step in what is undoubtedly a complicated multiphasic process.

Looking at factor structures, interitem analyses, coefficient alphas, and so forth for an instrument employed across cultures will give a sense of the instrument's reliability, a fundamental basis from which one can begin to look at validity. However, the fact that an instrument is reliable and its items seem to interrelate in comparable ways across cultures does not ensure that it is measuring the same construct across groups of people. Validity studies also must be undertaken.

Validity studies may take place within the context of the main study, either preceding it as in a preliminary validation study or following the main study as in the hierarchical approach recommended by Dohrenwend and Shrout (1981). In the former strategy, specific steps are taken to determine the extent to which the instrument is measuring the construct of interest prior to the initiation of the main study. In the latter approach, clinical interviews by those knowledgeable in the cultural manifestations of the targeted disorder may be used to substantiate the presence, absence, and severity of the disorder and correlate these findings with those observed using the instrument employed in the main study.

The second approach employed in cross-cultural studies is the development of *emic* instruments (see Kleinman & Good, 1985). An emic instrument is one that is consistent with the indigenous views of psychopathology in the culture to be studied. This approach addresses the need for precision in measurement of a psychological construct within a culture but presents additional problems when cross-cultural comparisons are attempted. An item that is meaningful in one culture may not at all represent another culture's perspective on deviance or pathology.

Some have recommended that outcome measurement (i.e., disorder) should be related in systematic ways to other variables and that theoretical models should be able to predict poor psychological functioning regardless of the precise symptoms or characteristics measured. For example, a measure of the psychological effects of rape in two cultures actually may include different symptoms and outcomes, but these outcomes would be related in certain predictable ways to societal functioning, interpersonal functioning, and psychological functioning. Models could be created to determine if a measure of rape's effects in one culture is related to functioning in that society as much as a second measure of rape's effects relates in functioning in that society.

The latter approach ultimately may prove to be the most accurate in comparing diverse societies on symptoms of psychopathology. Unfortunately, it has the limitation of extreme statistical and theoretical complexity, a problem of serious importance when the people using the data are policy makers, politicians, and citizens rather than social or behavioral scientists. Often, such individuals prefer a simple answer to complicated questions to justify any actions taken on behalf of the denizens of a country or a subculture. Providing realistically complex answers may be discouraged by those who are trying to make decisions about the actual distribution and use of resources.

Recommended Steps to Improve Ethnocultural Sensitivity

Marsella and colleagues (1985) summarized their thinking about the conduct of cross-cultural studies of psychopathology, recommending that scientists should (a) use relevant anthropological data to determine comparable life patterns and experiences in each culture, (b) develop glossaries and definitions of various deviant psychological experiences, (c) derive symptom patterns and interrelationships with statistical methods, (d) use similar sampling and case identification methods, (e) develop culturally based assessment instruments that optimize equivalence, and (f) establish baselines of normal functioning for the measures in different cultures.

These suggestions remain as pertinent today as they were a decade ago; yet there are few studies to date in the literature that employ these recommendations. Perhaps the cost associated with the conduct of such studies outweighs the benefits accrued. Perhaps the importance of cross-cultural research diminishes as society places greater emphasis on interventions for the individuals in need. Perhaps the demands of research within cultures exceeds the demand for comparisons across the cultures. Regardless of the problems, there will continue to be both a need and an interest in understanding how cultures experience psychopathology, how the members of a culture study it optimally within their culture, and how researchers can learn from other societies to minimize disorder and promote prosocial behavior on the part of individuals in all societies.

PSYCHOMETRIC CONSIDERATIONS IN ETHNOCULTURAL ASSESSMENT

Researchers and clinicians who embark on the study of psychopathology in general or PTSD in particular among populations that differ in cultural background must be prepared to apply the same standards to their work with these populations that they might with a majority population. Developing or using psychological tests or diagnostic instruments of any type requires an appreciation for the psychometric properties of an instrument. In this section, we present the notions of reliability and validity and how they should be used to evaluate the performance of a particular instrument in a specific population.

Validity

Validity is the extent to which an instrument is measuring what it purports to measure. To arrive at an estimate of validity one can employ several different procedures, depending on interest, resources, and available collateral measures. Criterion validity is the relationship of the individual's performance on the instrument to some external referent of interest or behavior of interest. If the criterion is a clinician's judgment of the presence of a psychological disorder (e.g., PTSD, the correlation of the instrument with the judgment is a measure of criterion validity. If these measures are taken at the same time, this form of criterion validity is referred to as *concurrent validity*. If one measure is used to predict a future status or condition, this is referred to as a *measure of predictive validity.*

The key to criterion validity is the credibility and accuracy of the criterion. Using the quidelines stated previously, it is crucial that the criterion be one that is acceptable to the culture under study, preferably even gendered by members of the culture who have relevant status to the criterion under investigation (e.g., health care professionals, spiritual healers). A focus group, as discussed in an earlier section, is one method used to generate acceptable criterion standards. In the mental health field, items to be included in the criterion should reflect the known expressions of the disorder, the idioms of expression for that disorder, and any additional ethnocultural considerations in describing the disorder in question. The test or instrument under development should then correlate with the domain of symptoms and behaviors identified by the specialists who have established the criterion.

Content Validity

Content validity is the extent to which the measurement tool represents the total domain of the criterion. Since it is difficult to employ a test that contains all symptoms possible, most tests and instruments contain a subsample of the available possibilities. Content validity is a measure of the instrument's relationship to the entire domain of symptoms. Does a test or instrument adequately sample the universe of possible symptoms? An evaluation of the content validity of a test is made on the basis of expert judgment.

Construct Validity

Construct validity is employed when there is no universally acceptable criterion with which to compare the instrument or test being developed. The methods employed in construct validation are comparisons between the measure of interest with other existing measures of the construct under investigation. Does the new measure behave as one would predict it should? If so, then it may well be measuring the important construct. The more measures with which one can compare performance, the stronger the claims one can make for achieving a high degree of construct validity. In the area of psychopathology, and PTSD especially, construct validity is the approach of choice when attempting to validate the performance of a measure to assess the psychological effects of exposure to massively stressful life experiences.

Construct validation has three distinct steps. First, the theoretical relationships among measures must be specified a priori. Second, the relationships among measures must be assessed properly using contemporary methods of statistical analysis. Third, the empirical relationships among measures must be interpreted in terms of clarifying the underlying construct of interest. These stages then can be repeated with different samples and under different conditions to increase the likelihood that the relationship observed in the earlier study is stable across time, samples, and conditions of administration.

Reliability

There are several methods of reliability (reproducibility) typically employed in studies of instrumentation development. Reliability sets an upper limit on validity. Thus, a thorough evaluation of reliability is a crucial step in the initial stages of developing a new instrument. Several different types of reliability might be assessed, each reflecting concerns about a different potential source of measurement error.

Test–Retest Reliability

Test–retest reliability addresses the replicability or stability of an instrument over time. It typically involves administering the same test to the same people at two different points in time and determining the relationship of performance at time 1 and time 2. A problem in using test–retest reliability in psychopathology research is that many disorders are cyclical and change over time. Thus, there is inherent change in symptom reporting, sometimes reflecting improvements in conditions and sometimes representing exacerbation of disorder. Selecting the appropriate interval for retesting becomes an important consideration. Most psychological disorders change gradually and, in the absence of treatment, an interval of a week or two typically would be optimal in assessing the stability of the measurement instrument over time.

Internal Consistency Reliability

Internal consistency methods are attempts to establish the replicability of scores obtained on multiple items in a test. Coefficient alpha is the most common form of internal consistency examined for psychological tests. It represents the relationship of scores on all items of a test to all other items on the test to provide an estimate of how consistently the individuals in the sample responded to the questions.

When a test consists of a single construct, responses to the test items should be highly interrelated. If, however, a test measures many different constructs (or factors), coefficient alpha should be calculated separately on items reflecting a different factor or construct to determine the reliability of each independently. Alphas above .80 generally are considered acceptable estimates of the reliability of an instrument or its components.

Utility Analysis

Psychiatric conceptualizations of human behavioral problems historically have employed a medical model of disease. One implication of this is that individuals are classified dichotomously as either having or not having a condition. The *DMS–III* (American Psychiatric Association, 1980) attempted to incorporate continuous and qualitative measures into the diagnostic process through the use of the multiaxial system. However, the current zeitgeist for psychiatric disorders is to consider them as categories that require certain minimal-symptom expressions in order to exceed threshold. Thus, measures that yield dichotomous ratings of disorders (e.g., the presence or absence of PTSD) have been developed.

Diagnostic instruments and tests used for the express purpose of arriving at a clinical diagnosis also must be subjected to rigorous evaluation to determine their adequacy. Kraemer (1992) described in detail the various ways in which one can examine the extent to which a test does what it was intended to do by its developers. Her description of utility analyses is now the standard in the field, explaining methods for understanding the relationship of scores on a test to a standard for determining diagnostic category membership.

Sensitivity and Specificity

Sensitivity is one measure of diagnostic utility, and it is the extent to which a measure can identify true cases of a condition such as PTSD. *Specificity* is another measure of utility, and it represents the extent to which a test can identify true noncases. For instance, a test that identifies all known cases of PTSD in a sample would have optimal sensitivity. If that test correctly identified all individuals who did *not* have PTSD, it would have optimal specificity. Of course, in practice it is rare for any type of test to have perfect sensitivity and specificity, especially in mental health. However, the research for instruments that will provide excellent sensitivity and specificity for the purposes at hand (i.e., clinical work or research) is a critical one in psychological work that extends across different cultures and ethnic groups.

Predictive Power

The predictive power of a positive test is also a measure of test utility, and it is defined as the true positives divided by the true positives plus false positives. In a similar way, the predictive power of a negative test is defined as true negative divided by true negatives plus false negatives. Efficiency is essentially a test's hit rate—that is, the proportion of cases that were correctly identified by the test. Each of the measures contained in a utility analysis provides incremental information about how a test performs.

Because there is a trade-off between sensitivity and specificity, the specific needs of an investigator or a clinician should determine which component of the utility analysis is more important given the particular assessment needs. If the goal is to maximize the detection of false negatives, a lower cutoff score usually would achieve this goal. This would lead to enhanced levels of sensitivity but lower specificity. If the goal is to minimize false positives, higher cutoffs would be used, resulting in greater specificity but lower sensitivity. Optimal sensitivity and specificity for tests generally is considered the goal for instruments (Kraemer, 1992), but these goals can vary depending on the needs of the investigator, the conditions of administration, and other variables impinging on the testing situation.

Summary of Psychometric Considerations

In constructing measures for culturally diverse populations, the primary considerations are the same as those for constructing any test with any population. Problems arise when researchers and clinicians attempt to overextend the known parameters of a test beyond the populations for which they were intended. Reliability and validity are primary concerns in understanding how an instrument will work with a specific population, and measures of reliability and validity will determine the quality of all work that will be accomplished subsequently with an instrument. In the case of psychiatric nosology, there is a definite need to incorporate comprehensive utility analyses so that the relative efficiency of a test can be determined on the samples or groups of individuals to be studied. To do less than this is to risk error in judgments about the presence, severity, and impact of psychological disorders in cultures of interest.

EXAMPLES OF RACIALLY AND CULTURALLY SENSITIVE ASSESSMENT INSTRUMENTS

There are may possible approaches that researchers and clinicians can take to increase the sensitivity of their assessment instruments to individuals from other cultures or subcultures within a majority culture. Existing effective instruments can be properly translated, instruments can be modified to reflect cultural nuances for a disorder, or entirely new instruments can be developed. We will review examples of each of these approaches to addressing the problem of ethnocentricity in assessing symptomatology.

Indochinese PTSD Screening Scale

Mollica, Wyshak, de Marneffe, Khuon, and Lavelle (1987) present three versions of the Hopkins Symptom Checklist-25 (HSCL-25) that was translated concurrently into Khmer, Laotian, and Vietnamese. These researchers were looking for an effective screening tool for their clinic, which serves Indochinese refugees living in the United States who were exposed to the ravages of the many years of war in their home countries.

They employed translation and back-translation for the 25 items of the HSCL using individuals who were fluent in both English and their native languages and knowledgeable about mental health concepts. The next step was to administer the instrument to patients, gathering experience with the reactions of patients who were representative of the types of people for whom the test was intended. Then a group of cultural experts reviewed the instrument to ensure that the literal translations and connotations were identical in English and the Indochinese languages.

Mollica and colleagues (1987) found excellent test–retest reliability ($r = .89$) and interrater agreement data ($r = .98$). Validational studies demonstrated that the scores on the test were correlated with *DSM–III* diagnoses given by a clinician blind to test scores, and the authors also provided information on the sensitivity and specificity of the test (.88 and .73, respectively). The construction of these tests in three languages combined the best of many of the techniques discussed previously. Attending to the issues of culture, language, and psychometric rigor, these authors made a significant contribution to the literature on cross-cultural assessment. However, there were several problems. Small sample sizes raised questions about generalizability. Further, the researchers failed to assess the extent of the subjects' ethnic identification or attachment to their native cultures. Thus, it was possible that the subjects were not good representatives of their cultural traditions.

Harvard Trauma Scale

This same research group (Mollica et al., 1992) developed the Harvard Trauma Questionnaire, which combines the assessment of traumatic stressors (e.g., torture, rape, murder, starvation, etc.) and traumatic responses (e.g., anxiety, depression, nightmares, alienation, etc.) in one instrument. The questionnaire was developed in English by subject matter experts and then it was translated into the three Indochinese languages of Khmer, Vietnamese, and Laotian by experienced mental health professionals. These professionals generated items for inclusion in the questionnaire based on their clinical experience with the refugees. The *DSM–III* criteria, supplemented by items from their knowledge of the refugee's condition, constituted the symptom items on the questionnaire. Unfortunately, little use was made of indigenous people in selecting the items. Thus, idiomatic expressions of problems were not included, resulting in possible false positives or negatives.

The scale was then back-translated to attain linguistic equivalence, and finally the entire group of experts engaged in a consensus discussion to create the final items for the questionnaire. Measures of test–retest reliability, interrater agreement, and internal consistency were computed following administration of the questionnaire to patients in a clinic. Test–retest reliability was .89 at 1 week; interrater agreement was .93; and coefficient alpha was .96 for the symptoms. The researchers then applied the HSCL-25 and the Harvard Team Questionnaire to their examination of the prevalence of mental health and health consequences for Indochinese refugees in a refugee camp in Thailand (Mollica et al., 1992). This sequence of studies demonstrated an approach to the development and use of both new instruments and modification of old assessment instruments for use across widely divergent cultures and populations.

Vietnamese Depression Scale

Kinzie and colleagues (1982) developed a depression measure for Vietnamese refugees initially using the Beck Depression Inventory (Beck, Ward, Mendelsen, Mock, & Erbough, 1961) and then adding cultural idioms and expressions for depressive mood. When applied to Vietnamese patients with known depression, the items from the inventory seemed less applicable to the patients than were the items related to cultural expression of depression. These researchers concluded that linguistic or semantic equivalence was inadequate in developing a measure of depression for this particular subculture within the United States. They included in their final instrument symptoms of depression that described affective, cognitive, and somatic components of depression within the context of the subjects' cultural experience of depression.

Measuring PTSD in African Americans

Penk and Allen (1991) described the relevant parameters for conducting a culturally sensitive assessment of African American veterans with PTSD. Their work represents a valuable description of the importance of distinguishing the effects of trauma on minority groups within Western societies. Penk and Allen (1991) argued that minorities who are exposed to potentially traumatic events experience the events in different ways than do members of the majority culture. The result of this differing experience is the need for incorporating specific assessment methods when evaluating minorities for PTSD. Recognizing the role of prejudice, discrimination, and socioeconomic factors in assessing the effects of potentially traumatic events, according to the researchers' thesis, will result in a more clinically sophisticated understanding of the person presenting for treatment or research. They recommended that the use of instruments developed for use on the majority culture be standardized on the minority cultures prior to their use and interpretation.

When developing measures for use across subcultures within a majority culture (e.g., African Americans), there are several approaches that can be taken. An issue of continuing importance in these situations is the extent to which minorities are acculturated into the majority culture. However, measures of acculturation are few and most are controversial as to their validity.

However, preliminary reports from Marsella and his colleagues (Marsella, Horvath, & Tsushima, 1995) suggested that a behavioral index consisting of behaviors that subjects engage in that are related to traditional cultural practices seems to have good psychometric properties for distinguishing various levels of acculturation. A sound strategy to adopt in creating measures that are to be used across subcultures within a society is to include sufficient numbers of minority individuals in the validational studies conducted with the instrument.

Mississippi Combat-Related PTSD Scale

In constructing the Mississippi Scale for Combat-Related PTSD, Keane, Caddell, and Taylor (1988) oversampled African Americans for inclusion in the initial study of reliability. Of the 362 subjects in the first study, 45% were African American. Principal component analysis and calculation of coefficient alphas for the six factors extracted did not differ depending on the race of the subjects studied. Test–retest data were collected in a second study in which 18% of the total sample were minority veterans. In the third study of the validity of the scale, 40% of the PTSD group was African American. Inspection of the data on the Mississippi Scale indicated that there were no differences among the racial groups of subjects in the initial reliability and validity studies on this instrument. This may account for the success of this scale in both the clinical and epidemiological studies in which it has been used (Kulka et al., 1988; McFall, Smith, MacKay, & Tarver, 1990). While this scale appears to work well in the United States, its use with samples from other cultures and in different languages would necessitate additional validational data.

In a similar way, the Keane PTSD (PK) scale of the MMPI (Keane, Malloy, & Fairbank, 1984) was validated on more than 35% of African American subjects with PTSD in a total sample of 100. Their responses were compared to Caucasians with PTSD and to a sample of 100 comparison subjects with general psychiatric disorders. Inspection of the clinical and validity scales of the MMPI in this study revealed few differences between the groups on the scales in general and on the PK scale specifically (Fairbank, Caddell, & Keane, 1985). The use of the PK scale with this minority group seems empirically warranted by the date that have been collected. Its use with other minority groups and in studies in different cultures awaits additional confirmatory data.

Clinician-Administered PTSD Scale

The Clinician-Administered PTSD (CAPS; Blake et al., 1990; 1995) is a structured diagnostic interview for PTSD designed to be a comprehensive measure of PTSD. It assesses the 17 core symptoms of the disorder and 8 associated features, as well as the effects of specific symptoms on social and occupational functioning. A major strength of this scale is its behaviorally based anchors for all ratings and its guidelines for evaluating current and lifetime PTSD. In a series of studies to examine the reliability and validity of the CAPS conducted by Weathers and colleagues (1992), 25% of the participants were minorities.

In addition to demonstrating the excellent psychometric properties of this instrument, the authors also inspected racial differences in performance with the scale. There were no differences between Caucasian and African American subjects in total scores on the CAPS or on any subscale of the instrument, indicating the capacity of the instrument to assess PTSD across racial groupings. Construct validity studies indicated that the CAPS correlated .91 with the Mississippi Scale, .77 with the PK of the MMPI, and .89 with symptoms endorsed on the Structured Clinical Interview for *DSM–III* (SCID; Spitzer, Williams, Gibbon, & First, 1990). Test–retest reliability was .90; sensitivity rates were 84%; specificity was 95%; efficiency was 89%; and kappa against the SCID was .78.

PTSD Checklist

Using the same approach to evaluating the usefulness of an assessment instrument across ethnic groups, Weathers and colleagues (1993) developed the PTSD Checklist (PCL), a simple questionnaire that included the 17 *DSM–III* and *DSM–IV* symptoms associated with PTSD. Employing a five-point ratings scale, the PCL displayed excellent psychometric properties with coefficient alphas equal to .97, test–retest reliability at .96, and strong relationships with the Mississippi Scale (.93), the PK Scale (.77), and the

Impact of Event Scale (.90; Horowitz, Wilner, & Alvarez, 1979). Diagnostic utility measures of sensitivity (82%) and specificity (83%) both were strong.

An inspection of the performance of different racial groups on this self-report measure indicated that African Americans, who made up 23% of the sample, did not differ from Caucasians in their scores. Further, there were no statistically significant interactions between race and PTSD status. It seems that both the CAPS and the PCL are excellent measures of PTSD and that the measures function comparably across ethnic subcultures in the United States.

In the context of studying the effects of World War II on Dutch resistance fighters, Hovens (1994) and his colleagues conducted a sequence of studies to determine the reliability, validity, and utility of various measures of PTSD. Recognizing that instruments translated from English might not competently measure the essence of PTSD in Dutch, they employed a strategy whereby they both translated instruments using back-translation to promote semantic equivalence and then developed their own instruments in Dutch. The CAPS, the Mississippi Scale, the PK scale of the MMPI, and the SCID were all translated into Dutch and then empirically examined. Each of the instruments was subjected to a series of reliability, validity, and utility studies during the course of the researchers study of the resistance fighters. Their efforts to conserve resources by using extant measures, coupled with developing measures in their own language, is a model for cross-cultural instrument development.

CONCLUSION

The issues raised regarding cross-cultural assessment of PTSD are indeed daunting ones. To adhere to the recommended procedures is expensive, time consuming, and difficult work. Moreover, rarely is there financial support for instrument development and validation in the mental health field. Psychometric studies have little glory associated with them. However, they are the cornerstones for all work in psychopathology; they are *sine qua non*.

The model we have proposed for assessing PTSD (Keane et al., 1987), suggested that a single PTSD instrument should not be the basis for conferring a PTSD diagnosis, even if it is developed and evaluated carefully. All instruments are subject to measurement error, and the use of multiple indicators is recommended—particularly when important clinical or policy issues are involved. Employing a multimethod approach combining structured interviews, psychological tests, relevant archival data, and even psychophysiological assessment (cf. Prins, Kaloupek, & Keane, 1995) ultimately will provide the most reliable information possible. The fundamental principle of using multiple measures for case identification is a necessity for cross-cultural research as well as research conducted within a single cultural context.

Further, simply translating instruments into the language of the targeted population is an inadequate strategy when conducting research or clinical work with diverse populations. Assessment of the translated instruments' psychometric properties is a minimal first step to determining the applicability of the instrument in the new language. Measures of reliability and validity must be collected to ensure that any data collected can be interpreted properly. When seeking a precise diagnosis for the purposes of a study, comprehensive utility analyses should be conducted to ascertain the extent to which the instruments employed are functioning in the desired manner.

There are no available assessment instruments for PTSD that can be used with impunity across all cultures and languages. There is much work to be done and much new knowledge needed before we can conduct successfully true cross-cultural studies. In the interim it would be wise for clinicians and researchers to appreciate the limits of our knowledge and to administer and interpret measures of personality and psychopathology in a cautious and culturally sensitive way. When opportunities present themselves to develop or modify instruments according to sound psychological principles, this should be the top research priority. Time and effort expended on instrumentation will yield huge benefits for the study at hand and for the entire field of cross-cultural psychology.

REFERENCES

American Psychiatric Association. (1980). *Diagnostic and statistical manual of mental disorders* (3rd ed.). Washington, DC: Author.

Beck, A. T., Ward, C. H., Mendelson, M., Mock, J., & Erbaugh J. (1961). An inventory of measuring depression. *Archives of General Psychiatry, 4,* 53–63.

Blake, D. D., Weathers, F. W., Nagy, L. N., Kaloupek, D. G., Gusman, F., Charney, D. S., & Keane, T. M. (1995). The development of a clinician-administered PTSD scale. *Journal of Traumatic Stress, 8,* 75–90.

Blake, D. D., Weathers, F. W., Nagy, L. N., Kaloupek, D. G., Klauminser, G., Charney, D. S., & Keane, T. M. (1990). A clinician rating scale for assessing current and lifetime PTSD: the CAPS-1. *Behavior Therapist, 18,* 187–188.

Dana, R. (1993). *Multicultural assessment perspectives for professional psychology.* Boston: Allyn & Bacon.

de Girolamo, G. (1992). International perspectives on the treatment and prevention of posttraumatic stress disorder. In J. P. Wilson & B. Raphael (Eds.),

International handbook of traumatic stress syndromes (pp. 935–946). New York: Plenum Press.

Dohrenwend, B. P., & Shrout, P. E. (1981). Toward the development of a two-stage procedure for case identification and classification in psychiatric epidemiology. *Research in Community and Mental Health, 2,* 295–323.

Fairbank, J. A., Caddell, J. M., & Keane, T. M. (1985, August). *Black–White differences on the MMPI and PTSD subscale.* Paper presented at the Annual Convention of the American Psychological Association, Los Angeles.

Flaherty, J. A., Gaviria, F. M., Pathak, D., Mitchell, T., Wintrob, R., Richman, J. A., & Birz, S. (1988). Developing instruments for cross-cultural psychiatric research. *Journal of Nervous and Mental Disease, 176,* 257–263.

Hathaway, S. R., & McKinley, J. C. Minnesota Multiphasic Personality Inventory — 2. Minneapolis: University of Minnesota.

Horowitz, M. J., Wilner, N. R., & Alvarez, W. (1979). Impact of Event Scale: A measure of subjective distress. *Psychosomatic Medicine, 41,* 208–218.

Hovens, J. E. (1994). *Research into the psychodiagnostics of posttraumatic stress disorder.* Amsterdam, Netherlands: Eburon Press.

Kameoka, V. A. (1985). Construct validation of psychological measures in cross-cultural research: Analysis of linear structural relationships. In R. Diaz-Guerrero (Ed.), *Crosscultural and national studies in social psychology* (pp. 88–99). Dordrecht, Netherlands: North Holland.

Keane, T. M., Caddell, J. M., & Taylor, K. L. (1988). Mississippi Scale for Combat-Related Posttraumatic Stress Disorder: Three studies in reliability and validity. *Journal of Consulting and Clinical Psychology, 56,* 85–90.

Keane, T. M., Malloy, P. F., & Fairbank, J. A. (1984). Empirical development of an MMPI subscale for the assessment of combat-related posttraumatic stress disorder. *Journal of Consulting and Clinical Psychology, 52,* 888–891.

Keane, T. M., Weathers, F. W., & Kaloupek, D. G. (1992). Psychological assessment of post-traumatic stress disorder. *PTSD Research Quarterly, 3,* 1–8.

Keane, T. M., & Wolfe, J. (1990). Comorbidity in post-traumatic stress disorder: An analysis of community and clinical studies. *Journal of Applied Social Psychology, 20,* 1776–1788.

Keane, T. M., Wolfe, J., & Taylor, K. L. (1987). Post-traumatic stress disorder: Evidence for diagnostic validity and methods of psychological assessment. *Journal of Clinical Psychology, 43,* 32–43.

Kinzie, J. D., Manson, S. M., Vinh, D. T., Tolan, N. T., Anh, B., & Pho, T. N. (1982). Development and validation of a Vietnamese-language depression rating scale. *American Journal of Psychiatry, 139,* 1276–1281.

Kleinman, A. (1977). Depression, somatization, and the "new" cross-cultural psychiatry. *Culture, Medicine, and Psychiatry, 6,* 1–39.

Kleinman, A., & Good, B. (Eds.). (1985). *Culture and depression.* Berkeley: University of California Press.

Kraemer, H. C. (1992). *Evaluating medical tests: Objective and quantitative guidelines.* Newbury Park, CA: Sage.

Kulka, R. A., Schlenger, W. E., Fairbank, J. A., Hough, R. L., Jordan, B. K., Marmar, C. R., & Weiss, D. S. (1988). *National Vietnam Veterans Readjustment Study (NVVRS): Description, current status, and initial PTSD prevalence estimates.* Research Triangle Park, NC: Research Triangle Institute.

Kulka, R. A., Schlenger, W. E., Fairbank, J. A., Jordan, B. K., Hough, R. L., Marmar, C. R., & Weiss, D. S. (1990). *Trauma and the Vietnam war generation: Report of findings from the National Vietnam Veterans Readjustment Study.* New York: Brunner/Mazel.

Marsella, A. J. (1987). The measurement of depressive experience and disorders across cultures. In A. J. Marsella, R. Hirshifield, & M. Katz (Eds.), *The measurement of depression: Biological, psychological, behavioral, and social aspects* (pp. 376–397). New York: Guilford Press.

Marsella, A. J., Friedman, M. J., & Spain, E. H. (1992). A selective review of the literature on ethnocultural aspects of PTSD. *PTSD Research Quarterly, 3,* 1–8.

Marsella, A. J., Horvath, A., & Nathan, J. (1995). *A behavioral index of ethnocultural identity.* Unpublished manuscript, University of Hawaii, Honolulu.

Marsella, A. J., Horvath, A., & Tshushima, S. (1995, January). The multimodel measurement of ethnocultural identity. Paper presented at the meeting of the Hawaii Psychological Association, Honolulu, HI.

Marsella, A. J., & Kameoka, V. A. (1988). Ethnocultural issues in the assessment of psychopathology. In S. Wetzler (Ed.), *Measuring mental illness: Psychometric assessment for clinicians* (pp. 229–256). Washington, DC: American Psychiatric Press.

Marsella, A. J., Kinzie, D., & Gordon, D. (1973). Ethnocultural variations in the expression of depression. *Journal of Cross-Cultural Psychology, 4,* 435–458.

Marsella, A. J., Sartorius, N., & Jablensky, A. (1985). Depression across cultures. In A. Kleinman & B. Good (Eds.), *Culture and depression* (pp. 299–324). Berkeley: University of California Press.

McFall, M. E., Smith, D. E., MacKay, P. W., & Tarver, D. J. (1990). Reliability and validity of Mississippi Scale for Combat-Related Posttraumatic Stress Disorder. *Psychological Assessment: A Journal of Consulting and Clinical Psychology, 2,* 114–121.

Mollica, R. F., Caspi-Yavin, Y., Bollini, P., Truong, T., Tor, S., & Lavelle, J. (1992). The Harvard Team Questionnaire: Validating a cross-cultural instrument for measuring torture, trauma, and posttraumatic stress disorder in Indochinese refugees. *Journal of Nervous and Mental Disease, 180,* 111–116.

Mollica, R. F., Wyshak, G., de Marneffe, D., Khuon, F., & Lavelle, J. (1987). Indochinese versions of the Hopkins Symptom Checklist-25: A screening instrument for the psychiatric care of refugees. *American Journal of Psychiatry, 144,* 497–500.

Newman, E., Kaloupek, D. G., & Keane, T. M. (in press). Assessment of PTSD in clinical and research settings. In A. C. McFarlane, B. van der Kolk, & L.

Weisaeth (Eds.), *Comprehensive text on posttraumatic stress*. Cambridge: Cambridge University Press.

Penk, W. E., & Allen, I. M. (1991). Clinical assessment of post-traumatic stress disorder (PTSD) among American minorities who served in Vietnam. *Journal of Traumatic Stress, 4,* 41–66.

Prins, A., Kaloupek, D. G., & Keane, T. M. (1995). Psychophysiological evidence for autonomic arousal and startle in traumatized adult populations. In M. J. Friedman, D. Charney, & A. Deutch (Eds.), *Neurobiological and clinical consequences of stress: From normal adaptation to PTSD* (pp. 291–314). New York: Raven Press.

Spitzer, R. L., Williams, J. B., Gibbon, M., & First, M. B. (1990). Structured Clinical Inventory for DSM–III–R. Washington, DC: American Psychiatric Press.

Sutker, P. B., Uddo-Crane, M., & Allain, A. N. (1991). Clinical and research assessment of posttraumatic stress disorder: A conceptual overview. *Journal of Consulting and Clinical Psychology, 3,* 520–530.

Weathers, F. W., Blake, D. D., Krinsley, K. E., Haddad, W., Huska, J. A., & Keane, T. M. (1992, November). *The Clinician-Administered PTSD Scale: Reliability and construct validity.* Paper presented at the 26th Annual Convention of the Association for Advancement of Behavior Therapy, Boston.

Weathers, F. W., Litz, B. T., Keane, T. M., Herman, D. S., Steinberg, H. R., Huska, J. A., & Kraemer, H. C. (1993). *The PTSD Checklist: Description, use, and psychometric properties.* Unpublished manuscript.

Wilson, J. P., & Raphael, B. (Eds.). (1993). *International handbook of traumatic stress syndromes.* New York: Plenum Press.

III

PTSD AMONG SPECIFIC
ETHNOCULTURAL GROUPS

8

PTSD AMONG
AFRICAN AMERICANS

IRVING M. ALLEN

THE AFRICAN AMERICAN EXPERIENCE

African Americans have coped with difficult and oppressive life circumstances from 1619 to present times. These circumstances have included
extremes of physical and psychological abuse, torture, humiliation, racial
intolerance and deprivation, and denial of all forms of freedoms. Ironically,
and quite tragically, the very freedoms that blacks have been deprived of
and denied are the very freedoms that have made this country a model for
individual freedoms and rights for the world.

At the end of slavery, an oppressive caste system was established that
continues to persist today. African Americans have made some progress
through legal and political, and economic action, but for most, the marginality and conditionality of being African American in America remains
a fact of everyday life.

During the past two decades, motivated by a "benign neglect" and
continued institutional racism, high rates of poverty, and frequent denigration and abuse have continued to wreak devastation on African American
culture and society, and ultimately, on the psyche of the individual African
American.

Health and Wellbeing

This chapter purports that the persistence of these oppressive factors creates life circumstances for African Americans that require a constant search and struggle for meaning, purpose, and presence within American society that is far beyond any ordinary or reasonable expectation. Therefore, when either natural or other types of disasters or traumatic events occur, these events may inflict on African Americans greater and more long-lasting devastation than on other people, documentable by persistent psychological and physiological changes.

The research on African Americans and posttraumatic stress disorder (PTSD) is not yet extensive, but to date the findings seem to indicate a positive relationship between African American status and an increase in the frequency and degree of PTSD suffering. Before proceeding with my review of the research on African Americans and PTSD, I would like to note that the findings reviewed in this chapter are the result of broad-scale statistical studies. In my opinion, the majority of African Americans do not suffer from PTSD nor do they consider themselves traumatized as individuals, in spite of the fact that many do experience numerous traumatic events. Many have learned to cope and survive despite difficult life experiences. It is part of Black heritage to, individually and collectively, demonstrate a rich complex of adaptations to the exigencies of American life. Traditionally, these adaptations have been rooted in strong family and community relational networks that function independently of European American influences.

I would, therefore, like to preface the discussion of studies on Blacks and PTSD with the following remarks by psychologist W. Nobles (1991):

> African American psychology is something more than the psychology of so-called underprivileged peoples, more than the experience of living in ghettoes or having been forced into the dehumanizing condition of slavery. It is more than the "darker" dimension of general psychology. Its unique status is from the positive features of basic African psychology which dictate the values, customs, attitudes, and behavior of Africans in Africa and the New World. (p. 47)

Nobles' thoughts help us avoid Kardiner and Oresey's (1941) error from the widely read *Mark of Oppression*, in which he concluded, despite obvious sympathy, that all African Americans lived stunted and miserable lives.

Chapter Purpose and Organization

This chapter will review and interpret some research, especially on Vietnam War veterans, that demonstrates a positive relationship between African American status and the development of PTSD. Three studies of civilian populations that have implications for African Americans will also be discussed, including a survey of PTSD in four Southern cities, a large survey of youth impacted by Hurricane Hugo, a devastating storm that swept the South in 1992, and a discussion of the Buffalo Creek disaster, the collapse of a West Virginia dam in 1972. Several viewpoints will offered to interpret these findings of the these studies.

The chapter will also discuss recent studies that document a huge increase in urban violence during the 1980s and the concomitant disturbing increase in obvious PTSD-related symptomatology in young people who are either witnesses or victims of this violence epidemic. This section will also review work that shows the disturbing incidence of domestic violence towards African American women. A context for understanding the epidemic of violence will be provided by an extensive discussion of the current status of African Americans that will cite health, unemployment, crime, and other data that document grim current life circumstances for the majority of African Americans. Throughout, history will be presented as interrelated with current social dilemmas to demonstrate the continuity between the traumatic experience of the slavery–segregation period, and the present post-Civil Rights era.

Finally, psychological theory, using the concept of projective identification, will be presented as a means of understanding the development and persistence of destructive, abusive, and racially discriminating behavior towards African Americans. The consequences of projective identification will also be applied to the processes of clinical diagnosis and treatment. Suggestions for further research and a proposal for the establishment of a "think tank" to study the relationship among racism, sexism, and poverty and trauma will conclude the chapter.

OVERVIEW OF RESEARCH

The Vietnam War Veteran

The study of Vietnam War combat veterans provided the first evidence that African Americans suffered a high PTSD rate when compared to veterans of European descent. A study of war veterans aptly referred to as the "Legacy Study" (Egendorf, Kadushin, Laufer, Rothbart, & Sloan, 1981), found that 70 percent of African American veterans who experienced heavy combat remained stressed several years after the war. Of these African American Vietnam veterans forty percent remained stressed for many years, compared to 20 percent of European American combat veterans.

Additionally, the Legacy Study found that African American veterans had a different "mind set." They were far more likely than European Americans to express positive or neutral feelings about the Vietnamese, and were even more likely to oppose the war itself. Work by other researchers supported these findings. For example, Yager and Laufer (1984) noted that African Americans were significantly more disturbed by abusive violence towards the Vietnamese; the authors speculated that this was so because African Americans were less able to dehumanize Vietnamese people. Laufer, Brett, & Gallops (1985) suggested that African Americans received less social support for abusive violence from their peers, and had closer relations with the Vietnamese. Parson (1984a) also wrote of the "powerful affinity" many African American veterans came to have for the suffering of the Vietnamese. Furthermore, Eisenhart (1975) found that the constant denigration of the Vietnamese, even during basic training, increased tensions between African Americans and European Americans.

In terms of exposure to stress, the Legacy Study also showed that African Americans were 12% more likely to be assigned to combat duty than European Americans. This fact should be considered in light of the disproportionate death rates. During the early days of war, African American combat participation was very high—their death rate approached 25% of the total American deaths by late 1965 (Johnson, 1968). Eventually, as the figures were released, a public outcry forced the Pentagon to reduce African American combat participation after 1965. (The final exposure rate downplayed the initial high combat exposure and casualty rates.) As if the stress of combat were not enough, many African American soldiers felt that their overrepresentation on the front lines was the result of a genocidal policy (Goff, Sanders, & Smith, 1982).

The results of the Legacy Study, as well as those from various clinical reports (e.g., Allen, 1986; Parson, 1990; Penk and Allen, 1991), indicated that prejudice intertwined with financial hardship compounded the adjustment problems faced by African American veterans. For many African American veterans, financial hardship was more likely to have been a problem before the war than it was for their European American counterparts. Racial prejudice was cited as an issue before, during, and after military experience.

Some years later, the National Vietnam Veterans Readjustment Study (NVVRS) (Kulka et al., 1990) yielded more data on African Americans and PTSD. At the time of the study, 20.6% of African Americans suffered from PTSD, compared with 13.7% of European Americans and 27.9% of Hispanics. This study, like the Legacy Study, showed a strong correlation between PTSD and the degree of combat exposure. The NVVRS also found that African Americans were assigned to combat duty with considerably greater frequency than European Americans. In addition, the NVVRS study found that four variables contributed to PTSD development: (a) growing up in an economically deprived family, (b) symptoms of drug abuse or dependence before the military, (c) symptoms of affective disorder prior to Vietnam, and (d) behavior problems in childhood.

The NVVRS study used what was termed a *demoralization scale* to compare veterans groups. This scale included symptoms of dread, anxiety, hopelessness, helplessness, poor self-esteem, psychophysiologic symptoms, confused thinking, and so forth. Both African American and Hispanic veterans showed significantly higher demoralization scores than European Americans.

Green, Grace, Lindy, and Leonard (1990) also found that African American combat veterans reported higher stress levels than European American veterans. They echoed Kulka et al.'s warnings that the race differences are complicated by other factors such as drug use and early life experience. Penk (1985, 1989) reported complex findings showing that African American Vietnam veterans seeking treatment for substance abuse were more disturbed than European American combat veterans. Laufer, Brett, & Gallops (1985) reported that war trauma interacts with race; European American soldiers experienced more intrusive imagery when they witnessed abusive violence, African American troops experienced more intrusive imagery and hyperarousal when they participated in abusive violence.

Some Civilian Studies: Buffalo Creek, Hurricane Hugo, and the Inner City

At least three studies of civilian African American populations report findings that are consistent with the studies of African American Vietnam War veterans (Lonigan et al., 1991; Norris, 1992; and Green et al., 1990). All of the studies cited, as well as those that will be discussed in the section on urban violence, indicate that degree of exposure to a traumatic event increases the likelihood of developing PTSD symptoms. Some of the civilian research suggests that exposure to stress may impact more severely on African Americans, with longer lasting sequelae. Both the research on veterans and the hurricane research find that exposures to similar stressors produce a greater impact on African Americans.

Several months after Hurricane Hugo struck in September 1989, Lonigan et al. (1991) surveyed over 5,000 South Carolina school children ranging in age from 9 to 19. Of those surveyed, 25.8% were African American. The African American children reported more symptomatology at all levels of exposure than the European American children. Furthermore, significantly more African American children were represented in the high-exposure group. This group was defined by multiple instances of parental job loss, moderate to severe home damage, and subjective experience of the hurricane.

The Buffalo Creek dam collapse occurred in Southern West Virginia in February 1972. It initially caused a lower incidence of stress among the

African American victims, according to Green and her colleagues (Green et al, 1990). However, in the second decade after the disaster, the authors found that race was the only variable differentiating 11% of the original sample that had developed PTSD more than 2 years afterwards. The African Americans' lower initial incidence did not preclude later emergence of long-term stress symptoms. The Buffalo Creek findings are particularly striking because the African Americans studied were less exposed to the traumatic event (Gleser, Green, & Winget, 1981) because they lived farther away from the dam and no African Americans had died. Also, African Americans were very involved in the lawsuits against the mining company responsible for the disaster and, moreover, reported feeling that God had spared them from the worst of the disaster. As for the subsequent emergence of PTSD, the authors surmised that over time, "the usual prejudicial attitudes resurfaced, raising the risk" of PTSD problems (p. 57).

Norris (1992) surveyed over 1,000 adults living in four southern cities. She investigated the impact of traumatic events in adults' lives. This study was equally divided between African Americans and European Americans. Norris reported complex findings pertaining to race. European Americans reported more occurrences of traumatic events (19% to 12% for African Americans). However, when the impact of trauma was considered, African Americans—especially African American men—showed the highest levels of stress.

Norris (1992) suggested three reasons for her complex findings concerning PTSD and race. One is that the traumatic incidents reported by African Americans were more serious in nature than those experienced by European Americans. The second is that greater economic resources of European Americans may have reduced the negative impact of traumatic events on them. The author cited studies that show that higher socioeconomic status buffers the negative impact of life events. Lastly, Norris, like Green and her coworkers (e.g., Green, Grace, Lindy, & Leonard, 1990), surmised that African Americans experiencing trauma may confront hostility, prejudice, and neglect, all of which serve to heighten the effects of a crisis.

These views coincide with those of several researchers and clinicians involved in work with African American Vietnam veterans. For example, Erwin Parson, probably the earliest and most prolific writer on PTSD and African American veterans, has discussed the *tripartite dilemma* (Parson, 1985), which complicates the readjustment task of African Americans. This dilemma includes: (a) undergoing the additional maturation burden of acquiring a dual African American and American identity (b) surviving as a member of a kinship of men and women who are slave descendants, and as such are despised and discriminated against; and (c) surviving the trauma of the Vietnam War.

The degree of exposure to a stressor provides some hints of common ground between the civilian and war studies. The Hurricane Hugo study and the war studies show that African Americans tended to experience relatively higher stress exposures, although for different reasons. The different *levels of exposure* to Hurricane Hugo may reflect the relative economic circumstances of the children surveyed. Applying Norris' views about the buffering effect of high socioeconomic status, the demographics of African American youth surveyed suggest they had relatively less socioeconomic support to withstand such events as parental job loss and home loss. Furthermore, if factors of prejudice are involved, such as those identified by Green, et al. (1990) in the Buffalo Creek disaster, the trauma effects of disasters like Hurricane Hugo would be compounded.

In summary, the veterans and civilian studies discussed suggest that there is a positive relationship between African American status and the development of PTSD. Furthermore, these studies suggest that African Americans' experience of traumatic stress is often characterized by greater exposure to stressors and more long-term adverse effects. Lack of economic resources, institutional racism, and prejudice often compound these problems.

URBAN VIOLENCE, AFRICAN AMERICANS, AND PTSD

Violence: Victims, Observers, and Perpetrators

Recent years have seen a dramatic increase in the occurrence of violence in many of our urban areas, with an associated increase in African American youth who have either witnessed or been victims of violence, or both. In a study conducted in Chicago, Bell and Jenkins (1991) reported survey findings that 26% of second-, fourth-, sixth- and eighth-grade students surveyed had seen someone get shot, and 29% had seen someone get stabbed. (The two surveys in this study included over 1,500 students.)

The Centers for Disease Control (CDC, 1991) reported that between 1978 and 1987, 20,315 African American young men died from homicides, and that the homicide rate of 84.6/100,000 in 1987 was a 40% increase from 1984. The homicide rate for young African American men was 4 to 5 times that of young African American women, 5 to 8 times that of young European American men, and 16 to 22 times that of young European American women. Homicide is the leading cause of death for African American males between ages 15 and 24 (CDC, 1991).

Fitzpatrick and Badizar (1993) reported that 21.7% of a survey of 221 inner-city African American youths reported symptoms of PTSD. These youths were 7 to 18 years old and were participants in a summer program in the Washington, DC area. Fitzpatrick also reported that 70% of the children were victims of violence such as house breaks, sexual assault, knife and gun attacks, and striking by family members. Of those studied, 85% had witnessed at least one violent attack, and astoundingly, 43.4% had witnessed a murder. Greater exposure to violence was found to be associated to a higher incidence of PTSD.

Shakoor and Chalmers (1991) conducted a violence screening survey of 1,035 children ages 10 to 19 in an African American area in the Chicago area, and found that 75% of the boys and 70% of the girls had seen someone get shot, stabbed, robbed, or killed. This study linked these experiences with deterioration in cognitive performance and both behavioral and emotional dysfunctions.

Domestic violence within African American families and between African American adults is a major source of coexisting problems among youth violence. Bell and Chance-Hill (1991) concluded that homicide from family violence is disproportionately higher among African Americans than among other ethnic groups. They cite studies that indicate high levels of spousal abuse and violence toward children. These authors underscore drug and alcohol abuse as strong risk factors in violence.

Consequences of Violence for Interpersonal Relationships

Urban violence, and its implications for PTSD, also wreaks havoc on personal relationships. Both the NVVRS and the Legacy studies show major interpersonal relationship disturbances among PTSD sufferers. Rosenheck and Nathan (1985), Haley (1985), and Williams and Williams (1985) all report that children of combat veterans have many adjustment problems, including academic difficulties, mood and anxiety problems, behavior disturbances, and even primary PTSD symptoms such as nightmares and ruminations. These findings are consistent with the many reports that children of Holocaust survivors suffer second-generation symptoms (e.g., Solkoff, 1992).

Understanding the Contexts and Consequences of African American Life as Traumatogenic

Unemployment and Underpayment

Urban Black-on-Black violence is characterized by Hacker (1992) as a kind of "self-inflicted genocide." The term *self-inflicted genocide*, while apt, should not stand alone lest it be misunderstood, and Hacker proceeds in his book to analyze the persistent racism in America and its expression in social and political policies that create life circumstances in which trauma and deprivation are endemic facts of life. According to Hacker

(1992), African Americans have had unemployment rates that are at least double those of the European American population since 1960. The 1990 African American unemployment rate of 2.76 times that of European Americans was the highest multiple recorded in the last 30 years. Moreover, when African American males are similarly educated and qualified, their incomes in the same jobs are 70 to 80% that of European Americans.

A related economic fact is that African Americans compose over 12% of the population, but earn about 8% of the total income. Hacker (1992) convincingly traces the impact of persistent employment difficulties faced by African American males on marital and family relationships, including child care. African American men between the ages of 35 and 54 who have had at least 5 years of posthigh-school education, are more than twice as likely as European American men to be separated or divorced; Hacker suggests that this is because of factors and forces thwarting the aspirations of Black Americans.

Unemployment is a well documented source of problems for both individuals and communities. A Group for the Advancement of Psychiatry (GAP, 1982) report cites Brenner's (1976) findings that a 1970 rise of 1.4% in unemployment (1,500,000 people nationally) over the following 5 years was linked to 51,570 deaths, including 1,740 additional homicides and 1,540 suicides. Brennan also reported rises in liver cirrhosis mortality, related to an increase in alcoholism, increases in cardiovascular–renal disease, and rises in state prison admissions. These findings, the GAP report states, apply to all ages, sexes, and races, and are consistent with similar European studies.

The African American community chronically struggles with an unemployment rate that is well known to be devastating to the community's well-being. When one recognizes that in the heart of urban areas the unemployment rate is considerably higher, it follows that the devastation there is even more pronounced. Hacker points out, too, that African Americans are estimated to constitute 30% of the so-called "discouraged worker" category and, therefore, are not even counted in the standard unemployment figures.

Social and Medical Problems

Hacker (1992) related African Americans' relative difficulty finding meaningful labor to the following endemic problems: excessive teenage pregnancies and out-of-wedlock births; single-parent families struggling at or below the poverty level; crime; and especially the absence of men as wage earners, reliable partners, and role models. Hacker reported that during a 60-year span, the percentage of African American men behind bars in the United States has doubled from 22 to 45%, a phenomenon he attributes to persistent poverty and the European Americans' upward movement on the economic ladder. Prothrow-Stith (1991) noted that one fourth of the African American male population between the ages of 20 and 29 is either in prison, on probation, or on parole. She further notes that there are more African American men in prison than in college. According to recent justice department figures (Butterfield, October 1995), the proportion of African American men in their twenties who are either in prison, on probation, or on parole has now reached one in three.

Health statistics provide even more disturbing evidence of the current interrelationship among racism, poverty, and traumatogenic life circumstances. A recent article, "History Shows Trends of African Americans' High Mortality Rates and Poor Health Care" (1993), noted that between 1984 and 1989, African Americans' life expectancy declined from 69.7 to 69.2 years, and that these figures are 5 to 7 years lower than European Americans' life expectancies. One of the most disturbing statistics reported in this article is a Centers for Disease Control estimate that the number of excess deaths among African Americans was 60,000 in 1989 and reached 75,000 in 1990.

The African American infant mortality rate of 17.9 per 1,000 is twice that of European Americans, and approaches that of many developing countries. The National Medical Association News article (1993) noted also that African Americans suffer twice the rates of low birth-weight, postneonatal mortality, tuberculosis, hypertension, stroke, diabetes, and heart disease. The author pointed out the historical continuity between these findings and the poor health conditions under slavery extending back into the 17th century.

Racial Discrimination and Health Care

The element of race, like the findings in the large PTSD studies, has been found to be a definite factor in the assessment and management of patients with acute chest pain. Johnson, Lee, Cook, Rowan, and Goldman (1993), in a study of 1,374 African Americans and 1,657 European Americans, found that African Americans, regardless of socioeconomic status, experienced a much lower rate of coronary bypass procedures than European Americans. This difference occurred despite similar clinical presentations.

Kasiske et al. (1991) found that fewer African Americans than European Americans received kidney transplants and noted that this finding holds true also for pancreas and liver transplants. While concluding that both biological and socioeconomic factors contribute to these differences, they noted that "any and all barriers imposed by ignorance or misunderstanding on the part of health care givers also must be identified and eliminated by an intensive educational process" (p. 309).

The notorious Tuskegee Syphilis Experiment (Jones, 1981) represents the absolute depths of medical dehumanization of African Americans; hundreds of African American men with tertiary syphilis were untreated for a 40-year period under the auspices of a study conducted by the United States Public Health Service. Further evidence for the problem of racism and American medicine is provided by Proctor's (1988) observation that Nazi "scientists" closely studied Americans' attitudes and policies toward African Americans, for possible application to their genocidal policies toward the European Jewish community.

AIDS has rapidly become a devastating illness in the African American community and is now the leading cause of death for Black men between ages 35 and 44, whereas it was the sixth leading cause of African American deaths in 1990 (Smith, 1992). Hutchinson (1992) has discussed this epidemic in terms of a slow government response, which she believes is partly determined by racism.

Racial Discrimination in Schools

Education has been traditionally thought by Americans to provide the means to upward mobility. Both Hacker (1992) and Kozol (1991) in his book *Savage Inequalities*, documented the hypersegregation that still exists in the vast majority of public schools in America. An integral part of the segregation pattern is the underfunding of schools primarily attended by African Americans, which in some cities profiled by Kozol seems to represent an intentional pattern.

Hacker (1992) has noted that even in integrated schools, tracking often enables the segregation of students by race even inside the same building. The funding for urban schools is a constant political struggle that sends the debilitating message that educating the poor is highly conditional. The consequences of this for African Americans are obvious.

Racial Discrimination in Financial Activities

A "man's home is his castle" is a widely held belief among Americans. The pervasive and often intentional blocking of African Americans' access to that dream has been increasingly documented by studies during the past decade of discrimination in banking and lending practices. In the Boston metropolitan area, African Americans with the same financial profiles were two to three times more likely to be turned down for mortgage loans than European Americans (Marantz, 1989).

Levine and Harmon's (1992) *Death of an American Jewish Community* describes a malignant interaction between race, private-sector greed, and governmental policies manipulated by banking and real estate interests. The authors describe how Jewish residents in three Boston neighborhoods were displaced by a red-lining policy that confined Blacks seeking housing to these three areas. As a result, racial tensions increased many-fold during the late 1960s as the Jewish population left its traditional neighborhoods, often selling their homes at below-market value. The incoming African Americans often bought these homes at high interest rates. Integration was not accomplished. This pattern was repeated in many urban areas around the country.

WHY DO THESE OPPRESSIVE CONDITIONS AND CIRCUMSTANCES PERSIST?

The Legacy of Slavery

Perhaps it is not necessary to point out that the slave trade was conducted over a 250-year period in this country and lasted even beyond the Civil War. The mortality rate for African American slaves was enormous. Curtin (1969) has estimated conservatively that 10 million African captives died in the slave boat trips from Africa or at various stages of their captivity.

Huggins (1990) hauntingly described the brutal process of enslavement that developed into one of the most profoundly totalitarian systems of control in history. African Americans had no rights. Men, women, and children could be sold away from their mates or parents at any time at the whim or economic need of their owners. This inhumanity was rationalized by the notion that slaves did not have the deeper feelings of attachment that whites were assumed to have. (See Thomas Jefferson's 1787 rationalization of slavery to a French nobleman in *Notes on the State of Virginia*.)

Movements of African Americans were strictly monitored, and among Whites a constant state of fear of African American revolutionary activity existed, despite the deep-set idea that African Americans were docile and even liked the dependency of slavery. Well-documented extremes of torture were applied to any who seemed defiant of the system, and medicine even provided a diagnostic category—*drapetomania*—for those slaves "crazy" enough to try to escape (Proctor, 1988). The education of an African American was illegal, and was considered one of the most treasonous acts for a European American person to allow. African Americans' physiological and psychological alertness had to be inordinately focused on the feelings, needs, and authority of European Americans.

Although slavery ended formally with the Civil War, African Americans continued to live in terror and degradation, enforced by lynching and burnings. By the time of World War I, over 1,000 lynchings had been documented in this country (Franklin, 1969). Despite innumerable brutalities, Carter's (1991) observation that in the entire history of the country, no European American has ever received capital punishment for the murder of a African American speaks volumes about the inequities of the criminal justice system in this country.

The nation and the world watched in astonishment and horror during the 1950s and 1960s as the naked power of Southern cities and towns used police and fire departments to suppress the aspirations of African Americans to have even the most basic of rights. Was it not for the media presence, the bloodshed would have been enormous.

Racism as Traumatic Stress

Establishing the continuity between the slavery/segregation past and the current political and social climate raises the following obvious question: Why does racism continue? The answer to that question is as important to the understanding of PTSD among Black Americans as the discovery of a virus is to an infectious disease. Racism is the ideological foundation for excessive stress in the lives of African Americans, which remains deeply ingrained in the American psyche, and has been relatively untouched by the legal changes to date.

The ideology of racism arose to rationalize the perpetual enslavement of human beings. Historian Franklin (1969) has extensively reviewed the elaboration of the ideology of racism, and Kovel (1971) has extensively discussed the intrapsychic nature of racist thinking from a psychoanalytic perspective. Pinderhughes (1979, 1986) has written extensively of projective mechanisms involved in racial stereotyping. Horsman (1981) thoroughly documented the rise in the belief in Anglo-Saxon superiority during the 19th century, a belief that was held throughout the country and that justified openly genocidal policies towards Native Americans and people of color in other lands. At the heart of this ideology was the belief in African inferiority.

Essentially, the ideology of racism allowed European Americans to dehumanize the African slaves. Scholars like Thomas Jefferson attributed to Blacks characteristics of low intelligence, low morality, incapacity for independence or self-governance, sexual depravity and incapacity for human relationships, docility, and so forth (See Jefferson's *Notes on the State of Virginia*).[1] These attributions permitted not only the enslavement of these human beings, but also numbed European Americans to the untold suffering that they were inflicting on the African captives and many generations of African Americans since.

The term *ideology of racism* implies a conscious, deliberately held set of systematic beliefs. Using a term like "numbing" suggests an additional "deeper" intrapsychic phenomenon. Consciously fabricated racist ideology

---

[1]On this subject, see also Woodson and Wesley, 1966 and Kovel, 1971.

shifted over generations to become resident in the internal psychic structures of Americans of European descent, although obviously with wide individual variation. The debasement of the African therefore altered the internal operations of European American colonists; to put it differently, debasing Africans altered and inflated the self-image of European Americans.

Projective Identification

This reciprocal relationship between object and subject describes the psychological process, *projective identification (PI)*. This mechanism is an essential factor in understanding the development and persistence of racism. It has various definitions, and there is no universal agreement about its application. My preferred definition is that of Zinner and Shapiro (1972)

> [PI] is an activity of the ego, which among its effects, modifies perception of the object, and in a reciprocal fashion, alters the image of the self. These conjoined changes may in fact govern behavior of the self towards the object. (p. 524).

The authors (Zinner & Shapiro, 1972) provide four important corollaries of PI: (a) the subject's perception of the object as if the object contained aspects of the subject's personality; (b) that the subject can evoke behavior or feelings in the object that conform with the subject's perceptions; (c) that the subject can experience vicariously the activity and feelings of the object; and (d) that participants in close relationships are often in close collusion with one another to sustain mutual projections. Ogden (1982) discussed the mechanism extensively, and Bion (1959) observed the mechanism in group processes.

As slaves, Africans acquired "value" primarily as workers, which set some limits on the extent of murderous violence towards them because European Americans were initially materially dependent on the slave population. (In contrast, once it was determined that American Indians could not be enslaved, they were ruthlessly uprooted and subjected to genocidal policies.) Ideological and psychological dependency evolved over generations as African Americans increasingly became the receptacles of attributes unwanted in the ideal American image such as passivity, low intelligence, hypersexuality, criminality, and so on. African Americans became drawn into the most intimate aspects of European Americans' lives.

The writer Toni Morrison (1992) brilliantly described the dialectical relationship between the hypertrophied sense of freedom shared by European Americans and the simultaneous debasement of those of African descent in her work *Playing in The Dark*. This dialectic speaks to a reciprocal projective process that could not be corrected because of the massive power disparity between European Americans and African Americans.

The Badness of Blackness

The "badness of blackness" became and remains a unifying and organizing theme or principle in the psychic lives of Americans of European decent. The projection of bad traits to African Americans seems to be at least one factor that has allowed Europeans of diverse and conflicting backgrounds to come together peacefully as "one nation indivisible." Class and caste divisions within this population have been muted relatively successfully by the African American presence, to which European Americans on even the lowest rungs of the socioeconomic ladder can favorably compare themselves and assign blame for their own ills (Morrison, 1992).

This interracial dynamic is not simply a delusional process as in pure projection. It is an interactive dynamic, enforced by the immense relative power held by Americans of European descent who, by overt means of terror (e.g., Rodney King beating) or through massive withholding of supports can effect changes in the African American population that appear to further justify the negative projections.

This is what is so alarming about the trauma-producing urban violence rate; rather than empathy and truly corrective actions, repressive measures (like imprisonment) are far more popular than constructive preventive measures, even though the cost of the law enforcement approach alone is in all aspects catastrophic. California, for example, will spend more on prisons in 1995 than for its two university systems (Butterfield, April 1995). Many psychiatrists recently received an upbeat letter from the federal prison system seeking job applicants for what was advertised as a growth industry. The increase in imprisonment rates will be costly in human financial terms: 50% of those expanding numbers are going to be people of color, and it is $25,000 per year to maintain minimum living standards for each imprisoned individual in these facilities. (Kerr, 1993; Reidy, 1993).

SELECTED DIAGNOSTIC AND TREATMENT CONSIDERATIONS

The Complexities of PTSD Treatment

"Putting the past behind" is the fervent goal of most individuals who have experienced a traumatic event, and African Americans are no exception. It might be said that collectively, African Americans have demonstrated considerable resilience in adapting to chronic untoward stress, including a repeatedly demonstrated capacity to sublimate and channel energies in positive directions.

The primary symptoms of PTSD, such as hyperautonomicity, reexperiencing, avoidance, or numbing, may be obscured in Black Americans (as in other sufferers) by more chronic behavior and characterological efforts to allay unpleasant states. These reactions may include substance and alcohol abuse or lifestyle changes (e.g., constriction or danger-seeking behavior). The diagnostic process alone can require several, if not many, sessions. Treatment can extend for many months and years. Trauma victims, especially after experiencing human violence, are understandably reluctant to trust a therapist or a therapeutic process requiring the direct recollection and examination of the very event that has been the source of such pain, terror, and helplessness, feelings that are all too easily reexperienced even years after the event. Counterdependency is common, and patients often take breaks from treatment, to the frustration of many therapists; these breaks often occur just at the times when one would expect the client to have the most need of therapeutic support.

These factors, along with others (such as lower financial status), can combine to make the treatment course of PTSD complicated and taxing for the therapist, which can result in countertransference feelings being evoked. These feelings in the long-term treatment of the chronic PTSD sufferer who has undergone reactive characterologic changes are the "meat" of the therapy, but can destroy the therapy if the clinician is not able to understand his own distress and apply its meaning to the patient's history. For African American clients who suffer from PTSD, the burden of race is superimposed at three levels of clinical assessment concern: (a) the patient's development prior to the trauma, (b) the traumatic incident, and (c) and the posttraumatic adaptation.

Racial Considerations in Treatment

When treatment involves a cross-racial interaction (e.g., European American therapist with African American patient), particular treatment-threatening stresses are expectable, which this section will address. (The reader will also be referred to other salient resources.) This is not to suggest that similar issues do not arise when African Americans treat other African Americans, but the likelihood of cross-racial misunderstanding is considerably lessened.

Penk and Allen (1991) strongly urged the development of racially integrated clinical settings for the effective treatment of African Americans and other minority clients. The therapy office is not a separate world, and the degree of integration of the clinic setting and the morale of that setting is something that an African American client with PTSD would notice. In fact, in my experience, PTSD sufferers (regardless of racial/ethnic backgrounds) are generally hyperaware of problematic clinical settings; African

Americans are certainly congizant of the racial and ethnic diversity among staff, whether or not they spontaneously express those impressions.

I have witnessed considerable overt and covert prejudice in a number of clinical settings; thus an underpinning of this section is that the same projective dynamic discussed in broader societal terms will operate in the clinical setting without active steps being taken to prevent it. These instances of ongoing situations of pervasive prejudice have included the antagonism toward Vietnam veterans who were characterized en masse as "losers", "hippies", or drug addicts during the early 1970s.

I have worked in clinics in which clients came from varied socioeconomic backgrounds, and very often, those from lower economic status were misdiagnosed and undertreated. I have witnessed the inappropriate labeling of African Americans as "entitled" or shunted away from "real" psychotherapy for reasons outside of their clinical needs. I have seen tearful African American men surrounded by security guards who were called in by clinicians who misdiagnosed their patients as paranoid and dangerous. I have also seen African American (and European American veterans also) almost castigated in clinical teaching conferences as passive–dependent and essentially "weak" of character. Lastly, I have seen, during the early days of my career, the reality of abuse towards children and women either totally denied treatment or minimized in importance.

These and many other experiences have informed me that diagnostic and treatment problems with African American patients are common, and may be especially so for those with PTSD and adjustment reactions. Problems associated with traumatic events increase the likelihood that conflicts endemic in the broader society will be reenacted in the clinical setting, either retraumatizing the patient or at least adding to his or her disillusionment. When combat veterans were met with hostility by Veterans Administration staff, they often reacted in ways that could then be labeled inappropriate, and the veterans, as a result, could not negotiate the system well or withdrew in frustration from the services to which they were entitled.

African Americans often experience hostile treatment, although sometimes more subtly expressed. The essence of prejudice is that all individuals are categorized by one negative description; the uniqueness of each client is thus lost. As Vietnam Era veterans were after the war, African American clients can be readily blamed for inappropriate behavior that in fact may be reactive to real or perceived slights.

African Americans represent a diverse group, not a monolithic group with uniform cultural characteristics. When present in integrated settings with enough numbers to form a "critical mass," African Americans may join together in what appears to be a unified cultural group, as combat troops did when they contrived unique handshakes, hairstyles, and so on.

This kind of group reaction usually arouses much consternation among those in authority, who typically take actions that further indicate to African Americans that there is a need to unify. The badness of blackness as a unifying theme for European Americans may provoke reactive unified responses among African Americans who actually come from very different backgrounds. My sense is that unified group responses may not simply be contrived reactions to the perceived oppressive presence of European Americans, but may also represent the awakening of African cultural traits from disparate groups.

African Americans come from rural and urban settings; they may live in communities that are integrated or entirely African American. Wide socioeconomic variations are now present, and these variations may occur within the same family system. A physician or professor may have a sibling or parents who are living on the margins of life. Tremendous migrations have occurred within this country during this century as African Americans have sought better lives away from the oppression in the South, although that trend is reversing recently. Many children who grow up in inner cities may spend their vacations visiting relatives in the deep South.

Included in the African American population are immigrants of African descent from the Caribbean, South America, and Africa. These people bring very different cultural styles that may be perplexing to the clinician unaware of the diversity of the African American population. Unexpected cultural differences include attitudes about psychotherapy and divulgence of personal concerns to strangers, and the holding of traditional views of healing mental and physical illness. Also, immigrants from Africa and the African diaspora may have adopted styles and manners of the colonizing countries that controlled their homelands. Attitudes about race and color may vary, with many immigrants of African descent having very complicated racial views. Furthermore, many of these immigrants have experienced trauma in their homelands or during their travels, and many, such as the Haitians, have certainly experienced significant trauma since arrival.

The Complexities of Diagnosis

Accurate diagnosis of African Americans has been highly problematic, as was pointed out by Adebimpe (1981). Recent articles by Worthington (1992) and Jenkins-Hall and Sacco (1991) confirm the persistence of this problem. Various factors, including prejudice, have been cited as possible causes. PTSD was a new diagnosis when Adebimpe first discussed this issue; I now wonder if PTSD and related stress factors account for some diagnostic error. PTSD can present in dramatic ways that mimic psychosis symptoms such as dissociative phenomena, behavioral hyperactivity, and social withdrawal.

Grier and Cobbs (1968) and Carter (1974) discussed the *black mask* appearance presumably "worn" or "put on" by many African American clients in the presence of European American professionals. Majors and Billson (1992) have more recently described the historical necessity for African Americans, especially men, to use a variety of "masks" for both intrapsychic protection and conveyance of a certain image to a dangerous world. African Americans historically have had every reason to be wary of self-disclosure with European Americans. The White therapist must be aware that either an extremely blunted or hyperactive appearance may say as much about the Black client's interactions with the clinician as about the clinician's basic diagnosis.

Herman's discussion of *complex PTSD*, (1992) or PTSD in those who have sustained abuse, stirs important questions relevant to understanding of African American patients. All of the factors of extreme political and social oppression have been in force until the very recent past. More recently, the politics of deprivation have created traumatogenic life circumstances in which disproportionate numbers of African Americans act out against each other, especially in male-to-female violence and youth violence.

My opinion is that considerable thought ought to be given to an expanded application of adjustment disorder and PTSD diagnostic categories as these can be applied to African American clients, including diagnoses made for compensation purposes (VA and social security). Due caution must be given, as pointed out by Herman (1992), that diagnostic labeling not have a "blaming-the-victim" effect. Framing initial treatment in terms of stress rather than on more internalized conflicts and character traits seems ultimately less victim-blaming and also allows for the possibility of a short-term goal-oriented alliance.

A direct implication of the PTSD/adjustment reaction diagnosis for African Americans is that appropriate therapist activity is indicated. The principle of therapist "neutrality" has been, in my experience, taken to mean silence and distance deliberately maintained by the clinician. PTSD patients need active empathy-driven involvement by the therapist. Poussaint (1980) has correctly noted that African American clients do not respond favorably to the neutrality stance. African Americans historically have experienced denial of services, detachment, and lack of interest or empathy in a variety of public and professional settings, including medical and mental health facilities; the initial wariness of these clients may be better addressed and reassured by appropriate therapist activity rather than by compulsive adoption of a style that may work for only a few patients of any race or diagnosis.

Integrating the African American Experience in PTSD Therapy

Daily Struggles

The experiences of those who suffer from PTSD, especially those whose trauma is the result of human behavior, can be excruciating for the therapist's system of values and trust. Therapists, like the PTSD sufferers, at times hope for short cuts without repeatedly "dredging up" the trauma. This seems to be especially so in cross-cultural or cross-racial therapy alliances (Parson, 1990). African Americans' lives, let alone traumatic experiences, may stir strong disturbing feelings in European therapists who may, for instance, learn that institutions that they trust are experienced very differently by their clients. This is similar to therapists who appropriately have strong reactions to veterans' stories of atrocities or officer misconduct. Distancing oneself from this kind of material or becoming overactive and interpretive are two common responses.

When disturbing material emerges in therapy, it is often accompanied by agitation or other symptomatology in the patient; thus, relational problems may also become more severe. Inappropriate use of medication may even occur at such a time—a major issue for African American clients who may see medication as a form of political control. Lastly, one of the most difficult areas for clinician restraint is allowing the patient to resolve at his or her own pace relationship problems that appear to be destructive. PTSD sufferers, if they have intimate relationships at all, frequently are engaged in and profoundly dependent on relationships that in fact seem to add to symptomatology rather than providing a safe haven.

Substance Abuse

The treatment of substance abuse and alcoholism is an integral part of PTSD treatment. Excessive use of alcohol may develop quickly after traumatic occurrences. Carter (1982) linked alcoholism to combat stress. Schneider, Greenberg, & Chol (1992) reported that a poll of over 300 African American health and political officials ranked alcoholism and substance abuse as the number one public health priority for this population. These problems require persistent educational and supportive involvement by the therapist who must be able to point out patiently how these patterns destructively affect the patient's life. Psychotherapists must also collaborate with primary care medical providers. PTSD clients often have accompanying medical illness that can be of life-threatening urgency (e.g., cardiovascular problems, hypertension, or gastrointestinal problems).

Shame and Guilt

PTSD patients invariably have powerful feelings of guilt and shame and, as a result, an overactive and brutal superego that is hypersensitive to outsiders—including therapists—who may seem to stand in harsh judgment of them. As long as a therapist stays deliberately on the side of the patient's ego capacity, the alliance can withstand confrontations during the months and even years such a therapy may require. Therapist activity based on the message "this behavior is destructive to your best interests" is much more conducive to long-term improvement than interventions that send the message "you're bad."

Avoiding sending judgmental and negative messages is extremely important in working with African American clients, especially youth who may almost deliberately adopt an antisocial facade under stressful circumstances. When Allen and colleagues (Allen, Brown, Jackson, & Lewis, 1977) examined the stresses of African American school children during Boston's 1974 school integration crisis, African American teenagers were seen during the first month to adopt defiant, belligerent stances that were most evident against the very African American adults who were their only allies. Moreover, several would even say, just as I often have heard combat veterans say, "I don't care whether I live or die." Black children from South Boston High were then treated by school administrators and police as if they were antisocial—not stressed and frightened—and they were treated punitively. This antisocial-facade mechanism is more broadly used by stress-weary youth who live in chronic life conditions of deprivation and stress, and can lead eventually to characterological changes (Prothrow-Stith, 1991). These changes would then include the typical PTSD signs such as lack of belief in a normal life span, constriction of activities and interests, and hyperarousal.

Group and Community Approaches

Whereas individual therapy is a basic modality in PTSD treatment along with medical treatments and behavior modification approaches to reduce stress responses, group therapies may have considerable and perhaps primary usefulness as a treatment modality for African Americans with PTSD. Prothrow-Stith's (1991) book contains many approaches to prevention of violence in urban neighborhoods that could readily be modified to include ongoing group therapy. Parson (1984b) discussed psychodynamic group therapy with combat veterans, as did Reid (1992) with African American combat veterans. Dyson (1992) reported the effectiveness of individual therapy with traumatized inner-city youth, but I wonder whether establishing a broader sense of trust and connectedness to the community can be accomplished equally well through a group process. I also wonder about groups that include different ages, given the fact that so many youths grow up in homes without fathers or with parents unavailable because of excessive work demands.

I propose that such therapy groups include a historical focus, both from the standpoint of general African American history, and from the biography of older members. Many youths have no awareness that events on the urban streets today have historical continuity with a violent overtly anti-Black past.

There is a growing number of references available for clinicians concerning treatment issues with African American patients. Elaine Pinderhughes (1989) has thoroughly discussed the interrelated issues of race, culture, and ethnicity. She has called for each clinician to confront his or her own ethnicity as the means to attain empathy and understanding of those from different cultures. She has also provided detailed suggestions for interactive workshops that are based on the assumption that clinicians' development of a cross-cultural capacity is an experiential process as well as an intellectual one.

Parson (1990) provided additional provocative ideas about the treatment of PTSD in African American combat veterans. His thoughts are also pertinent, in my opinion, to psychotherapy of African American civilians with PTSD. A broad range of subjects related to the stresses endured by African American individuals and families has been provided by Coner-Edwards and Spurlock (1988), Spurlock and Norris (1991), and Jones (1991).

SUGGESTIONS FOR RESEARCH AND CLOSING REMARKS

I have proposed in this chapter that the adverse sociopolitical climate of American life very likely accounts for the probable higher incidence and impact of PTSD on African Americans, and I have further suggested that the adverse climate is governed by the operation of a projective identification process. This proposition introduces several areas for further research on African Americans and PTSD.

African Americans are a Heterogenous Population

One needed research area is the subgroups that make up this population. For example, a comparative study of groups from the Caribbean Islands would be useful, especially those from Haiti. Haitians experience trauma in their country, trauma on the high seas, and disillusionment in this country after "safe" arrival. Although there are vast historical and experiential differences among Blacks, all of the studies cited in this article refer to "African Americans" as though this label defines a homogeneous population. Researchers would do well to attempt to describe the specifics of the African American population included in their studies. (This also may be a valid suggestion for other groups typically lumped together.)

Also, consider the civilian study by Norris in which European Americans reported a surprisingly higher (19% to 12%) traumatic event incidence than African Americans. Researchers should attend to differences between how these two broad groupings may vary in how questions about trauma are interpreted, and how they may have a demonstrably different threshold for defining trauma (e.g., possibly because of race-related birth-to-death vicissitudes, African Americans' trauma threshold may be higher).

Comparisons of African Americans across class boundaries would also be useful. One interest might be in examining PTSD rates among African Americans in lower, middle, and upper-class strata. If differences are found, are they as robust as those differences among different classes of European Americans? It is my guess that the marginality and conditionality of African American life extends throughout all socioeconomic strata, and I predict increased vulnerability to PTSD among African Americans.

PTSD and African Americans

Many other questions for research are prompted by the present work. Can the incidence of stress and PTSD in African Americans be studied clinically in reference to the diagnostic problems with African American patients? Can psychological as well as physiological factors be shown to influence the occurrence of diagnostic errors? Can the hypothesis that race-based projective mechanisms operate to maintain the historically conflicted relationship between African Americans and European Americans be studied?

Although additional PTSD studies on the African American population are indicated, can the European American population be studied? Why do these projective mechanisms develop and persist? Can European Americans respond to questions that evaluate their first awareness of racism in their parents, themselves, and their communities? Was this initial awareness disillusioning, or even traumatic? How does class affect views of race?

Ethnocentricism in Psychiatry and Mental Health Professions

Rugged individualism is a key element in American mythology, and is especially emphasized in male development. Taken to extreme expression, individualism and independence seem antithetical to universal human dependency/relational needs. Is this American ideal of adult development so psychologically burdensome to European Americans that its opposites—dependency and inadequacy—must be split off and projected to the African American collective? Can this be studied in a scholarly manner?

Can European American therapists and analysts who do intensive psychotherapy and analysis with European American patients shed some definitive light on the nature of their patients' usage of African Americans in their content and associations? Can biofeedback studies of physiological arousal patterns be devised that test the arousal patterns occurring during various interracial interactions? Is there a dissociative phenomenon that frequently occurs in interracial relations or conflicts? Again, the rationale for these kinds of studies by PTSD researchers is that relationships governed by projective identification can become violent when gross power disparities exist and corrective interaction is prevented.

A Time for New Thinking

It seems to me that the interrelated problems of race, poverty, sexism, violence, and trauma have reached heights in this country that justify the existence of a think tank that would have several purposes; One aim would be to analyze research that has already addressed some of the questions raised in this chapter but remains scattered, unpublicized, and unanalyzed by a consortium of researchers. Another purpose would be to promote future research on those issues fundamentally related to high incidence of PTSD. Also, a very important aim would be to disseminate important findings so as to better inform an American population that remains profoundly ignorant of the dimensions of these problems and, therefore, profoundly vulnerable to stereotypical fears that can be manipulated and exploited. Such a think tank also could be useful in an advisory capacity on matters such as urban violence and the long-term effects of PTSD. Lastly, such a think tank could provide advocacy and consultative support for those "front-line" people and agencies who are so often underfunded and underappreciated.

I have become aware during the past year that the community of trauma clinicians and researchers is not immune to the racial "blind spots" in the broader society. Recently, I expressed my deep disappointment (Allen, 1993) that in reading a definitive, much-needed work on trauma (Herman, 1992), I found that the element of race was completely excluded. It is not possible to understand the violence against women in this society without considering race. One justification for the subjugation of European American women has been their presumed need for protection from the African American man (see Kovel's *The Fantasies of Race*, 1995). I am concerned that researchers also may avoid specific focus on interracial factors.

The interpretation of findings pertinent to race is as important as the data collection. My concern is that trauma researchers may feel (or be) vulnerable to political influences if their findings are politically troublesome. The NVVRS study may be an example; although African Americans had a much higher exposure to combat rate, the most widely remembered bit of data might be the nonsignificant PTSD rate difference between African Americans and European Americans—primarily the result, as I understand it, of tiers of statistical controls.

Race permeates any subject related to trauma in American society; domestic violence against women, weapons control, health care, and so forth. The presence of African Americans in this country, as a group feared yet depended on, has predisposed this country to enormous internal conflict obscured by race. The conflict is intensified because the treatment of African Americans has been in violation of fundamental principles of human freedom, dignity, and opportunity.

Cornel West (1993) has written of nihilism among oppressed Black Americans

> Nihilism is to be understood here not as philosophic doctrine. . . . It is, far more, the lived experience of coping with a life of horrifying meaninglessness, hopelessness, and (most important) lovelessness. The frightening result is a numbing detachment from others and a self-destructive disposition toward the world. (p. 23)

West described a major feature of the PTSD complex, and this feature can be generalized to the life struggle of many African Americans. I believe trauma research has a place in examining this conflict. It is essential for PTSD researchers, programs and facilities to be integrated with African Americans, Native Americans, Hispanics, Asians, and other peoples of color so this subject can be pursued with sensitivity, insight, and boldness.

REFERENCES

Adebimpe, V. R. (1981). Overview: White norms and psychiatric diagnosis of Black patients. *American Journal of Psychiatry, 138*, 279–285.

Allen, I. M., Brown, J. L., Jackson, J. & Lewis, R. (1977). Psychological stress of young Black children as a result of school desegregation. *Journal of the American Academy of Child Psychiatry, 16*, 739–747.

Allen, I. M. (1986). Post-traumatic stress disorder among Black Vietnam veterans. *Hospital and Community Psychiatry, 37*, 55–61.

Allen, I. M. (1993, February). *PTSD: Are we Blacks invisible in this syndrome too?* Speech delivered at Judge Baker Guidance Center, Boston, Massachusetts.

Bell, C. C., & Chance-Hill, G. (1991). Treatment of violent families. *Journal of the National Medical Association, 83*, 203–208.

Bell, C. C., & Jenkins, E. J. (1991). Traumatic stress and children. *Journal of Health Care for the Poor and Underserved, 2*, 175–184.

Bion, W. R. (1959). *Experiences in groups.* New York: Basic Books.

Brenner, M.H. (1976). Estimating the social costs of national economic policy: Implications for mental and physical health and criminal aggression. *Joint*

Economic Committee of the Congress of the United States, Paper #5. Washington, DC: U.S. Government Printing Office.

Butterfield, F. (1995, April 12). New prisons case shadow over higher education. *The New York Times*, p. 21.

Butterfield, F. (1995, October 5). More Blacks in their 20's have trouble with the law. *The New York Times*, p. A-18.

Carter, J. H. (1974). Recognizing psychiatric symptoms in Black Americans. *Geriatrics, 29*, 95–99.

Carter, J. H. (1982). Alcoholism in Black Vietnam veterans: Symptoms of post-traumatic stress disorder. *Journal of the National Medical Association, 74*, 655–660.

Carter, S. L. (1991). *Reflections of an affirmative action baby*. New York: Basic Books.

Centers for Disease Control (1991). Homicide among young Black males — United States, 1978–1989. *Journal of the American Medical Association, 265(2)*, 183–184.

Coner-Edwards, A. F., & Spurlock, J. (1988). *Black families in crisis*. New York: Brunner/Mazel.

Curtin, P. D. (1969). *The Atlantic slave trade*. Madison: University of Wisconsin Press.

Dyson, J. L. (1992). The effects of family violence on children's academic performance and behavior. *Journal of the National Medical Association, 84*, 17–22.

Egendorf, A., Kadushin, C., Laufer, R., Rothbart, G., & Sloan, L. (1981). *Legacies of Vietnam: Comparative adjustment of veterans and their peers, Vols. 1–5*. Washington, DC: U.S. Government Printing Office.

Eisenhart, R. (1975). You can't hack it, little girl. *Journal of Social Issues, 31*, 13–23.

Fitzpatrick, K. M. & Boldizar, J. P. (1993). The prevalence and consequences of exposure to violence among African American youth. *Journal of Child and Adolescent Psychiatry, 32*, 424–430.

Franklin, J. H. (1969). *From slavery to freedom*. New York: Vintage Books.

Friedman, M. J. (1991). Biological approaches to the diagnosis and treatment of post-traumatic stress disorder. *Journal of Traumatic Stress, 4*, 67–91.

Gleser, G., Green, B. L., & Winget, C. (1981). *Prolonged psychosocial effects of disaster: A study of Buffalo Creek*. New York: Academic Press.

Goff, S., Sanders, R., & Smith, C. (1982). *Black soldiers in "The Nam."* Harrisburg, PA: Stackpole.

Green, B., Lindy, J., Grace, M., Gleser, G. C., et al. (1990). Buffalo Creek survivors in the second decade: Stability of stress symptoms. *American Journal of Orthopsychiatry, 60*, 43–54.

Green, B.L., Grace, M.D., Lindy, J. D., & Leonard, A. C. (1990). Race differences in response to combat stress. *Journal of Traumatic Stress, 3*, 379–393.

Grier, W., & Cobbs, P. (1968). *Black rage*. New York: Bantam Books.

Group for the Advancement of Psychiatry (1982). *Job loss — a psychiatric perspective*. Prepared by the Committee on Psychiatry in Industry. New York: GAP /Mental Health Materials Center.

Hacker, A. (1992). *Two nations*. New York: Charles Scribner Sons.

Haley, S. (1985). Some of my best friends are dead: Treatment of the post-traumatic stress disorder patient and his family. *Family Systems Medicine*, *3*, 17–26.

Herman, J. L. (1992). Complex PTSD: A syndrome in survivors of prolonged and repeated trauma. *Journal of Traumatic Stress, 5*, 377–391.

Herman, J. L. (1992). *Trauma and recovery*. New York: Basic Books.

History shows trends of African Americans' high mortality rates and poor health care. (1993, March/April). *National Medical Association News* (March/April). pp. 1, 8.

Horsman, R. (1981). *Race and manifest destiny*. Cambridge, MA: Harvard University Press.

Huggins, N. I. (1990). *Black odyssey*. New York: Vintage Books.

Hutchinson, J. (1992). AIDS and racism in America. *Journal of the National Medical Association, 84*, 119–124.

Jefferson, Thomas. (1787/1984) *Notes on the state of Virginia. Thomas Jefferson's writings* (pp. 123–326). New York: Literary Classics of the U.S.

Jenkins-Hall, K., & Sacco, W. D. (1991). Effect of client race and depression on evaluations by White therapists. *Journal of Social & Clinical Psychology, 10*, 322–333.

Johnson, P. A., Lee, T. H., Cook, E. F., Roman, G. W., & Goldman, L. (1993). Effect of race on the presentation and management of patients with acute chest pain. *Annals of Internal Medicine, 118*, 593–601.

Johnson, T. A. (1968). Negroes in "The Nam." *Ebony Magazine, 33* (10), 33–40.

Jones, J. H., (1981). *Bad blood*. New York: Free Press.

Jones, R. L. (Ed.) (1991). *Black psychology*. Berkeley, CA: Cobbs and Henry.

Kasiske, B. L., Neylan, J. F., III, Riggio, R. R., Danovich, G. M., Kahana, L., Alexander, S. R., White, M. G. (1991). The effect of race on access and outcome in transplantation. *New England Journal of Medicine, 324*(5), 302–307.

Kardiner, A., & Ovesey, L. (1966). *The mark of oppression*. New York: Meridan Books.

Kerr, P. (1993, June 27). The detoxifying of prisoner 88A0802. *The New York Times Magazine*, p. 23.

Kovel, J. (1971). *White racism: A psychohistory*. New York: Vintage Books.

Kozol, J. (1991). *Savage inequalities: Children in America's school's*. New York: Crown.

Kulka, R. A., Schlenger, W. E., Fairbank, J. A., Hough, R. L., Jordan, B. K., Marmar, C. R., & Weiss, D. S. (1990). *Trauma and the Vietnam war generation*. New York: Brunner/Mazel.

Laufer, R. S., Brett, E., & Gallops, M. S. (1985). Dimensions of post-traumatic stress disorder among Vietnam veterans. *Journal of Nervous and Mental Disease*, *173*, 538–545.

Levine, H., & Harmon, L. (1992). *The death of an American Jewish community*. New York: Free Press.

Lonigan, C. J., Shannon, M. P., Finch, A. J., Jr., Daugherty, T. F., & Taylor, C. M. (1991). Children's reactions to a natural disaster: Symptom severity and degree of exposure. *Advances in Behavioral Research and Therapy*, *13*, 135–154.

Majors, R., & Billson, J.M. (1992). *Cool pose*. New York: Simon and Schuster.

Marantz, S. (1989, January 11). Inequities are cited in hub mortgages. *The Boston Globe*. 1:1.

Morrison, T. (1992). *Playing in the dark*. Cambridge, MA: Harvard University Press.

Nobles, W. (1991). African philosophy: Foundations of black psychology. In R. Jones (Ed.). *Black psychology* (pp. 47–63). Berkeley, CA: Cobbs & Henry.

Norris, F. H. (1992). Epidemiology of trauma: Frequency and impact of different, potentially traumatic events on different demographic groups. *Journal of Consulting and Clinical Psychology*, *60*, 409–418.

Ogden, T. (1982). *Projective identification and the therapeutic technique*. Northvale, NJ: Jason Aronson.

Parson, E. R. (1984a). The gook-identification syndrome and post-traumatic stress disorders in Black Vietnam veterans. *The Black Psychiatrists of America Quarterly*, *13*, 14–18.

Parson, E. R. (1984b). The role of psychodynamic group therapy in the treatment of the combat veteran. In H. Schwartz (Ed.). *Psychotherapy of the combat veteran* (pp. 253–220). New York: Medical and Scientific Books.

Parson, E. R. (1985). The intercultural setting: Encountering Black Vietnam veterans. In S. Sonnenberg, A. Blank, & J. Talbott (Eds.). *The trauma of war: Stress and recovery in Vietnam veterans* (pp. 361–387). Washington, DC: American Psychiatric Press.

Parson, E. R. (1990). Post-traumatic psychocultural therapy (PTpsyCT): Integration of trauma and shattering social labels of the self. *Journal of Contemporary Psychotherapy*, *20*, 237–258.

Penk, W. E., Robinowitz, R., Dolan, M. P., Dorsett, D., Narga, L. & Black, V. (1985). *Ethnic difference in personality adjustment of Black and White male Vietnam combat veterans seeking treatment for substance abuse*. Paper presented at the 93rd Annual Meeting of the American Psychological Association, Los Angeles.

Penk, W. E., Robinowitz, R., Black, J., Dolan, M. D., Bell, W., Dorsett, D., Ames, M. & Noriega, L. (1989). Ethnicity: Post-traumatic stress disorder (PTSD) differences among Black, White, and Hispanic veterans who differ in degree of exposure to combat in Vietnam. *Journal of Clinical Psychology, 45,* 729–735.

Penk, W. E., & Allen, I. M. (1991). Clinical assessment of post-traumatic stress disorder among American minorities who served in Vietnam. *Journal of Traumatic Stress, 4,* 41–66.

Pinderhughes, C. A. (1979). Differential bonding: Toward a psychophysiological theory of stereotyping. *American Journal of Psychiatry, 2,* 5–14.

Pinderhughes, C. A. (1986). Paired differential bonding in biological, psychological, and social systems. *American Journal of Social Psychiatry, 2,* 5–14.

Pinderhughes, E. (1989). *Understanding race, ethnicity and power.* New York: Free Press.

Poussaint, A. F. (1980). Interracial relations and psychiatry. In A. Freedman, H. Kaplan, & B. Saddock, (Eds.). *Comprehensive textbook of psychiatry.* Baltimore, MA: Williams & Wilkins.

Proctor, R. N. (1988). *Racial hygiene: Medicine under the Nazis.* Cambridge, MA: Harvard University Press.

Prothrow-Stith, D. (1991). *Deadly consequences.* New York: Harper Perennial.

Reid, G. (1992). Clinical issues in a Black veterans group. *Vet Center Voice, 13*(3), 6–10.

Reidy, C. (1993, June 27). It costs to lock 'em up. *The Boston Globe,* p. 1.

Rosenheck, R., & Nathan, P. (1985). Secondary traumatization in children of Vietnam veterans. *Hospital and Community Psychiatry, 36,* 538–539.

Schneider, D., Greenberg, M. R., & Chol, D. (1992). Violence as a public health priority for Black Americans. *Journal of the National Medical Association, 84,* 843–848.

Shakoor, B. H., & Chalmers, D. (1991). Co-victimization of African American children who witness violence: Effects on emotional and behavioral development. *Journal of the National Medical Association, 84,* 837–840.

Smith, D. K. (1992). HIV disease as a cause of death for African Americans in 1987 and 1990. *Journal of the National Medical Association, 84,* 481–487.

Solkoff, N. (1992). Children of survivors of the Nazi holocaust: A critical overview of the literature. *American Journal of Orthopsychiatry, 62,* 342–358.

Spurlock, J., & Norris, D. M. (1991). The impact of culture and race on the development of African-Americans in the United States. In J. Oldham, A. Tasman, & S. Goldfinger (Eds.). *Review of Psychiatry, Volume 10* (pp. 594–607). Washington, DC: American Psychiatric Press.

Walker, B., Goodwin, N. J., & Warren, R. C. (1992). Violence: A challenge to the public health community. *Journal of the National Medical Association, 84,* 490–496.

West, C. (1993). *Race matters.* Boston, MA: Beacon Press.

Williams, C., & Williams, T. (1985). Family therapy for Vietnam veterans. In S. Sonnenberg, A. Blank, & J. Talbott (Eds.). *The trauma of war: Stress and recovery in Vietnam veterans* pp. 193–209. Washington, DC: American Psychiatric Press.

Woodson, C. G., & Wesley, C. H. (1966). *The Negro in our history.* Washington, DC: Associated Publishers.

Worthington, C. (1992). An examination of factors influencing the diagnosis and treatment of Black patients in the mental health system. *Archives of Psychiatric Nursing, 6,* 195–204.

Yager, T., & Laufer, R. (1984). Some problems associated with war experience in men of the Vietnam generation. *Archives of General Psychiatry, 41,* 327–333.

Zinner, J., & Shapiro, R. (1972). Projective identification as a mode of perception and behavior in families of adolescents. *International Journal of Psychoanalysis, 53,* 523–530.

9

CUMULATIVE TRAUMA AND PTSD IN AMERICAN INDIAN COMMUNITIES

ROBERT W. ROBIN, BARBARA CHESTER, and DAVID GOLDMAN

High rates of psychiatric disorder have been reported in many American Indian populations. Many of these disorders are found in various combinations (e.g., alcoholism and depression). It is often difficult to determine which comorbid disorder is the cause or precursor to the other or whether there is an underlying etiologic factor common to both.

Recent studies of non-Indian populations have shown associations between posttraumatic stress disorder (PTSD) and the psychiatric conditions of alcoholism, depression, and anxiety. These studies suggest that cumulative trauma and PTSD may be primary contributors to the development of other psychiatric disorders.

Since 1988, the Laboratory of Neurogenetics, National Institute of Alcoholism and Alcohol Abuse (NIAAA) has conducted studies in three North American Indian tribal communities to examine genetic and environmental contributors to alcoholism and other psychiatric disorders. While the NIAAA studies are ongoing, data from the Cheyenne Indian sample support and extend earlier findings of significantly higher rates of psychiatric disorder and comorbidity within American Indian populations as compared with non-Indian groups, including other ethnic minorities and impoverished groups.

Because of the reported high rates of trauma occurring in American Indian populations, we have recently begun to investigate the prevalence of PTSD and cumulative trauma in these three American Indian communities. This chapter will summarize what is known about the prevalence of psychopathology and multiple psychiatric disorders among American Indians, discuss how severe and cumulative trauma may be related or contribute to the occurrence of psychiatric disorders and clusters of psychiatric disorders, and discuss what steps are being taken to clarify these relationships.

PSYCHIATRIC DISORDERS AMONG AMERICAN INDIANS

The overall rate of lifetime psychiatric disorders in American Indian populations is substantial, estimated at between 20% and 63% of adult populations (McShane, 1987; Pelz, Merskey, Brant, Patterson, & Heseltine, 1981). Alcoholism and depression are reported to be the most commonly occurring psychiatric disorders among American Indians (Manson & Shore, 1981). Generally, psychiatric disorders appear to be more abundant in American Indians than among other minorities (Harris, 1968). Yet few studies investigating the relationship between substance abuse and psychiatric disorders have been conducted in American Indian populations (Westermeyer & Neider, 1984) and the occurrence of multiple psychiatric disorders within the same individual have not been adequately addressed (Robin et al., 1993).

In those studies that have been undertaken, subject populations have typically been inadequately described, or standardized measures for comparison across tribes have generally not been applied (Walker & Kivlahan, 1984). Cross-cultural factors reduce the validity of research on American Indians. For example, depression and schizophrenia may be overdiagnosed due to unfamiliarity with culture-specific mourning and grieving patterns and practices identified among several American Indian populations (Manson, Shore, & Bloom 1985; Pelz et al., 1981; Shen, 1986). Conversely, other disorders may be underreported, because of mistrust and misunderstanding (Rozynko & Ferguson, 1978; Ryan, 1979). These factors can be addressed by the participation of *culturally experienced* and local clinicians and interviewers (Manson, Shore, Bloom, Keepers, & Neligh 1987; Westermeyer, 1985).

All human cultures and societies have been found to have persons affected by depression and psychoses (Day et al., 1987; Marsella, 1980; World Health Organization, 1979). However, inherent within efforts to develop and use instruments with cross-cultural validity must be the recognition that assessment instruments and criteria are to some extent culture-bound. It is a fascinating but problematic aspect of cross-cultural studies that the context, frequency, and expression of psychiatric disorders vary across populations.

Currently, four epidemiological studies of psychiatric disorder have been conducted in American Indian populations. These studies were conducted in a Pacific Northwest Coast Village (Kinzie et al., 1992; Shore, Kinzie, Hampson, & Pattison, 1973), in 10 Saskatchewan reservations (Roy, Choudhuri, & Irvine, 1970), and in a Southern Baffin Island Native Alaskan settlement (Sampath, 1974). All of these studies indicated a greater prevalence of mental health problems in these communities than in non-Indian communities, even those in close geographical proximity to the groups being studied.

The most prevalent disorders—depression and adjustment reactions—were often seen in association with alcohol abuse (Manson & Shore, 1981). Other studies have indicated that prevalence estimates for depression and affective disorders in American Indians ranged from a high of 64% to a low of 14% (Bloom, 1972; Kinzie et al., 1992; Shore, Manson, Bloom, Keepers, & Neligh, 1987). In addition, studies of American Indians have suggested a relationship among alcoholism, depression, and other psychological factors, but little data is available (Hoffman & Jackson, 1973; Jones-Saumty, Hochhaus, Dru, & Zeiner, 1983).

Clustering of Alcoholism and Psychiatric Disorders in Cheyenne Indians

Findings have been reported from a total of 159 tribally enrolled Cheyenne Indians in Western and Central Oklahoma, who were aged 21 and older, and biologically related to one of five large Cheyenne families (Robin et al., 1993). A series of instruments was used, including a diagnostic interview—the Schedule for Affective Disorder and Schizophrenia (SADS-L; Spitzer & Endicott, 1978). The interview was administered either by a psychologist or by a clinically trained social worker, both with extensive clinical experience in American Indian communities. Interviews were blind-rated and data were separately analyzed across a subset of subjects who were not first degree relatives.

Data regarding comorbidity was striking (Robin et al., 1994). The risk for a Cheyenne alcoholic to develop a major lifetime psychiatric disorder was five times that of nonalcoholics. Specifically, an alcoholic had twice the risk of developing depression in his or her lifetime, and 10 times the risk of abusing drugs. Similar to other studies (Albaugh, & Washa, 1987), lifetime prevalence of alcoholism was 49% and 30% for depression. Alcoholics had high rates of psychiatric disorders (56%) and multiple major psychiatric disorders (20%) (Robin et al., 1993).

Interestingly, the largest group of nonalcoholics with a major psychiatric disorder was women with major depression. This finding remained constant when depressive episodes occurring in association with alcoholism were removed from the equation (Robin et al., 1993). Drug use disorder, anxiety disorder, and antisocial personality disorder also occurred significantly more frequently in alcoholics than in nonalcoholics.

The findings of this study (Robin et al., 1993) and others lead to some conclusions. In some American Indian communities where lifetime prevalence of substance abuse and mental health problems are high, more than half of the alcoholics are likely to develop at least one other major disorder, which is, most often, depression. The results indicating that major depression is found most often in nonalcoholic women are consistent with results of studies in non-Indian women (Baron, Manson, Ackerson, & Brenneman, 1990). This raises the possibility that environmental factors such as physical or sexual abuse may contribute with differential impact on men and women.

The issue of cause and effect pertaining to the relationship between alcoholism and other disorders (Schuckit, 1983) operates in American Indian communities like it does in other communities. The temporal sequence by which one disorder precedes another is sometimes unclear, particularly with disorders such as alcoholism, drug abuse, and depression, which can affect memory and concentration. It may be helpful, therefore, to examine specific factors that contribute to both the prevalence and relationship of these disorders. To clarify these relationships in American Indian communities, group-specific environmental and sociocultural factors need to be described and understood in a systematic way.

TRAUMA IN AMERICAN INDIAN POPULATIONS

There is good reason to postulate that both specific and cumulative trauma among American Indian people are significant contributory factors to high rates of alcoholism, drug abuse, and depression, and also to the relationships between these disorders. Evidence for these connections is found from three sources: studies of disorders that are comorbid with PTSD in non-Indian populations, suggestions that point to the existence of a specific traumatic depression, and data indicating high rates of physical and emotional trauma among American Indian people.

Studies of Comorbidity and PTSD

PTSD appears to be strongly related to substance abuse, anxiety, and depression—disorders with reported high rates of prevalence and comorbidity in studied American Indian communities. Upon reviewing several studies of high-risk cohorts, Davidson and Fairbank (1993) noted a high degree of comorbidity between PTSD and other disorders. Among three studies cited, rates of psychiatric disorders comorbid with PTSD ranged from 62 to 92%. A strong consistent relationship PTSD and anxiety disorders, depression or dysthymia, and substance abuse has been noted in the North Carolina and St. Louis ECA samples, (Weissman, Myers, & Ross, 1986), and the Mount St. Helens Study (Shore, Tatum, & Vollmer, 1986), although other disorders were also found to relate to PTSD.

Clinically identified severely traumatized individuals with PTSD also show a higher frequency of depression, anxiety, and substance abuse. Rates of concurrent major depressive disorder are 8 to 41% (Olivera & Fero, 1990). Green (1993) compared survivors of sexual assault with general population control groups and found that rates of comorbid major depression, alcohol and drug use, and phobia were significantly higher.

Solitary PTSD is rare among epidemiologically, clinically, or experimentally ascertained populations of Vietnam veterans (Kulka et al., 1988), battered women (Kemp, Rawlings, & Green, 1991), refugees (Garcia-Peltoniemi, 1991), and torture victims (Chester, 1994). After an exhaustive review of the literature, Green (1993) concluded that PTSD rarely occurred alone, and was most often comorbid with substance abuse, major depression, phobia, and generalized anxiety disorder. In addition, PTSD and associated problems tend to be long-lasting (Green, 1993).

There is little representation of American Indians among the epidemiologically or clinically based populations studied for PTSD (March, 1992; Maser & Dinges, 1993). The chapter by Manson et al. in this volume describes three ongoing studies of American Indian children and adolescents, as well as the first large-scale study of American Indian Vietnam Veterans. These studies and our ongoing NIAAA study of large families among three American Indian tribes will help elucidate the nature and extent of PTSD and comorbid conditions in American Indian communities.

Traumatic Depression

The issue of comorbidity raises several concerns about symptom clusters, including problems associated with a polythetic classification system (Maser & Dinges, 1993). Individuals, although diagnosed with the same condition, may have a vastly different symptom picture. However, it is possible that specific subconstellations of symptoms predict or account for the relationships among different disorders.

For example, Davidson and Fairbank (1993) noted:

> the possibility that there exists a subtype of depression following trauma ("posttraumatic depression") that differs in important ways from clinical major depression of non traumatic type. (p. 167).

However, if they are distinct, the subcategories of substance abuse and depression that are specifically associated with trauma remain to be defined.

Severe and Cumulative Trauma in American Indian Communities

Sociodemographic and mortality rates for American Indians reflect an astounding reality. American Indians have the highest infant mortality of any ethnic group in the United States, a rate of physical disability 4 to 6 times the national average, and out-of-home placements 5 to 20 times the national average. Almost three fourths of all American Indian households have a combined income that is below the federal poverty level for households of four or more, and a rate of suicide almost twice that of the US population in general (i.e. Blum, 1992; May, 1992, 1987; Robin, 1989).

At a time when the fastest growing part of the population cohort in the United States is over age 70, the average life expectancy for Native American people is under 50 years. For women, the situation is particularly alarming. American Indian women have a mortality rate 6 times higher for alcoholism, 3 times higher for homicide, 5 times higher for liver disease, and 3 times higher for motor vehicle accidents than women in the general US population (U.S. Department of Health and Human Sciences, 1988).

Within American Indian tribes, there are also large subpopulations that have experienced specific trauma. For example, since 1976, 921 off-reservation families in Coconino County in Northern Arizona have been traumatically displaced from homes in the former Navajo–Hopi Joint Use Area as a result of Public Law 93-531, the Navajo-Hopi Land Settlement Act (Navajo–Hopi Relocation Commission, 1993). These relocatees tend to be more traditional, lack cross-cultural skills, are less likely to speak English, and possess fewer employable skills than other reservation residents (Chester, Matalish, & Dans in press). Additionally, they are reported to experience high rates of symptoms indicative of depression, anxiety, and substance abuse. However, these symptoms may differ in important ways from similar symptoms that are experienced and expressed in groups of nontraumatized or traumatized but non-Indian people. For example, an elderly Navajo woman was relocated from her home which was in view of a mountain considered sacred to her people. Although her inability to sleep and loss of appetite were recognized as depressive symptoms, the cultural and spiritual basis of her loss are more indicative of a despair that is not easily described by Western systems of nomenclature or treated by normative psychiatric interventions.

Surprisingly, sociocultural and traumatic environmental factors specific to many American Indian communities that may be precursors to, or associated with, psychiatric disorders have rarely been studied. Many American Indians have been separated from their families and communities for extended lengths of time because of government policies and missionary placement programs (Robin, 1989). Many lived their formative years away from their homes and communities of birth, having been adopted away or placed into foster care (Shore & Nicholls, 1975). Involuntary placement in boarding schools is a phenomenon common to American Indian groups. However, only limited data have been collected to demonstrate the effects of involuntary placement (Manson, 1989).

Domestic violence has received no systematic study in American Indian populations (Chester, Robin, Koss, Lopez, & Goldman, 1994). Information on intimate violence comes primarily from anecdotal data. Whereas it has been suggested that domestic violence was almost unknown to American Indian communities until the introduction of alcohol (Allen, 1985), domestic violence has only been directly linked to future alcoholism in non-Indian populations.

For example, Miller, Downs, & Testa (1993) and Wolk (1982) reported that children who have been physically or sexually abused are more likely to become addicted to alcohol or other drugs. Other researchers have suggested that higher rates of depression for women might be related to their victimization by intimate male partners. A growing number of researchers have suggested that domestic violence is associated with PTSD (Koss, Koss, & Woodruff, 1992; Walker, 1991).

Researchers have also reported a high prevalence of child abuse and neglect of American Indian children, including sexual molestation (Lujan, DeBruyn, May, & Bird, 1989; Fischler, 1985; Piasecki, et al., 1989). The sharing of significant developmental and traumatic experiences by large segments of populations offers opportunities for relating these experiences to later behaviors. For example, symptoms of depression, PTSD, and substance abuse were found to correlate with experienced child sexual abuse (Roesler & McKenzie, 1993). These associations are similar to Los Angeles ECA findings that early childhood sexual abuse put individuals at higher risk to develop depression, alcohol or drug abuse, and anxiety disorders than those who reported no sexual abuse (Burnam, 1988).

However, in American Indians who show high rates of these disorders, the importance of the relationship between these events in childhood or adolescence to the development of adult psychiatric disorders is unclear. It is also likely that some of the traumas experienced by American Indian children and adolescents may be unique in quality and effect. For example, the existence of widespread child sexual molestation of children by Bureau of Indian Affairs teachers from outside of the community has been revealed within several tribes including the Havasupai, Hopi, Navajo, and Lakota (Chester, 1991).

Domestic violence, child abuse, forced relocation, and forced removal of children from their families are only three of many specific traumas that affect American Indian people and their communities. Multiple traumatic events frequently affect American Indian families, including mortality from motor vehicle and other accidents (May, 1992; Indian Health Service, 1989), and suicide attempts and completed suicides (Manson et al., 1989). Frequently, American Indian children have witnessed violent deaths of relatives and close friends from chronic medical conditions, drug overdoses, and homicides (Levy & Kunitz, 1987; Lujan et al., 1989; Nelson, McCoy, Stetter, & Vanderwagen, 1992). For American Indian people, the rates for these conditions greatly exceed the prevalence of trauma occurring in the general population of the United States.

Cumulative Trauma

Posttraumatic stress disorder is a concept that may be readily comprehensible to many American Indian people, particularly in relation to wartime experiences (i.e., Manson et al., this volume). However, as a diagnostic category, PTSD fails to describe the nature and impact of severe, multiple, repeated, and cumulative aspects of trauma common to many communities. Recent conceptualizations of trauma, such as complex PTSD or Disorders of Extreme Stress Not Otherwise Specified (DESNOS) (Herman, 1993), whereas more accurate in describing the complex nature of the stressor criteria for American Indian communities, focus more upon situations of prolonged victimization in captivity, as opposed to prolonged and repeated traumatization (Ochberg, 1988).

If the consequences of trauma and victimization in American Indian people are to be diagnosed or even described accurately, there are several aspects that require close scrutiny. First, the nature and extent of prolonged and repeated trauma in American Indian populations needs to be more extensively documented, so that non-Indian clinicians and researchers can better understand the history of trauma in American Indian populations. Mollica (1989) and others have described this process in Cambodian refugees, who as a group suffered from 16 major traumatic events that met the current PTSD stressor criteria. Second, the impact of a single, acute, traumatic incident within the context of cumulative, multigenerational trauma needs to be examined. Aron, Corne, Fursland, & Zelwer, (1991), for example, described significant clinical and conceptual differences between women who are raped in the context of civil war and repression, such as found in El Salvador, as opposed to women experiencing rape in the United States. Finally, the concept of community trauma, or trauma as experienced by entire communities, needs to be developed. This concept, introduced by clinicians working with survivors of political repression, recognizes the widespread and collective effects of trauma upon entire communities (Lira, Becker, & Catillo, 1988).

Community trauma is a particularly important consideration among American Indian people, given the extensive nature of their extended and well-integrated family and clan systems. American Indian reservation residents are often collectively affected by traumatic events because of the close and interwoven relationships that typify these communities. For example, the staggering reality depicted by numbers and statistics cannot illustrate the impact of one teacher over a period of 9 years on the small, closely knit villages of First Mesa on the Hopi Reservation. Within a community of 3,000 people, 144 boys were named as victims of sexual molestation by this teacher, making it unlikely that any family escaped direct confrontation with sexual abuse. As recently as November of 1991, former students of the teacher who were not identified as victims during the criminal investigation disclosed additional incidents of abuse. One parent stated, "After all these months we still don't know what to do or how we should help our boys. We all really hurt from this. We don't know who we should take our pain to." (Chester, 1991, p. 7). Unfortunately, this case of community trauma is not an isolated incident.

NIAAA STUDIES: METHODOLOGY OF STUDIES ON PTSD AND CUMULATIVE TRAUMA

In order to address issues pertaining to PTSD and cumulative trauma, the NIAAA has conducted studies in three American Indian communities over the past 5 years. Although these are not epidemiologic-based studies, participants have been recruited from large multigenerational genealogies identified on the basis of size and availability (not psychopathology) to determine individuals' vulnerability to alcoholism and other psychiatric disorders and to identify the role of genetic factors. Also, because subjects share membership in extended families, subgroups of subjects who are not first-degree relatives have been identified. These groups can then be used to confirm that findings made in the larger dataset are not due to the bias of including clusters of subjects who are closely genetically related.

Clinicians with extensive experience in psychiatric assessment with American Indian populations and specific familiarity with the Cheyenne administer the SADS-L. The SADS-L has been found to be reliable when used appropriately with American Indians (Manson, Shore, Baron, Ackerson, & Neligh, 1992).

Posttraumatic stress disorder is diagnosed by adding the PTSD component of the Structured Clinical Interview for *DSM–III–R* (Spitzer, Williams, Gibbon, & First, 1992) to the SADS-L interview. The PTSD component is presented within the section on anxiety disorders. To capture data on cumulative trauma and specific, multiple traumatic events, the Traumatic Events Booklet (Kulka et al., 1988) is administered to participating subjects by local interviewers. In this way, researchers will be able to evaluate trauma as it occurs within the context of a single event, as well as the cumulative trauma over the course of a person's lifetime.

Subjects are recruited and questionnaires administered by tribal, bilingual interviewers who reside in the areas of study. These individuals are trained and clinically supervised to administer instruments assessing acculturation, domestic violence, sociodemographic status, medical history, personality, out-of-home placement, and alcoholism. Psychiatric diagnoses are made by *DSM–III–R* and Research Diagnostic Criteria with several adjustments for sociocultural-specific factors including the "acceptable" time period for grieving and the appearance of hallucinations occurring within a cultural context. Blood samples are obtained for genetic studies, and when the research is completed, approximately 1,500 American Indian subjects will have participated.

CONCLUSION

Understanding the prevalence and expression of posttraumatic stress disorder and cumulative trauma in American Indians has important implications for both affected individuals and the communities in which they live. Further investigation into possible subcategories of depression and substance abuse, especially those conditions that are comorbid with PTSD, and clarification of the temporal relationships that occur among comorbid conditions may help refine assessment and diagnostic procedures for American Indians.

Improving assessment and diagnosis of PTSD and cumulative trauma should, in turn, lead to the enactment of more effective treatment regimens. In light of comorbidity findings, services should be delivered in an integrated manner for patients seeking help for substance abuse and mental health problems.

Finally, given the collective and interrelated nature of American Indian societies and the pervasive impact of trauma, public health policy might consider paradigms that focus not only on rehabilitation of the individual or the targeting of high-risk groups, but also on policy charges that can lead to community transformation.

REFERENCES

Albaugh, B. J., & Washa J. (1987). Cheyenne alcoholism from a Cheyenne perspective. *Report to the USPHS, Indian Health Research Center.* Tucson, AZ: Author.

Allen, P. G. (1985). Violence and the American Indian woman. In *Working together to prevent sexual and domestic violence, Volume 5, Issue 4.* Seattle, WA: Center for the Prevention of Sexual and Domestic Violence.

Aron, A., Corne, S., Fursland, A., & Zelwer, B. (1991). The gender-specific terror of El Salvador and Guatemala. *Women's Studies International Forum, 14 (1/2),* 37–47.

Baron, A., Manson, S. M., Ackerson, M., & Brenneman, D. (1990). Depressive symptomatology in older American Indians with chronic disease: Some psychometric considerations. In C. Attkisson & J. Zich (Eds.), *Depression in primary care: Screening and detection* (pp. 217–231). New York: Routledge, Kane & Co.

Bloom, J. D. (1972). Psychiatric problems and cultural transitions in Alaska. *Arctic, 25,* 203–215.

Blum, R., (Ed). (1992). *The state of Native American youth health.* Unpublished manuscript, Division of General Pediatrics and Adolescent Health, University of Minnesota Hospital and Clinic, Minneapolis, MN.

Burnam, M. A., Stein, J. A., Golding, J. M., Siegel, J. M., Sorenson, S. B., Forsythe, A. B., & Telles, C. A. (1988). Sexual assault and mental disorders in a community population. *Journal of Consulting and Clinical Psychology, 56,* 843–850.

Chester, B. (1991). *Evaluation: Hopi special child sexual abuse project.* Unpublished manuscript, Department of Behavioral Health Services, The Hopi Tribe, Kykotsmovi, AZ.

Chester, B. (1994). That which does not destroy me. In M. B. Williams & J. F. Sommer, Jr. (Eds.), *Handbook of post-traumatic therapy* (pp. 240–251). Westport, CT: Greenwood Press.

Chester, B., Mahalish, P., & Davis, J. (in press). A mental health needs assessment of off-reservation American Indian people in Northern Arizona. *American Indian and Alaska Native Mental Health Research.*

Chester, B., Robin, R., Koss, M., Lopez, J., & Goldman, D. (1994). Grandmother dishonored: Violence against women by male partners in American Indian communities. In A. Urquiza, G. Wyatt, & M. Root (Eds.), *Victims and violence, Vol. 9, No. 3.* New York: Springer.

Davidson, R. T., & Fairbank, J. A. (1993). The epidemiology of posttraumatic stress disorder. In R. T. Davidson & E. B. Foa (Eds.), *Post-traumatic stress disorder: DSM–IV and beyond* (pp. 147–169). Washington, DC: American Psychiatric Press.

Day, R., Nielsen, J., Korten, A., Ernberg, G., Dube, K., Gebhart, J., Jablensky, A., Leon, C., Marsella, A., Olatawura, M., Strömgren, E., Takahashi, R., Wig, N., and Wynne, L. C. (1987). Stressful life events preceding the acute onset of schizophrenia: A cross-national study from the WHO. *Culture, Medicine, and Psychiatry, 11,* 123–205.

Fischler, R. (1985). Child abuse and neglect in American Indian communities. *Child Abuse and Neglect, 9,* 95–106.

Garcia-Peltoniemi, R. E. (1991). Clinical manifestations of psychopathology. In Department of Health and Human Services (DHHS), *Mental health services for refugees* (pp. 42–55). Washington, DC: U.S. DHHS.

Green, B. L. (1993). *A review of the literature on posttraumatic stress disorder.* Paper presented at the 4th Annual European Society of Posttraumatic Stress Studies, Bergen, Norway.

Harris, F. (1968). Indian health: A Blue Cross report on the problems of the poor. Unpublished manuscript. Washington, DC.

Herman, J. L. (1993). Sequelae of prolonged and repeated trauma: Evidence for a complex posttraumatic syndrome (DESNOS). In R. T. Davidson & E. B. Foa (Eds.), *Posttraumatic stress disorder: DSM–IV and beyond* (pp. 213–228). Washington, DC: American Psychiatric Press.

Hoffman, H., & Jackson, D. N. (1973). Comparison of measured psychopathology in Indian and non-Indian alcoholics. *Psychological Reports, 33,* 793–794.

Indian Health Service (1989). *The trends in Indian health.* Unpublished manuscript, U.S. Department of Health and Human Services, Rockville, MD.

Jones-Saumty, D., Hochhaus, L., Dru, R., & Zeiner, A. R. (1983). Psychological factors of familial alcoholism in American Indians and Caucasians. *Journal of Clinical Psychology, 39,* 783–790.

Kemp, A., Rawlings, E. I., & Green, B. L. (1991). Post-traumatic stress disorder in battered women: A shelter sample. *Journal of Traumatic Stress, 4,* 137–148.

Kinzie, J. D., Leung, P., Boehnlein, J., Matsunaga, D., Johnson, R., Manson, S. M., Shore, J. H., Heinz, J., & Williams, M. (1992). Psychiatric epidemiology of an Indian village: A 19-year replication study. *Journal of Nervous and Mental Disorders, 180,* 33–39.

Koss, M., Koss, P., & Woodruff, J. (1992). Deleterious effects of criminal victimization on women's health and medical utilization. *Archives of Internal Medicine, 151,* 342–347.

Kulka, R. A., Schlenger, W. E., Fairbank, J. A., Hough, R. L., Jordan, B. K., Marmar, C. R., & Weiss, D. S. (1988). *Contractual report of findings from the National Vietnam Veterans Readjustment Study: Volume III: Survey interview questionnaires.* Research Triangle Park, NC: Research Triangle Institute.

Levy, J. E., & Kunitz, S. J. (1987). A suicide prevention program for Hopi youth. *Social Science and Medicine, 25,* 931–940.

Lira, E., Becker, D., & Catillo, M. I. (1988). *Psychotherapy with victims of political repression in Chile: A therapeutic and political challenge.* Paper presented at the meeting of the Latin American Institute of Mental Health and Human Rights, Santiago, Chile.

Lujan, C., DeBruyn, L. M., May, P., & Bird, M. E. (1989). Profile of abused and neglected American Indian children in the Southwest. *Child Abuse and Neglect, 13,* 449–461.

Manson, S. M., Beals, J., Dick, R. W., & Duclos, C. (1989). Risk factors for suicide among Indian adolescents at a boarding school. *Public Health Reports, 104,* 609–614.

Manson, S. M., & Shore, J. H. (1981). Psychiatric epidemiology among American Indians: Methodological issues. *White Cloud Journal, 2,* 48–56.

Manson, S. M., Shore, J. H., Baron, A. E., Ackerson, L., & Neligh, G. (1992). Alcohol abuse and dependence among American Indians. In J. E. Helzer &

G. J. Canino (Eds.), *Alcoholism in North America, Europe, and Asia* (pp. 113–130). New York: Oxford University Press.

Manson, S. M., Shore, J. H., & Bloom, J. D. (1985). The depression experience in American Indian communities: A challenge for psychiatric theory and diagnosis. In A. Kleinman & B. J. Good (Eds.), *Culture and depression* (pp. 331–368). Berkeley: University of California Press.

Manson, S. M., Shore, J. H., Bloom, J. D., Keepers, G., & Neligh, G. (1987). Alcohol abuse and major affective disorders: Advances in epidemiologic research among American Indians. *American Indians and Alaska Natives, 1,* 291–300.

March, J. S. (1992). The stressor criterion in *DSM–IV* post traumatic stress disorder. In J. R. T. Davidson & E. B. Foa (Eds.), *Posttraumatic stress disorder in review: Recent research and future development* (pp. 37–54). Washington, DC: American Psychiatric Press.

Marsella, A.J. (1980). Depressive affect and experience across cultures. In H. Triandis & J. Draguns (Eds.), *Handbook of cross-cultural psychology. Volume 6.* Boston: Allyn & Bacon.

Maser, J. D., & Dinges, N. (1993). Comorbidity: Meaning and uses in cross-cultural clinical research. *Culture, Medicine, and Psychiatry, 16,* 409–425.

May, P. A. (1987). Suicide and self-destruction among American Indian youths. *American Indian and Alaska Native Mental Health Research, 1,* 52–69.

May, P. A. (1992). Alcohol policy considerations for Indian Reservations and bordertown communities. *American Indian and Alaska Native Mental Health Research, 4,* 5–59.

McShane, D. (1987). Mental health and North American Indian/Native communities: Cultural transactions, education, and regulation. *American Journal of Community Psychology, 15,* 95–116.

Miller, B, Downs, W., & Testa, M. (1993). Interrelationships between victimization experiences and women's alcohol use. *Journal of Studies on Alcohol, 11,* 109–117.

Mollica, R. F. (1989). The social world destroyed: The psychiatric care of the refugee trauma survivor. In J. Gruschow & K. Hannibal (Eds.), *Health services for the treatment of torture and trauma survivors* (pp. 15–29). Washington, DC: American Association for the Advancement of Science Publication.

Navajo-Hopi Relocation Commission (1993). *Relocation program status statistical report.* Unpublished manuscript, Navajo-Hopi Relocation Commission, Flagstaff, AZ.

Nelson, S. H., McCoy, G. F., Stetter, M., & Vanderwagen, W. C. (1992). An overview of mental health services for American Indians and Alaska Natives in the 1990's. *Hospital and Community Psychiatry, 43,* 257–261.

Ochberg, F. M. (1988). *Post-traumatic therapy and victims of violence.* New York: Brunner/Mazel.

Olivera, A. A., & Fero, D. (1990). Affective disorders, DST, and treatment in PTSD patients: Clinical observations. *Journal of Traumatic Stress, 3*, 407–414.

Pelz, M., Merskey, H., Brant, C., Patterson, P. G., & Heseltine, G. F. (1981). Clinical data from a psychiatric service to a group of Native people. *Canadian Journal of Psychiatry, 26*, 345–348.

Piasecki, J., Manson, S. M., Biernoff, M., Hiat, A., Taylor, S., & Bechtold, D. (1989). Abuse and neglect of American Indian children: Findings from a survey of federal providers. *Journal of the National Center, 3*, 43–62.

Robin, R. W. (1989). Substitute care: Residential treatment, adoption, family foster care, day care. In E. Gonzalez-Santin (Ed.), *Collaboration — The key: A model curriculum on Indian child welfare* (pp. 185–219). Tempe: Arizona State University.

Robin, R. W., Brown, G. L., Albaugh, B. J., Goodson, S. G., Trunzo, M., & Goldman, D. (1993). Comorbidity of alcoholism and psychiatric disorders among Cheyenne Indians. Unpublished manuscript, National Institute of Health, Bethesda, MD.

Roesler, T., & McKenzie, N. (1993). Effects of trauma on psychological functioning in adults sexually abused as children. Unpublished manuscript. Study supported by grants from the van Derbur Family and the Hyman and Esther Krasne Foundation.

Roy, C., Choudhuri, A., & Irvine, D. (1970). The prevalence of mental disorders among Saskatchewan Indians. *Journal of Cross-Cultural Psychology, 3*, 383–392.

Rozynko, V., & Ferguson, L. C. (1978). Admission characteristics of Indian and White alcoholic patients in a rural mental hospital. *International Journal of the Addictions, 13*, 591–604.

Ryan, R. A. (1979). *American Indian/Alaska Native mental health research: A community perspective.* Paper presented at the meeting of the Society for the Study of Social Problems, Boston.

Sampath, B. M. (1974). Prevalence of psychiatric disorders in a Southern Baffin Island Eskimo settlement. *Canadian Psychiatric Association Journal, 19*, 303–367.

Schuckit, M. (1983). Alcoholic patients with secondary depression. *American Journal of Psychiatry, 140*, 711–714.

Shen, W. (1986). The Hopi Indian's mourning hallucinations. *Journal of Nervous and Mental Disorders, 174*, 365–367.

Shore, J. H., Kinzie, J. D., Hampson. D., & Pattison, M. (1973). Psychiatric epidemiology of an Indian village. *Psychiatry, 36*, 70–81.

Shore, J. H., Manson, S. M., Bloom, J. D., Keepers, G., & Neligh, G. (1987). A pilot study of depression among American Indian patients with research diagnostic criteria. *American Indian and Alaska Mental Health Research, 1*, 4–15.

Shore, J. H., & Nicholls, N. M. (1975). Indian children and tribal group homes: New interpretations of the Whipper Man. *American Journal of Psychiatry, 132*, 454–456.

Shore, J. H., Tatum, E., & Vollmer, W. M. (1986), Psychiatric reactions to disaster: The Mt. St. Helens experience. *American Journal of Psychiatry, 143*, 590–595.

Spitzer, R. L., & Endicott, J. (1978). *Schedule of affective disorders and schizophrenia: Lifetime version 3rd edition.* New York: Biometrics Research, New York State Psychiatric Institute.

Spitzer, R. L., Williams, J. B. W., Gibbon, M., & First, M. B. (1992). The structured clinical interview for *DSM–III–R* (SCID). *Archives of General Psychiatry, 49*, 624–629.

U.S. Department of Health and Human Services. (1988). *Indian health service: Chart series book.* Washington, DC: U.S. Government Printing Office.

Walker, L. E. (1991). Post-traumatic stress disorder in women: Diagnosis and treatment of battered woman syndrome. *Psychotherapy, 28*, 21–29.

Walker, R. D., & Kivlahan, D. R. (1984). Definitions, models, and methods in research on sociocultural factors in American Indian alcohol use. *Substance and Alcohol Actions/Misuse, 5*, 9–19.

Westermeyer, J. (1985). Psychiatric diagnosis across cultural boundaries. *American Journal of Psychiatry, 142*, 798–805.

Weissman, M. M., Myers, J. K., & Ross, J. C. (Eds.) (1986). *Commuity surveys of psychiatric disorders.* New Brunswick, NJ: Rutgers University Press.

Westermeyer, J., & Neider, J. (1984). Depressive symptomatology among Native American alcoholics at the time of a 10-year follow-up. *Alcoholism: Clinical and Experimental Research, 8*, 429–434.

Wolk, L. (1982). *Minnesota's American Indian battered women: The cycle of oppression* (A training manual). St. Paul, MN: St. Paul Indian center.

World Health Organization (1979). *Schizophrenia: An international follow-up study.* New York: John Wiley and Sons.

10

WOUNDED SPIRITS, AILING HEARTS: PTSD AND RELATED DISORDERS AMONG AMERICAN INDIANS

SPERO MANSON, JANETTE BEALS, THERESA O'NELL,
JOAN PIASECKI, DONALD BECHTOLD, ELLEN KEANE, and
MONICA JONES

TRAUMA AND THE AMERICAN INDIAN

Trauma and its consequences for individuals, families, and communities shadows the daily lives of American Indians and Alaska Natives. Both the popular press and professional literature offer ample evidence to this effect. Consider the suicide epidemic on the Wind River Reservation in Wyoming that claimed the lives of 9 Arapaho males in a brief 8 weeks (Bechtold, 1988); the revelation that a Bureau of Indian Affairs teacher—recently conferred a national teaching award—had, over a 9-year period, sexually abused more than 100 Hopi boys between 5 and 12 years of age; the *Exxon Valdez* oil spill and major disruption of economic, social, and psychological life among the Aleut inhabitants of Prince William Sound (Palinkas, Downs, Petterson, & Russell, 1993); the widespread prevalence of alcohol abuse, often accompanied by tragic violence to spouses and children (Bachman, 1992); the seldom recognized costs of combat among Indian and Native Vietnam veterans for whom military service is a time-honored tradition (Working Group on American Indian Vietnam Veterans, 1992); and most recently, a life-threatening viral illness initially

Preparation of this manuscript was supported in part by grants from the National Institute of Mental Health (R01 MH42473, K02 MH00833), National Institute on Alcohol Abuse and Alcoholism (R01 AA08747), and National Institute on Drug Abuse (R01 DA06076).

labelled the "Navajo flu" that plagues the Four Corners area of the American southwest.

Add to these examples a deeply ingrained sense of oppression spanning several centuries and the repeated violation of presumably ironclad agreements that displaced this special population from ancestral lands. It is not surprising, then, that once post-traumatic stress disorder (PTSD) entered the general vernacular, American Indian and Alaska Native people quickly adopted it as an idiom or metaphor for the consequences of the enormous social and psychological burdens under which they labor. But, despite the relative ease with which this construct has found a place in local lexicons, little systematic study of trauma, and PTSD in particular, has been conducted in these communities.

Purpose of Chapter

This chapter describes ongoing work of the National Center for American Indian and Alaska Native Mental Health Research (NCAIANMHR), which promises to shed light on the nature and extent of trauma among Indian and Native people, from latency-age children to middle-age adults. The four studies in question closely examine the phenomenological and cultural contexts of such experiences. The NCAIANMHR studies that speak to these experiences are (a) the Health Survey of Indian Boarding School Students, (b) the Flower of Two Soils Reinterview project, (c) the Foundations of Indian Teens project, and (d) the American Indian Vietnam Veterans Project.

The present chapter begins by describing the purpose, design, instrumentation, and samples of each of these four studies. In the discussion of relevant findings from works in progress, we present specific questions to guide ongoing analyses across a range of substantive concerns. The chapter closes by highlighting the importance of convergent investigative methods and the need to firmly ground the diagnosis, epidemiology, treatment, and prevention of trauma-related illnesses within the sociocultural contexts that give them meaning.

RELEVANT STUDIES: RESEARCH IN PROGRESS

The NCAIANMHR, one of five programs sponsored under the National Institute of Mental Health's Minority Mental Health Research Center initiative, has developed a multifaceted research agenda that builds progressively from basic studies in diagnostic assessment and psychiatric epidemiology to inquiries regarding service use and preventive intervention. This effort encompasses the developmental life span, with current emphasis on adolescence and middle adulthood. It incorporates qualitative as well as quantitative research methods, which frequently combine in a synergistic fashion, producing a richer interpretive framework than is possible by either method alone. The four studies relevant to this discussion of trauma and PTSD spring from this research agenda. These studies are focussed on children and yound adults; the fourth is concerned with middle-aged veterans of the Vietnam War.

Health Survey of Indian Boarding School Students

The Health Survey of Indian Boarding School Students was launched in 1988 to determine the prevalence and incidence of symptoms of depression, anxiety, suicidal behavior, and substance abuse among youth in a high-risk educational environment (Dick, Manson, & Beals, 1993; King, Beals, Manson, & Trimble, 1992). It was conducted in an accredited, tribally controlled secondary school located in the southeastern United States, where 96% of the approximately 200 grade 9–12 students live in dormitories throughout the academic year. The vast majority (92%) are from the region and belong to five local, culturally similar tribes. A self-report questionnaire is administered to the students twice each academic year, typically in October and April.

During the 1989–90 school year, 85 students were selected for clinical interviews from the 163 participants in the fall survey. They represented those scoring in the first ($n = 42$) and third quartiles ($n = 43$) of the Suicidal Ideation Questionnaire (representing students reporting very high and moderate levels, respectively, of suicide ideation; Dick, Beals, Manson, & Bechtold, 1994). Of these, 61 were successfully questioned about their mental health status, using the DISC–2.1C and its PTSD module (Shaffer et al, 1988)—the 43 scoring in the third quartile (21 female and 22 male participants), and only 18 of those from the first quartile (11 female and 7 male participants). This result was not surprising given the greater stress and symptomatology reported by the latter group, which predicts more frequent absence and school dropout. The students interviewed ranged from 14 to 20 years of age; all four grades (9–12) are represented.

The three most common diagnoses assigned across both groups were conduct disorder (18%), major depression (15%), and alcohol dependence (13%). Of additional clinical interest is that across both samples, 25% of the students indicated that they had made a previous suicide attempt—40% within the past 6 months. In comparing the two groups by specific diagnoses, individuals from the first SIQ quartile were significantly more likely to be diagnosed with any psychiatric diagnosis, any anxiety disorder, any mood disorder, and any behavior disorder.

Flower of Two Soils Reinterview

The Flower of Two Soils study was designed to investigate the potential relationship between risk of emotional disorder and school dropout among Indian youth in four culturally distinct reservation communities in the United States and Canada (Sack, Beiser, Clarke, & Redshirt, 1987; Sack, Beiser, Baker–Brown, & Redshirt, 1994). Beginning in 1984, cohorts of children in grades 2 and 4, drawn from Northern Plains, Southwest, Eastern woodlands, and Northwest coast communities, were assessed once annually for 3 years with a battery of measures of their intellectual abilities, academic achievement, and mental health status. In 1991, the NCAIANMHR sought to reinterview the 251 Northern Plains children who took part in the original study. Initially the children were between 8 and 10 years old; during the reinterview, they ranged from 13 to 18 years of age, a period when Indian youth seem to experience particularly high risk for developing emotional disorders (Beiser & Attneave, 1982). Of these teenagers, 119 (54 female and 55 male respondents; grades 8 to 11) were successfully followed up with the DISC–2.1C, which included the previously mentioned PTSD module.

Of the 109 respondents, 43% (43.1%; $n = 47$) received a DISC diagnosis of at least one major disorder: disruptive behavior disorders, 22%; conduct disorder, 9.5%; substance use disorders, 18.4%; alcohol dependence, 9.2%; anxiety disorders, 17.4%; affective disorders, 9.3%; major depression, 6.5%; posttraumatic stress disorders, 5%; and anorexia and bulimia 1%. Of these individuals, 20.2% qualified for a single diagnosis; the remainder were assigned multiple diagnoses. Almost half of the respondents with a disruptive behavior disorder or an affective disorder also qualified for a substance abuse disorder.

Foundations of Indian Teens

Despite general recognition of the influence of cultural factors on assessment methods, only limited progress has been accomplished in regard to American Indians (Ackerson, Dick, Manson, & Baron, 1990; Beals, Keane, Dick, & Manson, 1991; Manson, Ackerson, Dick, Baron, & Fleming, 1990; Manson, Shore, & Bloom, 1985; Manson, Walker, & Kivlahan, 1987). Hence, in 1992, the Foundations of Indian Teens project was initiated to develop more reliable and valid measures of psychopathology among Indian adolescents, with special emphasis on trauma.

The study proceeded in three phases. Focus groups were convened to discuss the nature of trauma in general, to elicit examples of particularly traumatic events, and to review a portion of a screening survey specific to the PTSD diagnostic criteria. A self–report survey, which included screeners for PTSD, depression, problem drinking, anxiety, and conduct disorder, subsequently was administered to 297 Indian adolescents in grades 9 through 12, attending a high school in a Southwestern Indian community. Students reporting a traumatic event plus 8 or more PTSD symptoms ($n = 65$) underwent a second stage clinical interview, which used a current version of the DISC (Version 2.3).

The PTSD screener included in the survey was a modified version of the PTSD Interview (PTSD– I), *DSM–III–R* version (Watson et al., 1991). The PTSD–I was chosen and adapted for self-report largely because of its close correspondence with diagnostic criteria. Considerable attention was devoted to describing the *DSM–III–R* criterion A. Drawing from the DIS, the DISC 2.3, and the PTSD–I, the following stimulus was developed for eliciting the traumatic event description:

> Have you ever experienced something that is so horrible that it would be very upsetting to almost anyone? Some examples might be: Situations in which you thought you were going to die, or where your life was seriously threatened. Other examples might be: You saw somebody killed, or get hurt very badly; or, someone you felt close to was killed or got hurt very badly. Has anything like that ever happened to you? How many things like that have happened to you? What was the worst thing like that you have experienced?

In response, nearly 51% ($n = 151$) of the students reported that they had experienced a traumatic event. Some (37%) described experiencing more than one such event, with 16% numbering four or more. Approximately half of those experiencing a traumatic event endorsed 8 or more PTSD symptoms (of 17 possible) on this self-report measure.

American Indian Vietnam Veterans Project

In 1991, Congress mandated that a nationwide study of PTSD and other readjustment problems among Vietnam war veterans, commonly referred to as the National Vietnam Veterans Readjustment Survey (NVVRS) (Kulka et al., 1990) be replicated among ethnic minority groups that had been significantly underrepresented in the original study. The American Indian Vietnam Veterans Project (AIVVP) is a part of this effort, and comprises four distinct but related stages of research taking place in two reservation communities situated in the Northern Plains and the Southwest.

The first stage of the AIVVP entailed an item-by-item review of the NVVRS instrumentation, using focus groups of Vietnam veterans, their family members, service providers, and elders, to identify means of improving comprehension. This effort has been augmented by longer-term ethnographic inquiry (life histories, key informant interviews, and participant observation) to illuminate the cultural construction of PTSD and local responses to it. The second stage involved the development of a sound, ecologically relevant sampling frame. Eligible participants were restricted to Vietnam combat veterans of the two tribes who are enrolled members and currently live on or near their reservations. Veterans from each community ($n = 300$) were randomly selected for interview. The third stage was a 5-hour lay-administered interview that covers childhood, family, and marital history; parenting; education; occupation; military service; physical health status; postservice experiences (M–PTSD); self-perceptions; attitudes; nonspecific distress; stressful and traumatic events; social support; health services use; experience in Vietnam; and psychiatric status (Composite International Diagnostic Instrument, CIDI). The fourth stage is a clinical reinterview of all participants deemed probable cases of PTSD based on their Mississippi–PTSD (M–PTSD) scores reported in the prior stage and a small control group screening below that threshold. Originally 30% of the 300 veterans at each site were presumed likely to screen positive on the M–PTSD (Keane, Caddell, & Taylor, 1988; Keane, Malloy, & Fairbank, 1984); however, actual rates currently approximate almost 70%. Experienced psychiatrists and clinical psychologists are conducting the follow-up Structured Clinical Interviews for Diagnosis (SCID), supplemented by measures of functioning and trauma (Impact of Life Events). At present, only preliminary data from the lay-administered interview conducted at the Northern Plains sites is available for discussion.

TRAUMA AND PTSD: PENDING QUESTIONS

Each of these NCAIANMHR studies expands, in various ways, our understanding of trauma and PTSD in American Indian populations. Let us briefly illustrate the nature of their contribution, and the questions that the research raises within a number of areas.

Definition and Perception of Trauma

What events are seen as outside the range of usual human experience that would be markedly distressing to almost anyone living in American Indian communities? Do these differ from those likely to receive the same attribution in other communities?

In the Health Survey of Indian Boarding School Students, only one student, belonging to the first SIQ quartile, received the diagnosis of PTSD, which presents several interesting diagnostic issues. One issue relates to the *DSM–III–R* Criterion A requirement that "the person has experienced an event that is outside the range of usual human experience and that would be markedly distressing to almost anyone (American Psychiatric Association, 1987, p. 247)." Although the *DSM–III–R* suggests examples of such stressors, there are no specific criteria as to what constitutes a sufficient stressor. Clinical experience, in fact, demonstrates considerable individual variability in response to a comparable stressor.

Temperamental, developmental, neurochemical, psychological, and cultural determinants interact to mediate posttraumatic responses. Attempts by an outside rater to assess the sufficiency of a given stressor to fulfill the *DSM–III–R* criterion A are at best difficult and complicated. They may in fact be naive, arbitrary, insensitive, or inaccurate given the multiplicity of determinants involved.

Data from this study nicely demonstrate the complexity of this issue. Most clinicians would concede that being personally involved in a severe auto accident, being shot, or being raped fulfills Criterion A. Many, however, would question whether taking an intentional overdose or suffering heat stroke represents a sufficient stressor. Likewise, few would argue that witnessing a severe auto accident, an auto–pedestrian accident, a drowning, a shooting, a stabbing, or a beating are insufficient to fulfill Criterion A. On the other hand, although some would question whether death by natural causes, illness, or surgery of a close acquaintance or family member constitutes a sufficient stressor, a number of students surveyed subjectively felt traumatized by events of this very nature.

Focus group discussion among youth participating in the Foundations of Indian Teens Project further elaborated on this issue. For example, the students in this study are members of a tribal group that views death, the afterlife, and witchcraft much differently than mainstream American society. Breaking one's leg is not typically thought of as especially traumatic. Yet, one youth described such an event in the context of a curse that had been visited upon her family. Great fear, constraints on behavior, and hypervigilance were strongly associated with her perception of this event and the meaning that it holds for herself and her family. Moreover, cultural values and taboos often limit the ability of an investigator or clinician to gather information relevant to these experiences: Witchcraft is not a subject for discussion, in general, and particularly not with nontribal members.

Given these difficulties in assessing the adequacy of a stressor to fulfill Criterion A, the remaining PTSD diagnostic criteria assume particular importance for establishing the presence or absence of the disorder. Again, data from the Health Survey of Indian Boarding School Students speak clearly to this issue. Numerous students ($n = 37$) reported experiencing a traumatic event or events; only one student fulfilled criteria for the PTSD diagnosis. An obvious interpretation of these data is that the trauma experienced by 36 of 37 students did not lead to persistent reexperiences of the event, persistent avoidance of stimuli associated with the event or psychic numbing, persistent symptoms of autonomic hyperarousal, or symptom duration of more than one month.

It is, however, not necessarily correct to infer that the majority of the stressors reported were insufficient to lead to posttraumatic clinical sequelae. These data argue for more latitude in allowing the individual to declare the sufficiency of the Criterion A stressor, trusting that other criteria will select out those cases in which Criterion A was not adequately fulfilled.

The Health Survey of Indian Boarding School Students data clearly suggest a need to revisit this diagnosis from a culturally sensitive perspective. Given the substantial amount and significant nature of trauma reported by the students, and the low prevalence of diagnosis of PTSD, one might question potential cultural bias in the manner by which the diagnostic criteria are operationalized. For example, is the obvious avoidance of stimuli associated with the trauma or the presence of psychic numbing masked by the interactional style of Indian people, which tends towards limited disclosure and stoicism? This style sometimes is perceived by non-Indian people as a lack of emotionality. So how does one recognize and identify psychic numbing? In the presence of threatened cultural disintegration, and high levels of cultural demoralization, how does one accurately assess loss of interest, feelings of detachment or estrangement, or a sense of a foreshortened future?

Similarly, in a population with documented high rates of both affective and anxiety disorders, might not comorbid PTSD be clinically obscured by preexisting symptomatology? Perhaps the degree of trauma itself is sufficiently greater in many Native communities so that the individual threshold for clinical response has been reset at higher levels as trauma has become more the norm than the exception.

The quantitative and qualitative data indicate that cultural and social factors are very important in assessing Criterion A. They point to the need for more explicit sensitivity to cultural issues. A short clinical vignette may serve to further exemplify the need for a culturally sensitive and informed application of current diagnostic technologies. The case is of a 15-year-old young Native woman who was a high school freshman at the time of interview. The traumatic event she describes is the death of a foster sibling who was driving while intoxicated. The foster sibling suffered immediate permanent disability from his injuries, and died several years after the accident. In examining the reported stressful event for adequacy as a Criterion A stressor, one might rightfully question its sufficiency. It could be argued that the relationship was peripheral insofar as it was a nonbiologic relative. The subject and the victim were by no means contemporaries in age; they were of opposite gender and were not interpersonally involved. Furthermore, the subject did not personally witness the accident, and the accident and the actual death of the victim were separated by several years.

In spite of these potential objections, however, the subject described a number of persistent reexperiences of the trauma, persistent efforts to avoid thinking about the trauma, interpersonal estrangement, sense of a foreshortened future, affective instability, and numerous symptoms of autonomic hyperarousal, all with onset subsequent to the traumatic event and greater-than-one-month duration.

An attempt must be made to integrate the clinically obvious appearance of posttraumatic symptomatology with the concerns first raised in regard to the sufficiency of the Criterion A stressor. It must be understood, for example, that the Native concept of "family" extends far beyond mere blood–relationships. More accurately, family to many Native people is a psychological construct that derives more from sharing a kindred spirit than from sharing genetic endowment. Family roles are operationally defined, not just biologically. A brother is "one who feels like a brother," and a brother so defined in many Native cultures is no less a brother than a sibling born of identical parents. In this sense, not only was the victim truly a brother to the subject, but their relationship was one of volition and choice. The disability and ultimate death of a broadly defined sibling in many ways becomes a shared experience in Native culture.

Frequency of Traumatic Events

How often do traumatic events occur in American Indian communities? What are their salient characteristics? Who are the most likely victims? Slightly more than 60% ($n = 37$) of the students in the Health Survey of Indian Boarding School Students project indicated that they had witnessed or experienced at least one traumatic event. The number of traumatic events witnessed or experienced per student ranged from 1 to 5. Traumatic events in which the student reported himself or herself as the victim included car accidents ($n = 1$), overdose ($n = 1$), shooting ($n = 2$), heat stroke ($n = 1$), and rape ($n = 1$). Traumatic events involving someone other than the student included car accidents ($n = 12$), death by natural causes ($n = 4$), shooting ($n = 4$), stabbing ($n = 4$), severe beating ($n = 4$), electrocution ($n = 2$), suicide ($n = 2$), surgery ($n = 2$), murder ($n = 1$), auto–pedestrian accident ($n = 1$), and drowning ($n = 1$).

Of the 66 students who reported a traumatic event in response to the DISC–2.1C PTSD module during the Flower of Two Soils Reinterview, nearly two thirds (62%) indicated experiencing two or more such events. The most frequent ones were car accidents ($n = 25$), death or suicide ($n = 29$)—86% of which involved someone close to the respondent, and violent beatings ($n = 10$).

As noted earlier, more than half (50.8%, $n = 151$) of the Foundation of Indian Teens students reported that they had experienced a traumatic event. Over one third of respondents (37%) described experiencing more than one such event, with 16% reporting four or more. Deaths, both accidental and natural, car accidents, stabbings, and sexual assault were the most frequently reported traumas.

Elicitation of *DSM–III–R* Diagnostic Criteria for PTSD

How well do American Indians understand the questions employed by the standard protocols (e.g., DISC–2.C, WHO–CIDI, SCID) to elicit relevant symptomatology? How can these questions be improved in terms of comprehension?

Questions of this nature long have been debated, typically under the rubric of the *emic/etic* distinction, an analogy drawn from descriptive linguistics that attempts to capture the important differences between "insider" and "outsider" views of phenomena and their meaning. There are clear methodological implications of this distinction, especially for highly structured forms of inquiries such as surveys and diagnostic protocols (Bravo, Canino, Rubio-Stepic, & Woodbury-Farina, 1991; Freidenberg, Mulvihill, & Caraballo, 1993; Kleinman, 1980; Manson et al., 1985; McNabb, 1990a; Rogler, 1989). Several of the studies that are the focus of the present discussion addressed such concerns. Illustrations from the American Indian Vietnam Veterans Project are particularly relevant.

A central goal of the American Indian Vietnam Veterans Project is to conduct a culturally sensitive epidemiological study that parallels the NVVRS. The ensuing effort recognizes the importance of standardized comparison as well as of possible cultural bias in the original survey instruments, which were designed largely for administration to White, African American, and Hispanic Vietnam veterans. Unfortunately, this dual concern with replication and cultural validity is problematic.

Although standardized instruments provide some of the best means for comparisons across subgroups within a given population, they possess significant deficiencies when used cross-culturally, especially in light of language differences. However, even when respondents from another culture speak English, the use of standardized instruments remains potentially problematic for several reasons.

First, questions that appear in standardized instruments may be incomprehensible to members of different ethnocultural groups. For example, among some American Indian respondents, a question that asks about "feeling as if you were going mad" may be interpreted as a question about anger rather than about one's sanity.

Second, some questions may be unacceptable to respondents from another culture. For example, asking whether an American Indian respondent has ever abused peyote—a powerful Indian medicine—must be approached with care and respect. It should not simply be included in a list of questions about other types of potentially abused drugs.

Third, some questions may prove irrelevant cross-culturally. Consider, for example, a typical query about social support: "About how often have you visited with friends at their homes during the past month? (Do not count relatives.)" Especially within reservation communities, the extent and importance of kin-based relationships dictate that most friends are relatives, and that friends are frequently referred to in familial terms. Indeed, within this setting, a friend who is not a relative has little meaning or relevance to the notion of social support.

Finally, other questions either may pose incomplete answers or fail to consider local equivalents. For example, an interview of Indian veterans' service use that asks extensively about state and Department of Veterans Affairs health services, but ignores the Indian Health Service, tribal programs, or even traditional healing options has disregarded critical elements in the local service ecology. Likewise, questions that inquire whether the respondent has told a health care professional about a particular problem, as an index of help-seeking behavior and subsequent criterion threshold but not a traditional healer, has overlooked an important local equivalent that carries similar implications for severity of an illness (cf Hispanics seeking care from priests; Hough, Canino, Abueg, & Gusman, this volume).

Failure to attend to the potential incomprehensibility, inappropriateness, irrelevance, and incompleteness of the questions posed by standardized instruments when used cross-culturally may have serious consequences. Misclassification, by confounding false-positive and false-negative attributions, can easily occur. Unexamined, the use of standardized instruments with American Indians, and other groups, can leading to significant under- and over-reporting of symptoms and syndromes, rendering comparisons with other groups highly tenuous.

As noted, in the interests of replication, the NCAIANMHR was required to use the instruments from the original NVVRS. However, in the interests of cultural validity, certain methods have been implemented to examine explicitly the capacities and limitations of these instruments. Specifically, two approaches have been adopted. Through key informant interviews with veterans, family members, and community members, and through the classic anthropological technique of participant observation, context and depth are added to the survey results. There is particular emphasis on the familial, community, and historical contexts within which the post war experience of American Indian Vietnam veterans have unfolded. Moreover, case descriptions of the phenomenological realities of the experiences of individual veterans are generated. The results of this work are discussed in greater detail under the last question in this section.

The second approach implemented by the NCAIANMHR more directly addresses the form and content of the instruments themselves. Here, a method known as *focus-group interviews* was used to obtain direct comment on and suggested revisions of the comprehensibility, acceptability, relevance, and completeness of interview items and areas of inquiry. In the American Indian Vietnam Veterans Project, one or two facilitators (represented among the authors) convened small groups of 3 to 10 participants at each of the study sites. Each group met from 8 to 10 2-hour sessions over a 2-month period. Participants were recruited from segments of the local communities: namely, Vietnam veterans, relatives of Vietnam veterans, service providers working with Vietnam veterans, and tribal elders. Each has a unique and important perspective on the area of concern. The focus groups were run on a classroom-like model, but reversed, with the participants as teachers and the facilitators as students. Participants were presented with the original NVVRS instrumentation and systematically asked a series of questions designed to elicit their reactions to the items and suggestions for improvement. These questions included the following:

> What does this question mean to me? Is the intended meaning easily understood? How would I ask this question of someone else? Might I encounter resistance in obtaining an answer to this question? How could I rephrase the question to reduce such resistance?

The lessons taught by these focus groups were wide ranging. However, the implications for assessing the validity of the interview are relatively straightforward. The general notion of war-related trauma as capable of adversely affecting soldiers—a central tenet of PTSD—clearly resonated with local understandings. Moreover, focus-group respondents had little difficulty recognizing many, if not most, of the specific symptoms of PTSD as the direct result of combat-related trauma. Stories of disturbed sleep, intrusive memories, avoidance, hypervigilance, isolation, and other such symptoms abounded.

Yet, despite these findings, it also became evident that certain items and constellations of items were problematic in these communities. Several of the problematic items are conveyed within the opening examples of this section. The research team labored arduously to identify such items, to articulate alternatives, to understand the implications that subsequent modifications might pose for issues of comparability, and to devise creative means for informing the instrumentation along such lines. The modifications can be summarized as changes in question wording, length and construction, and specificity. Debriefing and additional key-informant interviews more extensively elucidate the impact of such changes on respondent comprehension and acceptance of the items.

Performance Characteristics of Screeners and Diagnostic Interviews

What is the reliability and validity of self-report measures (M–PTSD, IES) and structured interview methods (DISC, CIDI, SCID) for ascertaining PTSD? Are these psychometric properties different among American Indians? Can they be improved?

Culture may place differential emphasis on particular symptoms, assign unique attributions to the intensity of their experience as well as expression, and shape the general tone of emotional life to which a person should aspire. Thus, distinguishing among mood, symptom, and disorder, which are presumed to vary along a continuum, is not as simple as it might seem (Kleinman & Good, 1985; Manson, in press). Although there is little empirical evidence to this effect, current diagnostic operations assume that such experiences are unidimensional, linear, and additive in nature, not unlike a ruler.

The cross–cultural literature suggests that the "markers" on the ruler may vary from one group to another akin to the difference between metric and nonmetric systems of measurement. Not only may the scale of measurement differ in terms of minimal unit(s), (e.g., millimeter vs. 1/32th of an inch), but the significant categories of aggregation may not correspond as well (e.g., centimeter and meter vs. inch, foot, and yard). Assessing the degree to which subjective conditions like dysphoria, anxiety, hyperarousal, and avoidance are present in cross-cultural settings, then, is not straightforward, as elegantly demonstrated by McNabb (1990b) in his recent article on determining the accuracy and meaning of self-reported satisfaction among the Eskimo, and by Iwata, Okuyama, Kawakami, and Saito (1989) in their report on the Japanese use of CES–D scalar values.

Assume that ways are developed to translate from one ruler to another—by no means an easy task even in the simplest form of the problem. This accomplishment does not take into account the normative uncertainty of psychiatric ratings (Chance, 1963; Good & Good, 1986; Guarnaccia, Angel, & Worobey, 1989; Jenkins, 1988; Manson et al., 1985; Murphy & Hughes, 1965; Robins, 1989). Specifically, the threshold at which *normal* is demarcated from *abnormal* may vary by gender and cultural group.

For example, the persistently higher prevalence of depressive symptoms reported among female than male study participants, and among Puerto Ricans than White, middle-class Americans (Guarnaccia, Rubio-Stipec, & Canino, 1989) may represent culturally patterned variations in the experiential levels of these phenomena and not necessarily higher rates of disorder. Consequently, such normative differences imply different cutoff points for distinguishing common, unremarkable episodes of mood from those that are unusual and noteworthy. Current *DSM* debate over the number of symptoms required to meet Criterion C (persistent avoidance or psychic numbing) for posttraumatic stress disorder reflects an analogous struggle to establish a viable cutoff point.

The *DSM–III–R* (and now the *DSM–IV*), however, uses more than just intensity or severity in rendering such judgments. Duration often figures into the diagnostic calculus, for example, 2 weeks of persistent dysphoria to meet criterion for major depressive episode, or 1 month for post-traumatic stress disorder. Nevertheless, the same problem arises. For example, among the Hopi, sadness and worry are so common and widespread that periods of 1 month or more may be required to reach a level of significance for the individual and fellow community members equivalent to that presupposed by the DSM (Manson et al., 1985). Even then, it appears as if duration is but a "proxy" measure of functional impairment: The sadness or worry experienced by a Hopi person becomes a concern when she or he begins to fail to meet deeply ingrained social expectations.

Further insight into the gender as well as cultural patterning of affect—in this case, symptoms of depression and anxiety—can be obtained from recent studies involving the Center for Epidemiologic Studies Depression Scale (CES–D). The CES–D is a composite measure that includes items from previously established scales, and was developed by researchers at the National Institute for Mental Health (NIMH) for use in epidemiological studies of depressive symptomatology (Radloff, 1977). The 20-item scale assesses the occurrence and persistence of the following symptoms in the past week: depressed mood, feelings of guilt and worthlessness, psychomotor retardation, loss of appetite, and sleep disturbance.

The scale (CES–D) has been shown to be psychometrically sound in terms of its reliability across diverse populations: adults (Radloff, 1977; Zich, Attkisson, & Greenfield, 1990); adolescents (Roberts, Andrews, Lewinsohn, & Hops, 1990); and certain racial and ethnic groups (Roberts, 1980; Ying, 1988). Radloff (1977) described factor analyses by gender and ethnicity (White vs. African-American) that yielded a consistent dimensional structure comprised of four factors that she labeled *depressed affect*, *somatic complaints*, *positive affect*, and *interpersonal*. Other researchers subsequently have reported important differences in the factor structures across gender and ethnic groups.

Analyses by Clark, Aneshensel, Frerichs, & Morgan, (1981), Guarnaccia et al., (1989), Garcia & Marks (1989), and Roberts et al. (1990) of a variety of different data sets incorporating the CES–D revealed significant factorial variation between male and female participants. Likewise, different factor structures have been observed among Chinese Americans (Kuo, 1984; Ying, 1989) and Hispanics (Guarnaccia et al., 1989; Garcia & Marks, 1989; Golding & Aneshensel, 1989).

Three studies have examined the performance of the CES–D among American Indian samples. Manson, Ackerson, Dick, Baron, and Fleming (1990) performed factor analyses on data collected from Indian adolescents attending a boarding school. They obtained a three-factor solution with a strong "general" factor that included items from Radloff's depressed affect, somatic complaints, and interpersonal factors. The remaining 2 factors encompassed additional items from the somatic complaints factor, as well as a distinct positive-affect factor.

In a study of older chronically physically ill American Indians, Baron, Manson, Ackerson, and Brenneman (1990) reported obtaining a four-factor solution, again with a strong general factor including both depressed affect and somatic complaints. The remaining three factors were not well defined. Beals, Keane, & Dick, and Manson (1991) examined the viability of the model tested by Golding and Aneshensel (1989) on a large sample of young adults. A three-factor model in which the somatic complaints and depressed-affect factors were collapsed was deemed the most appropriate for this data.

A number of studies have shown that the factor structures for other, similar self-report measures of symptoms of depression and anxiety (Brief Symptom Index, Zung Self-Rating Depression Scale, Beck Depression Inventory) also vary significantly by cultural populations (Good et al., 1985; Marsella, Kinzie, & Gordon, 1973; Tashakkori, Barefoot, & Mehryar, 1989). However, the evidence for the convergence of depressed affect and somatic complaints is not as strong as that which has recently emerged in the context of the CES–D.

There is good reason to anticipate, then, that similar dynamics may be at work in the performance of screeners used to identify individuals as probable cases of PTSD. Hence, the Foundations of Indian Teens and the American Indian Vietnam Veterans Project permit the careful analysis of the psychometric properties of the PTSD–I and M–PTSD, respectively, as they obtain among American Indians, in terms of dimensional structure as well as predictive ability. This is particularly important in light of the high percentages of respondents scoring above the scalar thresholds of these self-report measures. Furthermore, the latter study will enable researchers to determine the degree of concordance between a highly structured, lay-administered diagnostic interview (UM–CIDI) and a semistructured, clinician-administered protocol (SCID).

Symptomatological Patterns

Does the syndrome evidence distinct patterns among American Indians in terms of differential emphasis of emotional, cognitive, biological, and psychosocial symptoms?

Of those participating in the Health Survey of Indian Boarding School Students who reported a history of traumatic events, 64.9% fulfilled the DSM–III–R criterion of persistent reexperiences of the traumatic event. Almost 11% met the criteria of persistent avoidance of stimuli associated with the trauma and/or of psychic numbing. Slightly more than 16% of the students fulfilled the criterion of persistent symptoms of autonomic hyperarousal. Nearly 19% of the students reached the duration criterion of symptoms of at least 1 month.

Of the Flower of Two Soils Reinterview students who reported a past history of traumatic events, 50% fulfilled the *DSM–III–R* criterion of persistent reexperiences of the traumatic event, and 8% met the criteria of persistent avoidance of stimuli associated with the trauma and/or of psychic numbing. Furthermore, 17% of the students fulfilled the criterion of persistent symptoms of autonomic hyperarousal, and 9% reached the criterion of duration of symptoms of at least 1 month. In addition, 56% (n = 37) of the youth acknowledged having often thought about the precipitating event over the 6 months prior to interview, and 70% (n = 26) of these same individuals described these thoughts as upsetting. Sixty-two percent reported at least one symptom in association with the experienced trauma (M = 3.5; mode = 3; range = 1–14).

Of the Foundations of Indian Teens youth who reported a positive past history of traumatic events, regardless of the number of PTSD symptoms, 87.4% met the *DSM–III–R* criterion of persistent reexperiences of the traumatic event. Furthermore, two thirds (66.9%) fulfilled the criteria of persistent avoidance of stimuli associated with the trauma and/or of psychic numbing. Nearly 72% of the students reached the criterion of persistent symptoms of autonomic hyperarousal. No individual symptom was endorsed by less than 30% of the students experiencing trauma; 48.6% of the affected students described recent upsetting memories of the events. Approximately half of those experiencing a traumatic event endorsed 8 or more PTSD symptoms (of 17 possible) on this self-report measure.

Prevalence of Posttraumatic Stress Disorder

What is the prevalence of PTSD in American Indian communities? How many individuals who report experiencing one or more traumatic events subsequently meet diagnostic criteria?

As noted earlier, only one individual (1.6%) in the Health Survey of Indian Boarding School Students was diagnosed as suffering from PTSD. This represents slightly less than 3% of those reporting a qualifying trauma. Approximately 3% (n = 3) of the students participating in the Flower of Two Soils Reinterview met criteria for PTSD, comprising 4.5% of persons who experienced a traumatic event.

The available data from the Foundations of Indian Teens and American Indian Vietnam Veterans Project are based on screeners, rather than diagnostic protocols. In addition, the former was self-administered, as opposed to interview-based. More than a quarter (26.9%) of the students surveyed by the Foundations of Indian Teens project reached criteria for PTSD. The partial sample of Northern Plains Vietnam veterans scoring as probable cases on the M–PTSD is at least 50%.

Comorbidity With Other Disorders

To what extent and with which psychiatric disorders is PTSD likely to co-occur among American Indians? Are these associations similar to their non–Indian counterparts?

Other psychiatric disorders frequently are comorbid with PTSD (Davidson, Swartz, Storck, Krishnan, & Hammett, 1985; Escobar et al., 1983; Sierles, Chen, & McFarland, 1983). Helzer, Robins, and McEnvoy (1987), reporting adult Epidemiologic Catchment Area data, observed that men with PTSD were 5 times as likely as men without PTSD to have a *DSM–III* drug abuse or dependence disorder; women with PTSD were 1.4 times as likely to have drug abuse or dependence as women without PTSD. Breslau and Davis (1987) found the rate of drug abuse or dependence to be 86% among Vietnam veterans with PTSD. The NVVRS (Kulka et al., 1990) confirmed similar associations. Palinkas et al. (1993) observed significant comorbidity among PTSD, generalized anxiety disorder, and major depression in Alaska Native victims of the Exxon Valdez oil spill.

The nature of such relationships is complicated because non–PTSD disorders may precede the onset of PTSD, and thereby function as a risk factor by increasing vulnerability (Cottler, Compton, Mager, Spitznagel, & Janca, 1992; Smith, North, McCool, & Shea, 1990). Or these disorders may emerge in the course of the individual's attempt to cope with PTSD, for example, self-medication. Alternatively, other disorders may reflect gender- or culture-specific manifestations of stress-related syndromes, such as substance abuse among men and major depression among women. Nonetheless, the clinical picture underscores the frequent co-occurrence of other psychiatric disorders with PTSD.

The Flower of Two Soils Reinterview revealed that 52% (*n* = 34) of the students reporting a traumatic event met criteria for diagnosis of another disorder, either independent of or in addition to PTSD. The most common disorders were disruptive behavior disorders (32%), substance abuse and dependence disorders (24%), anxiety dsorders (18%), and mood disorders (17%). Further analyses indicated a direct relationship between the number of traumatic experiences reported and probability of assignment of a non–PTSD diagnosis.

Ethnographic inquiry conducted as a part of the American Indian Vietnam Veterans Project illustrates some of the forces at work in regard to the interaction of alcohol dependence and PTSD, at least in this population. Tony Two Bulls (a psuedonym), a Northern Plains tribal member, saw 22 months of combat while in the army. Talking about such experiences carries multiple risks for him and fellow Indian veterans—risks that are psychologically, historically, and culturally constructed. Few contexts are relatively free from these risks in their community. One of them, however, is group drinking, most often with other veterans or with family members. Recognition of the risks of talking and the culturally ascribed role of alcohol as providing courage to talk helps to explain, at one level, how and why Tony maintained a lifestyle of heavy drinking for close to 20 years after his return from Vietnam.

The resurrection of the agony, fear, guilt, sorrow, and horror associated with combat is done in a condition of being "blanked out," to use the local term. Veterans often have no memory of what transpires when they drink heavily, what they talked about, whether they wept, or who fought. In such situations, the veterans rely upon others to tell them what happened, which may not occur for many years. It is this ability of alcohol—to enable one to disclose intimate details about "Nam," and yet, at the same time, forget it, even for a brief moment—that many veterans, including Tony, cite as the most important reason for their drinking. Hence, motivations of this nature must be taken into account if PTSD is to be understood in association with other, frequently comorbid disorders.

Developmental Precursors

What factors prior to the precipitating event (e.g., exposure to other traumas and pretrauma adjustment) increase risk of PTSD among American Indians?

Questions of this nature introduce the issue of vulnerability and factors that, prior to the occurrence of a traumatic event, place an individual at increased risk of suffering from PTSD. Here, too, considerable debate is evident. For the most part, this debate has been over whether vulnerabilities exist and if they play a role in predisposing an individual to the disorder. The preponderance of findings to date suggests that such questions have been answered. Age, education, economic status, certain personality traits, personal psychiatric history, family psychiatric history, and prior traumatic events are among the most frequently cited risk factors (Atkeson, Calhoun, Resick, & Ellis, 1982; Cottler et al., 1992; Davidson et al., 1985; Solomon, Benbenishty, & Mikulincer, 1988; Solomon, Mikulincer, & Jakob, 1987).

Obviously, the high prevalence of traumatic events reported by youth in the Health Survey of Indian Boarding School Students, Flower of Two Soils Reinterview, and Foundations of Indian Teens invites speculation about their subsequent vulnerability at later points in the developmental life cycle. So does the extent of other, non-PTSD disorders observed in these samples. The American Indian Vietnam Veterans Project uses an extensive traumatic-events schedule that elicits relevant stressors over the lifetime. A key interest is the relative risk for PTSD that these events predict, and at what points in the developmental cycle they are likely to occur.

Mediators of Risk

What factors after the precipitating event (e.g., ethnic identification, self-concept, social support, spiritual beliefs) ameliorate risk of PTSD among American Indians?

Conceptually linked to questions of vulnerabilities, etiologic models of PTSD also consider factors that may serve protective functions. The literature presently champions at least two families of such models (Solomon, Mikulincer, & Waysman, 1991; Watson, Kucala, Manifold, & Vassar, 1989). The first can be construed as a modified stress-coping model in which the traumatic event is considered the major stressor; current life events, social support, and coping mechanisms are seen as important mediators. The second group of models seeks to explain PTSD in terms of family history of psychiatric illness, childhood traumas, dispositional features of personality, and, in the case of veterans, premilitary adjustment. Careful review of these conceptual frameworks suggests that there is no intrinsic barrier to their integration. Thus, the American Indian Vietnam Veterans Project quite purposefully gathers information relevant to both orientations. Model development and testing will proceed on empirical grounds.

More extensive inspection of the current literature revealed that certain aspects of American Indian personhood and life experience were, however, absent from past consideration. Examples are racial discrimination, identification with the enemy, ethnic affiliation, and salience of the self-as-warrior (Manson, in press). Special attention has been given to operationalizing and measuring these constructs to permit their inclusion in the aforementioned models.

Functioning and Domains of Impairment

What specific domains of American Indian life (e.g., physical health, school, work, family, peers, spirituality) does PTSD affect and how?

PTSD has enormous impact on a wide spectrum of activities of daily living. There appear, however, to be major differences between Native and non-Native victims in regard to the degree of such impact within certain domains. For example, focus-group interviews in the early phases of the American Indian Vietnam Veterans Project repeatedly underscored the devastating consequences that social isolation, avoidance, and psychic numbing—hallmark symptoms of this disorder—have for interpersonal relationships, notably with family and clan. Stories often were told by mothers, sisters, and wives of the communities' deep respect for their warriors, a status that is honored. Yet, virtually in the same breath, they voiced their frustration, despair, and fear, for these men proved to be distant, unconnected, and unpredictable. Caught in a dilemma—obliged to defer to and seek counsel from these latter day warriors, yet unable to relate to them in expected ways—family members find themselves at a loss.

This sense of loss is reflected in the case of Tony Two Bulls. Friends and relatives of Vietnam veterans claim that they can recognize veterans by the faraway look in their eyes. They say that many veterans are still in Vietnam, trying to finish the war. At a 1992 powwow that marked Tony's first step on this journey home, a local drum group sang a song that they composed for the Vietnam veterans they had gathered to honor. Above the mesmerizing beat of their upheld drum, as Grandmothers around the arena wiped tears from their eyes, the words of the singers rang out:

> Soldier, what is the matter? Your friends and family are talking. They say, "That war overseas is over. Come home! We are having a good time here."

The community cannot rest until the grandsons, sons, nephews, brothers, cousins, and husbands that it sent to Vietnam finally return. The loss is too great, for these men are of the generation who are now becoming grandfathers, who are destined to start assuming the roles of family and community leaders. In line with the warrior traditions of Northern Plains society, it is time for Vietnam veterans to transform their combat experiences, their courage and bravery, into wisdom to help guide their families and tribes. It is time for the *akicita*, or the warriors, to tame their aggressiveness and cultivate compassion for the people, to pick up the mantle of leadership.

Treatment

From whom do American Indians seek help for PTSD and related disorders? What factors affect these decision-making processes? Are indigenous forms of therapy available and used?

Issues such as these are closely examined within the context of the American Indian Vietnam Veterans Project. In addition to its epidemiological imperative, this study is charged with determining patterns of service use and facilitators as well as barriers thereof. The lay-administered interview contains an extensive section on help-seeking behavior across indigenous, tribal, state, and federal systems of care, for both physical and mental health problems. A wide range of factors are explored in regard to relevant decision-making processes, such as accessibility, acceptability, stigma, and racial discrimination.

Perhaps one of the more difficult forms of treatment to grasp, but which has considerable enduring character, is that which involves ceremonial activities to bring about a healing response in an afflicted individual, which may produce salutary effects for the nonafflicted members of the community. These have been defined as *healing ceremonies*, probably because that was the best available metaphor by which non-Natives could describe and understand of what was happening. But these ceremonies greatly exceed that which is commonly understood as healing by the biomedical perspective, and can have a positive social effect far beyond the individual who is the focus of the healing ritual. A few contrasts between biomedical and symbolic or cultural healing may clarify these differences.

With respect to the classification of the illness or affliction the American Indian view deals far more with the mythology or belief system of a particular culture (Farella, 1984; Sandner, 1979), as opposed to empirical facts and scientific principles. The particular healing technique is also based on cultural values and beliefs and can only be used in a specified area of cultural influence, as opposed to anatomical and physiological principles that are presumed to be transcultural.

Among the Navajo, with respect to Vietnam veterans, the most frequently mentioned healing ceremony of this nature is the Enemy Way, which explicitly evolved in response to the trauma experienced by warriors. This ceremony lasts for 7 days and 7 nights and employs ritual song by tribal medicine men. The ceremony seeks to return individual balance and harmony. The patient must actively believe in the treatment and carries most of the responsibility for the cure, as opposed to passively following treatment prescription for which the physician is responsible (Kluckhohm & Leighton, 1974). There is a substantial social function to the healing in which the extended family, clan, and surrounding community members actively participate, as opposed to being limited to the nonexistent social aspects of scientific healing practices. Many other contrasts have been noted in the literature, but the above serve as a limited set.

Perhaps the greatest relevance for such forms of healing lies in their *meaning-making* aspects and the coherence-engendering qualities of the healing ritual. Thus ceremonial healing approaches may accomplish the alleviation of physical symptoms for the patient while simultaneously reinforcing the idea that the world is predictably ordered as described by Antonovsky's (1979, 1987) sense of coherence.

Prevention

Are there ceremonies and ritual structures in American Indian communities that serve to protect individuals from the potentially harmful effects of traumatic experiences?

Clearly, there are such ceremonies and ritual structures. Another, specific example comes from the use of cultural ritual both to bring about healing and to increase spiritual well-being among Native Vietnam veterans experiencing PTSD (Wilson, 1988). This is a particularly apt example in light of the greatly expanded range of stressful life experiences for which long-term traumatic effects have been described. It is also pertinent because it suggests the psychophysiological mechanisms by which such cultural rituals may in part produce salutary effects on all the participants.

The cultural practice in this case involves the use of the sweat lodge purification ritual (*Inipi Onikare*), which is regarded as a "serious and sacred occasion in which spiritual insights, personal growth, and physical and emotional healing may take place. The purpose of purification is experienced on many levels of awareness, including the physical, psychological, social, and spiritual" (Wilson, 1988, p. 44). There are many symbolic aspects of the physical construction of the sweat lodge and the various objects that are part of the ritual (Brown, 1971).

Of more relevant concern are the psychological effects attributed to the ritual process, which includes a physically close circular arrangement of participants to increase unity and bonding, individual prayers involving self-disclosure of personal concerns and needs, as well as the needs and concerns of others, and the "opening" of the Four Doors through a cycle of prayers (actual opening of the sweat-lodge door with change in heat and light conditions). The ceremony is controlled by the medicine person who works to lead the group to

> see more fully the symbolic nature of the ritual as a paradigm of life's central struggles. The juxtaposition of darkness and light may then take on deeper symbolic values as the paradigms of life versus death; insight versus ignorance; growth versus stagnation; hope versus despair; relief versus suffering; renewal versus stasis; connection versus separation; communality versus aloneness, and will versus resignation. (Wilson, 1988, p. 54)

Other aspects of the ritual are designed to promote a sense of the continuity of the community and continuity of the individual in the culture, which may be particularly important to those who have struggled with adapting to stressful experiences outside of their Native communities. The conclusion of the ritual is typically accompanied by a number of positive psychological outcomes that include a sense of emotional release, and a feeling of renewal and inner strength.

Although the sweat-lodge ritual can be and often is used for otherwise relatively well-functioning persons, Wilson (1988) also describes the alleviation of the more prominent symptoms of posttraumatic stress disorder as among the positive benefits. In addition, Wilson provides an explanation of the psychobiological aspects of altered states of consciousness that have commonly been observed and measured during the ritual, and of the shifts in hemispheric dominance that are part of the altered states of consciousness commonly produced by ritual participation.

Collective Representations of and Responses to Traumatic Stress

How do social groups (e.g., families, peers, community) in American Indian communities make sense of the suffering associated with traumatic experiences? How are the resultant meanings negotiated within and between these groups? What do these cultural meanings imply for the matters noted above?

Returning to Tony Two Bulls, on an overcast day in June 1992, over 20 years after his return from Vietnam, he stepped forward for the first time in his life to be honored at the annual powwow for Vietnam veterans at his Northern Plains reservation. Tony, like many of his fellow combatants, still struggled with explosive anger. But his journey to (re)join the group was remarkable, for it conveys a great deal about how much he was willing to risk at this point in his life to come to terms with his Vietnam experiences, and their continuing hold on his life.

Tony has had difficulty speaking about that time in his life. In part, his reluctance derives from feelings "of hatred, of hurt, of death, of revenge" that he consistently prefers to keep at bay. This reluctance springs from participating in a war that suffers its soldiers a uniquely disvalued place in American history. It also derives from a deep ambivalence in Northern Plains culture regarding when it is appropriate to talk about oneself and when it is not. In the words of a World War II combat veteran, "War ain't nothing to brag about."

On one hand, there exists the Indian term and related institutions *waktoglaka*, meaning to retell one's own warlike exploits, to talk about one's accomplishments, or, in the past, to recount how many scalps one has helped to take. Usually, men are asked to retell their combat experiences at ceremonies honoring others, such as at a naming ceremony for one's niece or nephew. As such, honoring oneself honors others. Outside of specific settings such as these, however, the value of talking about war experiences is less straightforward. Rather than being judged as honorable speech, talking about one's combat experience might just as likely be understood in terms of *iglata*, meaning to praise yourself, to boast, or to brag. Negotiating these social and cultural shoals is a difficult but essential developmental task for Tony, his peers, and all others around him. It is, as described by the sister of one Indian Vietnam veteran, "the challenge of healing wounded spirits, and mending ailing hearts."

CONCLUSION

This chapter has woven threads from four quite different studies into a tapestry that, although far from complete, for the first time provides an empirically based rendering of trauma and PTSD among American Indians. The emerging picture spans significant portions of the developmental life cycle, and is stitched together by quantitative and qualitative research techniques. More suggestive than definitive, it provides a glimpse of the important contributions that future work in this area can offer to improving the mental health of Indian people as well as to the advancement of our understanding of PTSD as a serious psychiatric illness and of human suffering in general.

REFERENCES

Ackerson, L. M., Dick, R. W., Manson, S. M., & Baron, A. E. (1990). Depression among American Indian adolescents: Psychometric characteristics of the Inventory to Diagnose Depression. *Journal of the American Academy of Child and Adolescent Psychiatry, 29*(4), 601–607.

American Psychiatric Association. (1987). *Diagnostic and statistical manual of mental disorders* (3rd ed., rev.). Washington, DC: Author.

Antonovsky, A. (1979). *Health, stress, and coping.* San Francisco: Jossey-Bass.

Antonovsky, A. (1987). *Unraveling the mystery of health: How people manage stress and stay well.* San Francisco: Jossey-Bass.

Atkeson, B. M., Calhoun, K. S., Resick, P. A., & Ellis, E. (1982). Victims of rape: Repeated assessment of depressive symptoms. *Journal of Consulting and Clinical Psychology, 50,* 96–102.

Bachman, R. (1992). *Death and violence on the reservation.* Westport, CT: Auburn House.

Baron, A. E., Manson, S. M., Ackerson, L. M. & Brenneman (1990). Depressive symptomatology in older American Indians with chronic disease. In C. Attkisson & J. Zich (Eds.), *Screening for depression in primary care* (pp. 217–231). New York: Routledge, Kane & Co.

Beals, J., Keane, E. M., Dick, R. W., & Manson, S. M. (1991). The factorial structure of the CES–D among American Indian college students. *Journal of Consulting and Clinical Psychology, 3*(4), 623–627.

Bechtold, D. W. (1988). Cluster suicides in American Indian adolescents. *American Indian and Alaska Native Mental Health Research, 1*(3), 26–35.

Beiser, M., & Attneave, C. L. (1982). Mental disorders among Native American children: Rates and risk periods for entering treatment. *American Journal of Psychiatry, 139,* 193–198.

Bravo, M., Canino, G. J., Rubio-Stepic, M., & Woodbury-Farina, M. (1991). A cross-cultural adaptation of a psychiatric epidemiologic instrument: The Diagnostic Interview Schedule's adaptation in Puerto Rico. *Culture, Medicine and Psychiatry, 15,* 275–295.

Breslau, N., & Davis, G. C. (1987). Post-traumatic stress disorder: The etiologic specificity of wartime stressors. *American Journal of Psychiatry, 144,* 578–583.

Brown, J. E. (1971). *The sacred pipe: Black Elk's account of the seven rites of the Oglala Sioux*. Baltimore, MD: Penguin.

Chance, N. (1963). Conceptual and methodological problems in cross-cultural health research. *American Journal of Public Health, 52*, 410–417.

Clark, V. A., Aneshensel, C. S., Frerichs, R. R., & Morgan, T. M. (1981). Analysis of effects of sex and age in response to items on the CES–D scale. *Psychiatry Research, 5*, 171–181.

Costello, A. J., Edelbrock, C. S., Dulcan, M. K., Kalas, R., & Klaric, S. H. (1984). *Report to NIMH on the NIMH Diagnostic Interview for Children (DISC)*. Pittsburgh, PA: Authors.

Cottler, L. B., Compton, W. M., Mager, D., Spitznagel, E. L., & Janca, A. (1992). Post-Traumatic Stress Disorder among substance users from the general population. *American Journal of Psychiatry, 149*, 664–670.

Davidson, J., Swartz, M., Storck, M., Krishnan, R., & Hammett, E. (1985). A diagnostic and family study of post-traumatic stress disorder. *American Journal of Psychiatry, 142*, 90–93.

Dick, R. W., Beals, J., Manson, S. M., & Bechtold, D. W. (1994). *Psychometric properties of the Suicidal Ideation Questionnaire among American Indian adolescents*. Unpublished manuscript, National Center for American Indian and Alaska Native Mental Health Research, Denver, CO.

Dick, R. W., Manson, S. M., & Beals, J. (1993). Alcohol use among American Indian adolescents: Patterns and correlates of students' drinking in a boarding school. *Journal of Studies on Alcohol, 54*, 172–177.

Escobar, J. I., Randolph, E. T., Pruente, G., Spivak, F., Asamen, J., & Hill, M. (1983). Post-traumatic stress disorder in Hispanic Vietnam veterans. *Journal of Nervous and Mental Disease, 171*, 585–596.

Farella, J. R. (1984). *The main stalk: A synthesis of Navajo philosophy*. Tucson: University of Arizona Press.

Freidenberg, J., Mulvihill, M., & Caraballo, L. R. (1993). From ethnography to survey: Some methodological issues in research on health seeking in East Harlem. *Human Organization, 52*(2), 151–161.

Garcia, M., & Marks, G. (1989). Depressive symptomatology among Mexican-American adults: An examination of the CES–D scale. *Psychiatry Research, 27*(2), 137–148.

Golding, J. M., & Aneshensel, C. S. (1989). Factor structure of the Center for Epidemiologic Studies Depression Scale among Mexican-Americans and Non-Hispanic Whites. *Psychological Assessment, 1*(3), 163–168.

Good, B. J., & Good, M. J. (1986). The cultural context of diagnosis and therapy: A view from medical anthropology. In M. Miranda & H. Kitano (Eds.), *Research and practice in minority communities* (pp. 36–43). Washington, DC: U.S. Government Printing Office.

Good, B. J., Good, M. J., & Moradi, R. (1985). The interpretation of Iranian depressive illness and dysphoric affect. In A. Kleinman & B. J. Good (Eds.), *Culture and depression* (pp. 369–428). Berkeley: University of California Press.

Guarnaccia, P. J., Angel, R., & Worobey, J. L. (1989). The factor structure of the CES–D in the Hispanic Health and Nutrition Examination Survey: The influences of ethnicity, gender, and language. *Social Science and Medicine, 29*(1), 85–94.

Guarnaccia, P., Rubio-Stipec, M., & Canino, G. (1989). *Ataques de nervios* in the Puerto Rican Diagnostic Interview Schedule. *Culture, Medicine, and Psychiatry, 13,* 275–295.

Helzer, J. E., Robins, L. E., & McEnvoy, L. (1987) Post-traumatic stress disorder in the general population. *New England Journal of Medicine, 317,* 1630–1634.

Jenkins, J. H. (1988). Conceptions of schizophrenia as a problem of nerves: A cross-cultural comparison of Mexican-Americans and Anglo-Americans. *Social Science and Medicine, 26*(2), 1233–1244.

Iwata, N., Okuyama, Y., Kawakami, Y., & Saito, K. (1989). Prevalence of depressive symptoms in a Japanese occupational setting: A preliminary study. *American Journal of Public Health, 70,* 1486–1489.

Keane, T., Caddell, J., & Taylor, K. (1988). Mississippi Scale for Combat-related post-traumatic stress disorder: Three studies in reliability and validity. *Journal of Consulting and Clinical Psychology, 56,* 85–90.

Keane, T., Malloy, P., & Fairbank, J. (1984). Empirical development of an MMPI subscale for the assessment of combat-related post-traumatic stress disorder. *Journal of Consulting and Clinical Psychology, 52,* 888–891.

King, J., Beals, J., Manson, S. M., & Trimble, J. E. (1992). A structural equation model of factors related to substance abuse among American Indian adolescents. *Drugs and Society, 6*(3/4), 253– 268.

Kleinman, A. (1980). *Patients and healers in the context of culture.* Berkeley: University of California Press.

Kleinman, A., & Good., B. (Eds.). (1985). *Culture and depression.* Berkeley, CA: University of California Press.

Kluckhohn, C., & Leighton, D. (1974). *The Navaho* (Rev. ed.). Cambridge, MA: Harvard University Press.

Kulka, R. A., Schlenger, W. E., Fairbank, J. A., Hough, R. L., Jordan, B. K., Marmar, C. R., & Weiss, D. S. (1990). *Trauma and the Vietnam War generation: Report of findings from the National Vietnam Veterans Readjustment Study.* New York: Bruner/Mazel.

Kuo, W. (1984). Prevalence of depression among Asian-Americans. *Journal of Nervous and Mental Disease, 192,* 449–457.

Manson, S. M. (in press). Cross-cultural and multi-ethnic assessment of trauma. In J. P. Wilson & T. M. Keane (Eds.), *Assessing psychological trauma and PTSD: A handbook for practitioners.* New York: Guilford.

Manson, S. M. (in press). Culture and the *DSM–IV*: Implications for the diagnosis of mood and anxiety disorders. In J. Messich, A. Kleinman, H. Fabrega, & D. Parron (Eds.), *Culture and psychiatric diagnosis.* Washington, DC: American Psychiatric Press.

Manson, S. M., Ackerson, L. M., Dick, R. W., Baron, A. E., & Fleming, C. M. (1990). Depressive symptoms among American Indian adolescents: Psychometric characteristics of the Center for Epidemiologic Studies Depression Scale (CES–D). *Psychological Assessment, 2*(3), 231–237.

Manson, S. M., Shore, J. H., & Bloom, J. D. (1985). The depressive experience in American Indian communities: A challenge for psychiatric theory and diagnosis. In A. Kleinman & B. Good (Eds.), *Culture and depression* (pp. 331–368). Berkeley: University of California Press.

Manson, S. M., Walker, R. D., & Kivlahan, D. R. (1987). Psychiatric assessment and treatment of American Indians and Alaska Natives. *Hospital and Community Psychiatry, 38*(2), 165–173.

Marsella, A. J., Kinzie, J. D., & Gordon, P. (1973). Ethnocultural variations in the expression of depression. *Journal of Cross-Cultural Psychology, 4*, 453–458.

McNabb, S. L. (1990a). The uses of "inaccurate" data: A methodological critique and applications of Alaska Native data. *American Anthropologist, 92*, 116–129.

McNabb, S. L. (1990b). Self-reports in cross-cultural contexts. *Human Organization, 49*(4), 291–299.

Murphy, J. M., & Hughes, C. C. (1965). The use of psychophysiological symptoms as indicators of disorder among Eskimos. In J. M. Murphy & A. H. Leighton (Eds.), *Approaches to cross-cultural psychiatry* (pp 108–160). Ithaca, NY: Cornell University Press.

Palinkas, L. A., Downs, M., Petterson, J. S., & Russell, J. (1993). Social, cultural, and psychological impacts of the Exxon Valdez oil spill. *Human Organization, 52*(1), 1–13.

Radloff, L. S. (1977). The CES–D scale: A self–report depression scale for research in the general population. *Applied Psychological Measurement, 1*(3), 385–401.

Roberts, R. E. (1980). Reliability of the CES–D scale in different ethnic contexts. *Psychiatry Research, 2*, 125–134.

Roberts, R. E., Andrews, J. A., Lewinsohn, P. M., & Hops, H. (1990). Assessment of depression in adolescents using the Center for Epidemiologic Studies Depression Scale. *Psychological Assessment, 2*(2), 122–128.

Robins, L. N. (1989). Cross-cultural differences in psychiatric disorder. *American Journal of Public Health, 79*(11), 1479–1480.

Rogler, L. (1989). The meaning of culturally sensitive research in mental health. *American Journal of Psychiatry, 146*, 296–303.

Sack, W., Beiser, M., Baker–Brown, G., & Redshirt, R. (1994). Depressive and suicidal symptoms in Indian school children: Some findings from the Flower of Two Soils. In C. Wilson Duclos & S. M. Manson (Eds.), *Beyond the rim: Epidemiology and prevention of suicide among Indian and Native youth* (pp. 81–94). Niwot, CO: University Press of Colorado.

Sack, W., Beiser, M., Clarke, G., & Redshirt, R. (1987). The high achieving Sioux Indian child: Some preliminary findings from the Flower of Two Soils Project. *American Indian and Alaska Native Mental Health Research, 1*(1), 41–56.

Sandner, D. (1979). *Navajo symbols of healing: A Jungian exploration of ritual, image, and medicine*. Rochester, VT: Healing Arts Press.

Shaffer, D., Schwab-Stone, M., Fisher, P., Davies, M., Piacentinie, J., & Gioia, P. (1988). *A revised version of the Diagnostic Interview Schedule for Children (DISC-R): Results of a field trial and proposals for a new instrument (DISC-2)*. Report submitted to the National Institute of Mental Health. New York: Authors.

Sierles, F. S., Chen, J., & McFarland, R. E. (1983). Post-traumatic stress disorder and concurrent psychiatric illness: Preliminary report. *American Journal of Psychiatry, 140*, 1177–1179.

Smith, E. M., North, C. S., McCool, R., & Shea, J. M. (1990). Acute post-disaster psychiatric disorders: Identification of persons at risk. *American Journal of Psychiatry, 147*, 202–206.

Solomon, Z., Benbenishty, R., & Mikulincer, M. (1988). A follow-up of the Israeli casualties of combat stress reaction (battle shock) in 1982 Lebanon war. *British Journal of Clinical Psychology, 27*, 125–135.

Solomon, Z., Mikulincer, M., & Jakob, B. R. (1987). Exposure to recurrent combat stress: Combat stress reactions among Israeli soldiers in the Lebanon war. *Psychological Medicine, 17*, 433–440.

Solomon, Z., Mikulincer, M., & Waysman, M. (1991). Delayed and immediate onset post-traumatic stress disorder: The role of life events and social resources. *Journal of Community Psychology, 19*, 231–236.

Tashakkori, A., Barefoot, J., & Mehryar, A. H. (1989). What does the Beck Depression Inventory measure in college students? Evidence from a non-Western culture. *Journal of Clinical Psychology, 45*(4), 595–602.

Watson, C. G., Kucala, T., Juba, M., Manifold, V., & Andersen, P. E. D. (1991). A factor analysis of the *DSM-III* post-traumatic stress disorder criteria. *Journal of Clinical Psychology, 47*(2), 205–214.

Watson, C. G., Kucala, T., Manifold, V., & Vassar, P. (1989). Childhood stress disorder behaviors in veterans who do and do not develop post-traumatic stress disorder. *Journal of Nervous and Mental Disease, 177*(2), 92–95.

Wilson, J. (1988). Culture and trauma: The sacred pipe revisited. In J. Wilson, Z. Harel, & B. Kahana (Eds.), *Human adaptation to extreme stress: From holocaust to Vietnam* (pp. 38–71). New York: Plenum.

Working Group on American Indian Vietnam Veterans. (1992). *Untitled*. Report submitted to Readjustment Counseling Services, Department of Veterans Affairs. Washington, DC: Author.

Ying, Y. (1988). Depressive symptomatology among Chinese-Americans as measured by the CES-D. *Journal of Clinical Psychology, 44*(5), 739–746.

Zich, J., Attkisson, C., & Greenfield, T. (1990). Screening for depression in primary care clinics: The CES–D and the BDI. *International Journal of Psychiatry in Medicine, 20*(3), 259–277.

Zilberg, N., Weiss, D., & Horowitz, M. (1982). Impact of Event Scale: A cross-validation study and some empirical evidence supporting a conceptual model of stress response syndromes. *Journal of Consulting and Clinical Psychology, 50,* 407–414.

11

TRAUMATIZATION STRESS AMONG ASIANS AND ASIAN AMERICANS

FRANCIS R. ABUEG and KEVIN M. CHUN

The study of traumatic expriences among Asians and Asian Americans is characterized by a comparatively small body of literature. The subset of studies devoted specifically to the examination of posttraumatic stress disorder (PTSD) is very limited. Even the discussion of the application of the construct of PTSD has only recently been broached for such topics as Asian refugees (e.g., Friedman & Jaranson, 1994; Kinzie & Boehlein, 1989; Marsella, Friedman, & Spain, 1993; Mollica, 1994) and Asian war veterans (e.g., Kiang, 1991; Marsella, Chemtob, & Hamada, 1992). Nevertheless, this nascent research literature strongly demonstrates the vast suffering endured by members of various Asian ethnic minority groups. The aim of this chapter is to draw a clear link between ethnic-specific traumatization, psychopathology, and the fledgling literature concerned with PTSD, especially that concerning Southeast Asian refugees settled in North America and Asian American Vietnam veterans.

SOUTHEAST ASIAN REFUGEES

Southeast Asian refugees represent a high-risk population for mental illness because of their extensive exposure to traumatic events and stressors that typically span four time periods in the refugee experience: (a) pre-migration, (b) migration, (c) encampment, and (d) postmigration.

Premigration stressors include brutalization and death of family and friends, and loss of property and personal belongings associated with extensive and sustained warfare. Additionally, many Southeast Asians were subjected to government-sponsored intimidation and threats to their livelihood once the Communists gained power in their homelands in Vietnam, Cambodia, and Laos. *Migration stressors* encompass the separation from or deaths of family and relatives while fleeing one's home country under life-threatening conditions. Assaults by border guards while entering neighboring countries were also common occurrences for many refugees.

Encampment stressors are characterized by prolonged detainment in unsafe, overcrowded, and poorly sanitized refugee camps. Many detained refugees also faced uncertainty surrounding their future and the fate of separated family and friends. Finally, *postmigration stressors* involve building a new life in a foreign country, which necessitates the learning of new skills and cultural norms while dealing with the profound loss of loved ones, personal belongings, and even a familiar way of life. Because there is wide variability in the experiences and adjustment levels of Southeast Asians, the traumatic experiences, prevalence rates and high-risk correlates of psychopathology, and special treatment considerations will be presented for each refugee group.

The Vietnamese

The Vietnamese were one of the first Southeast Asian groups to flee their war-torn homelands and journey to the United States (see Mollica, 1994). Premigration stressors for the Vietnamese center around loss of and separation from family and friends, and destruction of personal property during the Vietnam War. Beginning in 1975, first-wave Vietnamese refugees migrated to the United States primarily in family units and represented the educated and professional classes of Vietnam. In contrast, second-wave Vietnamese refugees who fled Vietnam between 1977 and 1980 were mostly of rural and less educated backgrounds (Takaki, 1989). These refugees, most visibly known as the *boat people*, endured severe migration traumas. It is estimated that more than 200,000 of these refugees died at sea as they fled Vietnam on overcrowded and outdated vessels (Lee & Lu, 1989). Furthermore, over 80% of the boats were boarded by pirates who robbed, raped, assaulted, and killed its passengers (e.g., Lee & Lu, 1987; Mollica, 1994).

Those who succeeded in fleeing Vietnam often landed into refugee camps in Thailand, Hong Kong, Indonesia, Malaysia, and the Philippines. In Thailand, Vietnamese refugees faced what was considered the worst camp conditions and many were detained at Sikhiu, a former jail (Beiser, Turner, & Ganesan, 1989). The life situation of those who remained behind in Vietnam was also precarious at best as many faced the constant threat of indefinite imprisonment in reeducation camps where forced labor, starvation, and torture were commonplace. Past studies indicate that Vietnamese refugees exhibit high levels of psychological and physical distress resulting from their past traumas.

In a recent study (Felsman, Leong, Johnson, & Felsman, 1990), the baseline functioning of Vietnamese youths was examined prior to their exposure to postmigration stressors. Psychological distress among Vietnamese adolescents (13–17 yrs.), unaccompanied minors (13–18 yrs, without adult family members or relatives), and young adults (17.5–20 yrs.) was assessed using the General Health Questionnaire (GHQ), Hopkins Symptom Checklist-25 (HSCL), and the Vietnamese Depression Scale (VDS). Results from this study showed that although high anxiety levels and poor general health were clinically significant across all three groups, the young adult group was especially vulnerable to depression, anxiety, and poor general health.

One of the first studies on the general physical and mental health of first-wave Vietnamese refugees also reported high levels of psychological and physical distress using the Cornell Medical Index (CMI) (Lin, Tazuma, & Masuda, 1979). These researchers noted that 53% of their Phase I participants (data collection in 1975) and 55% of their Phase II sample (data collection in 1976, including both Phase I and new participants) manifested psychological problems. Overall dysfunction, which assessed both physical and psychological problems, was seen in 48% of the Phase I and 56% of the Phase II participants.

Lin, Tazuma, and Masuda (1979) concluded that the similarity of the CMI profiles seen in both phases demonstrates that the mental and physical problems exhibited by these Vietnamese refugees were consistent over time for a 1-year period. Furthermore, they noted that certain segments of the Vietnamese refugee population were significantly at risk for psychological and physical dysfunction. In particular, divorced–widowed female heads of households, individuals over 46 years old, individuals younger than 21 years old, and women between 21 and 45 years exhibited significant levels of dysfunction.

Demographic, premigration, and postmigration predictors of psychological distress were also established in a state-wide community sample of Vietnamese people living in California (Chung & Kagawa-Singer, 1993). In this study, both anxiety and depressive symptoms were associated with demographic variables that included being female, older age, and little or no formal education in one's homeland. Premigration factors predicting high levels of both anxiety and depression included multiple traumas and fewer years spent in a refugee camp.

The premigration variable—numerous deaths of family members— only predicted anxiety. Postmigration factors predicting both anxiety and depression included a low family income, whereas large family size only predicted depression. Protective factors of psychological well-being among Vietnamese refugees have also been investigated. For example, Tran (1989) found that greater memberships in ethnic social organizations, numerous ethnic confidants, high self-esteem, and high income all significantly con- tributed to positive psychological well-being for Vietnamese immigrants.

Chun (1991) examined the same statewide sample of Southeast Asians in Chung and Kagawa-Singer's study to investigate correlates of psychosocial dysfunction or impairment in daily living. This variable pro- vides important information beyond knowledge of symptoms alone. In this study, experiential correlates of psychosocial dysfunction included multiple premigration traumas and experiencing few reunions with separated family and relatives. Also, status variables such as being female or unemployed, having poor English-speaking skills, and relocating to a United States res- idence that is demographically different from one's native residence were correlated with dysfunction among Vietnamese refugees.

Prevalence rates of PTSD among Vietnamese refugees vary across studies. In a study of Southeast Asian patients seen at a specialized refugee clinic, 11% of the Vietnamese sample reportedly suffered from PTSD, a diagnosis that was established using the Diagnostic Interview Schedule (DIS) based on *DSM–III* criteria (Mollica, Wyshak, & Lavelle, 1987). Furthermore, results from this study indicated that multiple traumas was associated with greater susceptibility for PTSD. Kroll et al. (1989) reported that 8.1% of Vietnamese patients in a Southeast Asian psychiatric out- patient population exhibited PTSD. These findings were based on clinical interviews and a 19-item checklist comprising culturally relevant signs of depressive and anxiety symptoms based on *DSM–III* criteria.

This instrument was not cross-validated with other instruments. Women who were widows and increased age until 60 years were associated with increased risk for mental disorders among the general Southeast Asian population in this study. Kinzie et al. (1990) reported that 54% of a sample of Vietnamese psychiatric patients were diagnosed with PTSD using a *DSM–III–R* checklist. Moreover, PTSD was associated with advanced age, female gender, and a diagnosis of depression among this population.

Despite the high levels of psychological and physical distress mani- fested among the Vietnamese, they are generally better adjusted than other Southeast Asian refugee groups. Across the majority of studies, Vietnamese refugees have exhibited the lowest prevalence rate of PTSD compared with other Southeast Asian refugees. Chung and Kagawa-Singer (1993) also noted that a Vietnamese sample population was relatively well-adjusted compared with Cambodians and Laotians because community supports were already established upon their arrival to the United States by earlier well-educated and professional first-wave Vietnamese refugees. Along similar lines, past community-based studies have shown that Vietnamese refugees report greater happiness and less depression than Cambodian and Hmong refugees (Rumbaut, 1985) and less alienation than Cambodians, Hmong, and Laotians (Nicassio, 1983).

Cambodians (Khmer)

The Cambodians (Khmer) endured particularly severe premigration traumas beginning in 1975 with the rise of the Pol Pot regime. During this time, Pol Pot lead the Khmer Rouge on a bloody campaign of genocide to establish a Marxist agrarian society and rid the country of any Western influence. Mass executions, forced separations of family members, and confinement to work camps especially targeted at the professional and working classes were subsequently introduced on a national scale. Life in the work camps consisted of hard labor, torture, beatings, starvation, disease, and killings. Upon the Vietnamese invasion of Cambodia in 1979, a quarter of Cambodia's population was decimated and thousands fled to neighboring Thailand, where they were placed in refugee camps.

Cambodian refugees represent a special at-risk group for mental and physical illness because of their far-reaching history of premigration traumas. For instance, significantly higher levels of anxiety and depression have been seen in a nonpatient sample of Cambodians compared with Vietnamese and Vietnamese–Chinese refugees (Foulks, Merkel, Boehlin, 1992). Cambodian refugees also appear to have poorer self-perceptions and see themselves as more different from Americans to a greater extent than do Vietnamese, Laotian, and Hmong refugees (Mollica, 1994; Nicassio, 1983). Similarly, Rumbaut (1985) found that in a Cambodian community sample participants reported more depressive symptoms compared with any other Southeast Asian refugee group.

Chung and Kagawa-Singer (1993) likewise reported that participants from a community sample of Cambodian refugees exhibited the greatest psychological distress, as manifested by depressive and anxiety symptoms, than the Vietnamese and Laotians. In this study, less education and small family size in the United States predicted depression, whereas older age, multiple traumas, increased years spent in a refugee camp, and attendance in English as a Second Language (ESL) classes predicted both anxiety and depressive symptoms. Chung and Kagawa-Singer (1993) stated that this latter contradictory finding may reflect the ineffectiveness[1] of ESL classes for Cambodians. Correlates of psychosocial dysfunction among Cambodian refugees include older age, multiple traumas, numerous separations from family and relatives, frequent reunions with family and relatives (which may place added strain on limited household resources), and a prolonged stay in refugee camps (Chun, 1991).

The high rates of traumatization reported among Cambodian refugees also appear to be associated with elevated rates of PTSD. Mollica, Wyshak, and Lavelle (1987) reported that 57% of respondents in a Cambodian psychiatric patient sample suffered from PTSD according to *DSM–III* criteria. Moreover, Cambodians experienced the most traumas (M = 16.1 traumas) than the Vietnamese and Hmong/Laotian groups in this study. Of particular concern, Cambodian women who were separated, divorced, or widowed suffered the most traumas and displayed the most serious psychiatric and social impairments of all the patients. Kroll et al. (1989) likewise reported that 22% of Cambodians in a clinic population met *DSM–III* criteria for PTSD, which was the highest percentage of PTSD cases compared to those observed for Vietnamese, Hmong, and Lao refugees. Kinzie et al. (1990) also observed a high rate of PTSD (92%) among their clinic sample of Cambodians using *DSM–III–R* diagnostic criteria.

In a nonpatient sample of Cambodian refugees, a moderate correlation was found between trauma and psychiatric symptoms (Carlson & Rosser-Hogan, 1991). Nonetheless, 86% met modified *DSM–III–R* criteria for PTSD and emotional distress, whereas 96% experienced high levels of dissociation. The authors of this study concluded that the high rate of dissociation in this Cambodian population supports the universality of dissociation as a response to trauma. Kinzie and Boehnlein (1989) also noted that chronic psychotic symptoms may appear following massive psychological trauma among Cambodian refugees.

Past studies have examined Cambodian adolescents and young adults who were traumatized as children, to establish prevalence rates and correlates of PTSD in this population and examine the natural course of PTSD. Realmuto et al. (1992) reported high rates of traumatization among their nonpatient sample of Cambodian adolescents, especially among older youths. The authors stated that older youths may have reported more traumas for several reasons, namely because they were exposed to more traumas that were not applicable to the very young (e.g. forced labor), or simply because they were able to better comprehend or remember traumatic events than their younger counterparts. In any case, 87% of the Cambodian adolescents in this study met *DSM–III* criteria for PTSD, and 37% met the *DSM–III–R* PTSD criteria.

---

[1]These authors posit that the Cambodians may be suffering from trauma-related cognitive impairments that may contribute to their experience of psychological distress while attending ESL classes.

Realmuto et al. (1992) reasoned that the disparity between these prevalence rates can be attributed to fewer hyperarousal symptoms, which are required in the *DSM-III-R* classification of PTSD, among this population. Clarke, Sack, and Goff (1993) also found that a strong relationship exists between war trauma experienced in childhood and PTSD symptoms experienced in adolescence or young adulthood. Moreover, Cambodian adolescents and young adults reporting PTSD symptoms also reported greater amounts of resettlement stress than those without PTSD symptoms.

In a follow-up study of Cambodian adolescents who were traumatized as children, Kinzie, Sack, Angell, Clarke, and Ben (1989) found that 48% of their sample satisfied *DSM-III-R* criteria for PTSD. This finding was remarkable considering that over 10 years had elapsed since most of the children were traumatized. Kinzie et al., (1989) concluded that this demonstrated that PTSD was relatively stable and persistent over time. Nevertheless, they also mentioned that the Cambodian adolescents seemed to be functioning well in social, work, and family environments despite their high rates of PTSD.

Sack et al. (1993) examined the same population in Kinzie et al's (1989) study to chart the natural course of PTSD from adolescence to young adulthood. Results from this study indicated that 38% of the overall population exhibited a *DSM-III-R* diagnosis of PTSD. The authors stated that although PTSD persists, its symptoms become less intense and frequent over time. Furthermore, the overall functioning of these Cambodian young adults continued to be impressive; they were free of conduct problems, drug and alcohol abuse, and psychological breakdowns.

It is interesting to note that many Cambodians, with the exception of Cambodian women without spouses, are able to function in their social and occupational milieus despite their high rates of psychological and physical distress (Mollica, Wyshak, & Lavelle, 1987). This may be partly attributed to their general outlook on life and Buddhist beliefs. For example, Rumbaut (1985) noted that the Cambodians in a community sample of Southeast Asian refugees reported the most life satisfaction despite their significantly high levels of depressive symptoms and low self-reports of happiness.

Rumbaut (1985) credits this finding to an interaction between the extensive history of premigration traumas among many Cambodians and cultural appraisals of their life situation that are embedded in Buddhist values. In this case, postmigration stressors may be viewed as minor strains when compared with the severe traumas incurred in Cambodia. Furthermore, as will be discussed later in this chapter, many Cambodians frame their traumatic experiences within their Buddhist beliefs. For many Cambodians, life experiences are thus regarded as meaningful occurrences of fate or *kharma* which, from this spiritual perspective, may then contribute to positive adjustment to past traumas.

Laotians

Beginning with the Geneva Accords in 1954, civil discord erupted in Laos as the North Vietnamese-backed Pathet Lao fought the American-supported Royal Lao government for control of Laos, which had then gained independence from France (Takaki, 1989). As the Pathet Lao seized control of Laos in 1979 with the withdrawal of American troops from Southeast Asia, they embarked upon a massive campaign of retribution against former supporters of the Royal Lao government. During this time, thousands of Laotians of diverse social, educational, and economic backgrounds escaped to the adjacent country of Thailand where almost all were detained in refugee camps.

In general, the psychological and physical functioning of the overall Laotian refugee population was somewhat better than or equal to the functioning of other Southeast Asian refugee groups. Nicassio (1983) found that Laotians maintained the best self-perceptions compared with Vietnamese, Cambodian, and Hmong refugees. Furthermore, Laotians did not view themselves as highly different from Americans. Still, many Laotians have endured traumas that have contributed to mental and physical distress.

Chung and Kagawa-Singer (1993) established demographic, premigration, and postmigration predictors of psychological distress among a community sample of Laotian refugees. These researchers found that Laotian women were at higher risk for depression and anxiety than their male counterparts. Additionally, individuals who resided in the United States for a lengthy period were at risk for depression. The premigration variable—numerous traumatic events—predicted both depression and anxiety. Postmigration predictors of depression and anxiety include unemployment and receipt of public assistance. Finally, high family income predicted depression.

Chun (1991) found that the experiential factors—multiple premigration traumas, and few reunions with family and relatives—were correlates of psychosocial dysfunction among Laotian refugees. Status correlates of dysfunction among this group included being female, unemployment, poor English-speaking proficiency, and relocating to a United States residence demographically different from one's native residence.

Kroll et al. (1989) reported that 19.7% of their Laotian patients suffered from PTSD based on DSM–III criteria. Kinzie et al. (1990) reported a much higher prevalence rate of PTSD (68%) for a clinic sample of Laotian refugees. These researchers also stated that female and older Laotians were most susceptible for developing PTSD. Finally, Mollica et al. (1987) reported the highest prevalence rate of PTSD at 92% for a patient sample of Hmong/Laotian refugees. This latter finding, however, may be artificially inflated by combining traditionally highly traumatized Hmong refugees with the Laotian refugee sample (see also Mollica, 1994).

Hmong and Mien

Both the Hmong and Mien cultures are rooted in tribal, agrarian, and preliterate societies located in the mountainous regions of Laos and other Southeast Asian countries. The Hmong culture did not possess a written language until American and French missionaries developed one in the mid-1950's (Sherman, 1988). The majority of Hmong withstood premigration warfare during their tenure as CIA-sponsored soldiers whose mission was to combat Pathet Lao Communist guerrillas in the early 1960's (Cerhan, 1990). However, the Hmong became targets of deadly recriminations as the Royal Lao government fell to the Pathet Lao in 1979. Many Hmong were then forced to flee their highland homes and cross into Thailand under perilous circumstances and constant pursuit by Pathet Lao militia men.

Similar to the Hmong, the Mien's education and sociocultural tradition were transmitted orally until they formed a written language in 1982 (Moore & Boehnlein, 1991). The geographical location of the Mien's homeland also placed them in the middle of constant but "unofficial" warfare during the Vietnam War until their mass exodus into Thailand. Relatively little research has been conducted with the Mien in comparison with other Southeast Asian refugees. However, the few studies that exist show marked psychological impairment resulting from extensive premigration trauma and significant postmigration stressors.

Both the Hmong and Mien exhibit severe levels of psychological distress and impaired psychosocial functioning. Rumbaut (1985) found that the Hmong reported the least happiness and life satisfaction and the second most depression in his Southeast Asian community sample. Nicassio (1983) similarly reported that the Hmong exhibited much more alienation than other Southeast Asian refugees. Postmigration stressors may be particularly burdensome for the Hmong and Mien given their sociocultural backgrounds and lack of contact with Western technology and cultural norms. Westermeyer (1989) found that failure to acculturate may exacerbate and contribute to paranoid symptoms among Hmong refugees. Specifically, those who had more intense contacts within the Hmong community and more affiliation with Hmong culture exhibited more paranoid symptoms compared with their more Western-acculturated peers.

Westermeyer (1988) conducted a prevalence study to establish the rates and types of DSM–III diagnosis among a community sample of Hmong refugees. Results from this study showed that the majority of Hmong refugees (31%) suffered from adjustment disorder. However, none of the refugees were seeking treatment and half were able to function in their families and occupations despite the chronic nature of their symptoms. Westermeyer thus proposed that these refugees were not suffering from a psychological disorder per se, but rather from "refugee adjustment syndrome" or "refugee acculturation phenomenon."

Still, it appears that certain symptoms may subside over time. For instance, Westermeyer, Neider, & Callies (1989) found that depression, somatization, phobic anxiety, and self-esteem improved over time and with acculturation. However, anxiety, hostility, and paranoid ideations improved the least. Additionally, strong traditional ties, marital problems, and self-reported medical problems were associated with greater psychological distress, whereas older age was related to higher levels of depression. Chun (1991) also found that multiple premigration traumas and poor English proficiency placed Hmong refugees at risk for psychosocial dysfunction.

Both Hmong and Mien refugees traditionally exhibit some of the highest levels of PTSD. For instance, Mollica et al. (1987) reported that 92% of a sample of Hmong and Laotian patients suffered from a *DSM–III* diagnosis of PTSD. Similarly, Kinzie et al. (1990) found that 93% of a clinic population of Hmong refugees manifested PTSD, the highest rate of PTSD among all Southeast Asian groups. Lastly, Kroll et al. (1989) showed that 11.8% of the Hmong refugees seen in their clinic were PTSD sufferers.

General Conclusions for Southeast Asian Refugee Populations

In sum, there are only a few studies that have actually looked at the prevalence rate of PTSD among Southeast Asian refugees using valid instruments and diagnostic criteria. Also, past findings are often quite variable across studies partly because of differences in sample composition (e.g. patient vs. nonpatient samples) and diagnostic criteria (e.g. *DSM–III* vs. *DSM–III–R* PTSD criteria). Nonetheless, the reported prevalence rates of PTSD for Southeast Asian refugees are remarkably elevated because of nature and extent of their traumatization. Furthermore, these traumatized Asians manifest clinically significant levels of general anxiety and depressive symptoms.

Generally speaking, the Cambodians (Khmer), Hmong, and Mien refugees represent the three most traumatized groups, with the majority arriving within the last decade. Therefore, the immediate concerns of these refugees may center around their premigration traumas. In contrast, Vietnamese refugees have generally been here the longest, so postmigration stressors such as English speaking difficulties and unemployment may be their primary concern. Unfortunately, research on Lao refugees is lacking. Nonetheless, it appears that Lao refugees fall somewhere in the middle of Southeast Asian groups in regards to trauma exposure and overall adjustment levels. According to Gong-Guy (1987), 17% of the Lao sample population reported one or more premigration traumatic events. The percentage of traumatization among other groups is as follows: Cambodians (43%), Hmong (17%), and Vietnamese (14%).

ASIAN AMERICAN VIETNAM VETERANS

A handful of single-case studies and small-sample diagnostic investigations have directly examined the psychological effects of the Vietnam war on veterans of Asian American descent. Initial observations pointed toward some important consistencies among these ethnic minority veterans. Fighting an unpopular war in Southeast Asia during a period of great racial conflict provided the context for unique stressors and psychological consequences for these soldiers.

For example, it has been repeatedly observed that these American soldiers were subjected to racism typically reserved for the enemy, such as being called names such as "gook" and "dink" (e.g., Hamada, Chemtob, Sautner, & Sato, 1988; Marsella, Chemtob, & Hamada, 1990). Loo (in press) identified a number of other race-related stressors and cited a numerous anecdotal accounts: being mistaken for the Vietnamese on the battlefield, race-related physical assault or injury, unintended death or grief, near-death experiences, and nonverbal communications of prejudice.

The bicultural identification of many Asian American Vietnam veterans posed another set of stressors before, during, and after the war. One Japanese American patient described this problem to us as the "banana syndrome: being white on the inside and yellow on the outside" (Abueg & Gusman, 1991). To reaffirm his allegiance with his unit, his fellow soldiers, and his country, this patient would exaggerate his American identity. His Southern drawl would become more pronounced, and he became louder and more aggressive and would use racial epithets for the Vietnamese. These behaviors caused great internal conflict: guilt, shame, and a sense of betrayal of people who reminded him so much of his own family.

Chun and Abueg (1989) conceptualized similar conflicts of a Filipino American Vietnam veteran in a triadic fashion: the intersection among peer norms, parental norms, and cultural norms. Depending on the context (being in war or stateside) and salience of social influences (being close to family, friends; practicing traditions of Filipino culture), the axis of this veteran's identity was in a constant state of flux. Most disruptive to establishing some sense of a "centered self" was the fact that profound traumatic conditioning and PTSD had inhibited successful adaptation regardless of ethnic identity. It was hypothesized that the bicultural identity of this Filipino American exacerbated his sense of instability.

Matsuoka and Hamada (1991) made an important contribution to this literature in studying the variation in the expression of PTSD in Asian American Vietnam veterans across three subgroups: Japanese American, Chinese American, and Native Hawaiian. A fourth group comprised Koreans, Filipinos, and Samoans, each of which had a sample size too small to independently study. The first set of findings confirmed a high degree of ethnic identification with the enemy across a sizable proportion of the 44 veterans in the sample. Feelings of estrangement from fellow American soldiers were also commonly reported.

With regard to rates of PTSD, wide variation across subgroups was found (Matsuoka & Hamada, 1991): no Japanese Americans, 13% of Chinese Americans, 29% of Native Hawaiians, and 40% of the other "mixed" group cited earlier had PTSD diagnoses. Although the authors acknowledged the sampling limitations of their study, they speculated that these findings at least point toward more careful study of predisposing economic and social factors that may place certain groups at psychological risk for traumatization.

It is noteworthy that a major study of prevalence rates among Native Hawaiian and Japanese American Vietnam War veterans is currently in progress in Hawaii under the auspices of the National Center for PTSD of the Department of Veterans Affairs. This study is using methodologies similar to those used in the National Vietnam Veterans Research Study (NVVRS) (see chapter 16 by Schlenger & Fairbank in this volume). The results of the Hawaii Study will provide substantive research data on PTSD rates and expressive patterns for these two groups.

CULTURE-SPECIFIC CONCEPTUALIZATIONS OF TRAUMA TREATMENT

The power of the mental health's professional's conceptualization of PTSD (e.g., Friedman & Jaranson, 1994; Friedman & Marsella, this volume) is that the trauma becomes a centerpiece or touchstone upon which treatment can be based. The findings we have summarized in this chapter suggest that the traumatic experience is not homogeneous even within a specific region like Southeast Asia. Instead of simply paying lip service to the notion of cultural sensitivity (Sue & Sue, 1990), we suggest that the clinician must have a fine-grained understanding of the base rates of traumatization, by specific ethnic subgroups.

For those clinicians experienced with trauma, this may appear at face to be a superfluous or redundant recommendation. However, we believe this point needs particular attention because of the typically unavoidable cultural rifts between patient and therapist, subject and scientist. Hence, specific knowledge must include, for example, how premigration traumas varied between Cambodians and Vietnamese. Understanding these finer variations will undoubtedly have an impact on the empathic quality of interviewer questions; moreover, this knowledge may lead to creative interventions yet to be discussed in this literature. For example, Western therapists can begin to actively incorporate Buddhist principles into their practice for ethnic subgroups who adhere to such beliefs (Canda & Phaobtong, 1992). Creative integration of knowledge about subtle variations across and within these various cultures and subcultures will likely have direct impact upon patient disclosure and help-seeking, especially about experiences often so horrific and unspeakable. Many developmental (Loo, 1993) and constructivist (Gusman et al., this volume) approaches have begun to articulate such an integration for clinical work.

REFERENCES

Abueg, F. R., & Gusman, F. D. (1991). *Variability in the treatment of Asian Americans with Post-Traumatic Stress Disorder (PTSD): Four case histories.* Unpublished Manuscript. National Center for PTSD, VAMC (323 A8-MP), Palo Alto, CA.

Beiser, M., Turner, R., & Ganesan, S. (1989). Catastrophic stress and factors affecting its consequences among Southeast Asian Refugees. *Social Science Medicine, 28,* 183–195.

Canda, E. R., & Phaobtong, T. (1992). Buddhism as a support system for Southeast Asian refugees. *Social Work, 37,* 61–67.

Carlson, E. B., & Rosser-Hogan, R. (1991). Trauma experiences, posttraumatic stress, dissociation, and depression in Cambodian refugees. *American Journal of Psychiatry, 148,* 1548–1551.

Cerhan, J. U. (1990). The Hmong in the United States: An overview for mental health professionals. *Journal of Counseling & Development, 69,* 88–92.

Chun, K. M. (1991, August). *Correlates of psychosocial dysfunction among traumatized Southeast Asian refugees.* Paper presented at the Asian American Psychological Association convention, San Francisco, CA.

Chun, K. M., & Abueg, F. R. (1989). *An Ericksonian conceptualization of cultural factors in the adjustment of an Asian American Vietnam veteran.* Paper presented at the 18th Annual Western Psychology Conference for Undergraduate Research, Santa Clara University, Santa Clara, CA.

Chun, K. M., Chung, R., & Sue. S. (1994). *Correlates of psychosocial dysfunction among traumatized Southeast Asian refugees.* Unpublished manuscript. Department of Psychology, UCLA, Los Angeles, CA.

Chung, R., & Kagawa-Singer, M. (1993). Predictors of psychological distress among Southeast Asian refugees. *Social Science Medicine, 36,* 631–639.

Clarke, G., Sack, W. H., & Goff, B. (1993). Three forms of stress in Cambodian adolescent refugees. *Journal of Abnormal Child Psychology, 21,* 65–77.

Felsman, J. K., Leong, F. T. L., Johnson, M. C., & Felsman, I. C. (1990). Estimates of psychological distress among Vietnamese refugees: Adolescents, unaccompanied minors, and young adults. *Social Science Medicine, 31,* 1251–1256.

Friedman, M., & Jaranson, J. (1993). The applicability of the PTSD concept to refugees. In A.J. Marsella, T. Bornemann, S. Ekblad, & J. Orley (Eds.) *Amidst peril and pain: The mental health and wellbeing of the world's refugees* (pp. 207–227). Washington, DC: American Psychological Association.

Foulks, E. F., Merkel, L., & Boehlin, J. K. (1992). Symptoms in nonpatient Southeast Asian refugees. *Journal of Nervous and Mental Disease, 180,* 466–468.

Gong-Guy, E. (1987). *The California Southeast Asian mental health needs assessment* (Contract No. 85-76282A-2). Sacramento, CA: California State Department of Mental Health.

Hamada, R. S., Chemtob, C. M., Sautner, B., & Sato, R. (1988). Ethnic identity and Vietnam: A Japanese-American Vietnam veteran with PTSD. *Hawaii Medical Journal, 47,* 100–109.

Kiang, P. N. (1991). About face: Recognizing Asian and Pacific American Vietnam veterans in Asian-American studies. *Amerasia, 17,* 22–40.

Kinzie, J., & Boehnlein, J. J. (1989). Post-traumatic psychosis among Cambodian refugees. *Journal of Traumatic Stress, 2,* 185–198.

Kinzie, J., Boehnlein, J. K., Leung, P. K., Moore, L. J., Riley, C., & Smith, D. (1990). The prevalence of posttraumatic stress disorder and its clinical significance among Southeast Asian refugees. *American Journal of Psychiatry, 147,* 913–917.

Kinzie, J., Sack, W., Angell, R., Clarke, G., & Ben, R. (1989). A three-year follow-up of Cambodian young people traumatized as children. *Journal of the American Academy of Child & Adolescent Psychiatry, 28,* 501–504.

Kroll, J., Habenicht, M., Mackenzie, T., Yang, M., Chan, S., Vang, T., Nguyen, T., Ly, M., Phommasouvanh, B., Nguyen, H., Vang, Y., Souvannasoth, L., & Cabugao, R. (1989). Depression and posttraumatic stress disorder in Southeast Asian refugees. *American Journal of Psychiatry, 146,* 1592–1597.

Lee, E., & Lu, F. (1989). Assessment and treatment of Asian-American survivors of mass violence. *Journal of Traumatic Stress, 2,* 93–120.

Lin, K. M., Tazuma, L., & Masuda, M. (1979). Adaptational problems of Vietnamese refugees: I. Health and mental health status. *Archives of General Psychiatry, 36,* 955–961.

Loo, C. (1993). An integrative-sequential treatment model for posttraumatic stress disorder: A case study of the Japanese American internment and redress. *Clinical Psychology Review, 13,* 89–117.

Loo, C. (1994). The Asian American Vietnam veteran: Race-related trauma and PTSD. *Journal of Traumatic Stress, 7,* 637–656.

Marsella, A. J., Chemtob, C., & Hamada, R. (1992). (1990). Ethnocultural aspects of PTSD in Asian Vietnam war veterans. *National Center for PTSD Clinical Newsletter, 1*(1), 3–4.

Marsella, A. J., Friedman, M., & Spain, H. (1993). Ethnocultural aspects of PTSD. In J. Oldham, M. Riba, & A. Tasman (Eds.), *Review of psychiatry* (pp. 29–62). Washington, DC: American Psychiatric Press.

Matsuoka, J. & Hamada, R. (1991). The wartime and postwar experiences of Asian-Pacific American Vietnam veterans. *Journal of Applied Social Sciences, 16,* 23–36.

Mollica, R. (1994). Southeast Asian refugees: Migration history and mental health issues. In A. J. Marsella, T. Bornemann, S. Ekblad, & J. Orley (Eds.) *Amidst* peril and pain: The mental health and wellbeing of the world's refugees (pp. 83–100). Washington, DC: American Psychological Association.

Mollica, R., Wyshak, G., & Lavelle, J. (1987). The psychosocial impact of war trauma and torture on Southeast Asian refugees. *American Journal of Psychiatry, 144,* 1567–1572.

Moore, L. J., & Boehnlein, J. K. (1991). Treating psychiatric disorders among Mien refugees from highland Laos. *Social Science Medicine, 32,* 1029–1036.

Nicassio, P. M. (1983). Psychosocial correlates of alienation. *Journal of Cross-Cultural Psychology, 14,* 337–351.

Realmuto, G. M., Masten, A., Carole, L. F., Hubbard, J., Groteluschen, A., & Chhun, B. (1992). Adolescent survivors of massive childhood trauma in Cambodia: Life events and current symptoms. *Journal of Traumatic Stress 5,* 589–599.

Rumbaut, R. (1985). Mental health and the refugee experience: A comparative study of Southeast Asian refugees. In T. C. Owan (Ed.), *Southeast Asian mental health: Treatment, prevention, services, training, and research* (pp. 433–486). (Rockville, MD): National Institute of Mental Health.

Sack, W. H., Clarke, G., Him, C., Dickason, D., Goff, B., Lanham, K., & Kinzie, J. D. (1993). A 6-year follow-up study of Cambodian refugee adolescents traumatized as children. *Journal of the American Academy of Child & Adolescent Psychiatry, 32,* 431–437.

Sherman, S. (1988, October). The Hmong in America: Laotian refugees in the "land of the giants." *National Geographic,* 587–610.

Sue, S., & Sue, D. (1990). *Counseling the culturally different: Theory and practice.* New York: John Wiley & Sons.

Takaki, R. (1989). *Strangers from a different shore: A history of Asian Americans.* New York: Penguin.

Tran, T. V. (1989). Ethnic community supports and psychological well-being of Vietnamese refugees. *International Migration Review, 21,* 833–845.

Westermeyer, J. (1988). *DSM–III* psychiatric disorders among Hmong refugees in the United States: A point prevalence study. *American Journal of Psychiatry, 145,* 197–202.

Westermeyer, J. (1989). Psychological adjustment of Hmong refugees during their first decade in the United States: A longitudinal study. *Journal of Nervous and Mental Disease, 177,* 132–139.

Westermeyer, J., Neider, J., & Callies, A. (1989). Psychosocial adjustment of Hmong refugees during their first decade in the United States: A longitudinal study. *Journal of Nervous & Mental Disease, 177,* 132–139.

12

PTSD AND RELATED STRESS DISORDERS AMONG HISPANICS

RICHARD L. HOUGH, GLORISA J. CANINO, FRANCIS R. ABUEG,
and FRED D. GUSMAN

INTRODUCTION

This chapter attempts to summarize what is known about ethnocultural aspects of posttraumatic stress disorder (PTSD) among Hispanic populations. It addresses three topics. First, a research model and agenda is suggested for studies of ethnocultural variations in the origins, onset, and progression of PTSD. Second, the current literature on PTSD in Hispanic populations is reviewed in terms of its relevance to that research agenda. Finally, an overview is provided of some of the major issues that need to be addressed in future studies of the ethnocultural aspects of PTSD in Hispanic populations.

The Role of Ethnocultural Factors in PTSD

It has been suggested that some aspects of PTSD may be much the same across cultures. It may be that a relatively stable, invariant set of reflexive psychophysiological and neuropsychological symptoms (e.g., hyperarousal, startle responses, problems with sleep) follow traumatically stressful experiences across cultures (e.g., Friedman, 1991). However, the potential for ethnocultural variations in patterns of PTSD is great (e.g.,

Friedman, & Jaranson, 1992; Marsella, Friedman, & Spain, 1992; Marsella, Friedman, & Spain, 1993). Figure 1 provides an overview of various aspects of the development and course of PTSD, all of which may be affected by ethnic and cultural factors.

Figure 1 suggests that there are five stages in the development of PTSD: (a) the occurrence of a potentially traumatic stressor, (b) interpretation of the degree of threat posed by the event, (c) the development of symptomatology, (d) coalescence of the symptoms into a diagnosable disorder, and (e) the course of the disorder.

At most stages, there are particularly important variables inhibiting or promoting development to the next stage. For example, the degree of vulnerability or resilience to stress possessed by an individual will help determine the degree to which an event is interpreted as threatening and out-of-control. Similarly, the social support system and coping behavior repertoire of the individual will help determine the degree of symptom formation in the face of traumatic stress, and patterns of treatment and comorbidity may crucially affect the course and outcomes of the disorder.

It is the general contention of this chapter that to truly examine the effects of ethnocultural factors on PTSD, research is needed on their effects on each portion of the model. This suggests a research agenda focused on whether there are identifiable cultural differences in

1. the probability of experiencing traumatic stress;
2. social/structural characteristics (e.g., availability of safety, sustenance); personality characteristics; or cognitive belief systems (e.g., beliefs about stress, appropriate coping, mental illness) that make individuals more or less susceptible to stress;
3. attributional tendencies that interpret the degree of threat implied by particular types of traumatizing events, as well as their cause and how to control them;
4. coping behaviors or strategies and their effectiveness in ameliorating the probability that trauma may be attributed

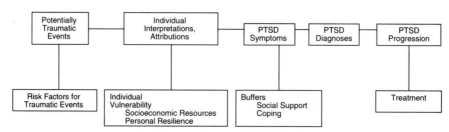

Figure 1. PTSD origins and outcomes.

to a particular stress, or the degree of felt distress and symptomatology that accompanies traumatic stressors;

5. patterns of social support and the degree to which they ameliorate the effects of trauma;
6. symptom patterns and syndromes that follow traumatic stress (e.g. endogenous syndromes or expression of symptoms of intrusive imagery, numbing and arousal symptoms);
7. onset and prevalence of PTSD;
8. comorbidity with other forms of mental disorders (e.g., anxiety, substance abuse, paranoia, depression) or physical disorders;
9. treatment; or
10. course of the disorder.

This chapter will explore the available literature on traumatic stress and posttraumatic stress disorder for evidence suggesting significant differences between Hispanics and others on these matters.

A major methodological assumption in this discussion is that the research agenda outlined above demands studies that, ideally, incorporate two often conflicting elements: (a) that they be truly comparative and (b) that they be truly sensitive to ethnocultural differences in the etiology, onset, and course of PTSD. Single-culture studies, unless there are data bases on comparative cultures that have used much the same design (sampling frame, measurement procedures, etc.) are essentially descriptive in that we do not know to what extent the findings are unique to the culture under study or to what degree the same findings might be found in other ethnic and cultural groups undergoing the same experiences.

To date, much of the literature concerning Hispanic populations and traumatic stress is descriptive in the latter sense. More purely descriptive studies in which similar populations are studied with similar instruments under similar conditions may be more satisfying in terms of drawing comparisons, but may be very incomplete and potentially misleading if they do not incorporate significant attention to the possibility that culturally endogenous etiologies, symptom patterns, diagnoses, and outcomes may exist. The few truly comparative studies reviewed in this chapter tend not to aggressively pursue this kind of ethnocultural sensitivity.

DESCRIPTIVE STUDIES

Descriptive studies concerning Hispanics in traumatically stressful circumstances have, for the most part, been limited to three substantive areas: (a) Latin American refugees and immigrants; (b) victims of natural and man-made disasters; and (c) Vietnam Veterans.

Latin American Refugees and Immigrants

A great deal of research literature has been focused on international migration and stress and particularly on the effects of trauma among refugees. Whereas most studies have focused on refugee and mental health status in general, some have focused more specifically on PTSD.

Table 1 summarizes the literature on Latino refugee groups. Several authors have studied Chilean or Argentinean refugee children in Mexico. Allodi (1980) reports on two studies of Chilean children whose parents had disappeared or had been persecuted, or detained. Predominant symptoms in these children were withdrawal, generalized fear and startle response, depression, and a sense of impotence and vulnerability. The author also reported on an unpublished study by Marzolla of Argentinean children and his own study of Chilean children in Mexico that report similar symptoms along with arrested development or regression and aggression (Allodi, 1980).

Hispanic Children and Political Trauma

A series of descriptive clinical reports on Chilean children who are victims of political repression and/or who are refugees in Denmark or Canada are available. The latter are from a Danish pediatric group working under the auspices of Amnesty International. The first report (Cohn, Holzer, Koch, & Severin, 1980) summarized preliminary data on the first 75 children seen by the group (ages 1 to 21 and examined 2 to 6 years after the children's father or mother had been released from prison and reunited with the child). Many symptoms characteristic of PTSD were found (e.g., 36% with anxiety and startle response, 35% with serious nightmares and sleep problems, 23% with secondary nocturnal enuresis, and 16% with introversion, depression, or difficulty establishing social relationships).

A second report (Cohn et al., 1985) concerns 85 children. Some 57 (two thirds) scored at or above the usual cut point (6+) on the 28-item version of the Hopkins Symptoms Checklist (HSCL-28). Upon clinical examination, some 58 of the 74 children and adolescents reported emotional disorders or somatic symptoms, most with anxiety (58%) and insomnia or nightmares (55%). Many somatic symptoms similar to those in Criterion D of the *DSM-III* were also noted. Allodi (1980) compared three studies of Chilean and Argentinean children, most under 6, who were either living in Santiago, Chile or who were refugees in Canada. A narrow repertoire of symptoms was noted, with social withdrawal, chronic fear, depressive moods, clinging and overdependent behavior, sleep disorders, somatic complaints, and arrest or regression in social habits and school

TABLE 1
Studies of Latin American Refugees and Immigrants

Authors	Participants	Measures	Findings
Allodi, 1980 (a)	203 Chilean children aged < 12 whose parents were detained or disappeared. Clinic population in Santiago, Chile, 1973–1977	clinical examinations, Goodenough test	withdrawal—78% generalized fear, startle response—78% depression—70%
(b)	9 Chilean children in Santiago clinic after parental persecution, disappearance, death	clinical examinations	predominant symptoms: fear, sense of impotence, vulnerability, paralysis
(c)	28 Argentinean children (0–4) of families exiled to Mexico in 1976, studied in 1979	interviews, drawing tests, play therapy, intelligence tests, Bender Psychomotor tests	predominant symptoms: feeding disorder behavioral regression or arrested development aggressiveness somatic complaints
(d)	40 Chilean child refugees from political persecution and torture	case records, interviews with mothers	social withdrawl, depression, fear, anxiety and irritability, severe behavioral, affective changes
Cohn, et al., 1980, 1985	75 Chilean child refugees in Denmark 6 years after reunited w/ tortured and/or imprisoned parents. (Most recent data on 58 from 1985)	clinical examinations	anxiety—51%, insomnia—35%, behavioral difficulties—28%, introversion—26%, nocturnal enuresis—26%, anorexia—22%, headaches—22%, stomach aches—21%

TABLE 1 (continued)

Authors	Participants	Measures	Findings
Weile et al., 1990	Followup on 58 subjects from Cohn study (above)	clinical examinations	number of symptoms rises significantly larger percentage of children have symptoms number of symptoms positively related to time in Denmark
Arroyo & Eth, 1985	28 Salvadoran and 2 Nicaraguan refugee children referred to Univ. of Southern California Clinic	clinical individual/family diagnostic interviews	PTSD—33%, adjustment disorders—30%, range of other diagnoses (2–3% each), most frequent symptoms vary by age
Cervantes et al., 1989	120 Central American refugees to United States 138 Mexican immigrants 188 Native-born Mexican Americans 141 Native-born Anglo-Americans	SCL-90-R CES-D PTSD scale	current PTSD prevalence: Central American refugees—52% Central American immigrants—49% Mexican immigrants—25%
Summerfield & Toser, 1990, 1991 Hjern et al., 1991	43 poor ex-Nicaraguan refugees in East Nicaragua 50 Chilean refugee children, 2/3 preschool, 36 w/ experience of violence & family separation, and 14 "spared"	GHQ28, clinical interviews clinical interviews	over GHQ cutpoint: M—62%, F—91% PTSD: M—25%, F—50% most common symptoms among persecuted: sleep disturbance—75%; anxiety—68%; defiance—58%; dependency—47%; depressed mood—42%; concentration difficulties—42%

performance. Aggressiveness was only considered a problem for older children.

Arroyo and Eth (1985) studied 28 Salvadoran and 2 Nicaraguan children and adolescents referred to the University of Southern California psychiatric unit. The children had been in the United States from 3 to 34 months, were evenly split by gender, and all had been exposed to warfare. One third were diagnosed with posttraumatic stress disorder. Some 30% were diagnosed with adjustment disorders. One or two cases each of separation-anxiety, atypical somatoform, conversion, major depressive, conduct, dysthymic, and schizophrenic disorders were also observed.

In the Arroyo amd Eth (1985) study, predominant symptoms varied somewhat by developmental stage. Younger children were generally more profoundly affected and typically had symptoms of regression, separation and stranger anxiety, frequent bed-wetting, irritability, and loss of acquired skills. Latency age children primarily reported difficulties in school and learning (often complicated by intrusive traumatic memories associated with parental separation and reunion) and conduct problems. Behavior changes such as inhibition, aggression, and somatic complaints were also reported. Adolescents were more likely to seriously act out aggressively toward other youth, new family members, and themselves. A few were psychotic, with paranoid delusions incorporating elements of their traumatic experience.

Adult Central American and Mexican Immigrants

In a more general study Cervantes, Salgado de Snyder, and Padilla (1989) examined PTSD and other symptoms of mental disorder in adult immigrant Central Americans and Mexicans compared with native-born Mexican Americans and Anglo-Americans. Again, approximately 50% of the Central American refugees and immigrants were found to have symptoms consistent with PTSD.

Although they do not assess the presence of PTSD or PTSD symptoms, several other surveys of the mental health status of immigrant or refugee populations should be noted. Vega, Kolody, Valle, and Hough (1986) surveyed 1,825 poor Mexican immigrant women in San Diego County, California and found that some 41.5% scored at or above the established cutpoint (16) on the Center for Epidemiologic Depression Scale (CES-D) (Radloff, 1977), with some 23% scoring at or above the extremely high score of 24. Similarly high numbers of depressive symptoms were found in surveys of Mexican American farmworkers (Vega, Warheit, & Palacio, 1985) and of some 1,000 residents of Tijuana, Mexico, many of whom had recently emigrated from elsewhere in Mexico (Vega, Kolody, Hough, & Figueroa, 1987).

The research studies described above report data from either clinical examinations or surveys of refugees or immigrants, generally in terms of predominant symptoms and symptom patterns. They are informative in that they establish that high rates of symptoms of PTSD and related disorders are found in Hispanic immigrants and refugees, particularly among those for whom immigration was associated with more traumatic events. These studies also begin to identify some particularly vulnerable subpopulations.

However, the value of the studies is limited for addressing the questions of whether culture-specific variations can be found in the experience of trauma or its aftermath. Neither the truly comparative nor the ethnocultural sensitivity elements of the overall research agenda suggested in the introduction to this chapter are directly represented. None of the studies were designed to compare various Hispanic populations or Hispanics to other ethnocultural groups. At the same time, none seriously probed for the existence of culturally endogenous expressions of traumatic stress or factors that might affect the course of emotional response to traumatic stress.

This is not to say that these descriptive studies are not useful. They do help to document the degree to which PTSD-like symptoms are found in traumatized populations. However, they have limited usefulness for addressing the truly comparative and ethnocultural sensitivity elements of our overall research agenda.

Victims of Natural and Man-Made Disasters

Table 2 summarizes data from studies of the mental health consequences of natural and man-made disasters for Latino populations. Lima and colleagues (Lima, Chavez, et al., 1989; Lima, Pai, Caris, et al., 1991; Lima, Pai, et al., 1989; Lima, Pai, Lozano, & Santacruz, 1990; Lima, Pai, Santacruz, et al., 1989; Lima, Pai, Santacruz, Lozano, & Luna, 1987) have conducted a series of studies of victims of the 1985 Colombian volcanic eruption and the 1988 earthquake in Ecuador.

Columbian and Ecuadorean Earthquakes

In these studies, clinician interviewers surveyed subjects from shelters, camps and health care clinics using Lima's Self Rating Questionnaire (SRQ). Data are presented on the proportion of participants scoring above a cut-point on the SRQ that categorizes them as *emotionally distressed*. The proportion of "emotionally distressed" was near or above 50% for the Colombian study groups, increasing to 78% 2 years following the volcanic eruption. These high rates are interpreted as the result of an incredibly

TABLE 2
Studies on the Effects of Natural Disasters on Hispanic Populations

Authors	Participants	Measures	Findings
Lima, Pai, Santacruz, Lozano, & Luna, 1987	200 adult victims 7 months after Columbian volcanic eruption. In shelters & camps.	Self Rating Questionnaire (SRQ)	emotionally distressed—56%, most common symptoms: nervous, tense, worried—82% easily frightened—59% headaches—56%
Lima, Chavez et al., 1989	150 adult victims 2 months after earthquake in Ecuador. From health care clinics.	SRQ	emotionally distressed—40%, most common symptoms: easily frightened—70% headaches—36% sleep badly—43% nervous, tense, worried—67% easily tired—43%
Lima, Pai, Santacruz et al., 1989b	100 adult primary care clients near Colombian volcanic eruption, 2 years later	SRQ	emotionally distressed—45%
Lima, Pai, Lozano, & Santacruz, 1990	Subsample of 40 victims of volcanic eruption in Columbia, after 2 years	SRQ	increase in emotionally distressed from 55% to 78%; more frequent symptoms; symptom profile the same.

TABLE 2 (continued)

Authors	Participants	Measures	Findings
Lima, Pai, Santacruz, & Lozano, 1991	Colombian volcanic eruption victims 8 months after—subsample of 102 (78%) of SRQ-positives and 34 (39%) of SRQ-negatives	Psychiatric interview & Helzer DSM–III Checklist	overall diagnostic rates: no diagnosis—41% any DSM–III diagnosis—59% PTSD—36%; GAD—3% major depression—11%
de la Fuente, 1990	573 adult Mexican earthquake victims living in shelters	Psychiatric DSM–III Questionnaire for PTSD, Depression, GAD, and Panic	PTSD—32% (m = 18%; f = 38%) GAD—19% (m = 9%; f = 24%) Depression—13% (m = 7%; f = 16%) Panic—2%
	208 Mexican women earthquake victims in shelters		no psychopathological symptoms—72% symptoms—18% severe decompensation—9.5%
Bravo, Rubio-Stipec, Canino, Woodbury, & Ribera, 1990	912 Puerto Rican flood victims (375 prospective & postflood data; 537 retrospective only)	DIS-DS	slight increase in depressive, somatic, alcoholic, and PTSD symptoms in both samples with greater increase for the more severely exposed

devastating natural disaster in which some 80% of the population were casualties.

By comparison, only 40% of the victims of the less severe Ecuadorean earthquake were classified as emotionally distressed. In a full psychiatric interview, with a subsample of the Colombian sample based on the Helzer *DSM–III* checklist, Lima, Pai, Santacruz, et al. (1991) found that nearly 60% met criteria for some *DSM-III* diagnosis. PTSD (36%), major depression (11%), and generalized anxiety disorder (3%) were the most common diagnoses.

Mexican Earthquake Victims

De la Fuente (1990) has reported on two studies of Mexican earthquake victims living in shelters. These studies, using a "Psychiatric *DSM–III* Questionnaire" found rates of 32% for PTSD, 19% for generalized anxiety, 13% for depression, and 2% for panic disorder. Rates were somewhat higher for males than females on the first three diagnostic categories mentioned.

Puerto Rican Flood Victims

In Puerto Rico, retrospective assessments of 912 adult victims of the 1985 torrential rains, floods, and mud slides were conducted (Bravo, Rubio-Stipec, Canino, Woodbury, & Ribera, 1990; Canino, Bravo, Rubio-Stipec, & Woodbury, 1990). Some 375 of the respondents were also prospectively assessed. The study used the Disaster Studies version of the Diagnostic Interview Schedule (DIS-DS).

Canino et al. (1990) reported significantly higher onset of depression (2.2%), generalized anxiety (9.7%), and posttraumatic stress disorder (3.7%) among those exposed to the disasters than among those not exposed (1.0, 0.7, and 6.1% respectively) in the retrospective data. The mean number of depressive, generalized anxiety, and somatic symptoms were also higher for exposed participants. Bravo et al., (1990) also noted that major depressive, somatic, alcoholic, and PTSD symptom counts varied by level of exposure. The link to exposure persisted after controlling for gender, age, education, predisaster symptom level, and interview status.

A Comparison With the Times Beach Studies in St. Louis

The Puerto Rico data differ in some respects from the Times Beach studies in St. Louis (Smith, Robins, Przybeck, Goldring, & Solomon, 1986), which also used the DIS-DS. No differences in the number of symptoms of PTSD were found in the St. Louis study by exposure levels, although the proportion with diagnosable PTSD did differ between the directly exposed (5.2%) and the unexposed (0.5%). It is unclear whether the similarity in number of symptoms may be cultural in origin, whether they may result from the relative degree of trauma involved in the two situations, or whether they may be due to some other methodological differences between the studies. Significantly higher rates of alcohol abuse or dependence (12.2%) and generalized anxiety (16.3%) were also reported for St. Louis respondents with direct exposure than for Puerto Ricans exposed to flooding and mud slides (1.3 and 9.7% respectively).

San Ysidro Massacre

A study belonging under the rubric of man-made disasters focused on the effects of the San Ysidro McDonald's Massacre in San Diego.[1] Hough et al. (1990) examined the potential for Hispanic women with no direct involvement in the traumatic incident to develop symptoms of PTSD. Some 303 immigrant, poor, Mexican American women 35 to 50 years of age were interviewed approximately 6 months following the massacre.

It was hypothesized that these women, although they were not directly involved in the massacre might, because of the strongly integrated nature of the community (particularly in the face of many "outsiders" wanting to report on, to study or to film the community) and the intense local publicity given the event, be traumatized to some degree by the incident. Approximately one third of the women reported being seriously affected, with some 12% reporting mild to severe levels of PTSD symptomatology since the incident. Some 6% still felt symptoms 6 to 9 months after. Those most affected had relatives or friends involved in the massacre or were very socially vulnerable (e.g., the widowed, separated or divorced, and unemployed as well as those with less income and only fair-to-poor health).

Comparative Studies of PTSD

Overall, these disaster studies move toward more truly comparative research. Lima's Colombian and Ecuadorean studies and de la Fuentes' Mexican study begin to use more standardized measures (the SRQ and a *DSM–III* Questionnaire) that could be replicated in other studies and therefore be of comparative interest. However, we are aware of no published comparative data. The Puerto Rican studies come closer to a research model that incorporates both comparative and culturally sensitive elements. They use the DIS-Disaster Supplement (DIS-DS) and random community samples, which has allowed some comparisons to the St. Louis studies of the Times Beach disasters.

The Puerto Rican study is also an example of how comparative studies can be combined with cultural sensitivity. For example Guarnaccia, Rubio-Stipec, and Canino, (1989) formulated a measurement for a culturally en-

---

[1]This incident occurred in 1984 when James Huberty walked into the restaurant with a small arsenal of weapons and began to shoot at employees and customers. During this incident—one of the largest of its kind in United States history–21 people were killed and 15 others were injured.

dogenous syndrome—*ataques de nervios*—that allows examination of how this culture-specific stress response may be related to PTSD symptoms and diagnoses. This kind of straightforward strategy for dealing with culturally diverse symptom syndromes that may be related to PTSD has, surprisingly, seldom been employed.

Brentwood VA Hospital Veterans Studies

Comorbidity Issues

In the early 1980s, two studies of Hispanic Vietnam veterans were conducted at the Brentwood VA Psychiatric Hospital in Los Angeles. The first (Escobar et al., 1983) was concerned primarily with comorbidity issues. In this study, 41 male Mexican American clients of a VA neighborhood clinic who were diagnosed with PTSD were enrolled. Medical record reviews were conducted on all, and an intensive interview assessment was conducted with a random subsample of 20. Considerable comorbidity was found with alcohol abuse and dependence (61%), drug abuse and dependence (32%), affective disorders (32%), suicide ideation and behavior (44%), violent behavior (49%), and antisocial personality (40%).

The research (Escobar et al., 1983) also examined social supports and found that participants with PTSD were more alienated from their families and culture than were schizophrenic participants or controls, and that the number of PTSD symptoms was negatively associated with the size of social network for the unacculturated respondents. In general, then, migrants with less attachment to their own culture and networks were most at-risk.

Chronicity and Comorbidity

The second study (Gongla et al., 1983; Hough, Gongla, Scurfield, Carr, & Corker, 1983) was of 99 male Hispanic Vietnam theater veterans, the great majority of whom were of Mexican descent. A purposive sample of clinical and nonclinical respondents was selected from VA medical centers, a VA outreach center, and other veterans' or social service agencies for a PTSD instrument development and nosological study. The subjects completed a structured, in-depth interview with a trained nonclinician interviewer concerning aspects of premilitary life, military experience, homecoming, and postmilitary life; the interview also included a DIS-like PTSD instrument. The study is of interest here because it addressed two issues relatively unexplored in the research literature—the chronicity of PTSD symptoms and the comorbidity of PTSD with other mental disorders.

To explore chronicity of PTSD symptoms in a retrospective manner, the interviews constructed a life chart detailing major occurrences in the respondent's life on a year-by-year basis (Hough, Gongla, et al., 1983). For every PTSD symptom endorsed on a lifetime basis, the respondent was then asked to identify, using the life-chart as a reference point, the onset and most recent experience of the symptom and its degree of severity by year. Annual diagnoses and criteria symptom counts were calculated. The findings were that, for the 49 Hispanic Vietnam veterans with a current diagnosis of PTSD, symptom onset tended to closely follow the traumatic event (87% within a year) and that diagnosis was constant across the years for most respondents (87%).

Specific symptom patterns across the years for PTSD positives were not as stable. Fourteen participants experienced mostly numbing symptoms and for 11 of these 14, the dominance was substantial and consistent across time. Only three respondents (6%) were clearly and consistently intrusive-imagery dominant. For 19% there were essentially no patterns of dominance. Numbing and intrusive imagery symptoms appeared year after year in approximately equal numbers. Finally, some 27% of the PTSD positives demonstrated a fluctuating numbing and intrusive imagery dominant pattern.

A second set of results was concerned with the degree to which PTSD can be distinguished from other disorders in an Hispanic Vietnam-veteran population (Gongla et al., 1983). PTSD diagnoses were most comorbid with major depression (83% PTSD-positive), obsessive–compulsive disorder (86% PTSD-positive), and schizophrenia (91% PTSD-positive), phobic disorders (61% PTSD-positive), and panic (72% PTSD-positive). Comorbidity with substance abuse disorders, antisocial personality, mania, and somatization were not statistically significant.

Given the comorbidity rates from the Gongla et al. (1983) study just noted, the question was raised of whether PTSD is really an independent syndrome. Therefore, analyses were conducted to determine whether there was significantly more comorbidity of PTSD with other disorders than there was for two other index diagnoses (schizophrenia and major depression) with other disorders. Factor analysis, case cluster analysis, and regression analyses were used to determine how well PTSD, schizophrenia, and major depression could be distinguished from each other and from other diagnoses.

The results consistently supported the conclusion that PTSD in this population is at least as distinct from other disorders as are schizophrenia and major depression. This suggests that though there may be considerable comorbidity of PTSD with other psychiatric disorders in an Hispanic population, the degree of comorbidity may not be more than is typically found between major mental disorders. The Brentwood studies are useful explorations of the nosology of PTSD in Hispanic veteran populations but, again, they do not help us to directly address the cross-cultural PTSD research agenda outlined in the introduction to this chapter. They are neither truly comparative nor very sensitive to potential cultural differences in reaction to trauma.

COMPARATIVE STUDIES

A second set of studies, discussed in this section, use the same methods across ethnocultural groups and can, therefore, be more extensively used to explore their differences.

The Los Angeles Epidemiologic Catchment Area (ECA) Studies

The National Institute of Mental Health (NIMH) Epidemiologic Catchment Area (ECA) research program (Eaton & Kessler, 1985; Regier et al., 1984; Robins & Regier, 1991) was designed to examine the prevalence and incidence of major mental disorders in five selected sites in the United States. Between 1978 and 1986, some 18,000 respondents were interviewed using the Diagnostic Interview Schedule (DIS) (Robins, Helzer, Croughan, & Ratcliff, 1981).

In the Los Angeles ECA study (Burnam, Hough, Escobar, et al., 1987; Hough, Karno, Burnam, Escobar, & Timbers 1983; Karno et al., 1987) interviews where conducted with over 3,000 participants including 1,305 Hispanics, the great majority of whom were Mexican Americans. The relevance of the ECA data to this overview of studies of posttraumatic stress disorder is unfortunately limited because a standard PTSD measure was not included in the original DIS. However, the Los Angeles ECA did include a PTSD module in their one-year follow-up survey. The Los Angeles ECA did also gather information concerning the prevalence and effects of a potentially traumatic event—sexual assault. These two aspects of the Los Angeles ECA are described in more detail below.

Perhaps the most remarkable finding of the ECA studies in general are the similarities of rates of disorder across the five sites and across ethnic groups. To some degree, African American respondents displayed higher rates of lifetime and current disorders than Hispanics or Whites, although these differences have been attributed (Robins & Regier, 1991) to the effects of age and socioeducational factors. Similar surveys using the DIS have been conducted in Puerto Rico (Canino et al., 1987) and Peru (Hayashi et al., 1985; Yamamoto, Silva, Sasao, Wang, & Nguyen, 1993). The Puerto Rican data is almost identical to that for the US-born data for the Los Angeles ECA and, in general, does not differ significantly from the ECA sites, with the exception that somatization disorder and symptoms were higher in Puerto Rico. The same is true for most of the Peruvian data except for slightly higher rates of phobia and lower rates of substance abuse.

However, Burnam, Hough, Telles, Karno, and Escobar (1987) found that US-born Mexican-origin Los Angeles ECA respondents had significantly higher rates of major depression, dysthymia, phobias, and alcohol and substance abuse disorders than their Mexican-born counterparts. These differences were not nearly so strongly linked to acculturation as to country of birth. It is not clear whether the differences may be due to greater mental health among immigrants and a subsequent regression in second-generation Mexicans, to adoption of majority mental health risk-behaviors (e.g., alcohol or substance abuse), or to increased despair over the effects of discrimination, minority status, or deprivation in the American environment.

Karno et al. (1987) examined the Los Angeles ECA data concerning anxiety disorders more closely and found that the higher US-born rates were due primarily to higher rates of phobias. For example, US-born Mexican-origin respondents reported a lifetime rate of 17.1 for all phobias, 12.7 for simple phobia and 7.6 for agoraphobia compared to 10.7, 7.8 and 4.7 for respondents born in Mexico and 10.4, 6.8, and 3.9 for non-Hispanic Whites. US-born Mexican Americans were also significantly higher on generalized anxiety (5.1) than Mexican-born respondents (2.9), but not as high as non-Hispanic Whites (10.0).

PTSD in the Los Angeles ECA Study

The Los Angeles ECA, in its one-year follow-up, assessed the prevalence of PTSD in the community using the Brentwood PTSD Instrument—a DIS-like measure created for the clinical research on PTSD at Brentwood VA Psychiatric Hospital described above (Gongla et al., 1983). Since data on this study (Hough & Golding, 1994) have not been previously reported, some description of the procedures and general findings are in order. The protocol first asked respondents whether they had ever been exposed to a traumatically distressing event, and then to describe the three worst such events and the approximate age at which they occurred. Next, respondents were asked whether they had ever experienced each DSM–III PTSD symptom. Each admitted symptom was then probed to determine after which traumatic event(s) it happened, its severity, the time of onset, and its most recent occurrence.

Overall, some 15.8% (380) respondents reported at least one traumatic event over their lifetime. The most common events reported by male respondents were seeing persons hurt or killed (3.1%), combat (3.0%), accidents (2.8%), and a threat or close call (1.6%). For female respondents (n = 1,300), the most common events were sexual assault (3.2%), natural disasters (2.9%), seeing persons hurt or killed (2.4%), other physical assault (1.4%), and accidents (1.2%). No significant differences in number or type of events were noted by ethnicity.

Table 3 summarizes the unweighted percentage of respondents meeting DSM–III criteria for PTSD in the Los Angeles ECA data using three different scoring paradigms. The top one third of the table uses the most

TABLE 3
Percentage of Respondents Meeting Various PTSD Criteria in the Los Angeles ECA Studies (Mexican American and Non-Hispanic White Respondents Only)

Criteria	Mexican American (*n* = 997)	Non-Hispanic White (*n* = 1,252)	Total (*n* = 2,249)
Full *DSM–III* Criteria			
within last 6 months	0.2	0.5	0.4
within last year	0.1	0.2	0.1
other lifetime	0.8	2.4	1.6
never	98.8	97.0	97.8
Full *DSM–III* Criteria Without Severity			
within last 6 months	0.4	0.5	0.4
within last year	0.1	0.2	0.1
other lifetime	1.3	3.3	2.4
never	98.2	96.0	97.0
Full *DSM–III* Criteria Without Severity and Event Specificity			
with last 6 months	0.2	0.6	0.4
within last year	0.1	0.2	0.1
other lifetime	1.9	3.2	2.7
never	97.8	96.0	96.8

Source: Hough & Golding, 1994.

stringent scoring, requiring (a) that each symptom meet severity criteria (the respondent saw a doctor or other professional or took medication for the symptom, or that the symptoms seriously interfered with his/her life) and (b) that the symptom be reported only after one of the three traumatic events named. The second scoring paradigm was more relaxed, dropping the severity criteria and only requiring that the symptoms be present and related to a specific stressor. The third paradigm was even more relaxed, in that it required only that the appropriate PTSD symptoms be present.

Using the most stringent criteria, somewhat more non-Hispanic Whites met criteria (0.7% within the last year and an additional 2.4% lifetime) than Mexican Americans (0.3% within the last year and an additional 0.8% lifetime). In the last two sections of Table 3, it can be observed that the numbers of respondents with PTSD diagnoses did not significantly increase as the criteria were relaxed. By comparison, the current rates found in the St. Louis ECA studies, using a very different DIS/PTSD scale, were 0.5% for men and 1.3% for women (Helzer, Robins, & McEvoy, 1987). This comparison suggests, in a preliminary fashion, that there may not be great ethnocultural differences in rates of PTSD.

Sexual Assault in the Los Angeles ECA Study

By *sexual assault*, the Los Angeles ECA study referred to a wide variety of sexual assault behaviors, not specifically to rape. Respondents were asked, "In your lifetime, has anyone ever tried to pressure or force you to have sexual contact? By sexual contact, I mean their touching your sexual parts, your touching their sexual parts, or sexual intercourse?" Respondents who answered affirmatively were asked a series of follow-up questions concerning the characteristics of the most recent assault. The data are summarized in Table 4.

The probability of experiencing a sexual assault was lower for Hispanics (8.1%) than for non-Hispanic Whites (19.9%) (Sorenson, Stein, Siegel, Golding, & Burnam, 1987). This finding was consistent across gender, age, and education levels. No ethnocultural differences were found in terms of the characteristics of the assault. Ethnicity also was not related to the number of victimizations following the initial assault (Sorenson et al., 1987) or in use of resistance strategies (Siegel, Sorenson, Golding, Burnam, & Stein, 1989).

No other significant differences were found between non-Hispanic White and Hispanic victims on such outcome variables as diagnosable

TABLE 4
Los Angeles ECA Studies Summary of Ethnic Differences
in Sexual Assault Data

	Hispanic	Non-Hispanic White	Data Source
Sexual assault victims:	81.%	19.9%	Sorenson et al., 1987
Hispanics born in Mexico	3.5%		
Hispanics born in the U.S.	11.4%		
men 18–39	6.8%	11.9%	
men 40+	8.2%	1.8%	
women 18–39	10.3%	26.3%	
women 40+	5.9%	15.5%	
Resistance Patterns	No differences		Siegel et al., 1989
Childhood sexual assault	3.0%	8.7%	Siegel et al., 1987
Emotional reactions	No differences		Siegel et al., 1990
Diagnosable mental disorder	No differences		Burnam et al., 1988
Use of social supports:			
talk with someone	61.1%	67.6%	Golding et al., 1989
talk with police	52.7%	62.8%	
talk to psychotherapist	8.8%	21.2%	
talk to clergy	7.2%	2.9%	
Use of mental health services by victims:			
men	19.0%	5.0%	Golding et al., 1988
women	21.2%	25.1%	

mental disorders (Burnam et al., 1988) or reports of emotional or behavioral distress (Siegel, Golding, Stein, Burnam, & Sorenson, 1990). Hispanics and non-Hispanic Whites tended to report similar patterns of use of social supports (Golding, Siegel, Sorenson, Burnam, & Stein, 1989), although non-Hispanic Whites were significantly more likely to talk with psychotherapists and Hispanics with clergy. Finally, Hispanic victims were less likely to use mental health services than non-Hispanic victims (Golding, Stein, Siegel, Burnam, & Sorenson, 1988).

Sorenson and Siegel (1992) suggest that cultural factors may influence rates of reported assault. Lower rates in the relatively unacculturated respondents may be partially due to more reticence to discuss sexual assault or that sexual assault is more specifically prohibited in Mexican culture. Supporting the latter notion is the fact that US-born Mexican Americans report higher rates of assault (11.4%) than those born in Mexico (3.5%) (Sorenson & Telles, 1991). The US-born rate approaches that of non-Hispanic Whites (16.2%), suggesting that cultural environment may influence rates of sexual assault. It may be, for example that the risk of sexual assault among Mexican heritage Hispanics may be reduced by machismo, which promotes, along with male dominance, dedication to the family and protection of female family members. On the other hand, it may simply be that those who have been sexually assaulted may have less energy and fewer resources to migrate to a new country, or that US-born sexual assault victims may be more likely to report assaults.

The National Vietnam Veterans Readjustment Study (NVVRS)

The NVVRS study (Kulka et al., 1991a) presents the most suggestive data to date that significant racial and ethnic variations in response to traumatic stressors may exist. The NVVRS was a Congressionally mandated study of national samples of 1,632 theater veterans (who served in the Vietnam theater of operations), 716 era veterans (who served in the military during the time of the Vietnam conflict but did not serve in the Vietnam theater), and 668 civilian controls who did not serve in the military during the Vietnam era but who were matched to the theater-of-operations sample on age, sex, and race and ethnicity. Participants were interviewed between 1986 and 1988. (Note that, though women were included in the sample, they are not included in the analyses reported here because the female sample was not large enough .to allow examination of racial and ethnic differences.)

The primary purpose of the study was to establish the prevalence of PTSD and other adjustment problems among Vietnam veterans. Stratified random samples for the two male veteran groups were selected from military personnel records of the more than 8.2 million living persons who had served on active duty during the Vietnam era. Overall, some 3,016 interviews were conducted.

Measurement of PTSD proved to be problematic. Only a brief summary of the diagnostic procedure can be reported here, but full detail can be found in Kulka et al. (1991a, 1991b) and Schlenger et al. (1992). A preliminary validation study had established a DIS-like PTSD measure constructed by the NVVRS as the instrument of choice for PTSD prevalence estimation. However, in the clinical reexamination portion of the survey, the DIS-like measure proved to be a relatively poor predictor of clinically identified PTSD. Because no one instrument appeared to be uniquely valid, researchers decided to use information from the 12 or so measures of PTSD incorporated in the design.

The Mississippi PTSD, MMPI-PTSD, and SCID-PTSD measures were taken as primary and differences between them were adjudicated by a team of clinicians to establish caseness in the clinical substudy. Because the three measures were not all available for the entire NVVRS sample, regression techniques were used to establish weighting for ratings on the seven or so measures available on the entire sample. The weights were then applied to the full sample to obtain a probability of PTSD caseness for each individual.

As can be seen in Table 5, Hispanic theater veterans were significantly more likely to have PTSD currently (27.9%) than Blacks (20.6%) or White/Others (13.7%). The proportionate differences remain by level of war zone stress. However, Hispanic era veterans were not statistically significantly different from Blacks and White/Others era veterans, suggesting that Hispanics may be more vulnerable to traumatic levels of military stress than other veterans. That is, if there are no significant differences in PTSD rates between Hispanic and White/Other era veterans not exposed to war trauma, but racial and ethnic differences emerge in theater veterans, it is reasonable to hypothesize that those differences may be due to cultural differences in response to war stress.

To examine this hypothesis further, racial and ethnic differences in PTSD prevalence were examined after controlling for over 80 potential predisposing variables including childhood and family background factors, premilitary factors and military factors. For theater veterans overall, the PTSD prevalence difference between Hispanic and Blacks was reduced 67.1%—from 7.3% to 2.4%. The difference between Hispanics and Whites was reduced 57%—from 14.2 percent to 6.1 percent—when these factors were controlled for. When war-zone stress was introduced, the difference between White/Other and Hispanic male respondents remained significant at 5.4%. The prevalence in Blacks was increased again (from 2.4 to 6.3%) controlling for all the predisposing variables.

In sum, racial and ethnic differences were reduced but not explained by introduction of predisposing variables in the analysis. It should be noted,

TABLE 5
Current Rates of PTSD and Other Psychiatric Disorders: NVVRS Data

	Hispanic	Black	White/Other
Current PTSD Prevalence Estimates			
Theater veterans	27.9 (2.5)	20.6 (2.0)	13.7 (1.2)
High war-zone stress	48.4 (3.9)	38.2 (3.7)	34.0 (3.6)
Low-moderate war-zone stress	17.9 (2.0)	9.9 (1.7)	7.8 (1.1)
Era veterans	2.1 (0.6)	4.4 (1.9)	2.3 (0.8)
Civilian controls	3.9 (2.2)	1.3 (0.9)	1.0 (0.5)
Current Rates of Other Psychiatric Disorders			
Depressive episode	4.8 (1.8)	4.8 (1.2)	2.4 (0.6)
Manic episode	0.6 (0.4)	0.8 (0.5)	0.7 (0.4)
Panic disorder	0.7 (0.4)	0.0	1.1 (0.4)
Obsessive–compulsive	2.9 (1.6)	0.9 (0.5)	1.5 (0.5)
Generalized anxiety	8.1 (3.1)	6.1 (1.4)	4.1 (0.9)
Alcohol abuse/dependence	15.2 (2.6)	11.7 (1.9)	10.9 (1.4)
Drug abuse/dependence	4.1 (1.8)	1.5 (0.7)	1.7 (0.6)
Antisocial personality	1.5 (0.6)	4.2 (1.2)	1.8 (0.6)
Any NVVRS/DIS disorder	25.7 (3.9)	20.2 (2.4)	16.2 (1.7)
Percent High (1.50+) On Readjustment Problems Index			
Theater veterans	36.8 (4.1)	39.1 (3.1)	24.1 (2.0)
High war-zone stress	47.2 (6.9)	53.6 (4.6)	39.3 (4.5)
Low-moderate war-zone stress	31.9 (5.2)	30.5 (3.8)	19.7 (2.2)
Era veterans	22.6 (6.9)	45.4 (7.0)	22.9 (3.8)

however, that all the aspects of premilitary vulnerability that might produce higher rates of PTSD in Hispanic Vietnam veterans may not have been effectively identified and measured in this study.

The clinical experience of two of the authors of this chapter with Hispanic Vietnam veterans suggests that the higher rates of PTSD in this population may be associated with particular vulnerabilities induced by the interactions of Hispanic culture and lifelong victimization. Their clinical experience also suggests that Hispanic veterans may have been more vulnerable to military stressors because they are more likely to construe the world from a victim stance, which results from a series of life experiences prior to and during Vietnam in which their minority status was associated with various forms of victimization.

Clinical reports of discrimination in the Vietnam theater of operations such as being given more dangerous duty, being refused promotions, and other, even lethal maltreatment have been common. The NVVRS data set is currently being reanalyzed by Drs. Gusman and Abueg at the National Center for PTSD laboratory in Palo Alto and Drs. Fairbank and Schlenger at Research Triangle Institute to more thoroughly explore these possibilities.

Jordan et al. (1991) reported on the prevalence of other psychiatric disorders among Vietnam theater veterans. Hispanics in this group tended to report more psychiatric problems. Overall, 25.7% of Hispanics met criteria for at least one disorder, compared to 20.2% for Blacks and 16.2% for Whites/Others. The Hispanic rates were significantly higher than for Whites and Others. On a lifetime basis, Hispanic rates were significantly higher than Whites on generalized anxiety disorder (22.4% vs. 17.2% for Blacks and 13.2% for Whites) and alcohol abuse and dependence (50.1% vs. 35.8% for Blacks and 38.9% for Whites).

The San Diego McKinney Homeless Mentally Ill Demonstration Research Project

The senior author of this chapter is the principal investigator on the San Diego McKinney Homeless Mentally Ill project, which has been funded by the NIMH and the Center for Mental Health Services to evaluate whether a mix of public housing and comprehensive case management services can stabilize severely mentally ill homeless individuals. The data reported here are preliminary, and have not been reported elsewhere. Some 362 participants have been referred to the project, evaluated, and placed in 1 of 4 experimental conditions (Hough, 1994). The study participants are being asked about traumatic experiences and symptoms at the 12-month follow-up, which has been completed on 226 participants.

As can be seen in Table 6, among the 78 female respondents, some 63% report a traumatic event and some 40% meet diagnostic criteria for PTSD on a lifetime basis. Unfortunately, the relative numbers of Hispanic and Black females in the study are so small as to make comparisons nonconclusive. However, five of the six Hispanic females (83%) reported no trauma and none met PTSD criteria. For the 56 non-Hispanic White fe-

TABLE 6
Percentage of San Diego Severely Mentally Ill Homeless
Reporting Trauma and Meeting *DSM–III–R* PTSD Criteria

| | Hispanic | | White | | Black | |
| | Male | Female | Male | Female | Male | Female |
Trauma status	(*n* = 26)	(*n* = 6)	(*n* = 94)	(*n* = 56)	(*n* = 35)	(*n* = 10)
No trauma	53.8%	83.3%	45.7%	30.4%	48.6%	40.0%
Trauma, does not meet PTSD criteria	15.4	16.7	25.5	25.0	40.0	20.0
Trauma, and meets PTSD criteria	30.8	0.0	28.7	44.6	11.4	40.0

Source: Hough, 1994.

males, 30% reported no trauma, 25% reported some trauma but did not meet criteria for diagnosis, and 45% reported trauma and met PTSD criteria. Data for the ten Black females is very similar to that for the White females.

Among the 164 male participants, some 52% report at least one traumatic event and 25% have met criteria for PTSD diagnosis at some point in their life. Approximately equal percentages of Hispanic (30.8) and White (28.7) male participants met criteria for diagnosis at some point in their life. Though the same percentage of Blacks reported a traumatic event, a significantly lower percentage (11.4) met diagnostic criteria. Overall, then, no remarkable differences in Hispanic and White rates of self-chreported traumatic experience and PTSD appear for this severely mentally ill homeless population. The low rates for Hispanic females are based on such a low sample size that no conclusions can be drawn.

CONCLUSIONS REGARDING PREVIOUS RESEARCH

This chapter began with three assertions. First, it was assumed that there is considerable potential for ethnocultural factors to affect variations in the development and course of PTSD. A second assumption was that to identify ethnocultural effects, research would have to examine whether there are culture specific risk factors for (a) experiencing trauma, (b) vulnerabilities to stress, (c) perceptions of what is to be experienced as traumatically stressful, (d) outcomes of trauma in terms of symptomatic and mental health effects, (e) course of symptoms and disorder, (f) effects of treatment, and (g) effects of coping styles and social support on all the above aspects of the aftermath of trauma.

Third, it was assumed that a research agenda addressing whether there are ethnocultural variations in all these aspects of traumatic stress and its outcomes would have to be both truly comparative (using common research designs and procedures on culturally different populations who have experienced the same types and levels of traumatic stress) and, at the same time, be truly sensitive to potential ethnocultural differences (using designs and procedures able to assess culturally endogenous interpretations of stress, stress response syndromes, diagnoses, and outcomes).

For the most part, the research reviewed above does not successfully meet many of these criteria. The studies of Latin American refugees and immigrants are largely descriptive rather than comparative, and are more focused on establishing the degree to which the target population meets standard diagnostic criteria than on identifying culturally unique response patterns. The same is true of most of the research on Latino responses to natural disasters. The major exceptions to this are the Puerto Rican studies (Bravo et al., 1990; Canino et al., 1990), in which efforts were made to use procedures comparable to the Times Beach research efforts in St. Louis and in which serious attention has also been paid to the culturally endogenous syndrome of *ataques de nervios*.

Among the more comparative studies reviewed, the Los Angeles ECA, the McKinney Homeless Demonstration Research Program, and the National Vietnam Veteran Readjustment Study all had the advantage of comparing culturally diverse populations using standardized assessment procedures and research methods. Among these comparative studies, the McKinney Homeless Demonstration Research Program reported no significant variations in the prevalence of traumatic events or disorders between homeless, mentally ill Hispanic, Black, and White men.

The Los Angeles ECA reported slightly lower (nonstatistically significant) prevalence of PTSD and sexual assault for Mexican Americans than Whites. The NVVRS provides the most convincing data to date that significant culturally endogenous reactions are to be found. Hispanic respondents, exhibited higher rates of diagnosable PTSD than Black or White respondents even after controlling for a wide range of predisposing factors. Although these "comparative" studies are of considerable interest, they still do not carry us far toward satisfying the research agenda proposed at the beginning of this chapter.

It should be noted first that all these comparative studies are of racial and ethnic subgroups in the United States, thereby limiting to some degree the extent of cultural variations. Also, these studies make no aggressive effort to take the ethnocultural aspects of PTSD seriously. Among these studies, there is no attempt, for example, to develop measures of culturally endogenous syndromes that may be related to traumatic stress, or to develop alternate culturally sensitive measures of the constructs used.

Most of the studies summarized in this chapter do not suggest that there are significant cultural differences between Hispanics and Whites or Others in the way in which they respond to trauma. Overall, it would appear that, in Hispanic PTSD research, we are far from developing strategies for blending standardized comparative and culturally sensitive elements in our research designs.

ISSUES FOR FUTURE RESEARCH

Some very difficult research issues must be addressed if we are to pursue truly comparative and culturally sensitive studies of PTSD in Hispanic populations and thereby determine whether significant cultural differences exist. Many of these research issues are generic to the field. For example, it is difficult to determine whether observed racial/ethnic/cultural differences in rates of PTSD are real differences unless the degree of traumatic experience is standardized.

For example, in comparisons of responses to natural disasters in different countries, it may be difficult to determine whether observed differences are reflective of cultural effects or differences in the level of trauma imposed by the event. There are also the standard cross-cultural research issues (e.g., instrument translation, interviewer training, etc.) to be considered. However, the attempt here is to focus on issues that all relate more specifically to cross-cultural studies of PTSD.

Assessing Culture-Specific Risk Factors in Exposure to Traumatic Events

In another chapter in this volume (de Girolamo & McFarlane) convincing evidence is provided that the prevalence of traumatic events is much higher in developing as opposed to developed countries. It may also be expected that traumas will also be more prevalent in disadvantaged sectors of developed countries. Canino (personal communication, June, 1993), for example, found that more adult Puerto Ricans were victims of mugging or robbery than adult residents of St. Louis. She also found that approximately 40% of Puerto Rican children have been victims of some kind of violence or have observed violence in their families, schools, or communities.

It has been suggested that Mexican American populations, for many reasons (e.g., migration and immigration experiences, prejudice and discrimination, few social resources, language barriers), could be expected to experience higher than normal levels of stress (Cervantes & Castro, 1985; Hough, Karno, et al., 1983). However, much more information is needed about cultural variations in exposure to such forms of traumatic violence as child maltreatment and battering of women, as well as to the traumas of crime, revolution, war, and terrorism, and natural and man-made disasters.

Are There Culture-Specific Interpretations of Potentially Traumatizing Events?

Cervantes and Castro (1985), among others, have suggested that the degree of stress imposed by a stressful event may be attenuated or intensified by culture-specific patterns of appraisal. Two major aspects of this question have been explored in the literature, but need future research.

First, there is some suggestion that Hispanic culture may "normalize" stress. Paz (1961), for example, has characterized the Mexican man as closed and defensive and as tending to express resignation, stoicism, and indifference to suffering—personality traits that would normalize stress and perhaps contribute to its being viewed as less traumatic.

The clinical experience of two of the authors at the clinical laboratory for PTSD in Palo Alto suggests that these characteristics may emerge in therapy as *alexithymia* (inability to label emotions), and may be more regularly found in Hispanics than other male clients. At the same time, they suggest that among some Mexican American men, a need to be in control may make traumatic events that induce helplessness especially challenging. A clinical generalization suggests that there may be two striking pathological adaptations to this situation—one that is passive, introspective, and severely depressed versus a highly reactive, angry, and potentially explosive response.

Second, although differences in the degree of felt stress for a given traumatic event have not been studied, there is some evidence that differences in perceptions of the degree of stress associated with more normal stressful life events do exist. In some studies of the severity of particular life events (Fairbank & Hough, 1981; Hough & Timbers, 1985), it was found that Mexican respondents in Ciudad Juarez rated events having to do with physical migration and upward mobility as more serious than Whites. Whites, in turn, saw events having to do with the breakup or alteration of the nuclear family as significantly more stressful than the Mexican respondents.

Much clinical and research work rests upon constructivist assumptions about how patients construe the meaning of trauma and loss. The assumptions of Western clinical thought may not always be applicable to Hispanic populations. What is needed is more careful and systematic attention to how Hispanic variations in cognitive style affect perceptions of potentially traumatic events and their outcomes in terms of mental health status.

Are There Cultural Variations in Individual Vulnerability to Traumatic Events?

There is some evidence that Mexican American populations may be more vulnerable to a larger range of traumatic events than others. For example, in the San Ysidro McDonald's massacre (Hough et al., 1990), it was found that general vulnerabilities (e.g., old age, low income, illness) were important in predicting PTSD-like symptoms. The study also suggested that in tightly knit Hispanic communities, the effects of traumatic events may extend beyond the immediate victims and witnesses. The same tendency was noted in the El Paso/Ciudad Juárez surveys (Hough, 1985), which reported that for Mexican Americans surveyed events happening to family significant others are more predictive of symptoms of mental disorder than for Whites. Research designs need to incorporate more sensitivity to particular sources of vulnerability or, alternatively, of resilience or strength in the face of traumatic events.

Coping and Social Support in Comparative PTSD Research

Solomon, Smith, Robins, and Fischbach (1987) found that emotional support lessened the amount of distress experienced following a disaster. The potential buffering effect of social support and, particularly, family support have often been assumed to take on more importance among Mexican Americans than for non-Hispanic Whites or persons from cultural settings in which friends and family are less extended (Cervantes & Castro, 1985; Escobar & Randolph, 1982).

Some data in the disaster research field (Bravo, Canino, Rubio-Stipec, & Serrano-García, 1991; Bravo, Serrano-García, Rubio-Stipec, & Canino, 1992; Solomon, Bravo, Rubio-Stepec, & Canino, 1993) support that contention. The Solomon et al. (1993) article is probably most important since it compares the role of emotional support from family following disaster in St. Louis and Puerto Rico. In that analysis, Puerto Rican disaster victims with lower support levels exhibited more symptoms of alcohol abuse, depression, and psychiatric symptomatology than those with more support. This relationship was not replicated in the St. Louis data. Several other studies (Vega, Kolody, & Valle, 1986; Vega, Kolody, Valle, & Hough, 1986) have found social support, and particularly confidant support, to be related to lower levels of depressive symptoms.

Although social support networks are generally assumed to be of greater extent in Hispanic populations, considerable data suggest that Mexican American friendship and kinship networks may, partially as a consequence of recent immigration, actually be smaller than others (Griffith, 1984; Vega & Kolody, 1985). For example, in their analysis of the Los Angeles ECA data set, Golding and Burnam (1990) found that Mexican Americans reported less marital, employment, friend, and relative social support than non-Hispanic Whites. However, Mexican Americans also reported less social conflict with potential sources of support. Overall, there was no evidence found that social support was related to depression symptoms scores independently from social strain for either population. However, low social conflict was associated with less depression for Mexican Americans.

Future researchers in this area needs to remain aware that, though social networks may provide the potential for emotional support, they may create demands as well (Vega & Kolody, 1985). Solomon et al. (1993) found that social network burden was related to higher numbers of symptoms in both St. Louis and Puerto Rico. Hough and Timbers (1985) found that events happening to others in the social network than self, spouse, or children, were important predictors of psychiatric symptoms for Mexican respondents in Ciudad Juárez but not for Mexican Americans or Whites in the United States.

Cultural Variations in Symptom Patterns in Response to Trauma

There are three areas in which cultural variations in symptom patterns have been explored—dissociation, culturally endogenous PTSD syndromes, and somatic complaints.

Dissociation

Dissociative symptoms are an important dimension of response to traumatic stress (Solomon & Canino, 1990). Guarnaccia et al. (1989) have noted the importance of *ataques de nervios* as an important culturally endogenous stress syndrome among Puerto Ricans and that *ataques* symptoms are heavily dissociative in nature. Therefore, one might expect Hispanic and particularly Puerto Rican populations to exhibit more dissociative symptoms in the face of trauma than other populations. However, Zatzick, Marmar, Weiss, and Matzler (1993) found no differences in the Dissociative Experiences Scale (DES) scores between ethnic groups in the NVVRS data by ethnicity, controlling for war-zone stress.

The relative importance of dissociative symptoms in Hispanic populations needs further exploration for at least two reasons. First, symptoms of dissociation are good predictors of later PTSD. Marmar et al. (1994) have suggested that

> the tendency to dissociate at the time a traumatic event is occurring, although affording the trauma victim some degree of detachment, distancing, and unreality concerning the horror of the event, does not confer long-term protection against posttraumatic stress disorder but rather constitutes a risk factor for subsequent PTSD. (p. 906)

This analysis of the NVVRS data finds a significant contribution of Dissociative Experiences Scale (DES) scores and Peritraumatic Dissociation Experiences Questionnaire, Rater Version (PDEQ-RV) scores to PTSD over and above ethnicity and level of war-zone stress exposure. To the degree that a given population is likely to dissociate, there is also the possibility that other types of symptoms may not be expressed and the capacity of the researcher to identify PTSD will be reduced (Solomon & Canino, 1990).

Somatic Complaints

A number of clinical and epidemiological population studies have shown that Hispanic populations tend to report significantly more somatic symptoms than non-Hispanic populations. Cross-cultural clinical studies performed in Columbia and Peru (Escobar, Burnam, Karno, Forsythe, & Golding, 1987; Mezzich & Raab, 1980) and population studies comparing Hispanics in United States communities with other ethnic groups (Dohrenwend & Dohrenwend, 1969) have consistently reported high levels of unexplained physical complaints for Hispanic populations. More recently, the distribution and comorbidity of functional somatic symptoms were examined in four community samples, three Hispanic (two Mexican American and one Puerto Rican), and one non-Hispanic white (Canino, Rubio-Stipec, Canino, & Escobar, 1992).

Of the four groups, Puerto Rican respondents reported the highest level of somatic symptoms, even after statistically controlling for socio-demographic factors. Various explanations have been given for the observed higher prevalence of somatization symptoms among Hispanics including societal views of mental illness and its treatment, and availability of mental health services (Canino et al., 1992; Escobar, Rubio-Stipec, Canino & Karno, 1989; Fabrega, 1991).

Given this evidence, one would expect that the symptomatic manifestations of PTSD should be somewhat different among Hispanic populations, particularly for Criterion D of *DSM–III–R*. Under this criterion the person has to have at least two out of six symptoms related to persistent arousal (hypervigilance, sleep disturbance, irritability, difficulty concentrating, memory impairment, startle response, and physiologic arousal caused by any stimulus that symbolizes or reenacts the traumatic event). These symptoms closely resemble complaints that may be somatic in character. Given their increased levels of somatization, one would expect that among Hispanic populations vulnerable to PTSD, physiological arousal would be more common. Cross-cultural research in this area is needed to provide empirical evidence regarding this hypothesis.

Culturally Endogenous Symptom Syndromes

Ataques de nervios, according to Canino and Canino (1993), have been described in the literature on Puerto Rican mental health for 30 years. Typically, episodes involve trembling, heart palpitations, difficulty moving limbs, memory loss, difficulty breathing, dizziness, and fainting spells. Trembling is usually followed by aggressive verbal and/or physical behavior and then falling to ground unconscious and/or convulsing (Canino & Canino, 1993; Guarnaccia et al., 1989).

That *ataques* may be associated with PTSD in Puerto Rican populations is suggested by Garrison's (1977) note that they are an "acceptable cry for help" when stress levels become intolerable. In appropriate cultural behavior, friends are required to help the victim deal with the unbearable level of stress. Canino et al. (1987) have noted the degree to which the syndrome is associated with psychosomatic symptoms, which suggests that the more psychosomatic aspects of PTSD may be confounded with symptoms of *ataques*.

Susto (also referred to as *espanto, espasmo, pasmo, miedo, saladera*) is usually translated into magical fright or soul loss. The cause of the syndrome is typically identified as a fear-inspiring event. Symptoms are typically those that can be associated with generalized anxiety, along with some startle response, trouble sleeping, worry, and fear (Martinez, 1993; Simons & Hughes, 1993).

Certainly, more studies that aggressively pursue the possibility of the existence of culturally endogenous syndromes of stress response is needed.

Patterns of Comorbidity

Escobar et al. (1983) found that PTSD was almost always mixed with other *DSM–III* diagnoses. Hough (1994) found that PTSD was highly correlated with schizophrenic and depressive disorders in a homeless mentally ill population. The pattern was interesting. Some 87.5% of Hispanics, 46.2% of Whites, and 62.5% of Blacks with PTSD were also schizophrenic. Some 12.5% of Hispanic, 53.4% of Whites, and 37.5% of Blacks with PTSD also had mood disorder (depression, manic/depressive, and mania).

Overall, there were no differences between paticipants with schizophrenia and mood disorder in terms of their likelihood of having PTSD. However, Hispanics with PTSD were less likely to have become diagnosable for mood disorders than other subjects with PTSD (8.3 Hispanic, 37.3 White and 13.6 Black). There were no significant racial and ethnic differences in the likelihood of PTSD subjects also being schizophrenic (35% for Hispanics, 32% for Whites, 22% for Blacks). Of subjects meeting PTSD criteria, 75% of Hispanics, 65% of White, and 50% of Blacks were also positive on alcohol or drug abuse or dependence disorder or both.

These studies could be seen as reporting rates of comorbidity so high as to question whether PTSD is a distinguishable, separate diagnosis in Hispanic populations. However, they should be viewed in the context of studies that generally demonstrate that most psychiatric diagnoses are highly comorbid with a range of other such diagnoses. The Brentwood studies (Gongla et al., 1983) described previously have suggested, however, that PTSD may actually be less predictable from other psychiatric disorders than are schizophrenia or major depression.

These findings suggest that the need for studies concerning possible cultural differences among Hispanic population and others in the effects of comorbidity on the long-term course and outcomes is badly needed.

Treatment for Hispanics

The Los Angeles ECA studies are the most conclusive in suggesting that Hispanics in general and, more specifically, Hispanics with diagnosable mental disorders, do not use mental health care resources nearly as frequently as other populations (Hough et al., 1987; Wells, Golding, Hough,

Burnam, & Karno, 1988). However, no significant differences were found between Hispanic and Black or non-Hispanic White Vietnam theater veterans in the NVVRS study (Kulka et al., 1991a).

When Hispanics do use mental health care resources, they may find treatment programs culturally insensitive. Dobkin de Rios and Friedmann (1987) have examined, for example, hypnotherapuetic intervention for traumatized Hispanic burn patients, and suggest that most do not respond to psychological interventions. Arredondo, Orjucla, and Moore (1989) point out the value of family therapy in treating Central American war refugees who have suffered trauma.

Culturally sensitive treatments may have to deal with what Parson (1985a, 1985b) calls the *tripartite adaptational dilemma* or "the triple effects of bicultural identity, institutional racism and residual stress from trauma" (1958a, p. 361). In terms of institutional racism, for example, minority veterans may well have faced racial stereotypes, ridicule, and inequitable treatment (Marsella et al., 1993). Penk and Allen (1991) similarly suggest that readjustment problems among minorities serving in the Vietnam war were compounded by prejudice and racism.

The degree to which Hispanics do not seek treatment or find culturally appropriate treatment effectively increases their risk for chronic PTSD and other psychiatric disorders. Understanding health-seeking behaviors and the effects of treatment on course of the disorder is crucial to the future agenda of research on PTSD in Hispanic populations.

CONCLUSION

In this chapter we have suggested that to most effectively isolate the role ethnocultural factors play in the development, progression, and outcomes of PTSD and related mental disorders in Hispanic populations, we need studies that are truly comparative and, at the same time, culturally sensitive.

Our overview of the literature suggests that to date studies in this area have generally fallen into one of two categories: (a) descriptive studies of PTSD symptoms and syndromes in disaster victims and refugees and (b) a few comparative studies of trauma and PTSD symptoms and diagnoses across ethnocultural groups. Neither set of studies has been terribly sensitive to the potential ethnocultural factors that affect PTSD and its course. They also have not provided much conclusive information concerning the hypothesis that ethnocultural groups will differ significantly in their propensities to experience trauma and serious deleterious mental health consequences. Finally, we have suggested a set of questions that need to be pursued in future research if cultural similarities and differences between Hispanic and other populations are to be carefully examined.

REFERENCES

Allodi, F. A. (1980). The psychiatric effects in children and families of victims of political persecution and torture. *Danish Medical Bulletin, 27,* 229–232.

American Psychiatric Association. (1980). *Diagnostic and statistical manual of mental disorders* (3rd. ed.). Washington, DC: Author.

Arredondo, P., Orjucla, E., & Moore, L. (1989). Family therapy with Central American war refugee families. *Journal of Strategic & Systematic Therapies, 8,* 38–35.

Arroyo, W., & Eth, S. (1985). Children traumatized by Central American warfare. In S. Eth & R. S. Pynoos (Eds.), *Posttraumatic Stress Disorder in children* (pp. 101–120). Washington, DC: American Psychiatric Press.

Bravo, M., Canino, G., Rubio-Stipec, M., & Serrano-García, I. (1991). Importancia de la familia como recurso de apoyo social en Puerto Rico [Importance of the family as social support resouce in Puerto Rico]. *Puerto Rico Health Sciences Journal, 3,* 149–156.

Bravo, M., Rubio-Stipec, M., Canino, G. J., Woodbury, M. A., & Ribera, J. C. (1990). The psychological sequelae of disaster prospectively and retrospectively evaluated. *American Journal of Community Psychology, 18,* 661–680.

Bravo, M., Serrano-García, I., Rubio-Stipec, M. & Canino, G. (1992). The impact of a disaster on social support networks in Puerto Rico. Unpublished paper. San Juan: University of Puerto Rico.

Burnam, M. A., Hough, R. L., Escobar, J. I., Karno, M., Timbers, D. M., Telles, C., & Locke, B. Z. (1987). Current psychiatric disorders: Mexican Americans and Nonhispanic Whites in Los Angeles. *Archives of General Psychiatry, 44,* 687–694.

Burnam, M. A., Hough, R. L., Telles, C. A., Karno, M., & Escobar, J. I. (1987). Acculturation and lifetime prevalence of DIS/DSM–III disorders among Mexican Americans in Los Angeles. *Journal of Health & Social Behavior, 28,* 89–102.

Burnam, M. A., Stein, J. A., Golding, J. M., Siegel, J. M., Sorenson, S. B., Forsythe, A. B., & Telles, C. A. (1988). Sexual assault and mental disorders in a community population. *Journal of Consulting & Clinical Psychology, 56,* 843–850.

Canino, G., Bird, H., Shrout, P. E., Rubio-Stipec, M., Bravo, M., Martinez, R., Sesman, M., & Guevara, L. M. (1987). The prevalence of specific psychiatric disorders in Puerto Rico. *Archives of General Psychiatry, 44,* 127–133.

Canino, G. C., Bravo, M., Rubio-Stipec, M., & Woodbury, M. (1990). The impact of disaster on mental health: Prospective and retrospective analyses. *International Journal of Mental Health, 19,* 51–69.

Canino, I. A., & Canino, G. J. (1993). Psychiatric care of Peurto Ricans. In A. C. Gaw (Ed.), *Culture, ethnicity, and mental illness.* Washington, DC: American Psychiatric Press.

Canino, I., Rubio-Stipec, M., Canino, G., & Escobar, J. (1992). Functional somatic symptoms: A cross-ethnic comparison. *American Journal of Orthopsychiatry, 62,* 605–612.

Cervantes, R. C., & Castro, F. G. (1985). Stress, coping and Mexican American mental health: A systematic review. *Hispanic Journal of Behavioral Science, 7,* 1–73.

Cervantes, R. C., Salgado de Snyder, V. N., & Padilla, A. M. (1989). Post traumatic stress in immigrants from Central America and Mexico. *Hospital & Community Psychiatry, 40,* 615–619.

Cohn, J., Danielsen, L., Holzer, K. I. M., Koch, L., Severin, B., Thorgersen, S., & Aalund, O. (1985). Repercussions of torture: A study of Chilean refugee children in Denmark. *Lancet, 2,* 437–438.

Cohn, J., Holzer, K. I. M., Koch, L., & Severin, B. (1980). An investigation of Chilean immigrant children in Denmark. *Danish Medical Bulletin, 27,* 238–239.

De la Fuente, R. (1990). The mental health consequences of the 1985 earthquakes in Mexico. *International Journal of Mental Health, 19,* 21–29.

Dobkin de Rios, M., & Friedmann, J. K. (1987). Hypnotherapy with Hispanic burn patients. *International Journal of Mental Health, 19,* 21–29.

Dohrenwend, B. P., & Dohrenwend, B. S. (1969). *Social status and psychological disorder: A causal inquiry.* New York: John Wiley.

Eaton, W. W., & Kessler, L. G. (Eds.). (1985). *Epidemiologic field methods in psychiatry: The NIMH Epidemiologic Catchment Area Program.* New York: Academic Press.

Escobar, J. I., Burnam, M. A., Karno, M., Forsythe, A., & Golding, J. M. (1987). Somatization in the community. *Archives of General Psychiatry, 44,* 710–726.

Escobar, J. I., & Randolph, E. T. (1982). The Hispanic and social networks. In R. M. Becerra & M. Karno (Eds.), *Mental health and Hispanic-Americans: Clinical perspectives.* New York: Grune & Stratton.

Escobar, J. I., Randolph, E. T., Puente, G., Spivak, F., Asamen, J. K., Hill, M., & Hough, R. L. (1983). Post-traumatic stress disorder in Hispanic Vietnam veterans: Clinical phenomenology and sociocultural characteristics. *Journal of Nervous & Mental Disease, 171,* 585–596.

Escobar, J., Rubio-Stipec, M., Canino, G., & Karno, M. (1989). Unfounded physical complaints in the community: Further validation of an abridged somatization construct. *Journal of nervous and mental disease, 117,* 140–146.

Fabrega, H. (1992). Culture and the psychosomatic tradition. *Psychosomatic Medicine, 54,* 561–566.

Fairbank, D. T., & Hough, R. L. (1981). Cultural differences in perceptions of life events. In B. S. Dohrenwend & B. P. Dohrenwend (Eds.), *Stressful life events and their contexts* (pp. 63–84). New York: PRODIST (Neal Watson Academic Publications).

Friedman, M. (1991). Biological approaches to the diagnosis and treatment of post traumatic stress disorder. *Journal of Traumatic Stress, 4,* 67–91.

Friedman, M., & Jaranson, J. (1992). PTSD among refugees. In A. J. Marsella, T. Borneman, J. Orley, & S. Ekblad (Eds.), *Amidst peril and pain: The mental health and well-being of the world's refugees*. Washington, DC: American Psychological Association.

Garrison, V. (1977). The Puerto Rican syndrome. In V. Crapanzano (Ed.), *Psychiatry and spiritism: Case studies in spirit posession*. New York: Wiley.

Golding, J. M., & Burnam, M. A. (1990). Stress and social support as predictors of depressive symptoms in Mexican Americans and non-Hispanic Whites. *Journal of Social & Clinical Psychology, 9*, 268–286.

Golding, J. M., Siegel, J. M., Sorenson, S. B., Burnam, M. A., & Stein, J. A. (1989). Social support sources following sexual assault. *Journal of Community Psychology, 17*, 92–107.

Golding, J. M., Stein, J. A., Siegel, J. M., Burnam, M. A., & Sorenson, S. B. (1988). Sexual assault history and use of health and mental health services. *American Journal of Community Psychology, 16*, 625–644.

Gongla, P. A., Hough, R. L., Carr, C., Corker, T. J., Forsythe, A. B., & Scurfield, R. M. (1983). *Post-Traumatic Stress Disorder: Is it a separate diagnosis?* Unpublished manuscript. Vietnam Veteran Research Laboratory, Brentwood VA Medical Center, Los Angeles, California.

Griffith, J. (1984). Emotional support providers and psychological distress among Anglo and Mexican Americans. *Community Mental Health Journal, 20*, 182–201.

Guarnaccia, P., Rubio-Stipec, M., & Canino, G. (1989). *Ataques de nervios* in the Puerto Rican Diagnostic Interview Schedule: The impact of cultural categories on psychiatric epidemiology. *Cultural Medical Psychiatry, 13*, 275–295.

Hayashi, S., Perales, A., Sogi, C., Wharton, D., Llanos, R., & Novara, J. (1985). *Prevalencia de vida de trastornos mentales en Independencia* [Lifetime prevalence of mental health problems in Independencia] (Lima, Peru). *Anales de Salud Mental* [Annals of Mental Health], *1*, 206–222.

Helzer, J. E., Robins, L. N., & McEvoy, L. (1987). Posttraumatic Stress Disorder in the general population. *The New England Journal of Medicine, 317*, 1630–1634.

Hjern, A., Birgitta, A., & Jojer, B. (1991). Persecution and behavior: A report of refugee children from Chile. *Child Abuse and Neglect, 15*, 139–148.

Hough, R. L. (1985). Life events and stress in Mexican-American culture. In W. A. Vega & M. R. Miranda (Eds.), *Stress and Hispanic mental health: Relating research to service delivery* (pp. 110–146). Rockville, MD: National Institute of Mental Health.

Hough, R. W. (1994). [San Diego McKinney Homeless Mentally Ill Demonstration Project]. Unpublished raw data.

Hough, R. W., & Golding, J. H. (1994). [Los Angles ECA post-traumatic stress disorder estimates]. Unpublished raw data.

Hough, R. L., Gongla, P. A., Scurfield, R. W., Carr, C., & Corker, T. (1983). *Natural history of post-traumatic stress disorder.* Paper presented at the meeting of the American Psychological Association, Anaheim, California.

Hough, R. L., Karno, M., Burnam, M. A., Escobar, J. I., & Timbers, D. M. (1983). The Los Angeles Epidemiologic Catchment Area Research Program and the epidemiology of psychiatric disorders among Mexican Americans. *Journal of Operational Psychiatry, 14,* 42–51.

Hough, R. L., Landsverk, J. L, Karno, M., Burnam, M. A., Timbers, D. M., Escobar, J. I., & Regier, D. R. (1987). Utilization of health and mental health services by Los Angeles Mexican Americans and Nonhispanic Whites. *Archives of General Psychiatry, 44,* 702–709.

Hough, R. L., & Timbers, D. M. (1985). Social network support and demand: Implications for prevention. In R. L. Hough, P. A. Gongla, V. B. Brown, & S. E. Goldston (Eds.), *Psychiatric epidemiology and prevention: The possibilities* (pp. 191–206). Los Angeles: Neuropsychiatric Institute, University of California at Los Angeles.

Hough, R. L., Vega, W., Valle, R., Kolody, B., Griswold del Castillo, R., & Tarke, H. (1990). The prevalence of symptoms of Posttraumatic Stress Disorder in the aftermath of the San Ysidro massacre. *Journal of Traumatic Stress, 3,* 71–92.

Jordan, B. K., Schlenger, W. E., Hough, R., Kulka, R. A., Weiss, D., Fairbank, J. A., & Marmar, C. R. (1991). Lifetime and current prevalence of specific psychiatric disorders among Vietnam veterans and controls. *Archives of General Psychiatry, 48,* 207–215.

Karno, M., Hough, R. L., Timbers, D. M., Escobar, J. I., Burnam, M. A., Santana, F., & Burke, J. B. (1987). Lifetime prevalence of specific psychiatric disorders among Mexican Americans and Nonhispanic Whites in Los Angeles. *Archives of General Psychiatry, 44,* 695–701.

Kulka, R. A., Schlenger, W. E., Fairbank, J. A., Hough, R. L., Jordan, B. K., Marmar, C. R., & Weiss, D. S. (1991a). *Trauma and the Vietnam war generation: Report of findings from the National Vietnam Veterans Readjustment Study.* New York: Brunner/Mazel.

Kulka, R. A., Schlenger, W. E., Fairbank, J. A., Hough, R. L., Jordan, B. K., Marmar, C. R., & Weiss, D. S. (1991b). Assessment of PTSD in the community: Prospects and pitfalls from recent studies of Vietnam veterans. *Psychological Assessment: A Journal of Consulting & Clinical Psychology, 3,* 547–560.

Lima, B. R., Chavez, H., Samaniego, N., Pompei, M. S., Pai, S., Santacruz, H., & Lozano, J. (1989). Disaster severity and emotional disturbance: Implications for primary mental health care in developing countries. *Acta Psychiatrica Scandinavica, 79,* 74–82.

Lima, B. R., Pai, S., Caris, L., Haro, J. M., Lima, A. M., Toledo, V., Lozano, J., & Santacruz, H. (1991). Psychiatric disorders in primary health care clinics one year after a major Latin American disaster. *Stress Medicine, 7,* 25–32.

Lima, B. R., Pai, S., Lozano, J., & Santacruz, H. (1990). The stability of emotional symptoms among disaster victims in a developing country. *Journal of Traumatic Stress, 3*, 497–505.

Lima, B. R., Pai, S., Santacruz, H., & Lozano, J. (1991). Psychiatric disorders among poor victims following a major disaster: Armero, Colombia. *Journal of Nervous & Mental Disease, 179*, 420–427.

Lima, B. R., Pai, S., Santacruz, H., Lozano, J. Chavez, H., & Samanicgo, N. (1989). Conducting research on disaster mental health in developing countries: A proposed model. *Disasters 3*, 177–184.

Lima, B. R., Pai, S., Santacruz, H., Lozano, J., & Luna, J. (1987). Screening for the psychological consequences of a major disaster in a developing country: Armero, Colombia. *Acta Psychiatrica Scandinavica, 76*, 561–567.

Marmar, C. R., Weiss, D. S., Schlenger, W. E., Fairbank, J. A., Jordan, B. K., Kulka, R. A., & Hough, R. L. (1994). Peritraumatic dissociation and post-traumatic stress in male Vietnam Theater veterans. *American Journal of Psychiatry, 46*, 902–907.

Marsella, A., Friedman, M., & Spain, E. (1992). A selective review of the literature on ethnocultural aspects of PTSD. *PTSD Research Quarterly, 2*, 1–7.

Marsella, A. J., Friedman, M. J., & Spain, E. H. (1993). Ethnocultural aspects of posttraumatic stress disorder. In J. M. Oldham, M. B. Riba, & A. Tasman (Eds.), *Review of psychiatry* (pp. 157–182). Washington, DC: American Psychiatric Press.

Martinez, C., Jr. (1993). Psychiatric care of Mexican Americans. In A. Gaw (Ed.), *Culture, ethnicity, and mental illness* (pp. 431–466). Washington, DC: American Psychiatric Press.

Mezzich, J., & Raab, E. (1980). Depressive symptomatology across the Americas. *Archives of General Psychiatry, 37*, 818–823.

Parson, E. R. (1985a). Ethnicity and traumatic stress: The intersecting point in psychotherapy. In C. R. Figley (Ed.), *Trauma and its wake: The study and treatment of post-traumatic stress disorder* (pp. 314–337). New York: Brunner/Mazel.

Parson, E. R. (1985b). The intercultural setting: Encountering Black Viet Nam veterans. In S. M. Sonnenberg, A. S. Blank, Jr., & J. A. Talbott (Eds.), *The trauma of war: Stress and recovery in Viet Nam veterans* (pp. 360–387). Washington, DC: American Psychiatric Press.

Paz, O. (1961). *The labyrinth of solitude, life and thought in Mexico.* New York: Grove Press.

Penk, W. E., & Allen, I. M. (1991). Clinical assessment of post-traumatic stress disorder (PTSD) among American minorities who served in Vietnam. *Journal of Traumatic Stress, 4*, 41–66.

Radloff, L. (1977). The CES-D scale: A self report depression scale for research in the general population. *Applied Psychological Measurement, 1*, 385–401.

Regier, D. A., Myers, J. K, Kramer, M., Robins, L. N., Blazer, D. G., Hough, R. L., Eaton, W. W., & Locke, B. Z. (1984). The NIMH Epidemiologic Catchment Area (ECA) Program: Historical context, major objectives and study population characteristics. *Archives of General Psychiatry, 41,* 934–941.

Robins, L. N., & Regier, D. A. (Eds.). (1991). *Psychiatric disorders in America.* New York: Free Press.

Robins, L. N., Helzer, J. E., Croughan, J., & Ratcliff, K. (1981). National Institute of Mental Health Diagnostic Interview Schedule: Its history, characteristics and validity. *Archives of General Psychiatry 38,* 381–389.

Schlenger, W. E., Kulka, R. A., Fairbank, J. A., Hough, R. L., Jordan, B. K., Marmar, C. R., & Weiss, D. S. (1992). The prevalence of post-traumatic stress disorder in the Vietnam generation: A multimethod, multisource assessment of psychiatric disorder. *Journal of Traumatic Stress, 5,* 33–363.

Siegel, J. M., Golding, J. M., Stein, J. A., Burnam, M. A., & Sorenson, S. B. (1990). Reactions to sexual assault: A community study. *Journal of Interpersonal Violence, 5,* 229–246.

Siegel, J. M., Sorenson, S. B., Golding, J. M., Burnam. M. A., & Stein, J. A. (1987). The prevalence of childhood sexual assault: The Los Angles epidemiologic catchment area project. *American Journal of Epidemiology, 126,* 1141–1153.

Siegel, J. M., Sorenson, S. B., Golding, J. M., Burnam, M. A., & Stein, J. A. (1989). Resistance to sexual assault: Who resists and what happens? *American Journal of Public Health, 79,* 27–31.

Simons, R. C., & Hughes, C. C. (1993). Culture-bound syndromes. In A. Gaw (Ed.), *Culture, ethnicity, and mental illness* (pp. 75–79). Washington, DC: American Psychiatric Press.

Smith, E. M., Robins, L. N., Przybeck, T. R., Goldring, E., & Solomon, S. D. (1986). Psychosocial consequences of a disaster. In J. H. Shore (Ed.), *Disaster stress studies: New methods and findings.* Washington, DC: American Psychiatric Press.

Solomon, S. D., Bravo, M., Rubio-Stipec, M., & Canino, G. (1993). Effect of family role on response to disaster. *Journal of Traumatic Stress, 6,* 255–269.

Solomon, S. D., & Canino, G. J. (1990). Appropriateness of *DSM–III–R* criteria for posttraumatic stress disorder. *Comprehensive Psychiatry, 31,* 227–237.

Solomon, S. D., Smith, E. M., Robins, L. N., & Fischbach, R. L. (1987). Social involvement as a mediator of disaster-induced stress. *Journal of Applied Social Psychology, 17,* 1092–1112.

Sorenson, S. B., & Siegel, J. M. (1992). Gender, ethnicity, and sexual assault: Findings from a Los Angeles study. *Journal of Social Issues, 48,* 93–104.

Sorenson, S. B., Stein, J. A., Siegel, J. M., Golding, J. M., & Burnam, M. A. (1987). The prevalence of adult sexual assault: The Los Angeles Epidemiologic Catchment Area Project. *American Journal of Epidemiology, 126,* 1154–1164.

Sorenson, S. B., & Telles, C. A. (1991). Self-reports of spousal violence in a Mexican-American and non-Hispanic White population. *Violence and Victims, 6,* 3–15.

Summerfield, D., & Toser, L. (1990). Nicaragua: The psychological impact of "low intensity" warfare. *Lancet, 336,* 638–679.

Summerfield, D., & Toser, L. (1991). "Low intensity" war and mental trauma in Nicaragua: A study in a rural community. *Medicine and War, 7,* 84–89.

Vega, W. A., & Kolody, B. (1985). The meaning of social support and the mediation of stress across cultures. In W. A. Vega & M. R. Miranda (Eds.), *Stress and Hispanic mental health: Relating research to service delivery* (pp. 48–75). Rockville, MD: National Institute of Mental Health.

Vega, W. A., Kolody, B., Hough, R. L., & Figueroa, G. (1987). Depressive symptomatology in northern Mexican adults. *American Journal of Public Health, 77,* 1215–1218.

Vega, W. A., Kolody, B., & Valle, J. R. (1986). The relationship of marital status, confidant support, and depression among Mexican immigrant women. *Journal of Marriage & the Family, 48,* 597–605.

Vega, W. A., Kolody, B., Valle, R., & Hough, R. (1986). Depressive symptoms and their correlates among immigrant Mexican women in the U.S. *Social Science & Medicine, 22,* 645–652.

Vega, W. A., Warheit, G., & Palacio, R. (1985). Psychiatric symptomatology among Mexican American farmworkers. *Social Science & Medicine, 20,* 39–45.

Wells, K. B., Golding, J. M., Hough, R. L., Burnam, M. A., & Karno, M. (1988). Factors affecting the probability of use of general and medical health and social/community services for Mexican Americans and non-Hispanic Whites. *Medical Care, 26,* 441–452.

Weile, B., Wingender, L. B., Bach-Mortensen, N., Busch, P., Lukman, B., & Holzer, K. I. M. (1990). Behavioral problems in children of torture victims: A sequel to cultural maladaptation or to parental torture? *Developmental and Behavioural Pediatrics, 11,* 79–80.

Yamamoto, J., Silva, J. A., Sasao, T., Wang, C., & Nguyen, L. (1993). Alcoholism in Peru. *American Journal of Psychiatry, 150,* 1059–1062.

Zatzick, D. F., Marmar, C. R., Weiss, D. S., & Matzler, T. (1993). *Trauma, ethnicity and dissociation.* Manuscript presented at the meeting of the American Psychiatric Association, San Francisco, California.

IV

ETHNOCULTURAL ASPECTS OF PTSD AMONG SPECIFIC VICTIM POPULATIONS

13

CROSS-NATIONAL AND ETHNOCULTURAL ISSUES IN DISASTER RESEARCH

BONNIE L. GREEN

Presently, disaster research does not focus on ethnocultural and cross-national issues. Almost no studies exist that have attempted to compare directly responses of one culture or nation to another to determine a potentially different extent or type of reaction to such events. A few studies in the United States have compared African American and European American subjects to examine differences in responses (e.g., Gleser, Green, & Winget, 1981), and one study has compared Native Alaskans to non-Natives (Palinkas, Downs, Patterson, & Russell, 1993). However, no studies were found examining the same outcomes in equivalent populations from one country to another.

To some extent, this reflects the lack of attention to cultural aspects of disaster in general. However, it also reflects real difficulties in comparing one event to another, even within a nation or culture. Further, as pointed out by Marsella, Friedman, and Spain (1993, see also chapter 4, this volume), these methodologic problems are even more difficult in the context of working with different ethnocultural groups, which may be differentially vulnerable to trauma, have different personal and social resources for coping, and different exposure to other traumas.

At the present time, no conclusions may be drawn about the impact of cultural factors in determining response to disasters. In this chapter I will address suggestive findings in disaster studies, present specific studies of disaster that may provide hypotheses for future investigators, focus on appropriate questions for disaster researchers to address in the future, and draw attention to the importance of sensitivity to the specific experiences and ethnocultural context of disaster events that may affect the quality of research data obtained, even in settings in which the backgrounds of investigators and subjects are not extremely different.

SOME QUESTIONS AND GOALS FOR CROSS-CULTURAL RESEARCH ON TRAUMAS AND DISASTERS

Marsella and colleagues (chapter 4, this volume) have suggested several types of questions that would be appropriate foci for cross-cultural studies of posttraumatic stress disorder (PTSD). These include (a) exploring symptom frequencies in different settings, (b) exploring symptom patterns among different ethnocultural groups with a common diagnosis, (c) surveying symptomatology in patients from different countries exposed to trauma, (d) matching samples from different groups on important demographic variables then comparing symptom profiles, (e) studying symptom expressions via culture-specific disorders, and (f) conducting factor analytic studies of symptom patterns in different ethnocultural groups.

An additional question of interest might be the extent to which factors that were most predictive of a particular outcome vary depending on the cultural context. For example, social support may predict outcome in one culture but not in an other if, for example, social conditions were quite different in the two settings or if ranges of support varied greatly from one group to the next. Another question would be whether members of different groups viewed what happened to them in sufficiently different ways to affect their own views of the possibility of recovery and the nature of the recovery process. This social construction of reality by both the society and the person must be considered in interpreting the findings.

For example, a recent study of immigrant farm workers in California showed that more than half of the laborers believed that cancers were mostly the result of unavoidable exposures (e.g., substances in the air or water), compared to surveys of the general public in which fewer than one third of individuals had this belief (Vaughn, 1993). Further, the perceived unavoidability and lack of control of the threat from pesticides among these immigrant farm workers was associated with self-protective behavior, such that those who perceived themselves as having less control were much less likely to engage in self-protective behavior to control exposure. This effect was independent of education or degree of knowledge about exposure risk (Vaughn, 1993). Whereas this study described attitudes toward future risk, it is reasonable to hypothesize that similar factors could affect exposure to disaster agents or coping responses to such events.

As noted previously, the equivalence of symptoms and their meanings across cultures should be a focus of research in this area. Certain symptoms may have an entirely different meaning in one culture than in another (e.g., Kortmann, 1987, found the question "Is your appetite poor?" did not make sense to a group of Ethiopians who struggled daily to get enough food to stay alive). Thus, merely translating an instrument does not ensure measurement of equivalent syndromes.

It is unclear at this point whether the most likely and salient outcomes in one culture are necessarily the most salient outcomes in another culture. Therefore, learning for each setting what the most important issues, concerns, and outcomes are may be as important as employing the same measures in two settings (which may be quite important in its own right).

What qualifies as traumatic also could vary by culture, perhaps for reasons of expectation or of the particular experiences of the individuals involved. It seems likely, however, that certain types of experiences would be universally stressful, such as a severe life threat, violent loss of loved ones, being the victim of a deliberate injury or violation (Green, 1990).

As a slight variant of issues mentioned earlier (see chapter 4, this volume), the characteristics of the stressors (i.e., disasters) may differ from one location to the next. That is, disasters actually may be more devastating or deadly in some locations than in others, so that the events experienced may be qualitatively different, making cross-cultural research even more difficult.

Finally, also a variation on the points made by Marsella et al. (see chapter 4, this volume), the characteristics of the populations affected and the quality of the local response to a disaster (e.g., relief efforts) may vary qualitatively from one setting to the next, further reducing the ability of investigators to make meaningful comparisons. Whereas the latter points stand as potential barriers to cross-cultural research in the arena of disaster, they also may be legitimate factors on which to focus study.

METHODOLOGIC PROBLEMS IN DISASTER RESEARCH WITHIN CULTURES

In earlier publications, my colleagues and I have pointed out methodological problems that have made assessing disaster effects from one event to the next difficult (Green, 1982, 1985, 1991; Solomon, 1989). Some of these methodological problems, initially noted more than a decade ago, have improved considerably. These include use of standardized instruments and nonclinical populations. There are now numerous studies of general population samples (e.g., Bromet, Parkinson, & Dunn, 1990; Canino, Bravo, Rubio-Stipec, & Woodbury, 1990; Phifer & Norris, 1989;

Shore, Tatum, & Vollmer, 1986; Smith, Robins, Przybeck, Goldring, & Solomon, 1986) following disasters that have used accepted, standardized instruments. Common interview instruments, as well as self-report measures, allow direct comparison on equivalent measures in many cases (Green, 1991). Along these lines, there are readily agreed-on criteria for defining who receives a diagnosis or who would meet a certain criterion for severity of disorder, both of which can be accomplished if the same cutoffs are used with the same instruments.

The Timing of Assessment

Other methodologic factors continue to make it more difficult to compare one study to the next. One of these is the *timing of assessment*. For a variety of reasons, few studies are conducted at the same points in time following the disaster. Since negative disaster responses tend to drop off over time, with some notable exceptions, comparisons would only be equivalent if the same time periods were compared. This issue, too, is improving in that new studies are beginning earlier and earlier (and in a few cases, there is a predisaster database) and more standard time periods are being used, so that comparisons are more easily linked to time period.

Identifying the Target Population

Further methodologic factors, however, as well as some real differences among events, make it even more difficult to draw comparisons, and the likelihood of these factors improving is lower. **First**, in most disasters, the population to be studied is not necessarily clear-cut. In a natural disaster, for example, the population may be all residents who suffered damage from a storm or a flood, everyone living in a certain area whether or not they suffered individual damage, everyone in the county, and so on. Which of these original populations was chosen to be studied would likely influence estimates of the number of people affected by the event.

In a technological disaster, the population may be even more difficult to define. For example, in a restaurant fire, the disaster population might be defined as all those at the restaurant the night of the fire, individuals living in the community of the fire, friends and family of those at the fire or those killed or injured, off-duty employees who no longer have employment, and so on.

How the population is defined influences estimates of those negatively affected. In studying the Three Mile Island radiation leak, for example, investigators chose different radii around the plant from which to draw their sample to represent the resident population (e.g., 20 miles; Dohrenwend et al., 1981; 10 miles; Bromet et al., 1990; 5 miles; Baum, Gatchel, & Schaffer, 1983). Until generic parameters are developed, it will be difficult to overcome these differences in definitions of the population to draw conclusions about what proportion of individuals are affected by such events.

Defining Exposure

A related issue is that of defining exposure to an event. As noted elsewhere (Green, 1990, 1993; March, 1993), studies usually show a significant relationship between exposure severity (e.g., degree of life threat, extent of loss, disruption, etc.) and PTSD or other stress response syndromes). However, the deadliness or the extent of devastation of the landscape differ broadly from one event to the next, to the point that they may be almost qualitatively different. While this is a difficult issue even within a culture or country, it may become even more salient when examining events across cultures.

For example, Lima, Pai, Santacruz, Lozano, and Luna (1987) have pointed out, based on statistics from the U.S. Agency for International Development, that in this century (through 1986), there have been nearly 2,400 disasters worldwide (excluding the United States), but 86% of them have occurred in developing nations, producing 42 million deaths and 1.4 billion individuals affected. Seventy-eight percent of all deaths occurred in developing countries where more than 97% of affected individuals are located. Further, the ratio of affected to killed individuals is threefold in developed nations but tenfold in developing countries, so that each disaster in a developing country leaves more affected individuals in need of disaster relief and other services, likely under conditions of fewer available resources.

Another study by the International Federation of Red Cross and Red Crescent Societies (1993) has shown the same trends. The total number of disaster events reported for the time period between 1967 and 1991 was 7,766, with more than 7 million people killed in these events and nearly 3 billion affected. However, the distribution by geographic area was not random. It was the poorest countries and those with the largest populations that sustained the most deaths during this period, and the people in the least-developed countries continued to run the greatest risk of dying from disaster. For example, whereas Africa had 15% of the total disaster events, it had 50% of the deaths. Asia had 42% of the events and 43% of the deaths, but it had 68% of the injuries and 85% of people affected.

An example is the disaster studied by Lima and his colleagues (eg., Lima et al., 1987; Lima et al., 1993), in which a volcanic eruption in Armero, Columbia, destroyed the town and killed 22,000 people or 80% of the area inhabitants. Disasters of this scope are difficult to imagine in the United States, where citizens found Hurricane Andrew (a disaster of much lower magnitude) significantly taxing. Individuals who live in developing countries may have a different overall experience than those living in areas with fewer such events, and expectations and attitudes about such natural events may differ from country to country.

Differential Vulnerability to Disasters

As noted by Oliver-Smith (1993), a disaster involves the combination of a potentially destructive agent from the natural or technological environment and a vulnerable population. That is, disasters may affect populations that are differentially vulnerable to begin with. Seaman (1984, cited in Lima, Santacruz, Lozano, & Luna, 1988) noted that disasters are more likely to affect socioeconomically disadvantaged populations because the fast rise in some city populations, the pressure on the land, and deteriorating economic conditions have forced underprivileged populations into more hazardous areas in which they are more likely to encounter disasters.

Oliver-Smith (1993) also suggested that low income groups, even if they have information that certain areas are more prone to hazards, may not have a choice about where they live because more dangerous areas may be all that they can afford. These points suggest that some disasters may be confounded with the populations that they affect and that research attempting to address impacts related to cultural issues alone (beliefs, customs, etc.) may be difficult because similar types of exposure may not fall equally on different populations.

Variables that Mediate Responses to Disasters

A great deal is now known about the types of variables that mediate the responses to disaster stressors, including community level mediators, social mediators, individual predispositions, and formal interventions (Green & Solomon, 1995; Solomon, 1989). Although these factors have been studied at an individual level as risk factors predicting response and recovery, it is more difficult to study them across events because a number of aspects of a disaster are likely to vary between events, and isolating the impact of a particular factor is thus made more difficult.

Further, the availability of interventions, and in particular community mediators (e.g., extent of disruption, scope, setting) and social mediators (e.g., kin and network support), are likely to differ from one cultural community to the next. Although certain of these aspects are the target of cross-cultural research (e.g., supportiveness and availability of kin), others may vary with culture but be more tangential to hypotheses regarding mental health (i.e, availability of disaster relief services).

The major point of these observations is that in many, and perhaps most, studies comparing ethnocultural groups with regard to their mental health responses to disaster, cultural factors are likely to be influenced by, and confounded with, elements of geography, government, and so forth, that are not aspects of culture per se but may have a huge impact on individual responses. These points are valid for other areas of mental health and trauma/PTSD as well; however, disaster may be one of the most difficult areas in which to do cross-cultural research. Further complicating these drawbacks is that disasters, by definition, are not predictable, so that preplanning such research is extremely difficult.

STUDIES OF PTSD IN OTHER COUNTRIES FOLLOWING DISASTER

A number of studies have examined the question of whether PTSD symptoms, or the syndrome, are found in other than North American cultures, where the diagnosis originated. These studies generally support the idea that PTSD and its symptoms indeed can be found in the other settings following disaster. For example, Lima and colleagues (1987; Lima, Pai, Santacruz, Hozaw, 1991) identified "cases" of psychiatric distress following a volcano eruption and mudslides in Columbia, and when many of these individuals were reassessed specifically for PTSD shortly afterward by a psychiatrist, 54% of them met criteria.

Following an earthquake in Mexico City at 10 weeks, de la Fuente (1990) found that 32% of his sample met criteria for PTSD (not present prior to the event). Fairley, Langeluddecke, and Tennant (1986) estimated, by using the results of a questionnaire, that 66% of their exposed sample had partial PTSD within a few months of exposure to a cyclone in the Fiji Islands; however, cases meeting full diagnostic criteria were rare. Canino and colleagues (1990) and Bravo, Rubio-Stipec, Canino, Woodbury, and Ribera (1990) found PTSD diagnoses (3.7% at 2 years) in survivors of mudslides in Puerto Rico that killed 180 people. A number of these studies also showed a significant relationship between severity of exposure to the disaster and PTSD-type outcomes, further indicating the validity of this syndrome in other settings. Weisaeth (1989) found a relationship between exposure and PTSD symptoms in a sample of Norwegian factory workers following an explosion. Thus, there is evidence that the PTSD syndrome has some validity in Western cultures outside of the United States.

STUDIES OF ETHNOCULTURAL DIFFERENCES IN DISASTERS IN THE UNITED STATES

Under the auspices of the National Institute of Mental Health (Green, 1993), I reviewed English-language studies on disasters to determine whether they examined race differences in response to disaster events.

Only a handful of studies took up this question at all, even in its most simplistic version (i.e., mean differences between samples for African Americans vs. Caucausians), and the results were mixed.

It is not clear whether investigators have these data and do not examine them because of low numbers of subjects in certain subgroups, whether it is a sensitive topic that investigators are not comfortable discussing, whether samples tend to be homogeneous for race, or some combination of these and other factors. However, I will present four studies that did examine differences between African Americans and European Americans, three at some length because they examined the question in some detail and illustrate some of the problems in doing research in this area. I also will describe a recent study of different cultural groups in Alaska.

A Texas Tornado Study

Bolin and Klenow (1988) studied a random sample of Black and White elderly and nonelderly victims who had damaged residences from a tornado in Texas in 1982, about 8 months after the event. Approximately 212 White subjects were studied along with 219 African American subjects. Overall findings showed that elders within each racial group were more likely to be psychosocially recovered (measured via interview questions) than were those between the ages of 18 to 64. This fits well with other studies examining age effects (e.g., Green, Gleser, Lindy, Grace, & Leonard, in press). However, there were differences by race in recovery rates that were evident primarily in the samples of elderly adults.

Among the broader sample under 65, the recovery rates were similar (38% Whites recovered, 33% African Americans recovered), but the discrepancy was larger for the elderly victims (53% Whites recovered, 37% African Americans recovered). Although the rates of damage to the housing of the two groups was nearly identical, the African American and White samples differed by social class, with African Americans showing lower socioeconomic status on a number of indicators. Thus, differences attributed to race are just as likely to be a result of social class.

These investigators also looked at differences in predictors of recovery by race (as well as age), an unusual approach in disaster research, and took social class into account at this point. The results were complex but showed that determinants of outcome varied only slightly by race. For all groups (both races and ages), positive predictors of recovery were higher social class (related to resources available to subjects), married status, number of friends or relatives in the community, extent of available social and material support, and adequacy of federal aid. The number of moves to temporary housing predicted lower recovery, whereas percentage of home destroyed and insurance adequacy did not add unique variance to the recovery prediction.

Family size was the variable that most differentiated subgroups. For the younger groups, larger families were associated with less recovery, whereas for older victims, family size predicted differently depending on race. Family was not associated with recovery for White subjects but was positively associated for African Americans. The authors did not discuss the negative association for younger victims, but it is likely because of the increased burdens that middle-aged families have for both children and aging parents (Green et al., in press). For White elderly subjects, family size was less important because they were less likely to live in extended families and had to rely on extrafamilial kin for social support. For African American elderly subjects, more family (i.e., living with children) predicted better recovery. These differences are interesting, but subtle, and more complex than just comparing one ethnic group with another.

Hurricane Hugo

As part of a large, epidemiologic study of traumatic events in the general population, Norris (1992) studied 1,000 African American and White community subjects from four southeastern cities. In her overall study, Norris found that Whites were significantly more likely to be exposed to robbery, physical assault, tragic death, or disaster than African Americans, in spite of the fact that Whites were more likely to be socioeconomically advantaged. African Americans were more likely to be exposed to a motor vehicle crash. Exposure to these various events decreased with age. African American men showed the highest stress responses to recent hazards and other traumatic events. Included in the study were questions about exposure and responses to Hurricane Hugo. Differences in exposure to the hurricane were stratified in the study.

Norris (1992) also determined which subjects were likely to meet current criteria for PTSD (using various questions from different instruments and matching them to DSM criteria). The rate of current PTSD from Hurricane Hugo was about 5% in the total population and 5.8% for all hazards combined. The rate of PTSD for subjects exposed to any type of traumatic event was 7.3%. Race did not predict rates of PTSD following exposure to these events. There were also no differences by race within gender groups. She concluded that the impact of race on reactions to traumatic events is quite complex and may be a result of the unique social dynamics associated with a particular event, highlighting the importance of specifying cultural context.

Beverly Hills Supper Club Fire

In our study of the Beverly Hills Supper Club fire of 1977, which killed 165 patrons, comparisons among the middle-class subjects studied showed that African Americans were more impaired on several measures (Green, 1980). However, this was a convenience sample and many of the African American subjects (about 9% of the total sample of 147) were members of a choral union attending a yearly outing at the supper club. Two of their members died in the fire and were the last two bodies to be identified several days later. Thus, in this case, race differences were deemed attributable to somewhat idiosyncratic circumstances of the sample recruitment (and perhaps the population studied).

The Buffalo Creek Disaster

In 1972, heavy rains and poor dam construction caused a dam collapse that killed 125 people in a small Appalachian mining community; this became known as the Buffalo Creek disaster. The original sample studied at 2 years after the disaster consisted of 381 plaintiffs in a lawsuit—again, not a random group from the community (Gleser et al., 1981). African Americans represented a larger proportion in the sample (about 21%) than in the community (about 10%).

In the original studies, African Americans overall showed significantly less disaster-related impairment than Whites. This was in part because of the differences in stressors suffered. African Americans tended to live further down the valley than Whites so their neighborhoods were less destroyed and individuals were less exposed and displaced. No African Americans died in the disaster, and lawyers and research investigators were told by some residents that God had protected African Americans during the disaster. There were no socioeconomic differences between the two groups. When extent of disaster exposure was controlled statistically, the differences between the races disappeared for women, but African American men continued to be doing better than White men. At the time, we interpreted this to be most likely related to the leading role played by African American individuals, particularly men, in organizing the lawsuit and in other community activities following the disaster (attempts to incorporate the valley, attempts to build recreational facilities).

When a follow-up study was conducted 14 years after the disaster (Green et al., 1990a; 1990b), the survivors had improved, on the average, although they were still more impaired than their nonexposed neighbors. However, 11% of the sample had no PTSD diagnosis at 2 years but did have a PTSD diagnosis at 14 years. The only variable that predicted this delayed group was race: More African Americans had a delayed version of PTSD and relatively fewer were in the recovered group.

We hypothesized at the follow-up that the original situation surrounding the African American subjects (their protection from death and destruction during the event, their role in the lawsuit and the community following the disaster) was initially protective, but suggested that as the memory of the disaster and the lawsuit faded over time, more usual prejudicial attitudes resurfaced, and risk for PTSD symptoms reappeared. This is speculative, of course, and these case studies only suggest the importance of looking beyond single categorical variables when examining ethnocultural differences. However, in line with Norris (1992), the findings in from the Beverly Hills and Buffalo Creek disasters also suggest that ethnocultural factors may interact with specific aspects of a disaster event to produce risk for one subgroup or another.

Exxon Valdez Oil Spill

In a recent study by Palinkas and colleagues (1993) examining different ethnocultural groups—taking into account cultural explanations for the outcomes—the researchers studied nearly 600 community residents exposed to the Exxon Valdez oil spill in Alaska. Both Native and non-Native groups participated. They found a dose-response relationship between exposure severity and outcome (psychiatric diagnoses of PTSD, generalized anxiety and depression). Exposure also predicted declines in quality of social relationships, a perceived increase in health problems, increased reports of substance abuse and domestic violence, and a decline in subsistence activities (production and distribution).

More relevant to the present context, however, is the fact that the Alaskan Natives were at much higher risk (two or more times higher) for PTSD and generalized anxiety disorder than the non-Natives. Several explanations for these differences were considered, including the higher exposure of the Natives and generally higher rates of certain psychological symptoms in Native Alaskans in the general population. It also was suggested that the meaning to the two subpopulations of the lost subsistence activities may have played a role. These were particularly salient for the Alaska Natives because the destroyed natural resources were not simply a means of economic sustenance but also a way of transmitting traditional values and culture to the next generation; they were at the core of Native identity, ideology, and social organization. This study also suggests that the subgroup at risk in a particular event may depend on the specific aspects of the event and its context.

THE ARMERO DISASTER: A CASE STUDY IN A DEVELOPING COUNTRY

The Armero disaster, studied by Lima and colleagues, offers an example of disaster in a different cultural and sociopolitical context than most of those studied in the United States. These investigators paid attention to issues that might be specific to developing countries and that therefore would be appropriate to a discussion of cross-cultural issues in disaster research.

As noted earlier, the Armero disaster was a devastating volcanic eruption, followed by mudslides, which killed 22,000 people or about 80% of the entire population around the town. Two small neighboring towns of about 3,000 people each had to assimilate approximately 6,000 homeless victims. Survivors were mostly unskilled workers with limited possibility for alternative gainful employment (Lima et al., 1988). The individuals who participated in the study were several hundred survivors in shelter camps.

At 7 months after the disaster, the investigators found that 56% of the survivors (compared to norms developed in other communities in Latin America, including Colombia, in which the disaster took place) met cutoffs for *caseness* (Lima et al., 1987). When a subsample of these individuals was interviewed by psychiatrists a month later and diagnosed according to *DSM–III* criteria, 54% of the cases met criteria for PTSD and 91% met criteria for some formal diagnosis, suggesting that the screening instrument indeed identified distressed individuals (Lima et al., 1991). Studies over time (up to 5 years) showed that for a longitudinal sample ($N = 113$), rates of caseness decreased from 65% at 7 months to 31% at 5 years (Lima et al., 1993).

Two-year rates on a small subsample were 78%, an increase over the 7-month figures. These rates are quite high but do seem to be supported by the psychiatric interviews at 8 months indicating that 91% of the cases had diagnosable *DSM–III* disorders, compared to 26% of the below-cutoff subjects.

The authors acknowledged that all of the problems might not have been a result of the disaster itself but a result of the continuing difficult living situation, poor housing, unemployment, and disrupted family and social support systems (Lima et al., 1987) They noted, however, that in developing countries, this combination of factors is more often the rule than the exception and should be seen as an integral component of the disaster and its impact over time.

The point to be made here is not one about specific rates, because the studies can be criticized from several perspectives. However, the more salient point for a decision of cross-cultural issues is the overwhelming nature of the event and the ratio of needs and demands to resources in this setting (Lima et al., 1993), which may not be comparable with disaster events studied in more developed countries.

Guarnizo (1991) studied this same disaster from a community planning perspective and noted several aspects of the event that are potentially important to consider in recovery efforts but that also have implications for mental health consequences. She focused on the relationship between the aid provider and aid user (victim) in the Armero disaster, suggesting that the relief effort created a dependency relationship that had the effect of continuing psychosocial and economic problems.

This dependency relationship was primarily created by external factors (i.e., the nature of the recovery effort, in which resources flowed in from the outside and created a traditional patron–client relationship). It then was maintained or exacerbated by the characteristics of the survivor population (socioeconomic status, education, skills). The predisaster economic situation, in combination with the disaster impact itself, left the survivors with few individual or social resources with which to face recovery. Even so, an estimated 87% of the survivors managed to survive outside of shelters (Guarnizo, 1991).

In analyzing this event, Guarnizo suggested that the relief providers were caught in a *poor victim* syndrome in which they believed that the disaster survivors were helpless. Thus, providers continued to care for survivors even after survivors were able to care for themselves (based on providers' role definitions, rather than any intent to create or maintain dependency). The camp residents, conversely, came to rely on the aid and yielded personal responsibility. As the relief stage was prolonged, some began to feel that the agency's provision of relief was an obligation and should continue indefinitely. This dynamic is more likely to ensue when an outsider enters the relationship than when the relief efforts are internal to an area (Guarnizo, 1991).

Tierney and Baisden (1979) make a similar observation that worse mental health and other psychosocial consequences may ensue when victims outnumber nonvictims and help must be imported from the outside. Guarnizo (1991) used her study of the Armero disaster to develop guidelines for practice regarding relief intervention programs and subsequent development efforts that will minimize these problems.

This example is relevant because, although these problems could apply in developed countries if the event is devastating enough, they are likely to be part and parcel of large scale events in developing countries. Thus, cross-cultural research efforts need to take into account this entire complex of issues that may impinge on individuals exposed to disaster events that may interact with, and not be easily disentangled from, cultural issues.

INTERNATIONAL AND CROSS-CULTURAL STUDIES
OF DISASTERS

A few disaster studies that attempted to address cross-national or cross-cultural issues were found, although, as mentioned, there were few. I will review their findings as examples of the types of studies that might be done in this area.

Earthquakes in Ecuador and Colombia

In addition to the Armero volcano eruption and mudslides, Lima and colleagues (1989) also studied a major earthquake in Ecuador, which allowed a cross-national comparison of survivors' mental health in these separate disasters in South America. In the Ecuador earthquake, which caused a few deaths, the subject sample was recruited from primary care clinics in the affected area. Every third patient was studied. The same screening instrument, the Self-Reporting Questionnaire (SRQ), was used. Data were collected at 2 months after the earthquake. Rates of caseness were 40% for this sample of 250 individuals, a rate three times higher than that for individuals screened in other primary care settings in South America in which no disaster had occurred. The most frequent symptoms in this group were being easily frightened; feeling nervous, tense, or worried; and feeling easily tired or sleeping badly.

In comparing the two disasters, the authors also reported a rate of caseness for survivors in the Armero area not in tent camps but recruited from primary care settings, as in the Ecuador study. The authors noted that for all of the comparisons, the severity of symptoms was the same for individuals with a positive SRQ score cutoff, and the symptom profiles for the cases were nearly identical, suggesting that the disasters produced similar symptom constellations for those individuals who were affected.

Although the authors do not point this out, the time frames were different for the two evaluations, which may indicate that the discrepancies between levels of problems for the two events are more pronounced than the authors assumed (i.e., there were higher rates for Armero victims at 8 months than for the Ecuador victims at 2 months, suggesting possibly even larger differences when both samples reached 8 months). While these two studies were indeed cross-national, they demonstrate some of the problems with this type of research. The strengths were that the same instruments were used in both settings, and similar analyses were conducted for both groups.

However, the situations were different in a number of ways—in particular, in defining the affected population for study. In one case, it was residents of a tent camp, and in the other, it was patients in a primary care medical setting. The findings were strengthened by the addition of a sample of primary care patients in Armero as an additional comparison group. The authors used the differences in the severity of the two events to interpret their findings—in other words, that severity accounted for differences in rates of caseness between the two events.

These authors drew attention to the potentially qualitative differences between disasters in developing countries compared to those in industrialized nations, but they did not use their studies to investigate cross-cultural differences. Rather, they assumed cultural similarities between individuals in the two studies and rather conceptualized their findings as a comparison of different disasters (and different disaster severities) taking place in similar settings. Thus, these comparative studies do not add a great deal to our understanding of cultural factors in disaster response.

Earthquakes in California and Chile

Durkin (1993) conducted a study that did a more direct cross-cultural comparison of the same type of disaster. This investigator studied two disaster samples, one in Coalinga, California, exposed to a 6.7-magnitude quake, and one in Santiago, Chile, exposed to a 8.2-magnitude quake. Individuals from 404 households were interviewed, at 14 to 24 months after the disaster in California and at 8 to 12 months after the disaster in Chile. Subjects were stratified by damage levels to their property and were interviewed using the Diagnostic Interview Schedule (in Chile, the Spanish translation was used). The samples represented the entire Coalinga community, and in the Chile sample, a group inhabiting a housing complex.

Both samples had rates of major depression and postdisaster PTSD (*DSM–III–R* criteria) that were considerably higher than comparable rates in the Los Angeles Epidemiologic Catchment Area (ECA) study of a general California sample, thus indicating the negative impact of the quakes. The two disaster groups had roughly equivalent rates of major depression: 18% in Chile ($n = 116$) and 15% for California ($n = 228$). Rates of PTSD, however, were quite different, with a rate of 19% in Chile and only 3% in California.

The author's explanations of the difference in PTSD rates were primarily noncultural. He noted that the Chile residents *all* had to relocate after the earthquake, whereas a third of the California sample did. The earthquake was also stronger and more devastating in Chile, and the Chileans had a more severe history of quakes. Some findings on individual symptoms such as guilt and sexual disturbance suggested potential cultural differences, but cultural differences in PTSD rates were not discernable. Indeed, the difference in the disaster stressors is the most parsimonious explanation for differential rates of PTSD, and the findings suggested more similarities than differences across cultures. Of course, one must consider the fact that culturally senstive indices of PTSD and psychopathology were not used in Chile, and thus the distress levels may not have been assessed adequately.

A Flood in Puerto Rico

Guarnaccia, Canino, Rubio-Stipec, and Bravo (1993) took a different approach—one that may be more directly relevant to cultural issues in disaster work. Subjects were evaluated for standard Western diagnoses following a disaster and other life stressors, while simultaneously being evaluated for the experience of a specific syndrome indigenous to the culture, and the two modes of assessment were compared for the same subjects. This study addressed the different definitions of mental health applying in the same subjects, the overlap of these discrepant definitions, and whether these different ways of assessing subjects found the same individuals to be psychologically distressed.

The study was based on epidemiologic surveys conducted in Puerto Rico in 1984 and 1987, the latter to assess the impact of a 1985 flood and mudslide disaster that killed 180 people. The predisaster data had been collected as part of a general epidemiologic survey conducted there earlier. A Spanish version of the Diagnostic Interview Schedule (DIS) was used to gather information on a representative sample of island residents between the ages of 17 and 68. Following the disaster, the investigators were able to reevaluate 375 of the initial respondents and 537 new respondents about 2 years after the disaster. Exposed subjects were compared to unexposed controls on panic disorder, major depression, dysthymic disorder, and alcohol abuse. Comparing predisaster to postdisaster symptom reporting they found significantly increased symptoms only for the depression diagnoses in the prospective sample. In the postdisaster wave, PTSD, generalized anxiety disorder (GAD), and drug abuse also were assessed. In the larger, retrospective sample, they found significantly increased GAD symptoms and diagnoses associated with exposure and new PTSD cases. The exposed group showed higher use of health care services as well.

Ataques de Nervios

The cross-cultural aspect of the study was accomplished by gathering information about *ataques de nervios*, a culturally sanctioned response to acute stressful experiences, particularly relating to grief, threat, and family conflict (Guarnaccia et al., 1993). They are characterized by trembling, heart palpitations, a sense of heat in the chest rising into the head, faintness, and seizure-like episodes. They typically occur during funerals, at the scene of an accident, or during a family argument or fight. The person usually loses consciousness and does not remember the attack (Guarnaccia et al., 1993).

To assess this syndrome in the earlier epidemiologic study, the authors created a scale using 12 relevant symptom items from a somatization factor from the DIS, which they developed and which was unique in their sample (compared to the Los Angeles ECA data). They found that 23% of their sample fit the category created, with older women most highly represented, along with those of lower socioeconomic status. They found particularly high rates of major depression, dysthymia, agoraphobia, phobic disorder, and panic disorder among the *Ataque* group (Guarnaccia et al., 1989).

In the later, postdisaster study, the investigators added a question on *ataques de nervios* to the somatization section of the DIS/Disaster Schedule, inquiring about whether the person had ever experienced such an *ataque*, and if so, to describe it and the situation that provoked it. Of the 912 people interviewed, 16% reported experiencing an *ataque de nervios*, and 12% met additional criteria for a positive symptom on the DIS (functional impairment or consulting a physician). All 16% were used in the analysis because severity did not differ between the groups. This translated into a population estimate of the syndrome of 13.8%.

Many of the associated symptoms reported were already in the DIS, but a number of others were not. The *ataques* were associated with the disaster but were also associated with arguments with close family members, drunkenness of a family member, death of a close family member, and experiencing a life-threatening accident. Those reporting such an attack were more likely to be female, over the age of 45, have less than a high school education, be formerly married, and be out of the labor force.

Individuals reporting *ataques de nervios* were more than 25 times as likely to experience panic disorder than the general population sample. They were about 10 times as likely to experience depression diagnoses and between 5 and 8 times as likely to qualify for PTSD and to report suicidal thoughts and suicidal attempts. In addition, 63% of those reporting an *ataque* met diagnostic criteria for one or more psychiatric disorders in the DIS, being overall 4.35 times more likely to meet diagnostic criteria than the general sample.

Including Indigenous Syndromes and Symptoms in Research

The authors pointed out that, contrary to popular belief, those experiencing *ataques de nervios* do meet criteria for mental disorders. Further, this syndrome did not correlate with one particular psychiatric disorder, although it was associated with anxiety and depression diagnoses. When information was available, it indicated that *ataques* more often preceded, rather than followed, psychiatric disorders, although the two usually occurred together.

The authors discussed their findings carefully with regard to possible interpretations and implications, including avenues for future research. Among the research implications was the importance of including culturally salient categories in future cross-cultural studies. The investigators also pointed out that their findings lent support to the use of a combined anxiety and depression diagnosis that currently exists in the international nosology of *ICD–10*, but is not represented in the American nosology of *DSM–III–R*.

CONCLUSION

The Puerto Rican study on *ataques de nervios* addresses an extremely important genre of question in cross-cultural research—that of whether syndromes that are defined in one culture apply to other cultures and the extent of overlap between symptoms and categories in different cultures. These questions, and others raised earlier, although potentially applicable to disaster research, can be answered in a variety of settings and do not need to wait until a disaster occurs to be addressed. As a matter of fact, addressing such questions might be better done initially in careful cross-cultural studies that are not disaster oriented and later used as a basis for developing disaster studies across cultures.

Such work might be most applicable to disaster research, however, if background work was done specifically with trauma survivors, because findings about the congruence of categories and so on will be more informative if syndromes and symptoms associated with severe stress are the foci of study. Such questions are also not limited to differences between subjects in different countries but are potentially applicable to subgroups within countries that share ethnocultural experiences that may differ from the dominant culture.

REFERENCES

Baum, A., Gatchel, R., & Schaeffer, M. (1983). Emotional, behavioral, and physiological effects of chronic stress at Three Mile Island. *Journal of Consulting and Clinical Psychology, 51*, 565–572.

Bolin, R., & Klenow, D. J. (1988). Older people in disaster: A comparison of Black and White victims. *International Journal on Aging and Human Development, 26*, 29–43.

Bravo, M., Rubio-Stipec, M., Canino, G., Woodbury, M., & Ribera, J. (1990). The psychological sequelae of disaster stress prospectively and retrospectively evaluated. *American Journal of Community Psychology, 18*, 661–680.

Bromet, E., Parkinson, D., & Dunn, L. (1990). Long-term mental health consequences of the accident at Three Mile Island. *International Journal of Mental
Health*, 19, 48–60.

Canino, G., Bravo, M., Rubio-Stipec, M., & Woodbury, M. (1990). The impact
of disaster on mental health: Prospective and retrospective analyses. *International Journal of Mental Health*, 19, 51–69.

de la Fuente, R. (1990). The mental health consequences of the 1985 earthquakes
in Mexico. *International Journal of Mental Health*, 19, 21–29.

Dohrenwend, B. P., Dohrenwend, B. S., Warheit, G., Barlett, G., Goldstein, R.,
Goldsteen, K., & Martin, J. (1981). Stress in the community: A report to the
president's commission on the accident at Three Mile Island. *Annals of the
New York Academy of Sciences*, 365, 159–174.

Durkin, M.E. (1993). Major depression and post-traumatic stress disorder following
the Coalinga (California) and Chile earthquakes: A cross-cultural comparison. In R. Allen (Ed.), *Handbook of disaster interventions*. New York: Select
Press.

Fairley, M., Langeluddecke, P., & Tennant, C. (1986). Psychological and physical
morbidity in the aftermath of a cyclone. *Psychological Medicine*, 16, 671–676.

Gleser, G., Green, B., & Winget, C. (1981). *Prolonged psychosocial effects of disaster*.
New York: Academic Press.

Green, B. L. (1980). *Prediction of psychosocial functioning following the Beverly Hills
fire*. Unpublished doctoral dissertation, Department of Psychology, University
of Cincinnati, Ohio.

Green, B. L. (1982). Assessing levels of psychological impairment following disaster: A consideration of actual and methodological dimensions. *Journal of
Nervous and Mental Disease*, 170, 544–552.

Green, B. L. (1985). Conceptual and methodological issues in assessing the psychological impact of disaster. In B. J. Sowder (Ed.), *Disasters and mental health:
Selected contemporary perspectives* (NIMH/DHHS Publication No. ADM
85–1408) pp. 179–195. Rockville, MD: National Institute of Health.

Green, B. L. (1990). Defining trauma: Terminology and generic stressor dimensions. *Journal of Applied Social Psychology*, 20, 1632–1642.

Green, B. L. (1991). Evaluating the effects of disasters. *Psychological Assessment:
A Journal of Consulting and Clinical Psychology*, 3(4), 538–546.

Green, B. L. (1993). *Mental health and disaster: Research review*. Unpublished manuscript.

Green, B. L., Gleser, G. C., Lindy, J. L., Grace, M. C., & Leonard, A. C. (in
press). Age related reactions to the Buffalo Creek dam collapse: Second decade effects. In P. Ruskin & J. Talbott (Eds.), *Aging and post traumatic stress
disorder*. Washington, DC: American Psychiatric Press.

Green, B. L., Grace, M., Lindy, J., Gleser, G., Leonard, A., & Kramer, T. (1990a).
Buffalo Creek survivors in the second decade: Comparison with unexposed
and nonlitigant groups. *Journal of Applied Social Psychology*, 20, 1033–1050.

Green, B. L., Lindy, J., Grace, M., Gleser, G., Leonard, A., Korol, M., & Winget, C. (1990b). Buffalo Creek survivors in the second decade: Stability of stress symptoms. *American Journal of Orthopsychiatry, 60*, 43–54.

Green, B. L., & Solomon, S. D. (1995). The mental health impact of natural and technological disasters. In J. R. Freedy & S. E. Hobfoll (Eds.), *Traumatic stress: Theory to practice* (pp. 163–180). New York: Plenum.

Guarnaccia, P. J., Canino, G., Rubio-Stipec, M., & Bravo, M. (1993). The prevalence of *ataques de nervios* in the Puerto Rico disaster study. *The Journal of Nervous and Mental Disease, 181*(3), 157–165.

Guarnaccia, P. J., Rubio-Stipec, M., & Canino, G. J. (1989). *Ataques de nervios* in the Puerto Rico Diagnostic Interview Schedule: The impact of cultural categories on psychiatric epidemiology. *Culture, Medicine, and Psychiatry, 13*, 275–295.

Guarnizo, C. C. (1991). *Integrating disaster and development assistance after natural disasters: Lessons from PVO response in the third world.* Unpublished doctoral dissertation, Department of Urban Studies and Planning, Massachusetts Institute of Technology, Boston.

International Federation of Red Cross and Red Crescent Societies (1993). *World disaster report 1993.* Dordrecht, Netherlands: Author.

Kortmann, F. (1987). Problems in communication in transcultural psychiatry: The self reporting questionnaire in Ethiopia. *Acta Psychiatrica Scandinavica, 75*, 563–570.

Lima, B. R., Chavez, H., Samaniego, N., Pompei, M. S., Pai, S., Santacruz, H., & Lozano, J. (1989). Disaster severity and emotional disturbance: Implications for primary mental health care in developing countries. *Acta Psychiatrica Scandinavica, 79*, 74–82.

Lima, B. R., Pai, S., Santacruz, H., & Lozano, J. (1991). Psychiatric disorders among poor victims following a major disaster: Armero, Colombia. *The Journal of Nervous and Mental Disease, 179*, 420–427.

Lima, B. R., Pai, S., Santacruz, H., Lozano, J., & Luna, J. (1987). Screening for the psychological consequences of a major disaster in a developing country: Armero, Colombia. *Acta Psychiatrica Scandinavica, 76*, 561–567.

Lima, B. R., Pai, S., Toledo, V., Caris, L., Haro, J. M., Lozano, J., & Santacruz, H. (1993). Emotional distress among disaster victims: A follow-up study. *The Journal of Nervous and Mental Disease, 181*, 388–393.

Lima, B. R., Santacruz, H., Lozano, J., & Luna, J. (1988). Planning for health/mental health integration in emergencies. In M. Lystad (Ed.), *Mental health responses to mass emergencies* (pp. 371–393). New York: Brunner/Mazel.

March. J. S. (1993). What constitutes a stressor? The "criterion A" issue. In J. Davidson & E. Foa (Eds.), *Post traumatic stress disorder: DSM-IV and beyond.* Washington, DC: American Psychiatric Press.

Marsella, A. J., Friedman, M. J., & Spain, E. H. (1993). Ethnocultural aspects of posttraumatic stress disorder. In J. M. Oldham, M. B. Riba, & A. Tasman

(Eds.), *Review of Psychiatry Vol. 12*. Washington, DC: American Psychiatric Press.

Norris, F. H. (1992). Epidemiology of trauma: Frequency and impact of different potentially traumatic events on different demographic groups. *Journal of Consulting and Clinical Psychology, 60*, 409–418.

Oliver-Smith, A. (1993) Anthropological perspectives in disaster research: A review of the literature. In E. Quarantelli & K. Popov (Eds.), *Proceedings of the Former Soviet Union Seminar on social sciences research on litigation for and recovery from disasters and large scale hazards. Volume I: American participation*. Newark: University of Delaware Disaster Research Center.

Palinkas, L., Downs, M., Patterson, J., & Russell, J. (1993) Social, cultural, and psychological impacts of the *Exxon Valdez* oil spill. *Human Organization, 52*, 1–13.

Phifer, J., & Norris, F. (1989). Psychological symptoms in older adults following natural disaster: Nature, timing, duration and course. *Journal of Gerontology & Social Sciences, 44*, 207–217.

Shore, J., Tatum, E., & Vollmer, W. (1986). Psychiatric reactions to disaster: The Mount St. Helens experience. *American Journal of Psychiatry, 143*, 590–595.

Smith, E., Robins, L., Przybeck, T., Goldring, E., & Solomon, S. (1986). Psychosocial consequences of a disaster. In J. Shore (Ed.), *Disaster stress studies: New methods and findings*. Washington, DC: Clinical Insights.

Solomon, S. D. (1989). Research issues in assessing disaster's effects. In R. Gist & B. Lubin (Eds.), *Psychosocial aspects of disaster* (pp. 308–340). New York: Wiley.

Tierney, K. J. & Baisden, B. (1979). *Crisis intervention programs: A source book and manual for smaller communities* (DHEW Publication No. ADM 79-675). Washington, DC:

Vaughan, E. (1993). Individual and cultural differences in adaptation to environmental risks. *American Psychologist, 48*, 673–680.

Weisaeth, L. (1989). The stressors and the post-traumatic stress syndrome after an industrial disaster. *Acta Psychiatrica Scandinvica, 80* (Suppl. 355), 25–37.

14

WOMEN OF COLOR AND TRAUMATIC STRESS IN "DOMESTIC CAPTIVITY": GENDER AND RACE AS DISEMPOWERING STATUSES

MARIA P. ROOT

Consider these statistics (Koss, Gidycz, & Wisniewski, 1987; Koss, Goodman, Browne, Fitzgerald, Keita, & Russo, 1994; Straus & Gelles, 1990): In the United States, women are more frequently killed by intimates than by all other forms of violence combined; 2,000 women annually are murdered by their husbands; yearly, 1.8 million wives are physically battered by their husbands; 1 woman is raped every minute; 1 out of 4 adults reports being the target of sexual abuse as a child. Despite living in a technologically advanced society, some researchers suggest that on a daily basis, the United States is one of the most violent nations in the world (Lore & Schultz, 1993). Despite our nation's leadership in advocacy for women and children's rights, some researchers suggest that we may be a dishonorable leader in the incidences of violence against women and children of any technologically advanced nation (Allison & Wrightsman, 1993). Furthermore, the majority of these acts of violence are nonrandom; they are perpetrated primarily by male intimates such as parents, relatives, husbands, and boyfriends. Consequently, many women, and girls more than boys, are held in *domestic captivity* through the repeated violent experiences of rape, sexual abuse, child physical abuse, and domestic violence. However, domestic captivity extends beyond the limits of one's house or neighborhood as the very real threat of violence against women and girls includes them as targets of random sexual aggression. Subsequently, many girls and women experience a "captivity" or limitation to the degree they are not free to move about in their daily lives.

Commonly, psychological explanations of male domination and subordination of women and children across ethnic groups, social class, and cultures are associated with the abuse of power, the objectification of women, and the association of individualism with interpersonal violence (Brownmiller, 1975; Hall, Hirschman, Graham, & Zaragoza, 1993; Herman, 1990; Holtzworth-Munroe, Beatty, & Anglin, 1995; Koss et al., 1994; Triandis, Bontempo, Villareal, Assai, & Lucca, 1988). In patriarchal societies, male privilege and entitlement has driven the definition of female gender (Levi-Straus, 1969). Furthermore, White male entitlement since colonial times has also driven the social construction of gender and racial identity toward the subordination of the female gender and non-White ethnic and racial group members (Lerner, 1986).

In a matrix of gender (male vs. female) and racial status (White vs. not-White), women of color are at the bottom of a ladder of subordination (Sandoval, 1990). The lower one's status, the more invisible that individual and her distress, and the more likely she is to be objectified. It is the objectification of others that allows individuals to commit atrocities against other individuals (Root, 1992). It appears that these less valued members of society are often those at economic disadvantage. Unfortunately, poverty is associated with higher levels of violence (Sampson, 1993); a disproportionate number of women of color are disproportionately represented at high rates among those living in poverty (cf. White, 1990). At a systemic level, these environmental facts recapitulate the risk factors for women being targets of male violence within their homes. Furthermore, whereas poor women of color have fewer personal economic resources for escaping violent environments they may simultaneously have more obstacles in obtaining protection from this violence, that is, their voices may be more inaudible.

These conditions of marginalization can result in despair and anger. Whereas many women of color are leading middle-class lives, thus apparent economic barriers are not as formidable, the others remain; social and institutional barriers remain astonishingly similar, founded again in the intersection of subordination of the female gender by race. To ignore the topic of violence against women of color, particularly regarding violence in domestic captivity, is to imply that women of color's lives are not as important as White women's lives, or that poor women's needs can be denied.

Despite more than a decade of conclusive research about the toll and long-term sequelae that result from violence against women, specific research on violence against women of color is just emerging (e.g., Hine, 1989; Ho, 1990; Koss et al., 1987; O'Keefe, 1994; Lockhart, 1985; Schroeder & Wallace, 1990; Sorenson & Telles, 1991; Urquiza, Wyatt, & Root,

1995; Wyatt, 1985). The emerging research primarily focuses on African American women. This lack of attention to the most frequent crimes against women is a significant omission and a subtle sign of how the intersection of gender and racial oppression manifests itself in our society (Hine, 1989). However, without this data, we cannot have a full understanding of the dynamics and variables that account for outstanding rates of violence against women. Research on women of color and traumatic stress would provide a deeper and broader determination of which aspects of posttrauma responses and symptoms are more universal across culture and gender, and which might be more culturally specific to both ethnicity and gender as is the focus of this chapter.

This chapter offers information about male violence directed toward women in general, and specifically toward women of color. Because of the absence of research on the latter, the coverage is more limited in scope. I will focus on sexual abuse, rape, and domestic violence because these are the most common forms of violence against women that limit women's freedom to move around without fear of personal safety violations on a daily basis.

THE HISTORICAL CONTEXT

Some scholars suggest that the transformation of gender into a class category originated with the concept of private property in which women's reproduction and sexuality became an important commodity of clans and tribes wherein ownership was eventually held by male elders (cf. Lerner, 1986). Historically, this ownership was manifested in rape of women and lack of punishment of rapists: rape of African female slaves in colonial America (Hine, 1989; Tenzer, 1990) and rape of American Indian women during dislocation and genocide of Native Americans (LaDue, personal communication, 1993). In current times ownership of female sexuality is manifested in sexual abuse of undocumented workers seeking refuge from atrocities in their countries of origin (Cole, Espin, & Rothblum, 1992), sexual slavery (paid or unpaid), arranged marriages, concubinage, and acquaintance or stranger rape and sexual abuse in general.

Abuse of power, particularly in the form of male dominance, has been documented cross-culturally for centuries. For example, Shon and Ja (1982), observe that much is said in a Confucian saying that outlines three paths that a Chinese woman follows in her lifetime; "In her youth, she must follow her father. In her adulthood, she must follow her husband. In her later years, she must follow her oldest son" (pp. 211–212). Similar observations across disciplines by historians such as Lerner (1986), anthropologists such as Levi-Strauss (1969), and feminist scholars such as Brownmiller (1975) have led to the conclusion that abusive forms of male psychological dominance are not likely to be biological, but represent the transformation and abuse of arrangements that eventually objectified women.

In general, people of color in this country have experienced the cumulative effects of abuses of power through disenfranchisement, dislocation, and objectification. These experiences comprise a foundation for insidious trauma that results in a decreased sense of optimism, risk for displaced anger, and sometimes a turn toward individualism for survival of the spirit (Root, 1992). None of these experiences constructively empowers a person or community. People of color are objectified when they are used as commodities for exchange. Historically, people of color were kidnapped or indentured as slave labor (Takaki, 1993); Africans were kidnapped and sold into slavery for plantation work, Chinese were imported for mining and railroad work, and Japanese and Filipinos for farming. Native Hawaiians, Native Americans, and people of Mexican descent were displaced from homelands and often put to work as slaves. Economic parity with White men was prevented and people of color were depersonalized as various legislation was promoted and enacted to prevent economic parity, civil rights, personal control, or regard as equal human beings (Takaki, 1993). It has taken decades and, in the case of African Americans and Native Americans, centuries for this government to enact legislation to extend equal protection of civil rights to these communities. And in some cases this protection was not extended to women. In the gender by race matrix, the reenactment of male dominance in communities of color has led women of color to be subjected further to oppression both in the society at large and by men in their respective ethnic communities. Simultaneously, the risk of women's safety in domestic captivity and the historically very real risk of men of color being treated more harshly by representatives of law enforcement has suppressed the voice of women of color speaking out about their plights in their respective communities (Hine, 1989; Ho, 1990). To speak out even contemporarily can be misguided and manipulatively interpreted as lack of commitment to the solidarity of the ethnic community.

Legal statutes in this country have had to overturn the thinking that women are men's property. In fact even as consciousness regarding women's equality in rights has increased, many states had difficulty ratifying the Equal Rights Amendment in the 1980s.

THE INCIDENCE OF ACTS OF VIOLENCE AGAINST WOMEN

The reports that millions of women in this country are affected by malicious violence are staggering. We now know that psychological and physical violence against women, accompanied by threats to loved ones and threats to personal safety are anything but rare experiences. Regardless of ethnic community, violence against women of color appears to originate in male dominance of women in society at large as well as communities of color. In this country, the manifestation of male domination in violence has been hypothesized to be correlated with an engendered culture that allows and supports violence (Ho, 1990; Sorenson & Siegel, 1992). Most forms of violence are committed by a person the victim knows. Thus, these acts threaten the victim's safety and well-being on physical, psychological, interpersonal, and spiritual levels.

Rape

Koss (1992) reviewed rape incidence statistics and concluded that 1 out of 5 women have experienced a completed rape. Koss and her colleagues (1987) are among the first to attempt to look at rape statistics by social–racial designation. They found that the rates of rape were numerically dissimilar in a national sample of college students who were socioeconomically more homogenous than the general population. A rape experience was reported by 16% of European American women, 10% of African American women, 12% of Latina women, 7% of Asian American women, and 40% of Native American women. However, Koss and colleagues (1987) suggested that obstacles to reporting may bias these figures and that the difference among groups may be less important than other variables predicting sexually violent behavior towards women.

Wyatt (1985), also a forerunner in empirically studying rape and sexual abuse in African American communities, found similar figures to Russell's (1986) data based on a study in the San Francisco area. Conducting her study in Los Angeles County, Wyatt found that 1 out of 5 African American women and 1 out of 4 White women said they had been raped. She and her colleagues continued this research (Wyatt, Newcomb, & Riederle, 1993). Sorenson and Siegel (1992) found that 13.5% of the sample of 766 Hispanic women in a Los Angeles catchment area study reported sexual assault after age 15. Although the empirical studies have not been conducted, the reports of sexually aggressive behavior are low for Asian Americans compared to other groups (Federal Bureau of Investigation [FBI], 1994).

Whereas sexually aggressive behavior is purportedly intraracial (Hall, 1995), it is noteworthy to consider that rising racial tensions in the United States (simultaneous with progress of racial integration) may give rise to tactics that are associated with design of war. As women have been considered men's property in a host of cultures (Rozee, 1993), one of the consequences war is that women are raped. With increased rates of interracial dating and intermarriage, particularly in metropolitan areas, race of the perpetrator may also become an important research variable.

Child Sexual Abuse

The experience that most frequently has been correlated with increased risk for adult sexual victimization is childhood sexual abuse (Koss & Harvey, 1991). Herman (1981) reviewed five surveys of nonrepresentative samples throughout the United States. She found that from 1 out of 3 to 1 out of 5 women had had a sexual encounter as a child with an adult man. Finkelhor (1984) has suggested a more conservative estimate that 10 to 30% of girls are sexually abused in the United States. Estimates from both Wyatt (1985) and Russell (1986) in two of the best known community studies of women's unwanted sexual experiences, suggest that 1 in 5 women has had at least one sexual experience with a relative before she reaches 18 years of age. If familial and nonfamilial sexual abuse are combined (excluding noncontact abuse), the rates jump to approximately 40% (Russell, 1986; Wyatt, 1985). The rates were not significantly different for Whites and Blacks in these two studies, and Russell (1986) found that rates of reporting sexual abuse were lower among Asians.

In a large community study of the Los Angeles catchment area, Sorenson and Siegel (1992) found that Euro-American women in their sample had 2.5 times the lifetime prevalence of sexual assault than Hispanics in their sample. An interesting finding, however, was that rates of sexual assault for Hispanics born in the United States were not significantly different than for non-Hispanic White women (11.4% vs. 16.2%, respectively) but were much higher than for Hispanic women born in Mexico. Their results stand in contrast to a Texas sample of Latinas in which combined rates of intra- and extrafamilial abuse were higher for Latinas (22%) than for Euro-American women (10%) (Kercher & McShane, 1984). Schroeder and Wallace (1990) conducted sexual abuse workshops for Native American women in Juneau, Alaska and found informal rates of sexual abuse in village women similar to those of national samples.

With an increasing population, Asian American women in university settings are the subjects of studies attempting to seek contemporary estimates of sexual abuse experiences. However, these studies remain primarily the subject of masters and dissertation studies ongoing. The results of these studies will be important for futhering our understanding of social and cultural factors that give rise to sexual abuse of children.

Schroeder and Wallace (1990) have provided a group treatment protocol for helping Native American women to heal their experiences of sexual abuse. The Swinomish Tribal Mental Health Project out of Washington state has addressed policy and contextual issues in the mental health of Native American people. Empirically based rates of sexual abuse in Native communities are not available at this time, though they are greatly needed to further the understanding of the sociocultural context of sexual abuse in this country.

Domestic Violence

Domestic violence also cuts across all economic classes. However, ethnic and class stereotypes have relegated domestic violence to mythic disproportions in communities of color and among the poor; there is a concurrent mythic invisibility about domestic violence among middle and upper middle class families of European descent. According to a 1980 National Crime Survey, victims of domestic violence sustain injury and more serious injury than victims of physical attacks by strangers (cf. Browne, 1987). The dynamics and consequences of these attacks are similar to those of child sexual abuse; domestic violence crimes usually are perpetrated by a person with whom the victim is intimately related, and they occur in the home and most often at night.

In 1975, the largest national community survey of violence among married couples was undertaken by Straus, Gelles, and Steinmetz (1980). Repeated approximately 10 years later by Straus and Gelles (1986), the results remained unchanged. Over one fourth of the respondents (28%) reported physical violence in their relationship, 75% of the time in the direction of male to female. (Crime surveys have consistently shown that the vast majority of the violence was in the direction of men to women.) In Straus and colleagues' sample, 16% of participants reported physical violence in the year preceding the first survey, similar to a finding by a Harris poll (cf. Straus et al., 1980). The level of violence was potentially lethal, involving guns, knives, and other objects, as well as kicking and punching.

African Americans

Three significant variables are emerging that appear to mediate the characteristics of violence in Black samples and are different between White and Black couples: income bracket, social support, and lethality of the violence. First, Cazenave & Straus (1990) reanalyzed the the original data from Straus et al. (1980). They found that racial differences between African Americans and Whites were hard to compare because class differences were profound (Cazenave & Straus, 1991). While African Americans had lower rates of domestic violence in three of the four household income brackets, 40% of the sample fell into the $6–12,000 income bracket, in which they had a higher incidence of domestic violence than Whites. The socioeconomic class factor has been found to be an important mediating factor in domestic violence in a subsequent study of African American women by Lockart and White (1989). Reported assaults were much higher among middle (46%) and lower (44%) income groups than upper income groups (18%). Second, whereas the presence of family members and an extended family network appeared to have little effect on domestic violence in White families, it did lessen the incidence in Black families (Cazenave & Straus, 1991). Third, Stark (1990) found that compared to Whites, domestic violence in Black couples is more frequently lethal. Lethality was attributed to a lack of police response to the violence.

Southeast Asians

Using a culturally sensitive methodology of the focus group, Ho (1990) studied attitudes towards domestic violence in four Southeast Asian groups: Laotians, Khmers, Vietnamese, and Southeast Asian Chinese. She was also sensitive to gender issues within culture and conducted gender-segregated focus groups. Group participants offered estimates of violence in their communities that were in line with those of Straus et al. (1980). Ho (1990) found that both genders in the Khmer, Laotian, and Vietnamese accepted domination of women by men; women openly talked about being considered men's property. However, opinions of what could be tolerated varied by ethnic group and support the importance of analyzing inter-ethnic differences.

Asian American

Rimonte (1989) found that in a community shelter for battered women specifically serving Pacific Islander and Asian Americans in Los Angeles, 3,000 women were served between 1978 and 1985. Although by no means a random sample, the data she reports are important because they underscore that domestic violence does indeed occur within Asian American groups.

The first and only systematic study of Asian American battered women was recently conducted by Song (1986). However, it is a nonrandom sample of 150 immigrant Korean American married women in Chicago, Illinois. She found that 60% of the women reported being battered. The majority of the abused women reported that the abuse started after they immigrated to the United States during the period of adjustment to the new culture.

Mexican Americans

Sorenson and Telles (1991) used the Los Angeles Environmental Catchment Area data to study domestic violence rates in Mexican Americans. They found similar rates of domestic violence between Euro-Americans and Mexican Americans. Although similar to the sexual abuse data derived from the same data set, Mexican-born Hispanics reported lower rates of violence than White or US-born Mexican Americans, who reported similar rates to one another.

Despite the incredible growth of controlled, empirical studies on violence against women, most of them have focused either primarily on White women, or included few women of color in the samples. This absence of knowledge about violence against women points to how our racially and gender stratified society can render certain segments of the population invisible. Whereas the traumatic events reviewed may be the same, one finding consistent across several studies is that the degree of trauma was significantly different by ethnicity, with ethnic minority women—particularly African American and Latina women—reporting greater mental health consequences (Russell, 1986; Sorenson & Siegel, 1992; Wyatt, 1985).

DOUBLE JEOPARDY: ETHNIC AND GENDER BURDENS

Lerner (1986), in her tome, *The Creation of Patriarchy*, suggests that out of White male dominance, people of color are constructed in the feminine gender with all its disparity in power, privilege, and implicit worth of life in contrast to the White-male status. Implicit in the construction of female gender is the objectification or dehumanization of this part of the population. The implications of Lerner's work and many others is that the woman of color holds dual roles and identities, both of which have ascribed secondary status, that is, *double jeopardy*, for gender and ethnic status. In the matrix, women of color have the least power (Sandoval, 1990).

This grid of power by gender and ethnicity is dangerous to women of color. By placing women of color at the bottom of the ladder of power, they become potential targets for the anger of all those subordinate to White men: White women and men of color. That is, the oppressed can become oppressors as a way of asserting status in their own lives. Simultaneously, the disempowerment that results from gender and ethnicity for women of color also muffles the voice of the woman of color and prevents her from being taken seriously. Furthermore, Hine (1989) suggests that many African American women use their appearance of openness to actually hide the truths about their inner lives and selves. This tactic as a defense against the oppressor ironically results in silence on traumatic issues. Furthermore, those who speak for the woman of color, particularly the one who is poor, may be her middle class sisters who are removed from the violence and insidious trauma of poverty, street life, crowding, and underclass invisibility, but not from harm entirely, as violence against women cuts across classes.

Existing negative stereotypes derived from a combination of stereotypes of women and cultural groups in this country further minimize the power of women of color to be taken seriously. The portrayals of women of color by those in power results in a destructive form of social control (Fiske, 1993). Many of the stereotypes portray women of color as sexual objects to possess and conquer though simultaneously having little value. Casting women of color as "bad women," the stereotyped character is both considered less worthy of sympathy and help and more deserving of violence directed her way as she is reduced to a sexualized charicature with reduced value. Stereotypical constructs of women of color include the exotic, conniving, and diabolical Asian woman (aka "dragon lady"), the hooker-with-a-heart-of-gold Suzie Wong; the hysterical Latina; the drunken Indian and the Indian princess or squaw, subservient to the White man's needs (LaDue, personal communication, 1993); or the sexually promiscuous and "willing" Black woman.

The stereotypes, internalized by several generations, are subsequently used to blame a woman of color's personal or cultural characteristics for the awful things that are directed her way. That is, outsiders apply a just-world hypotheses (Lerner, 1980) to justify the bad things that happen to "bad" women; this twisting of reality subsequently absolves society from social responsibility for crimes against women of color.

PSYCHIATRIC DIAGNOSIS AND VIOLENCE AGAINST WOMEN

Women's Experience and Psychiatric Symptomatology

Barely a decade has passed since researchers have connected psychiatric symptomatology of women with the sequelae related to being traumatically violated: depression, anxiety, dissociation, problems of impulse control, and so on. Recent studies demonstrate that a significant number of women admitted for psychiatric hospitalizations have histories of sexual assault either in childhood or adulthood (Carmen, Mills, & Rieker, 1984), ranging from approximately half (Beck & van der Kolk, 1987) to 81% (Jacobson & Richardson, 1987).

Suppressing the reality of the commonness of trauma in girls' and women's lives has led women to seek help for posttrauma symptoms, often seemingly disconnected from the original events, rather than for the traumas themselves. A disproportionate number of women compared to men are psychiatrically diagnosed related to the sequelae of abuse (Hamilton & Jensvold, 1992).

Figure 1 shows the gender ratios of diagnoses that are more frequently made of women than men and are associated with violence, particularly of

- **Axis I: Gender Ratio (Women to Men)**
  Eating Disorders [1] 9:1
    Anorexia nervosa with bulimia
    Bulimia nervosa
  Depression [2] 2:1
  Anxiety Disorders
    Panic disorder [3] 2:1
    Agoraphobia[4] 7:1
    PTSD [5] 13:5
  Dissociative Disorders
    Multiple Personality Disorder[6] 5:1
- **Axis II**
  Personality Disorders
    Borderline [7] 7:3

Sources: [1] Halmi (1987); [2] Weissman & Klerman (1977); [3] Coryell & Winokur (1991); [4] Fodor (1992); [5] Helzer, Robins, & McEvory (1987); [6] Putnam (1989); [7] Linehan (1993).

Figure 1. *DSM–III–R* Diagnoses Prevalent Among Women Who Have Been Sexually Assaulted as Compared to Men

a sexual nature. Disordered eating, particularly bulimia nervosa (there is no diagnosis for compulsive eating), depression, anxiety disorders, multiple personality disorder, and borderline personality are all more frequently observed in women than in men (American Psychiatric Association [APA], 1987). Substance abuse and dependence has different patterns in women and men, but in women is often correlated with a previous history of sexual victimization (Russell & Wilsnack, 1991).

Blaming the Victim

The very nature of the current diagnostic system (*DSM–IV*) and nomenclature makes it easy to use, albeit unwittingly, as a tool of oppression for persons phenomenologically different in social experience than the originators of the diagnostic system, whether the lived experience is gender or race. For example, although the perpetrators of violent crimes are often thought to be deviant, the victims of violence are most often the ones diagnosed and their victim status hypothesized to originate in individual pathology (Wardell, Gillespie, & Leffler, 1983); thus, in effect the system protects those most similar to its creators.

Furthermore, this system of diagnosis does not necessarily reflect the reality of White women or women of colors' lives wherein many of the traumas affecting women are common, repeated, and current. These traumas include contextual threats through the interplay of domination by gender or race or ethnicity that threaten the safety, limit the mobility, and denigrate the self-worth of an individual by virtue of a status she is born into. Even the notion of "post"-trauma responding largely originates in the White male experience of time-limited events, often singular in nature versus the prolonged, everyday effects of rape, and sexual and physical assault.

PTSD and Women

Ironically, the fact that the *DSM–IV* diagnostic system is largely acontextual places women and people of color at a disadvantage when personal history and the history of those that have gone before shape a worldview that is context-driven. Without the consideration of context, clinicians do not know to what extent behavior manifested in our clinics and offices are situation-specific, are trait characteristics, or are normal responses to environmental conditions or devalued status that pose risk of harm to the individual.

Nevertheless, the diagnosis of posttraumatic stress disorder (PTSD) represents two significant accomplishments in representing women. First, it is the first diagnosis that incorporated much of the feminist literature on violence against women; as such it recognized the depth of distress and psychological toll that violence against women takes in the form of rape, domestic violence, and sexual abuse. Second, it is one of the few diagnoses within the *DSM-IV* system (APA, 1994) that acknowledges an outside environmental event as the cause of the psychological distress. As such, it moves one step away from the individual model of responsibility that pathologizes a human response to intensely frightening experiences.

Insidious Trauma

Root (1992) suggests that the concept of *insidious trauma* is important to understanding the experiences and cognitive schemas that determine one's subjective experiences that define a traumatic event. Insidious trauma is characterized by repetitive and cumulative experiences. It is perpetrated by persons who have power over one's access to resources and one's destiny, and directed towards persons who have a lower status on some important social variable. The types of experiences that form insidious traumas are repeated oppression, violence, genocide, or femicide—both historical and contemporary. The effects of insidious trauma can be passed down transgenerationally through stories of atrocities about what has been done to those who have come before (LaDue, personal communication, 1993; Hine, 1989) to prepare or protect the next generation from an unrealistically naive view of the world.

Over time, the nature of this type of trauma manifests itself in one's reactivity to certain environmental stimuli, as one carries not only one's own direct experiences, but also the unresolved traumatic experiences of those who went before. Given that the dynamics of domination by gender and race are similar, one's own experiences may easily make come alive the stories of those who went before.

Unlike the types of traumas that were originally considered in the *DSM–III–R* (APA, 1987), insidious traumas shape reality and reinforce the subsequent construction of reality. Unlike Janoff-Bulman's (1992) assumption that traumatic events shatter assumptions about how the world operates, insidious traumas create and reinforce assumptions that the world and life is unfair, White people are malevolent, and one's life has little worth and meaning in the whole scheme of things, for example. Consider America's history of treatment of all groups of people of color (Takaki, 1993).

Like many of the traumas that are levied against people of the female gender, insidious traumas in context are often perceived as malicious and personal. Janoff-Bulman (1992) noted that traumas that are perceived as person-perpetuated tend to result in negative self-evaluation and a tendency to view the world as a malevolent environment. Thus, part of the damage of this type of trauma is difficulty in trusting others and even self (Root, 1992).

Insidious trauma's imprint rests in an acute self-awareness that one's safety is very tentative. One comes to this conslusion by experiences that show that a fundamental, unchangeable aspect of one's identity is used to justify unequal worth and lack of protection from danger. The result is that most women are at times acutely aware of being female and the risk associated with it. This is manifested in a fear of being raped, fear of walking to one's car alone, choosing apartments off ground-level, and so on. Likewise, in order to protect themselves some women of color are daily aware that they are not-White and that this status is unsafe. Like other persons of color, they may consciously or unconsciously perform a "head count" in certain environments to note the presence of other persons of color to assess the safety of a situation. Law enforcement agents may not be considered "friends" of the community, particularly in interracial situations. Casual comments about race or class will be noticed and much meaning attributed to these comments. This awareness aids survival.

THREATS TO DIMENSIONS OF SECURITY

In reviewing the literature on violence against women, Root (1992) elaborated on four dimensions of security that allow us to compare and understand why one category of traumatic event (e.g., a rape) may be similar to a seemingly different trauma (e.g., combat experience) or dissimilar to a seemingly similar trauma (e.g., another rape). Figure 2 displays these dimensions of security that are potentially threatened that distinguish a stressor from a trauma: physical, psychological, interpersonal, and spiritual realms. All four dimensions are important to understanding what about trauma changes one's personal construction of reality—and what needs to be addressed in treatment. From many cultural perspectives these four fac-

- **Physical**
  Stimulus deprivation
  Pain
  Injury
  Starvation
- **Psychological**
  Confrontation with mortality
  Dislocation
  Isolation
  Perceived malicious intent
  Helplessness/loss of control
  Diminished value of life
- **Interpersonal**
  Betrayal
  Abuse of power
  Violation of personal space
  Invalidation
  Loss of attachments
- **Spiritual**
  Crushing of spirit
  Loss of meaning to life
  Diminished life force
  Connectedness

Source. Root, M. (1992).

Figure 2. Dimensions of Security and Violations of Security

tors are "inseparably connected and continuously interacting" (Swinomish Tribe, 1991; p. 127).

Physical Security

The physical dimension at a concrete level threatens one's physical survival. Across different types of trauma, threat to life has been designated a part of the cognitive appraisal of an experience that defines trauma (e.g., Foa, Steketee, & Rothbaum, 1989). If we believe that the mind and body act in concert and often are inseparable, it helps us to understand and even anticipate that there will be kinesthetic memories associated with certain traumas (e.g., rape, torture, battering, and other assaults that usually involve force and temporary if not permanent injury). It helps us form different hypotheses as to why many more women than men have disorders of sexual desire and arousal when we consider the numbers of women affected by sexual abuse and rape (Heiman, Epps, Ellis, 1995; Russell, 1986). It helps us understand why a scar or permanent disability is a constant reminder of what one has been through.

Psychological Security

The psychological dimension of security represents the issues that we focus on in psychology, particularly in response to a threat to life. A threat to life may instigate a cognitive confrontation with one's assumptions about (a) the "rules" that order one's environment, (b) good and evil, (c) personal control and the locus of responsibility, (d) the meaning of life, and (e) one's own mortality. Damage on this dimension leaves one with quite shattered assumptions about how life works and one's relationships to the order of the world and others (Janoff-Bulman, 1992).

Interpersonal Security

The interpersonal dimension of security points to our social nature as human beings (i.e., we need other people). The construction of the self is substantiated through the reflection, connectedness, and affirmation of our existence by others. The damage to interpersonal connections often sustained by people who experience trauma at the hands of other people may result in damage to trust in others and in one's self—a brokenness that is often irreparable. It results in acute feelings of isolation (Root, 1992) from the experiences of betrayal, abuse of power, violation or stolen personal space, invalidation of the self, and broken attachments. It also manifests itself in situation-specific paranoia, and causes people to view the world malevolently (Janoff-Bulman, 1992).

Spiritual Security

Lastly, an overlooked dimension of security essential to our well-being and the victim's ability to transform a traumatic experience and integrate it into growth is the spiritual dimension. No less abstract than the psychological or interpersonal dimensions, psychologists have been much more reluctant to tackle the life of the *soul*, the life-force, *chi*, *mana*, and so on—or that which can be hypothesized to connect us to and define our self and our connectedness to others (Swinomish Tribe, 1991). Spirituality may continue to play an important part in people of colors' lives, as it often provides a framework for finding meaningfulness in a life that is pointedly unfair, and enables one to believe one counts and to restore and repair interpersonal connectedness (Myers, 1992).

This spiritual dimension of security is threatened by (a) physical dislocation from ancestral lands as Native Americans, Native Hawaiians, and African Americans have experienced; (b) diminished value placed on one's life (e.g., with gender and racial biases); and (c) obstacles to restoring hope. The Swinomish Tribal Mental Health Project (1991) reflects on spirituality being connected to both beliefs and to how one lives one's life. It is this life force, *chi* energy in Asian philosophies, that connects the physical, psychological, and interpersonal dimensions that form the self. Damage to this dimension results in a disconnectedness from self and others as though the individual is no longer truly connected to the present but lives in the past and temporarily forays into the present only when absolutely necessary for survival. Folklore from different cultures speaks to the importance of damage to this dimension of security for understanding what has happened to the individuals who have "lost their soul," are "wandering souls," or are "walking death."

Examining how different types of security may be differentially threatened by each trauma as perceived by each individual provides a way of beginning to compare and contrast traumas. It allows us an understanding of why not all people respond to a rape in the same way without having to postulate preexisting psychopathology in the individual. It may help us to understand why the data on sexual assault of women of color suggests that the mental health consequences are more severe (Russell, 1986; Wyatt, 1985). Finally, examining the various threats to security also allows us to understand the similarity between traumas that lead to similar reactions to superficially dissimilar events.

BARRIERS TO RESEARCH ON VIOLENCE AGAINST WOMEN OF COLOR

There are several factors that must be considered in increasing the likelihood of obtaining valid estimates of sexual abuse, rape, and domestic violence in communities of color, and the interplay among race, gender, and trauma. Briefly, structural, conceptual, and cultural barriers will be described. These barriers suggest the need to reexamine the methodological paradigms used to obtain data. Lockhart (1985) makes suggestions for obtaining comparative racial analyses. Any methodology should also consider the assumptions a researcher makes in using race as an independent versus dependent variable for analysis.

Structural Barriers

Structural barriers that must be considered are our country's history of race relations, language, economic disenfranchisement, methodology, and gender relations. Our country's history of race relations has made it difficult for women of color to feel safe in reporting crimes within our communities of color for fear of negative stereotypes of the community, fear of abuse by authorities, and fear that one will not be taken seriously given negative stereotypes about the sexuality of women of color that grant many of us less than equal and human status. Hostile race relations have also led many women to believe that reporting the crimes will make no difference in their safety as women and minorities. Wyatt (1985) pointed out that in United States history, during slavery, it was not illegal for White men to rape Black women. The transgenerational transmission of this lack of justice has resulted in many Black women believing that society at large questions whether or not Black women really can be raped, which deters many Black women from reporting. Likewise, LaDue (personal communication, 1993) pointed out that the degree to which Native American women have been rendered invisible, asexual, and worthless make it doubtful in many persons' minds that a Native woman can really be violated. Reporting of crimes also entails contact with law enforcement, which has a legacy of racial discrimination and unequal protection for people of color.

Language Barriers

Language barriers can make research and reporting difficult. Lack of English skills presents both a barrier to communication and a denigrated class status that in turn provokes fear of being misperceived. The presence of researchers and research assistants who have language facility of the population to which outreach is offered is important.

Economic Disenfranchisement

In this nation, poverty and race are confounded (see U.S. Bureau of the Census, 1991). Poverty renders many people invisible. Perhaps as a defense against landing among the economically disenfranchised, people are often blamed for their poverty. Joblessness, childcare costs, illness, and hopelessness are not considered as contexts making it difficult to move out of poverty. As stated earlier, the economic berth of poverty is occupied by more women than men, and proportionately more women of color than any other group. Economic status is a critical variable in understanding risk for violent behavior (Cazenave & Straus, 1990; Lockhart & White, 1989; Sampson, 1993), lack of systemic intervention such as law enforcement, and hopelessness.

Research Barriers

The method and personnel used to collect data are also important (Lockhart, 1985). Many ethnic minority individuals distrust how data will be used (i.e., for or against the community). Given cultural barriers discussed, it will be important to have women researchers of similar ethnic backgrounds prominent in the data collection. Some studies will need to consider qualitative methodologies (Ho, 1990). Privacy in asking about sensitive material will be extremely important—not only privacy from one's family, but privacy from anyone else so that there is no loss of face.

Gender segregation in focus groups would be important to eliminate the possibility of men dominating or shaping information that will be released. It is also important that this segregation is guaranteed because the research is asking girls and women to violate a structural hierarchy in male–female relationships, particularly in Asian and Hispanic cultures. In terms of gender dominance, there is an implicit barrier in asking women in all cultural groups to report on the very men who have violated and abused them with force and coercion and to whom they return home.

Conceptual Barriers

It is not only tempting to use conventional methodology to obtain data, it is also tempting to use culturally circumscribed interpretations of the data consistent with the existing mainstream literature. However, conceptual barriers include, for example, considering what is valid data and understanding and accurately interpreting what is perceived as abusive or violent behavior. Researchers must conceptualize problems and treatment in ethnoculturally credible, thus valid ways. Researchers will need to distinguish the possible culturally protective factors against trauma from proscriptions that require silence (Hall, 1995).

At this point in time, there are few well designed studies by conventional methodology. It is important that we be open to obtaining information from less mainstream resources to begin our formulation of the problems of violence against and trauma among women of color. For example Rimonte (1989) and Ho's (1990) research on domestic violence in Asian American communities is valuable in that it confirms that violence is a significant problem in Asian American communities. The authors also provide us the foundation for reconceptualizing male dominance in culturally sensitive ways. Cultural perspectives and differences on seemingly violent and abusive behavior is also important; Sorenson and Siegel (1992) pointed out that within the Mexican Amerian population in the Los Angeles area, there are differences in what is considered domestic violence between US-born and Mexican-born Latinos.

It is important that data be analyzed responsibly. Correlational studies are tempting for better understanding of what factors are correlated. But in the midst of intrigue about culture, many correlations may be transformed into causal relationships without the necessary investigation.

Whereas few, if any, cultural groups believe that violence against women is desirable and proper (Ho, 1990), it is important that the dominant perspective not be overlayed on a culturally different group without an in-depth understanding of the culture. Ho (1990) found that the focus group methodology facilitated an understanding of why it was difficult for many Southeast Asian women to report violence, which in turn gave her work-group ideas of how better to obtain data about violence inside the Southeast Asian America community.

Cultural Barriers

Cultural barriers to investigating violence revolve around the structure of male–female relationships, respect for elders, issues considered private, the role and meaning of suffering, and degrees of responsibility and
loyalty to ancestors. The structure of male–female relationships is complex
cross-culturally. It is important to note that not all ethnic minority groups
have patriarchal structures. For example, many of the Southwest, Northwest Coastal, and some plains tribes of Native Americans have matrilineal
structures (Allen, 1986). Some Pacific Island cultures were originally or
still are matrilineal.

However, in observing the numerous United States ethnic groups in
which patriarchal gender structure exists, it includes not only the extent
to which women and children implicitly or explicitly are considered men's
property, but also includes gender role proscriptions that prohibit women
and men from even considering the inhumanity of the violence perpetrated
against women. For example, Rimonte (1989) noted that many Asian
American women seen at their Los Angeles center hesitated to leave their
partners or returned to abusive relationships because of cultural proscriptions about what makes a good wife.

Furthermore, but sometimes more explicitly, women are often assigned responsibility for maintaining relationship harmony and order even
at the cost of self-sacrifice (Ho, 1990) regardless of the source of dishar-
mony. Partially related to the hierarchical arrangement of genders is respect
for elders. Thus, while there is a structural barrier to women reporting the
men they fear, this reporting may also violate rules of respect for elders, a
status that comes with age in many cultures—regardless of an elder's behavior.

Talking about sex may also run counter to religious, spiritual, or gender training. Admitting to having been sexually abused may render a
woman worthless in the eyes of members of her community. It is even
possible in many ethnic groups that once violated, a woman may believe
that she deserves anything that happens to her or that her complaints are
not real.

Lastly, many cultures have normalized the suffering and sacrificing of
its women and made this a proscription consistent with being a "good"
woman (Ho, 1990) or a "strong" woman. LaDue (personal communication,
1993) has pointed out that the stereotype of the good Native American
woman images of Pocahantas and Sacajewa are of women who were self-
sacrificing for the White man's service. Suffering through many generations, many women have come to associate suffering with the female role
and internalized the notion that their ability to tolerate and endure suffering imparts virtue. Unfortunately, many religions indiscriminately rein-

force this. Already feeling disempowered by gender and race, many people of color resist seeing themselves in a victim role. Also, in some Asian, Hispanic, and African American cultures, suffering has taken on a value for ultimate salvation, that is, the plight of women has been normalized and transformed to have positive meaning in an afterlife.

CONCLUSION

If we consider the significance of insidious traumas, whether they be in the form of the impact of a lifetime of racism or poverty or exposure to the threat of violence often associated with inner-city living, we have a backdrop of variables and previous experiences that may help us better understand the impact of cumulative traumas acquired from two devalued statuses that women of color hold in our society. The two core cultural and demographic identities of *race* and *gender* have been transformed by a legacy of male domination that discounts those who are less powerful. Subsequently, these identities become liabilities in a social system that victimizes those who are viewed as less powerful.

Male dominance exerts control through the combination of abuse of power and stereotyping. Fiske (1993) observed, "People in power stereotype in part because they do not need to pay attention, they cannot easily pay attention, and they may not be personally motivated to pay attention" (p. 621).

To research traumatic experiences with an ethnocultural sensitivity, it is important that we move toward historical views of trauma and transgenerational effects; we must reconsider the embeddedness of current notions of trauma in conceptual frameworks that may exclude many of the current traumas of women of color and insidious trauma sustained by many people of color and women. We need to have an understanding of both the actuarial data on reactions to traumatic events, and we need to have a willingness to hear about traumatic events that have not been medicalized or legitimized by the diagnostic system.

Ethnoculturally sensitive research on traumas sustained by women of color will need to consider how to overcome structural barriers to data collection; perceptions of what constitutes valid data; cultural conceptualizations for understanding violence between people of unequal stature (i.e., parents and children, men and women); and cultural barriers to disclosing violence that, when kept secret, prevents victims from reclaiming their lives. Furthermore, the concept of posttrauma responding may need to be expanded symptomatically, and the nature of ongoing versus posttrauma responding compared.

REFERENCES

Allen, P. G. (1986). *The sacred hoop*. Boston: Beacon Press.

Allison, J. A. & Wrightsman, L. S. (1993). *Rape: The misunderstood crime*. Newbury Park: Sage.

American Psychiatric Association (1987). *Diagnostic and statistical manual of mental disorders* (3rd ed., rev.). Washington, DC: American Psychiatric Press.

American Psychiatric Association (1994). *Diagnostic and statistical manual of mental disorders* (4th ed.). Washington, DC: American Psychiatric Press.

Beck, J. C., & van der Kolk, B. (1987). Reports of childhood incest and current behavior of chronically hospitalized psychotic women. *American Journal of Psychiatry, 144*, 1474–1476.

Browne, A. (1987). *When battered women kill*. New York: The Free Press/Macmillan.

Brownmiller, S. (1975). *Against our will: Men, women and rape*. New York: Bantam Books.

Carmen, E., Mills, T., & Rieker, P. P. (1984). Victims of violence and psychiatric illness. *American Journal of Psychiatry, 141*, 378–383.

Cazenave, N. A. & Straus, M. A. (1990). New theory and old canards about family violence research, *Social Problems, 38*, 180–198 .

Cole, E., Espin, O. M., & Rothblum, E. D. (Eds.). (1992). *Refugee women and their mental health: Shattered societies, shattered lives*. New York: The Haworth Press.

Coryell, W., & Winokur, G. (1991). *The clinical management of anxiety disorders*. New York: Oxford University Press.

Federal Bureau of Investigation (1994). *Uniform crime reports for the United States, 1993*. Washington DC: U.S. Government Printing Office.

Finkelhor, D. (1984). *Child sexual abuse: New theory and research*. New York: Free Press.

Fiske, S. T. (1993). Controlling other people: The impact of power on stereotyping. *American Psychologist, 48*, 621–628.

Fodor, I. G. (1992). The agoraphobic syndrome: From anxiety neurosis to panic disorder. In L. S. Brown & M. Ballou (Eds.), *Personality and psychopathology* (pp. 177–205). New York: Guilford Press.

Hall, G. C. N. (1995). Presidential Address for Division 45. *Prevention of sexual aggression: Sociocultural risk and protective factors*. Division 45, American Psychological Association, New York.

Hall, G. C. N., Hirschman, R., Graham, J. R., & Zaragoza, M. S. (1993). *Sexual Aggression: Issues in etiology, assessment, and treatment*. Bristol, PA: Taylor & Francis.

Halmi, K. A. (1987). Anorexia nervosa and bulimia. *Annual Review of Medicine, 38*, 373–380.

Hamilton, J. A., & Jensvold, M. (1992). Personality, psychopathology, and depressions in women. In L. S. Brown & M. Ballou (Eds.), *Personality and psychopathology: Feminist reappraisals* (pp. 116–143). New York: Guilford Press.

Heiman, J. R., Epps, P. H., & Ellis, B. (1995). Treating sexual desire disorders in couples. In N. S. Jacobson and A. S. Gurman (Eds.), *Clinical Handbook of Couple Therapy* (pp. 471–495). New York: Guilford.

Helzer, J., Robins, L., & McEvory, M. (1987). Post-traumatic stress disorder in the general poulation. *New England Journal of Medicine, 317,* 1630–1634.

Herman, J. L. (1981). *Father-daughter incest.* Cambridge, MA: Harvard University Press.

Herman, J. L. (1990). Sex offenders: A feminist perspective. In W. L. Marshall, D. R. Laws and H. E. Barbaree (Eds.), *Handbook of sexual assault: Issues, theories, and treatment of the offender* (pp. 177–193). New York: Plenum Press.

Herman, J. L. (1992). *Trauma and recovery.* New York: Basic Books.

Hine, D. C. (1989). Rape and the inner lives of Black women in the Middle West: Preliminary thoughts on the culture of dissemblance. *Signs, 14,* 912–920.

Ho, C. K. (1990). An analysis of domestic violence in Asian American communities: A multicultural approach to counseling. In L. S. Brown & M. P. P. Root (Eds.), *Diversity and complexity in feminist therapy* (pp. 129–150). Binghamton, NY: The Haworth Press.

Holtzworth-Munroe, A., Beatty, S. B., & Anglin, K. (1995). The assessment and treatment of marital violence: An introduction for the marital therapist. In N. S. Jacobson and A. S. Gurman (Eds.), *Clinical handbook of couple therapy* (pp. 317–339). New York: Guilford.

Jacobson, A., & Richardson, B. (1987). Assault experiences of 100 psychiatric inpatients: Evidence of the need for routine inquiry. *American Journal of Psychiatry, 144,* 908–913.

Janoff-Bulman, R. (1992). *Shattered assumptions: Towards a new psychology of trauma.* New York: The Free Press/Macmillan.

Kercher, G., & McShane, M. (1984). The prevalence of child sexual abuse victimization in an adult sample of Texas residents. *Child Abuse and Neglect: The International Journal, 8,* 495–501.

Koss, M. P. (1992). The underdetection of rape: A critical assessment of incidence data. *Journal of Social Issues, 48,* 61–76.

Koss, M. P., Gidycz, C. A., & Wisniewski, N. (1987). The scope of rape: Incidence and prevalence of sexual aggression and victimization in a national sample of higher education students. *Journal of Consulting and Clinical Psychology, 55,* 162–170.

Koss, M. P., Goodman, L., Browne, A., Fitzgerald, L. F., Keita, G. P., & Russo, N. F. (1994). *No safe haven: Violence against women at home, at work, and in the community.* Washington, DC: American Psychological Association.

Koss, M. P., & Harvey, M. R. (1991). *The rape victim: Clinical and community interventions* (second edition). Newbury Park, CA: Sage.

Lerner, G. (1986). *The creation of patriarchy*. New York: Oxford University Press.

Lerner, M. J. (1980). *The belief in a just world*. New York: Plenum.

Levi-Strauss, C. (1969). *The elementary structures of kinship*. Boston: Beacon.

Linehan, M. (1993). *Cognitive behavioral treatment of borderline personality disorder*. New York: Guilford.

Lockhart, L. (1985). Methodological issues in comparative racial analyses: The case of wife abuse. *Social Work Research & Abstracts, 21,* 35–41.

Lockhart, L. & White, B. W. (1989). Understanding marital violence in the Black community. *Journal of Interpersonal Violence, 4,* 421–436.

Lore, R. K., & Schultz, L. A. (1993). Control of human aggression: A comparative perspective. *American Psychologist, 48,* 16–25.

Myers, L. J. (1992). Transpersonal psychology: The role of the Afrocentric paradigm. In A. K. H. Burlew, W. C. Banks, H. P. McAdoo, & D. A. Y. Azibo (Eds.), *African American psychology: Theory, reearch, and practice*. Thousand Oaks, CA: Sage.

O'Keefe, M. (1994). Racial/ethnic differences among battered women and their children. *Journal of Child & Family Studies, 3,* 283–305.

Putnam, F. W. (1989). *Diagosis and treatment of multiple personality disorder*. New York: Guilford.

Reid, P. T. (1988). Racism and sexism: Comparisons and conflicts. In P. A. Katz & D. A. Taylor (Eds.), *Eliminating racism: Profiles in controversy* (pp. 203–221). New York: Plenum.

Rimonte, N. (1989). Domestic violence against Pacific Asians. In Asian Women United of California (Eds.), *Making waves* (pp. 327–337). Boston: Beacon.

Root, M. P. P. (1992). Reconstructing the impact of trauma on personality. In L. S. Brown & M. Ballou (Eds.), *Personality and psychopathology* (pp. 229–265). New York: Guilford.

Rozee, P. D. (1993). Forbidden or forgiven? Rape in cross-cultural perspective. *Psychology of Women Quarterly, 17,* 499–514.

Russell, D. E. (1986). *The secret trauma: Incest in the lives of girls and women*. New York: Basic Books.

Russell, S. A., & Wilsnack, S. (1991). Adult survivors of childhood sexual abuse: Substance abuse and other consequences. In P. Roth (Ed.), *Alcohol and drugs are women's issues: Volume I—A review of the issues* (pp. 61–70). Metuchen, NJ: Women's Action Alliance and The Scarecrow Press.

Sampson, R. J. (1993). The community context of violent crime. In W. J. Wilson (Ed.), *Sociology and the public agency* (pp. 259–286). Newbury Park, CA: Sage.

Sandoval, C. (1990). Feminism and racism: A report on the 1981 National Women's Studies Association Conference. In G. Anzaldua (Ed.), *Making face, making soul (Haciendo caras): Creative and critical perspectives by women of color* (pp. 55–71). SF: Aunt Lute Foundation.

Schroeder, E., & Wallace, L. (1990). *Workshops for Alaska Native women with histories of sexual abuse: A training manual for leaders*. Juneau, AK: Author.

Shon, S. P., & Ja, D. Y. (1982). Asian families. In M. McGoldrick, J. K. Pearce, & J. Giordano (Eds.), *Ethnicity and family therapy* (pp. 208–229). New York: Guilford Press.

Song, Y. I. (1986). *Battered Korean women in urban America: The relationship of cultural conflict to wife abuse*. Unpublished Doctoral Dissertation, Department of Psychology, Ohio State University, Columbus, Ohio.

Sorenson, S. B., and Siegel, J. M. (1992). Gender, ethnicity, and sexual assault: Findings from a Los Angeles study. *Journal of Social Issues, 48*, 93–104.

Sorenson, S. B., and Telles, C. A. (1991). Self-reports of spousal violence in a Mexican-American and non-Hispanic White population. *Violence and Victims, 6*, 3–15.

Stark, E. (1984). The battering syndrome: Social knowledge, social therapy and the abuse of women. Dissertation Abstracts International.

Straus, M. A., & Gelles, R. J. (1986). Societal change and change in family violence from 1975–1985 as revealed by two national surveys. *Journal of Marriage and the Family, 48*, 465–479.

Straus, M. A., & Gelles, R. J. (1990). How violent are American families? Estimates from the national family violence resurvey and other studies. In M. A. Straus & R. J. Gelles (Eds.), *Physical violence in American families: Risk factors and adaptations to violence in 8,145 families* (pp. 95–112). New Brunswick, NJ: Transaction.

Straus, M. A., Gelles, R. J., & Steinmetz, S. (1980). *Behind closed doors: Violence in the American family*. Garden City, NY: Anchor Press/Doubleday.

Swinomish Tribal Mental Health Project (1991). *A gathering of wisdoms: Tribal Mental Health—A cultural perspective*. LaConner, WA: Author.

Takaki. R. (1993). *A different mirror: A history of multicultural America*. Boston: Little, Brown & Company.

Tenzer, L. R. (1990). *A completely new look at interracial sexuality: Public opinion and select commentaries*. Manahawkin, NJ: Scholars' Publishing House.

Triandis, H. C., Bontempo, R., Villareal, M. J., Assai, M., & Lucca, N. (1988). Individualism and Collectivism: Cross-cultural perspectives on self-ingroup relationships. *Journal of Personality and Social Psychology, 54*, 323–338.

Urquiza, A. J., Wyatt, G., & Root, M. P. P. (Eds.). (1995). [Special Issue] *Violence and Victims: Violence Against Women of Color, 10*.

Wardell, L., Gillespie, D., & Leffler, A. (1983). Science and violence against women. In D. Finkelhor, R. J. Gelles, G. T. Hotaling, & M. J. Strauss (Eds.), *The dark side of families* (pp. 69–84). Newbury Park, CA: Sage.

Weissman, M. M., & Klerman, G. L. (1977). Sex differences and the epidemiology of depression. *Archives of General Psychiatry 34*, 98–111.

White, E. C. (1990). Love don't always make it right: Black women and domestic violence. In E. C. White (Ed.), *The Black women's health book: Speaking for ourselves* (pp. 92–97). Seattle, Washington: Seal Press.

Wyatt, G. (1985). The sexual abuse of Afro-American and White women in childhood. *Child Abuse and Neglect, 9,* 507–519.

Wyatt, G. E., Newcomb, M. D., & Riederle, M. H. (1993). *Sexual abuse and consensual sex: Women's developmental patterns and outcomes.* Thousand Oaks, CA: Sage.

15

ETHNOCULTURAL ASPECTS OF PTSD AND RELATED DISORDERS AMONG CHILDREN AND ADOLESCENTS

VINCENZO F. DINICOLA

We are all of us emigrants from a country we can remember little of . . . because we know so little, we feel the heavy responsibility of not understanding—horror happening to a child seems twice the horror because we don't know what he feels and can't help him. . . .

Graham Greene (1990, p. 9)

Cross-cultural therapy for mental disorders of children and adolescents presents many challenges. The young people may seem strangers to us because they are from different places (culture), because they have disturbing and alienating experiences (mental disorder), and because as adults, we have become strangers to the their world of childhood, as Graham Greene's childhood reminiscence cited above suggests.

Working with children, adolescents, and their families who are in cultural transition is one of the most complex and rewarding tasks for the health care provider (Canino & Spurlock, 1994; Vargas & Koss-Chioino, 1992). The task is complex because several lines of growth and development are moving simultaneously: the growing child, the move of the family

Preparation of this chapter was supported in part by grants from Queen's University Faculty of Medicine and the Department of Psychiatry. I am grateful to Stephanie Fortin for her assistance in the literature search and to Juris Draguns, Solvig Ekblad, and Richard Hough for their helpful comments on early drafts of this chapter.

group from one culture to another, and the differential rates of adaptation of individual family members (Bullrich, 1989; Rakoff, 1981; Westermeyer, 1991). It is also rewarding because of the opportunity to construct new metaphors for child development and family experience and to develop new tools for treatment.

When the clinical problem is posttraumatic stress disorder (PTSD), there are the added concerns of the survival of family members and the community, the overall survival of the family and community itself, and the separation of the child or adolescent from these living contexts. These living contexts infuse meaning into children's views of the world (the eth-nocultural dimension) and structure their expectations of the future (the developmental dimension).

In this overview of PTSD in children and adolescents, I will examine the concept of PTSD through two perspectives—the developmental perspective and the ethnocultural perspective. The first section examines the developmental perspective through a review of key studies on PTSD in children and adolescents. The second section focuses on the ethnocultural perspective through reference to current knowledge and practices identified with transcultural child psychiatry. The third section integrates current knowledge regarding the cross-cultural study of PTSD in children and adolescents.

PTSD IN CHILDREN AND ADOLESCENTS: THE DEVELOPMENTAL PERSPECTIVE

Exhibit 1 outlines the stressors that have been documented to result in PTSD in children and adolescents. In the discussion of the diagnostic features of PTSD in *DSM–IV* (American Psychiatric Association, 1994), traumatic events are conceptualized as either directly or vicariously experienced. A potentially important distinction is drawn between vicariously experienced events that are witnessed personally and events experienced by significant others who convey their traumatic experiences. This may be especially salient for children given their usually trusting and dependent relationships to family members.

DSM–IV emphasizes that the risk for PTSD "may increase as the intensity of and physical proximity to the stressor increase" (American Psychiatric Association, 1994, p. 424). Because of the dependence of children and adolescents on their families, one should note that the risk may increase correspondingly as the traumatic events involve closer attachment figures. It is helpful in working with children that *DSM–IV* now explicitly recognizes developmental and family factors in the discussion of PTSD.

Based on her extensive clinical work with children, Terr (1991b) proposed two forms of PTSD. Type I results from a sudden, unexpected

EXHIBIT 1
Stressors Resulting in PTSD in Children and Adolescents

1. Directly experienced events
   Violent personal assault (including sexual assault, physical attack, robbery, mugging)
   Kidnapping and hostage situations
   Exposure to violence (including terrorism, gang violence, sniper attacks, and war atrocities)
   Incarceration as a prisoner of war and concentration camps
   Severe accidental injury (including burns and hit-and-run accidents)
   Major disasters (natural or human-made)
   Train, airplane, ship, and automobile accidents
   Life-threatening diseases and life-endangering medical procedures

2. Vicariously experienced events
   A. Personally witnessed events
   Observing serious injury or unnatural death of another person as a result of violent assault (including sexual assault and murder), accident, war, or disaster
   Witnessing self-injury and suicidal behavior in others
   Unexpectedly observing a dead body or body parts
   B. Events experienced and conveyed by significant others
   Violent personal assault
   Serious accident or injury experienced by a family member or close friend
   Learning about the sudden, unexpected death of a family member or close friend
   Learning that one's family member or close friend has a life-threatening disease

Note. Adapted from "Post-traumatic Stress Disorder in Children and Adolescents," by R. S. Pynoos, 1990, in B. D. Garfinkel, G. A. Carlson, & E. G. Weller (Eds.), Psychiatric Disorders in Children and Adolescents, pp. 48–63 and the *DSM–IV*, American Psychiatric Association, 1994. Adapted with permission of the publishers.

single-impact traumatic event. In this type of PTSD in children, reexperiencing phenomena are typical. Many of the stressors in Exhibit 1 are examples of Type I PTSD. Type II results from a series of traumatic events or from exposure to a prolonged traumatic stressor. Denial, dissociation, and numbing are especially characteristic of this type of PTSD. Some of the stressors in Exhibit 1 are examples of ongoing stressors producing Type II PTSD. The prototype would be chronic physical or sexual abuse of a child (see Adam, Everett, & O'Neal, 1992.; Miller-Perrin & Wurtele, 1990). Adaptations to a Type II stressor (e.g., chronic sexual abuse) may produce symptoms associated with borderline and multiple personality disorders. This typology may be relevant for the study of PTSD in children and adolescents because young people are quite likely to be exposed to Type II stressors due to their dependence on adult caregivers. A methodological problem is that Type II stressors likely produce a diversity of psychiatric disturbances rather than a coherent syndrome (Corwin, cited in

McNally, 1991) with blurred boundaries between Type II PTSD and borderline and multiple personality disorders.

Pathogenesis

How traumatic stress produces PTSD in children and adolescents is
still unknown. Most theories tend to focus on the etiological event—in
other words, the trauma—and on the experience of traumatic helplessness
(as with adults). In her view of theories of PTSD in children, Koverola
(1995) noted that each theoretical framework focuses on the symptoms it
best explains, while ignoring the others. Psychodynamic explanations in-
voke information overload to account for alternating symptoms of denial
and intrusive reexperiencing while ignoring symptoms of physiological
arousal. Behavioral models account for symptoms of arousal as involuntary
responses associated with classical conditioning and symptoms of avoidance
as learned by operant conditioning but do not explain why PTSD patients
reexperience trauma. The addition of cognitive elements of meaning to
cognitive–behavioral explanations elucidates the cognitive and affective
components of fear. This formulation suggests that as events become unpredictable and out of control, the patient develops avoidance symptoms,
but it does not account for symptoms of physiological arousal or traumatic
reexperiencing. Biological explanations based on neurobiological learning
models propose that extended shock and norepinephrine (NE) depletion
become conditioned, leading to NE receptor hypersensitivity. NE depletion
leads to symptoms of numbing and constriction, whereas NE receptor hypersensitivity creates symptoms of hyperactivity (nightmares, startle reflex,
intrusive thoughts). A criticism of this intriguing model is that it does not
account for avoidance or chronic aspects of PTSD.

Developmental processes are invoked in rather vague generic terms,
restating age response patterns (discussed in a later section). Koverola
(1995) reported that she is dismayed by the portrayal of children in the
PTSD as "miniature adults" who can be treated in the same way as adults
with minor modifications. More research is needed to establish the value
of Terr's proposed distinction between Type I and Type II PTSD. Is it simply
a way of categorizing pathways to PTSD, or is it an etiological model with
prognostic value? A reasonable conclusion from clinical research with
young people is that extent of exposure determines risk for the development of PTSD (Pynoos, 1990), and that chronic trauma heralds a more
profound level of dysfunction with longer lasting impacts (Koverola, 1995).

Clinical Presentation

PTSD does occur in young people and its presentation strongly
resembles the disorder in adults (Eth & Pynoos, 1985; March & Amaya-

Jackson, 1993). The differences appear to be related to some diverse stressors, developmental themes, and collateral symptoms (Pynoos, 1993). Exhibit 2 sets out the symptom criteria of PTSD in children and adolescents, outlining four main symptoms. Most clinical descriptions concentrate on age-related behavioral responses (see Pynoos, 1990; Terr, 1990). Each age group has particular vulnerabilities. Thus, preverbal children aged 28 to 36 months or younger are unable to put trauma into words. Instead, they have long lasting perceptual memories that are evident in play activity or expressed through fears. As children approach preschool age, they respond to trauma with decreased verbalization, cognitive confusion, increased anxious attachment behavior, and other more immature (regressive) symptomatology. School-age children often respond to trauma with aggresive or inhibited behavior and psychosomatic complaints. Their behavior becomes

EXHIBIT 2
Symptom Criteria of PTSD in Children

1. Child experiences unusual event(s) that would be markedly distressing to almost anyone (see Exhibit 1)
    A. Directly experiences events
    B. Vicariously experiences events
        i. Personally witnesses events
        ii. Events experienced and conveyed by significant others

2. Reexperiencing phenomena
    A. Intrusive recollections/images
    B. Traumatic dreams
    C. Repetitive play
    D. Reenactment behavior
    E. Distress at traumatic reminders

3. Psychological numbness/avoidance
    A. Avoidance of thoughts, feelings, locations, situations
    B. Reduced interest in usual activities
    C. Feelings of being alone/detached/estranged
    D. Restricted emotional range
    E. Memory disturbance
    F. Loss of acquired skills
    G. Change in orientation toward the future

4. Increased state of arousal
    A. Sleep disturbance
    B. Irritability/anger
    C. Difficulty concentrating
    D. Hypervigilance
    E. Exaggerated startle response
    F. Autonomic response to traumatic reminders

Note. Adapted from "Post-traumatic Stress Disorder in Children and Adolescents," by R. S. Pynoos, 1990, in B. D. Garfinkel, G. A. Carlson, & E. G. Weller (Eds.), Psychiatric Disorders in Children and Adolescents, pp. 48–63. Adapted with permission of the publisher.

more inconsistent or reckless and there may be obsessive retelling of the event. By adolescence, the response pattern resembles adult responses rather than those of younger children. Because adolescents play less than younger children, they do not exhibit posttraumatic play. However, teenagers exhibit more sleeplessness, inattentiveness, and irritability. They often express premature independence or increased dependence, which may lead to school drop-out, early marriage, radical changes in career choice, a decision to never leave home. Acting out behavior includes school truancy, precocious sexual activity, substance abuse, delinquency, and self-endangering reenactment behavior. Teenagers are vulnerable to narcissistic rage and taking revenge. In war time, for example, a young person might respond to the killing of a combat friend by committing an atrocity.

Detection and Screening

A study of PTSD in children by Yule and Williams (1990) concluded that children 8 to 16 years of age show similar problems to adult PTSD but these are not picked up by commonly used screening instruments. The Impact of Events Scale (Horowitz, Wilner, & Alvarez, 1979) is valuable for children aged 8 and older, but the authors recommended that screening instruments be backed up with detailed interviews with the children.

Saigh (1988, 1989) reported two studies in Lebanese children and adolescents. His method was to test three groups (PTSD, simple phobia, nonclinical controls) of Lebanese children or adolescents in Beirut. Saigh used the Revised Children's Manifest Anxiety Scale (RCMAS), the Children's Depression Inventory (CDI), and the Conners Teacher Rating Scale (CTRS). In the adolescent study, Saigh (1988) sampled 13-year-olds. PTSD cases showed higher levels of anxiety, depression, and behavior problems. The results supported the *DSM–III* PTSD classification for adolescents. In the children's study, Saigh (1989) sampled Lebanese children aged 9 years to 12 years, 11 months. PTSD cases had markedly higher RCMAS, CDI, and CTRS scores than both other groups. This group of tests differentiated PTSD cases from other clinical cases and nonclinical subjects and supported the validity of classifying children with PTSD. Four approaches to assessment have been reported (McNally, 1991), and I will review these in turn in the subsections that follow.

Structured Interviews With Children.

There are several structured interviews for assessing childhood PTSD. The common feature is that they are based on *DSM* criteria. Directly interviewing children about their traumatic experiences seems both unavoidable and the best approach. Interviewing parents misses subjective symptoms. This parallels the problems encountered in diagnosing mood disorders in young people. Questionnaires about specific symptoms pick only the associated features and do not establish caseness of PTSD (see McNally, 1991).

Structured Interviews With Parents

Early research on childhood trauma revealed that parents and teachers typically underestimate the suffering of children. There are several reasons; parents may be unfamiliar with posttraumatic symptoms; they may misinterpret numbed silence as *fortitude* (researchers may call it *invulnerability*); or they may be unwilling to acknowledge symptoms in children they believe they should have protected from harm. Nonetheless, parents can provide adjunctive information on their traumatized children. The Child Post-Traumatic Stress Disorder Inventory (CPTSD-I) is a structured interview for parents (Nader & Pynoos, cited by McNally, 1991). In a comparison of children's and parents' reports, children reported more subjective symptoms (e.g., intrusive thoughts), whereas parents reported more objective symptoms (e.g., irritability).

Questionnaires

Questionnaires measure associated features: depression, anxiety, low self-esteem, or general behavioral disturbance. As for PTSD measures, Horowitz's Impact of Events Scale is the best questionnaire available as a measure of childhood PTSD (McNally, 1991).

Psychophysiological Assessment

One study of disturbed startle reflex in childhood PTSD showed that psychic trauma can produce lasting physiological disturbance (Ornitz & Pynoos, 1989).

Garmezy and Rutter (1985) made a number of useful observations on the assessment of traumatized children that should be taken into account. Because of the inherent difficulties in assessing children, Garmezy and Rutter emphasized the value of multimethod assessment. They argued that part of such an assessment should be the study of Potential Trait–Situation Interactions, noting that in situations in which *courage* under stress is valued by adults, children minimize their reports of fear. Children's stress response must be interpreted within the context of the stressful event and the ongoing activities it evokes in the significant adult figures in the child's life. Parental reaction to the stress is seen as crucial because children under stress model parental responses to the trauma.

Impact on Child Development

Much is made of the interaction between trauma and developmental stage. However, in the absence of clearer and more specific models of pathogenesis, these are really restatements of what is known about age-specific reactions (Trad, 1989). A recurring theme in the literature is that post-traumatic stress influences developmental processes in the areas of cognitive functioning, trust, initiative, interpersonal relationships, personality style, self-esteem, outlook, and impulse control.

Concrete reminders of traumatic events can restrict the child's use of symbolic expression, and imaginative play can become constricted and less enjoyable through the repetition of trauma-related themes. Traumatic avoidant behavior can lead to inhibitions and altered interests, whereas irritability and diminished modulation of aggression can interfere with peer relationships. Prominent personality changes are observed even in very young children. Indeed, observers often remark on profound changes in the children's views of the world and their futures.

Biological Correlates

Neurophysiological disturbances are part of the sequelae of PTSD. Freud postulated a breakdown in the stimulus barrier that protects an organism from excessive external stimulation. Key physiological sequelae include sleep disturbance and exaggerated startle reaction. PTSD appears to have a distinct biological profile that is different than depression, based on research with adults. However, more research with children and adolescents is needed, such as the study on startle reaction by Ornitz and Pynoos (1989).

Clinical Course

DSM–IV (American Psychiatric Association, 1994) requires a duration of the disturbance of more than 1 month to make the diagnosis of PTSD. This was meant to exclude transient stress reactions. However, this is less of an issue in children and adolescents for several reasons. Youth who face severe situations are likely to suffer a prolonged course. In school-age children and adolescents, there is no apparent delay in onset of severe PTSD symptoms. Furthermore, in younger people the initial exposure is more predictive of later course. *DSM–IV* has added the new category of acute stress disorder to describe acute reactions to extreme stress (i.e., occurring within 4 weeks of the stressor and lasting from 2 days to 4 weeks). It is hoped that this new category will assist in case-finding, as acute stress disorder may lead to PTSD.

Multiple adversities after massive trauma modify the complex of symptoms, their duration, and their resolution. This occurs specifically by increasing comorbidity, especially concurrent PTSD, depression or generalized anxiety disorder (in younger children, separation anxiety disorder). War traumas are even more complex because the traumatic experiences are superimposed on deprivation, malnutrition, family disruption, loss, immigration, and resettlement.

An important clinical issue is discriminating effects of acute trauma from chronic or repetitive trauma such as child abuse (Famularo, Kinsdnerff, & Fenton, 1990). As noted earlier, Terr (1991b) proposed Type I and II PTSD to distinguish causal pathways. Additional research needs to address whether a similar distinction is valid and reliable in describing the clinical courses of these two types of PTSD. Alternatively, does the clinical course converge, regardless of the type of traumatic stressors? All clinical discussions mention intrinsic factors in the child, often under the rubric of vulnerability or resilience. This is addressed in the discussion that follows on the developmental approach.

Differential Diagnosis

The main considerations in the differential diagnosis of PTSD in children and adolescents include (a) simple phobia; (b) hallucinations/schizophrenia; (c) generalized anxiety disorder (or separation anxiety disorder); and (d) major depressive episode. Adjustment disorder and closed head injury also should be considered (Lyons, 1987).

Treatment

The first principle of treatment is early detection. There should be triage and screening for children and adolescents at risk. Multimethod assessment is the best approach. Saigh's (1988, 1989) work suggested that standard screening tests can discriminate PTSD from other clinical and nonclinical groups. However, Yule and Williams (1990) cautioned that it is important to add detailed clinical interviews when PTSD is suspected.

Little is known about the relative effectiveness of different treatments for young people with PTSD. The literature is filled mostly with case reports from committed clinicians applying creative strategies to troubled youngsters. Clinical rationales have been given for cognitive–behavioral therapy for single-incident trauma (Saigh, 1992) and for sexual abuse (Deblinger, McLeer, & Henry, 1990). Most treatment is modeled on the treatment of other children's problems—in other words, it is not specifically tailored to PTSD. Given the emphasis by clinicians on family and social relationships and on cultural adaptation, the clinical literature is remarkable for the lack of application of family therapy, group approaches, and culture-responsive therapies.

Clinicians tend to agree on a prevention–intervention model including triage for acutely exposed children (March & Amaya-Jackson, 1993). Intervention aims at strengthening individual and family coping capacities for anticipated trauma responses (Garbarino, 1993) and treating other disorders that develop or worsen in the face of PTSD. Brief focused psychotherapy is aimed at chronic PTSD symptoms (Pynoos, Nader, & March, 1991). In the short term, key goals are survival, coping, and preventing hazardous behavior. In the long term, the issues are preventing interference of PTSD with normal child development and treating maladjustments in family life, peer relationships, and school performance (see Garbarino, Kostelny, & Dubrow, 1991).

Future Directions

A major problem with available findings is that PTSD research is conducted largely on adult males in the mainstream of European and North American societies. Larger, younger, and more culturally diverse samples of both sexes are needed to corroborate the validity of the PTSD classification (Saigh, 1988) for children and adolescents around the world.

Terr (1991a) suggested several important areas for further research: Epidemiological studies are needed to help identify how much trauma goes undetected, as well as longitudinal follow-through studies. The latter would investigate the impact of earlier traumatic events on child development and promote better understanding of the clinical course of early traumatic stress. In addition, Terr advocated further study of the mechanisms of brain response to trauma, suggesting that studies of tragically killed children may reveal neurotransmitters released during psychic traumas. Finally, she called for a *psychology of the external* to complement the current *psychologies of the internal*. The comprehensive study of PTSD in young people must move beyond an emphasis on the individual's intrapsychic responses, or *internal* psychology, to include such *external* aspects as the family, social, and cultural contexts of the individual experiencing the trauma.

PTSD in childhood and adolescence is a major, but underrecognized, mental health problem. The full extent of childhood trauma still may be unappreciated. We do not know how many children and adolescents are traumatized, by which particular experiences, what their reactions are, or how they cope, and as adults, we do not appreciate the impact on their lives. As much of our information concerns the presentation of PTSD in young people at various ages, there are still gaps in our knowledge of the sex, familial, geographic, and ethnocultural parameters. We need epidemiological studies to identify the incidence of traumatizing events among young people and longitudinal studies to track their efforts. As important as age effects are, the impact of trauma on children and adolescents needs to be addressed in a broad, comprehensive way, extending beyond the individual to the family, social, and ethnocultural contexts.

TRANSCULTURAL CHILD PSYCHIATRY: ETHNOCULTURAL ISSUES

Ethnocultural context does more than add to the clinical picture of PTSD. Examining PTSD across cultures may well paint an entirely different picture. Marsella, Friedman, and Spain (see chapter 4) caution that little is known about the relationship between ethnocultural factors and PTSD. This reveals two things: the paucity of research on ethnocultural aspects of PTSD and the need for outlining the conceptual basis for such research, fleshing out what Terr (1991a) calls the psychology of the external.

With young people, we have to examine the ways childhood and adolescence are constructed in a given society and perceived in the social sciences. Each society values children in different ways: as part of the family life cycle, for the transmission of core values, and so on. Societies also differ in the ways that young people are expected to behave, reflecting its core values. These values and expectations need to be examined within the culture of each family. The social sciences have misused the construct of childhood in two important ways. In the comparative approach, age is treated as just another control variable in the search for universals. For example, there was a time when a doctoral student in psychology with an interesting hypothesis, measurement, or intervention would be asked—for the sake of scholarly completeness—"What would the study yield with children or across cultures?" This approach looks for universals, not particulars. The danger is that the particulars may get explained away when they do not fit the search for universals. In the so-called *developmental approach*, childhood is tested as a pathway for how adults arrive at some specified state. For example, in much of the work in the human sciences, ranging from anthropology to psychology, *childhood* is used as a testing ground for some imagined typical person, usually an adult male from the dominant culture of Western society. The danger is that in the interest of adult outcomes, the distresses of childhood be minimized or ignored. For example, the literature on resilience or invulnerability values children's capacities to keep functioning and their eventual good outcome.

Combined with other problems in child psychiatry, these approaches have resulted in a paucity of information about children's experiences, a lack of interest in their experiences, and the unrepresentativeness of the information available. To move the field forward, researchers must work across disciplines and other boundaries. I have proposed transcultural child psychiatry (DiNicola, 1992) as a field of studies that has much to offer by combining clinical specialties (clinical psychology and psychiatry, pediatrics, and social work) with developmental studies (child psychiatry, developmental psychology) and cultural and social branches of the human sciences. This approach builds on an important new paradigm for the study of children—*culture-inclusive developmental psychology* (Valsiner, 1989).

By employing a rich interdisciplinary approach, transcultural child psychiatry (TCP) offers new tools for study and treatment of young people: (a) a historical analysis of developmental metaphors—the Western metaphors of development have become reified as scientific facts, when little more has happened than that stories about the human life cycle have changed their clothing from folk tales to psychological theories; (b) a culture-inclusive methodology for the study of children's development—detailed proposals for the inclusion of cultural variables in child studies are available in psychology (Valsiner, 1989) and psychiatry (DiNicola, 1992); (c) a methodological critique of child psychiatry research that excludes culture—there is strong evidence demonstrating cultural variation in the constructs we use to understand child and family phenomena (e.g., attachment, parenting styles, gender differences, child temperament, child abuse; DiNicola, 1992). Many research reports ignore or discount this cultural variation; (d) TCP recognizes culture-reactive child psychiatric problems and disorders—there are many culturally shaped problems and practices in the field of child psychiatry (e.g., children's vocal nodules, school refusal, and adolescent suicidal behavior and self-mutilation) (DiNicola, 1992). A number of disorders also show cultural reactivity (e.g., anorexia nervosa, elective mutism, and disruptive behavior disorders) (DiNicola, 1992); (e) TCP fosters the construction of culture-responsive therapeutics for children and their families.

Three key propositions for transcultural child psychiatry are (DiNicola, 1992)

1. Culture is integral to self-identity: Culture is not a perceptual barrier obscuring some supposedly fundamental reality such as biology but one of the integral sources of the self.
2. Child development is contingent and contextual: The key concept for transcultural work with children is that childhood and adolescence are social, cultural, and historical constructs.
3. Familism is normative: The family is a living context that defines the stages of life; it is the key context for redefining life stages and adapting to new social and cultural realities.

The challenge of working with children and adolescents across cultures is an opportunity to construct new metaphors for child development and family experience and new tools for working with children, adolescents, and their families (see DiNicola, 1985a, 1985b, 1985c, 1986, 1992, 1993). Constructing new metaphors requires a reworking of our notions of culture, child development, and family. Valuable work is being done on transcultural aspects of child psychiatry (Canino, 1988; DiNicola, 1992; Earls & Eisenberg, 1991; Grizenko, Sayegh, & Migneault, 1992; Mc-Dermott, 1991); in cultural aspects of family therapy (DiNicola, 1985a, 1985b, 1985c, 1986, 1994, in press; Falicov, 1983; Tseng & Hsu, 1991), and psychotherapy with children (Vargas & Koss-Chioino, 1992).

Elsewhere I have referred to children and adolescents who experience traumatic events as *changelings* (DiNicola, in press). This seems to be an appropriate metaphor for what Erikson (1960) described as a *transitory identity* that is assumed by children in response to the crises of uprootedness and loss of assigned or expected identity. The image of the changeling is an updated version of the fairy tale notion of a strange child who has replaced a family's own valued child.

Child psychiatrists and social scientists use Erikson's notion of transitory identity as a working assumption when children's cultural backgrounds are in flux and their core identities are less grounded. With the mass movement of refugees around the world and the increasing mobility and diversity of developed nations, however, such transitoriness may be more normative, and the child as a cultural changeling may have more positive connotations. For example, bicultural children may develop a personal synthesis of worldviews reflecting the different cultures they have lived in to form a *third culture*. According to Werkman (1978), such children are part of an international population with loosened ties to a home country that is not fully integrated within the host country. My positive construal of children undergoing profound cultural change as changelings is an invitation to identify and build on their adaptive capacities, which include their ability to adapt to and even to create new cultural syntheses. Nonetheless, multiple dislocations and traumas may be additive or multiplicative, overwhelming the young person's coping ability.

THE CROSS-CULTURAL STUDY OF PTSD IN CHILDREN AND ADOLESCENTS

The ultimate changelings may be children who experience PTSD through stressors that dislocate them from their ethnocultural roots. When all the ethnocultural issues are compounded by the chain of traumas associated with war and other severe stressors, understanding these children as changelings emphasizes the extent to which their lives have multiple dislocations. These children experience changes in their developmental paths; their family life cycle; their culture, language, religious traditions;

and the whole supportive context that make their lives meaningful. In the study of PTSD in children and adolescents, these factors are crucial to situate the work in a way that is responsive to ethnocultural context and developmental processes.

Studies of Childhood PTSD in Diverse Populations

The study of the impact of war on children began in Britain during World War II, with researchers examining child evacuees from the cities and child refugees from continental Europe (Alcock, 1941; Garmezy & Rutter, 1985). This work continued with the study of children from Nazi concentration camps (see Garmezy & Rutter, 1985) and later with much work on what have become two national laboratories for traumatic stress: Israel and Northern Ireland (Garmezy & Rutter, 1985).

Studies are now available about many other parts of the world, including Lebanon (Saigh, 1988, 1989), South Africa (Dawes, Tredoux, & Feinstein, 1989; Straker, Moosa, & Sanctuaries Counselling Team, 1988), and the former Yugoslavia (Zivcic, 1993). Important studies are also available about refugee children: Latin American refugees in Canada (Allodi, 1980, 1989) and in Denmark (Cohn et al., 1985; Weile et al., 1990); Southeast Asian refugees in the United States (Kinzie, Sack, Angell, & Manson, 1986; Kinzie, Sack, Angell, Clarke, & Ben, 1989; Westermeyer, 1991); and refugees from the former Yugoslavia in Sweden (Ekblad, 1993). In addition, Boothby's account of the experiences of refugee children in Africa offers a moving portrayal of trauma in children and youth (Boothby, 1993).

Jensen and Shaw (1993) reviewed the emerging issues on children as victims of war, noting that research has shifted from psychopathology to social awareness, values, and attitudes. This growing body of research adds to the already established literature on the impact of disasters and other major trauma on children and adolescents (Marsella, Bornemann, Ekblad, & Orley, 1994; Saylor, 1993; Terr, 1990).

Some objections and concerns regarding the use of the PTSD concept in non-Western contexts have been articulated (see chapter 4, this volume). Punamaki (1989) argued that stress models are inappropriate for conceptualizing trauma from political repression because they reduce social, political, and historical problems to the individual level. Eisenbruch (1991) offered an alternative *cultural bereavement model* for refugees, arguing that coping strategies are normal and healthy reactions. The thrust of both critiques is that larger social forces trigger coping strategies that can be considered normal adaptations to abnormal situations. A parallel feminist argument could be made against constructing the sequelae of incest, family violence, and rape as PTSD.

However, if the concept of PTSD has value in describing the final common pathway of severe stress, then the challenge is to enhance the validity of the term by expanding the study of PTSD to include all the variables that are meaningful for subjective, sociocultural, and historico-political reasons to the victims, at the same time improving its reliability by including these variables in its operational criteria (cf. Burges Watson, 1990; Garbarino et al., 1991; Weile et al., 1990).

Furthermore, the PTSD rubric can help to mobilize therapeutic resources for populations not otherwise served by mainstream psychiatry and related clinical fields. This is especially relevant for children and adolescents; (a) their stresses simply may go unheeded, understood as part of their dislocation or vulnerability because of their age. This danger is addressed in a study of children of torture victims by Weile and colleagues (1990), who question whether the worsening of the children's behavioral problems at 4-year follow-ups was a result of cultural maladaptation or to the influence of the parents' problems. As a result, not only PTSD but other problems associated with culture change may be missed; (b) their resilient adaptations may be healthy in the short term but create negative *sleeper* effects in the longer term (this is a metaphor from research on the sleeper effect in social psychology; see Zimbardo and Leippe, 1991).

The concerns expressed by Eisenbruch (1991), Marsella, Friedman, and Spain (see chapter 4, this volume), and Punamaki (1989) do not invalidate PTSD as a construct. They do suggest that we shore up the individually oriented *psychologies of the internal* with the insights of more socially oriented interpersonal approaches from epidemiology, cross-cultural, and social psychology and social and transcultural psychiatry to develop the *psychology of the external*. To progress in the study of traumatic stress, we must challenge the dichotomy between stress conceived as external and social life events and resilience or vulnerability conceived as internal and individual qualities to construct a more complete account of both personal and social being (as in the more comprehensive psychology outlined by Harré, 1979, 1984). With this more complete account of traumatic stress, we need to construct therapeutics that are responsive to developmental processes and cultural context.

Two Cross-Cultural Cases of PTSD in Young People

What follows is two cases of young people with PTSD across cultures.

Nur: A Train of Traumas

Nur was a 10-year-old boy, a Somalian refugee, with the presenting complaint of bed-wetting. Nur sat in my office drawing pictures as any other Canadian boy would. The difference was in the details—vivid and realistic pictures of bombs exploding and bodies strewn in their wake. He explained one picture as "planes dropping bombs on my country."

Nur's father had worked for the president of his country and had been able to provide well for his family. However, when civil war broke out, Nur's father was accused of plotting against the government, and he was tortured subsequently. Nur's mother said that her husband no longer could recognize her or their children. They escaped with their lives and little else, leaving family and friends behind. Along the way, Nur and his family experienced many cruelties and deprivations, as they sought to escape from Somalia. They experienced additional cruelties in a refugee camp in Ethiopia.

At his new home in Canada, Nur lived with his mother and siblings in subsidized housing near train tracks. At night, he was awakened by the nearby trains, which the mother believed caused his bed-wetting. When the child awoke, he related nightmares to his mother, who had her own terrifying memories with which to contend. From the noise of the train to bed-wetting and nightmares to memories of their civil war, for this family one trauma summons another in a train of traumas.

One could tease out the individual components: The bed-wetting was diagnosed as functional enuresis, secondary type—regressive behavior caused by war trauma and now triggered by the noise of the train in the night (Garfinkel, 1990). Because enuresis occurs during nondreaming sleep, the nightmares were probably flashbacks that occurred after Nur was awakened in the night, and he understood them as dreams.

The child waking up fearfully in the night was in turn a disturbing trigger for the mother's own traumatic memories, although during the day, she appeared remarkably poised. Over the months of therapy, the mother's poise was better described as a combination of a survivor's coping strategy and posttraumatic numbing. The components add up in each case—mother and child—to symptoms of PTSD. This probably would have occurred in any setting, but their move away from their homeland is another factor. The loss of their familiar cultural context was in itself a trauma, but settling in a safe and secure new country was experienced with great relief by the mother.

Treatment with Nur and his mother was aimed first at explaining his bed-wetting and symptom relief. Two months' treatment with imipramine (a tricyclic antidepressant), cured the enuresis. Gently, over time, while focusing on concrete issues such as bed-wetting, housing, and other practical needs, I was able to develop a working relationship with Nur's mother. During this process, I consulted a female social worker who spoke French to work with her. We learned that she had married young to an ambitious man who brought her to Marseilles, France, where he pursued an education for several years. As a result, she spoke French fluently. Our family sessions (child, mother, and therapists) were quite complex because there was no language we all had in common. Mother and child communicated in Somali, the therapists spoke English with the child and French with the mother.

As a result of marrying young and going abroad, she managed to avoid female circumcision (clitoridectomy or surgical removal of the clitoris). However, she did undergo infibulation (sewing up of most of the vulva leaving only a small opening for the passing of fluids). She told us that several young Canadian doctors who examined her had obviously never encountered women from North Africa because they were shocked by what appeared to be lacerations across her vulva from the sutures (for a discussion of female circumcision in the context of self-mutilation in culture and psychiatry, see Favazza, 1987).

As we treated her depression and other symptoms of PTSD, this intelligent woman who had survived the ordeal of civil war entered a rapid process of culture shock and acculturation. She spoke at great length about her perception of the freedom of women in Canada, which she contrasted to her upbringing, her arranged marriage, her forced infibulation, and the ruses she had had to use to avoid a clito-ridectomy. She was molting a layer of culture as we witnessed her going through a rejection of her culture of origin, mostly aimed at men in Somalia and Ethiopia and how they had treated her. This became concrete when she sought a divorce from her husband who was a chronic patient at a psychiatric hospital. We were concerned that in rejecting her culture of origin so vehemently and so quickly, she would create a great void in her life. But she was propelled forward by the clarity of the experiences from which she wanted to distance herself. And this was the source of her apparent resilience.

The therapeutic process shifted from Nur to his family, from individual symptoms to the complex predicament described as PTSD, and finally, from clinical psychiatry to a cultural encounter. Both Nur and his mother were like changelings: Their world was in rapid flux that required constant new adaptations and adjustments. The flux was not only in their new world, but perhaps even more profoundly, in their redefinitions of the one from which they had come.

A Girl of Color: Culture as a "Dirty Window"

Jasmine was a 15-year-old girl referred by a community agency. The presenting complaint concerned behavior problems at her group home and at school. Jasmine came from Guyana where her family was well-off and her father was politically prominent. When her father was murdered, the family lost its center, and her large nuclear family drifted to other countries, so she had siblings all over North America. She arrived in Canada with her mother, who later left her with Jasmine's older sister. The sister became physically abusive to her. This was sus-pected at school and the children's agency became involved, placing her in a group home. The agency sought psychiatric help when the placement was breaking down.

The assessment included a detailed history over several clinical interviews, a mental status examination, rating scales, and a consultation for further diagnostic psychological tests. Treatment included antidepressant medication for her depression, which had become complicated by a variety of losses including bereavement over her father, abandonment by her mother, abuse by her sister, and the loss of her home, her homeland, and her culture. Jasmine had witnessed the beating of her father, which led to his death, and she exhibited sequelae typical of PTSD: nightmares, anxiety, depression, and a numbed response to her social world.

Her social worker was active, supportive, warm, deeply interested in her, and spent a disproportionate amount of time with her despite a heavy case load. I attempted to meet the important people in Jasmine's life but was unable to meet either her mother or her sister. Eventually, I arranged to meet her foster mother, despite Jasmine's objections. When the foster mother came to the interview, I met a group home manager who lectured Jasmine for most of the session. I could make nothing of it. As the weeks went by, Jasmine lost weight despite her treatment, and I suspected an eating disorder. When I questioned her about her eating habits, I learned she was not eating because she disliked the food at her group home.

I have not mentioned Jasmine's ethnic or racial background. Jasmine was of East Indian descent. Her foster mother was a Black woman from the West Indies. The agency had thought that in placing this girl of color with a Black foster mother, they had made an inspired match. However, Jasmine liked neither this Black woman nor the food she cooked. Her contact with Blacks in her own country was mostly with servants in her home. She was never asked what she would think of living with this woman. In fact, it was assumed that she shared their view of herself as a cultural and racial outsider to Canadian society. In this view, immigrants are homogenized as undifferentiated others with a presumed sense of community among themselves.

With this information, some practical interventions were made. Jasmine was given money to buy her own food and shops were located that sold the foodstuffs of her culture. Within a week, she started gaining weight. After several weeks, she was transferred to a new group home, and she worked on writing about her family and cultural history. We learned that she identified herself as an Indian, which had been understood as aboriginal rather than East Indian. She joined a church group with people from her own country and faith. Finally, she was transferred to Toronto where members of her family lived and there is a sizable community from her home country.

In this case, the skills of a child psychiatrist were needed to diagnose and manage the elements of depression, conduct disorder, and PTSD. However, in the final analysis, none of those skills could fully elucidate her predicament. Jasmine's story illustrates the fact that cultural misperceptions often act like a dirty window, obstructing our ability to perceive clearly. Transcultural child psychiatry aims to clarify a particular child's predicament by integrating crosscultural considerations into the clinical protocol.

Cultural Family Therapy: A Model

One therapeutic model for children and adolescents is cultural family therapy (see DiNicola, 1990, 1993, 1994, in press; Falicov, 1983; Tseng & Hsu, 1991). The salience of a family approach to PTSD in children is clear from the literature: "Evidence from World War II and from the Middle East indicates that the level of emotional upset displayed by adults in a child's life, not the war situation *per se*, was most important in predicting the child's response" (Garbarino, 1993, p. 8; see also Garbarino et al., 1991). Koverola (1995) went even further, noting that parental psychopathology or distress can be impediments to the assessment and treatment of children.

Cultural family therapy, as I construct it (DiNicola, 1985c, 1986, 1993, 1994, in press) is a synthesis of family therapy and transcultural psychiatry (DiNicola, 1985a, 1985b) and becomes a *cultural encounter* between the family and the therapist (DiNicola, 1994) in which everything can be negotiated—from the family system's definitions of self and family and what constitutes problems and solutions, to the assumptions, methods, and goals of the therapeutic system. This does not occur routinely in Western models of family therapy, in which the cultural determinants of the family's identity, construction of their problems, and culturally sanctioned solutions are either assumed or ignored altogether. Furthermore, only by explicitly describing therapy as a *cultural encounter* between the family and the therapist will therapists also be prepared to examine their culture as a starting point for conducting therapy. The fundamental attitude and the most basic tool in cultural family therapy is *cultural translation* (DiNicola, 1986).

Conducting cultural therapy requires an active involvement motivated by curiosity about cultural differences or the desire to build bridges across these differences. The effort to translate and work across cultural differences encourages both parties—families and therapists—to relinquish clichés, myths, and stereotypes and together to explore new perceptions, explanations, and ways of being. The more I work with diversity across age, cultural, gender, and religious differences, the more I confirm my belief that, "All therapy is a form of translation—of language, of culture, and of family process (DiNicola, 1986, p. 189).

The practice of cultural family therapy raises the issue of the family's adaptive strategies (DiNicola, 1992). These strategies can be examined in various ways. I have suggested that the perspectives of *insiders* and *outsiders* (DiNicola, 1986) usefully capture a lot of information and can help to predict how the encounter of different cultural values is resolved. The language of insiders and outsiders helps to place where both the family and the host culture position each other and, in turn, where therapists are placed in their cultural encounters with the family. To Nur and his mother, I was a welcome outsider, a teacher about a world they wanted to enter. In expanding therapy beyond the presenting symptoms to deal with their cultural and social problems, I became a resource for solutions, not just problems. For Jasmine, her cultural encounters meant being seen through a series of cultural misperceptions. My clinical role was to remove this perceptual barrier as a cultural interpreter, again looking further than a narrow definition of her trauma or even her family predicament that re-quired a foster replacement.

Another approach is to examine how families negotiate culture change, which depends on how they carry their culture of origin, how they experience the host culture, and what models each of those cultures makes available to that particular family. If cultures provide a smorgasbord of choices, the subculture of the family, their class, caste, religion, and atti-tudes will determine their adaptive style.

One adaptive style is to develop a *creole culture* (DiNicola, 1992)—a local blend of two or more cultures created through the layer-by-layer build-up of cultural elements, much like the syncretic religions of Brazil and the Caribbean. When this strategy is not possible in the face of cultural differences, family members sometimes employ *double description*. Within the family culture, members endorse one set of cultural values, while out-side the family they experiment with and learn another.

In summary, cultural family therapy (CFT) has these key features (DiNicola, 1994, in press) that are useful in dealing with PTSD: (a) CFT deals with families across cultures or that are in cultural transition. When PTSD occurs in the midst of culture changes, the experience must be framed in its full context to minimize retraumatizing affected individuals; (b) CFT emphasizes that constructing a therapeutic system is a cultural encounter. This establishes a dialogue about models for coping with trauma in a new society; (c) CFT adds cultural complexity to family therapy. As a cultural encounter, CFT continues the expression of therapy from the individual to the family to ethnicity, society, and culture. This gives trau-matized families permission to discuss their problematic experiences in a new society; (d) CFT recognizes that all therapeutics are cultural products that need to be adapted for application in different cultures. Family therapy needs to be adapted outside the Western world and with immigrants and refugees (see DiNicola, 1985a, 1985b, 1985c) and for traumatized popula-tions (e.g., with families dealing with intergenerational sexual abuse); (e) CFT examines the family's *presenting culture*, much as a doctor examines the patient's *presenting complaint*. In CFT, culture is not a dirty window or an opaque screen, obscuring the view of the other side; rather, culture provides the *grounding locus* for traumatic experiences; (f) CFT attends to *emic* or *insider* perspectives. By directly observing the family's presenting culture, CFT allows one to examine culturally sanctioned definitions of the self and the family and what constitutes a problem and what constitutes a solution. Especially with PTSD, it is critical to negotiate constantly what is meaningful to foster the recovery from trauma to healing.

Cultural Family Therapy Tools

Cultural family therapy employs these tools (DiNicola, 1994, in press):

1. Cultural translation: CFT works on the translation of culture as well as language, making family therapy into a process of cultural translation;
2. Multiple descriptions: CFT uses multiple descriptions, including symbolic language, to exploring cultural metaphors to convey diverse experiences.
3. Insiders and outsiders: CFT maps out the family's boundaries, using the perspectives of *insiders and outsiders* to identify who is part of their world, who is not, and what their attitudes to others are.
4. Cultural strategies: CFT explores the family's strategies for adapting to its new culture.
5. Family life cycle in cultural context: CFT places the individual child within the family life cycle, which is in turn viewed in cultural context. This allows the therapist to normalize even potentially explosive issues such as adolescent turmoil, differential rates of adaptation, and generational differences as normative family events in the face of change.

CONCLUSION

The cross-cultural study of PTSD in children and adolescents must integrate complex developmental and ethnocultural perspectives. In identifying the literature on PTSD in diverse populations of children and adolescents, the scarcity of information is evident. Knowledge of the general patterns of PTSD among young people is rather vague, being most detailed about the expression of PTSD at different ages, but not in different cultures and ethnic groups nor between genders.

Objections to the cross-cultural construct of PTSD can be met by expanding research and clinical work to consider the wider ethnocultural context. This can strengthen the validity of PTSD as a classification. Furthermore, by recognizing the symptoms of PTSD, therapeutic resources can be mobilized for populations not otherwise served by clinicians. This is especially relevant for children and adolescents, whose experiences are easily ignored, misunderstood, or misrepresented. The two cases in this chapter of PTSD in non-Western youth outline how culture-responsive therapeutics can be constructed by clinicians. Cultural family therapy is offered as a model for working with children and adolescents with PTSD.

For the further study of PTSD in children and adolescents, (a) we need larger, younger, and more culturally diverse samples of both sexes to corroborate the validity of the PTSD classification in children and adolescents around the world; (b) we need to employ culture-inclusive developmental psychology and transcultural child psychiatry to redefine the questions of study and the methods of treatment in ethnocultural work with young people.

REFERENCES

Adam, B. S., Everett, B. L., & O'Neal, E. (1992). PTSD in physically and sexually abused psychiatrically hospitalized children. *Child Psychiatry and Human Development, 23*, 3–9.

Alcock, A. T. (1941). War strain on children. *British Medical Journal, 1*, 124.

Allodi, F. (1980). The psychiatric effects in children and families of victims of persecution and torture. *Danish Medical Bulletin, 27*, 229–232.

Allodi, F. (1989). The children of victims of political persecution and torture: A psychological study of a Latin American refugee community. *International Journal of Mental Health, 18*, 3–15.

American Psychiatric Association. (1994). *Diagnostic and statistical manual of mental disorders* (4th ed.). Washington, DC: Author.

Boothby, N. (1993). Trauma and violence among refugee children. In A. J. Marsella, T. Bornemann, S. Ekblad, & J. Orley (Eds.), *Amidst peril and pain: The mental health and well-being of the world's refugees* (pp. 239–262). Washington, DC: American Psychological Association Press.

Bullrich, S. (1989). The process of immigration. In L. Combrinck-Graham (Ed.), *Children in family contexts: Perspectives on treatment* (pp. 482–501). New York: Guilford Press.

Burges Watson, I. P. (1990). "Is violence a contagious disease?" The social implications of post-traumatic stress disorder. *Irish Journal of Psychological Medicine, 7*, 47–52.

Canino, I. A. (1988). The transcultural child. In C. J. Kestenbaum & D. T. Williams (Eds.), *Handbook of clinical assessment of children and adolescents, Vol. II* (pp. 1024–1042). New York: New York University Press.

Canino, I. A., & Spurlock, J. (Eds.). (1994). *Culturally diverse children and adolescents: Assessment, diagnosis, and treatment.* New York: Guilford Press.

Cohn, J., Danielson, L., Holzer, K. I. M., Koch, L., Severin, B., Thogorsen, S., & Aalund, O. (1985). A study of Chilean refugee children in Denmark. *Lancet, 2,* 437–438.

Dawes, A., Tredoux, C., & Feinstein, A. (1989). Political violence in South Africa: Some effects on children of the violent destruction of their country. *International Journal of Mental Health, 18,* 16–43.

Deblinger, E., McLeer, S. V., & Henry, D. (1990). Cognitive behavioral treatment for sexually abused children suffering post-traumatic stress: Preliminary findings. *Journal of the American Academy of Child and Adolescent Psychiatry, 29,* 747–752.

DiNicola, V. F. (1985a). Family therapy and transcultural psychiatry: An emerging synthesis. Part I: The conceptual basis. *Transcultural Psychiatric Research Review, 22,* 81–113.

DiNicola, V. F. (1985b). Family therapy and transcultural psychiatry: An emerging synthesis. Part II: Portability and culture change. *Transcultural Psychiatric Research Review, 22,* 151–180.

DiNicola, V. F. (1985c). Le tiers-monde à notre porte: Les immigrants et la thérapie familiale (The Third World in our own backyard: Family therapy with immigrants). *Systèmes Humains, 1,* 39–54.

DiNicola, V. F. (1986). Beyond Babel: Family therapy as cultural translation. *International Journal of Family Psychiatry, 7,* 179–191.

DiNicola, V. F. (1990). Family therapy: A context for child psychiatry. In J. G. Simeon & H. B. Ferguson (Eds.), *Treatment strategies in child and adolescent psychiatry* (pp. 199–219). New York: Plenum Press.

DiNicola, V. F. (1992). De l'enfant sauvage à l'enfant fou: A prospectus for transcultural child psychiatry. In N. Grizenko, L. Sayegh, & P. Migneault (Eds.), *Transcultural issues in child psychiatry* (pp. 7–53). Montréal, Canada: Éditions Douglas.

DiNicola, V. F. (1993). The postmodern language of therapy: At the nexus of culture and family. *Journal of Systemic Therapies, 12,* 49–62.

DiNicola, V. F. (1994). The strange and the familiar: Cultural encounters among families, therapists and consultants. In M. Andolfi & R. Haber (Eds.), *Please help me with this family: Using consultants as resources in family therapy* (pp. 34–54). New York: Brunner/Mazel.

DiNicola, V. F. (in press). Changelings: Children and their families in cultural transition. In S. O. Okpaku (Ed.), *Clinical methods in transcultural psychiatry.* Washington, DC: American Psychiatric Press.

Earls, F., & Eisenberg, L. (1991). International perspectives in child psychiatry. In M. Lewis (Ed.), *Child and adolescent psychiatry: A comprehensive textbook* (pp. 1189–1196). Baltimore: Williams & Wilkins.

Eisenbruch, M. (1991). From post-traumatic stress disorder to cultural bereavement: Diagnosis of Southeast Asian refugees. *Social Science and Medicine, 33,* 673–680.

Ekblad, S. (1993). Psychosocial adaptation of children while housed in a Swedish refugee camp: Aftermath of the collapse of Yugoslavia. *Stress Medicine, 9,* 159–166.

Erikson, E. H. (1960). Identity and uprootedness in our time. In *Uprooting and resettlement.* Geneva, Switzerland: World Federation for Mental Health.

Eth, S., & Pynoos, R. S. (Eds.). (1985). *Post-traumatic stress disorder in children.* Washington, DC: American Psychiatric Press.

Falicov, C. J. (Ed.). (1983). *Cultural perspectives in family therapy.* Rockville, MD: Aspen.

Famularo, R., Kinscherff, R., & Fenton, T. (1990). Symptom differences in acute and chronic presentation of childhood post-traumatic stress disorder. *Child Abuse & Neglect, 14,* 439–444.

Favazza, A. R. (1987). *Bodies under siege: Self-mutilation in culture and psychiatry.* Baltimore: Johns Hopkins Press.

Garbarino, J. (1993). Beyond PTSD: How to help children in chronic danger cope with their world. *Child and Adolescent Behavior Letter, 9,* 1, 7–8.

Garbarino, J., Kostelny, K., & Dubrow, N. (1991). What children can tell us about living in danger. *American Psychologist, 46,* 376–383.

Garfinkel, B. D., Carlson, G.A., & Weller, E. B. (1990). *Psychiatric disorders* in children and adolescents. Philadelphia: W. B. Saunders.

Garmezy, N., & Rutter, M. (1985). Acute reactions to stress. In M. Rutter & L. Hersov (Eds.), *Child and adolescent psychiatry: Modern approaches* (2nd ed., pp. 152–176). Oxford: Basil Blackwell.

Greene, G. (1990). *Reflections.* Toronto, Canada: Lester & Orpen Dennys.

Grizenko, N., Sayegh, L., & Migneault, P. (Eds.). (1992). *Transcultural issues in child psychiatry.* Montréal, Canada: Éditions Douglas.

Harré, R. (1979). *Social being: A theory for social psychology.* Oxford: Basil Blackwell.

Harré, R. (1984). *Personal being: A theory for individual psychology.* Cambridge, MA: Harvard University Press.

Horowitz, M. J., Wilner, N., & Alvarez, W. (1979). Impact of events scale: A measure of subjective stress. *Psychosomatic Medicine, 41,* 209–218.

Jensen, P. S., & Shaw, J. (1993). Children as victims of war: Current knowledge and future research needs. *Journal of the American Academy of Child and Adolescent Psychiatry, 32,* 697–708.

Kinzie, J. D., Sack, W., Angell, R., Clarke, G., & Ben, R. (1989). A three-year follow-up of Cambodian young people traumatized as children. *Journal of the American Academy of Child Psychiatry, 28,* 501–504.

Kinzie, J. D., Sack, W., Angell, R., & Manson, S. (1986). The psychiatric effects of massive trauma on Cambodian children: I. The children. *Journal of the American Academy of Child Psychiatry, 25*, 370–376.

Koverola, C. (1995). Posttraumatic stress disorder. In R. T. Ammerman & M. Hersen (Eds.). *Handbook of child behavior therapy in the psychiatric setting* (pp. 389–408). New York: Wiley-Interscience.

Lyons, J. A. (1987). Posttraumatic stress disorder in children and adolescents: A review of the literature. *Developmental and Behavioral Pediatrics, 8*, 349–356.

March, J. S., & Amaya-Jackson, L. (1993). Post-traumatic stress disorder in children and adolescents. *PTSD Research Quarterly, 4*, 1–7.

Marsella, A. J., Bornemann, T., Ekblad, S., & Orley, J. (Eds.) (1994). *Amidst peril and pain: The mental health and well-being of the world's refugees.* Washington, DC: American Psychological Association Press.

Marsella, A. J., Friedman, M. J., & Spain, E. H. (1993). Ethnocultural aspects of posttraumatic stress disorder. In J. M. Oldham, M. B. Riba, & A. Tasman (Eds.), *Review of psychiatry, Volume 12* (pp. 157–181). Washington, DC: American Psychiatric Press.

McDermott, J. F., Jr. (1991). The effects of ethnicity on child and adolescent development. In M. Lewis (Ed.), *Child and adolescent psychiatry: A comprehensive textbook* (pp. 408–412). Baltimore: Williams & Wilkins.

McNally, R. J. (1991). Assessment of posttraumatic stress disorder in children. *Psychological Assessment, 3*, 531–537.

Miller-Perrin, C. L., & Wurtele, S. K. (1990). Reactions to childhood sexual abuse: Implications for post-traumatic stress disorder. In C. L. Meek (Ed.), *Post-traumatic stress disorder: Assessment, differential diagnosis, and forensic evaluation* (pp. 91–135). Sarasota, FL: Professional Resource Exchange.

Ornitz, E. M., & Pynoos, R. S. (1989). Startle modulation in children with post-traumatic stress disorder. *American Journal of Psychiatry, 146*, 866–870.

Punamaki, R. (1989). Political violence and mental health. *International Journal of Mental Health, 17*, 3–15.

Pynoos, R. S. (1990). Post-traumatic stress disorder in children and adolescents. In B. D. Garfinkel, G. A. Carlson, & E. B. Weller (Eds.), *Psychiatric disorders in children and adolescents* (pp. 48–63). Philadelphia: W. B. Saunders.

Pynoos, R. S. (1993). Traumatic stress and developmental psychopathology in children and adolescents. In J. M. Oldham, M. B. Riba, & A. Tasman (Eds.), *Review of psychiatry, Volume 12* (pp. 205–238). Washington, DC: American Psychiatric Press.

Pynoos, R. S., Nader, K., & March, J. (1991). Posttraumatic stress disorder. In J. Weiner (Ed.), *Textbook of child and adolescent psychiatry* (pp. 339–348). Washington, DC: American Psychiatric Press.

Rakoff, V. (1981). Children of immigrants. In L. Eitinger & D. Schwarz (Eds.), *Strangers in the world* (pp. 133–146). Bern, Switzerland: Hans Hueber.

Saigh, P. A. (1988). The validity of the DSM-III posttraumatic stress disorder classification as applied to adolescents. *Professional School Psychology, 3,* 283–290.

Saigh, P. A. (1989). The validity of the DSM-III posttraumatic stress disorder classification as applied to children. *Journal of Abnormal Psychology, 98,* 189–192.

Saigh, P. A. (1992). The behavioral treatment of child and adolescent posttraumatic stress disorder. *Advances in Behaviour Research and Therapy, 14,* 247–275.

Saylor, C. F. (Ed.). (1993). *Children and disasters.* New York: Plenum Press.

Straker, G., Moosa, F., & Sanctuaries Counselling Team. (1988). Post-traumatic stress disorder: A reaction to state-supported child abuse and neglect. *Child Abuse and Neglect, 12,* 383–395.

Terr, L. (1990). *Too scared to cry: Psychic trauma in childhood.* New York: Basic Books.

Terr, L. (1991a). Acute responses to external events and posttraumatic stress disorders. In M. Lewis (Ed.), *Child and adolescent psychiatry: A comprehensive textbook* (pp. 755–763). Baltimore: Williams & Wilkins.

Terr, L. (1991b). Childhood traumas: An outline and overview. *American Journal of Psychiatry, 148,* 10–20.

Trad, P. V. (1989). Stress and child development. *Advances, 6,* 42–49.

Tseng, W.-S., & Hsu, J. (1991). *Culture and family: Problems and therapy.* New York: Haworth Press.

Valsiner, J. (Ed.). (1989). *Child development in cultural context.* Toronto, Canada: Hogrefe and Huber.

Vargas, L. A., & Koss-Chioino, J. D. (Eds.). (1992). Working with culture: Psychotherapeutic interventions with ethnic minority children and adolescents. San Francisco: Jossey-Bass.

Weile, B., Wingender, L. B., Bach-Mortensen, N., Busch, P., Lukman, B., & Holzer, K. I. M. (1990). Behavioral problems in children of torture victims: A sequel to cultural maladaptation or to parental torture? *Developmental and Behavioral Pediatrics, 11,* 79–80.

Werkman, S. (1978). A heritage of transience: Psychological effects of growing up overseas. In E. J. Anthony & C. Chiland (Eds.), *The child in his family* (pp. 117–133). New York: Wiley-Interscience.

Westermeyer, J. (1991). Psychiatric services for refugee children: An overview. In F. L. Ahearn & J. L. Athey (Eds.), *Refugee children: Theory, research, and services* (pp. 127–162). Baltimore: Johns Hopkins University Press.

Yule, W., & Williams, R. M. (1990). Post-traumatic stress reactions in children. *Journal of Traumatic Stress, 3,* 279–295.

Zimbardo, P. G., & Leippe, M. R. (1991). *The psychology of attitude change and social influence.* New York: McGraw-Hill.

Zivcic, I. (1993). Emotional reactions of children to war stress in Croatia. *Journal of the American Academy of Child and Adolescent Psychiatry, 32,* 709–713.

16

ETHNOCULTURAL CONSIDERATIONS IN UNDERSTANDING PTSD AND RELATED DISORDERS AMONG MILITARY VETERANS

WILLIAM SCHLENGER and JOHN FAIRBANK

The purpose of this chapter is to summarize current knowledge regarding the occurrence of posttraumatic stress disorder (PTSD) among ethnocultural subgroups exposed to one extreme event: participation in a war. By focusing on war veterans, we control, to some extent, the nature of the event to which the subgroups were exposed; consequently, we can examine ethnocultural variations in the prevalence and characteristics of PTSD among defined subgroups. This is important because exposure to specific trauma is one of the defining determinants of PTSD (Fairbank, Schlenger, Caddell, & Woods, 1993).

It is important to study the experiences of war veterans for several reasons. First, there have been, and continue to be, so many wars that the number of people exposed to war zone trauma is extremely large. De Girolamo (1993) noted, for example, that since World War II there have been 127 wars and more than 20 million war-related deaths in the world.

Second, it was largely through observation and documentation of the postwar experiences of soldiers exposed to combat that the syndrome known today as PTSD came to be recognized. Although scattered accounts of the postwar problems of those exposed to combat have appeared following many of recorded history's numerous wars, the medical and scientific communities' efforts to describe and understand these problems did not achieve critical mass until World War I. Although many of the postexposure symptoms of World War I veterans were observed and acknowledged, the syndrome was described as *shell shock* and attributed to neurological damage resulting from proximity to exploding shells. However, there was little systematic study of those exposed, the nature of their exposures, or the course of their subsequent symptoms and disorders.

Building on what had been learned through observation of the veterans of World War I, the postwar psychological problems of World War II veterans were studied more systematically, with follow-ups at 5 years (Brill & Beebe, 1956), 10 years (Futterman & Pumpian-Midlin, 1951), 15 years (Archibald & Tuddenham, 1965), 24 years (Keehn, Goldberg, & Beebe, 1974), 30 years (Klonoff, McDougall, Clark, Kramer, & Horgan, 1976), and 40 or more years (Sutker, Allain, & Winstead, 1993). Although these studies contain important methodological limitations (e.g., all involve samples of convenience rather than probability samples), they demonstrate that soldiers exposed to combat or other stressors of war (e.g., prisoner of war experiences) manifest a variety of stress-related symptoms long after the exposure. None of these studies, however, focused on ethnocultural differences.

In this chapter we will examine the experiences of those exposed to combat trauma, although research conducted in recent years has demonstrated that PTSD is not specific to combat but rather can result from exposure to a variety of extreme events. These include criminal victimization (Kilpatrick et al., 1985), sexual assault (Nadelson, Notman, Zackson, & Gornick, 1982; Winfield, George, Swartz, & Blazer, 1990), and exposure to natural or humanmade disasters (Gleser, Green, & Winget, 1981; Green, Lindy, Grace, et al., 1990; McFarlane, 1988; Shore, Tatum, & Volmer, 1986; Smith, North, McCool, & Shea, 1990; Steinglass & Gerrity, 1990).

Evidence (Breslau, Davis, Andreski, & Peterson, 1991) also demonstrates that exposure to a variety of extreme events is much more prevalent in the general population than was thought previously. Although combat veterans are a large and identifiable subgroup that is at risk for development of PTSD, it is clear, as has been discussed throughout this book, that this is by no means the only such subgroup.

In addition to limiting ourselves to PTSD among war veterans, we will also limit our examination to questions of prevalence to address the general questions: Does the prevalence of PTSD among subgroups of veterans defined by race or ethnicity vary, and if so, why? We will focus on prevalence and potential etiologic issues because many of the other important issues concerning PTSD in ethnocultural subgroups, such as case identification and appropriate treatment, are the focus of other chapters in this book and some previous publications (e.g., Marsella, Friedman, & Spain, 1993; and chapter 4, this volume).

PTSD AMONG VIETNAM VETERANS

Although there have been wars throughout human history, PTSD was not studied intensively or systematically among war veterans until the Vietnam war. Study of PTSD among Vietnam veterans was facilitated by the publication in 1980 of *DSM–III* (American Psychiatric Association, 1980) because: (a) it included PTSD as a diagnostic category defined by a specific cluster of symptoms and (b) its emphasis on behavioral criteria improved the chances that PTSD diagnoses could be made reliably, even outside of clinical settings.

In the decade following the publication of *DSM–III*, estimates of the prevalence of PTSD among Vietnam veterans based on several major epidemiologic studies were reported. These include findings from the (a) National Vietnam Veterans Readjustment Study (Kulka, Schlenger, Fairbank, et al., 1990a; Kulka, Schlenger, Fairbank, et al., 1990b), (b) The Centers for Disease Control's Vietnam Experience Study (1988), (c) The Department of Veterans Affairs' Twin Study (Goldberg, True, Eisen, & Henderson, 1990), (d) the St. Louis site of the National Institute of Mental Health's Epidemiologic Catchment Area Program (Helzer, Robins, & McEvoy, 1987), (e) the American Legion Study (Snow, Stellman, Stellman, & Sommer, 1988) and (f) a study conducted by the Traumatic Stress Study Center at the University of Cincinnati (Green, Grace, Lindy, Gleser, & Leonard. 1990).

There are a number of methodological differences among these studies that impact on their utility. First, PTSD prevalence estimates from many of these studies are based on small or nonrepresentative samples of Vietnam veterans. Second, most of the studies employed PTSD case identification procedures whose relationship to clinical diagnosis, or to any other criterion of assessment method, is unkown.

The most comprehensive examination of the prevalence of PTSD among Vietnam veterans comes from the National Vietnam Veterans Readjustment Study (NVVRS), a congressionally mandated study of the prevalence of postwar psychological problems among Vietnam veterans. The NVVRS included nationally representative samples of veterans who served in Vietnam or its surrounding waters or airspace when the war was being fought (theater veterans; $n = 1,632$); veterans who served in the military during the war period but not in the war zone (era veterans; $n = 716$); and civilian counterparts ($n = 668$) who did not serve in the military and who were matched to the theater veterans on age, sex, and race and ethnicity. Hispanic and African American men were oversampled so that the potential differential impact of the war on these subgroups could be studied reliably. Cases of PTSD were identified on the basis of a comprehensive multimeasure assessment that included both self-report scales and structured clinical interviews.

NVVRS findings (Schlenger et al., 1992) indicated that 15.2% of men and 8.5% of women Vietnam theater veterans were current cases of PTSD (i.e., met the *DSM–III–R* criteria in the 6 months prior to the interview) at the time the study was conducted (1987). By contrast, the current prevalence among comparable era veterans was 2.5% among men and 1.1% among women, and for nonveterans 1.2% among men and 0.3% among women. Lifetime prevalence rates (i.e., the percentage who had met the criteria at some time during their lives) among Vietnam veterans was 30.9% for men and 26.9% for women.

In spite of the substantial methodological differences among the various studies of Vietnam veterans, however, a thorough review (Kulka et al., 1991) of the findings of seven major epidemiologic studies of the prevalence of PTSD among Vietnam veterans demonstrated surprisingly good agreement of findings. Although the estimates of current PTSD prevalence in the seven studies ranged from 1.8% to more than 25%, the estimates from the majority of the studies lie very nearly within the 95% confidence interval of the NVVRS estimates (13.0% to 17.4%). This suggests that PTSD among Vietnam veterans is an important and continuing public health problem.

Prevalence of PTSD Among Racial and Ethnic Subgroups

Of the approximately 3.2 million U.S. veterans who served in the Vietnam war, about 170,000 (5%) were Hispanic men and about 350,000 (11%) were African American men (Kulka et al., 1990b). These two subgroups were oversampled in the NVVRS, as were women veterans, to ensure that they would be included in adequate numbers to support detailed analysis. No other racial or ethnic subgroups were oversampled, and for analysis purposes members of any such subgroups were classified with White subjects.

NVVRS findings (Schlenger et al., 1992) indicated that there are significant differences in the prevalence of current PTSD among African American, Hispanic, and White/other male Vietnam veterans. The prevalence for White/other men was 13.7% (2.3% for White/other era veterans, 1.0% for White/other civilian counterparts), 20.6% for African American men (4.4% for African American era veterans and 1.3% for African American civilian counterparts), and 27.9% for Hispanic men (2.1% for Hispanic era veterans, 3.9% for Hispanic civilian counterparts). The prevalence of current PTSD for Vietnam veteran women, more than 95% of whom were White, was 8.5%.

One of the major findings of the NVVRS was that Vietnam veterans with PTSD are much more likely than those without PTSD to have experienced a wide variety of life adjustment problems (Kulka et al., 1990a). This finding holds for African American and Hispanic subgroups as well as for Vietnam veterans as a whole. Both African American and Hispanic theater veterans reported more overall adjustment problems than White/others. Although there were only a few differences between the subgroups in the prevalence of other (non-PTSD) psychiatric disorders, both African American and Hispanic men reported significantly more problems with marital relationships and violent behavior than White/others.

In terms of marital relationships, African American Vietnam veterans were significantly less likely to be currently married compared to Hispanics or White/others and were more likely to be living as though married or to be separated. However, no significant racial or ethnic differences were found on number of divorces, number of parental problems, and family adjustment. Both African American and Hispanic Vietnam theater veterans reported higher mean numbers of violent acts in the past year than White/others. Both minority groups also reported lower levels of happiness and life satisfaction than White/others.

There were no other readjustment problems on which Hispanics were higher than either African Americans or White/others. African Americans, however, were more likely than White/other veterans to report lower levels of educational attainment, to be currently unemployed, and to have had some involvement with the criminal justice system.

One other important finding emerged from comparisons between African American Vietnam theater and era veteran men. Specifically, many of the problems examined for which African American theater veterans were significantly higher than White/others and Hispanics were also quite prevalent among male African American era veterans. As a result, significant differences between theater and era veteran men frequently observed among White/others and Hispanics were rarely observed among African Americans. Rather than indicating that African American theater veterans are relatively well adjusted, the lack of such differences emphasizes instead an especially high level of adjustment problems among African American era veterans, problems that they appear to share with the African American men who served in Vietnam.

Overall, it appears that African American and Hispanic veterans have experienced more mental health and life adjustment problems subsequent to their service in Vietnam than White/other veterans. These subgroups shared a number of problems, including elevated rates of PTSD, overall adjustment problems, and lower levels of life satisfaction. For Hispanics, problems were particularly manifested in high rates of PTSD and other psychiatric disorders (e.g., alcohol abuse and dependence and generalized anxiety). Among African Americans, the more serious problems (in addition to PTSD) appeared to be in social readjustment, particularly educational and occupational achievement, marital status, and negative involvement with the criminal justice system.

Understanding Differences Among Ethnocultural Groups in PTSD Prevalence

The literature contains descriptions of a variety of conceptual approaches that have been proposed to explain the development and maintenance of psychiatric and other adjustment problems following exposure to trauma. Examples of psychological approaches include psychodynamic models (Horowitz, 1974; Horowitz & Kaltreider, 1980), conditioning and learning models (Keane, Zimering, & Caddell, 1985), and cognitive and information-processing models (Chemtob, Roitblat, Hamada, Carlson, & Twentyman, 1988; Foa, Steketee, & Rothbaum, 1989; Litz & Keane, 1989). Biological models, however, emphasize the role of neurochemical systems (Krystal et al., 1989) and genetic influences (Davidson, Smith, & Kudler, 1989).

The conceptualization that guided the design of the NVVRS is the *diathesis-stress model* (Escobar, 1987; Keane, 1989; Meehl, 1962; Zubin & Spring, 1977). As applied to the study of reactions to traumatic stress, the diathesis-stress model is a biopsychosocial conceptualization that describes the interpersonal variability in reactions to extreme events in terms of the interactions of internal and external factors. The model posits that extreme events may elicit crisis in almost everyone, but, depending on the intensity of the stressor and the individual's threshold for tolerating it, the trauma will be either contained homeostatically or lead to an episode of disorder (Zubin & Spring, 1977).

In a similar way, Lazarus and Folkman (1984) and their colleagues have advanced the position that the patterns of adjustment after stress exposure differ because they are influenced by the variance in characteristics of both the stressor and the individual. Comprehensive biopsychosocial models have been proposed that incorporate a range of variables that may act as vulnerability, protecting, or potentiating factors (e.g., Foy, Osato, Houskamp, & Neumann, 1992; Jones & Barlow, 1990).

The NVVRS findings presented earlier indicate that the prevalence of PTSD is higher among African American and Hispanic Vietnam veterans than among White/others. Why is this so? Biopsychosocial and diathesis-stress models suggest the answer lies in an assessment of the interaction of characteristics of the person, characteristics of the exposure, and characteristics of the periexposure and postexposure environments as determinants of postexposure adjustment.

In principle, then, the observed differences among the subgroups might be a result of three kinds of factors: (a) differences in characteristics or exposures that they brought with them to the war (i.e., differential "predisposition"), (b) differences in the nature or magnitude of their exposure to trauma during their service in Vietnam, or (c) differences in their postexposure experiences. The NVVRS database affords the unusual opportunity to examine in a multivariate framework the relationships of a wide range of stressor characteristics, individual characteristics that may have rendered one more (or less) vulnerable to stressors, and postexposure experiences in determining postexposure adjustment.

Differences in Preexposure Characteristics

Many powerful social forces interacted during the Vietnam era to determine which soldiers went to Vietnam and what kinds of experiences they had while they were there. As a result, it is possible that differences in one or more kinds of vulnerability to PTSD existed between the race and ethnicity subgroups and that those differences account for the observed differences in PTSD prevalence.

To examine the role of *potentially predisposing factors*, the NVVRS investigators (Schlenger et al., 1992) selected more than 80 characteristics and experiences that predate military or Vietnam experience and that might conceivably account for differences in current PTSD prevalence rates between the study groups. The major categories of factors that were included and some illustrative examples of variables from each category are shown in Table 1.

The impact of these factors was assessed via a series of multiple regression analyses that provided estimates of the difference in current prevalence for each of the race and ethnicity subgroup contrasts with the effects of the predisposing factors controlled. Potential predisposing factors became candidates for inclusion in the analyses if they were related significantly to the probability of being a current case of PTSD and related significantly to the specific group contrast being modeled (the two conditions that define a statistical confound; Cochran, 1983). The models were fit via a backward elimination procedure, starting with all predisposing factors that met these requirements.

The adjustment for predisposing factors had a substantial impact on the contrasts of race and ethnicity subgroups of male Vietnam veterans. The adjustment reduced the current PTSD prevalence difference between White/others and African Americans by 10%, the difference between White/others and Hispanics by 57%, and the difference between African American and Hispanics by 67%.

Despite these reductions in group prevalence differentials, the adjusted current PTSD prevalence for White/others remained about 6 percentage points lower for White/others than for African Americans or Hispanics. The difference in current PTSD prevalence between African American and Hispanic males became statistically nonsignificant, however, when adjusted for predisposing factors. This means that if African American and Hispanic Vietnam veterans had had the same profile of predisposing characteristics when they went to Vietnam, there would be no difference in current PTSD prevalence between the groups today.

TABLE 1
Major Categories of NVVRS Potential Predisposing Factors

Category	Example Variables
Childhood and Family Background Factors	
Demographic characteristics	Age, race, family religious background
Family socioeconomic status	Parents' education, father's occupation
Family social environment	Relationship with parents, health/mental health problems of family/household members, child abuse
Biopsychosocial factors	Health/mental health problems among first-degree relatives
Childhood behavior problems	Delinquent behaviors index
Childhood health and mental health status	Health/mental health symptoms during childhood/adolescence
Premilitary Factors	
Role status	Age, educational attainment, marital status at time of entry into military
Health and mental health status	Health and mental health problems prior to entry into military
Military Factors	
General, non-Vietnam	Non-Vietnam combat duty, other overseas military duty
Pre-Vietnam role status	Age, educational attainment at beginning of Vietnam service
Pre-Vietnam health and mental health status	Health/mental health problems prior to beginning of Vietnam service
Vietnam	War zone stress exposure indices

Note. Adapted by permission from Schlenger et al., 1992.

Differences in War Zone Stress Exposure

A second factor that might contribute to differences between the subgroups in PTSD prevalence is their relative levels of exposure to war zone stress. That is, if the groups were unequally exposed to trauma and other stressors of the war zone, we would expect them to differ in PTSD prevalence.

Measurement of Exposure. Measurement of exposure to war zone stress was an important aspect of the NVVRS for several reasons. First, the basic hypothesis underlying the study's quasiexperimental design was that involvement in combat leads to exposure to trauma, which in turn may lead to the development of PTSD, so the contrasts of most interest involve comparing combat veterans to other veterans or to nonveterans. Since those who served in Vietnam were not equally exposed to combat or other war zone stressors, the NVVRS research team sought to develop a war zone stress exposure measure that would allow theater veterans to be divided into relative-exposure groups and thereby improve the internal validity of the study's comparisons.

Because prior research also has demonstrated that exposure to war zone stress is a multidimensional phenomenon (Laufer, Gallops, & Frey-Wouters, 1984), it was important that the overall exposure measure reflect the basic underlying dimensions. Thus, while exposure to firefights and other direct combat experiences is an important element of war zone stress, it is not the only element. Other elements that have been shown to be related to postwar adjustment include exposure to people who are wounded, dying, or dead, and exposure to (or participation in) violence (Egendorf, Kadushin, Laufer, Rothbart, & Sloan, 1981; Laufer et al., 1984).

In addition, prior research with combat veterans has shown that the various dimensions of war zone stress exposure may be related differentially to subsequent development of stress reaction symptoms and that the impact of stress exposure may differ among subgroups of the veteran population (Laufer, Brett, & Gallops, 1985). Thus it was important that the exposure measure be sensitive to the full range of stressors to which theater veterans might have been exposed.

The NVVRS team began with a set of nearly 100 items from the NVVRS survey interview covering eight broad stressor content areas that prior research suggested should be included in a comprehensive assessment and used principal components analysis to derive empirically a set of specific measures of the underlying dimensions. This resulted in identifying four war zone stress dimensions for men and six for women. Examples of the kinds of items included on each of the scales for men and women are shown in Table 2.

Internal consistency reliabilities of the scales ranged from .70 to .94 (Mdn = .87). Second-order principal components analyses indicated that for both sexes the specific dimensions could be combined statistically into a single overall index of exposure. Doing so allowed the variability from all of the important dimensions of war zone stress exposure to be reflected in a single index separately for men and women veterans. These overall indices were used to define *high* and *low/moderate* stress exposure groups.

Levels of Exposure. NVVRS findings (Kulka et al., 1990b) indicated that exposure to war zone stress was not equally distributed among the race and ethnicity subgroups. About 23% of White/other males were classified by the multidimensional index as *high exposure*, but significantly higher percentages of African American and Hispanic men were so classified: 37% of African American men and 33% of Hispanic men. The difference in exposure between African American men and Hispanic men was not statistically significant.

In addition, there was a substantial differential in the prevalence of PTSD between the high and low/moderate exposure groups. For all Viet-

TABLE 2
Example Items From NVVRS War Zone Stress Exposure Scales

Gender	Scale	Example Items
Men	Exposure to combat	Frequency of receiving enemy small arms fire
		Frequency of encountering mines and booby traps
		Frequency of firing weapon at enemy
		Frequency of personally killing enemy
		Ever wounded or injured in combat
	Abusive violence and related conflicts	Involvement in mutilation of bodies
		Involvement in killing/injuring civilians
		Involvement in torturing/wounding prisoners
	Deprivation	Lack of shelter from weather
		Lack of food/water/supplies
		Frequency of fatigue/exhaustion
		Frequency of exposure to insects, disease, etc.
	Loss of meaning and control	Sense of purposelessness
		Feeling out of touch with the world
		Loss of freedom of movement
		Feeling unimportant as an individual
Women	Exposure to dead and wounded	Frequency of giving care to people who later died
		Saw soldiers wounded in combat
		Responsible for care of casualties
		Frequency of exposure to wounded/dying/dead
	Exposure to enemy fire	Frequency of being under enemy fire
		Frequency of being in danger of being killed
		Frequency of being in unsafe or hostile territory
	Direct combat involvement	Frequency of firing weapon in combat situation
		Frequency of seeing enemy being killed
		Ever killed enemy
	Exposure to abusive violence	Saw or heard of Americans tortured
		Saw American bodies mutilated by enemy
		Involved in torturing/wounding/killing enemy
	Deprivation	Lack of shelter from weather
		Lack of food/water/supplies
		Frequency of fatigue/exhaustion
		Frequency of exposure to insects, disease, etc.
	Loss of meaning and control	Sense of purposelessness
		Feeling out of touch with the world
		Loss of freedom of movement
		Feeling unimportant as an individual

Note. Adapted by permission from Schlenger et al., 1992.

nam veterans, the current prevalence of PTSD was 36% in the high exposure group versus 9% for the low/moderate exposure group. Similar differentials held for the race and ethnicity subgroups. Among White/others, the differential was 34% versus 8%; for African Americans, 38% versus 10%; and for Hispanics, 48% versus 18%.

Accounting for Predisposition and Exposure. Could these differences in exposure levels account for the remaining differences in current PTSD prevalence rates among the race and ethnicity subgroups? To clarify the role of war zone stress exposure, we added the war zone stress exposure index to the predisposition adjustment models for the male theater veteran racial and ethnic subgroup contrasts. This allowed us to compare current prevalence rates among the race and ethnicity subgroups while controlling for predisposing characteristics and war zone stress exposure.

With the predisposing factors and exposure to war zone stress controlled, the difference in current PTSD prevalence between White/other and African American theater veterans was reduced to statistical nonsignificance. That is, if White/other and African American Vietnam veterans had had the same background characteristics when they went to Vietnam and had been exposed to similar levels of war zone stress, there would be no difference in the prevalence of PTSD today.

The effect on the contrasts of Hispanics with White/others and with African Americans, however, was different. The difference in current prevalence between White/other and Hispanic males was reduced slightly, from 6.1% (adjusted for predisposition) to 5.4%, but remained statistically significant. The difference for the African Americans versus Hispanics contrast, which had been reduced to statistical nonsignificance when only predisposing factors were controlled, was increased to a statistically significant 6.3% (Hispanics higher than African Americans) when war zone stress exposure was controlled also. Thus, although the adjustment for both predisposition and exposure eliminated the prevalence differential between White/others and African Americans, even when both are controlled the current PTSD prevalence for Hispanics is significantly higher than for White/others or for African Americans.

Differences in Postexposure Experiences. The third domain of variables that might influence PTSD prevalence rates are the experiences of exposed individuals after the exposure. These include such factors as the availability of social support, the effects of differing coping strategies, and the impact of the occurrence of subsequent stressful and traumatic events in Vietnam veterans' lives. Analyses of such factors are necessary to provide a more complete understanding of the roles that pretrauma experiences and background variables, characteristics of the stressor, and posttrauma experiences play in shaping the response to traumatic stress.

There are several reasons why these factors were not examined as part of the initial NVVRS analyses. First, they had limited relevance to the

NVVRS' congressional mandate, in that the multivariate analyses conducted for the NVVRS report to Congress (Kulka, et al., 1990a) were aimed at: (a) ruling out the hypothesis that differences in PTSD prevalence between study groups could be fully explained by differences in predisposing factors, and (b) determining whether Vietnam experience factors contributed significantly to the observed differences in PTSD prevalence even after predisposing factors were controlled.

Second, these variables have a somewhat fuzzy status. Because all are measured retrospectively and no independent source is available against which the validity of those retrospective self-reports can be assessed (such as the military records that were used as a validity check for self-reported war zone stress exposure), and because the potential for confounding of these variables with the outcomes is high, we have been somewhat wary of them. However, we plan to analyze them, though the findings must be interpreted cautiously.

There are several general types of candidate posttrauma environment variables available in the NVVRS database. First, there are a number of variables reflecting aspects of the veteran's military service and the immediate postservice period, such as reported coping strategies while in Vietnam, negative experiences while in the military, homecoming experiences, social support at the time of return to civilian life, and membership in veterans' organizations.

Second, there are a number of more general indices of postservice life. These include the report of exposure to *traumatic events* at any time during the postservice period, report of stressful life events during the past 12 months, current social support (existence of social relationships, social isolation, availability of a confidante, and perception of support availability), a family environment scale (adaptability and cohesion), unemployment status and history, history of marital separations and divorces, mental and emotional problems of the spouse or partner, mental and emotional problems of the veteran's children, and the occurrence of mental or emotional problems in the veteran's family of origin after the veteran became an adult.

Analyzing these and other postexposure variables will help elucidate the extent to which characteristics and events in the postexposure environment contribute to the development of PTSD among Vietnam veterans. As noted previously, however, these findings will be less definitive than other NVVRS findings because of the methodological limitations.

PTSD AMONG VETERANS OF OTHER WARS

Although there have been, and unfortunately will probably continue to be, many other wars, there have been few methodologically sound epidemiologic studies of PTSD among veterans of those wars and little information about differences among ethnocultural subgroups of those exposed (see chapter 4, this volume). One important reason for this is that prior to the publication of *DSM–III*, there did not exist a widely agreed on, operationalizable definition of the disorder.

Probably the best studied combat-exposed group other than Vietnam veterans is Israeli war veterans. Solomon and her colleagues have studied extensively the development of PTSD in groups of participants in the 1982 Lebanon war and more recently among those exposed to the Gulf War. Concerning the Lebanon war, Solomon, Weisenberg, Schwarzwald, and Mikulincer, (1987) reported a PTSD prevalence rate of 16% 1 year after the war among soldiers who had not experienced an acute combat stress reaction during the war, a rate comparable to findings for Vietnam veterans. The rate among soldiers who had experienced a combat stress reaction, however, was 59%. Solomon and her colleagues subsequently studied these veterans at 2 (Solomon & Mikulincer, 1988) and 3 (Solomon, 1989) years postwar.

In addition, they have studied extensively the contributions of exposure and postexposure factors to the development of PTSD in Israeli veterans, focusing particularly on social cognitive variables such as self-efficacy, attributional style, and coping (Mikulincer & Solomon, 1988; Solomon, Mikulincer, & Benbenishty, 1989; Solomon, Benbenishty, & Mikulincer, 1991), and more recently the effects of a specialized intervention aimed at treating chronic PTSD in these veterans (Solomon, Bleich, Shoham, Nardi, Kotler, 1992). None of these studies, however, has included analyses aimed at identifying differences among ethnocultural subgroups of Israelis.

Although the prevalence of the PTSD syndrome as defined in *DSM–III* was not studied well among World War II and Korean War veterans, (for the obvious reason that the *DSM–III* wasn't published until 1980), studies of PTSD among combatants and others exposed to those wars recently have been conducted. Sutker and her colleagues (Sutker et al., 1993) studied samples of World War II prisoners of war and combat veterans about 40 years after their war experience and found current PTSD prevalence rates of 18% for combat veterans and 70% for former prisoners of war. In a similar way, in a follow-up study of former prisoners of war from World War II, Kluznick, Speed, Van-Valkenburg, and Magraw (1986) found that two thirds had had PTSD at some time following their imprisonment and about 21% still had at least moderate residual PTSD symptoms about 40 years after the end of the war. Also, Weisaeth and Eitinger (1991a; 1992b) have summarized findings from studies conducted in Europe.

Although all of these studies add to our understanding of the epidemiology of PTSD following exposure to war trauma, none examined the role of ethnocultural factors. It is interesting to note, however, the consistency with which PTSD prevalence estimates for the various war trauma exposure groups from different countries and different wars fall within the 95% confidence interval of the NVVRS estimates.

CONCLUSION

In this chapter we have summarized what is currently known about ethnocultural differences in PTSD among war veterans. Our efforts were hampered to some extent by two factors. First, it was not possible to study the PTSD syndrome as defined in *DSM–III* prior to 1980, so the only available studies have been relatively recent. Second, many of the studies that do exist, particularly studies of veterans of wars other than Vietnam, did not include analyses of ethnocultural subgroups.

As a result, we focused our attention on Vietnam veterans, and particularly on multivariate analyses from the NVVRS. These findings demonstrated the significant role of war zone stress exposure in the etiology of PTSD in Vietnam veterans and highlight the fact that those who were most heavily involved in the war are those who are most likely to be experiencing adverse emotional sequelae today.

This finding, in which a variety of background characteristics were controlled statistically, complements and is consistent with findings of the Twin Study (Goldberg et al., 1990) in which potential genetic contributions were controlled by comparing the prevalence of PTSD in male monozygotic twins who served in Vietnam with the prevalence among their identical siblings who served in the military but not in Vietnam. Both studies showed a strong dose-response relationship between exposure to war zone stress and the current prevalence of PTSD.

The NVVRS analyses of background and exposure factors only begin to address, however, the important scientific question of etiology. NVVRS findings indicate that even after taking into account differences in preexposure characteristics and levels of exposure to war zone stress, the current PTSD prevalence among Hispanics is higher than among African Americans or White/others. Further analysis is needed to identify the factors that account for these differences.

Social Support, Coping, and Impact of Subsequent Exposure

Among the potentially important factors that have not yet been examined are the postwar experiences of Vietnam veterans, including the availability of social support, the effects of differing coping strategies, the effect of contextual variables (e.g., unit cohesion), and the impact of the occurrence of subsequent stressful and traumatic events in Vietnam veterans' lives. Analyses of such factors are necessary to provide a more complete understanding of the roles that pretrauma background variables, characteristics of the stressor, and posttrauma experiences play in shaping the response to traumatic stress.

The NVVRS experience highlights an important logistical problem associated with the study of ethnocultural differences in the context of large-scale epidemiologic research. As we have discussed, by design, the NVVRS oversampled African American and Hispanic men so that the overall sample would contain enough veterans from these subgroups to support reliable analysis. Oversampling was required because African Americans and Hispanics represented 11% and 5% respectively, of the soldiers who served (Kulka et al., 1990b).

But African Americans and Hispanics are not the only race and ethnicity subgroups of interest. Other subgroups of interest made up still smaller proportions of the Vietnam veteran population—for example, American Indians and Alaska Natives about 1.5%, Asian Americans about 0.8%, Pacific Islanders about 0.3% (Kulka et al., 1990b). Because membership in these subgroups was not recorded in military records (which formed the frame from which the NVVRS sample was drawn), oversampling them on the basis of information from their records was not feasible.

There is reason to believe, however, that the Vietnam War may have affected some other ethnocultural subgroups differentially as well. For example, Marsella, Chemtob, and Hamada (1992) and Hamada, Chemtob, Sautner, and Sato (1988) argued on the basis of clinical experience that the prevalence of PTSD among Asian American Vietnam veterans may be disproportionately high and that their PTSD may be misdiagnosed because of cultural factors. In a similar way, Loo (in press) described a conceptual framework of race-related stressors to which Asian American veterans were uniquely exposed in the Vietnam-era military because of their subgroup membership that may have made them more likely to develop PTSD (e.g., similarities in appearance to the enemy).

Because of the NVVRS finding of differences between African American, Hispanic, and White/other veterans that could not be explained by background or exposure factors, however, and because of the accumulating anecdotal evidence of the type just described, Congress has mandated that studies of PTSD in some additional subgroups be conducted. Community epidemiologic studies of the prevalence of PTSD among Japanese American veterans, Native Hawaiian veterans, and Sioux and Navajo veterans currently are being conducted under the auspices of the Department of Veterans Affairs' National Center for PTSD. These studies are important steps in the advancement of the PTSD literature and will provide important information about the role of ethnocultural factors in the etiology of PTSD.

Other steps are also clear. Longitudinal studies of war veterans of all races and ethnicities are needed to examine how PTSD symptoms are expressed over the lifespan. In particular, such studies could begin to provide answers to questions about the course of PTSD as a disorder, the temporal relationship between PTSD reexperiencing and avoidance and numbing symptoms, and the temporal relationships among PTSD symptom patterns, other psychiatric disorders—such as substance abuse and major depression—and functional adaptation and impairment.

In addition, longitudinal studies of veterans of different races, ethnicities, and cultures could provide much needed empirical information on the prevalence and effects of exposure to other kinds of extreme events, especially adverse events that minorities are more likely to experience, such as racism and urban violence. Examining how these variables might interact with severity of exposure to war zone stress and other background and pre- and postwar characteristics could help to explain further the complex etiology of higher PTSD rates among African American and Hispanic Vietnam veterans.

Another important step in ethnocultural research on PTSD should be the development and psychometric evaluation of instruments intended to assess exposure to a broad range of potentially traumatic conditions to which ethnic minorities are exposed in the military and in the war zone. Loo's (1994) recent work with Asian American Vietnam veterans, for example, suggests that constructs of race- and ethnicity-related trauma are likely to be multidimensional, including factors such as ethnic isolation and cultural deprivation, exposure to racial harassment and discrimination, racial stigmatization, and mistaken identity experiences.

Penk and Allen (1991) have identified race-related issues that can interfere in accurate diagnosis and appropriate treatment of combat veterans from minority groups. Developing reliable and valid measures of constructs such as race-related trauma and using ethnoculturally appropriate assessment techniques are necessary conditions for research aimed at understanding potential ethnocultural contributions to adverse and resilient postwar adjustment and coping (see chapter 4, this volume).

Research on war trauma, race and ethnicity, and PTSD also could benefit greatly from the use of comparable measurement strategies across studies. Adoption of core measures of critical variables (e.g., stress exposure, PTSD case identification) across studies would go a long way toward enhancing the communication and dissemination of findings to scientists and clinicians, as well as to those government and military officials whose policy decisions about the waging of war may disproportionately affect ethnocultural minorities.

Thus, although much progress has been made in the empirical study of differences among ethnocultural groups in response to exposure to combat trauma, many questions remain unanswered. Bell (1994) noted that the variable called *race* in many research studies may be a proxy for a variety of other variables (e.g., genetic influences, cultural influences, exposure to racism), and that researchers should both include more racial groups in their studies and define specifically their use of race-related variables. Adebimpe (1994) recommended guidelines for methods that will provide an improved basis for studying racial differences.

Green and her colleagues (Green et al., 1990), in discussing racial differences in response to combat stress exposure, noted the sensitivity of the topic. They speculated that this sensitivity may cause some investigators to shy away from it, a view shared by Bell (1994). They further noted, however, that all could "learn from a more open discussion and more empirical scrutiny of the data we have collected" (Green et al., 1990; p. 392).

We concur with this sentiment. We also recognize that issues of cause and effect with respect to ethnocultural variables are tremendously complicated. We also believe, however, that the most effective antidote for harmful stereotypes is careful and sensitive analysis of systematically collected evidence.

REFERENCES

Adebimpe, V. R. (1994). Race, racism, and epidemiological surveys. *Hospital & Community Psychiatry, 45,* 27–31.

American Psychiatric Association. (1980). *Diagnostic and statistical manual of mental disorders (3rd ed.).* Washington, DC: Author.

American Psychiatric Association. (1987). *Diagnostic and statistical manual of mental disorders* (3rd ed., rev.). Washington, DC: Author.

Archibald, H. C., & Tuddenham, R. D. (1965). Persistent stress reaction after combat: A 20-year follow-up. *Archives of General Psychiatry, 12,* 475–481.

Bell, C. C. (1994). Race as a variable in research: Being specific and fair. *Hospital & Community Psychiatry, 45,* 5.

Breslau, N., Davis, G. C., Andreski, P., & Peterson, E. (1991). Traumatic events and post-traumatic stress disorder in an urban population of young adults. *Archives of General Psychiatry, 48,* 216–222.

Brill, N., & Beebe, G. (1956). *A follow-up study of war neuroses* (VA Medical Monograph). Washington, DC: U.S. Government Printing Office.

Centers for Disease Control Vietnam Experience Study. (1988). Health status of Vietnam veterans: I. Psychosocial characteristics. *Journal of the American Medical Association, 259,* 2701–2707.

Chemtob, C., Roitblat, H. L., Hamada, R. S., Carlson, J. G., & Twentyman, C. T. (1988). A cognitive action theory of post-traumatic stress disorder. *Journal of Anxiety Disorders, 2,* 253–275.

Cochran, W. G. (1983). *Planning and analysis of observational studies*. New York: Wiley & Sons.

Davidson, J., Smith, R., & Kudler, H. (1989). Familial psychiatric illness in chronic posttraumatic stress disorder. *Comprehensive Psychiatry, 30*, 339–345.

de Girolamo, G. (1993). International perspectives on the treatment and prevention of posttraumatic stress disorders. In J. P. Wilson and B. Raphael (Eds.), *International handbook of traumatic stress syndromes*. New York: Plenum.

Egendorf, A., Kadushin, C., Laufer, R. S., Rothbart, G., & Sloan, L. (1981). *Legacies of Vietnam: Comparative adjustment of veterans and their peers*. Washington, DC: U.S. Government Printing Office.

Escobar, J. (1987). Commentary: Post-traumatic stress disorder and the perennial stress-diathesis controversy. *Journal of Nervous and Mental Disease, 175*, 265–266.

Fairbank, J. A., Schlenger, W. E., Caddell, J. M., & Woods, M. G. (1993). Posttraumatic stress disorder. In P. B. Sutker & H. E. Adams (Eds.), *Comprehensive handbook of psychopathology* (2nd ed.). New York: Plenum Press.

Foa, E. B., Steketee, G., & Rothbaum, B. O. (1989). Behavioral/cognitive conceptualizations of post-traumatic stress disorder. *Behavior Therapy, 20*, 155–176.

Foy, D. W., Osato, S. S., Houskamp, B. M., & Neumann, D. A. (1992). PTSD etiology. In P. A. Saigh (Ed.), *Post-traumatic stress disorder: A behavioral approach to assessment and treatment*. New York: Pergamon Press.

Futterman, S., & Pumpian-Midlin, E. (1951). Traumatic war neuroses five years later. *American Journal of Psychiatry, 108*, 401–408.

Gleser, G., Green, B., & Winget, C. (1981). *Prolonged psychosocial effects of disaster: A study of Buffalo Creek*. New York: Academic Press.

Goldberg, J., True, W. R., Eisen, S. A., & Henderson, W. G. (1990). A twin study of the effects of the Vietnam war on posttraumatic stress disorder. *Journal of the American Medical Association, 263*, 1227–1232.

Green, B. L., Grace, M. C., Lindy, J. D., Gleser, G. C., & Leonard, A. (1990). Risk factors for PTSD and other diagnoses in a general sample of Vietnam veterans. *American Journal of Psychiatry, 147*, 729–733.

Green, B. L., Grace, M. C., Lindy, J. D., & Leonard, A. (1990). Race differences in response to combat stress. *Journal of Traumatic Stress, 3*, 379–393.

Green, B. L., Lindy, J. D., Grace, M. C., Gleser, G. C., Leonard, A. C., Korol, M., & Winget, C. (1990). Buffalo Creek survivors in the second decade: Stability of stress symptoms. *American Journal of Orthopsychiatry, 60*, 43–54.

Hamada, R. S., Chemtob, C. M., Sautner, B., & Sato, R. (1988). Ethnic identity and Vietnam: A Japanese-American Vietnam veteran with PTSD. *Hawaii Medical Journal, 47*, 100–109.

Helzer, J. E., Robins, L. N., & McEvoy, M. A. (1987). Post-traumatic stress disorder in the general population: Findings of the Epidemiologic Catchment Area Survey. *New England Journal of Medicine, 317*, 1630–1634.

Horowitz, M. (1974). Stress response syndromes: Character style and dynamic psychotherapy. *Archives of General Psychiatry, 31,* 768–781.

Horowitz, M. J., & Kaltreider, N. B. (1980). Brief psychotherapy of stress response syndromes. In T. B. Karasu & L. Bellak (Eds.), *Specialized techniques in individual psychotherapy.* New York: Brunner/Mazel.

Jones, J. C., & Barlow, D. H. (1990). The etiology of posttraumatic stress disorder. *Clinical Psychology Review, 10,* 299–328.

Keane, T. (1989). Post-traumatic stress disorder: Current status and future directions. *Behavior Therapy, 20,* 149–153

Keane, T., Zimering, R., & Caddell, J. (1985). A behavioral formulation of post-traumatic stress disorder in Vietnam veterans. *The Behavior Therapist, 8,* 9–12.

Keehn, R. J., Goldberg, I. E., & Beebe, G. W. (1974). Twenty-four year mortality follow up of Army veterans with disability separations for psychoneurosis in 1944. *Psychosomatic Medicine, 36*(1), 27–46.

Kilpatrick, D., Best, C. Veronen, L., Amick, A., Villeponteaux, L, & Ruff, G. (1985). Mental health correlates of criminal victimization: A random community survey. *Journal of Consulting & Clinical Psychology, 53,* 866–873.

Klonoff, H., McDougall, G., Clark, C., Kramer, P., & Horgan, J. (1976). The neuropsychological, psychiatric, and physical effects of prolonged and severe stress: 30 years later. *The Journal of Nervous & Mental Disease, 163,* 246–252.

Kluznick, J. C., Speed, N., Van-Valkenburg, C., & Magraw, R. (1986). Forty-year follow-up of United States Prisoners of War. *American Journal of Psychiatry, 143,* 240–245.

Krystal, J. H., Kosten, T. R., Southwick, S., Mason, J. W., Perry, B. D., & Giller, E. L. (1989). Neurobiological aspects of PTSD: Review of clinical and preclinical studies. *Behavior Therapy, 20,* 177–198.

Kulka, R. A., Schlenger, W. E., Fairbank, J. A., Hough, R. L., Jordan, B. K., Marmar, C. R., & Weiss, D. S. (1990a). *The National Vietnam Veterans Readjustment Study: Tables of findings and technical appendices.* New York: Brunner/Mazel.

Kulka, R. A., Schlenger, W. E., Fairbank, J. A., Hough, R. L., Jordan, B. K., Marmar, C. R., & Weiss, D. S. (1990b). *Trauma and the Vietnam War Generation: Report of findings from the National Vietnam Veterans Readjustment Study.* New York: Brunner/Mazel.

Kulka R. A., Schlenger, W. E., Fairbank, J. A., Hough, R. L., Jordan, B. K., Marmar, C. R., & Weiss, D. S. (1991). Assessment of PTSD in the community: Prospects and pitfalls from recent studies of Vietnam veterans. *Psychological Assessment, 3,* 547–560.

Laufer, R., Brett, E., & Gallops, M. (1985). Symptom patterns associated with post-traumatic stress disorder among Vietnam veterans exposed to war trauma. *American Journal of Psychiatry, 142,* 1304–1311.

Laufer, R. S., Gallops, M. S., & Frey-Wouters, E. (1984). War stress and trauma: The Vietnam veteran experience. *Journal of Health & Social Behavior, 25,* 65–85.

Lazarus, R., & Folkman, S. (1984). *Stress, appraisal, and coping.* New York: Springer.

Litz, B. T., & Keane, T. M. (1989). Information processing in anxiety disorders: Application to the understanding of post-traumatic stress disorder. *Clinical Psychology Review, 9,* 243–257.

Loo, C. M. (in press). The Asian American Vietnam veteran: Race-related trauma and PTSD. *Journal of Traumatic Stress.*

Marsella, A. J., Chemtob, C., & Hamada, R. (1992). Ethnocultural aspects of PTSD. *National Centers for PTSD Newsletter, 1,* 1–2.

Marsella, A. J., Friedman, M., & Spain, H. (1993). Ethnocultural aspects of PTSD: Issues and directions. In J. Oldham, M. Riba, & A. Tasman (Eds.), *Review of psychiatry.* Washington, DC: American Psychiatric Press, 157–181.

McFarlane, A. (1988). The etiology of PTSD following a natural disaster. *British Journal of Psychiatry, 152,* 116–121.

Meehl, P. (1962). Schizotaxia, schizotypy, schizophrenia. *American Psychologist, 17,* 827–838.

Nadelson, C., Notman, M., Zackson, H., & Gornick, J. (1982). A follow-up study of rape victims. *American Journal of Psychiatry, 139,* 1266–1270.

Penk, W. E., & Allen, I. M. (1991). Clinical assessment of post-traumatic stress disorder among minorities who served in Vietnam. *Journal of Traumatic Stress, 4,* 41–66.

Schlenger, W. E., Kulka, R. A., Fairbank, J. A., Hough, R. L., Jordan, B. K., Marmar, C. R., & Weiss, D. S. (1992). The prevalence of post-traumatic stress disorder in the Vietnam generation: A multimethod, multisource assessment of psychiatric disorder. *Journal of Traumatic Stress, 5,* 333–363.

Shore, J., Tatum, E., & Vollmer, W. (1986). Evaluation of mental effects of disaster: Mount St. Helens eruption. *American Journal of Public Health, 76(Suppl. 3),* 76–83.

Smith, E., North, C., McCool, R., & Shea, J. (1990). Acute postdisaster psychiatric disorders: Identification of persons at risk. *American Journal of Psychiatry, 147,* 202–206.

Snow, B. R., Stellman, J. M., Stellman, S. D., & Sommer, J. F. (1988). Post-traumatic stress disorder among American Legionaires in relation to combat experience in Vietnam: Associated and contributing factors. *Environmental Research, 47,* 175–192.

Solomon, Z. (1989). Psychological sequelae of war: A 3-year prospective study of Israeli combat stress reaction casualties. *Journal of Nervous & Mental Disease, 177,* 342–346.

Solomon, Z., Benbenishty, R., & Mikulincer, M. (1991). The contribution of wartime, pre-war, and post-war factors to self-efficacy: A longitudinal study of combat stress reaction. *Journal of Traumatic Stress, 4,* 345–361.

Solomon, Z., Bleich, A., Shoham, S., Nardi, C., & Kotler, M. (1992). The "Koach" project for treatment of combat-related PTSD: Rationale, aims, and methodology. *Journal of Traumatic Stress, 5,* 175–193.

Solomon, Z., & Mikulincer, M. (1988). Psychological sequelae of war: A 2-year follow-up study of Israeli combat stress reaction casualties. *Journal of Nervous & Mental Disease, 176,* 264–269.

Solomon, Z., Mikulincer, M., & Benbenishty, R. (1989). Locus of control and combat-related post-traumatic stress disorder: The intervening role of battle intensity, threat appraisal, and coping. *British Journal of Clinical Psychology, 28,* 131–144.

Solomon, Z., Weisenberg, M., Schwarzwald, J., & Mikulincer, M. (1987). Post-traumatic stress disorder among frontline soldiers with combat stress reaction: 1982 Israeli experience. *American Journal of Psychiatry, 144,* 448–454.

Steinglass, P., & Gerrity, E. (1990). Natural disasters and post-traumatic stress disorder: Short-term vs. long-term recovery in two disaster-affected communities. *Journal of Applied Social Psychology, 20,* 1746–1765.

Sutker, P. B., Allain, A. N., & Winstead, D. K. (1993). Psychopathology and psychiatric diagnoses of World War II Pacific theater prisoner of war survivors and combat veterans. *American Journal of Psychiatry, 150,* 240–245.

Weisaeth, L., & Eitinger, L. (1991a). Research on PTSD and other post-traumatic reactions: European literature. *PTSD Research Quarterly, 2,* 1–7.

Weisaeth, L., & Eitinger, L. (1991b). Research on PTSD and other post-traumatic reactions: European literature (Part II). *PTSD Research Quarterly, 2,* 1–8.

Winfield, I., George, L., Swartz, M., & Blazer, D. (1990). Sexual assault and psychiatric disorders among a community sample of women. *American Journal of Psychiatry, 147,* 335–341.

Zubin, J., & Spring, B. (1977). Vulnerability: A new view of schizophrenia. *Journal of Abnormal Psychology, 86,* 103–126.

V

ETHNOCULTURAL CONSIDERATIONS IN THERAPY AND MENTAL HEALTH SERVICES FOR PTSD

17

A MULTICULTURAL DEVELOPMENTAL APPROACH FOR TREATING TRAUMA

FRED. D. GUSMAN, JUDITH STEWART, BRUCE HILEY YOUNG,
SHERRY J. RINEY, FRANCIS R. ABUEG, and DUDLEY DAVID BLAKE

INTRODUCTION

The ability to treat trauma victims is enhanced when the clinician fully integrates an appreciation of cultural differences. This chapter draws upon decades of direct clinical experience with victims of a wide range of catastrophic stress including natural disaster, child abuse, sexual assault, and combat. To elucidate our approach, we begin with case examples drawn from (a) the Japanese American internment experience and (b) the Vietnam war. These extreme traumas of isolation, terror, and fear of death highlight the convergence of social, moral, and political issues in the minority experience of victimization.

The Case of "Pat"

Pat was 15 years old in 1942 when President Franklin D. Roosevelt signed the order for the internment of all Japanese Americans. Pat and his family were forced to move, and as a result, Pat and his family lost their home, their community's support, their friendships, and their sources of livelihood and recreation. As internees, their multicultural identity as Japanese Americans was instantaneously redefined as untrustworthy enemies of the state. Furthermore, they were viewed as

439

people who were somehow less than the German or Italian immigrants whose countries of national origin were equally at war with the United States but who were not interned. Common responses to the internment included feelings of betrayal, outrage, shame, and helplessness.

In addition, the adverse conditions of the internment camps worsened the violations of Pat's sense of self and dignity. Victimized by violence and lack of privacy, Pat recalls shifting from being socially active to increasingly withdrawn and apathetic. As his preinternment Japanese American identity was being destroyed, the resulting void left Pat an adolescent without an integrated identity. Perceiving himself as neither American, Japanese, nor Japanese American, Pat was left with the impossibility of finding or developing an acceptable identity in place, culture, and time. In retrospect, this formidable developmental task remained incomplete for the 15-year-old Pat, and a loss of self-cohesion ensued.

Fifty years later, when a flood destroyed much of Pat's home and personal possessions, like other flood victims, he showed the common signs of posttraumatic stress. In addition, as the federal application process to repair his home became increasingly complicated by bureaucratic procedures, Pat experienced overwhelming anxiety. The cognitions associated with his anxiety included suicidal ideation, helplessness, and the existential angst of questioning who he was and where he belonged. Unlike other victims who are commonly irritated by the application process, in Pat's case the governmental procedures precipitated a reactivation of the intense psychological sequelae of the internment: feelings of mistrust, shame, alienation, and a tenuous sense of identity.

Pat sought therapy, and although the therapeutic process is not complete, he has reported more manageable levels of anxiety, has overcome his apathy (completing the federal relief application process), and has begun to experience a positive sense of identity again as a Japanese American. The clinical regimen of exploring and affirming the affect associated with his traumatic experiences, combined with providing support for redeveloping his multicultural identity, appear to promote Pat's experience of greater self-cohesion.

The Case of "Clay"

Clay is an American Indian war veteran raised in San Francisco. During his military service, he was nicknamed *Chief* by his fellow squad members and, because of his ethnicity and appearance, was believed to have stereotypical American Indian traits (e.g., keen senses and an ability to track). Based on this assumption, he was selected to *walk point* (i.e., walk at the front of his squad when on patrol) and, wanting to be a team member, agreed to do so. He accepted the role of point man as a challenge and learned to do the job well without realizing the potential challenge to his identity issues. Clay struggled with conflicting feelings regarding the squad's assumptions of his abilities to sense and to track and his desire to take on the role as part of his American Indian identity.

While he was point man, there were no enemy encounters, thereby reinforcing his own and the squad's perceptions of his exceptional abilities. During a time when another squad member was in the point position, the squad walked into an ambush and experienced several casualties. Clay felt guilty and responsible for the encounter because he was not walking point at the time. Thereafter, he and the squad incurred numerous casualties from a series of catastrophic engagements with enemy units.

Following his discharge from the military, Clay returned to San Francisco where he eventually sought treatment for intrusive war memories, nightmares, and rage. His therapist learned that Clay was raised in an urban environment, with little exposure to traditional American Indian culture. The treatment process began with helping Clay to identify who he was prior to the military and combat, recognizing that he was an urban American Indian whose family was well assimilated into general society. Clay's parents encouraged him to view himself as a member of the larger society so that he might accomplish more in his life without the potential restrictions of his ethnicity. His military and combat experiences directly conflicted with those parentally instilled mainstream culture views because he was labeled *Chief* and was expected to have the special talents and abilities of a stereotypical American Indian. Clay accepted this label in direct opposition to stronger self-identification with his Americanized self.

The therapist assisted Clay in examining his life using a developmental perspective, identifying connections between events and his evolution into adulthood and evaluating pretrauma circumstances that helped shape his identity. In addition, Clay was able to experiment with an increasingly more complex cultural identity in the context of a war trauma group (with 8 members) as well as the larger community of patients in the center (more than 80 other war veteran patients). This process helped Clay to reorganize and begin to understand his beliefs, values, expectations, and fears at the time he entered the military and later when he was walking point in the bush. While reviewing the traumatic events, the therapist helped Clay to find new and positive meanings of the events (e.g., a greater appreciation for and connection with his heritage), providing a sense of control in his life and over his past.

THE ETHNOCULTURAL FACTOR IN PTSD

The population of the United States is multicultural. Each person in America is part of several cultures shaped by ethnic, religious, or political values; and exposure to metropolitan or rural, educational, or biotechnological environments. In addition, each person in the United States has ancestors that have immigrated to America or, in the case of American Indians, has ancestry who were forced to live within a culture other than their own. Any one individual, therefore, may have a multicultural identity or several self-conceptualizations that may or may not form a unified, culturally coherent identity (Madsen, 1964). Mental health treatment provided to individuals diagnosed with PTSD should address the points of interaction between victims' multicultural identity and their traumatization (e.g., Marsella, Chemtob, & Hamada, 1990; Westermeyer, 1989; Young & Erickson, 1988, see also chapter 4, this volume).

Traditional acculturation and bicultural models (e.g., Berry, 1990; Gordon, 1964; Sue & Sue, 1990) assume that an individual moves toward the dominant culture and away from their culture of origin. Numerous important findings, especially in the area of immigrant adjustment, have emerged from this model. In contrast, the multicultural model proposed by Oetting and Beauvais (1990) suggests that a unidimensional description of race or ethnicity is not tenable in the study of the complexities of American culture. With immigration and blending of various ethnic origins, sole dominant identifications do not provide for an adequate understanding of mixed heritage. Indeed, for many Americans several independent identities with separate origins may coexist and may be maintained behaviorally and cognitively over time (Boehlein, 1987).

This multicultural perspective also is rooted in role theory and suggests that a person can hold simultaneously a number of ethnic identities, each composed of a dynamic network of attitudes and beliefs (Goode, 1960; Gove & Tudor, 1973; Pearlin, 1983; Sarbin, 1954). When one's primary ethnic identity is different than that of the dominant culture, and when a situation draws on a multitude of identities (such as in the case of Pat) or when others in the society define an individual as having unique nondominant identities (such as in Clay's case), one may be seen as having the status of an ethnic minority.

Primary and Secondary Crisis Intervention

This chapter describes a multicultural conceptual framework for guiding interventions with traumatized individuals. Relevant here is our belief that two principal opportunities for intervention exist that may occur at numerous points during an individual's life. The first opportunity occurs immediately after the traumatic events and involves helping the individual to begin dealing with the trauma and its implications at an occasion more proximal to that event. Intervening at this point may be critical for circumventing long-range adverse effects of trauma exposure (i.e., chronic posttraumatic stress disorder or PTSD).

As an example, the research literature both with war veterans and rape victims suggests that failing to intervene or provide a supportive environment may prolong or exacerbate PTSD-related symptoms (Barrett & Mizes, 1988; Coates, & Winston, 1983; Keane, Scott, Chavoya, Lamparski, & Fairbank, 1985; Lindenthal, Thomas, Claudwell, & Myers, 1971; Steiner & Neumann, 1978). Treatment provided at this juncture can be construed as *primary crisis intervention*. Critical incident stress debriefing (CISD; Mitchell, 1983) is an example of this form of crisis intervention.

When traumatized individuals request assistance in dealing with catastrophic experiences and their effects (e.g., sleep disturbance, isolation, hypervigilance, etc.), the conventional intervention involves supporting the victims by listening to their experiences and attempting to normalize their feelings. In some cases, this type of debriefing provides immediate relief. This brief cathartic treatment arrests some symptoms in those who are mildly or moderately affected by the events but may have little impact on those who are severely affected or who have a history of multiple traumas that remain unresolved (and for which related symptoms may have been reactivated by the recent event). Brief interventions of this type do not *typically* address the event's impact on an individual's unique sociocultural identities.

A second opportunity for intervention occurs later in the traumatized person's life during times of stress related to major turning points in life (e.g., divorce, death of loved ones, debilitating injuries, etc.). Because stressful life events can be expected to occur more frequently than traumatic events, this treatment condition may be the most frequent point of intervention. Treatment at this juncture can be construed as *secondary crisis intervention*. Inpatient treatment and longer-term outpatient therapy are prime examples of this type of crisis intervention. Both primary and secondary crisis interventions should include the cultural and identity considerations presented in this book and can follow the developmental and constructivist framework described in this chapter.

The Challenge of Treating PTSD in Ethnocultural Minorities

Ongoing treatment of the ethnic minority patient with PTSD presents an important and unique challenge to the mental health professional. To a significant degree, PTSD involves social avoidance and isolation (American Psychiatric Association, 1987; Wilson & Zigelbaum, 1986). The experience of PTSD often is described by patients as "feeling different from others" or "feeling like no one can really understand."

Individuals who grow up and live in a culture that is not congruent with aspects of their cultural identity often experience conflicts centered on belongingness, trust, and safety (Rodriguez, 1987). Furthermore, mainstream American society, for example, also tends to undergo relatively rapid changes that can compound the significant challenges inherent in acculturating to that mainstream culture (see Young & Erickson, 1988).

Therefore, identity conflicts, compounded by traumatization, may enhance the severity or breadth of life problems experienced by the ethnic minority patient with PTSD (Brende & Parson, 1985). We agree with others that PTSD and ethnic minority status often interact to produce a heightened sense of isolation, disenfranchisement, and shame (Young & Erickson, 1988). The treating therapist is aided significantly by adopting a working model that addresses these multiple and interactive factors that contribute to subjective experience.

A Constructivist and Developmental Perspective

We approach the challenge of PTSD treatment with assumptions based on a constructivist and developmental framework. A *constructivist perspective* is founded on a belief in the proactive and self-organizing features of human experience. This perspective assumes that there is a form-giving, meaning-making part to each of us, so that for every waking moment of our lives an account is produced of who we are, what we are doing, and why we are doing it. Trauma stresses this meaning-making component to the extreme, at times leading to a rigidity and inflexible repetitiveness in the process of meaning-making. The trauma therapist needs to assume the constructive meaning-making function, thus aiding traumatized persons in their progress toward regaining the willingness and ability to be active, interpretive agents engaged in an exploratory process of meaning-making (Stewart, 1992).

A *developmental perspective* within the constructivist framework assumes that the self-organizing features of human knowing at any moment in the individual's life arise from the accumulation and, most important, the organization of experiences and interpretations of self and world across the entire life of the person (Mahoney, 1991; Carlsen, 1991). Such a developmentally informed constructivist view assumes that learning, knowing, and memory are phenomena that reflect the ongoing attempts of body and brain to reorganize continually action patterns and experience patterns—namely, prior learning—that are intimately related to highly dynamic, momentary experiencing.

Therefore, (a) the meaning of trauma or how trauma is construed varies widely from patient to patient, even within a single ethnic minority subgroup; (b) these meanings are accessible to the therapist through careful questioning, for example, understanding the developmental history of the patient, recognizing cultural factors and previous traumatization, and accessing the complex system of meaning networks associated with the trauma and posttrauma; and (c) posttraumatic symptoms often are expressed differently among different ethnic subgroups, and the symptoms exhibited may not be represented adequately in our diagnostic taxonomy.

A DEVELOPMENTAL MODEL FOR VIEWING TRAUMATIZATION

To understand the relationship between the traumatic event and its impact on the self, it is important to take an in-depth approach. This approach involves explicitly recognizing that trauma is a violation of self; a developmental meaning-based model can be applied to illuminate the ways in which the self has been violated. The developmental model encompasses the individual's *entire* life history, including the traumatic experiences. Using the model helps the therapist move beyond extinction of symptoms by helping the individual identify a full range of variables related to the origin of the symptoms and how these variables interact with the nature of the traumatic events.

The developmental model also provides the opportunity for the victim to identify personal coping mechanisms and their point of origin. These coping mechanisms may be initiated prior to, during, or immediately following the traumatic event; they may be healthy or they may be maladaptive. The evolution of how the individual perceives self prior to, during, and after the traumatic events and how these self-perceptions are overtly and covertly modified can assist the individual in meaningfully integrating the traumatic experience.

To implement the developmental model, it is essential that a preliminary psychosocial evaluation be completed to determine severity of posttraumatic stress, possible comorbidities, and sociocultural influences. Educating the victim about posttraumatic stress and its potential impact at this juncture sets the foundation for going beyond crisis management to understanding how the traumatic experiences have affected the victim's self-perception.

Assumptions About Self

We view traumatic experiences as violations of the self. We do not assume any particular theoretical position on whether a self exists and what that entails (cf. Dennett, 1978); rather, we understand that people, for whatever reason, believe that they have a self and that certain behavior is predictable from it. This self has several components, three of which are particularly important when dealing with issues of cross-cultural sensitivity.

First, there is the self as the accumulation of learned probabilities based on how the person has acted in the past. The self contains all of the expectations for self-action and anticipation about world responses, both of which are weighted for their subjective importance. For example, I may expect that I will brush my teeth with my right hand but if I happen to use my left, it will not be significant for me or for those in my world. However, if I am usually a person who expresses anger verbally but I resort to physical violence when someone has angered me, a significant violation of my anticipations or expectations for my behavior will occur and will have more profound consequences for those in my world.

Second, there is the self as the idealization of what the person *ought* or *wants* to be. Such aspects of self may be historically based, as in the individual's idealization of a parent, but also they may be idealizations of a culturally transmitted group member ideal. Third, there are what we have come to call *self-fragments*. These also may be historically based expectations or idealizations, but they do not fit within a structured, multidimensional self-system. The person may have incorporated only one action directive as a cultural ideal without this fitting into a larger unifying framework.

In extreme situations in which expectations about how the world works fail, the anticipations of how a person will respond based on past experiences also may be invalidated. This may shift the person into attempting to behave like the ought-or-want-to-be ideal or may facilitate the person's reliance on fragmented behaviors. Stress occurs when the historically based anticipations and the idealized expectations conflict with the domain in which the person is acting. In particular, when no action can satisfy environmental demands and maintain all aspects of self, the person may feel extreme frustration. An example of this is provided via the following clinical vignette.

The Case of Alice

Alice is a female Vietnam veteran of American Indian heritage. She dresses and is groomed in a way that does not express her Indian heritage, is married to a non-Indian, works in a large metropolitan area with a non-Indian population, and on coming into inpatient treatment did not avail herself of the counseling offered by a nurse specialist who has worked with Indian populations and is considered knowledgeable and approachable. Alice had stated on admission that she liked to go driving to deserted areas as a way to be alone and escape from her problems and that one day she would attempt suicide by driving off a high mountain. One of her early requests for a weekend pass was to go for a drive alone, on a holiday weekend when her family had decided not to visit her, along the mountain ridges not far from the hospital. This request was denied based on program policy; that is, it involved isolative behavior that was connected to stated suicidal ideation.

Alice became furious when her pass was denied, despite extensive discussion and feedback by staff and peers as to its apparent dysfunctional basis. The anger was excessive, including physical acting out by a normally mild-mannered woman, such that it appeared that some deeper, more meaningful issue had been activated. A culturally uninformed view might have assumed that the patient's plans for isolation, and possible suicide, had been thwarted and that alone explained the magnitude of the angry response. However, the clinician responded to the patient's consistency in speaking of the mountain as a *high place*, and wondered whether this term had a special meaning.

Initially, the patient denied any special meaning and said she just talked funny at times. However, by maintaining the focus on the meaning of going to a high place, the clinician, with the aid of the patient's peers, came to see that this action was part of an idealized, and to some degree, historically based anticipation derived from this apparently highly acculturated woman's Indian heritage.

The meaning structures that were discovered were as follows: "To fit in I must be a good Indian"; "To be a good Indian means giving up Indian ways"; "Going to a high place means being an Indian"; "Acting like an Indian means being cast out by the group (e. g., authorities, peers)"; "Therefore, going to the mountain means being cast out (loss of the non-Indian aspect)"; "Not going to a high place means feeling like I am dying (loss of the Indian aspect)."

The tension between these choices resulted in extreme frustration and, eventually, anger. Alice had hoped to be allowed to have a pass without discussion of its meaning to her—in other words, to be able to allow the Indian aspect to be present without threatening the non-Indian aspects of her self. However, addressing this dilemma in fact was an important key to the war-zone-related trauma work because in the war zone her Indianness had contributed to her being locked out of a compound because she was mistaken for a Vietnamese person.

A significant part of the healing for Alice arose from her being able to acknowledge both the Indian and the non-Indian anticipations, idealizations, and fragments of her self without being rejected by the staff or her non-Indian peers. The therapist's approach to this situation was informed by the constructivist–developmentalist therapy framework described earlier.

CULTURALLY SENSITIVE TREATMENT OF PTSD

To concretize the conceptual framework used at the Clinical Laboratory of the National Center for PTSD, we will outline a working model for culturally sensitive trauma treatment. In assessing a trauma victim across the lifespan, it is valuable to track the origin, development, and maintenance of the full range of self-components and of unique personal, cultural, and social identifications. The individual's identity or set of identities is entwined, often intimately, in current expressions of PTSD and, thus, in its treatment. In the next section, we will provide guidelines for the elicitation of patients' unique constructions of their traumatic experiences and the cognitive–affective reconstructions that occur in treatment.

The Three-Way Mirror: A Therapy Heuristic

In our trauma work, we employ a heuristic, the Three-Way Mirror, for elucidating the complexities of multiple identities for the patient in therapy. This heuristic incorporates both constructivist and developmental tenets within a life narrative framework (Schafer, 1992; Stewart, 1992). The Three-Way Mirror (see Figure 1) provides a reflection of the individual's pretrauma, trauma, and posttrauma contexts. This visual aid is used also with patients to enhance their ability to understand the connections between the trauma and their multiple identifications.

The pretrauma panel represents the significant events prior to the individual's traumatic experiences and serves as a reference point. A number of important developmental themes and issues tend to emerge and can and should be addressed in the therapeutic context. Pretrauma themes include cultural practices, control, power, vulnerability, fear, relationships, intimacy, family, gender roles, sexuality, and religion. Within each of these themes the individual's beliefs, values, expectations, fears, and behaviors are explored and examined.

The middle panel focuses on the traumatic experience. In particular, specific processes are acknowledged, including: (a) attempts to suppress recollections of the event (e.g., numbing or denial) to escape from the stress and anxiety, (b) aggression as an attempt to gain control over the experience and emotion, and (c) survival coping mechanisms that can be interpreted as appropriate during the traumatic experience but can lead to maladaptive behavior.

The third panel represents the accumulation of one's life experiences, both before and during the traumatic events, that overtly or covertly influence how one functions and how one relates to new experiences. The three panels cover related issues discussed by Westermeyer (1987) in a six-point model for eliciting information about PTSD symptoms and the implications of these symptoms to the individual.

The Different Selves

Three important additional features of the three-way mirror are the experiential self, the observing self, and the new integrated self-representation. The experiential self represents the individual subjectively viewing and affectively processing life experiences both in isolated panels

THREE-WAY MIRROR

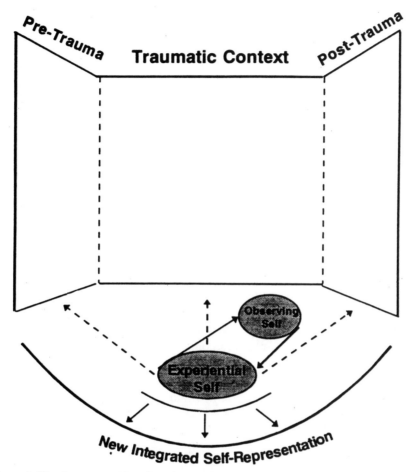

Figure 1. The three-way mirror is a therapy heuristic. The three panels of the mirror represent our developmental orientation. Affective and cognitive processing allows for a new, more intergrated self-representation.

and in total. The observing self represents the opportunity that arises for the individual to assess experiences and behaviors and their meanings objectively when some psychological distance from the emotional content of all the experiences represented in the panels, including the traumatic events, is obtained.

As the individual becomes able to move flexibly between the experiential and observing modes of processing, a new integrated self-representation can be developed. This new integrated self-representation represents the working through and incorporation of traumatic experiences within a unified and continuous life narrative such that the individual experiences self-cohesion and some degree of meaningfulness and integration across life experiences.

New Self-Representations

The three-way mirror is a vehicle for helping the patient adopt a new, integrated self-representation. Through experiencing and observing one's life course, the patient makes connections and draws conclusions with respect to pretrauma, trauma, and posttrauma contexts, resulting in a reframing of the traumatic experiences and self. These stages of treatment are embedded in an overall program that is integrated and sequential in nature. Such integrative and sequential treatment is well suited to trauma work in general, but particularly when dealing with the complexities introduced in the treatment of trauma when multiple cultural selves (i.e., learned probabilities, idealizations, and fragments) are present (Loo, 1993).

Alice: An Application of the Treatment Model

To illustrate the three-way mirror, we will return to the case of Alice, the American Indian patient introduced earlier. As noted, she identified primarily with the dominant, Anglo-American culture. Psychosocial evaluations supported this impression. Alice exhibited moderate to severe PTSD symptoms with sporadic alcohol abuse. However, she had been employed continuously since the war, had been married for more than 20 years, and had raised two college-age children with whom she reportedly had a good relationship. Her relationship with her husband had become progressively more troubled, and at the time of her seeking intensive treatment, she feared that a divorce was imminent.

In the extensive assessment, completed during the first 2 weeks of her stay in the program, Alice did not refer to cultural practices associated with her Indian heritage. Conventional psychological assessment (e.g., the Clinician Administered PTSD Scale [CAPS; Blake et al., 1990] or the Structured Clinical Interview for *DSM–III–R* Patient Edition [SCID-R; Spitzer, Williams, Gibbon, & First, 1989]) may not elicit this information and, furthermore, it is not uncommon for individuals strongly identified with multiple cultures to assign different meanings to the symptoms in question (e.g., visions as part of religious practices as opposed to visual hallucinations).

However, when turning to the work of exploring themes, patterns, and self-conceptions across the lifespan, hints of a greater complexity of self-patterning and cultural affiliation begin to unfold. A useful tool for initiating exploration of the pretrauma self is the written pretrauma autobiography. A list of questions is provided that helps the individual begin to reflect on the pretrauma environment and what expectations were developed around such issues as family; how to act and think given the individual's gender and religious and cultural practices; and ideas of self and self in relationships. Writing the autobiography begins the process of identifying the learned probabilities of self, the idealizations of how the person *ought* or *wants* to be, and at times can provide hints to fragments of self.

In the case of Alice, the writing of the pretrauma autobiography clarified the cultural split that had been introduced early in her life and offered explanation for her determined attempt to present only the non-Indian side in the institutional context of the hospital. She had been raised on a reservation within a large, extended, loving family, with clear culturally congruent gender role differentiation.

At about 8 years of age, it was decided that Alice should go to Catholic boarding school. At that school, the split and accompanying tension was established. She was made to feel that Indian ways were "evil" uncivilized, and un-Christian, and she was punished by practices of rejection and condemnation whenever she allowed some Indian aspect of herself to surface. Thus, that which was "good" was non-Indian; that which was spiritually and interpersonally rich was "bad." As a result, Alice developed fear that others might see core aspects of her self; thus, to show Indian aspects of self became entwined with the danger of being harmed (e.g., rejected and abandoned).

During the trauma focus work, it became clear that this split was operative in the war zone. Newly arrived in country, she found herself outside the compound without identification and was denied entry because she looked like the enemy. Thus, as in her youth, being identified as *different* equated with being dangerous and bad.

Throughout her time in Vietnam, she appears to have engaged with these two selves, at times flaunting her identification with the enemy and rebelling against military constraints, in what were occasionally quite dangerous activities. These behaviors can be seen as instances of denial and of coping by reconstruing reality. Thus, we see a core theme established as critical for self-definition in childhood is central to understanding trauma-related behavior (i.e., the second panel of the Three-Way Mirror).

During the latter period of treatment, Alice participated in a group that focused on the entire lifespan, particularly on identifying reenactments in the posttrauma period (Stewart, 1993). Such reenactments can be a result of the dysfunctional extension of trauma-related coping mechanisms or the desire to redo the trauma with a different conclusion. It is in the work of this period that the themes that are continuous across the lifespan are identified and the subtle and not so subtle modifications of these themes via experience, particularly traumatic experiences, are reflected.

In a graph of her posttrauma life, in which she traced the emotional and functional ups and downs of this period with the use of icons to represent recurrent influences (e.g., trees represent periods of spiritual reconnection with high places), the two selves generally entwined and hovered in an emotionally neutral plane of the graph. However, for a period of 3 years she had allowed herself to work on a reservation and to live once again following Indian ways. At this point the two selves separated, with clearly differentiated emotional tones associated with each. The happy, joyful self was the Indian one; the sad, restless self was the other. The association of the Indian self with badness continued to some degree because her residence on the reservation far from home adversely affected her nuclear, Anglo family.

Despite this, she felt that this brief period post-Vietnam was the only time that she had had moments of happiness, calm, and contentment. She could assume an observing stance with regard to these two selves and could talk about the different anticipations and idealizations of each and how they often were in conflict. This focused her healing and recovery on finding a resolution so that she could more readily embrace and integrate both self-components.

RELATED MULTICULTURAL PERSPECTIVES ON TRAUMA AND RECOVERY

Catherall (1989) provided a valuable reference for the clinical implications of multiculturalism and PTSD treatment. Two central clinical issues were conceptualized: (a) conflicts in self-integration and (b) the loss of self-cohesion. In conflicts in self-integration the victim is intact characterologically but cannot assimilate or tolerate the feelings associated with the trauma. In such cases, the victim's self-identity is not a primary clinical issue. However, in cases of the loss of self-cohesion, characterized by the misalignment and dysynchrony between victims and their social environment, the psychological impact is more severe and results in social withdrawal, feelings of mistrust and alienation, identity disturbance, and interpersonal difficulties.

These symptoms amount to a *disorder of the multicultural self*. Here, as in the case examples of Pat, Clay, and Alice, the clinical issues and therapeutic tasks involving multicultural identity become essential to facilitating the victim's capacity to reconstitute a sense of self. The therapeutic process facilitates an integration between the victim's perception of self (i.e., the self as a personal construct comprised of propositions related to beliefs, values, and expectations), with the cognitive–emotional meaning assigned to the events and to other significant psychosocial events or developments in the victim's life history.

Hiley-Young (1992) proposed a framework for differentiating between subtypes of trauma reactivation as a guide to client treatment-matching that is applicable to the disorder of the multicultural self. In cases that involve a disorder of self, treatment initially emphasizes process rather than content and, initially, at helping the patient to feel understood—first about current stressors and then about other significant life events. An account of early memories of childhood and adolescence is obtained.

A pretrauma review serves to encourage the patient's sense of control, in addition to providing valuable information. This review takes into account moment-to-moment events during earlier significant events and afterward. When appropriate, information regarding stress response syndromes is interjected. The effect of orchestrating information giving with encouraging emotional ventilation bolsters the patient's tolerance for increasing amounts of traumatic-linked affect and its assimilation.

Therapeutic structures and procedures necessary for treating the traumatized self include the provision of a *holding environment* to facilitate self-cohesion (e.g., clear therapeutic contract, appointment times). Concerted attention to the therapeutic relationship and to relevant cultural, contextual cues is necessary for the adequate development of rapport (Parson, 1985; Pina, 1985).

In addition, therapy must help examine the relationship between the patient's behavior and feelings (e.g., apathy, hopelessness, identity diffusion), facilitate the patient's perceptual differentiation between current and past threats, facilitate cognitive restructuring of events, teach problem solving and stress management skills as they apply to current problems, provide information regarding stress–response syndromes, and link the individual to other trauma survivors and their organizations. A treatment provider who attributes the individual's dysfunction as precipitated solely by the trauma and trauma-related stressors likely would err by ignoring the individual's multicultural identity issues.

Most PTSD treatments aim to enable the traumatized individual to become as self-sufficient as possible. Thus, these treatments *empower* the individual to lead a productive and fulfilled life. Empowered individuals have learned adaptive and generalizable skills with which to manage symptoms, emotions, and the exigencies of life. These skills might involve managing distress from PTSD symptoms or negotiating the cultural barriers to trauma recovery (e.g., recovery from a psychiatric breakdown during battle by individuals from relatively stoic cultures or from rape in cultures in which discussion of sexual activities is discouraged). Empowerment of this type provides the individual with the capabilities to manage PTSD and related symptoms and resume a normal life.

The developmental–constructivist model described in this chapter was developed as an empowering approach for application in cross-cultural PTSD treatment. In the model viewing individuals as being a product of a single cultural context is seen as being too narrow and that a multicultural perspective is considerably more helpful. We introduce the Three-Way Mirror as a method of integrating lifespan data and as a formal intervention technique (and visual aid) to be used with the patient. We also encourage working through reactivation issues as well as uncovering layers of meaning structures.

CONCLUSION

Several conclusions can be reached from the information presented in this chapter. It is clear that clinicians and researchers working with traumatized individuals need to be cognizant of and sensitive to the multicultural influences that have direct implications for a range of identities. Graduate and continuing education should include exposure to multicultural issues; supervised training in cross-cultural treatment may be an essential complement to classroom exposure (Westermeyer, 1989). Each PTSD patient should be evaluated and treated with these identifications in mind. In clinical work, adopting a constructivist framework that includes a developmental perspective (e.g., the Three-Way Mirror) allows for greater consideration of an individual's multiculturality.

Ethnicity and trauma in America are likely to overlap increasingly in the future. Evidence for this increase can be found in the well publicized stories about U.S. immigrants from around the world and the efforts made to make more culture-fair and culture-sensitive our employment practices and access to education and health care services. In this evolving context, the challenges for PTSD treatment are formidable.

Marsella, Chemtob, and Hamada (1990), for example, cited three broad areas of ethnocentrism and bias in current psychiatric practice: (a) inappropriate standards of normality and abnormality; (b) lack of knowledge about the expression, course, diagnosis, assessment, and outcome of psychiatric disorders; and (c) the use of inappropriate therapy procedures, including pharmacotherapy (i.e., some medications work differently for different cultural groups). Marsella, Friedman, and Spain (see chapter 4, this volume) also point out the limitations in much of the cross-cultural research on PTSD and the need to conduct research that considers the ethnocultural context of the patient. Advances in each of these areas are critical for the future of cross-cultural PTSD treatment.

We recommend that information about the interplay of ethnicity and PTSD treatment be obtained and integrated into research as well as practice. Development of measurement tools, for example, that simultaneously assess different roots to a complex identity, is needed. It also remains unclear what patient–treatment matches are best for various ethnic groups. Perhaps different techniques from different schools of therapy may produce a better fit with a given ethnic group. In the same way, how members of one cultural group tend to view mental health treatment and treatment providers is likely to influence the determination of optimal patient–treatment matching (Westermeyer, 1989).

A second recommendation can be made at the organizational level. Agencies and institutions that provide services to PTSD patients should develop multicultural initiatives. Included here are initiatives pertaining to service delivery, such as those that will enhance interagency communication and maximize the availability of mental health services and treatment and service providers to cultural groups located in geographically remote areas (e.g., American Indians who reside on reservations and Pacific Islanders who live away from urban areas). Other initiatives include developing theories and treatments for PTSD that take into account cultural pluralism, increasingly becoming the rule rather than exception in American society.

In this chapter, we have outlined a model for addressing multiculturality in PTSD treatment. Although we have experienced success following this model, it is clear to us that PTSD professionals have only begun to recognize the considerable influence of culture on trauma recovery. As with most constructs, recognition is a first and necessary step toward fuller understanding. It is our hope that with our growing awareness of cultural influences will come more efficacious treatment for this multifaceted and multicultural disorder.

REFERENCES

American Psychiatric Association. (1987). *Diagnostic and statistical mnual, of mental disorders* (3rd ed., rev.). Washington, DC: Author.

Barrett, T. W., & Mizes, J. S. (1988). Combat level and social support in the development of posttraumatic stress disorder in Vietnam veterans. *Behavior Modifications, 12,* 100–115.

Berry, J. W. (1990). Psychology of acculturation. In J. J. Berman (Ed.), *Cross-cultural perspectives* (pp. 201–234). Lincoln: University of Nebraska Press.

Blake, D. D., Weathers, F., Nagy, L. M., Kaloupek, D. G., Klauminzer, G., Charney, D. S., & Keane, T. M. (1990). A clinician rating scale for assessing current and lifetime PTSD: The CAPS-1. *The Behavior Therapist, 13,* 187–188.

Boehlein, J. K. (1987). Culture and society in post-traumatic stress disorder: Implications for psychotherapy. *American Journal of Psychotherapy, 41*(4), 519–530.

Brende, J. O., & Parson, E. R. (1985). Special veteran groups: Women and the ethnic minorities. In J. O. Brende & E. R. Parson (Eds.), *Vietnam veterans: The road to recovery* (pp. 125–165). New York Plenum Press.

Carlsen, M. B. (1991). *Creative aging: A meaning-making perspective.* New York: Norton.

Catherall, D. R. (1989). Differentiating intervention strategies for primary and secondary trauma in post-traumatic stress disorder: The example of Vietnam veterans. *Journal of Traumatic Stress, 2,* 289–304.

Coates, D., & Winston, T. (1983). Counteracting the deviance of depression: Peer support groups for victims. *Journal of Social Issues, 39,* 169–194.

Dennett, D. C. (1978). *Brainstorms: Philosophical essays on mind and psychology.* Montgomery, VT: Bradford Books.

Goode, W. J. (1960). A theory of role strain. *American Sociological Review, 25,* 483–496.

Gordon, M. (1964). *Assimilation in American life: The role of race, religion, and national origins.* New York: Oxford University Press.

Gove, W., & Tudor, J. (1973). Adult sex roles and mental illness. *American Journal of Sociology, 78,* 812–835.

Hiley-Young, B. (1992). Trauma reactivation and treatment: Integrated case examples. *Journal of Traumatic Stress, 5*(4), 545–555.

Keane, T. M., Scott, O. N., Chavoya, G. A., Lamparski, D. M., & Fairbank, J. A. (1985). Social support in Vietnam veterans with post-traumatic stress disorder: A comparative analysis. *Journal of Consulting and Clinical Psychology, 53,* 95–102.

Lindenthal, J., Thomas, J., Claudwell, S., & Myers, J. K. (1971). Psychological status and the perception of primary and secondary support from the social milieu in time of crisis. *Journal of Nervous & Mental Disease, 153,* 92–98.

Loo, C. M. (1993). An integrative-sequential treatment model for posttraumatic stress disorder: A case study of the Japanese American internment and redress. *Clinical Psychology Review, 13,* 89–117.

Madsen, W. (1964). The Mexican-Americans of South Texas. G. Spindler & L. Spindler (Eds.), *Case studies in cultural anthropology* [Monograph series]). New York: Holt, Reinhart, & Winston.

Mahoney, M. J. (1991). *Human change processes: The scientific foundations of psychotherapy.* New York: Basic Books.

Marsella, A. J., Chemtob, C., & Hamada, R. (1990). Ethnocultural aspects of PTSD in Vietnam War veterans. *National Center for PTSD Clinical Newsletter, 1*(1), 3–4.

Marsella, A. J., Friedman, M., & Spain, E. H. (1993). Ethnocultural aspects of PTSD. In J. Oldham, M. Riba, & A. Tasman (Eds.) *Review of psychiatry* (pp. 157–181). Washington, DC: American Psychiatric Press.

Mitchell, J. T. (1983). When disaster strikes: The critical incident stress debriefing. *Journal of Emergency Medical Services, 8,* 36–39.

Oetting, G. R., & Beauvais, L. L. (1990). Orthogonal cultural identification theory: The cultural identification of minority adolescents. *International Journal of the Addictions, 25,* 655–685.

Parson, E. R. (1985). The intercultural setting: Encountering Black Viet Nam veterans. In S. M. Sonnenberg, A. S. Blank, Jr., & J. A. Talbot, (Eds.), *The trauma of war: Stress and recovery in Vietnam veterans* (pp. 363–387). Washington, DC: American Psychiatric Press.

Pearlin, L. I. (1983). Role strains and personal stress. In H. B. Kaplan (Ed.), *Psychosocial stress: Trends in theory and research* (pp. 3–32). New York: Academic Press.

Pina, G., III. (1985). Diagnosis and treatment of post-traumatic stress disorder in Hispanic Vietnam veterans. In S. M. Sonenberg, A. S. Blank, Jr., & J. A. Talbot (Eds.), *The trauma of war: Stress and recovery in Vietnam veterans* (pp. 389–402). Washington, DC: American Psychiatric Press.

Rodriguez, O. (1987). *Hispanics and human services: Help-seeking in the inner city.* New York: Hispanic Research Center, Fordham University, Bronx.

Sarbin, T. (1954). Role theory. In G. Lindzey (Ed.), *Handbook of social psychology Vol. 1* (pp. 223–255). Reading, MA: Addison-Wesley.

Schafer, R. (1992). *Retelling a life: Narration and dialogue in psychoanalysis.* New York: Basic Books.

Spitzer, R. L., Williams, J. B., Gibbon, M., & First, M. B. (1989). *Structured Clinical Interview for DSM III(R)—Patient edition (SCID-P).* New York: Biometrics Research Department, New York State Psychiatric Institute.

Steiner, M., & Neumann, M. (1978). Traumatic neurosis and social support in the Yom Kippur War returnees. *Military Medicine, 143,* 866–868.

Stewart, J. (1992, July). *Reconstruction of self: Lifespan-oriented group psychotherapy.* Paper presented at the Fifth Conference of the North American Personal Construct Network, University of Washington, Seattle.

Stewart, J. (1993, July). *Retraumatization issues in the assessment of trauma survivors.* Workshop presented at the Continuing Education Course "Women Veterans Health and Issues of Sexual Trauma," Department of Veterans Affairs, Baltimore.

Sue, D. W., & Sue, D. (1990). *Counseling the culturally different* (2nd ed.). New York: Wiley.

Westermeyer, J. (1989). Cross-cultural care for PTSD: Research, training, and service needs for the future. *Journal of Traumatic Stress, 2*(4), 515–536.

Wilson, J., & Zigelbaum, S. (1986). PTSD and the disposition to criminal behavior. In C. Figley (Ed.), *Trauma and its wake: Traumatic stress theory, research, and intervention* (Vol. II, pp. 305–322). New York: Brunner/Mazel.

Young, M. B., & Erickson, C. A. (1988). Cultural impediments to recovery: PTSD in contemporary America. *Journal of Traumatic Stress, 1*(4), 431–443.

18

ETHNOCULTURAL CONSIDERATIONS IN THE TREATMENT OF PTSD: THERAPY AND SERVICE DELIVERY

JURIS G. DRAGUNS

There is a compelling and imperative need for crossing the culture gulf in extending meaningful and appropriate interventions at the sites of traumatic stress around the world. Yet no substantive knowledge base has come into being that would permit treatment techniques to be matched adequately with the stressful experience endured within a specific cultural context. It is possible only to proceed toward elucidating the current state of the field in a piecemeal and indirect fashion. The major question is, "What is the weight of cultural factors on the manifestations of posttraumatic stress disorder (PTSD) and on the techniques for its remediation?" There currently is no basis for the definitive resolution of this problem, but I will seek a provisional and partial clarification of this objective by attempting to disentangle the humanly universal and the culturally distinctive components of therapeutic intervention with PTSD. To this end, it will be necessary to turn to the experience of those clinicians who have pursued therapeutic intervention with the victims of PTSD from culturally different backgrounds. On the basis of this information, I will advance tentative generalizations pertaining to the relationship between cultural characteristics and the preferred, promising, and potentially useful modes of therapy. It is recognized that, given the current state of knowledge, they rest more on informed speculation than on demonstrated evidence.

459

PRELIMINARY CONSIDERATIONS: THE STATE OF THE FIELD

On the basis of rational considerations, PTSD appears to be an ideal syndrome for the incorporation of cultural factors into its treatment. The traumatic events inflicted on the person originate in a specific physical locale. With the exception of physical catastrophes, such as earthquakes and hurricanes, these events are caused or influenced by the cultural milieu in which they occur. And the responses of the persons affected by the stressful event are determined by their accumulated social experience and learning and cultural construction of reality (see Marsella, 1993).

Figure 1 presents the sequence of steps in outline form that are traversed in observable behavior and in personal experience as the person exposed to stress attempts to come to grips with it; every one of these steps is subject to cultural shaping. Culture impinges at all of the stages of attempted coping and experience following a stressful event (Marsella & Dash-Scheur, 1988). The arrows in the figure indicate that both the behavioral and the experiential steps of this progression are triggered by an external, usually traumatic event—for example, war, assault, earthquake, fire, flood, and so on. The arrows also show that the various components of the response to stress stand in a mutual relationship of feedback and interaction. What the figure does not convey is that the several steps overlap or even occur contemporaneously.

What sense is made of the traumatic event, what resources are brought to bear on coping with it, how affect is mobilized and modulated, what social support and solace are sought—all of these features and more are embedded in the person's culturally mediated experience. Similarly affected by culture are the person's expectations, whether vague or specific, of therapeutic help.

Proceeding from these considerations, a simple and direct research design can be envisaged to disentangle the interplay of disorder, technique, and culture on the symptoms in the aftermath of a disaster, such as the 1985 earthquake in Mexico City. Reporting on the psychiatric effects of this catastrophic event and on the emergency measures instituted to alleviate them, de la Fuente (1990) made naturalistic observations based on the behaviors that occurred at a specific point in space and time. However, the tragic effects of earthquakes have been experienced at countless other times and places. The culturally oriented investigators of PTSD are faced with the challenge of first recording and then comparing both the symptoms and the treatment responses in Mexico with the manifestations and interventions after comparable events elsewhere—for example, in China, Italy, or Japan. Such a study has not been undertaken. Disasters, caused by human beings or by forces of nature, are unanticipated, unique events. They demand immediate relief; there is no time or opportunity to gather

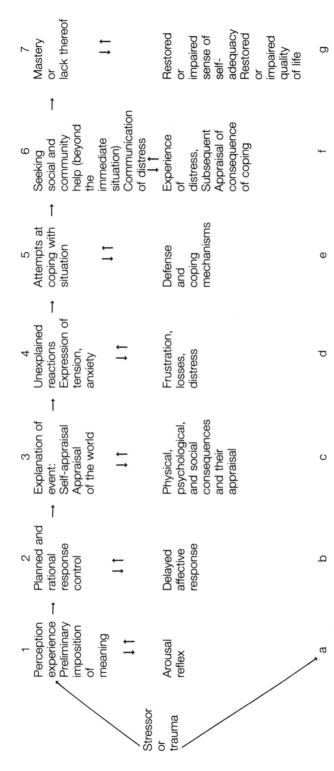

1	2	3	4	5	6	7
Perception experience Preliminary imposition of meaning	Planned and rational response control	Explanation of event: Self-appraisal Appraisal of the world	Unexplained reactions Expression of tension, anxiety	Attempts at coping with situation	Seeking social and community help (beyond the immediate situation) Communication of distress	Mastery or lack thereof
Arousal reflex	Delayed affective response	Physical, psychological, and social consequences and their appraisal	Frustration, losses, distress	Defense and coping mechanisms	Experience of distress, Subsequent Appraisal of consequence of coping	Restored or impaired sense of self-adequacy Restored or impaired quality of life
a	b	c	d	e	f	g

Stressor or trauma

Figure 1. Experience of a traumatic event and its aftermath. The numbered entries on the upper line represent at least partially observable and public occurrences. The entries designated by letters on the lower line are reserved for the subjective and internal processes corresponding to these events. At least an approximation of simultaneity is envisaged for numbers and letters.

and process data or to institute meaningful cross-cultural comparisons, even on a post hoc basis.

In the past few decades, the United States, the Soviet Union, and France were involved in protracted, unpopular foreign wars (in Vietnam, Afghanistan, and Algeria, respectively). Each of these conflicts generated substantial psychiatric casualties. The problems of the U.S. veterans of the Vietnam conflict are well documented and are presented in several chapters in this volume. A substantial body of psychiatric writing also has emerged on the French veterans of the Algerian war (Porot, 1956), and reports on the effects of the Afghanistan experience on Russian and other participants are beginning to appear (e.g., Tsygankov, 1991). However, no comparisons of the manifestations of PTSD experienced as a result of these three wars have been undertaken, nor has there been any attempt to examine treatment techniques that have been effective with the veterans of these three conflicts.

The staggering complexity of attempting to link culture, disorder, and intervention is illustrated by the review by Rubonis and Bickman (1991) who presented a meta-analysis of the available quantitative data on the effects of disasters and their relationships with psychopathology. Most of the events included in the analysis occurred in the United States, although Australia, Canada, Great Britain, Russia, and Sri Lanka also were represented. The authors could not include ethnic or cultural variables in their analyses, and their conclusions about the effect of victims' social and demographic characteristics were cautious and limited. In a similar way, Boehnlein (1987, p. 519) concluded on the basis of his observation and other relevant clinical data that "there exists virtually no literature on cross-cultural factors that may make possible the patient's and clinician's understanding of the trauma and the specific system complex."

UNIVERSAL COMPONENTS IN EFFECTIVE INTERVENTION WITH PTSD

General Formulations

Universally applicable features of intervention can possibly be discerned through the examination of clinical writings. On the basis of their extensive experience and knowledge of the clinical literature, Everstine and Everstine (1993) proposed a general model of intervention for all kinds of trauma response. They considered one of the therapist's primary tasks "to facilitate the traumatized person's entry into the recovery process, a natural psychological passage that is similar to grief" (Everstine & Everstine, 1993, p. 9).

This goal is achieved during the preliminary stabilization phase. Victims are guided gently from the initial shock and the subsequent denial to the acceptance of the reality of their traumatic experience. Only then are they ready to embark on psychotherapy in the narrow sense of the term. This phase entails dealing with depression, anger, and other affects, helping victims achieve optimal distance from the acceptable meaning of their experiences by philosophizing, and enabling them to close the books on the traumatic event.

These formulations are based on clinical work with clients in the United States. Everstine and Everstine's scheme, however, is sufficiently flexible to be potentially applicable regardless of its locale. The extent to which their specific techniques would require modification across cultural frontiers is unknown.

Pioneering Interventions

In contrast to the Everstines, Kinzie's (1978) ideas on the components of universally effective psychotherapy in PTSD emerged in the course of clinical work with victims of perhaps the most savage political oppression suffered anywhere in the past two decades, the Cambodian Holocaust under Pol Pot's regime in 1975–1979. Kinzie identified three valid principles of therapeutic intervention: (a) appropriate use of the medical model; (b) recognition of the nonverbal modes of communication, especially those of affect and distress; and (c) sensitivity to the subjective meanings of the patient's life. The first point emphasizes the nonjudgmental aspects of the medical model and accepts the reality of the patient's somatic complaints. The remaining two points address the universal and the culturally unique aspects of personal experience, respectively. Ekman and Friesen's (1971) well known demonstration of the worldwide recognition of the facial expression of basic human emotions highlighted the possibility of realistic communication of affect across cultures. The concept of subjective culture, as developed by Triandis (1972) and applied to cross-cultural psychotherapy by Vassiliou and Vassiliou (1973), emphasized cultural divergence in the interrelationship of concepts, objects, and behaviors and introduced the cultural diversity of meanings.

Kinzie's formulations were general and flexible. He did not advise or counsel against the use of any particular technique. The implication of Kinzie's proposal is that in effective cross-cultural intervention with traumatized patients, general orientation is more important than technique. It should be kept in mind that these formulations were offered at an exposure to the effects of stress in other cultures. Given the early point of Kinzie's writing, it is not surprising that his tenets are not further specified. Almost a decade later, Kinzie and Fleck (1987) made their suggestions more concrete. Drawing on their extensive experience with severely traumatized Cambodian refugees, they emphasized the therapeutic value of fostering long-term supportive relationships, recognizing the role of recent stressors in symptom development, relieving patients' complaints with medication, and strengthening traditional values and social ties.

It should be kept in mind that these suggestions were made on the basis of therapy with a specific group of trauma victims. Thus the universality of these proposals is neither claimed nor demonstrated. There is, however, an apparent plausibility to all of the above points. If not universal, they appear to be widely applicable.

Extreme Traumas

The rule of terror by the Khmers Rouges in Cambodia is a matter of historical record and copious documentation (e.g., Ablin & Hood, 1987; Kiljunen, 1984). The entire country was transformed into a network of forced labor camps in which terror was ever present, brutal executions were routine, toil was back breaking, and near starvation was the rule. Following the collapse of Pol Pot's government, some of the survivors succeeded in fleeing from Cambodia and eventually in being admitted to the United States. Given the unique and extreme stress experienced by these refugees, it is necessary to describe their characteristics in some detail.

Kinzie and colleagues (1990) diagnosed PTSD in 90% of a group of Cambodian refugees in the United States on the basis of a checklist of symptoms derived from *DSM–III–R* criteria. The manifestations of PTSD were missed at the initial psychiatric examination of these refugees. They never spontaneously brought up their traumatic experiences in Cambodia, nor did they speak of their reactions in the aftermath of their flight. Only by systematic inquiry into the presence or absence of *DSM–III–R* signs for PTSD was the nature and the extent of the massive posttraumatic reaction elicited (Kinzie, Frederickson, Ben, Fleck, & Carls, 1984). In this group, PTSD was comorbid with depression, which was mostly expressed through vegetative symptoms (e.g., sleep disturbance, loss of appetite). These observations were paralleled in the reports of other clinicians who worked with Cambodian and other Southeast Asian immigrants (Beiser, Turner, & Gandsen, 1989; Mollica, Wyshak & Lavelle, 1987; Mollica et al., 1990; Moore & Boehnlein, 1991).

On the basis of his observations, Kinzie (1987) described the features of the concentration camp syndrome among Cambodian refugees. Three kinds of symptoms were found in at least 75% of the cases: (a) disturbance of sleep, appetite, or concentration; (b) avoidance of painful memories and of events or activities that might arouse such memories; and (c) recurrent dreams and thoughts. Survivor guilt was found in fewer than 25% of the cases; it may be a less prominent component of posttraumatic experience of Cambodian survivors than in their Jewish post-World War II counterparts (Eitinger, 1961; Matussek, 1971; Trautmann, 1961). Among the survivors of Hitler's death camps, "survivor guilt was a 'given'—a background to their lives that was taken for granted, and not talked about. Self-reproach for not having saved someone close could virtually always be found, but generally was covered by the 'conspiracy of silence'" (Krystal & Danieli, 1994, p. 4).

Important Principles of Therapy: Provisional Formulation

The list of cross-culturally valid features of therapeutic intervention is by no means exhausted by the points proposed by Kinzie and Fleck (1987). Table 1 lists eight characteristics of experiencing a traumatic event; they appear to be valid regardless of social context and geographical locale. They are derived from points contained in the therapy effectiveness literature (e.g., Lambert, Shapiro, & Bergin, 1986) and the writings on workable interventions in PTSD (Deitz, 1986; Everstine & Everstine, 1993; Figley, 1986; van de Veer, 1992). Other principles have originated in theoretical formulation, such as Rogers' (1957) well known necessary and sufficient conditions of personality change.

Promptness and Immediacy

Promptness and immediacy constitute an uncontroversial feature of intervention in PTSD and are especially important when therapy is conducted across culture lines. Stress-related disorders are not among the conditions that can be helped by techniques that bring about substantial improvement in the long run without reducing distress expeditiously. Moreover, the impact of this recognition is increased in those cases in which the therapeutic procedures are culturally unfamiliar and are administered by a therapist from another culture. Under these circumstances,

TABLE 1
Universal Components of Effective Intervention in Posttraumatic Stress
Disorder

1. Intervene immediately or promptly after the traumatic event
2. Focus on presenting complaints or current distress
3. Use specific and possibly directive techniques
4. Deal with any guilt and self-blame early and directly
5. Experience and communicate empathy readily
6. Strengthen the client's sense of competence, autonomy, and self-worth
7. Help clients make sense of the traumatic event in the context of their lives (including culture)
8. Deal with any object losses early and directly

demonstrating the benefits of psychotherapy quickly and tangibly is highly desirable, if not indispensable.

Removal of Distressing Symptoms

Focusing the therapist's efforts on the removal of distressing or disabling symptoms appears to be associated with improved functioning, an accelerated pace of therapeutic change, an optimistic outlook, and satisfaction with psychotherapy. However, burdened by painful and terrifying experiences, distressed and suffering clients are frustrated by what may appear to them to be a rudderless therapy—diffuse, erratic, and without any apparent direction.

This recognition coalesces with two major contemporary trends: directive behavioral intervention and time-limited psychotherapy. Behaviorally, cognitively, and socially oriented approaches are targeted to specific changes in the patient's symptoms and deficits. The movement in the past two decades toward brief psychotherapy, with circumscribed objectives to be attained within a specified time frame, may well be extended across cultures, especially in cases of PTSD. Room should be allowed for modifying the specific techniques and couching them in a culturally meaningful manner. This precaution, however, does not alter the more general impression that these techniques are more flexible in their range of cultural usefulness than the traditional and open-ended varieties of verbal psychotherapy.

The need-based strategies of intervention promoted by Garbarino (1992a, 1992b) with children and adolescents in Kuwait after the Persian Gulf War and with Vietnamese refugees in detention camps in Hong Kong suggest another set of promising suggestions animated by the sensitive recognition of the constants of human suffering and stress. Specifically, the question was asked: "What are the unmet needs of these children? What are their painful concerns?" Their experiences—for example, the uncertainty inherent in being an unwelcome refugee potentially subject to forcible repatriation or in being overwhelmed by having witnessed death, danger, and destruction—were then dealt with on the basis of knowledge and understanding of and empathy with these specific instances of the universals of human condition.

Neki, Joinet, Hogan, Hauli, and Kilonzo (1985) have shared instances of their experiences in some extremely challenging triads of therapist, client, and setting, in which all three represented different cultures. Faced with this kind of extreme complexity, these therapists adopted a directive and active stance in engaging clients from the start and in gratifying their dependency needs in a situation of subjective helplessness and disorientation.

Communication of Empathy

Experience and communication of empathy is another essential component of psychotherapy, both within and across cultures (cf. Rogers, 1957). An unknown, but presumably substantial proportion of cross-cultural therapy failures is traceable to disruptions of empathy. Either the therapist does not sufficiently empathize with the client or the therapist's empathy, though experienced, is not effectively transmitted to the client. In the aftermath of extreme trauma, this challenge is magnified. Therapist have neither experienced the patient's suffering and pain nor do they possess first-hand knowledge of the social context in which they have occurred. This two-fold gulf has been bridged many times, albeit with difficulty (Ridley & Lingle, 1995). Moreover, little or nothing is known about the success and veridicality of these endeavors. Has empathy indeed been achieved and has it contributed to a more positive outcome of intervention? As Kleinman and Kleinman (1991) have shown, suffering by human beings at remote places and in different cultures is all too easily transformed from experience into category, at a point of intersection between cultural and psychopathological dimensions. Empathy gets lost in the process. Yet, in my opinion, it would appear that empathy is a sine qua non of successful therapy, whereas the modes of expressing it are widely variable across cultural lines.

The other hypothetical conditions can be dispensed quickly. PTSD requires dealing with guilt, object loss, and trauma directly, intelligibly, and efficiently. Dealing with these painful experiences should go hand in hand with strengthening clients' senses of self-efficacy and competence and bolstering their self-esteem. All of these objectives should be accomplished in a culturally sensitive and meaningful way that, quite often, poses a major challenge of technique and communication.

An additional generalization that aspires to, but as yet has not attained, the status of universality (and is therefore omitted from Table 1) is the caution that experienced therapists have expressed concerning the usefulness and efficacy of reconstructing, and helping the victims of PTSD relive, their traumatic experiences. Kinzie (1987) has reported that Cambodian refugees rarely, if ever, volunteered accounts of what they had gone through during Pol Pot's reign of terror. With a clientele of a different cultural background, contemporary therapists working with Jewish Holocaust survivors and other survivors of Nazi concentration camps described the gamut of complex emotional reactions and entangled therapist–client relationships that recollection of the concentration camp trauma provokes (Krystal & Danieli, 1994; Yehuda, 1994; Yehuda, Kahana, Southwick, & Giller, 1994). Also relevant are the results of Kaminer and Lavie (1991), who found a negative correlation between dream recall and adjustment in

Holocaust survivors. Perhaps the extremes of inhumanity, as perpetrated in Nazi Germany and by the Khmers Rouges in Cambodia, have tapped the limits of human ability to reconstruct and to relive traumatic events and to benefit from this experience.

CULTURALLY VARIABLE COMPONENTS OF EFFECTIVE INTERVENTION IN PTSD

The considerations mentioned previously, even if they are valid, leave ample room for the operation of cultural factors in arresting and reversing PTSD. As shown in Table 2, culture enters the loop at every point in the transaction. As shown in this table, culture impinges on the coping process in content and in style. With the exception of natural catastrophes, the traumatic event is shaped by its culture, as are the various steps in attempting to counteract the effects of stress.

How the various stimuli are construed, labeled, and categorized is a matter of cultural mediation experienced within the person's lifetime. Somewhat less obvious, what coping and defense mechanisms are used and how, what is perceived, accentuated, or glossed over, how the information pertaining to the stressful event and its effect is processed, and what avenues for its processing are obstructed are in part influenced by cultural factors (see Marsella, 1993, for an overview of cultural factors in treatment).

Horowitz (1986, 1990) has proposed a phasic model of coping with extreme and unexpected stress during which intrusions and omissions alternate. In the former phase, the person is flooded and overwhelmed by uncontrollable memories and emotions associated with them. In the latter phase, rigid over-control is exercised in the form of freezing and blocking. In their pure forms, both mechanisms result in obstructing the person's attempts at readaptation by obliterating awareness of the traumatic event or imposing an intolerable information overload. In reality, these two phases not only alternate but overlap and stand in a shifting mutual dominance–submission relationship. Individual differences in emphasis on either of these two contrasting styles in dealing with stress may exist and conceivably may be related to such constructs as repression–sensitization (Byrne, 1964), augmenting–reducing (Petrie, 1967), and leveling–sharpening (Klein, 1970).

Cognition or Affect

Cultures may emphasize either affect or cognition as the principal mode of coping with traumatic stress. Leff (1988) has provided illustrative evidence to that effect in the form of intense, undifferentiated emotional

TABLE 2
Cultural Components of Experiencing a Traumatic Event

1. Stressors:
   External vs. internal
   Natural vs. humanmade
   Universal vs. particular
   Individual vs. collective
   a. Arousal
      Nature and degree of arousal
      Kind and intensity of affect
2. Experience:
   Extrapunitive vs. intropunitive
   Random vs. lawful
   Culturally prepatterned vs.
      individually structured
   Meaningful vs. meaningless
   b. Delayed affect:
      Kind of affect
      Minimization vs. maximization
      Style of affective expression
3. Response:
   Active vs. passive
   Overt vs. covert
   Complex vs. simple
   Quick vs. slow
   Intense vs. weak, etc.
   c. Expression vs. suppression
      Alloplastic vs. autoplastic
         response
      Fantasy vs. reality, etc.
4. Explanation:
   Acceptance vs. rebellion
   Confusion vs. meaning
   Low self-esteem vs. unchanged self-
      esteem
   Unchanged self-esteem vs.
      increased self-esteem, etc.
   d. Rational vs. magical
      Denial vs. awareness
      Optimism vs. pessimism
      Realism vs. illusion, etc.

5. Residues:
   Acceptance of incongruity vs. denial
      of incongruity
   Awareness of anxiety vs. denial of
      anxiety
   Sensitivity to discomfort vs.
      insensitivity to discomfort, etc.
6. Coping;
   Effective vs. ineffective
   Real vs. imaginary
   Confidence vs. doubt
   Low energy vs. high energy, etc.
   e. Defense and coping mechanisms:
      Repression v. sensitization
      Field-dependence s. field-
         independence, etc.
7. Help Seeking:
   Trustful vs. distrustful
   Personal vs. impersonal
   Open vs. closed
   Mutual vs. unilateral, etc.
   f. Personal Sense:
      Competent vs. incompetent
      Helpless vs. self-sufficient
      Interdependent vs. autonomous,
         etc.
8. Outcome:
   Balance restored vs. balance lacking
   g. Effect on self-concept and well-
      being:Enhanced vs. impaired
      Strengthened vs. weakened, etc.

Note. Entries marked by numbers, refer to the more public and concrete events; the lower entries, provided with letters, pertain to the more personal resources and to their role in the more subjective aspects of coping.

expression in some cultures. This pattern is complicated by the culturally prescribed demand characteristics of various situations. Conspicuous but ritualized suspension of controls over emotional expression is a culturally sanctioned or even prescribed component of the grief experience, at funerals and elsewhere. There are also cultures—for example, in Mexico—in which the traditional norm is to endure stoically and unexpressively any and all suffering, even unto arbitrary and violent death (cf. Diaz-Guerrero, 1970).

These considerations apply to the exercise of social influence in psychotherapy, at the service of alleviating the impact of stress and its resulting complications. Table 3 contains a provisional listing of therapy experiences in which cultures are expected to differ.

Interpretations of Actions, Feelings, and Experiences

An important source of cultural variation is the importance assigned to interpretations of the patient's actions, feelings, and experiences. The principle of psychodynamic therapies that posits the therapeutic value of imposing meaning and understanding on personal experience is probably sound and widely applicable. The question remains open, however, on how important these interpretations are, from the perspective of the person and the culture. In a related manner, how much words matter may be a matter of divergence between, for example, Japanese and American psychotherapists as well as between their respective clients (Doi, 1985; Kimura, 1972; Roland, 1988).

Social Distance Between Therapist and Client

The social distance between the therapist and the client and the nature and differentiation of their respective roles also are affected by the culture. The attention paid to psychological discomfort as opposed to somatic distress has emerged as a major contrast of symptom presentation and the therapist's response to it between China and North America. In some traditional cultures, indigenous therapeutic interventions are ceremonial and ritualized, with a prescribed sequence of the therapist's and patient's actions.

In modern psychotherapy in Euro-American cultures, spontaneity is prized, ambiguity is fostered, and conventional expectations are called into

TABLE 3
Culturally Variable Components of Intervention in Posttraumatic Stress Disorder

1. Use of interpretations and their rationale and basis
2. Extent and nature of verbal interaction between client and therapist
3. Role of verbal communication
4. Role differentiation between client and therapist
5. Respective weights of physical and somatic and psychological distress
6. Role of ritual in psychotherapy
7. Use of metaphor, imagery, myth, and storytelling in psychotherapy
8. Nature of relationship between therapist and client

question deliberately. Yet positive results are achieved, in as yet unknown proportions, in both cases, and the challenge is to find a culturally fitting balance between ritual and spontaneous experience. Of particular moment for the pancultural panorama of psychotherapy is the role of mythical ir-rational images, which loom large in the subjective experience of some cultures, as opposed to the rational, empirical, and naturalistic arguments and rhetoric that dominate the psychotherapy discourse among modern urban North Americans (Draguns, 1975; Nathan, 1994; Prince, 1920).

Uses of Metaphor

The proposals for story telling in psychotherapy by Peseschkian (1986), a psychiatrist born in Iran and practicing in Germany, may provide an avenue for reaching clients who are more at home in metaphorical representations of interpersonal relations and of the human condition. Pesechkian (1986) described the rationale of story-telling therapy as fol-lows:

> Stories that can be used as mediator between therapist and patient are an important help. They give the patient a basis for identification, and at the same time they are protection for him; by associating with the story he talks about himself, his conflicts and his desires. (p. xiv)

Marsella (1985) and Nathan (1994) called attention to the emotional power of these visual and symbolic condensations of basic human dilem-mas. Moreover, Marsella argued that these vivid sensory representations loom larger in traditional non-Western cultures than they do in modern, fast changing, cosmopolitan Euro-American milieus. In Marsella's (1985) words,

> a metaphorical language provides a rich immediate sensory experience of the world which is not diluted by being filtered through words which distantiate the cognitive understanding from the experience. In a met-aphorical language system, the understanding and the language are one. (p. 294)

These considerations remain to be linked with therapy in PTSD. None of the points mentioned previously are unique to this condition, yet all of them are potentially germane to the practical objective of developing and implementing culturally appropriate intervention programs for PTSD. As the clinical literature on PTSD grows, attention may be increasingly concentrated on the subtler aspects of the culture–disorder–therapy triad.

PTSD: ITS WIDELY EXPERIENCED COMPLICATIONS

In focusing on the culturally variable features of PTSD and interven-tions for it, one should not lose sight of the common elements of experiencing PTSD across cultures. In clinical settings, modern Western therapists often encounter cases of PTSD among immigrants, sojourners, and refugees to their countries (cf. van de Veer, 1992). The paradox is that by providing shelter from the threats and dangers in their homelands, the host countries inevitably, though inadvertently, impose new kinds of stress on these victims of trauma.

Acculturation is a difficult, stressful process even under optimal circumstances; its adverse effects are compounded when it occurs in the aftermath of losses, injuries, and perils to life and limb. Moreover, some clinicians (e.g., Kinzie & Fleck, 1987) have observed that the effect of the original trauma in refugees' homelands may make them less adaptable and more rigid and may stultify their learning ability, temporarily or for an indefinite period of time. Westermeyer (1989) coined the term *acculturation stress syndrome* to describe a condition combined of depressive, paranoid, and anxiety symptoms. This disorder responds sluggishly to psychological, milieu, or pharmacological interventions. Jilek (1982) referred to *anomic depression*, which is an overlapping state of distress and impairment.

However, these two overlapping reactions have been observed under conditions of less sudden, although still painfully disruptive social change, as experienced by traditional indigenous cultures in North America and elsewhere. Both acculturation stress syndrome and anomic depression may or may not be preceded by the experience of PTSD, but the prior history of PTSD increases the difficulty of effectively counteracting the more recent acculturative disorder. Best results have been achieved by combining therapeutic sophistication with cultural sensitivity. For the most part, this has been done on a semiintuitive basis, and a prescriptive, focused psychotherapy for acculturative stress is several steps removed from implementation.

EMIC THERAPIES FOR PTSD: AN UNCHARTED TERRITORY

A few words remain to be said about emic interventions, indigenous approaches, or folk therapies in treating PTSD. Since PTSD is a relatively newly classified disorder, not yet firmly rooted in psychiatric tradition, the literatures on indigenous intervention and on the cultural aspects of PTSD have not had the chance to coalesce. In fact, there appears to be no point of contact between these two bodies of writing. The typical account in the literature about PTSD in other cultures contains the description of one or more cases and relates the interventions of a nonindigenous therapist who, to varying degrees, has attempted to accommodate the patient's culture.

Culture-Bound Syndromes and Trauma

The rich and detailed literature on culture-bound psychiatric syndromes (e.g., Pfeiffer, 1994; Simons & Hughes, 1985; Yap, 1974) is devoted to the description of the manifestations of these syndromes, with little information on either the antecedents of these disturbances or the therapeutic or other attempts to reverse them. *Amok* is a dramatic state of aggressive arousal, often accompanied by violence toward self or others. Yap (1974) noted that *amok* often was precipitated by object loss or other emotionally intense disappointment experiences, which seemingly would place it in the posttraumatic stress category. The state is described as spontaneously reversible (Yap, 1974), and the community's task is not so much to *cure* the patients as it is to protect them and others from agitation and violence.

Latah in Malaysia has been described by Simons (1985) as the cultural elaboration of the startle reflex. Its manifestations include echolalia and an automatic imitation of the movements and gestures of other people, especially those imbued with greater prestige and power. In reference to *latah*, Hughes (1985, p. 111) stated that "the presentation of a stimulus of the given person is so traumatic that it precipitates an episode of unusual and involuntary behavior." Westermeyer (1985) investigated the antecedents of *amok* in 18 Laotians. Major losses were featured in several cases, but the level of situational stress varied from slight to extreme. It is noteworthy that, even though this study was conducted during a period of intense warfare in Indochina including aerial bombing, these traumatic events triggered disturbed behavior in only one case.

In describing the culture-bound syndrome of *pibloqtoq* of the Inuit, also referred to as Arctic hysteria in early sources, Gussow (1985, p. 282) wrote that it "represents reactions of the polar Eskimo to situations of unusually intense, but culturally typical stress." The examples given by Gussow include finding oneself in unfamiliar surroundings or at sea, without being able to see the coastline.

In light of these descriptions, typical instances of culture-bound disorders do not meet the current criteria for diagnosis of PTSD, even though they are preceded by subjectively intense stressful experiences. These stimuli, however, are defined culturally and do not involve events of catastrophic proportions. The innovative approaches, based on tradition but applied to contemporary problems, that Manson et al. reported in chapter 10, probably constitute the most detailed and factual description of emic interventions in PTSD in the literature.

Indigenous Therapies

Even if the paucity of authentic information on treatment procedures for these syndromes is discounted, grave doubts remain about the scope of application of traditional healing practices for the treatment of PTSD at this time. The worldwide trends toward urbanization, modernization, and secularization may have made the traditional healing ceremonies obsolete or irrelevant for many of their potential contemporary participants.

The Swiss psychiatrist Scharfetter (1985) has raised the issue of the future of the tradition healer. A note of skepticism also has been sounded from Côte d'Ivoire in West Africa (Claver, 1976). It may be more promising to incorporate creatively elements of traditional ceremonies into preventive cultural reinterpretation proceedings, as the authors of the reports cited by Manson and colleagues have done. Less realistic would be any attempts to transpose mechanically the rituals of a premodern age and to apply them automatically in a different cultural and historical context.

Where these rituals still occur in real life, as among the Salish Indians of British Columbia, they should be studied to increase understanding of the effective ingredients of psychotherapy. These procedures also can be incorporated fruitfully into flexible and innovative treatment programs. Jilek (1982) and Jilek and Todd (1974) have described the Salish winter spirit dance ceremony and have recorded its therapeutic effects. Even though their case material does not include any clear-cut instances of PTSD, they have reported that this emic ritual is particularly effective in psychophysiological and psychoreactive states, which would suggest its potential relevance for counteracting PTSD.

On the basis of his observations, Jilek (1982) found himself in an implicit disagreement with the skeptics on the prospects of emic interventions. Indeed, he reported a revival of traditional rituals among the Salish, which augurs well for the future of their healing ceremonies and their potential extension to PTSD (see also chapters 9 and 10, this volume).

CULTURAL FEATURES AND TECHNIQUES FOR DEALING WITH PTSD: HYPOTHESES FOR THE FUTURE

Different as the therapist–patient interactions are across cultures in dealing with PTSD, a pattern of regularity may be discerned. In earlier reports, psychopathological manifestations (Draguns, 1990b) and psychotherapeutic interventions (Draguns, 1990a) have been linked to four basic cultural dimensions.

These dimensions were derived by Hofstede (1980) in the course of a comparison of work behavior encompassing 40 countries in all regions of the world. This method involved the sequential use of multivariate statistics, including factor analysis. The end result of this mammoth effort was the identification of four maximally independent dimensions that Hofstede labeled *individualism–collectivism, power distance, uncertainty avoidance,* and *masculinity–femininity*. Moreover, Hofstede (1991) took steps to extend the potential relevance of these four dimensions to a variety of domains of experience, from social interaction within educational organizations to private constructions of the self. It is conceivable, then, that Hofstede's four dimensions may be applicable to psychotherapy, specifically in the aftermath of stressful experience. Introductory descriptions of these four variables follow, based on Hofstede's (1980, 1991) writings, together with preliminary hypotheses about their role in intervention with PTSD. Table 4 presents this information schematically.

Individualism–Collectivism

Individualism–collectivism refers to the degree to which individuals experience themselves as autonomous units or as members of a social entity. The contrast is between the primacy of self-experience and the imperative of social integration. Individualism is expected to be associated with self-actualization as the ultimate goal of intervention, whereas collectivistic

TABLE 4
Hofstede's Dimensions in Psychotherapy

Individualism:	Collectivism:
Insight, self-understanding	Alleviation of suffering
Guilt, alienation, loneliness	Relationship problems, shame
Therapist as father figure	Therapist as nurturant mother
Development of individuality	Social integration
Development of responsibility	Acceptance of controls
Interpersonal conflict and its resolution	Harmonious relationships
High-Power Distance:	**Low-Power Distance:**
Directive psychotherapy	Person-centered psychotherapy
Therapist as expert	Therapist as sensitive person
Therapist as change-agent	Therapist as catalyst
Conformity and social effectiveness	Self-discovery and actualization
Differentiation of therapist and client roles	Dedifferentiation of therapist and client roles
Emphasis upon professional credentials	Promotion of self-improvement
	Patient movements
High-Uncertainty Avoidance:	**Low-Uncertainty Avoidance:**
Biological explanations	Psychological explanations
Behavioral techniques	Experiential psychotherapy
Medical orientation	Multiprofessional orientation
Few schools of therapy	Many schools of therapy
Tightly regulated therapy practice	Loosely regulated therapy practice
Masculinity:	**Femininity:**
Prosociety orientation	Properson orientation
Responsibility, conformity, adjustment	Expressiveness, creativity, empathy
Guilt	Anxiety
Enabling	Caring

societies would strive for the attainment of harmonious relationships through therapeutic experience. Both of these objectives are inherently desirable and are probably simultaneously pursued in widely different cultures, but their respective prominence would constitute a source of differences. Other factors follow from this dichotomy: loneliness, guilt, and alienation as hallmarks of negative psychological states in individualistic milieus; conformity and stifling of personal strivings as the obverse side of the sense of belonging that collectivistic cultures in the ideal case ensure.

Power Distance

Power distance has to do with the importance of authority and the nature of its exercise. The gulf between the therapist and client in the high power distance cultures is wide. The therapist knows and directs; the client follows, gratefully or resentfully, submissively or rebelliously. By contrast, the room for cooperative, egalitarian psychotherapy is ample in low power distance cultures, but when it comes to implementing focused, directive psychotherapy, which may be important in PTSD, such cultures may be at a disadvantage. Role differentiation and social distance in high power distance cultures would stand in the way of developing intense, compassionate interpersonal relationships that may provide a valuable shortcut in psychotherapy with PTSD.

Uncertainty Avoidance

Uncertainty avoidance may stifle innovation but breeds respect for facts, science, certainty, and clarity. The cultist fringes of the therapy movement and the untried and verified techniques would be swept away in high uncertainty avoidance cultures. Conversely, self-help would thrive in situations in which uncertainty avoidance is low. Both professional and bureaucratic requirements are expected to be stringent in high uncertainty avoidance milieus; they would be assigned much less importance in low uncertainty cultures. Biology would be preferred over psychology and behavioral interventions over experiential and psychodynamic therapies.

Masculinity–Femininity

Femininity is associated with caring and masculinity with coping, and these two modalities would be reflected in the therapeutic interventions preferred in the two kinds of cultures. Masculine cultures are expected to be concerned with the restoration of productivity and efficiency; feminine cultures would cater to the inner person and would promote the experience of satisfaction with self and others, contentment, and happiness. The role of the therapist in masculine cultures would be distinctly fatherly;

therapist–client interaction in feminine cultures would partake of maternal features and experience.

Somatization Across Cultures

Beyond Hofstede's four dimensions, the balance between the person's somatic experience (*le corps vécu* of French phenomenologists; see Merleau-Ponty, 1962 and Minkowski, 1966) and its cognitive representation must be considered. One of the major themes of modern cross-cultural research on psychopathology is the complex role of bodily sensations, including pain. Western therapists and many of their clients construe personal experience on a psychological basis, whereas other cultures—for example, the Chinese—take the somatic sensations more seriously and report them more readily (Cheung, 1986; Kleinman, 1980).

It would be a gross oversimplification to reduce this complex and subtle state of affairs to a dichotomy. It is misleading to say that the Chinese somatize while the Americans psychologize discomfort and distress. A precarious and shifting structure can be envisaged as a subjective representation of body, self, sensation, perception, thought, communication, and action; it may undergo shifts and modifications in the course of psychotherapy.

CONCLUSION

There is a disappointing paucity of objective, research-based data on the interplay of cultural variables and psychotherapeutic procedures in PTSD. The available fragments of information suggest that PTSD is a highly malleable disorder and that its symptoms are shaped to a substantial extent by cultural practices and experiences. There is ample room for both noting cultural characteristics in response to psychotherapy and for incorporating culturally oriented techniques into psychotherapy programs.

Clinical experience and rational considerations make it possible to identify on a tentative basis the culturally invariant and variable features of psychotherapeutic interventions. It is also possible to discern commonalities in PTSD and related manifestations across cultures and in the responses of individuals affected by it to acculturative stress. In light of all of these factors, preliminary suggestions for culturally sensitive and pragmatic intervention of PTSD across cultural boundaries have been formulated.

A special problem pertains to indigenous or emic approaches to healing, which have been featured prominently in the clinical literature but have not as yet been applied extensively to PTSD. Moreover, there has been a disappointing absence of links between the concepts and findings of cross-cultural psychology and the practical enterprise of intervening in and counteracting the manifestations of PTSD. Such concepts include subjective culture, metaphoric experience and communication of subjective cognitive–affective states, interplay of somatic and psychological experiences in personal distress, and relationships of Hofstede's four cultural dimensions to the practice and mode of psychotherapy.

It is possible only to speculate on the potential relevance of these constructs in psychotherapeutic intervention with victims of PTSD. It is hoped that these speculations will generate hypotheses that, in turn, will result in incremental information. In the optimal case, the end result of this effort will be the development of more efficient and effective procedures for the reversal of PTSD, wherever it may occur.

REFERENCES

Ablin, D. A., & Hood, M. (Eds.). (1987). *The Cambodian agony*. Armonk, NY: M. E. Sharpe.

Beiser, M., Turner, R. J., & Gandsen, S. (1989). Catastrophic stress and factors affecting its consequences among Southeast Asian refugees. *Social Science and Medicine, 25*, 183–195.

Boehnlein, J. K. (1987). Culture and society in post-traumatic stress disorder: Complications for psychotherapy. *American Journal of Psychotherapy, 16*, 519–530.

Byrne, D. (1964). Repression–sensitization as a dimension of personality. In B. A. Maher (Ed.), *Progress in experimental personality research*. New York: Academic Press.

Cheung, F. M. C. (1986). Psychopathology among Chinese people. In M. H. Bond (Ed.), *The psychology of the Chinese people* (pp. 171–212). Hong Kong: Oxford University Press.

Claver, B. G. (1976). Problèmes de guérissage en Côte d'Ivoire (Problems of healing in Ivory Coast). *Annales Médico-Psycholoqiques, 134*(1), 23–30.

de la Fuente, R. (1990). The mental health consequences of the 1985 earthquake in Mexico. *International Journal of Mental Health, 19*, 21–29.

Deitz, L. J. (1986). Time-limited psychotherapy for posttraumatic stress disorder: The traumatized ego and its self-reparative function. *American Journal of Psychotherapy, 40*, 290–299.

Díaz-Guerrero, R. (1970). *Estudios de psicologia del Méxicano* (2nd ed.) (Studies of psychology of the Mexican). Mexico CA: Trillas.

Doi, T. (1985). Psychotherapy: A cross-cultural perspective from Japan. In P. B. Pedersen, N. Sartorius, A. J. Marsella (Eds.), *Mental health services: The cross-cultural context* (pp. 267–279). Thousand Oaks, CA: Sage.

Draguns, J. G. (1975). Resocialization into culture: The complexities of taking a worldwide view of psychotherapy. In R. W. Brislin, S. Bochner & W. J. Lonner (Eds.). *Cross-cultural perspectives on learning* (pp. 273–289). Beverly Hills, CA: Sage.

Draguns, J. G. (1990a). Applications of cross-cultural psychology in the field of mental health. In R. W. Brislin (Ed.), *Applied cross-cultural psychology* (pp. 302–324). Thousand Oaks, CA: Sage.

Draguns, J. G. (1990b). Culture and psychopathology: Toward specifying the nature of the relationship. In J. Berman (Ed.), *Cross-cultural perspectives: Nebraska Symposium on Motivation 1989* (pp. 235–277). Lincoln: University of Nebraska Press.

Eitinger, L. (1961). Pathology of the concentration camp syndrome. *Archives of General Psychiatry, 5,* 371–379.

Ekman, P., & Friesen, W. V. (1971). Constants across cultures in the face and emotion. *Journal of Personality and Social Psychology, 17,* 124–129.

Everstine, D. S., & Everstine, L. (1993). *The trauma response: Treatment for emotional injury.* New York: Norton.

Figley, C. R. (Ed.), (1986). *Trauma and its wake. Volume II: Traumatic stress theory, research, and intervention.* New York: Brunner/Mazel.

Garbarino, J. (1992a). *Interviews with Vietnamese minors in detention camps in Hong Kong.* Unpublished manuscript.

Garbarino, J. (1992b). *The experience of children in Kuwait: Occupation, war, and liberation.* Unpublished manuscript.

Gussow, Z. (1985). Pibloktoq (hysteria) among the Polar Eskimo: An ethnopsychiatric study. In R. C. Simons & C. C. Hughes (Eds.), *The culture-bound syndromes: Folk-illnesses of psychiatric and anthropological interest* (pp. 271–288). Dordrecht, Netherlands: D. Reidel.

Hofstede, G. (1980). *Culture's consequences: International differences in work-related values.* Newbury Park, CA: Sage.

Hofstede, G. (1991). *Culture and organizations.* London: McGraw-Hill.

Horowitz, M. J. (1986). *Stress response syndromes* (2nd ed.). Northvale, NJ: Jason Aronson.

Horowitz, M. J. (1990). Post-traumatic stress disorders: Psychosocial aspects of the diagnosis. *International Journal of Mental Health, 19,* 21–36.

Hughes, C. C. (1985). Commentary: The startle matching taxon. In R. C. Simons & C. C. Hughes (Eds.), *The culture-bound syndromes: Folk illnesses of psychiatric and anthropological interest* (pp. 111–114). Dordrecht, Netherlands: D. Reidel.

Jilek, W. G. (1982). *Indian healing: Shamanistic ceremonialism in the Pacific Northwest today.* Surrey, Canada: Hancock House.

Jilek, W. G., & Todd, N. (1974). Witchdoctors succeed where doctors fail: Psychotherapy among coast Salish Indians. *Canadian Psychiatric Association Journal, 19,* 351–356.

Kaminer, H., & Lavie, P. (1991). Sleep and dreaming in Holocaust survivors. Decrease in dream recall in well-adjusted survivors. *Journal of Nervous and Mental Disease, 179*, 664–669.

Kiljunen, K. (1984). *Kampuchea: A decade of genocide.* London: Zed Press.

Kimura, B. (1972). Mitmenschlichkeit in der Psychiatrie (Empathic attitude in psychiatry). *Zeitschrift für Klinische Psychologie. 20,* 3–13.

Kinzie, J. D. (1978). Lessons from cross-cultural psychotherapy. *American Journal of Psychotherapy, 32,* 510–520.

Kinzie, J. D. (1987). The concentration camp syndrome among Cambodian refugees. In D. A. Ablin & M. Hood (Eds.), *The Cambodian agony* (pp. 332–353). Armonk, NY: M. E. Sharpe.

Kinzie, J. D., Boehnlein, J., Leung, P., Moore, L., Riley, C., & Smith, D. (1990). The prevalence of posttraumatic stress disorder and its clinical significance among Southeast Asian refugees. *American Journal of Psychiatry, 147,* 913–917.

Kinzie, J. D., & Fleck, J. (1987). Psychotherapy with severely traumatized refugees. *American Journal of Psychotherapy, 41,* 82–94.

Kinzie, D., Frederickson, R., Ben, R., Fleck, J., & Karls, W. (1984). Posttraumatic stress disorder among survivors of Cambodian concentration camps. *American Journal of Psychiatry, 141,* 645–650.

Klein, G. S. (1970). *Perception, motives, and personality.* New York: Random House.

Kleinman, A. (1980). *Patients and healers in the context of culture.* Berkeley: University of California Press.

Kleinman, A., & Kleinman, J. (1991). Suffering and its professional transformation: Toward an ethnography of interpersonal experience. *Culture, Medicine and Psychiatry, 15*(3), 275–301.

Krystal, H., & Danieli, Y. (1994). Holocaust survivor studies in the context of PTSD. *PTSD Research Quarterly, 5*(4), 1–5.

Lambert, M. J., Shapiro, D. A., & Bergin, A. E. (1986). The effectiveness of psychotherapy. In S. L. Garfield & A. E. Bergin (Eds.), *Handbook of psychotherapy and behavior change* (3rd ed., pp. 157–212). New York: Wiley.

Leff, J. P. (1988). *Psychiatry around the globe, a transcultural view* (2nd ed.). London: Gaskell.

Marsella, A. J. (1985). The self, adaptation, and adjustment. In A. J. Marsella, G. DeVos, & F. L. K. Hsu (Eds.), *Culture and self: Asian and Western perspectives* (pp. 281–308). New York: Tavistock.

Marsella, A. J. (1993). Counseling and psychotherapy with Japanese Americans: Cross-cultural considerations. *American Journal of Orthopsychiatry, 63,* 200–208.

Marsella, A. J., & Dash-Scheur, A. (1988). Coping, culture, and healthy human development: A research and conceptual overview. In P. Dasen, J. W. Berry, & N. Sartorius (Eds.), *Cross-cultural psychology and health: Toward applications* (pp. 162–178). Beverly Hills, CA: Sage.

Marsella, A. J., Friedman, M., & Spain, H. (1993). Ethnocultural aspects of PTSD: An overview of conceptual, methodological, and clinical research and directions. In R. Oldham, M. Riba, & A. Tashman (Eds.), *Review of Psychiatry, 12*, 29–62.

Matussek, P. (1971). *Die Konzentrationslagerhaft und ihre Folgen* (Incarceration in concentration camps and its consequences). Berlin: Springer-Verlag.

Merleu-Ponty, M. (1962). *Phenomenology of perception*. New York: Humanities Press.

Minkowski, E. (1966). *Traité de psychopathologie* (Textbook of psychopathology). Paris: Presses Universitaires de France.

Mollica, R., Wyshak, G., & Lavelle, J. (1987). The psychosocial impact of war trauma and torture on Southeast Asian refugees. *American Journal of Psychiatry, 144*, 1567–1572.

Mollica, R., Wyshak, G., Lavelle, J., Truang, T., Tor, S., & Yang, T. (1990). Assessing symptom change in Southeast Asian refugee survivors of mass violence and torture. *American Journal of Psychiatry, 147*, 83–88.

Moore, L. J., & Boehnlein, J. K. (1991). Posttraumatic stress disorder, depression, and somatic symptoms in U.S. Mien patients. *Journal of Nervous and Mental Disease, 179*, 728–733.

Nathan, T. (1994). *L'influence qui quérit* [The healing influence.] Paris: Editions Odile Jacob.

Neki, J. S., Joinet, B., Hogan, M., Hauli, J. G., & Kilonzo, G. (1985). The cultural perspective of therapeutic relationship—A viewpoint from Africa. *Acta Psychiatrica Scandinavica, 71*, 543–550.

Peseschkian, N. (1986). *Oriental stories as tools in psychotherapy*. Berlin: Springer-Verlag.

Petrie, A. (1967). *Individuality in pain and suffering*. Chicago: University of Chicago Press.

Pfeiffer, W. G. (1994). *Transkulturelle Psychiatrie* (2nd ed.) (Transcultural psychiatry). Stuttgart, Germany: Thieme.

Porot, M. (1956) Les rétentissements psychologiques des évènements d'Algérie [Psychological reverberations of Algerian events]. *Annales Médico-Psychologiques, 116*(2), 622–636.

Prince, R. (1980). Variations in psychotherapeutic procedures. In H. C. Triandis & J. G. Draguns (Eds.), *Handbook of cross-cultural psychology. Volume 6: Psychopathology* (pp. 291–349). Boston: Allyn and Bacon.

Ridley, C. R. & Lingle, D. W. (1996) Cultural empathy in multicultural counseling: A multidimensional process model. In P. B. Pedersen, J. G. Draguns, W. J. Lonner, & J. E. Trimble (Eds.), *Counseling across cultures*. (4th ed., pp. 21–46). Thousands Oaks, CA: Sage.

Rogers, C. R. (1957) Necessary and sufficient conditions of personality change. *Journal of Consulting Psychology, 21*, 95–103.

Roland, A. (1988). *In search of self in India and Japan*. Princeton, NJ: Princeton University Press.

Rubonis, A. V., & Bickman, L. (1991). Psychological impairment in the wake of disaster: The disaster-psychopathology relationship. *Psychological Bulletin, 109,* 384–399.

Scharfetter, C. (1985). Der Schamane: Zeuge einer alten Kultur—wieder belebbar? (The shaman as witness of an old culture: Can he be brought back to life?). *Schweizer Archiv der Neurologie und Psychiatrie, 136,* 81–95.

Simons, R. C. (1985). Introduction: The startle matching taxon. In R. C. Simons & C. S. Hughes (Eds.), *The culture-bound syndromes: Folk illnesses of psychiatric and anthropological interest* (pp. 41–42). Dordrecht, Netherland: D. Reidel.

Simons, R. C., & Hughes, C. S. (Eds.) (1985). *The culture-bound syndromes: Folk illnesses of psychiatric and anthropological interest.* Dordrecht, Netherlands: D. Reidel.

Trautmann, E. C. (1961). Psychiatrische Untersuchungen an Überlebenden der nationalsozialistischer Vernichtungslager 15 Jahre nach der Befreiung (Psychiatric investigations of survivors of the nationalist socialist death camps 15 years after liberation). *Nervenarzt, 32,* 545–559.

Triandis, H. C. (1972). *The analysis of subjective culture.* New York: Wiley.

Tsygankov, B. (1991, May). *PTSD in Soviet veterans of the war in Afghanistan.* Paper at the annual meeting of the American Psychiatric Association, New Orleans.

van de Veer, G. (1992). *Counselling and therapy with refugees: Psychological problems of victims of war, torture, and repression.* Chichester, England: Wiley.

Vassiliou, G., & Vassiliou, V. G. (1973). Subjective culture and psychotherapy. *American Journal of Psychotherapy, 27,* 42–51.

Westermeyer, J. (1985). Sudden mass assault with grenade: An epidemic amok form from Laos. In R. C. Simons & C. C. Hughes (Eds.), *The culture-bound syndromes: Folk illnesses of psychiatric and anthropological interest* (pp. 225–236). Dordrecht, Netherlands: D. Reidel.

Westermeyer, J. (1989). *Mental health for refugees and other migrants: Social and preventive approaches.* Springfield, IL: Thomas.

Yap, P. M. (1974). *Comparative psychiatry: A theoretical framework.* Toronto: University of Toronto Press.

Yehuda, R. (1994). Comments on the lack of integration between the Holocaust and PTSD literatures. *PTSD Research Quarterly, 5*(4), 5–8.

Yehuda, R., Kahana, B., Southwick, S. M., & Giller, E. L. (1994). Depressive features in Holocaust survivors with post-traumatic stress disorder. *Journal of Traumatic Stress, 7,* 699–704.

19

ETHNOCULTURAL VARIATIONS IN SERVICE USE AMONG VETERANS SUFFERING FROM PTSD

ROBERT ROSENHECK and ALAN FONTANA

SERVICES TO VETERANS

For as long as there have been civilizations, from the time of Odysseus's long journey home from the Trojan War to the modern day pilgrimages of American veterans to the Vietnam Veterans Memorial in Washington, nations have searched for ways to heal the physical and psychological wounds of war. Self-reliance and a distaste for government assistance, especially as the latter involves the federal government, have long been central values in American political culture (Marmor, Mashaw, & Harvey, 1990). The sense of obligation to the nation's veterans, however, has been the major exception to this principle (Adkins, 1967).

As described in a recent monograph (Skocpol, 1992), federal assistance to veterans was the largest and perhaps the most important forerunner of the federal social welfare programs that proliferated in America during the twentieth century; and the nation's vast complex of federal, state, and voluntary veterans assistance programs is still our longest running effort in the area of welfare democracy.

One of the distinctive features of our democratic nation state, in contrast to the European monarchies from which it emerged, is that military service, at all levels, is the responsibility and obligation of the citizenry, not of an aristocratic elite (Berryman, 1988). In principle, if not always in fact, our nation adheres to the ideal that the armed forces should reflect the universality of opportunity and the respect for diversity that are among our most cherished national ideals. Racial minorities and women have been the largest growing segments of our armed forces since the end of the Vietnam conflict. Recent controversies over the participation of women in combat roles specifically, and of gay men and lesbians in the military more generally, illustrate the incompleteness with which we have achieved the ideal of a representative military, but also the continued efforts to attain that ideal.

MENTAL HEALTH SERVICE USE AMONG ETHNOCULTURAL MINORITY VETERANS: MYTHS AND FACTS

Previous Research

Empirical studies conducted in recent decades have suggested that ethnocultural minorities make less use of both physical and mental health services than other Americans, either because they lack the resources needed to pay for such services, because they are personally reluctant to use such services, or because they have encountered service providers who are insensitive to their distinctive values and traditions (Acosta, 1980; Lefley, 1990; Snowden & Cheung, 1990).

There have been many accounts of the exceptionally painful and alienating experiences of members of ethnic minority groups who served in the armed forces (Parson, 1985a, 1985b; Silver & Wilson, 1988; Terry, 1984). Minority troops have often found themselves risking their lives for a society that accorded them only second-class status at home, and as a result, many felt deeply alienated from their government and from its leaders (Parson 1985b). In a 1980 survey of Vietnam veterans, for example, 29% of African American veterans and 27% of Hispanic veterans agreed with the statement, "My country took unfair advantage of me," as compared with only 20% of Whites (Veterans Administration, 1980).

Those who are responsible for serving America's veterans are thus confronted with the challenge of providing assistance to a clearly entitled but ethnoculturally diverse, often politically alienated, and geographically dispersed population. There has been virtually no empirical examination of how successful we have been at delivering health care and other benefits to members of ethnocultural minorities who have sustained injuries and other hardships as a result of their military service.

Leading scholars have expressed concern at the lack of attention to ethnocultural and minority issues in the treatment of PTSD specifically (Marsella, Friedman, & Spain, 1994; Westermeyer, 1989) and in psychiatric treatment generally (Lawson, 1986). Specific attention to services provided to ethnocultural minorities is especially warranted in the evaluation of the nation's treatment of its wartime veterans.

Previous Research in the Department of Veterans Affairs

In a previous study (Rosenheck & Fontana, 1994), we used data from a national community sample of veterans who served during the Vietnam conflict (the National Vietnam Veterans Readjustment Study [NVVRS]; Kulka et al., 1989, 1990) to test two hypotheses: (a) that veterans from ethnocultural minority groups were less likely than other veterans to use services of mental health professionals and (b) that because of their alienation from the government, these veterans were especially less likely to use VA mental health services.

Contrary to these hypotheses, no differences were observed in rates of professional mental health service use among five different ethnocultural groups (Whites, African Americans, Puerto Rican Hispanics, Mexican Hispanics, and others) until adjustments were made for severity of need or resource availability. When adjustments were made for these other factors, African American and Mexican Hispanic veterans were less likely to use professional mental health services than other veterans, but they were also less likely to make use of self-help groups such as Alcoholics Anonymous.

Minority groups were just as likely as Whites, however, to use VA mental health services, even after adjustment was made for factors such as income, health insurance, and receipt of VA financial benefits. In contrast, after adjusting for these factors, African American and Mexican Hispanic veterans were less likely than White veterans to use non-VA mental health services.

We concluded from those findings that in spite of the central role of the federal government in the initiation and conduct of the Vietnam conflict, feelings of alienation among minority veterans of the Vietnam era have not dissuaded them from turning to VA for help. Perhaps more important than its involvement in the Vietnam conflict is the fact that the federal government has played a visible and often leading role in the expansion of civil rights, from the 14th Amendment to the Constitution in 1868, to the desegregation of the Armed Forces in 1948, to the Voting Rights Act of 1965. It appears that embittered minorities feel that even if American society remains unjust, they get the fairest chance at treatment from an institution operated by the federal government. The forces of affiliation with VA thus appear to be more important than the forces of alienation.

A NATIONAL STUDY OF MENTAL HEALTH SERVICES

Background of Study

In this report, we extend our examination of ethnocultural factors in the treatment of combat-related PTSD through a detailed examination of treatment received by veterans who came to VA for help with psychological problems related to their war zone experiences. Data for this study were derived from structured interviews conducted as part of the national evaluation of the implementation of the Department of Veterans Affairs PTSD Clinical Teams (PCT) Program. Fifty-three teams were established across the country by VA between 1989 and 1992, with the task of providing war zone veterans with treatment of PTSD in specialized outpatient clinical settings.

This study explores differences among ethnocultural minority groups in five related domains: (a) sociodemographic status and baseline clinical presentation, (b) self-identified service needs, (c) past service use, (d) prospectively examined use of team services during the year after first contact with the program, and (e) clinical improvement as assessed by team clinicians at the time of the last clinical contact. We, thus, hoped to determine whether there were differences among minority groups in clinical problems and self-identified needs, in receipt of services, and in benefit from services.

Note that the data used in this study were not collected specifically to evaluate the influence of ethnocultural background or current ethnocultural orientation on the use or effectiveness of mental health treatment. Consequently, the information on ethnocultural identity available in these studies is rudimentary, and the categorizations of illness and health care services are those of conventional American culture, not, as one might prefer, those of the informants themselves (Kleinman, 1988).

Methods

As part of the national evaluation of the implementation of the PCT program, the first 100 veterans seen at 53 VA sites received a formal assessment using a structured interview instrument, the War Stress Interview, Part 1 (WSI–1; Fontana, Rosenheck, & Spencer, 1990, 1993). The WSI–1 was administered by program clinicians during the implementation phase of the program. The progress of veterans in treatment was documented for 1 year thereafter using the Clinical Process Form (CPF), a structured clinical summary completed by PCT clinicians 2, 4, 8, and 12 months after each veteran entered treatment.

Instruments

The WSI–1 assessed veterans' baseline characteristics in five broad domains: (a) sociodemographic characteristics (age, race, marital status, employment, income, and receipt of VA compensation benefits), (b) exposure to war zone trauma, (c) clinical status (PTSD and other psychiatric symptoms, substance abuse disorders, and medical problems), (d) past VA and non-VA mental health service use, and (e) areas of clinical need, as identified by the veteran.

CPF reports allowed determination of (a) the length of veterans' participation in treatment with the team up to 1 year, (b) the number of treatment sessions, (c) the clinicians' assessment of regularity of attendance and commitment to treatment during the first 2 months of treatment, (d) the overall content focus of treatment, and (e) the clinicians' assessment of improvement in 16 areas at the time of last contact.

Key Research Variables

Six ethnocultural groups were distinguished: Whites, African Americans, Puerto Rican Hispanics, Mexican Hispanics, American Indians, and others). Unfortunately, WSI–1 did not ask specifically about Hispanic subgroup identification. Using residence data from the NVVRS as a guide, we made a determination by site location between Hispanics who were likely to be of Puerto Rican descent and those who were likely to be of Mexican descent.

Exposure of the veteran to war zone stressors was assessed by two variables: exposure to combat, as measured by the Revised Combat Scale (Laufer, Yager, Frey-Wouters, & Donnellan, 1981), and participation in abusive violence.

We measured PTSD symptoms as the mean of responses to the Structured Clinical Interview for Diagnosis (Spitzer & Williams, 1985) concerning the *DSM–III–R* criteria for PTSD, whereas we assessed general psychiatric problems by means of the Psychiatric Composite Scale of the Addiction Severity Index (ASI; McLellan et al., 1985). Alcohol abuse was assessed with the four "CAGE" items (Ewing, 1984); drug abuse was assessed with selected items from the Diagnostic Interview Schedule (DIS; Robins, Heizer, & Croughan, 1981; Vernez, Burnam, McGlynn, Trude, & Mittman, 1988). We determined the presence of medical problems with a single question asking if the veteran suffered from a serious medical problem.

An extensive series of questions addressed past use of VA and non-VA inpatient and outpatient services for psychiatric, substance abuse, and medical problems, as well as overall satisfaction with VA mental health services. At the conclusion of the WSI–1 interview, each veteran was presented with a list of 15 clinical and social adjustment problem areas and was asked to identify all areas in which he or she felt a need for additional help.

Treatment provided by the team was tracked with the CPF. General patterns of attendance were assessed after 2 months by means of a three-level question (1 = *attended only once or twice,* 2 = *attendance has been continuing but irregular,* 3 = *attendance quite regular*). Commitment to working with the team was also assessed after 2 months, on a 5-point scale (0 = *not at all committed,* 2 = *slightly committed,* 2 = *moderately committed,* 3 = *highly committed,* 4 = *maximally committed*). Content focus was addressed through a question that asked, overall, how much of the total clinical time was spent on 21 general clinical modalities and 10 specific clinical activities (0 = *no time,* 1 = *a little time (less than 10%),* 2 = *some time (between 10% and 50%),* and 3 = *a lot of time (more than 50%)*).

Clinical improvement since initiation of contact with the program was measured for 16 domains on a 5-point scale (0 = *substantial deterioration,* 1 = *some deterioration,* 2 = *no change,* 3 = *some improvement,* 4 = *substantial improvement*). Only those who were identified as having a problem in each domain were rated. Because there could be more than one CPF per veteran, data on therapeutic content focus were averaged across all CPFs for each veteran. The improvement rating used was the one reported on the last CPF for each veteran.

Data Analyses

We used one-way analysis of variance (ANOVA), with Tukey multiple-range tests, to evaluate the statistical significance of differences in various measures of clinical status and service use. In the analysis of veterans' assessment of their own needs, of past service use, and of clinician-assessed improvements, the potentially confounding influence of sociodemographic and clinical factors that differed significantly across ethnocultural group membership, as well as site differences, was statistically controlled by analysis of covariance (ANCOVA).

Results

Ethnocultural Group Membership

The sample included 3,879 Whites (70.8%), 918 African Americans (16.8%), 249 Puerto Rican Hispanics (4.5%), 195 Mexican Hispanics (3.6%), 124 American Indians (2.3%), and 110 others (2.0%). Comparisons of the proportions of minority groups in this sample with the proportions seen among veterans treated for PTSD in other VA programs revealed only modest differences. Specifically, data gathered in a national VA survey (Ronis, Bates, & Wolff, 1992) showed that among Vietnam era veterans treated for PTSD at VA medical centers during a 2-week period in 1990 ($N = 9,853$), 74.9 % were White, 16.1% African American, 8.1% Hispanic (Puerto Rican and Mexican Hispanics were not differentiated in the survey), and 0.8% American Indian.

Among Vietnam era veterans seen for PTSD in VA's Vietnam Veterans Readjustment Counseling Center Program (Blank, 1993), a storefront, community-based VA program that emphasizes outreach to minorities ($N = 4,436$), 78.3% of those surveyed were White, 12.5% African American, 6.9% Hispanic and 1.1% American Indian. The proportion of minorities in this sample was, thus, only slightly greater than the proportion seen in other VA programs.

Veteran Characteristics

As shown in Table 1, veterans from different ethnocultural groups differed significantly on several sociodemographic and baseline measures. Whites were older than other veterans. African Americans were less likely to be married, had lower incomes, and were less likely to be receiving VA compensation payments than other groups. Clinically, African Americans had higher levels of alcohol and drug abuse but were less likely to have attempted suicide. Note that there were no significant differences among groups in reports of combat exposure, although a greater proportion of Puerto Rican Hispanics than Whites or Mexican Hispanics reported participating in abusive violence. Puerto Rican Hispanics reported more PTSD symptoms than did either Whites or African Americans, and both Puerto Rican and Mexican Hispanics scored higher than all other groups on psychiatric problems and symptoms. There were no differences among groups in the proportion of veterans reporting medical problems.

Veterans' Identified Needs for Additional Services

Data on veterans' perceived needs are presented in Table 2. The most consistent finding is that, as one would expect from their lower incomes, African Americans were more likely than other groups to express a need for assistance in the domains of basic resources, finances, and employment. In keeping with the data reported above on their clinical status, African Americans were also more likely than members of other groups to express a need for assistance with legal problems, alcohol, and drug abuse. Puerto Rican Hispanics expressed greater need for assistance with interpersonal relationships than did Whites or African Americans, perhaps because a higher proportion were married. In general, Whites expressed less need for help with PTSD symptoms than did minority groups.

TABLE 1
Predictors of Service Use by Ethnocultural Group (53 PCT Sites)

Predictor	White (1)	Black (2)	Puerto Rican Hispanic (3)	Mexican Hispanic (4)	American Indian (5)	Other (6)	F_a	Significant differences
n	3,879	918	249	195	124	110		
Sociodemographic characteristics								
Years of age	46.27	43.82	43.63	45.50	44.00	51.35	30.7****	1>2,3,5;6>1,2,3,4,5
Married (percentage)	0.50	0.30	0.59	0.54	0.43	0.55	30.1****	2<1,3,4,6;3<1,5
Working (percentage)	0.56	0.47	0.47	0.53	0.46	0.32	3.4**	
Personal income	$1,179	$755	$1,053	$947	$901	$1,297	35.2****	2<1,3,6
VA compensation	0.58	0.52	0.63	0.55	0.55	0.59	3.5**	2<1,3
War zone stress								
Combat exposure	10.52	10.73	10.91	10.55	10.58	10.50	1.6	
Abusive violence in VN (percentage)	0.29	0.31	0.38	0.21	0.37	0.31	4.2**	3<1,4;5<4
Illness characteristics								
PTSD (SCID sum)	1.51	1.52	1.66	1.59	1.60	1.47	8.2****	3>1,2,6
Psychiatric problems (ASI)	0.56	0.57	0.63	0.61	0.54	0.53	7.6****	3>1,2,5,6;4>1,2,5,6
Alcoholism (CAGE)	1.22	1.66	1.07	1.12	1.53	0.84	15.3****	2>1,3,4,6;5>6
Drug abuse (DIS)	0.46	0.88	0.49	0.55	0.52	0.53	27.2****	2>1,3,4,5,6
Ever attempted suicide (percentage)	0.38	0.32	0.48	0.38	0.47	0.35	5.6****	2<1,3,5;3>1
Medical problems	0.53	0.56	0.49	0.51	0.58	0.65	2.3*	

Note. PCT = PTSD Clinical Teams Program, VA = Department of Veterans Affairs; VN = Vietnam, PTSD = posttraumatic stress disorder, SCID sum = mean of responses to Structural Clinial Interview for Diagnosis, ASI = Addiction Severity Index, CAGE = CAGE Questionnaire, DIS = Diagnostic Interview Schedule. Statistical comparisons are based on ANOVAs with Tukey multiple-range test for paired comparisons (p<.05). All entries are scale scores unless otherwise noted. $_a$ df = 5, 5238 * p<.01. ** p<.01. *** p<.001. **** p<.0001.

Service Use

Table 3 shows the proportion of veterans in each ethnocultural group who had used each of 21 categories of VA and non-VA health services. Because differences both in clinical practice style and in the supply of services exist across sites independently of the ethnocultural status of veterans, ANCOVAs included dichotomous dummy-coded site variables for $N - 1$ sites. By controlling for the influence of sociodemographic characteristics, clinical status, site-specific practice variation, and supply effects, the statistical analyses reflect the best estimate possible of the relationship of ethnocultural status to service use.

As shown in Table 3, African Americans made less use than other groups of outpatient psychiatric services and psychotropic medications, whereas Puerto Rican Hispanics made more use than other groups of psychotropic medications, particularly anxiolytics and sleep medications. Corresponding to their higher scores on substance abuse measures and self-expressed needs for substance abuse treatment, African Americans made greater use than other groups of all types of substance abuse treatment, with the exception of outpatient treatment for alcoholism. American Indians made greater use of inpatient alcoholism treatment than other groups, with the exception of African Americans. There were no differences among groups in the use of specialized PTSD services.

The differential rates of psychiatric and substance abuse service use among various groups appear to cancel each other out, producing no significant differences among Whites, African Americans, Hispanics, or American Indians in their use of all types of psychiatric and substance abuse services. There were also no differences in recent use of any medical services (VA and non-VA), in the use of VA medical services alone, or in overall satisfaction with mental health services received from VA.

Use of PCT Services

Table 4 shows that duration of involvement in the PCT program was significantly shorter for African Americans than for other groups and that African Americans were more likely than Whites or Hispanics to terminate treatment within 2 months of program entry. Corresponding to their greater rate of early termination, African Americans had fewer individual sessions than did Whites or Hispanics, and clinicians described African Americans' attendance as less regular and their commitment to therapy as less strong.

There were few significant differences among groups on the clinicians' ratings of the content focus of treatment. Clinicians treating African Americans, however, reported spending less time on insight-oriented therapy, on deconditioning negative affects, and on discussions of war traumas. These activities are usually associated with substantial and prolonged in-

TABLE 2
Percentage Veterans Reporting Clinical Needs When Assessed for Treatment by VA's PTSD Clinical Teams Program (53 Sites)

Clinical needs	White (1)	Black (2)	Puerto Rican Hispanic (3)	Mexican Hispanic (4)	American Indian (5)	Other (6)	F_a	Significant differences
n	3,879	918	249	195	124	110		
Community/social adjustment								
Basic needs (food, shelter, and clothing)	32.5	55.2	35.5	35.6	42.0	37.7	36.5*****	2>1,3,4,5,6
Financial support	51.3	73.4	57.4	58.2	59.7	55.7	38.6*****	2>1,3,4,5,6
Employment	42.6	58.6	43.4	49.5	46.2	34.9	20.0*****	2>1,3,6
Legal problems	11.7	14.1	7.9	11.9	15.1	10.4	2.0*	2>3
Interpersonal relationships	54.6	53.6	64.5	53.6	54.6	50.9	2.4**	3>1,2
Daily social activities	56.7	58.3	64.5	53.1	59.7	48.1	2.6**	3>6
Health care problems								
Alcohol abuse	22.7	32.0	20.2	17.5	35.3	15.1	18.7*****	2>1,3,4,6;5>1,3,4,6
Drug abuse	10.0	25.6	11.2	14.9	15.1	17.9	50.3*****	2>1,3,4,5;6>1
War-related stress	92.0	94.5	93.8	96.9	93.3	92.5	3.2***	1<2,4
Reliving experiences	84.0	88.5	92.1	90.2	89.1	81.1	7.8*****	3>1,6;2>1
Numbing of emotions	82.3	84.3	81.0	82.4	84.0	68.8	4.5*****	6<1,2,3,4,5
Violent impulses	66.6	71.3	76.4	70.1	63.9	74.5	5.1*****	1<3,2
Sleep problems	82.4	88.2	88.8	91.7	89.9	81.1	9.5*****	1<2,3,4
Another psychiatric condition	27.3	25.7	18.6	31.4	30.5	19.8	3.2***	3<1,4
Medical condition	41.9	45.1	43.0	45.4	48.7	47.2	1.6	

Note. VA = Department of Veterans Affairs. PTSD = posttraumatic stress disorder. Statistical comparisons are based on ANCOVAs with Tukey multiple-range tests ($p<.05$), controlling for the influence of age, combat exposure, marital status, current employment, medical problems, PTSD symptoms, psychiatric problems, alcohol abuse, drug abuse, income, and site specific practice patterns. $_a$ df = 67,5176 * $p<.05$. ** $p<.10$. *** $p<.01$. **** $p<.001$. ***** $p<.0001$.

TABLE 3

Percentage of Veterans Reporting Past Use of Services When Assessed for Treatment by VA's PTSD Clinical Teams Program (53 Sites)

Service	White (1)	Black (2)	Puerto Rican Hispanic (3)	Mexican Hispanic (4)	American Indian (5)	Other (6)	F	Significant differences
n	3,879	918	249	195	124	110		
Psychiatric treatment								
Psychiatric inpatient	51.7	49.9	57.0	47.9	52.1	43.4	1.6	
Psychiatric inpatient (VA)	45.3	43.8	52.1	43.8	47.1	37.7	0.9	
Psychiatric outpt. (VA or non-VA)	69.3	57.9	74.4	74.2	62.2	62.3	4.8***	2<1,3,4
Psychiatric outpt. (VA)	69.3	57.9	74.3	74.2	62.2	62.3	4.7****	2<1,3,4
Any psychiatric treatment (IP or OP)	77.8	69.2	81.8	77.8	70.6	67.9	4.6***	2<1,3; 3>2,6
Any VA psychiatric treatment (IP or OP)	76.2	66.8	80.2	77.3	68.9	67.0	4.9***	2<1,3,4
Specialized PTSD treatment	33.9	29.7	28.9	38.7	36.1	35.8	0.9	
Psychotropic medications	57.3	47.9	69.0	60.8	52.9	47.2	4.6***	2<1,3,4; 3>1,2,5,6
Anxiolytics	26.3	18.0	49.2	26.8	19.3	17.0	5.2****	3>1,2,4,5,6; 1>2
Antidepressants	40.4	30.2	43.6	42.3	37.0	23.6	4.4***	2<1,3,4; 6<1,3,4
Sleep medications	8.6	10.3	29.3	11.3	6.7	13.2	0.6	3>1,2,4,5,6
Substance abuse								
Alcohol inpatient	36.9	43.4	25.2	29.4	53.8	18.9	2.7*	2>1,3,4,6; 5>1,3,4,6; 1>3,6
Alcohol outpatient	39.6	42.8	27.3	34.0	48.7	21.7	3.3**	3<1,2,5; 6<1,2,5; 4<5
Drug inpatient	14.8.	34.7	16.1	15.5	18.5	20.8	16.4****	2>1,3,4,5,6
Drug outpatient	12.8	30.8	13.6	17.5	14.3	18.9	13.7****	2>1,3,4,5,6
Substance abuse inpatient (A or D)	41.1	57.1	30.6	32.5	56.3	29.2	4.0**	2>1,3,4,6; 5>1,3,4,6; 1>3,6
Substance abuse outpatient (A or D)	42.6	53.3	31.4	38.1	51.3	27.4	2.8*	2>1,3,4,6; 3<1,2,5; 6<1,2,5;
Any substance abuse (IP or OP)	49.9	64.7	38.0	42.8	64.7	34.0	4.4***	2>1,3,4,6; 5>1,3,4,6; 3<1,2,5; 6<1,2,5
Total for mental health	89.0	89.1	89.7	84.0	85.7	71.7	6.4*****	6<1,2,3,4,5
Medical treatment	42.1	43.3	38.4	42.3	46.2	44.3	1.1	
VA medical treatment	33.2	36.5	35.1	35.6	38.7	34.0	1.5	
Satisfaction with VA services	1.76	1.74	1.85	1.79	1.76	1.73	0.2	

Note. VA = Department of Veterans Affairs, PTSD = posttraumatic stress disorder, IP = inpatient, OP = outpatient, A = alcohol, D = drugs. Statistical comparisons are based on ANCOVAs with Tukey multiple-range test ($p<.05$), controlling for the influence of age, combat exposure, marital status, current employment, medical problems, PTSD symptoms, psychiatric problems, alcohol abuse, drug abuse, income, and site specific practice patterns. [a]df = 67,5176 * $p<.05$. ** $p<.01$. *** $p<.001$. **** $p<.0001$.

TABLE 4
Use of PCT Services by Ethnocultural Groups

Use of service	White (1)	Black (2)	Puerto Rican Hispanic (3)	Mexican Hispanic (4)	American Indian (5)	Other (6)	F_a	Significant differences
n	3,879	918	249	195	124	110		
Participation in treatment:								
Duration of involvement (in months)	5.45	4.58	7.66	6.16	5.27	5.35	1.84*	2<1,3,4; 3>1,2,5
Terminated before 2 months	0.35	0.41	0.24	0.26	0.37	0.38	2.59**	1>3,4; 2>1,3,4
Total sessions	23.00	17.99	21.78	20.79	24.03	22.87	3.31***	1>2
Individual sessions	11.11	8.42	11.65	11.63	10.57	9.16	6.86***	2<1,3,4
Group sessions	11.80	9.73	9.44	9.04	13.63	13.76	1.23	
Attendance	1.63	1.37	1.59	1.46	1.55	1.67	6.61****	2<1,3,6
Commitment	2.55	2.18	2.47	2.44	2.48	2.51	8.3****	2<1,2,4
Clinical time committed to:								
Current social adjustment	1.79	1.79	1.63	1.86	1.71	1.59	1.60	
Vocational counseling	0.11	0.15	0.04	0.05	0.14	0.04	0.72	
Social skills training	0.62	0.61	0.49	0.51	0.64	0.36	0.24	
Crisis intervention	0.31	0.31	0.20	0.29	0.29	0.33	1.82	
Benefits counseling	0.22	0.22	0.14	0.16	0.18	0.12	0.33	
Working toward psychological insight	1.42	0.97	1.28	1.06	1.13	1.14	2.81**	2<1,3
Directive therapy	0.85	0.89	0.90	0.84	0.92	1.18	5.10****	6>1,2,4
Deconditioning negative affects	0.49	0.38	0.52	0.56	0.55	0.39	3.33****	2<1,4
Abreacting negative trauma-related affects	0.74	0.66	1.14	0.69	0.71	0.84	2.75**	3>1,2,4,5
Discussing war traumas	1.98	1.09	1.24	1.36	1.09	1.40	3.95***	2<1,4,6
Substance abuse treatment	0.38	0.53	0.27	0.20	0.47	0.47	2.09*	2>1,3,4; 4<1,5
Physical illness	0.40	0.37	0.55	0.39	0.38	0.60	1.57	

Note. PCT = PTSD Clinical Teams Program, PTSD - posttraumatic stress disorder. Statistical comparisons are based on ANCOVAs with Tukey multiple-range tests ($p<.05$), controlling for the influence of age, combat exposure, marital status, current employment, medical problems, PTSD symptoms, psychiatric problems, alcohol abuse, drug abuse, income, and site specific practice patterns. $_a$ df = 67, 5176 * $p<.10$. ** $p<.05$. *** $p<.01$. **** $p<.0001$.

volvement in therapy and may be less prominent among African Americans because of their briefer involvement with the PCT program and reportedly lower levels of commitment to therapy. Clinicians reported spending more time with African Americans, however, on issues related to substance abuse. Clinicians reported spending more time with Puerto Rican Hispanics than with Whites, African Americans, or Mexican Hispanics in therapies involving abreacting traumatic affects.

Clinicians' Evaluation of Improvement

Significant differences among ethnocultural groups in the clinicians' ratings of improvement were evident for 4 of 16 measures (Table 5). Whites were judged to have made more improvement than Mexican Hispanics in employment and more improvement than African Americans in social isolation, overall PTSD symptomatology, and sleep problems.

Early Termination, Duration of Involvement Among African American Veterans

In view of the results presented above regarding the lesser service use and improvement by African Americans, we conducted an additional series of analyses to explore possible explanations for these differences. First, duration of involvement was added as a covariate to the analysis of number of sessions received. With duration of involvement controlled, there were no statistical differences between ethnocultural groups in the total number of sessions, in the number of individual sessions, or in the number of group sessions. The smaller number of treatment sessions received by African Americans was, thus, shown to be a consequence of their briefer involvement in treatment.

Second, both duration of involvement and total number of sessions were added as covariates to models of attendance, commitment, attention to various content areas, and improvement. When these measures of involvement were included as covariates, African Americans were still significantly less regular in their attendance and less committed to treatment, and their treatment focused less on war zone traumas and deconditioning of negative affects than for either Whites or Puerto Rican Hispanics. Differences in improvement between African Americans and Whites, however, were no longer significant. Differences between ethnocultural groups in reported improvement, thus, appear to be primarily a function of differences in the duration of involvement in treatment.

Third, we attempted to determine whether the briefer duration of involvement of African Americans could be explained by the less frequent use of medications before treatment or by the less intensive focus on war traumas. It seemed plausible that veterans who obtain regular prescriptions for medications are more likely to stay involved in treatment than others

TABLE 5
Clinical Improvement as rated by PCT Clinicians at Time of Last Contact (Among Those With Each Problem): PTSD Clinical Teams Program (53 Sites)

Domain of Improvement	n	White (1)	Black (2)	Puerto Rican Hispanics (3)	Mexican Hispanic (4)	American Indian (5)	Other (6)	F_a	Significant differences
Community/social adjustment									
Basic needs (food, shelter, and clothing)	1,519	3.24	3.23	3.15	3.20	3.13	3.25	0.2	
Financial support	2,147	3.23	3.15	3.04	3.12	3.13	3.13	1.7	
Employment	2,106	3.17	3.11	2.96	2.88	3.06	3.26	3.4***	1>4
Legal problems	669	3.14	3.11	2.91	3.00	3.00	3.06	0.4	
Interpersonal relationships	2,878	3.37	3.20	3.26	3.19	3.23	3.37	1.6	
Social isolation	2,911	3.38	3.26	3.27	3.26	3.20	3.41	2.6**	1>2
Health care problems									
Substance abuse	1,665	3.43	3.43	3.49	3.25	3.34	3.23	0.6	
Alcohol abuse	1,489	3.44	3.39	3.48	3.32	3.41	3.21	0.4	
Drug abuse	767	3.42	3.52	3.50	3.37	3.22	3.29	0.6	
PTSD symptoms	3,783	3.50	3.40	3.49	3.37	3.40	3.52	2.7**	1>2
Reliving experiences	3,583	3.39	3.29	3.44	3.30	3.24	3.35	1.3	
Numbing of emotions	3,543	3.45	3.32	3.41	3.36	3.39	3.47	1.7	
Violent impulses	3,069	3.51	3.41	3.51	3.40	3.51	3.46	0.7	
Sleep problems	3,530	3.41	3.30	3.38	3.30	3.31	3.36	2.0*	1>2
Another psychiatric condition	1,234	3.30	3.28	3.18	3.26	3.26	3.16	0.3	
Medical condition	1,778	3.06	3.04	3.31	2.94	3.16	2.82	1.5	

Note. PCT = PTSD Clinical Teams Program, PTSD = posttraumatic stress disorder. Statistical comparisons are based on ANCOVAs with Tukey multiple-range tests ($p < .05$), controlling for the influence of age, combat exposure, marital status, current employment, medical problems, PTSD symptoms, psychiatric problems, alcohol abuse, drug abuse, income, and site specific practice patterns. $_a$ df = 67, (n-68) using n from n column. * $p < .10$. ** $p < .05$. *** $p < .01$.

and that those whose war experiences are not addressed as extensively might feel less understood and therefore drop out. With use of medication before PCT treatment and attention to war traumas controlled, there were no significant differences between ethnocultural groups in duration of involvement or total number of sessions of treatment received, although differences in regularity of attendance and commitment were still significant.

It must be acknowledged that extensive discussion of war experiences may be as much a result of extended treatment as a cause of it, and we cannot, therefore, interpret the meaning of this finding unambiguously. These data, nevertheless, suggest that part of the explanation for the briefer involvement of African Americans in treatment could be that they were prescribed medication less often and that their treatment focused on war zone trauma less extensively than others.

Fourth, we explored the possibility that the higher level of substance abuse among African Americans might also contribute to their briefer involvement in treatment. Previous analyses demonstrated that substance abuse was associated with briefer involvement in the program but that it did not fully account for the shorter duration of involvement in the program by African Americans. In this series of analyses, we added an interaction term to the analyses to evaluate whether substance abuse was associated with greater attrition from treatment among African Americans than among other veterans. These analyses showed that veterans who suffer from substance abuse disorders participated in treatment about 1 month less than non-substance abusers but that there was no significant interaction between ethnocultural group membership and substance abuse in predicting duration or other measures of program involvement.

Differences between African Americans and both Whites and Puerto Rican Hispanics in services received from the PCT program are, thus, partly attributable to differences in duration of involvement in the program, in the use of prescribed medications, in the amount of time devoted to discussion of war traumas, and in the prevalence of substance abuse problems. These factors do not, however, entirely account for the differences between African Americans and others in use of team services.

Discussion

Some Differences and Similarities

In a previous study, we analyzed data from a national survey of veterans and identified a significant difference in the frequency with which minority veterans used mental health services. As suggested by other studies, African Americans and Mexican Hispanics were less likely than Whites to use professional mental health services. This underutilization, however, was limited to use of non-VA mental health services. It did not characterize use of VA services. The current study examined the use of VA services in greater detail.

Using data on over 5,000 veterans assessed in VA's national PCT program, several important differences were found among ethnocultural groups in health service use and in clinical improvement. These differences were most striking for African Americans, Puerto Rican Hispanics, and American Indians.

African Americans were, in several respects, less well-off than other groups. They were least likely of all groups to be married and had the lowest incomes and the highest rates of alcohol and drug abuse. Concomitantly, they reported a greater need for help with financial support, employment, and alcohol and drug abuse. In keeping with their expressed needs, they made greater use of substance abuse services. Prospective examination of their use of PCT services showed that African Americans were less intensively involved in treatment and showed less improvement than other groups in several areas.

Puerto Rican Hispanics reported the highest levels of PTSD symptoms, and Puerto Rican and Mexican Hispanics had the highest levels of general psychiatric symptoms. Puerto Rican Hispanics also used psychotropic medications more than other groups, were involved in PCT treatment longer than members of other groups, and spent more time in abreactive therapeutic modalities.

American Indians had significantly higher levels of alcohol problems than all groups except African Americans and, correspondingly, reported higher levels of need for alcoholism treatment and used inpatient alcoholism treatment more frequently than any other group except African Americans.

Again, there were no differences in the ethnocultural proportions of veterans who had made prior use of at least one type of psychiatric or substance abuse service, nor were there any differences in prior use of specialized PTSD services, in overall satisfaction with VA services, or in clinical improvement in the majority of domains.

These findings confirm the general conclusion of our previous study, that ethnocultural minorities do not appear to be at any general or consistent disadvantage in access to, or use of, VA health care services. They also demonstrate that although differences between Whites and minorities were not found in overall use of services, there are clear differences among ethnocultural minority groups in use of specific mental health services. African Americans, in particular, appear to be less involved in treatment than either Whites or Puerto Rican Hispanics.

Some Possible Explanations of Differences

These differences between ethnocultural groups in specific service use and clinical improvement may be explained in three ways. First, the differences may reflect epidemiologic differences in the type or severity of the disorders for which ethnocultural groups seek help. Second, differences in service use and outcome may reflect differences in receptiveness or responsiveness to the treatments offered, whether ethnoculturally or socioeconomically determined. Third, there may be differences among groups that are attributable to the way providers treat them, either by providing different amounts or types of services or by providing a different quality of services. It remains for us to draw on the data available here, and on other published studies, to evaluate the role of these explanations in generating the minority group use patterns observed above.

Both the greater proportion of unmarried African American veterans and their substantially lower incomes reflect national trends that are well demonstrated in studies such as the NVVRS (Rosenheck & Fontana, 1994). Higher rates of alcohol and drug use among African Americans, although reported from several studies conducted in urban centers (Sutocky, Shultz, & Kizer, 1993; Williams, 1986), have not been confirmed in national surveys such as the NVVRS (Rosenheck & Fontana, 1994) or the Epidemiologic Catchment Area (ECA) study (Robins & Regier, 1991).

We cannot, therefore, determine whether the high rate of substance abuse among African American veterans in the VA sample reflects a greater rate of substance abuse among African American veterans generally or whether it reflects a tendency for African American veterans suffering from substance abuse to seek help or, more specifically, to seek help from VA. The lower rate of use of medications among African Americans probably reflects both a general reluctance among African Americans to take medication (Lefley, 1990) and a reluctance among clinicians to prescribe medications to veterans who have a history of substance abuse (Fontana et al., 1993).

Briefer Involvement in Therapy Among African Americans: Some Speculations

It is more difficult to explain the briefer involvement of African Americans and other differences in their participation in the PCT program. Several interpretations are possible, some of which receive partial support from our analyses. First, African Americans are less likely to use medications, are less likely to spend time discussing their war experiences in treatment, and are more likely to have substance abuse problems than other veterans. We have shown, above, that these factors partially explain their briefer involvement in PCT treatment. Second, important service needs of African Americans veterans in the area of financial support and employment may not be adequately met by the PCT program because of its central focus on mental health services. African Americans may terminate earlier from the program because it does not completely meet these needs.

Third, because the majority of VA mental health professionals are White, it is also possible that African American veterans find it more difficult to sustain involvement in therapy with clinicians who are White or, alternatively, that White clinicians are less successful at engaging African American veterans in treatment. Although differential rates of service use have been identified between African Americans and Whites in some, but not all, studies of mental health care (Acosta, 1980; Blendon, Aiken, Freeman, & Corey, 1989; Mollica, Blum, & Redlich, 1980; Soloman, 1988; Sue, 1991) and in many studies of physical health care (Cowie, Fahrenbruch, Cobb, & Hallstrom, 1993; Escarce, Epstein, Colby, & Schwartz, 1993), the relationship of these findings to racial differences between patient and clinician has been addressed in only one large clinical study.

In that study (Sue, 1977), clients with ethnically matched clinicians were less likely than clients with ethnically unmatched clinicians to drop out after one session and received a greater number of treatment sessions, although there was no relationship between ethnic matching and clinical outcome. However, among African Americans, ethnic matching did not affect dropping out after one session, although it was associated with having a greater number of sessions. Note, however, that in a separate study of veterans treated by two PCTS that had both White and African American clinicians, we found no differences in duration of involvement or number of sessions related to the racial match of clinicians and patients.

Like others who have found evidence of relative underutilization of health care services among African Americans, even after adjustment for socioeconomic and clinical factors (Bergner, 1993), we have no ready explanation for our findings. In a recent overview of the situation of African Americans, Princeton theologian Cornel West echoed the thoughts of many other scholars and social scientists in suggesting that centuries of racial oppression have generated a pervasive nihilism, pessimism, and hopelessness among African Americans (West, 1993). It is possible that this nihilism or some related phenomenon, unmeasured in our study, may account for the lesser use among African Americans of available mental health services.

Puerto Rican Symptomatology and Service Use

Findings of increased symptomatology and greater use of abreactive therapies among Hispanics, especially Puerto Rican Hispanics, are in keeping with an extended series of epidemiologic studies that have shown (a) that Puerto Rican Hispanics report higher frequencies of psychiatric symptoms than do other groups; (b) that among Puerto Ricans living on the mainland, reporting psychological symptoms is relatively socially desirable; (c) that increased symptom reporting among Puerto Ricans reflects an acquiescent response style; and (d) that among Puerto Ricans, somatization is a socially conventional way of expressing psychological distress (Guarnaccia, Good, & Kleinman, 1990).

Our observations that Puerto Rican veterans are prescribed psychotropic medications more frequently than other groups and have more sustained involvement in treatment are also in keeping with findings of other researchers that Puerto Ricans are more likely to remain in treatment when they are prescribed medications (Dworkin & Adams, 1987) and that they have a greater affinity for medical services than Mexican Hispanics (Schur, Bernstein, & Berk, 1987).

American Indians

The high level of alcohol-related problems and inpatient alcohol service use observed among American Indian veterans is in keeping with epidemiologic data describing high levels of alcoholism in some, although not all, American Indian tribes (Fleming, 1992; U.S. Department of Health and Human Services, 1987).

Summary

This study of veterans seeking treatment for PTSD identified several differences among ethnocultural groups in service use and clinical improvement. Most of these differences can be explained by epidemiologic and cultural factors that exist independently of service system characteristics and are similar to findings reported in other studies. The evidence of less involvement in treatment among African Americans, however, was not fully explained by any of the factors we examined and calls for additional study.

REFERENCES

Acosta, F. X. (1980). Self-described reasons for premature termination of psychotherapy by Mexican American, Black American, and Anglo-American patients. *Psychological Reports, 47,* 435–443.

Adkins, R. (1967). *Medical care for veterans.* Washington, DC: U.S. Government Printing Office.

Bergner, L. (1993). Race, health and health services. *American Journal of Public Health, 83,* 948–954.

Berryman, S. E. (1988). *Who serves? The persistent myth of the underclass army.* Boulder, CO: Westview Press.

Blank, A. S., Jr. (1993). Vet centers: A new paradigm in delivery of services for victims and survivors of traumatic stress. In J. S. Wilson & B. Raphael (Eds.),

International handbook of traumatic stress syndromes (pp. 915–924). New York: Plenum.

Blendon, R. J., Aiken, L. H., Freeman, H. E., & Corey, C. R. (1989). Access to medical care for Black and White Americans. *Journal of the American Medical Association, 261,* 278–281.

Cowies, M. R., Fahrenbruch, C. E., Cobb, L. E., & Hallstrom, A. P. (1993). Out-of-hospital cardiac arrest: Racial differences in outcome in Seattle. *American Journal of Public Health, 83,* 948–954.

Dworkin, R. J., & Adams, G. L. (1987). Retention of Hispanics in public sector mental health services. *Community Mental Health Journal, 23,* 204–216.

Escarce, J. J., Epstein, K. R., Colby, D. C., & Schawrtz, J. S. (1993). Racial differences in the elderly's use of medical procedures and diagnostic tests. *American Journal of Public Health, 83,* 948–954.

Ewing, J. A. (1984). Detecting alcoholism: The CAGE Questionnaire. *Journal of the American Medical Association, 252,* 1905–1907.

Fleming, C. M. (1992). American Indians and Alaskan Natives: Changing societies past and present. In M. A. Orlandi, R. Weston, & L. G. Epstein (Eds.), *Cultural competence for evaluators: A guide for alcohol and drug abuse prevention practitioners working with ethnic/racial communities* (pp. 147–172). Rockville, MD: U. S. Department of Health and Human Services.

Fontana, A., Rosenheck, R., & Spencer, H. (1990). *The long journey home: The first progress report on the Department of Veterans Affairs PTSD Clinical Teams Program.* West Haven, CT: Northeast Program Evaluation Center, Evaluation Division of the National Center for PTSD, Department of Veterans Affairs Medical Center.

Fontana, A., Rosenheck, R., & Spencer, H. (1993). *The long journey home: III. The third progress report on the Department of Veterans Affairs PTSD programs.* West Haven, CT: Northeast Program Evaluation Center, Evaluation Division of the National Center for PTSD, Department of Veterans Affairs Medical Center.

Guarnaccia, P. J., Good, B. J., & Kleinman, A. (1990). A critical review of epidemiological studies of Puerto Rican mental health. *American Journal of Psychiatry, 147,* 1449–1456.

Kleinman, A. (1988). *Rethinking psychiatry.* New York: Free Press.

Kulka, R. A., Schlenger, W. E., Fairbank, J. A., Hough, R. L., Jordan, B. K., Marmar, C. R., & Weiss, D. A. (1989). *Trauma and the Vietnam war generation: Report of findings from the National Vietnam Veterans Readjustment Study.* New York: Brunner/Mazel.

Kulka, R. A., Schlenger, W. E., Fairbank, J. A., Hough, R. L., Jordan, B. K., Marmar, C. R., & Weiss, D. A. (1990). *The National Vietnam Veterans Readjustment Study: Tables of findings and technical appendices.* New York: Brunner/Mazel.

Laufer, R. S., Yager, T., Frey-Wouters, E., & Donnellan, J. (1981). *Legacies of Vietnam: Vol. III. Postwar trauma: Social and psychological problems of Vietnam veterans and their peers* (House Committee Print No. 14). Washington, DC: U.S. Government Printing Office.

Lawson, W. (1986). Racial and ethnic factors in psychiatric research. *Hospital and Community Psychiatry, 37*, 50–54.

Lefley, H. P. (1990). Culture and chronic mental illness. *Hospital and Community Psychiatry, 41*, 277–286.

Marmor, T. R., Mashaw, J. L., & Harvey, P. L. (1990). *America's misunderstood welfare state*. New York: Basic Books.

Marsella, A. J., Friedman, M. J., & Spain E. H. (1994). Ethnocultural aspects of PTSD: An overview of issues, research and directions. In J. M. Oldham, A. Tasman, & M. Riba (Eds.), *Review of Psychiatry* (pp. 157–181). Washington, DC: American Psychiatric Press.

McLellan, A. T., Luborsky, L., Cacciola, J., Griffith, J., Evans, F., Barr, H. L., & O'Brien, C. P. (1985). New data from the Addiction Severity Index: Reliability and validity in three centers. *Journal of Nervous and Mental Disease, 173*, 412–423.

Mollica, R. F., Blum, J. D., & Redlich, F. (1980). Equity and the psychiatric care of the Black patient, 1950–1975. *Journal of Nervous and Mental Disease, 168*, 279–286.

Parson, E. R. (1985a). *The Black Vietnam veteran: His representational world*. In W. E. Kelley (Ed.), *Post-traumatic stress disorder and the war veteran patient* (pp. 170–192). New York: Brunner/Mazel.

Parson, E. R. (1985b). Ethnicity and traumatic stress: The intersecting point in psychotherapy. In C. R. Figley (Ed.), *Trauma and its wake*: (Vol. 1, pp. 314–337). New York: Brunner/Mazel.

Robins, L. N., Helzer, J. E., & Croughan, E., (1981). The National Institute of Mental Health Diagnostic Interview Schedule. *Archives of General Psychiatry, 38*, 381–389.

Robins, L. N., & Regier, D. A. (1991). *Psychiatric disorders in America: The epidemiologic catchment area study*. New York: The Free Press.

Ronis, D., Bates, E. W., & Wolff, N. W. (1992). *Survey of outpatient mental health and readjustment counseling services: Analyses of diagnoses and problems*. Ann Arbor, MI: VA Great Lakes HSR&D Field Program.

Rosenheck, R., & Fontana, A. (1994). Utilization of mental health services among minority veterans of the Vietnam era. *Journal of Nervous and Mental Disease, 182*, 685–691.

Schur, C. L., Bernstein, A. B., & Berk, M. L. (1987). The importance of distinguishing Hispanic subpopulations in the use of medical care. *Medical Care, 25*, 627–641.

Silver, S. M., & Wilson, J. P. (1988). Native American healing and purification rituals for war stress. In J. M. Wilson, Z. Harel, & B. Kahana (Eds.), *Human adaptation to extreme stress: From the Holocaust to Vietnam* (pp. 337–356). New York: Plenum.

Skocpol, T. (1992). *Protecting soldiers and mothers: The political origins of social policy in the United States.* Cambridge, MA: Harvard University Press.

Snowden, L. R., & Cheung. F. K. (1990). Use of inpatient mental health services by members of ethnic minority groups. *American Psychologist, 45,* 347–355.

Solomon, P. (1988). Racial factors in mental health service utilization. *Psychosocial Rehabilitation Journal, 11,* 3–12.

Spitzer, R. L., & Williams, J. B. W. (1985). *Structured clinical interview for diagnosis.* New York: New York State Psychiatric Institute.

Sue, S. (1977). Community mental health services to minority groups. *American Psychologist, 32,* 616–624.

Sue, S. (1991). Community mental health services for ethnic minority groups: A test of the cultural responsiveness hypothesis. *American Psychologist, 59,* 533–540.

Sutocky, J. W., Shultz, J. M., & Kizer, K. W. (1993). Alcohol-related mortality in California, 1980–1989. *American Journal of Public Health, 83,* 817–823.

Terry, W. (1984). *Bloods: An oral history of the Vietnam War by Black veterans.* New York: Random House.

U.S. Department of Health and Human Services. (1987). *Alcohol and health.* Washington, DC: U.S. Government Printing Office.

Vernez, G., Burnam, M. A., McGlynn, E. A., Trude, S., & Mittman, B. S. (1988). *Review of California's program for the homeless mentally disabled.* Santa Monica, CA: Rand Corporation.

Veterans Administration. (1980). *Myths and realities: A study of attitudes towards Vietnam era veterans.* Washington, DC: U.S. Senate.

West, C. (1993). *Race matters.* Boston: Beacon Press.

Westermeyer, J. (1989). Cross-cultural care for PTSD: Research, training and service needs for the future. *Journal of Traumatic Stress, 2,* 515–536.

Williams, D. (1986). The epidemiology of mental illness in Afro-Americans. *Hospital and Community Psychiatry, 37,* 42–49.

20

ETHNOPSYCHOPHARMACOLOGY AND THE TREATMENT OF PTSD

KEH-MING LIN, RUSSELL E. POLAND, DORA ANDERSON,
and IRA M. LESSER

Pharmacotherapy represents an important part of the care of patients suffering from PTSD and related problems and has been the focus of intense research efforts in recent years. As a clear reflection of progress in this regard, a large number of psychotropic agents have become available for the treatment of these conditions, and the majority of PTSD patients benefit from such interventions. These pharmacotherapeutic agents include tricyclic antidepressants, (TCAs), neuroleptics, benzodiazepines, and lithium (Smith, Cartaya, Mendoza, Lesser, & Lin, in press). Recent literature has clearly indicated that ethnicity and culture often exert important influences on the clinical effects of these potent therapeutic agents. These issues are highly relevant for the clinical care of PTSD patients with ethnic minority backgrounds.

In this chapter, we first review the principles of how ethnicity may interact with drug metabolism and drug action. Next, the role that ethnicity plays in relation to the specific classes of medications that are commonly used to treat PTSD—antidepressants, neuroleptics, benzodiazepines, and lithium—is covered. Finally, we briefly discuss future research directions and the applicability of this research to clinical practice.

This research was supported in part by Research Center on the Psychobiology of Ethnicity Grant MH47193, National Institute of Mental Health Research Scientist Development Award MH00534 (to Russell E. Poland), and National Institutes of Health Clinical Research Center Grant RR00425.

ETHNICITY AND PSYCHOPHARMACOLOGY

It has been well documented that there are differential interethnic pharmacologic responses with nonpsychoactive medications (e.g., Kalow, Goedde & Agarwal, 1986). Recent research developments reveal significant interethnic differences in response to various psychotropic drugs as well (e.g., Lin, Poland, Smith, Strickland & Mendoza, 1991; Mendoza, Smith, Poland, Lin & Strickland, 1991; Strickland et al., 1991; Wood & Zhou, 1991). The interplay of ethnicity and pharmacology can be studied with reference to basic principles of pharmacology: pharmacogenetics, pharmacodynamics, environmental influences, and plasma protein binding.

Pharmacogenetics

Pharmacogenetics refers to the interplay of genetic factors in the metabolism of a particular medication. In the 1950s, experience with the antitubercular drug isoniazid led to the clinical observation that there were ethnic differences in side effect profiles. This, in turn, led to the identification of populations showing genetically controlled slow versus rapid acetylation (Weber, 1987). Acetylation status has subsequently been found to determine the metabolism of a large number of medicinal agents, including some frequently prescribed psychotropics (Lin et al., 1991; Mendoza et al., 1991).

Another example was experience with "primaquine hemolysis" among African American soldiers fighting in Southeast Asia, which was found to be related to an inborn deficiency of glucose-6-phosphate dehydrogenase (Dern, Beutler, & Alving, 1955). Yet another example was the discovery of atypical alcohol dehydrogenase and the genetic basis of aldehyde dehydrogenase deficiency, which are related to cross-ethnic variations in response to alcohol and to the "flushing response" (Argawal & Goedde, 1990; Yoshida, 1993). With recent developments in molecular biology, a large number of ethnically specific, genetically determined variants of these enzymes have been identified.

A specific example of the importance that pharmacogenetics has in pharmacologic treatment relates to the fact that many pharmacologically active agents require two metabolic steps (functionalization and conjugation) to be rendered sufficiently water soluble for excretion. Phase 1 of the process, involving the addition of a functional group into the substrate, is predominantly carried out by the cytochrome P-450 isozymes (Shen & Lin, 1990).

This enzyme system may be regarded as one of the most important defense systems that have evolved in animals through the millennia to protect themselves against potentially harmful xenobiotics to which they are routinely exposed in their habitat (Gonzalez & Nebert, 1990). Their ubiquity and broad spectrum allow for the P-450 isozymes to metabolize and usually detoxify modern chemotherapeutic agents that are mostly synthetic and, thus, not the original targets for these enzymes.

Similar to the other examples discussed above, two of the P-450 isozymes, debrisoquine hydroxylase and mephenytoin hydroxylase, are not unimodally distributed. Therefore, members of a given population can be classified as extensive metabolizers (EM) and poor metabolizers (PM); Gonzalez, 1989; Kalow, 1991; Meyer, Zanger, Grant, & Blum, 1990; Wilkinson, Guengerich, & Branch, 1989; Wood & Zhou 1991). Molecular genetic studies have revealed that such differences in the enzyme activities are genetically controlled. The enzymes are defective in PM because of mutations in the nucleic acid sequence in the DNA, with a consequent alteration in the amino acid structure in the enzyme.

Studies involving these two enzymes may be of particular significance for psychiatry because they are responsible for the metabolism of many commonly used psychotropics. These include medications particularly important in the treatment of anxiety disorders—including TCAs (Bertilsson & Aberg-Wistedt, 1983; Bertilsson et al., 1980; Mellstrom, Bertilsson, Lou, Sawe, & Sjoqvist, 1983; Skjelbo, Brosen, Hallas, & Gram, 1991); benzodiazepines (Bertilsson et al., 1989; Wilkinson et al., 1989); and propranolol (Shaheen, Biollaz, Koshakji, Wilkinson, & Wood, 1989; Ward, Walle, Walle, Wilkinson, & Branch, 1989); as well as neuroleptics (Dahl-Puustinen, Liden, Alm, Nordin, & Bertilsson, 1989) and barbiturates (Kupfer & Preisig, 1984).

Substantial cross-ethnic differences in the frequency of PM phenotype exist with these enzymes. For example, the frequency of PM of debrisoquine varies from less than 3% in the Cuna Amerindians, Egyptians, and Saudi Arabians, as well as in several Asian subgroups (Chinese, Japanese, Malayans, and Thai) to 3%–10% in Caucasians and Hispanics in Europe and North America (Lin, Poland, & Silver, 1993). A wider range of frequencies is found in Black Africans; 0%–8% of Saharan Africans, 4% of Venda in South Africa, 1.9% of African Americans, and 19% of Sans Bushmen are classified as PM. Table 1 shows the percentage of PMs in some of the major ethnic groups.

Mephenytoin hydroxylation displays a discrete phenotypy from that of debrisoquine (Table 1). In contrast to findings that PMs of debrisoquine are more frequent in Caucasians than in Asians, PMs of mephenytoin are more prevalent in Asian populations, with approximately 20% of Japanese being classified as PM (Horai et al., 1989; Nakamura et al., 1985).

Chinese in their native land also demonstrate a high frequency of PM (Horai et al., 1989), whereas Chinese in Canada display a much lower frequency (Jurima, Inaba, Kodar, & Kalow, 1985), similar to that of Caucasians (Inaba, Jurima, Nakano, & Kalow, 1984; Jurima et al., 1985; Nakamura et al., 1985; Sanz, Villen, Alm, & Bertilsson, 1989). There is no

TABLE 1
Ethnicity and the Percentage of Poor Metabolizers of Debrisoquine
Hydroxylase and Mephenytoin Hydroxylase

Ethnic group	Debrisoquine hydroxylase	Mephenytoin hydroxylase
African American	1.9	18.5
Caucasian	3–9.2	2.5–6.7
East Asian	0–2.4	17.4–22
Amerindians	0–5.2	0
Hispanic	4.5	4.8
Sub-Saharan African	0–8.1	–

clear-cut answer to the question of why ethnic variations exist in these vitally important enzymes. However, it is quite possible that they reflect differences in diet and other environmental factors to which they were exposed and forced to adapt for hundreds of thousands of years.

Pharmacodynamics

Pharmacodynamics refers to the mechanism of action of a pharmacologic compound affecting a physiologic system. A good example of ethnic differences in drug response, which is probably a result of pharmacodynamic factors, is the pupillary response to topical mydriatics. Impaired mydriasis has been repeatedly observed in African Americans and Asians after standard doses of epinephrine, cocaine, and atropine (Angenent & Koelle 1953; Garde, Aston, Endler, & Sison, 1978). This reduction in the mydriatic effect appears to be correlated with the degree of pigmentation of the irises and is not seen among albino Africans. African Americans also have been shown to be significantly less responsive than Caucasians to intramuscular atropine and scopolamine (Garde et al., 1978).

Another prominent example of how ethnicity and pharmacodynamics interact is found for beta blockers such as propranolol, which have been found to be relatively ineffective in treating hypertension in African American patients (Moser & Lunn, 1981). In contrast, the doses of propranolol required for the effective treatment of hypertension in Asians were substantially smaller than those required for Caucasians (Zhou, Koshakji, Siolberstein, Wilkinson, & Wood, 1989).

Subsequent studies objectively demonstrated that the effects of propranolol on blood pressure and heart rate are most prominent in Asians, and least apparent in African Americans, with Caucasians falling in between (Dimsdale, Ziegler, & Graham, 1988; Johnson, Burlew, & Sullivan, 1992). These differences could not be explained by pharmacokinetic factors

(Zhou et al., 1989). Studies have suggested that African Americans may have a higher degree of beta$_2$-adrenoceptor activity (Rutledge, Steinberg, & Cardozo, 1989), leading to the hypothesis that differences in the sensitivity of adrenoceptors may be the major cause for the differential effects of propranolol and other beta blockers in various ethnic groups (Kalow, 1989).

Observations of the ethnic differences in therapeutic concentrations of various psychotropics (Hu, Lee, Yang & Tseng, 1983; Takahashi 1979; Yamashita & Asano 1979) and their neurohormonal effects have led to speculation about the existence of ethnic differences in pharmacodynamics of these drugs. These are discussed below, in relation to specific classes of psychotropics.

Environmental Influences

In addition to genetic control, the activity of some cytochrome P-450 enzymes can be quite sensitive to environmental changes—including exposure to different diets, environmental toxins, and other drugs. The role of the cytochrome P-450s in the induction and inhibition of the metabolism of various drugs, including psychotropics, has been reviewed in detail elsewhere (Murray & Reidy, 1990) and is not repeated here. Not as well known is the fact that diet also can influence the rate of metabolism of various drugs and thus might also contribute to the observed ethnic differences in drug response.

For example, Branch, Salih, & Homeida (1978) compared the rate of the biotransformation of antipyrine and found a significantly longer antipyrine half-life among Sudanese living in their home villages as compared both with Sudanese residing in Britain and with Caucasian British subjects. The latter two groups metabolized antipyrine at similar rates, suggesting that environmental factors, such as diet, were responsible for the pharmacokinetic differences. Similar findings were reported in subsequent studies involving Asian Indians living in India, Asian Indian immigrants residing in Britain, and Caucasian British subjects (Fraser et al., 1979).

Plasma Protein Binding

Most psychotropics rely on plasma proteins for their transportation in blood to their site of action (Reidenberg & Erill, 1986). Variations in the concentration of these drug-binding proteins in the plasma can significantly influence the effect of the drug by changing the free fraction and, thus, the amount of the unbound (free) drug concentrations in the plasma (DeLeve & Piafsky, 1981; Levy & Moreland, 1984; Routledge, 1986).

Because only the free (unbound) fraction of the drugs is usually pharmacologically active and capable of crossing the blood–brain barrier, changes in the concentrations of drug-binding proteins may have profound clinical significance (Crabtree, Jann, & Pitts, 1991; Routledge, 1986). Theoretically, ethnic differences in plasma protein binding could occur, because of genetic or environmental factors. The structures of these plasma proteins are genetically determined and have been shown to vary across ethnic groups in several studies (Fukuma, Kashimura, Umetsu, Yuasa, & Suzuki, 1990; Juneja, Weitkamp, Stratil, Gahne, & Guttormsen, 1988; Umetsu, Yuasa, Nishimura, Sasaki, & Susuki, 1988). It is presently unclear whether these structural differences could lead to differences in the plasma proteins' drug-binding capacities; so far, only a few studies have addressed this possibility.

ETHNICITY AND THE ANTIDEPRESSANTS

Action Mechanisms and Processes

Tricyclic antidepressants, widely used for the treatment of depression, often are medications of choice for patients with PTSD and related disorders. After oral administration, TCAs undergo extensive first pass metabolism to both active and inactive metabolites. Both genetic and environmental variables (e.g., concomitant drug therapy, diet, smoking, caffeine intake, and exposure to alcohol) may influence TCA metabolism.

Tricyclic antidepressants are extensively protein bound, and as noted above, it is the unbound fraction that is biologically active, contributing to both clinical efficacy and side effects. However, ethnic variations in protein binding, which have been found for nonpsychiatric medications, have not been clearly demonstrated for the TCAs (Rudorfer, Lane, Chang, Zhang, & Potter, 1984).

Drug concentrations are determined in part by activity of the P-450 isozymes that catalyze the hydroxylation and demethylation of the TCAs, and as described above, both genetics and environment may alter activity of these enzymes. Specifically, the hydroxylation of a number of TCAs and their metabolites has been found to correlate highly with debrisoquine hydroxylas activities, and the demethylation of these drugs has been shown to be primarily determined by mephenytoin hydroxylase activities (Lin, Poland and Nakasaki, 1993). In addition, the P-450 1A2 isozyme also appears to be involved (Brosen, Skjelbo, Rasmussen, Poulsen & Loft, 1993). Because the activity of the debrisoquine hydroxylase and mephenytoin enzymes vary cross-ethnically, this may contribute to ethnic variations in metabolism of TCAs.

Antidepressants and Asians

Of the various ethnic groups studied with regard to differences in prescribing practices and clinical efficacy and side effects of TCAs, the most extensively studied group has been Asian patients. Surveys of prescribing practices (Yamashita & Asano, 1979) and studies of the "therapeutic threshold dose" of multiple TCAs in Chinese living in China (Kleinman, 1981) and in the West (Rosenblat & Tang, 1987) all reveal that Asian patients need less TCA, or that they are more sensitive to TCAs than are Caucasians. Regarding plasma levels, most (Kishimoto & Hollister 1984; Rudorfer et al., 1984; Schneider et al., 1991), but not all, investigators found significant differences in TCA kinetics when comparing Asian with Caucasian subjects (Pi, Simpson, & Cooper, 1986; Pi et al., 1989). These differences remained statistically significant after controlling for body weight.

Antidepressants and African Americans

Although African Americans have not been studied as extensively as Asians in this regard, a number of observations have demonstrated that response to antidepressants may differ between African Americans and Caucasians. Generally, these studies indicate that African American patients show higher plasma TCA levels and tend to respond better and faster to TCAs but that African American patients manifest more toxic side effects than do Caucasian patients.

In 1969, Overall, Hollister, Kimball, and Shelton, in a multicenter VA study of patients treated with TCAs, found that African American patients improved more rapidly than did Caucasian patients—a finding replicated by Raskin, Thomas, and Crook (1975). Similarly, Henry, Overall, and Markette (1971) found that African American and Hispanic American patients responded better to pharmacotherapy than did Caucasian patients. This finding held for treatment with TCAs, but even more strongly for treatment with benzodiazepines.

In studies of depressed patients treated with amitriptyline (AMI) and nortriptyline (NT), results showed no ethnic difference in the rate of demethylation of AMI to NT or in the steady-state levels of AMI (Ziegler & Biggs, 1977; Ziegler, Clayton, & Biggs, 1977). However, African American patients had significantly higher (50%) steady-state NT plasma levels than did Caucasians.

This difference is proposed to underlie the more rapid response of African Americans to TCAs in this as well as other studies. In a chart-review investigation (Livingston, Zucker, Isenberg, & Wetzel, 1983), African Americans were noted to be significantly overrepresented among depressed inpatients taking TCAs who developed delirium. In a retrospective investigation of patients who had overdosed on AMI, it was reported that there was a significant racial difference in the level/dose ratio between African American and Caucasian females and that the plasma concentrations were higher in African Americans than in Caucasians (Rudorfer & Robins, 1982).

Although these clinical reports suffer from significant methodological problems (Strickland et al., 1991), taken together, they do consistently suggest that African American patients with depression may be more sensitive to the effect of TCAs. Findings derived from some of these studies further suggest that this may be mediated through ethnic differences in TCA pharmacokinetics. This hypothesis, however, remains to be tested, because to the best of our knowledge, no vigorously designed pharmacokinetic or pharmacogenetic studies have been conducted with African Americans.

Antidepressants and Hispanics

Even fewer data are available regarding the Hispanic population, another ethnic group which has been understudied. Similar to what was found in surveys of dose requirements in Asians, it has been reported that the mean maximum daily dosage of a group of depressed Hispanic women treated with a variety of TCAs was only about half of the mean maximum daily dosage of a Caucasian group, yet a higher percentage of the Hispanic patients complained of side effects, a finding which the authors ascribe to the Hispanic tradition of expressing depression in somatic terms (Marcos & Cancro, 1982). Despite the lower dosages prescribed for Hispanic patients, the two groups had very similar treatment outcomes.

No data were available on TCA concentrations, thus, it is impossible to ascertain whether the differences found with regard to dosage and side effects were related to TCA pharmacokinetics. One study with NT (Gaviria, Gil, & Javaid, 1986) demonstrated a lack of kinetic variation between Hispanics and Caucasians and suggested that if Hispanics do respond more favorably to lower dosages, this response may be due to pharmacodynamic differences.

ETHNICITY AND NEUROLEPTICS

Neuroleptics and Asians

Similar to the TCAs, most neuroleptics also are metabolized extensively by the P-450 isozymes and are highly bound to plasma protein. A large number of clinical reports and surveys have suggested that large ethnic differences exist in terms of the dosage requirements and side effect profiles of the neuroleptics. Most of these reports suggested that Asians required significantly smaller doses of neuroleptics. These clinical impressions have been supported by several pharmacokinetic and pharmacodynamic studies conducted recently.

Lin, Poland, Lau, and Rubin (1988) studied the pharmacokinetics of haloperidol (HL) in 12 Caucasian, 11 American-born Asian and 11 foreign-born Asian healthy male volunteers. Haloperidol (1.0 mg po or 0.5 mg im) was administered in random order on 2 separate days at least 2 weeks apart. Repeated blood samples were obtained for the measurement of HL and prolactin concentrations, each by specific radioimmunoassays. The HL (after both intramuscular and oral administrations) and prolactin (after intramuscular administration) concentrations of both Asian groups were significantly higher than those of the Caucasians. The differences in HL concentrations remained highly significant after controlling for body surface area in the oral administration portion of the study.

Furthermore, when the influence of HL was controlled statistically, the differences in prolactin concentration after intramuscular HL remained statistically significant. Time lapse between drug administration and peak concentration (T_{max}) for HL and prolactin were consistently shorter for the foreign-born as well as American-born Asians than for the Caucasians. These differences reached statistical significance for HL concentrations after oral administration, and for prolactin concentrations after intramuscular HL administration. Although foreign-born Asians had slightly higher HL and prolactin concentrations than did American-born Asians in most of these measurements, as well as shorter T_{max}, these differences were not statistically significant for any of the comparisons.

Thus, the study demonstrated that there are clear-cut pharmacokinetic differences for HL between Asians and Caucasians that could at least partially explain why Asians require smaller doses of HL for similar clinical effects. The fact that the two Asian groups had similar pharmacokinetic profiles suggests that the ethnic pharmacokinetic difference may be more genetically rather than environmentally determined, although similar dietary habits between the two Asian groups also could contribute to the findings.

Because single-dose pharmacokinetic results are highly predictive of steady-state blood levels (Cooper, 1978; May & Goldberg, 1978), the findings reviewed above should lead one to expect similar occurrences in subjects treated chronically with HL. This, in fact, has been reported by Potkin et al. (1984), who compared the steady-state serum HL concentrations in 18 Chinese chronic schizophrenic patients and 18 matched non-Asian American patients (17 Caucasians, 1 African American), after each had received 0.4 mg/kg HL for 5 weeks. They reported that at the end of the study, the serum HL levels of the Chinese patients were, on average, 52% higher than those observed in their American counterparts.

Findings from another recent study also demonstrated significant differences between Asians and Caucasians in responding to neuroleptics. Lin et al. (1989) prospectively and sequentially treated 13 Caucasian and 16 Asian schizophrenic patients over a 3-month period with both weight-adjusted fixed doses (0.15 mg/kg) and clinically determined (variable) doses of HL. During the initial fixed-dose phase, Asians had slightly higher serum HL concentrations and significantly higher ratings of extrapyramidal symptoms (EPS). During the subsequent clinically determined phase, Asian patients required significantly smaller doses (6.5 vs. 11.5 mg/day for the EPS threshold; 5.1 vs. 14.3 mg/day for the optimal point), resulting in lower serum HL concentrations for the first emergence of EPS (4.3 vs. 7.8 ng/ml) and for optimal clinical responses (3.6 vs. 7.6 ng/ml), as determined by Brief Psychiatric Rating Scale (BPRS) scores.

These results further support previous clinical observations of ethnic differences between Asians and Caucasians in terms of therapeutic dose ranges and side effect profiles. Additionally, these findings suggest that brain receptor responsivity may be more important than kinetic factors in determining such differences.

Reduced HL (RH) has been identified as a major metabolite of HL, which has about one fifth to one tenth of the dopamine blocking potency of HL and appears to be readily convertible to HL in vivo (Chang, Chen, Lee, Hu, & Yeh, 1987). Chang et al. (1987) measured HL and RH concentrations in 21 Chinese chronic schizophrenic patients in Taiwan treated with 20 mg/day of HL over 7 weeks. They found that these Chinese patients had a much lower RH/HL ratio as compared with those reported by American researchers. The researchers further suggested that this may be the reason for the higher HL concentrations and lower therapeutic dose range of HL observed among Asians in previous studies.

In a subsequent study conducted by the same research group, Jann et al. (1989) reported that the mean RH level of their Chinese patients was only about one third of their age-matched non-Chinese counterparts. Although the Chinese patients received substantially lower doses of HL (18.8 vs. 31.6 mg/day), the mean HL concentrations were comparable between the two groups.

In summary, the results of these carefully designed studies are in congruence with one another and together demonstrate that pharmacokinetic factors are at least partially responsible for ethnic differences in response to HL as observed clinically. The lower RH/HL ratio in Asians, caused either by a slower rate of reduction of HL or a more active oxidation process converting RH back to HL, could significantly affect the clearance of HL resulting in a higher level of HL.

Neuroleptics and African Americans and Hispanics

In comparison with studies conducted with Asians, much less information has been available in regard to African Americans and Hispanics. A number of survey studies have demonstrated that African Americans as well as Blacks in other parts of the world (Afro-Caribbeans in England and Blacks in South Africa) were treated with significantly higher doses of neuroleptics (D'Mello, McNeil, & Harris, 1989; Marcolin, Stiers, & Chung, 1991). Midha, Hawes, Hubbard, Korchinski, and McKay (1988a, 1988b), however, found no pharmacokinetic differences between African American, and Caucasians in studies involving trifluoperazine and fluphenazine.

The reason for the discrepancy between pharmacokinetic and clinical findings remains to be further clarified. However, because African Americans have also been found to receive neuroleptic treatment significantly more often than Caucasians, regardless of diagnosis (D'Mello et al., 1989), and are much more likely to be treated with depot neuroleptics (Price, Glazer, & Morgenstern, 1985), it appears that this dosage differential between African Americans and Caucasians is not determined by pharmacological factors but is predominantly the result of prescription biases.

ETHNICITY AND BENZODIAZEPINES

Benzodiazepines and Asians

Ethnicity has been identified by several clinical and survey reports as being an important factor in determining benzodiazepine responses (Kumana, Lauder, Chan, Ko, & Lin, 1987; Murphy, 1969; Rosenblat & Tang 1987). As with TCAs, the majority of reports regarding benzodiazepines have been based on Asian/Caucasian comparisons.

Murphy (1969) first suggested that as compared with Caucasians, Asians may be more sensitive to the effects of various psychotropics, including anxiolytics. This was supported by recent surveys of the prescription patterns of psychiatrists who regularly treat both Asian and non-Asian patients (Kumana et al., 1987; Rosenblat & Tang, 1987). Results of these studies showed that the mean dosages of benzodiazepines received by Asians were about one half to two thirds of those prescribed for their Caucasian counterparts.

Ghoneim et al., (1981) studied the kinetics and behavioral effects of diazepam in healthy Caucasian and Asian volunteers. The results showed that the two ethnic groups diverged substantially in their pharmacokinetic, but not pharmacodynamic, responses to diazepam. When extrapolated to the steady state, this difference in the rate of metabolism could lead to

Asians having (on the average) 40%–50% higher drug concentrations in serum and in tissue. There was no difference in the proportion of protein binding between the two ethnic groups (98%), which was comparable to previous reports on Caucasians.

Lin, Lau, Smith, and Poland (1988) examined plasma alprazolam concentrations and acute behavioral effects in 14 American-born Asian, 14 foreign-born Asian, and 14 Caucasian healthy male volunteer participants. When compared with the Caucasians, both Asian groups had a higher area-under-the-plasma concentration curve (AUC), peak plasma concentration (C_{max}), and smaller total plasma clearance after both oral and intravenous administration of alprazolam. These differences either reached or approached statistical significance.

In contrast to the differences between Asians and Caucasians, the pharmacokinetic parameters of the two Asian groups were remarkably similar. There was no significant statistical difference between the two groups in any of the parameters examined. Although the results derived from pharmacodynamic measurements consistently revealed greater pharmacological effects of alprazolam on Asians as compared with Caucasians, on behavioral tests, only the differences in the mean sedation scores reached statistical significance. Foreign-born Asians experienced significantly more sedation as compared with both the Caucasians and the American-born Asians. Substantial variability, a characteristic of studies of this nature, was thought to be the main reason for these results.

Bertilsson et al., (1989) demonstrated a high correlation between the metabolism of diazepam and the phenotype status of S-mephenytoin in Caucasian participants. This finding led to the hypothesis that the higher percentage of S-mephenytoin-type enzyme deficiency among Chinese may be mainly responsible for the slower metabolism of diazepam in this ethnic group.

This theory, however, was not supported by a recent report, in which diazepam and desmethyldiazepam concentrations measured over 21 days in 16 healthy Chinese volunteers in Beijing showed no differences between EM and PM participants of S-mephenytoin and (Zhang, Reviriego, Lou, Sjoqvist, & Bertilsson, 1990). Other than desmethyldiazepam concentrations, which were significantly higher in Chinese EM participants than in Chinese PM participants for the entire duration of the study, the two phenotype groups showed no significant difference in most of the pharmacokinetic parameters, including the plasma half-life and clearance of diazepam.

The majority of studies involving Asians and Caucasians demonstrated significant kinetic differences between the two ethnic groups. Because they were conducted at different geographic sites (two in North America, one in Hong Kong, one in mainland China) and possibly included different Asian subcultural groups, questions could be raised regarding the generalizability of the findings. At the same time, the consistency in these reports of a slower metabolism of benzodiazepines in Asians is quite remarkable, suggesting that genetic factors contribute more strongly to benzodiazepine pharmacokinetics than do environmental influences.

Benzodiazepines and African Americans

In the African American population, controlled studies using benzodiazepines are just beginning to be conducted. Our group recently conducted a study of the pharmacokinetics and pharmacodynamics of adinazolam, a triazolo-benzodiazepine currently being investigated as an anxiolytic and antidepressant, with 8 African American and 8 Caucasian normal volunteers. The analysis of the pharmacokinetic dose proportionality and pharmacodynamics in the total population has been published (Fleishaker & Phillips 1989), and the results have been reanalyzed to assess ethnic differences in kinetics and dynamics.

The results showed that African Americans had increased clearance of adinazolam, which resulted in a lower AUC, lower C_{max}, and a longer half-life, as compared with Caucasians. Concurrently, however, the C_{max} and AUC of N-desmethyladinazolam, a metabolite of adinazolam, were significantly higher in African Americans. Along with these pharmacokinetic findings, African Americans also manifested a significantly greater drug effect on psychomotor performance. Adinazolam is almost exclusively eliminated by hepatic oxidation to N-desmethyladinazolam, so these findings suggested that African Americans may have a higher metabolic capacity for adinazolam. Because N-desmethyladinazolam is cleared directly by renal excretion in addition to hepatic metabolism, increases in oxidative capacity are expected to have a lesser effect on N-desmethyladinazolam AUC values.

The increased C_{max} and AUC of N-desmethyladinazolam in African Americans may be due to increased first-pass conversion of adinazolam to N-desmethyladinazolam. N-desmethyladinazolam has been shown primarily to mediate the benzodiazepine-like side effects, including effects on psychomotor performance, after adinazolam administration (Fleishaker, Smith, Friedman, & Hulst, 1992). This may be responsible for the larger drug effects on African Americans despite their higher metabolic capacity for adinazolam.

As noted above, only a few studies have looked at Asians and African Americans, and to our knowledge, no study has been conducted with other major ethnic groups in this country, such as the Hispanics and American Indians.

A number of cross-national comparison studies have consistently indicated that Asian bipolar patients respond clinically to substantially lower doses as well as lower plasma levels of lithium as compared with Caucasians. In contrast to the situation with TCAs and neuroleptics, this ethnic differential in response to lithium appears to not be related to pharmacokinetic factors.

In two studies conducted separately in Shanghai and in Taipei, Chang and colleagues (Chang, Pandey, Yang, Yeh, & Davis, 1985; Chang, Pandey, Zhang, Ku, & Davis, 1984) reported remarkably similar therapeutic lithium concentrations for these two Chinese groups residing in drastically divergent socioeconomic environments. These were significantly lower than the mean level of 0.98 mEq/L for the matched Caucasian American patients, as well as the 0.8 to 1.2 mEq/L therapeutic levels generally reported in Europe and North America and recently confirmed in a longitudinal follow-up study.

Similar to the studies on Asians, Shelley (1987) also found no significant differences between 10 Afro-Caribbean and 11 Caucasian healthy male volunteer participants in terms of lithium pharmacokinetics. However, an important aspect of the distribution of lithium, the red blood cell/serum lithium ratio, has been reported to differ significantly between Blacks and Caucasians (Bunker, Mallinger, Adams, & Kuller, 1987; Okpaku, Frazer, & Mendels, 1980; Ostrow et al., 1986; Trevisan, Ostrow, Cooper, Sempos, & Stamler, 1984). This ratio is quite likely correlated with intracellular concentration of lithium, which may have important meaning in terms of not only the genetic control of cell membrane permeability of lithium but also the clinical effects and side effect status of lithium.

Thus, the difference between Blacks and other ethnic groups in the red blood cell/serum lithium ratio may have important clinical significance. In a recent study, Strickland, Lin, Fu, Anderson, and Zheng (1995) replicated this difference between African American and Caucasian bipolar patients. This study further demonstrated a higher rate of central nervous system–related side effects in African American patients, suggesting that the the higher lithium ratio in this group may indeed lead to higher central toxicity. There has been no study for Hispanics or Amerindians on lithium kinetics or clinical effects.

CONCLUSION

Psychotropic responses, and, more broadly, responses to pharmacological agents in general, are complex phenomena that are simultaneously influenced by biological, psychological, and sociocultural determinants. Interindividual variations in responses to most psychotropics (as well as nonpsychotropics) are substantial. Ethnicity represents one of the most important variables that contribute to such variations in drug response.

Ethnic differences in pharmacokinetics have been observed between Asians and Caucasians in regard to HL and some benzodiazepines, but not to lithium. The results involving TCAs have been inconsistent in this regard. In addition, pharmacodynamic factors and plasma protein binding may also contribute to differences in psychotropic responses between these two ethnic groups.

Fewer studies have been focused on African Americans and Hispanics. However, clinical and research data suggest that African Americans may be more sensitive to TCAs and adinazolam for kinetic as well as dynamic reasons. Hispanics have been reported to require lower doses of TCAs for the clinical treatment of depression. In addition, significantly higher red blood cell/plasma lithium ratios have been observed in African Americans. The clinical significance of this phenomenon, however, remains to be determined. Studies on cross-ethnic comparisons of tardive dyskinesia and other psychotropic side effects have thus far yielded inconsistent findings.

Aldehyde dehydrogenase deficiency and flushing response to alcohol among Asians, Eskimos, and Amerindians represent the most dramatic and well-studied example of genetically determined ethnic differences in response to a psychoactive agent. Recent reports have also demonstrated a negative association between this trait and risk for the development of alcoholism.

Despite the progress and achievement, many issues await clarification. To address these admittedly complicated issues, integrated research efforts with diverse designs and strategies are needed. New techniques in pharmacogenetics should allow researchers to combine the genotyping and phenotyping of drug-metabolizing enzymes with traditional pharmacokinetic studies. The contribution of protein binding to ethnic and individual variations in drug responses could be further clarified by the simultaneous measurement of the free fractions of the drugs and their metabolites, on the one hand, and the concentrations of plasma proteins involved in the binding of the drugs, such as the $alpha_1$ acid glycoproteins and albumins, on the other.

In terms of pharmacodynamics, it is also very likely that advances in brain-imaging technology will make it possible for researchers to directly assess drug–receptor interactions. These exciting new advances in biotechnologies, combined with developments in clinical and cross-cultural psychiatric research methodologies, will ensure that the field will progress at an increasingly accelerated fashion, leading to information that will enable clinicians to provide culturally and ethnically sensitive pharmacotherapy for conditions related to PTSD as well as other psychiatric conditions.

REFERENCES

Angenent, W. J., & Koelle, G. B. (1953). A possible enzymatic basis for the differential action of mydriatics on light and dark irises. *Journal of Physiology, 119*, 102–117.

Argawal, D. P., & Goedde, H. W. (1990). *Alcohol metabolism, alcohol intolerance and alcoholism.* Berlin: Springer-Verlag.

Bertilsson, L., & Aberg-Wistedt, A. (1983). The debrisoquine hydroxylation test predicts steady-state plasma levels of desipramine. *British Journal of Clinical Pharmacology 15*, 388–390.

Bertilsson, L., Eichelbaum, M., Mellstrom, B., Sawe, J., Schulz, H. U., & Sjoqvist, F. (1980). Nortriptyline and antipyrine clearance in relation to debrisoquine hydroxylation in man. *Life Sciences, 27*, 1673–1677.

Bertilsson, L., Henthorn, T. K., Sanz, E., Tybring, G., Sawe, J., & Villen, T. (1989). Importance of genetic factors in the regulation of diazepam metabolism: Relationship to S-mephenytoin, but not debrisoquine, hydroxylation phenotype. *Clinical Pharmacology & Therapeutics, 45*, 348–355.

Branch, R. A., Salih, S. Y., & Homeida, M. (1978). Racial differences in in drug metabolizing ability: A study with antipyrine in the Sudan. *Clinical Pharmacology & Therapeutics, 24*, 283–286.

Brosen, K., Skjelbo, E., Rasmussen, B. B., Poulsen, H. E., & Loft, S. (1993). Fluvoxamine is a potent inhibitor of cytochrome P450 1A2. *Biochemical Pharmacology, 45*, 1121–1214.

Bunker, C. H., Mallinger, A. G., Adams, L. L., & Kuller, L. H. (1987). Red blood cell sodium–lithium countertransport and cardiovascular risk factors in Black and White college students. *Journal of Hypertension, 5*, 7–15 .

Chang, S. S., Pandey, G. N., Yang, Y. Y., Yeh, E. K, & Davis, J. M. (1985, May). *Lithium pharmacokinetics: Inter-racial comparison.* Paper presented at the 138th Annual Meeting of the American Psychiatric Association, Dallas.

Chang, S. S., Pandey, G. N., Zhang, M. Y., Ku, N. F., & Davis, J. M. (1984). Racial differences in plasma and RBC lithium levels. In *Continuing medical education syllabus and scientific proceedings* (Paper No. 27, pp. 239–240). Washington, DC: American Psychiatric Association.

Chang, W.-H., Chen, T.-Y., Lee, C.-F., Hu, W. H., & Yeh, E. K. (1987). Low plasma reduced haloperidol/haloperidol ratios in Chinese patients. *Biological Psychiatry, 22*, 1406–1408.

Cooper, T. B. (1978). Plasma level monitoring of anti-psychotic drugs. *Clinical Pharmacokinetics, 3*, 14–38.

Crabtree, B. L., Jann, M. W., & Pitts, W. M. (1991). Alpha$_1$ acid glycoprotein levels in patients with schizophrenia: Effects of treatment with haloperidol. *Biological Psychiatry, 29*, 43A–185A.

Dahl-Puustinen, M. L., Liden, A., Alm, C., Nordin, C., & Bertilsson, L. (1989). Disposition of perphenazine is related to polymorphic debrisoquine hydroxylation in human beings. *Clinical Pharmacology & Therapeutics, 46*, 78–81.

DeLeve, L. D., & Piafsky, K. M. (1981). Clinical significance of plasma binding of basic drugs. *Trends in Pharmacological Sciences, 2*, 283–284.

Dern, R. J., Beutler, E., & Alving, A. S. (1955). The hemolytic effect of primaquine: The natural course of the hemolytic anemia and the mechanism of its self-limited character. *Journal of Laboratory & Clinical Medicine, 44*, 171–176.

Dimsdale, J., Ziegler, M., & Graham, R. (1988). The effect of hypertension, sodium, and race on isoproterenol sensitivity. *Clinical & Experimental Hypertension—Theory and Practice, A10*, 747–756.

D'Mello, D. A., McNeil, J. A., & Harris, W. (1989, May). *Multi-ethnic variance in psychiatric diagnosis and neuroleptic dosage.* Paper presented at 142th Annual Meeting of the American Psychiatric Association, San Francisco.

Fleishaker, J. C., & Phillips, J. P. (1989). Adinazolam pharmacokinetics and behavioral effects following administration of 20–60 mg oral doses of its mesylate salt in healthy volunteers. *Psychopharmacology, 99*, 34–39.

Fleishaker, J. C., Smith, T. C., Friedman, H. L., & Hulst, L. K. (1992). Separation of the pharmacokinetic/pharmacodynamic properties of oral and IV adinazolam mesylate and N-desmethyladinazolam mesylate in healthy volunteers. *Drug Investigations, 4*, 155–165.

Fraser, H. S., Mucklow, J.C., Bulpitt, C. J., Kahn, C., Mould, G., & Dollery, C. T. (1979). Environmental factors affecting antipyrine metabolism in London factory and office workers. *British Journal of Clinical Pharmacology, 7*, 237–243.

Fukuma, Y., Kashimura, S., Umetsu, K., Yuasa, I., & Suzuki, T. (1990). Genetic variation of alpha-2-HS-glycoprotein in the Kyushu district of Japan: Description of three new rare variants. *Human Heredity, 40*, 49–51.

Garde, J. F., Aston, R., Endler, G. C., & Sison, O. S. (1978). Racial mydriatic response to belladonna premedication. *Anesthesia and Analgesia, 57*, 572–576.

Gaviria, M., Gil, A. A., & Javaid, J. I. (1986). Nortriptyline kinetics in Hispanic and Anglo subjects. *Journal of Clinical Psychopharmacology, 6*, 227–231.

Ghoneim, M. M., Korttila, K., Chiang, C. K., Jacobs, L., Schoenwald, R. D., Newaldt, S. P., & Lauaba, K. O. (1981). Diazepam effects and kinetics in Caucasians and Orientals. *Clinical Pharmacology & Therapeutics, 29*, 749–756.

Gonzalez, F. J. (1989). The molecular biology of cytochrome P450s. *Pharmacology Review, 40*, 243–288.

Gonzalez, F. J., & Nebert, D. W. (1990). Evolution of the P450 gene superfamily: Animal–plant "warfare," molecular drive, and human genetic differences in drug oxidation. *Trends in Genetics, 6*, 182–186.

Henry, B. W., Overall, J. E., & Markette, J. (1971). Comparison of major drug therapies for alleviation of anxiety and depression. *Diseases of the Nervous System, 32*, 655–667.

Horai, Y., Nakano, M., Ishizaki, T., Ishikawa, K., Zhou, B., Liao, C., & Zhang, L. (1989). Metoprolol and mephenytoin oxidation polymorphisms in Far Eastern Oriental subjects: Japanese versus mainland Chinese. *Clinical Pharmacology & Therapeutics, 46*, 198–207.

Hu, W. H., Lee, C. F., Yang, Y. Y., & Tseng, Y. T. (1983). Imipramine plasma levels and clinical response. *Bulletin of Chinese Society of Neurology and Psychiatry, 9*, 40–49.

Inaba, T., Jurima, M., Nakano, M., & Kalow, W. (1984). Mephenytoin and sparteine pharmacogenetics in Canadian-Caucasians. *Clinical Pharmacology & Therapeutics, 36*, 670–676.

Jann, M. W., Chang, W. H., Davis, C. M., Chen, T. Y., Deng, H. C., Lung, F. W., Ereshefsky, L., Saklad, S. R., & Richards, A. L. (1989). Haloperidol and reduced haloperidol plasma levels in Chinese versus non-Chinese psychiatric patients. *Psychiatry Research, 30*, 45–52.

Johnson, J. A., Burlew, B. S., & Sullivan, J. M. (1992). Racial differences in blood pressure response to increased forearm vascular resistance. *Clinical Pharmacology & Therapeutics, 51*, 141.

Juneja, R. K., Weitkamp, L. R., Stratil, A., Gahne, B. & Guttormsen, S. A. (1988). Further studies of the plasma α_1 B-glycoprotein polyorphism: Two new alleles and allele frequencies in Caucasians and in American Blacks. *Human Heredity, 38*, 267–272.

Jurima, M., Inaba, T., Kodar, D., & Kalow, W. (1985). Genetic polymorphism of mephenytoin p(4') hydroxylation: Differences between Orientals and Caucasians. *British Journal of Pharmacology, 19*, 483–487.

Kalow, W. (1989). Race and therapeutic drug response. *New England Journal of Medicine, 320*, 588–589.

Kalow, W. (1991). Interethnic variation of drug metabolism. *Trends in Pharmacological Sciences, 12*, 102–107.

Kalow, W., Goedde, H. W., & Agarwal, D. P. (Eds.). (1986). *Ethnic differences in reactions to drugs and xenobiotics.* New York: Alan R. Liss.

Kishimoto, A., & Hollister, L. E. (1984). Nortriptyline kinetics in Japanese and Americans [Letter to the editor]. *Journal of Clinical Psychopharmacology, 4*, 171–172.

Kleinman, A. (1981). Culture and patient care: Psychiatry among the Chinese. *Drug Therapy, 11*, 134–140.

Kumana, C. R., Lauder, I. J., Chan, M., Ko, W., & Lin, H. J. (1987). Differences in diazepam pharmacokinetics in Chinese and White Caucasians: Relation to body lipid stores. *European Journal of Clinical Pharmacology, 32*, 211–215.

Kupfer, A., & Preisig, R. (1984). Pharmacogenetics of mephenytoin: A new drug hydroxylation polymorphism in man. *European Journal of Clinical Pharmacology, 26*, 753–759.

Levy, R. H., & Moreland, T. A. (1984). Rationale for monitoring free drug levels. *Clinical Pharmacokinetics, 9* (Suppl. 1), 1–9.

Lin, K. M., Lau, J. K., Smith, R., & Poland, R. E. (1988). Comparison of alprazolam plasma levels and behavioral effects in normal Asian and Caucasian male volunteers. *Psychopharmacology, 96,* 365–369.

Lin, K. M., Poland, R. E., Lau, J. K., and Rubin, R. T. (1988). Haloperidol and prolactin concentrations in Asians and Caucasians. *Journal of Clinical Psychopharmacology, 8,* 195–201.

Lin, K. M., Poland, R. E., & Nakasaki, G. (1993). *Psychopharmacology and psychobiology of ethnicity.* Washington, DC: American Psychiatric Press.

Lin, K. M., Poland, R. E., Nuccio, I., Matsuda, K., Hathuc, N., Su, T. P., & Fu, P. (1989). Longitudinal assessment of haloperidol dosage and serum concentration in Asian and Caucasian schizophrenic patients. *American Journal of Psychiatry, 146,* 1307–1311.

Lin, K. M., Poland, R. E., & Silver, B. (1993). Overview: The interface between psychobiology and ethnicity. In K. M. Lin, R. E. Poland, & G. Nakasaki (Eds.), *Psychopharmacology and psychobiology of ethnicity* (pp. 11–36). Washington, DC: American Psychiatric Press.

Lin, K. M., Poland, R. E., Smith, M. W., Strickland, T., & Mendoza, R. (1991). Pharmacokinetic and other related factors affecting psychotropic responses in Asians. *Psychopharmacology Bulletin, 27,* 427–439.

Livingston, R. L., Zucker, D. K., Isenberg, K., & Wetzel, R. D. (1983). Tricyclic antidepressants and delirium. *Journal of Clinical Psychiatry, 44,* 173–176.

Marcolin, M. A., Stiers, W., & Chung, Y. S. (1991, May). Racial differences in schizophrenia when controlling for economic status. *Continuing Medical Education Syllabus and Scientific Proceedings,* pp. 80–81. American Psychiatric Association, 144th Annual Meeting, May 11-16, New Orleans, Louisiana.

Marcos, L. R., & Cancro, R. (1982). Pharmacotherapy of Hispanic depressed patients: Clinical observations. *American Journal of Psychotherapy, 36,* 505–512.

May, P. R., & Goldberg, S. C. (1978). Prediction of schizophrenic patients' response to pharmacotherapy. In M. Lipton, A. DiMascio, & K. Killam (Eds.), *Psychopharmacology: A generation of progress* (pp 1139–1154). New York: Raven Press.

Mellstrom, B., Bertilsson, L., Lou, Y. C., Sawe, J., & Sjoqvist, F. (1983). Amitriptyline metabolism: Relationship to polymorphic debrisoquine hydroxylation. *Clinical Pharmacology & Therapeutics, 34,* 516–520.

Mendoza, R., Smith, M. W., Poland, R. E., Lin, K. M., & Strickland, T. (1991). Ethnopsychopharmacology: The Hispanic and Native American perspective. *Psychopharmacology Bulletin, 27,* 449–461.

Meyer, U. A., Zanger, U. M., Grant, D., & Blum, M. (1990). Genetic polymorphisms of drug metabolism. *Advances in Drug Research, 19,* 197–241.

Midha, K. K., Hawes, E. M., Hubbard, J. W., Korchinski, E. D., & McKay, G. (1988a). A pharmacokinetic study of trifluoperazine in two ethnic populations. *Psychopharmacology, 95,* 333–338.

Midha, K. K., Hawes, E. M., Hubbard, J. W., Korchinski, E. D., & McKay, G. (1988b). Variation in the single dose pharmacokinetics of fluphenazine in psychiatric patients. *Psychopharmacology, 96*, 206–211.

Moser, M., & Lunn, J. (1981). Comparative effects of pindolol and hydrochlorothiazide in Black hypertensive patients. *Angiology, 32*, 561–566.

Murphy, H. B. M. (1969). Ethnic variations in drug responses. *Transcultural Psychiatric Research Review, 6*, 6–23.

Murray, M., & Reidy, G. F. (1990). Selectivity in the inhibition of mammalian cytochromes P-450 by chemical agents. *Pharmacology Review, 42*, 2.

Nakamura, K., Goto, F., Ray, W. A., McAllister, C. B., Jacqz, E., Wilkinson, G. R., & Branch, R. A. (1985). Interethnic differences in genetic polymorphism of debrisoquine and mephenytoin hydroxylation between Japanese and Caucasian populations. *Clinical Pharmacology & Therapeutics, 38*, 402–408.

Okpaku, S., Frazer, A., & Mendels, J. (1980). A pilot study of racial differences in erythrocyte lithium transport. *American Journal of Psychiatry, 137*, 120–121.

Ostrow, D. G., Dorus, W., Okonek, A., Desai, P., Bauer, J., Bresolin, L. B., & Davis, J. M. (1986). The effect of alcoholism on membrane lithium transport. *Journal of Clinical Psychiatry, 47*, 350–353.

Overall, J. E., Hollister, L. E., Kimball, I., Jr., & Shelton, J. (1969). Extrinsic factors influencing responses to psychotherapeutic drugs. *Archives of General Psychiatry, 21*, 89–94.

Pi, E. H., Simpson, G. H., & Cooper, M. A. (1986). Pharmacokinetics of desipramine in Caucasian and Asian volunteers. *American Journal of Psychiatry, 143*, 1174–1176.

Pi, E. H., Tran-Johnson, T. K., Walker, N. R., Cooper, R. B., Suckow, R. F., & Gray, G. E. (1989). Pharmacokinetics of desipramine in Asian and Caucasian volunteers. *Psychopharmacology Bulletin, 25*, 483–487.

Potkin, S. G., Shen, Y., Pardes, H., Phelps, B. H., Zhou, D., Shu, L., Korpi, E., & Wyatt, R. J. (1984). Haloperidol concentrations elevated in Chinese patients. *Psychiatry Research, 12*, 167–172.

Price, N. D., Glazer, W. M., & Morgenstern, H. (1985). Race and the use of fluphenazine decanoate. *American Journal of Psychiatry, 142*, 1491–1492.

Raskin, A., Thomas, H., & Crook, M. A. (1975). Antidepressants in Black and White inpatients. *Archives of General Psychiatry, 32*, 643–649.

Reidenberg, M. M., & Erill, S. (Eds.). (1986). *Drug–protein binding*. New York: Oxford University Press.

Rosenblat, R., & Tang, S. W. (1987). Do Oriental psychiatric patients receive different dosages of psychotropic medication when compared with Occidentals? *Canadian Journal of Psychiatry, 32*, 270–274.

Routledge, P. A. (1986). The plasma protein binding of basic drugs. *British Journal of Clinical Pharmacology, 22*, 499–506.

Rudorfer, M. V., Lane, E. A., Chang, W. H., Zhang, M. D., & Potter, W. Z. (1984). Desipramine pharmacokinetics in Chinese and Caucasian volunteers. *British Journal of Clinical Pharmacology, 17*, 433–440.

Rudorfer, M. V., & Robins, E. (1982). Amitriptyline overdose: Clinical effects on tricyclicantidepressant plasma levels. *Journal of Clinical Psychiatry, 43,* 457–460.

Rutledge, D. R., Steinberg, M. B., & Cardozo, L. (1989). Racial differences in drug response: Isoproterenol effects on heart rate following intravenous metoprolol. *Clinical Pharmacology & Therapeutics, 45,* 380–386.

Sanz, E. J., Villen, T., Alm, C., & Bertilsson, L. (1989). S-mephenytoin hydroxylation phenotypes in a Swedish population determined after coadministration with debrisoquine. *Clinical Pharmacology & Therapeutics, 45,* 495–499.

Schneider, L., Pawluczyk, S., Dopheide, J., Lyness, S. A., Suckow, R. F., & Copper, T. B. (1991). Ethnic differences in nortriptyline metabolism. *New Research Program and Abstracts* (p. 206), American Psychiatric Association, 144th Annual Meeting, New Orleans, Louisiana.

Shaheen, O., Biollaz, J., Koshakji, R. P., Wilkinson, G. R., & Wood, A. J. (1989). Influence of debrisoquine phenotype on the inducibility of propranolol metabolism. *Clinical Pharmacology & Therapeutics, 45,* 439–443.

Shelley, R. K. (1987). Are there ethnic differences in lithium pharmacokinetics and side effects? *International Clinical Psychopharmacology, 2,* 337–342.

Shen, W. W., & Lin, K. M. (1990). Cytochrome P-450 monooxygenases and interactions of psychotropic drugs. *International Journal of Psychiatry in Medicine, 21,* 21–30.

Skjelbo, E., Brosen, K., Hallas, J., & Gram, L. F. (1991). The mephenytoin oxidation polymorphism is partially responsible for the N-demethylation of imipramine. *Clinical Pharmacology & Therapeutics, 49,* 18–23.

Smith, M., Cartaya, O. J., Mendoza, R., Lesser, I., & Lin, K. M. (in press). Psychopharmacologic treatment of torture victims. In J. M. Jaranson & M. Poplin (Eds.), *The role of psychiatrists and other physicians in caring for victims of torture.* Oxford, England: Refugee Studies Program.

Strickland T. L., Lawson, W., Lin, K. M. & Fu, P. (1993). Interethnic variation to lithium therapy among African-American and Asian-American populations. In K. M. Lin, R. Poland, & G. Nakasaki (Eds.), *Psychopharmacology and psychobiology of ethnicity* (pp 107–121). Washington, DC: American Psychiatric Press.

Strickland, T. L., Lin, K. M., Fu, P., Anderson, D., & Zheng. Y. P. (1995). Comparison of lithium ratio between African American and Caucasian bipolar patients. *Biological Psychiatry, 37,* 325–330.

Strickland, T. L., Rangananth, V., Lin, K. M., Poland, R. E., Mendoza, R., & Smith, M. (1991). Psychopharmacologic considerations in the treatment of Black American populations. *Psychopharmacology Bulletin, 27,* 441–448.

Takahashi, R. (1979). Lithium treatment in affective disorders: Therapeutic plasma level. *Psychopharmacology Bulletin, 15,* 32–35.

Trevisan, M., Ostrow, D., Cooper, R. S., Sempos, C., & Stamler, J. (1984). Sex and race differences in sodium–lithium countertransport and red cell sodium concentration. *American Journal of Epidemiology, 120,* 537–541.

Umetsu, K., Yuasa, I., Nishimura, H., Sasaki, H., & Suzuki, T. (1988). Genetic polymorphisms of orosomucoid and alpha-2-HS-glycoprotein in a Philippine population. *Human Heredity, 38*, 287–290.

Ward, S. E., Walle, T., Walle, U. K., Wilkinson, G. R., & Branch, R. A. (1989). Propranolol's metabolism is determined by both mephenytoin and debrisoquine hydroxylase activities. *Clinical Pharmacology & Therapeutics, 45*, 72–79.

Weber, W. W. (1987). *The acetylator genes and drug responses.* New York: Oxford University Press.

Wilkinson, G. R., Guengerich, F. P., & Branch, R. A. (1989). Genetic polymorphism of S-mephenytoin hydroxylation. *Clinical Pharmacology & Therapeutics, 43*, 53–76.

Wood, A. J. J., & Zhou, H. H. (1991). Ethnic differences in drug disposition and responsiveness. *Clinical Pharmacokinetics, 20*, 1–24.

Yamashita, I., & Asano, Y. (1979). Tricyclic antidepressants: Therapeutic plasma level. *Psychopharmacology Bulletin, 15*, 40–41.

Yoshida, A. (1993). Genetic polymorphisms of alcohol-metabolizing enzymes related to alcohol sensitivity and alcoholic diseases. In K. M. Lin, R. E. Poland, & G. Nakasaki (Eds.), *Psychopharmacology and psychobiology of ethnicity* (pp 169–186). Washington, DC: American Psychiatric Press.

Zhang, Y., Reviriego, J., Lou, Y., Sjoqvist, F., & Bertilsson, L. (1990). Diazepam metabolism in native Chinese poor and extensive hydroxylators of S-mephenytoin: Interethnic differences in comparison with White subjects. *Clinical Pharmacology & Therapeutics, 48*, 496–502.

Zhou, H. H., Koshakji, R. P., Siolberstein, D. J., Wilkinson, G. R, & Wood, A. J. (1989). Altered sensitivity to and clearance of propranolol in men of Chinese descent as compared with American Whites. *New England Journal of Medicine, 320*, 565–570.

Ziegler, V. E., & Biggs, J. T. (1977). Tricyclic plasma levels—effect of age, race, sex, and smoking. *Journal of the American Medical Association, 238*, 2167–2169.

Ziegler, V. E., Clayton, P. J., & Biggs, J. T. (1977). A comparison study of amitriptyline and nortriptyline with plasma levels. *Archives of General Psychiatry, 34*, 607–612.

VI

CONCLUSION

21

ETHNOCULTURAL ASPECTS OF PTSD: SOME CLOSING THOUGHTS

ANTHONY J. MARSELLA, MATTHEW J. FRIEDMAN,
ELLEN T. GERRITY, and RAYMOND M. SCURFIELD

In our opinion, this book has served three functions. First, it has brought together scholars and researchers from many different disciplines who have common interests in mental health, but who have not often interacted with one another in a true interdisciplinary manner. The contributors to this volume have included clinical psychologists, medical anthropologists, psychiatrists, and sociologists. Some of the contributors (e.g., cross-cultural psychologists and medical anthropologists) have been dedicated to defining idioms of distress, normative behavior, and psychopathological states in an ethnoculturally sensitive context. Others (e.g., clinical psychologists, clinical psychiatrists) have focused their attention on understanding a clinical syndrome that has been operationalized primarily in a Euro-American, Western, industrialized context, but that came to be used on an international basis without, in many instances, consideration of ethnocultural factors. The convergence of these different disciplines and concerns has offered this book a unique vantage point for understanding both PTSD and interdisciplinary perspectives.

Second, this book has synthesized and presented most of the conceptual and empirical information currently available on ethnocultural aspects of PTSD. The patient and careful reader should now be familiar with the current state of the art regarding ethnocultural aspects of PTSD in particular, and posttraumatic syndrome in general.

Third, this book has identified current controversies in the field and generated an agenda for future research that we believe are encapsulated by the following questions:

1. Can PTSD be diagnosed in people from non-Western cultures?
2. Is such a diagnosis clinically meaningful?
3. How do ethnocultural considerations affect interpretations of human experience as traumatic or nontraumatic?
4. Do PTSD diagnostic criteria encompass both universal and culture-specific responses to trauma?
5. Is PTSD the best transcultural conceptualization of the psychological impact of trauma?
6. Are there other diagnostic formulations (syndromes) that provide a better reflection of trauma-induced distress?
7. Does the PTSD concept distort or ignore sociopolitical realities that may contribute to or precipitate the subjective distress experienced by PTSD patients?
8. Should PTSD be considered a culture-bound syndrome?
9. What are the major assessment and methodological challenges in cross-cultural PTSD research?
10. Should treatment be transcultural, culture-specific, or both, or which under what circumstances?

The story is told that Gertrude Stein, the famous American author, went dramatically to her death by rejecting the call for answers and instead with her last breath asked, "What is the question?" Let us elaborate on these questions in a final effort to summarize the contents of this book for the reader.

SOME SUMMARY QUESTIONS AND ANSWERS

1. Can PTSD be Diagnosed in People From Non-Western Cultures?

Yes, as shown in many chapters, PTSD can be diagnosed in Southeast Asian refugees, Latin American disaster survivors and immigrants, Navajo and Sioux Vietnam veterans, and other non-Western cohorts, even when there is minimal acculturation to Western orientations and life styles. In some cases the assessment of PTSD was made using instruments that have been previously used and standardized with Euro-American cohorts. In other instances, there has been an effort to translate specific questionnaire items with culturally sensitive and relevant inquiries (see chapter by Manson, et al.).

We are not aware of any ethnocultural cohort in which PTSD could not be diagnosed, although prevalence rates have varied considerably from one setting to another. Where such differences have been found, it is unclear whether they represent ethnocultural differences in the prevalence of PTSD per se or differences in the cultural sensitivity of the assessment instruments employed. Concerns about the adequacy of instrumentation cut both ways, because it is just as important to avoid overdiagnosis as underdiagnosis of PTSD. However, it is clear that diagnostic validity could be improved if greater attention was given to culturally sensitive issues such as idioms of distress and concepts of personhood and trauma. With improved understanding of these factors, treatment and prevention activities could be improved.

2. Is Such a Diagnosis Clinically Meaningful?

In our opinion, PTSD is a clinically meaningful diagnosis because of universals in human experience in response to trauma. Any individual who meets diagnostic criteria is a person who has been unable to recover from the traumatic experience(s) to which s/he was exposed. Such continuous psychological involvement with the relentless recycling of traumatic material through reexperiencing, avoidant, numbing, and arousal symptoms is often a major source of subjective, interpersonal, social, and functional distress. It is absolutely necessary, however, to understand this cluster of symptoms in its proper ethnocultural context in order to identify an appropriate intervention. The ethnocultural variations in the perceptual and experiential aspects of responses to trauma can only assist in treatment and prevention efforts.

3. How do Ethnocultural Considerations Affect Interpretations of Human Experience as Traumatic or Nontraumatic?

Several authors (see chapters by Kirmayer; Manson et al.; Robin et al.; Jenkins) have identified aspects of traumatic experiences often suffered by people from many non-European cultures that they believe are not adequately encompassed by the PTSD construct. They are

- prolonged and repeated trauma;
- acute traumatic episodes that can only be properly understood in a sociopolitical or multigenerational context; and
- collective trauma as experienced by a whole community in the context of political repression, war, or a natural disaster.

Since 1980, as mental health professionals have gained more experience with trauma-focused assessment and treatment, there has been growing concern within the field about possible differences between acute and prolonged repetitive traumatic events. Even within a Euro-American context, there was enough dissatisfaction with the PTSD construct among clinicians working with adult survivors of repetitive child sexual abuse that they proposed a new diagnosis—*complex PTSD*.

This construct focused less on subjective PTSD symptoms than on interpersonal relations, dissociation, somatic symptoms, and alterations in one's worldview in terms of trust, hope, and meaning. The same dissatisfaction with the PTSD construct is evident in several chapters in this book. Although PTSD may not encompass all of the symptoms that may be clinically relevant among certain trauma survivors, many would argue that it does identify those symptoms that are most distinctive. It is clearly an issue for future research whether we need additional posttraumatic syndromes in order to do nosologic justice to the variety and complexity of psychological expressions of distress following exposure to trauma. This may be particularly relevant in an ethnocultural context in which differences in social constructions of reality have profound implications for concepts of health and disease.

There are two ways to address the criticism that PTSD does not encompass the full range of posttraumatic syndromes. On the one hand, it can be argued that in the *DSM–IV* the stressor criterion has been modified so that an overwhelming event must produce a strong emotional response in order to be considered traumatic. Individual appraisal of any given event will depend greatly upon that individual's ethnocultural perspective. Therefore, it can be argued that PTSD is now open to any idiosyncratic or ethnocultural definitions of trauma. In this case, the task of assessment is to insure that the diagnostician understands both the ethnocultural context in which an event has occurred and the ethnocultural options through which a strong emotional response to that event might be expressed.

On the other hand, one can argue that there is a spectrum of posttraumatic syndromes in which PTSD is only one of several disorders that may result from experiencing trauma. Such a strategy compels PTSD researchers to employ ethnographic methodologies to identify discrete syndromes that may be applicable to certain ethnocultural groups and not to others. It is an open question at this time and a challenge to future research whether such additional posttraumatic syndromes can be reliably identified and codified.

The same comments apply to the second concern, the impact of an acute traumatic event in its ongoing sociopolitical and multigenerational context. Unless it can be shown that there is something so unique about such occurrences that they generate a unique psychological expression and demand a unique clinical intervention, there is not much to be gained by searching for a distinct syndrome for such an experience. We can certainly identify differences between rape in the context of genocide and rape following a date with someone well-known to the victim beforehand. What we don't know is whether these differences mitigate, exacerbate, or promote different expressions of the psychological response to these specifically similar events. Again, it is a matter for future research.

Finally, it has been argued that the stronger sense of community and spiritual connectedness seen in non-Western societies in contrast to the individualistic subjective focus found in Euro-American cultures produces crucial differences in the psychological impact and expression of such traumatic encounters. If this is the case, one might search for posttraumatic symptoms and idioms of distress that cannot be understood through the standard PTSD construct. This is certainly an important question for future research that we hope this book will help stimulate.

The philosophy that one must accept events in life, regardless of their impact, is an important topic that needs better understanding within cultural contexts that emphasize personal control and personal responsibility. It should be noted, in this regard, that trauma seems well understood by people from non-Western cultural backgrounds, as noted throughout this book, even in the face of variations in concepts of health and illness. We are hopeful that more research can be conducted in non-Western cultures where religious systems such as Buddhism, Hinduism, and Islam dominate.

Finally, we must emphasize our belief that collective and individual trauma are not mutually exclusive. Experiencing sociopolitical events such as war, genocide, or disaster in a cultural, national, or community context does not mean that one will not also experience such events as an individual. The fact that trauma may occur on a social or collective level in no way obviates the subjective distress precipitated by such events. One can suffer the private torment of PTSD and the social anguish of sociopolitical events simultaneously.

4. Do PTSD Diagnostic Criteria Encompass Both Universal and Culture-Specific Responses to Trauma?

There is a growing body of evidence suggesting that a number of PTSD symptoms may have a hard-wired biological basis. PTSD reexperiencing symptoms, such as flashbacks and arousal symptoms, can be precipitated by drugs that act on the central adrenergic (e.g. yohimbine) or serotonergic (e.g., m-chlorophenylpiperazine, MCPP) systems. Furthermore, studies of different traumatized ethnocultural cohorts have usually been able to detect reexperiencing and arousal symptoms more easily than avoidant/numbing symptoms. Indeed, such patients most often fail to meet PTSD diagnostic criteria because they lack avoidant/numbing symptoms despite the presence of reexperiencing and arousal symptoms.

These experimental observations suggest to us that there may be a universal biologic response to trauma that can be detected in humans from every sort of ethnocultural background. Although the frequency, severity, and phenomenology of such symptoms may be modified by ethnocultural and genetic factors, the weight of research at this time suggests that activation of the biologic response system is at least partially responsible for PTSD reexperiencing and arousal symptoms.

On the other hand, there appears to be less evidence to support a biological basis for avoidant or numbing symptoms. For this reason, we believe that this symptom cluster may be most susceptible to culture-specific influences. Taking this argument one step further, we believe that ethnocultural settings in which avoidant and numbing behaviors are more common expressions of distress are those ethnocultural settings in which PTSD prevalence rates will be the highest.

Furthermore, as noted in the chapter by Friedman and Marsella, ethnocultural factors may be important determinants of vulnerability to trauma (by shaping concepts of what constitutes a trauma); personal and social resources for dealing with traumata; early childhood experiences; exposure to multiple trauma; premorbid personality disease profiles (e.g., substance abuse, alcoholism); and treatment options that successfully contain and control the trauma experience.

5. Is PTSD the Best Transcultural Conceptualization of the Psychosocial Impact of Trauma?

Because there has been little systematic research that addresses this question, we don't know for sure whether PTSD is the best transcultural conceptualization for trauma impact. A number of authors (see chapters by Kirmayer; Jenkins; Manson et al.; Hough et al.; and Robin et al.) have suggested, however, that somatization and dissociation are very prominent components of posttraumatic distress among traumatized individuals from non-Western cultures.

Although dissociation is one of many potential *DSM–IV* symptoms of PTSD, it is not a prominent aspect of the syndrome. Indeed, one can meet diagnostic criteria for PTSD without any evidence of dissociation. Perhaps the low prominence of dissociation is because of the Euro-American focus of the *DSM–IV*. It is apparent that norms within certain non-Western cultures regarding the nature of personhood and religious practices may increase the likelihood that dissociation will be used as a coping strategy in these ethnocultural settings.

Somatic expressions of distress are likewise frequently observed following trauma. Traumatized individuals may exhibit a syndrome like *DSM–IV* somatization disorder, conversion disorder, or more culturally specific somatic syndromes such as *calor* or *ataques de nervios*. Clearly future research must monitor these syndromes as well as PTSD among traumatized individuals in order to identify those syndromes that are most representative of posttraumatic distress within a given ethnocultural setting.

6. Are There Other Diagnostic Formulations (Syndromes) That Provide a Better Reflection of Trauma-Induced Distress?

Complex PTSD (Herman, 1992) has been promoted as a better diagnostic construct than PTSD for posttraumatic distress among different ethnocultural groups. Advocates for complex PTSD point out that this construct fills in a number of gaps in the *DSM–IV* PTSD construct. First, complex PTSD was formulated to encompass the symptoms observed in victims of repetitive trauma. Second, its array of symptoms is supposed to represent those seen clinically in victims of repetitive sexual trauma and political torture—two conditions often encountered among non-Western trauma survivors, especially political refugees. Third, dissociation and somatization are much more prominent as symptom clusters in complex PTSD than in the *DSM–IV* PTSD diagnostic criteria.

Before getting too enthusiastic about complex PTSD, however, several points are worth noting. First, the complex PTSD diagnosis grew out of clinical work with (mostly) American female adult survivors of childhood sexual abuse. It has not been systematically studied in non-American cohorts and is therefore open to all the cross-cultural concerns previously expressed regarding PTSD. Second, complex PTSD has not been shown to be a distinct and robust diagnostic entity in its own right. In the *DSM–IV* field trials, only 8% of all individuals with complex PTSD failed to meet PTSD diagnostic criteria. In other words, it is not at all clear that complex PTSD is diagnostically distinct from PTSD. It is a matter that certainly merits further research. Rather than seeking yet another Western-derived syndrome, we suggest that a better approach is to retain PTSD as the frame of reference and to use cross-cultural techniques to assess the applicability of this construct to the diverse ethnocultural expressions of posttraumatic distress.

7. Does the PTSD Concept Distort or Ignore Sociopolitical Realities That May Contribute to or Precipitate the Subjective Distress Experienced by PTSD Patients?

We have addressed this matter previously (see Question 3). We believe that rather than distorting them, the PTSD concept is very sensitive to sociopolitical realities that produce subjective distress. Indeed, each individual's appraisal of an event as either traumatic or nontraumatic is a psychological exercise that depends entirely on how she or he interprets her or his experience. Ethnocultural factors will certainly influence that process and sociopolitical realities will be factored into that appraisal process to the extent that they are perceived as important aspects of that experience.

8. Should PTSD be Considered a Culture-Bound Syndrome?

It can be said that all disorders are essentially culture-bound syndromes because no one can escape the influence of cultural factors in their conceptualization, experience, display, and treatment responsivity. However, the challenge for clinicians and researchers alike is to pursue an understanding of each disorder so that ethnocultural similarities and differences can be identified and mapped to the advantage of the individual patient and the society.

We believe that the PTSD construct has both culture-bound and universal dimensions. We have addressed elsewhere the need for culturally sensitive assessment techniques and the need to identify other posttraumatic expressions of distress (e.g., somatization, dissociation) that may be particularly pertinent to non-Western individuals. The fact remains, however, that PTSD has been detected in traumatized cohorts from very different ethnocultural backgrounds, and that refugees from non-Western cultures who meet PTSD diagnostic criteria appear to show a similar clinical course and response to treatment as do Euro-American individuals who have been traumatized.

Diagnosis is most useful if it suggests a therapeutic strategy that would not be implemented without such a given diagnosis. In the case of PTSD, it appears that non-Western traumatized individuals with PTSD can benefit greatly from a trauma-oriented treatment approach. Within the context of PTSD-focused treatment, there is plenty of room for therapeutic strategies that are culturally sensitive and that incorporate specific treatments for individuals from specific ethnocultural backgrounds. To summarize, the PTSD construct appears to be useful and applicable to individuals from ethnocultural backgrounds.

9. What are the Major Assessment and Methodological Problems in Cross-Cultural PTSD Research and Practice?

The major assessment and methodological problems in cross-cultural PTSD research and practice are mainly related to the concept of *cross-cultural equivalence*. Cross-cultural equivalence means the extent to which phenomena are "equal" or "similar" across cultures. As was pointed out in the chapter by Keane et al., linguistic, conceptual, scale, and normative equivalence are all essential for valid cross-cultural assessment and measurement.

This area is one of real challenge for researchers and clinicians because it is the basis of our data. Clearly, it would be valuable if instruments could be developed that are sensitive to cultural factors including the cultural concept of the person, the culture's idioms of distress, and the culture's social construction of reality—particularly trauma. One can imagine that future instruments will address not only Western criteria (i.e., *DSM–IV*), but also symptoms and clinical parameters specific to particular cultural groups. Cross-cultural research designs that compare patients on the basis of similarities in personal demographics, diagnosis, clinical symptoms, and trauma experiences would also be important for furthering our understanding of PTSD. Lastly, one cannot ignore the importance of approaching ethnocultural aspects of PTSD from the viewpoint of ethnographies and other research strategies that are sensitive to indigenous perspectives (e.g., ethnosemantics).

10. Treatment of PTSD: Transcultural, Cultural-Specific, and Interactive Options?

If one imposes rigorous methodological standards upon the PTSD treatment literature, then few conclusions seemed warranted. There have been few cross-cultural studies of treatment efficacy using cultural-specific therapies (e.g., morita therapy for Japanese Americans, sweat-lodge therapy for American Indians), although there are a growing number of publications on these indigenous practices.

At this point in time, the challenge for therapy researchers is to conduct therapy process and outcome studies that compare nontraumatized individuals and trauma victims from different ethnocultural groups. If possible, there should be a careful matching or selective study of therapist ethnicity because this has been shown to be important in therapy and counseling outcome. Designs that consider therapeutic approach, therapist ethnicity, patient ethnicity, and culturally sensitive outcome concepts of health and disorder would be ideal. Certainly, the chapter by Gusman et al. in the present volume offers a number of tantalizing hypotheses regarding ethnocultural aspects of PTSD.

Psychopharmacological treatments have been addressing ethnocultural variations outcome in recent years (see chapter by Lin et al.). These studies deserve more attention, and with the addition of improved measures of ethnicity and ethnic identification it may be possible to uncover some important racial or ethnic factors in the therapy of PTSD and related stress disorders.

CONCLUSION

It is always wise—and thus, always warranted—to call for more research at the end of any scholarly or clinical article or book. This is certainly the case for the present book on ethnocultural aspects of PTSD. Clinical and research studies indicate that ethnocultural factors must be considered in the conceptualization, diagnosis and classification, and treatment of PTSD. That this should be the case is not surprising because research has indicated that all patterns of psychopathology are intimately related to the cultural context in which they emerge, are defined, and are treated. Culture is an important factor in the etiology, expression, course, and outcome of psychopathology. Researchers and clinicians need to understand its influences, especially its interactions with biology, psychology, and the social formation.

Clinical, field, and treatment studies of PTSD have contributed much toward an international and transcultural understanding of PTSD and related stress disorders. There are substantive reasons to believe that the experience of trauma has similar biopsychosocial consequences and correlates in spite of the fact that different cultural traditions may define and experience reality, personhood, and trauma in different ways.

Thus, the study of ethnocultural aspects of PTSD offers clinicians and scientists alike the delightful and unlimited opportunity to test their assumptions and hypotheses about the nature, causes, and treatment of PTSD through cultural comparisons and, in the process, to better identify and understand the complex forces that shape and determine human disease, health, and well-being.

AUTHOR INDEX

Ball, W. A., 18, 29
Ballenger, J. C., 61
Banerjee, G., 136, 161
Barefoot, J., 269, 282
Barger, S. J., 153, 161
Barlett, G., 359
Barley, S. R., 155, 156
Barlow, D. H., 420, 433
Baron, A., 242, 247, 249
Baron, A. E., 250, 258, 268, 269, 278, 281
Barr, H. L., 503
Barrett, T. W., 443, 455
Barse, H., 111, 122
Barsky, A. J., 138, 149, 156
Basoglu, M., 50, 60
Bass, C., 137, 140, 162
Bates, E. W., 503
Bateson, G., 142, 156, 170, 178
Bauer, G. B., 50, 51, 62
Bauer, J., 524
Bauer, M., 60
Baum, A., 344, 358
Baum, M., 92, 102
Baumgartner, D., 113, 122
Bavington, J. T., 160
Beagley, G., 17, 29
Beals, J., 250, 257, 258, 269, 278, 279, 280
Beatty, S. B., 364, 384
Beauvais, L. L., 442, 456
Becerra, R., 111, 122
Bechtold, D. W., 252, 255, 257, 278, 279
Beck, A. T., 198, 202
Beck, J. C., 372, 383
Becker, D., 246, 250
Becker, J., 92, 99
Becker, M., 122
Beebe, G., 416, 431
Beebe, G. W., 166, 179, 433
Beeman, W. O., 169, 178
Beiser, M., 107, 108, 122, 258, 278, 281, 287, 297, 464, 478
Bell, C. C., 215, 216, 233, 430, 431, 431
Bell, P., 51, 60, 62
Bell, W., 112, 128, 236
Ben, R., 291, 298, 402, 412, 464, 480
Benbenishty, R., 272, 282, 427, 434, 435
Benedikt, R. A., 52, 60
Bergin, A. E., 465, 480
Bergner, L., 500, 501
Berk, M. L., 501, 503
Bernstein, A. B., 501, 503

Berry, J. W., 442, 455
Berryman, S. E., 484, 502
Bertelsen, A., 158
Bertilsson, L., 507, 516, 520, 521, 523, 525, 526
Best, C., 433
Best, C. L., 65, 68, 92, 101
Beutler, E., 506, 521
Bharati, A., 134, 156
Bhatia, M. S., 134, 156
Bhatnagar, K. S., 160
Bickman, L., 58, 69, 462, 482
Biernoff, M., 252
Biggs, J. T., 511, 526
Billson, J. M., 227, 236
Biollaz, J., 507, 525
Bion, W. R., 222, 233
Bird, H., 332
Bird, M. E., 245, 250
Birgitta, A., 334
Birket-Smith, M., 158
Birz, S., 203
Bittner, E., 127
Bjornson, L., 161
Black, J., 112, 128, 236
Black, V., 236
Blackburn, T. C., 153, 163
Blake, D. D., 60, 200, 202, 205, 450, 455
Blanchard, E. B., 16, 18, 25, 52, 64
Blank, A., 20, 25
Blank, A. S., Jr., 502
Blascovitch, J., 25
Blazer, D., 416, 435
Blazer, D. G., 22, 30, 46, 63, 135, 162, 336
Bleich, A., 56, 64, 70, 91, 99, 427, 434
Blendon, R. J., 67, 500, 502
Blikra, G., 109, 126
Bloom, J., 114, 125
Bloom, J. D., 240, 241, 249, 251, 252, 258, 281
Blow, F. C., 44, 49, 61
Blum, J. D., 500, 503
Blum, M., 507, 523
Blum, R., 244, 249
Boccellari, A., 108, 126
Boddy, J., 141, 156
Boehlein, J. K., 442, 455
Boehlin, J. K., 289, 298
Boehnlein, J., 108, 114, 115, 122, 125, 127, 250, 462, 464, 480
Boehnlein, J. J., 290, 298

Boehnlein, J. K., 51, 67, *101*, 134, *160*, 285, 293, 298, 299, *478, 481*
Boldizar, J. P., 215, *234*
Bolin, R., 348, *358*
Bollini, P., *127, 204*
Bontempo, R., 364, *386*
Boon, S., *61*
Booth, B. M., 44, *61*
Boothby, N., 402, *410*
Bornemann, T., 22, *28*, 40, 67, 98, *101*, 402, *413*
Bouafuely, M., 134, *163*
Boudewyns, P. A., 93, 96, *99*
Bourbeau, R., 42, *61*
Bourguignon, E., 144, 145, *156*
Bourne, E., 168, *181*
Bowers, K. S., 143, 150, *156*
Bownes, I. T., 52, *61*
Boyd, H., 17, *30*
Boyd, J., 89, *101*
Brailey, K., *71*
Branch, R. A., 507, 509, *520, 524, 526*
Branchey, M., *61*
Brant, C., 240, *252*
Braun, B. G., 142, *157*
Braun, P., 91, *99*
Bravo, M., 48, *62*, 134, 147, *157, 158*, 264, *278*, 311, 323, 327, *332, 337*, 343, 347, 355, *358, 360*
Brawman-Mintzer, O., 50, *61*, 67
Breckenridge, A., 114, *125*
Bremner, D., 17, 18, *30, 70*
Bremner, J. D., *25*
Brende, J. O., 444, *455*
Brenneman, D., 242, *249*, 269, *278*
Brenner, M. H., 217, *234*
Breslau, N., 14, 22, *25*, 46, *61*, 88, *99*, 110, *122*, 271, *278*, 416, *431*
Bresolin, L. B., *524*
Brett, E., 212, 213, *236*, 423, *433*
Bridges, K. W., 140, *156*
Briggs, J., 169, *178*
Brill, A., 166, *179*
Brill, N., 416, *431*
Brom, D., 34, 57, *61*, 93, 94, *99*
Bromet, E., 343, 344, *359*
Brooks, N., *61*
Brosen, K., 507, 510, *520, 525*
Brown, G. L., *252*
Brown, J. E., 276, *279*
Brown, J. L., 229, *233*
Brown, P. J., 21, *30, 71*

Browne, A., 363, 369, *383, 384*
Brownmiller, S., 364, 365, *383*
Bryant, B., 52, 67
Bucsela, M. L., 21, *30*
Bullrich, S., 390, *410*
Bulpitt, C. J., *521*
Bunker, C. H., 518, *520*
Burge, S. K., 52, *61*
Burgess, P., 17, *25*
Burges Watson, I. P., 50, *61*, 403, *410*
Burke, J., 89, *101*
Burke, J. B., *335*
Burlew, B. S., 508, *522*
Burnam, M. A., 245, 249, 315, 318, 319, 327, 328, 331, *332, 333, 334, 335*, 337, 338, 487, *504*
Busch, P., *338, 414*
Butterfield, F., 218, 223, *234*
Buydens-Branchey, L., *61*
Byrne, D., 468, *478*

Cabugao, R., 66, *298*
Cacciola, J., *503*
Caddell, J., 92, 93, *100*, 260, 280, 415, 420, *433*
Caddell, J. M., 17, *27, 101*, 199, 200, 203, *432*
Caldwell, M. F., *61*
Calhoun, K. S., 272, *278*
Callen, K. E., *61*
Callies, A., 134, *163*, 294, *299*
Campbell, D., 19, *25*
Cancro, R., 512, *523*
Canda, E. R., 296, *297*
Canino, F., 134, *157*
Canino, G., 48, 54, 59, *62*, 70, 135, 147, *156, 158*, 264, 267, *278, 280*, 311, 312, 315, 323, 325, 327, 328, 329, *332, 333, 334, 337*, 343, 347, 355, *358, 360*
Canino, I. A., 135, *156*, 329, *332–333*, 389, 400, *410–411*
Cannon, W. B., 17, *25*
Caraballo, L. R., 264, *279*
Caraveo, J., 13, *25*, 48, *62*
Card, J. J., *62*
Cardeña, E., 141, 152, *156, 162*
Cardozo, L., 509, *525*
Caris, L., 48, 66, 308, *335, 360*
Carlsen, M. B., 444, *456*
Carlson, E. B., 51, *62*, 141, *157*, 290, *297*
Carlson, G. A., 391, 393, *412*

Figley, C. R., 11, 12, *26*, 465, *479*
Figueroa, G., 307, *338*
Finch, A. J., Jr., *236*
Finder, K., 115, *126*
Fingerhut, L. A., 42, *63*
Fink, R., 146, *162*
Finkelhor, D., 368, *383*
First, M. B., 200, *205*, 247, *253*, 450, *457*
Fischbach, R. L., 327, *337*
Fisher, N., *64*
Fisher, P., *282*
Fishler, R., 245, *249*
Fiske, S. T., 372, 382, *383*
Fitterling, J. M., 17, *26*
Fitzgerald, L. F., 363, *384*
Fitzpatrick, K. M., 215, 216, *234*
Flaherty, J. A., 186, *203*
Fleck, J., 108, 114, 115, *122, 125,* 463, 464, 465, 472, *480*
Fleishaker, J. C., 517, *521*
Fleming, C. M., 258, 268, *281,* 501, *502*
Flores, L. P., 50, *67*
Foa, E. B., 15, 20, 21, *26,* 52, 69, 91, 92, 93, 96, *100, 101, 102,* 376, *383,* 420, *432*
Fodor, I. G., 373, *383*
Folkman, S., *27,* 420, *433*
Folnegovic-Smalc, V., *66*
Fontana, A., 23, *26,* 485, 486, 499, *502, 503*
Foreman, C., 52, *67*
Forgue, D. F., 16, *29*
Forsythe, A., 328, *333*
Forsythe, A. B., *249, 332, 334*
Foulks, E. F., 289, *298*
Foy, D., 21, *28*
Foy, D. W., *65,* 420, *432*
Fram, D. H., 91, *102*
Frances, A. J., 52, *68*
Frank, J. B., 91, *100*
Frankel, F. H., 143, 146, 152, *157, 162*
Frankel, M., *67*
Franklin, J. H., 220, 221, *234*
Fraser, G. A., *161*
Fraser, H. S., 509, *521*
Frazer, A., 518, *524*
Frederick, C., *29*
Frederickson, R., 108, *125,* 464, *480*
Freeman, H. E., 500, *502*
Freidenberg, J., 264, *279*
Freimer, N., 115, *123*
Frerichs, R. R., 268, *279*

Frey-Wouters, E., 110, *125,* 423, *433,* 487, *503*
Friedman, H. L., 517, *521*
Friedman, J., 114, *123*
Friedman, M. J., 12, 13, 17, 18, 19, 20, 21, 22, 23, *26–29,* 44, 60, *61,* 67, 69, 90, 91, 98, *100, 101,* 106, 107, 108, 111, *123, 126,* 174, *181,* 184, *204,* 234, 285, 296, 297, 298, 301, 302, *333–334,* 336, 341, 360, 399, 403, *413,* 416, *434,* 454, 456, *481,* 485, *503*
Friedmann, J. K., 331, *333*
Friesen, W. V., 463, *479*
Frieze, I. H., 90, *100*
Frischholz, E. J., 142, *157*
Frye, S., *64*
Fu, P., 518, *523, 525*
Fukuma, Y., 510, *521*
Funari, D. J., *69*
Fursland, A., 246, *248*
Futterman, S., 416, *432*

Gahne, B., 510, *522*
Gallops, M. S., 110, *125,* 212, 213, *236,* 423, *433*
Gandsen, S., 464, *478*
Ganesan, S., 108, *122,* 287, *297*
Garb, B., 91, *99*
Garbarino, J., 398, 403, 407, *412,* 466, *479*
Garcia, M., 268, *279*
Garcia-Peltoniemi, R. E., 107, *123–124,* 243, *249*
Garde, J. F., 508, *521*
Garfield, B. D., 391, *393*
Garfinkel, B. D., 404, *412*
Garmezy, N., 395, 402, *412*
Garrettson, L. K., *69*
Garrison, V., 329, *334*
Gatchel, R., 344, *358*
Gaviria, F. M., *203*
Gaviria, M., 512, *521*
Gaw, A., *124*
Gearing, M. L., *69*
Gebhart, J., *249*
Geertz, C., 168, *179*
Gelder, M., *157*
Gelles, R. J., 369, *386*
Gelsomino, J., 21, *27*
George, L., 416, *435*
George, L. K., 22, *30,* 46, *63,* 135, *162*
Gerardi, R. J., 16, *25*

Hough, R. L., 65, 66, *204, 236, 250, 280,*
    312, 313, 315, 322, 325, 326, 327,
    330, *332, 333, 334, 335, 336,*
    337, 338, 433, 434
Hough, R. P., *27*
Hough, R. W., 316, *334*
Houskamp, B. M., 65, 420, *432*
Hovens, J. E., 63, *201, 203*
Hryvniak, M. R., 44, 52, 65
Hsu, F. L. K., 168, *181*
Hsu, J., 401, 407, *414*
Hu, W. H., 509, 514, *520, 522*
Hua, C., 13, *28*
Hubbard, J., 68, *299*
Hubbard, J. W., 515, *523, 524*
Huberty, J., 312n1
Huggins, N. I., 220, *235*
Hughes, C. C., 267, *281, 330, 337, 473,*
    479
Hughes, C. S., 473, *482*
Hughes, D., 46, *63*
Hughes, S. J., 68
Hulsey, T. L., 151, *161*
Hulst, L. K., 517, *521*
Hunt, M., *71*
Hunt, M. F., 63
Hunt, T., *162*
Huska, J. A., *205*
Hussain, Y., *160*
Hutchinson, J., 219, *235*
Huxley, P., 139, *157*
Hyatt-Williams, A., *67*
Hyer, L., 96, 99

Ifabumuyi, O. I., 174n5, *180*
Ihle, L., 108, *125*
Ilechukwu, S. T. C., 139, *158*
Inaba, T., 507, *522*
Incesu, C., *60*
Indian Health Service, 245, *250*
International Federation of Red Cross and
    Red Crescent Societies, 35, 36,
    38, 39, 65, *345, 360*
Irvine, D., 241, *252*
Isenberg, K., 511, *523*
Ishikawa, K., *522*
Ishiyama, F. I., 138, *158*
Ishizaki, T., *522*
Iwadate, T., 13, *28*
Iwata, N., 267, *280*

Ja, D. Y., 365, *386*

Jablensky, A., 119, *127, 204, 249*
Jackson, D., 170, *178*
Jackson, D. N., 241, *250*
Jackson, J., 229, *233*
Jacobs, L., *521*
Jacobsberg, L., 52, 68
Jacobson, A., 372, *384*
Jacoby, R., *64*
Jacqz, E., *524*
Jakob, B. R., 272, *282*
James, W., 17, *27*
Janca, A., 46, 62, 271, *279*
Janet, P., 166, 167, *180*
Jann, M. W., 510, 514, *521, 522*
Janoff-Bulman, R., 90, *100, 375, 377, 384*
Jaranson, J. M., 13, 22, 26, 106, 107, 108,
    113, 114, 115, *123, 124,* 285, 296,
    297, 302, *334*
Jarrell, M. P., *61*
Javaid, J. I., 512, *521*
Jeanneret, O., 42, 65
Jeavons, A., *157*
Jefferson, T., 220, 221, *235*
Jenkins, E. J., 215, *233*
Jenkins, J. H., 267, *280*
Jenkins, P. H., 168, 169, 170, 170n3, 171,
    172, 173n4, 174, 177, *180*
Jenkins-Hall, K., 226, *235*
Jensen, P. S., 402, *412*
Jensvold, M., 372, *384*
Jilek, W. G., 472, 474, *479*
Johnson, D. R., 29, *70*
Johnson, J. A., 508, *522*
Johnson, M., *61*
Johnson, M. C., 287, *297*
Johnson, P. A., 218, *235*
Johnson, R., *250*
Johnson, R. E., 18, *25*
Johnson, T. A., 212, *235*
Joinet, B., 466, *481*
Jojer, B., *334*
Jones, J. C., 420, *433*
Jones, J. H., 219, *235*
Jones, R. L., 230, *235*
Jones-Saumty, D., 241, *250*
Jordan, B. K., 27, 49, 65, 66, *204, 236,*
    250, 280, 322, 335, 336, 337,
    433, 434, 502
Jordan, K., 111, *124, 125*
Joshi, S., 141, *161*
Juba, M., *282*
Julkunen, J., 137, *158*

Leonard, A. C., 48, 64, 213, 214, *234, 360*
Leong, F. T. L., 287, *297*
Lerer, B., 91, 99, *102*
Lerner, G., 364, 365, 371, *385*
Lerner, M. J., 372, *385*
Lerner, P. M., 142, *162*
Lesser, I., 23, 505, *525*
Lesser, M., 115, *126*
Leung, P., 108, 115, *125, 250, 480*
Leung, P. K., *101, 298*
Levine, H., 219, *236*
LeVine, R. A., 168, 169, *180, 181*
Levi-Strauss, C., 365, *385*
Levy, J. E., 246, *250*
Levy, R., 168, 169, *180*
Levy, R. H., 509, *523*
Lewinsohn, P. M., 268, *281*
Lewis, R., 229, *233*
Lewis-Fernandez, R., 141, 147, *160*
Liao, C., *522*
Liden, A., 507, *521*
Lifton, R. J., 16, *27*
Lightcap, P. E., 48, *68*
Lima, A. M., 66, *335*
Lima, B., 109, *125*
Lima, B. R., 13, *27–28*, 48, 66, 308, 311,
    312, *335–336*, 345, 346, 347, 352,
    353, 354, *360*
Lin, E., 108, 115, *125*
Lin, H. J., 515, *522*
Lin, K., 115, *126*
Lin, K. M., 23, 287, *298*, 505, 506, 507,
    510, 513, 514, 516, 518, *523, 525*
Lindal, E., 46, *66*
Lindberg, F. H., *66*
Lindenthal, J., 443, *456*
Lindy, J., 110, *124*
Lindy, J. D., 48, 57, 64, 66, 213, 214, *234*,
    416, 417, *432*
Lindy, J. L., 348, *360*
Linehan, M., 373, *385*
Lingle, D. W., 467, *481*
Lipman, L. S., 142, *157*
Lipper, S., *100*
Lira, E., 246, *250*
Li-Shuen, L., *163*
Litz, B. T., 17, *28*, 205, 420, *434*
Livingston, R. L., 511, *523*
Li-Wah, O., *163*
Llanos, R., *334*
Lock, M., 169, *181*
Locke, B. Z., *332, 336*

Lockhart, L., 364, 369, 378, 379, *385*
Loft, S., 510, *520*
Long, D., 166, *178*
Long, N., *66*
Lonigan, C. J., 213, *236*
Loningan, C. J., *213*
Loo, C., 297, *298*
Loo, C. M., 429, 430, *434*, 450, *456*
Lopez, A., 108, *126*
Lopez, G., 52, *66*
Lopez, J., 245, *249*
Lore, R. K., 363, *385*
Lorenzo, J., *27*
Lou, Y., 507, 516, *526*
Lou, Y. C., *523*
Loughrey, G., 51, *62*
Loughrey, G. C., *60*
Low, S., 174, *181*
Lozano, J., 13, *28*, 48, 66, 109, *125*, 308,
    335, 336, 345, 346, 347, *360*
Lu, F., 113, 115, *123, 125*, 286, *298*
Lu, F. G., *64*
Luborsky, L., *503*
Lucca, N., 364, *386*
Lujan, C., 245, 246, *250*
Lukach, B. M., 52, *67*
Lukman, B., *338, 414*
Luna, J., 13, *28*, 308, *336*, 345, 346, *360*
Lung, F. W., *522*
Lunn, J., 508, *524*
Lutz, C., 169, *181*
Ly, M., 66, *298*
Lydiard, B., *61*
Lygren, S., *69*
Lyness, S. A., *525*
Lynn, S. J., 142, 143, 150, 151, *160, 162*
Lyons, J. A., 60, 397, *413*

Macher, J. P., 50, *62*
MacKay, P. W., 67, 199, *204*
MacKenzie, T., 66, 108, *125, 298*
Macklin, M. L., *68*
MacLean, D. G., 52, *62*
Madakasira, S., 48, *66*
Madsen, W., 442, *456*
Mager, D., 45, *62*, 271, *279*
Mager-Stellman, J., 50, *70*
Magraw, R., 50, 65, 427, *433*
Mahalish, P., 244, *249*
Mahoney, M. J., 444, *456*
Mahorney, S., *100*
Majors, R., 227, *236*

Makanjuola, R. O. A., 139, *160*
Malik, S. C., 134, *156*
Mallinger, A. G., 518, *520*
Malloy, P., 260, *280*
Malloy, P. F., 16, *28*, 200, *203*
Maloney, J. P., *70*
Malt, U., 52, 66, 109, *126*
Manifold, V., 273, *282*
Manolias, M. B., *67*
Manson, S. M., 24, 51, 65, 111, *123, 203,*
     240, 241, 242, 245, 247, *249–252,*
     257, 258, 264, 267, 268, 269, 273,
     278–281, 402, 413, 473
Marantz, S., 219, *236*
March, J., 392, 398, *413*
March, J. S., 243, *251, 345, 360, 413*
Marcolin, M. A., 515, *523*
Marcos, L. R., 512, *523*
Markette, J., 511, *522*
Markidis, M., 136, *162*
Marks, G., 268, *279*
Marks, I., *60*
Marmar, C., *124, 125*
Marmar, C. R., 21, *27, 28*, 65, 66, *204,*
     250, 280, 328, 335, 336, 337,
     338, 433, 434, 502
Marmor, T. R., 483, *503*
Marsella, A. J., 12, 13, 19, 22, *28*, 40, 60,
     67, 98, *101*, 106, 110, 111, 117,
     118, 119, *123, 126–127*, 135,
     160, 168, 169, 174, *181*, 184, 186,
     188, 190, 192, 199, *204*, 240, *249,*
     251, 269, *281*, 285, 295, 296, 298,
     302, 331, *336*, 341, 342, 343, *360,*
     399, 402, 403, *413*, 416, 429, *434,*
     442, 454, 456, 460, 468, 471,
     480–481, 485, 503
Martin, J., *359*
Martin, M., *157*
Martin-Baro, I., 177, 177n6, *181*
Martinez, C., Jr., 330, *336*
Martinez, R., *332*
Marusic, A., *66*
Marzolla, *304*
Maser, J. D., 243, *251*
Mashaw, J. L., 483, *503*
Mason, J. W., *30, 433*
Masserman, J. H., 17, *28*
Massion, A. O., *71*
Masten, A., 68, *299*
Masuda, M., 287, *298*
Matsuda, K., *523*

Matsunaga, D., *250*
Matsuoka, J., 295, 296, *298*
Matussek, P., 465, *481*
Matzler, T., 328, *338*
Maxwell, M. J., *61*
May, P., 244, 245, *250*
May, P. A., *251*
May, P. R., 513, *523*
Mayhew, P., 40, 41, *71*
Mayou, R., 52, *67*
McAllister, C. B., *524*
McCammon, S. L., 52, *63*
McCarthy, E., *67*
McCool, R., 271, *282*, 416, *434*
McCool, R. E., 48, 52, 68, *70*
McCoy, G. F., 246, *251*
McDermott, J. F., Jr., 401, *413*
McDougall, G., 416, *433*
McDougle, C. J., 91, *101*
McEnvoy, L., 271, *280*
McEvory, M., 373, *384*
McEvoy, L., 14, *27*, 45, 64, 317, *334*
McEvoy, M. A., 417, *432*
McFall, M. E., *67*, 199, *204*
McFarland, B. H., *61*
McFarland, R. E., 271, *282*
McFarlane, A., 416, *434*
McFarlane, A. C., 13, 22, *28*, 47, 48, 59,
     67, 148, 152, *160*, 325
McGlynn, E. A., 487, *504*
McGorry, P. D., 52, *67*
McKay, G., 515, *523, 524*
McKenzie, D., *67*
McKenzie, N., 245, *252*
McKinlay, W., *61*
McKinley, J. C., 189, *203*
McKinley, R., *124*
McLeer, S. V., 397, *411*
McLellan, A. T., 487, *503*
McNabb, S. L., 264, 267, *281*
McNally, R. J., 52, *67*, 148, *160*, 392, 394,
     395, *413*
McNeil, J. A., 515, *521*
McShane, D., 240, *251*
McShane, M., 368, *384*
Medina-Mora, E. M., 13, *25*
Medina Mora, M. E., 48, *62*
Meehl, P., 420, *434*
Mehryar, A. H., 269, *282*
Mellman, T. A., 50, *67*
Mellstrom, B., 507, *520, 523*
Mendels, J., 518, *524*

Mendelson, M., 198, *202*
Mendoza, R., 505, 506, *523, 525*
Menkes, D. B., 91, 99
Merkel, L., 289, *298*
Merlou-Ponty, M., 477, *481*
Merskey, H., 240, *252*
Meyer, U. A., 507, *523*
Mezzich, J., 328, *336*
Middleton, H., *157*
Midha, K. K., 515, *523–524*
Migneault, P., 401, *412*
Mikulincer, M., 50, *70*, 112, *128*, 272, 273, *282*, 427, *434, 435*
Milanes, F. J., 50, *67*
Miller, B., 245, *251*
Miller, C., 166, *178*
Miller, S. D., *161*
Miller-Perrin, C. L., 391, *413*
Mills, T., 372, *383*
Minkowski, E., 477, *481*
Miranda, J., *64, 158*
Mirza, S., *160*
Mitchell, J. T., 23, *28*, 443, *456*
Mitchell, T., *203*
Mittman, B. S., 487, *504*
Mizes, J. S., 443, *455*
Mock, J., 198, *202*
Modestin, J., 145, *160*
Mollica, R., 107, 108, 112, 114, *124, 127*, 285, 286, 288, 289, 290, 291, 292, 294, *298–299*, 464, *481*
Mollica, R. F., 51, *67*, 134, *160*, 197, 198, *204*, 246, *251*, 500, *503*
Moore, L., 108, 114, *122, 125, 127*, 331, 332, 464, *480*
Moore, L. J., 51, *67, 101*, 134, *160*, 293, *298, 299, 481*
Moosa, F., 402, *414*
Mora, C., *60*
Moradi, R., *279*
Moreland, T. A., 509, *523*
Morgan, A., *70*
Morgan, T. M., 268, *279*
Morgenstern, H., 515, *524*
Morita, S., *138*
Morrison, T., 222, 223, *236*
Moser, M., 508, *524*
Mould, G., *521*
Mowrer, O. H., 17, *28*, 92, *101*
Mucklow, J. C., *521*
Muff, A., 87, *102*
Muff, A. M., 21, *29*

Muller, U. F., *70*
Mulvihill, M., 264, *279*
Mumford, D. B., 133, 134, 152, *160*
Munster, A. M., 52, *69*
Murdock, T., 21, *26*, 52, *69*
Murdock, T. B., 93, *100*
Murphy, H. B. M., 139, *161*, 515, *524*
Murphy, J. M., 267, *281*
Murray, A., *62*
Murray, H., 116, *125*
Murray, M., 509, *524*
Musngi, G., 52, *68*
Myers, F., 169, *181*
Myers, J. K., 243, *253*, 336, 443, *456*
Myers, L. J., 377, *385*

Nadelson, C., 416, *434*
Nader, K., *29*, 395, 398, *413*
Nagy, L. M., *70, 455*
Nagy, L. N., *202*
Nakamura, K., 507, *524*
Nakano, M., 507, *522*
Nakasaki, G., 510, *523*
Nandi, D. N., 136, *161*
Nandi, P., 136, *161*
Nandi, S., 136, *161*
Narasimhachari, N., *69*
Nardi, C., 427, *434*
Narga, L., *236*
Nash, M. R., 142, 151, *161, 162*
Nathan, J., *204*
Nathan, P., 216, *237*
Nathan, T., 471, *481*
National Center for PTSD, 107, *127*
National Center on Child Abuse and Neglect, 97, *101*
Navajo-Hopi Relocation Commission, 244, *251*
Nebert, D. W., 506, *521*
Neider, J., 134, *163*, 240, *253*, 294, *299*
Neki, J. S., 466, *481*
Neligh, G., 240, 241, 247, 250, *251, 252*
Neller, G., *62*
Nelson, S. H., 246, *251*
Neumann, D. A., 420, *432*
Neumann, M., 443, *457*
Newaldt, S. P., *521*
Newcomb, M. D., 367, *387*
Newman, E., 185, *205*
Newman, J. P., 52, *67*
Newton, J., 18, *29*
Neylan, J. F., III, *235*

Nguyen, H., 66, *298*
Nguyen, L., 315, *338*
Nguyen, N., 108, *129*
Nguyen, T., 66, *298*
Nicassio, P. M., 108, *127*, 289, 292, 293, 299
Nicholls, N. M., 244, *252*
Nichter, M., 133, *161*
Nicolaou, A. L., 70
Nielsen, J., *249*
Niem, T., 114, *127*
Nisbett, R. E., 155, *162*
Nishimura, H., 510, *526*
Nobles, W., 210, *236*
Nolen-Hoeksema, S., 176, *181*
Nordin, C., 507, *521*
Noriega, L., *236*
Norris, D. M., 230, *237*
Norris, F., 88, 89, *101*, 343, 349, 351, *361*
Norris, F. H., 42, 68, 213, 214, *236*, *361*
North, C., 43, 48, 52, 56, 58, 59, 70, 416, *434*
North, C. S., 68, 271, *282*
Norton, H. S., 63
Notman, M., 416, *434*
Noumair, D., *61*
Novara, J., *334*
Noy, S., 112, *128*
Nuccio, I., *523*
Nuñez, F., *29*

Obeyesekere, G., 134, 144, 153, *161*, 174, *181*
O'Brien, C. P., *503*
O'Brien, K. F., 48, 66
O'Brien, L. S., 68
Ochberg, F. M., 246, *251*
Ochs, E., 168, 169, *181*
Odaira, T., 13, *28*
O'Donnell, I., 63
Oetting, G. R., 442, *456*
Ogden, T., 222, *236*
O'Gorman, E. C., 52, *61*
Ohnuki-Tierney, E., 138, *161*
O'Keefe, M., 364, *385*
Okonek, A., *524*
Okpaku, S., 518, *524*
Okuyama, Y., 267, *280*
Olasov Rothbaum, B., 92, 93, *100*, *101*
Olatawura, M., *249*
Olivera, A. A., 243, *252*
Oliver-Smith, A., 346, *361*

O'Neal, E., 391, *410*
O'Nell, C. W., 140, *162*
Onstad, S., 69
Oppenheimer, B., 112, *128*
Orjucla, E., 114, *122*, 331, *332*
Orley, J., 22, 28, 40, 67, 98, *101*, 109, *123*, 402, *413*
Orner, R. J., 68
Ornitz, E. M., 16, 18, *28*, 395, 396, *413*
Orr, S. P., 16, *29*
Osato, S. S., 420, *432*
Ostrow, D., 518, *525*
Ostrow, D. G., *524*
Ostwald, P., *127*
Ots, T., 168, *181*
Ottoson, J. O., *158*
Overall, J. E., 511, *522*, *524*
Ovesey, L., 210, *235*
Owan, T., 22, *28*
Ozmen, E., 60

Padilla, A. M., 51, *62*, 108, 307, *333*
Pai, S., 13, *27*, *28*, 48, 66, 109, *125*, 308, 311, *335*, *336*, 345, 347, *360*
Paige, S., 18, *29*
Pakaslahti, A., *158*
Paker, M., 60
Palacio, R., 307, *338*
Palinkas, L. A., 48, 52, 68, 255, 271, *281*, 341, 351, *361*
Pallmeyer, B. A., 16, *25*
Pandey, G. N., 518, *520*
Pardes, H., *524*
Paris, J., 137, 142, *159*, *163*
Parker, J. D. A., 137, *162*
Parkinson, D., 343, *359*
Parson, E. R., 110, 113, 115, *127*, 212, 214, 228, 229, 230, *236*, 331, *336*, 444, 453, 455, 457, 484, *503*
Pathak, D., *203*
Patrick, V., 13, *29*
Patrick, W. R., 13, *29*
Patterson, D. R., 52, 68
Patterson, E. T., 69
Patterson, J., 341, *361*
Patterson, P. G., 240, *252*
Pattison, M., 241, *252*
Pattison, P., 17, *25*
Pawluczyk, S., *525*
Payeur, R., *61*
Paz, O., 325, *336*
Pearlin, L. I., 442, *457*

Regier, D. R., 335
Reid, G., 18, 29, 229, 237
Reid, P. T., 385
Reidenberg, M. M., 509, 524
Reidy, C., 223, 237
Reidy, G. F., 509, 524
Reist, C., 91, 101
Resick, P. A., 272, 278
Resnick, H. S., 60, 65, 68
Rettersól, N., 158
Retterstól, N., 145, 157
Reviriego, J., 516, 526
Rhue, J. W., 143, 160
Ribera, J., 347, 358
Ribera, J. C., 311, 332
Richards, A. L., 522
Richardson, B., 372, 384
Richman, J. A., 203
Ridley, C. R., 467, 481
Riederle, M. H., 367, 387
Rieker, P. P., 372, 383
Riggio, R. R., 235
Riggs, D. A., 52, 69
Riggs, D. S., 21, 26, 52, 69, 93, 100
Riley, C., 101, 298, 480
Rimonte, N., 370, 380, 381, 385
Robbins, J. M., 132, 134, 137, 138, 140, 149, 151, 159, 161
Roberts, J., 61
Roberts, R. E., 268, 281
Roberts, W. R., 69
Robin, R., 240, 241, 242, 244, 245, 249
Robin, R. W., 252
Robinowitz, R., 69, 112, 128, 236
Robins, E., 512, 525
Robins, L., 344, 361, 373, 384
Robins, L. E., 271, 280
Robins, L. N., 14, 27, 45, 48, 64, 69, 70, 267, 281, 311, 315, 317, 327, 334, 336, 337, 417, 432, 487, 499, 503
Robinson, R., 52, 68
Roca, R. P., 52, 69
Rocke, L. G., 62
Roddy, R., 51, 62
Roddy, R. J., 60
Rodriguez, O., 443, 457
Roesler, T., 245, 252
Rogers, C. R., 465, 467, 481
Rogler, L., 264, 281
Roitblat, H. L., 420, 431

Roland, A., 470, 481
Roman, G. W., 218, 235
Ronis, D., 503
Root, M. P. P., 364, 366, 374, 375, 376, 377, 385, 386
Rosaldo, M., 168, 169, 181
Rosenberg, S. D., 23, 29, 69
Rosenblat, R., 511, 515, 524
Rosenheck, R., 20, 21, 23, 26, 27, 70, 216, 237, 485, 486, 499, 502, 503
Ross, C. A., 141, 142, 161
Ross, J. C., 243, 253
Ross, L., 155, 162
Ross, R. J., 18, 29
Rosser, R., 114, 128
Rosser-Hogan, R., 141, 157, 290, 297
Roth, S., 92, 100
Rothbart, G., 211, 234, 423, 432
Rothbaum, B. O., 15, 21, 26, 52, 69, 376, 383, 420, 432
Rothbaum, F. M., 153, 163
Rothblum, E. D., 365, 383
Routledge, P. A., 509, 510, 524
Roy, C., 241, 252
Roy-Byrne, P. P., 141, 158
Rozee, P., 108, 128
Rozee, P. D., 367, 385
Rozynko, V., 240, 252
Rubel, A. J., 140, 162
Rubin, R. T., 513, 523
Rubio-Stipec, M., 48, 62, 134, 135, 147, 156, 157, 158, 264, 267, 278, 280, 311, 312, 327, 329, 332, 333, 334, 337, 343, 347, 355, 358, 359
Rubonis, A. V., 58, 69, 462, 482
Rudd, M. D., 52, 69
Rudorfer, M. V., 510, 511, 512, 524–525
Ruff, G., 433
Rumbaut, R., 289, 291, 293, 299
Russell, D. E., 363, 367, 368, 371, 376, 378, 385
Russell, J., 48, 68, 255, 281, 341, 361
Russell, S. A., 373, 385
Russo, N. F., 384
Rutledge, D. R., 509, 525
Rutter, M., 395, 402, 412
Ryan, R. A., 240, 252

Sacco, W. D., 226, 235
Sachs, R. G., 142, 157

556   AUTHOR INDEX

Young, A., 155, *159, 163, 166*n1, *182*
Young, K., *163*
Young, M. B., 442, 444, *457*
Yuasa, I., 510, *521, 526*
Yule, W., 394, 397, *414*

Zackson, H., 416, *434*
Zanger, U. M., 507, *523*
Zaragoza, M. S., 364, *383*
Zatzick, D. F., 328, *338*
Zeiner, A. R., 241, *250*
Zelwer, B., 246, *248*
Zenberg, R., 15, *26*
Zhang, L., *522*
Zhang, M. D., 510, *524*
Zhang, M. Y., *520*
Zhang, Y., 516, *526*

Zheng, Y. P., 518, *525*
Zhou, D., *522, 524*
Zhou, H. H., 506, 507, 508, 509, *526*
Zich, J., 268, *283*
Ziegler, M., 508, 511, *521*
Ziegler, V. E., *526*
Zigelbaum, S., 443, *457*
Zilberg, N., *283*
Zimbardo, P. G., 403, *414*
Zimering, R., 420, *433*
Zimering, R. T., 92, 93, *100, 101*
Zimering, Z. T., 17, *27*
Zinner, J., 222, *237–238*
Zivcic, I., *414*
Zubin, J., 420, *435*
Zucker, D. K., 511, *523*
Zweig-Frank, H., 142, *163*
Zwi, A. B., 39, *71*

SUBJECT INDEX

Burn patients, Hispanic, 114

California
    earthquake victims in, 355
    farm workers in, 342
Calor, 171–172
Cambodians, 115, 289–291, 463–465
Category fallacy, 174–175
Center for Epidemiologic Studies Depression Scale (CES-D), 268–269, 307
Checklists, PTSD symptom, 55
Cheyenne Indians, 241
Chicago, 216
Childhood trauma, dissociative disorders related to, 142
Children and adolescents, PTSD in, 389–410
    developmental aspects of, 390–399
        biological correlates, 396
        clinical course, 396–397
        clinical presentation, 392–394
        detection/screening, 394–395
        differential diagnoses, 397
        impact, 396
        pathogenesis, 392
        treatment, 397–398
    ethnocultural issues, 399–401
    stressors, 391
    studies of, 401–409
        case studies, 403–407
        in diverse populations, 402–403
        family therapy model, use of, 407–409
Child sexual abuse, 368–369
Chileans, 304, 307, 356
China, 139
Chronic fatigue syndrome, 139
Civil strife, 36
Classification of PTSD. *See* Diagnosis of PTSD
Clinical issues related to PTSD, 20–21
    comorbidity, 20
    longitudinal course/chronicity, 20–21
Clinician-Administered PTSD Scale, 200
Clonidine, 115
CMI (Cornell Medical Index), 287
Cognition, affect vs., as culturally variable component of interventions, 468–470

Cognitive-behavioral treatment of PTSD, 21
Cognitive therapy, 93
Collective responses to trauma, 177–178
    among American Indians, 276
    treatment, implications for, 475–476
Colombia, 13, 48, 345, 354
Community trauma, among American Indians, 246–247
Comorbidity, 20, 58–59
    in American Indians, 242–243, 271–272
    in children and adolescents, 397
    in Hispanics, 313–314, 330
    and pharmacotherapy, 91
Complex PTSD, 227
Conceptual equivalence in PTSD measures, 188
Construct validity, 193–194
Content equivalence in PTSD measures, 187
Content validity, 193
Conversion symptoms, 136–137
Coping, 327
Cornell Medical Index (CMI), 287
Crime, 41–42
Cultural bereavement model, 402
Cultural family therapy, 407–409
Culture
    definition of, 116–117
    and experience of emotion, 168–170

Debrisoquine, 507–508
Depression
    among American Indians, 241–243
    cross-cultural approach to studying, 190
    somatic presentation of, 140–141
DES (Dissociative Experiences Scale), 328
Desipramine, 91
Desmethyldiazepam, 516
DESNOS (disorder of extreme stress not otherwise specified), 19
Detroit, 46
Developmental aspects of PTSD, 390–401
    biological correlates, 396
    child development, impact on, 396
    clinical course, 396–397
    clinical presentation, 392–394
    detection/screening, 394–395

Mexican, 311, 460
South America, 354–355
ECA. *See* Epidemiologic Catchment Area Program
Economic factors in PTSD
    African Americans, 216–217, 219–220
    women of color, 379
Ecuador, 354–355
Education, African Americans and discrimination in, 219
Emic instruments, 191, 264
Emic interventions, 472–474
Emotion
    cognition vs., as culturally variable component of interventions, 468–470
    cognized, 169–170
    culture and experience of, 168–170
    vehement, 166–167
Empathy, therapist's communication of, 467–468
Enemy Way ceremony, 24
Epidemiologic Catchment Area Program (ECA), 14, 45–47
    Los Angeles, 315–319
Epidemiology of PTSD, 13–14, 33–60, 119
    comorbidity issues, 58–59
    and dose–response relationship, 59
    future research needs, 53
    instruments, diagnostic sensitivity of, 54–55
    lifetime prevalence estimates, 57–58
    literature review, 43–53
        prevalence studies, 45–48
        strategy for, 43–45
        victim studies, 50–53
        war veteran studies, 48–50
    and method of assessment, 58
    natural vs. technological disasters, 58
    and nature/prevalence of traumatic events, 35–43
        classification of disasters, 35
        definition of disasters, 35
        Glickman review of, 39
        man-made violence, 39–43
        mortality rates, increases in, 37–39
        most frequent disasters, 36–37

prevalence rates, difficulties in comparing, 56–57
and somatization research, 151–152
timing of diagnosis, 56
and variations in diagnostic criteria, 53–54
Ethnocentricity, 116
Ethnocentrism, in psychiatry and mental health professions, 231–232
Ethnocultural identity, 117–118
Ethnosemantic methods, 118
Excerpta Medica Psychiatry CD-ROM, 43
Exposure to traumatic events, defining, 345–346
Exxon Valdez oil spill, 351

Family therapy, cultural, 407–409
Fiji, 13, 347
Flashbacks, PTSD, 15
Flood victims, 36, 311, 355–357
Flower of Two Souls study, 258, 263, 270, 271
Folk disorders, 119
Foundations of Indian Teens project, 258–259, 261, 263, 270
Fright illness *(susto)*, 140, 329
Functional impairment criterion for PTSD, 16–17

General Health Questionnaire (GHQ), 287
GHQ (General Health Questionnaire), 287
Group therapy, 94, 229–230
Guilt feelings, in African Americans, 228–229

Haloperidol, 513–514
Harvard Trauma Questionnaire, 197–198
Health care, African Americans and discrimination in, 218–219
Health Survey of Indian Boarding School Students, 257–258, 261, 263, 269–270
Hispanics and PTSD, 301–331. *See also* Mexicans and Mexican Americans
    burn patients, 114
    comorbidity patterns, 313–314, 330
    comparative studies, 315–323

Post-traumatic psychocultural therapy (PTpsyCT), 113
Power distance, as cultural dimension in treatment, 476
Predictive power of tests, 196
Predisposing factors, potentially, 421–422
Prevalence rates of PTSD, 45–48
    among American Indians, 270
    among Vietnamese refugees, 288–289
    by country (table), 72–85
    studies of, 47–48
Prisoners of war, 50–51
Projective identification, 222
Propranolol, 91
Psychic numbing, 16
Psychic trauma, 166
Psychodynamic therapy, 93–94
Psychological automatisms, 167
Psychometry. *See* Measurement
Psychopharmacology, 90–91, 95–96, 505–520
    antidepressants, 510–512
        with African Americans, 511–512
        with Asians, 511
        with Hispanics, 512
    benzodiazepines, 515–517
        with African Americans, 517
        with Asians, 515–517
    environmental influences on, 509
    lithium, 518
    neuroleptics, 512–515
        with African Americans and Hispanics, 515
        with Asians, 512–514
    and pharmacodynamics, 508–509
    and pharmacogenetics, 506–508
    plasma protein binding, 509–510
    therapy studies, 114–115
Psychotherapy, 92–94
    behavior therapy, 92–93
    cognitive therapy, 93
    group therapy, 94
    hypnotherapy, 94
    psychodynamic therapy, 93–94
    therapy studies, 113–114
PTpsyCT (post-traumatic psychocultural therapy), 113
PTSD Checklist, 200–201
PTSD flashbacks, 15
Puerto Ricans, 48

flood victims, 311, 356–357
service use, among military veterans, 500–501
somatization disorder among, 135–136

Questionnaires, with children, 395

Racism, as traumatic stress, 221–223. *See also* Violence against women of color
Rape, 367
Reactive psychoses, 145–146
Refugees, 40
    from Latin America, 304–308
    Salvadoran women, 170–175
    studies of, 51–52, 107–108
Relapses, 20–21
Reliability, 194–195
Research issues, 165–166
    design, 19
    methods, 116–119
        and definition of culture, 116–117
        and epidemiology, 119
        and equivalence in assessment, 118
        and ethnocentricity, 116
        and ethnocultural identity, 117–118
        ethnosomatic methods, 118
    strategies, 190–192
Responsibility, 175
Risk factors for PTSD, 22–23, 325
Ritual, 24, 275–276, 473–474

SADS-L (Schedule for Affective Disorder and Schizophrenia), 241, 247
Salvadoran women refugees, 170–175
San Diego McKinney Homeless Mentally Ill project, 322–323
San Ysidro Massacre, 312
Scale/technical equivalence in PTSD measures, 188–189
Schedule for Affective Disorder and Schizophrenia (SADS-L), 241, 247
SCL-90-R, 55
Self, assumptions about, 445–450
Self-Rating Questionnaire (SRQ), 308
Sensitivity, as measure of diagnostic utility, 195

and intensity of trauma, 22
postwar experiences of, 428–430
predisposition and exposure, accounting for, 425–426
preexposure characteristics, 421–422
research design issues, 19
risk factors for, 22, 23
studies of, 109–112
war zone stress exposure among, 422–425
Violence against women of color, 363–382
barriers to research on, 378–382
conceptual barriers, 380
cultural barriers, 381–382
economic barriers, 379
language barriers, 379
structural barriers, 378–379
domestic violence, 369–371
and ethnicity, 371–372
historical context, 365–366
incidence of, 366–371
child sexual abuse, 368–369
domestic violence, 369–371
rape, 367
and psychiatric diagnosis, 372–375

blaming of victim, 373
insidious trauma, 374–375
symptomatology, 372–373
security, threats to, 375–378
interpersonal security, 377
physical security, 376
psychological security, 376–377
spiritual security, 377–378
Violent deaths, 42
Vulnerability, 175–176
to disasters, 346–347
to PTSD, 23–24

Wars, 39–40
War Stress Interview, Part 1 (WSI-1), 486–488
War veterans. *See* Military veterans
Women, violence against. *See* Violence against women of color
World War I veterans, 415–416
World War II veterans, 20, 415, 416
WSI-1 (War Stress Interview, Part 1), 486–488

Yohimbine, 16

ABOUT THE EDITORS

Anthony J. Marsella, PhD, is a professor of psychology and director of the clinical studies program at the University of Hawaii, Honolulu. He is also director of the World Health Organization Field Psychiatric Research Center. He is an internationally recognized scholar in the areas of ethnocultural studies of psychpathology and psychotherapy, and has published 110 journal articles and book chapters and 10 books, including *Amidst Peril and Pain: The Mental Health and Well-being of the World's Refugees* (with T. Bornemann, S. Ekblad, and J. Orley).

Matthew J. Friedman, MD, PhD, is director of the National Center for Post-Traumatic Stress Disorders, Veterans Affairs Medical and Research Center, White River Junction, Vermont. He is also professor of psychiatry and pharmacology at Dartmouth Medical School in Hanover, New Hampshire. Dr. Friedman is an internationally known scholar in clinical and biological PTSD studies, and is the former president of the International Society for Traumatic Stress Research. He has published numerous journal articles, book chapters, and books, including *Neurobiological and Clinical Consequences of Stress: From Normal Adaptation to PTSD* (with A. Deutsch and D. Charney).

Ellen T. Gerrity, PhD, is Acting Chief, Violence and Traumatic Stress Research Branch of the Epidemiology and Services Research Division, Institute of Mental Health in Rockville, Maryland. She is also the program chief for emergency research at NIMH, where she is responsible for administering funds regarding trauma responses associated with natural and technological disasters, combat, rape, and sexual assault. Dr. Gerrity also serves as associate research professor in the Department of Psychiatry and Behavioral Sciences at the George Washington University Medical Center in Washington, DC. She has published numerous journal articles and book chapters on traumatic stress and behavioral medicine.

Raymond M. Scurfield, DSW, is director of the Pacific Center for Post-Traumatic Stress Disorders, Veterans Affairs Medical Center, Honolulu, Hawaii. He has published numerous journal articles and book chapters on PTSD among military veterans. He is an adjunct professor of psychology in the Department of Psychology, University of Hawaii, Honolulu. Dr. Scurfield is also a Vietnam War veteran, and has worked with the federal government for more than 25 years.